He Usually

With a Fe......

Garrigues, a fine reporter, did an exceptionally good job in running down the facts in the sensational John P. Mills asserted rape case. . . . Where he has gone since those thrilling days of Los Angeles' "fantastic era," the writer does not know. But he is glad to salute his courageous memory, with a like tribute to all newspaper men of his sturdy breed.
—Guy W. Finney, *Angel City in Turmoil*

G

He Usually Lived With a Female

By George Garrigues

THE STORY OF CALIFORNIA NEWSPAPERMAN
CHARLES HARRIS (BRICK) GARRIGUES

Quail Creek Press
2006

HE USUALLY LIVED WITH A FEMALE
Copyright 2006 by George Garrigues

For information and correspondence:
http://www.ULWAF.com

Cover painting by Irving Sussman
Cover design by Wilsted & Taylor
Printed in the United States of America

Edited by Vivian Garrigues

PUBLICATION DATA
Garrigues, George
He Usually Lived With a Female
1. California; 2. Biography
1. Title
ISBN 0-9634830-1-3

Seek here neither thesis nor theory.
Behold in this work merely the inner history of a life that is
sincere, long, fertile in joys and sorrow,
not exempt from contradictions, abounding in errors,
yet always struggling to attain,
in default of the inaccessible Truth,
that harmony of spirit which is our supreme truth.

—Romain Rolland, *Jean-Christophe*

I am thirty-odd years old, an American and a newspaperman,
and I have a son.
And some time — before long, whether it is tomorrow or
forty years—I shall be nothing, as my father is nothing now,
upon the earth. And my son will remain for a while in his turn.
Now. What does that mean? . . .
This child will be here after me, following, without knowing,
where I have been before him. And he will hurt himself and
those whom he loves, just as I have; and some day he will
come to the place where I am now.
And maybe he will remember me then . . .

—Michael Foster, *American Dream*

Any man's childhood years are the most important.

—Frank Harris, *On Bernard Shaw*

Contents

A Word in Front

The Author Talks With His Editor   *ix*

Narcissus

The Mysterious Letter	*2*
Roots	*11*
Imperial	*14*
Westward	*27*
Waiting	*33*
Los Angeles	*45*
Why Herbert Hoover Beat Al Smith	*61*
Janet	*77*
The Devil Considerably Less Black	*88*
Passions	*113*
The Dream Ranch	*130*
Naomi	*149*
Usually Lives With a Female	*162*

Amaryllis

San Francisco	*180*
Extra-Specials	*194*
The Kids	*212*
Sunrise Over the Next Hill	*240*
The Role to Which She Was Assigned	*251*
Love's Old Sweet Song	*258*
The Hearts of Women and Men	*273*

Foxglove

284 Full Stop
292 The Family Divided
314 To Dig Furiously in the Earth
334 To Think That Two and Two
354 The Characters Begin to Live and Move
365 How to Live Within Your Income
379 The Boy on the Wagon
395 Legacies
409 Running the Eggfield
419 Fathers and Sons
438 The Answer

Oak

450 Chuck
460 I Do Not Know the Truth, Not Yet
478 There Came a Feeling of Finality I Cannot Shake
490 What Clarale Typed at the Big Desk

Ivy

498 Grieving
506 Peggy
514 Letting Go
524 Period Pieces
535 Neither Five Nor Three
542 The Name, When I Find It, Will Be Much Easier
     to Pronounce
547 There's Not Enough Time
550 Nineteen Years Later

A Word in Front
The Author Talks With His Editor

After I had completed the first draft of this book, I was able to secure the services of one of the best editors I know. She told me she was giving me a big discount from her usual price, and instead of thinking, "Yeah, sure!" I actually believed her because we were once married and we had shared not only the upbringing of our three children but also a joint bank account.

So when Vivian Garrigues had given the manuscript a good read, she asked me to come to her place, gave me a cup of coffee, looked at her notes and said: "Let's sum up: This is a book of your dad's letters — of Brick's letters. They begin in 1925, and the reader starts tentatively with 'This man is fascinating, but insensitive and arrogant. Who the hell does he think he is?' Then we watch him changing, sometimes awkwardly, sometimes with an amiable acceptance, and finally — over a half century — he eases into maturity. At the end the reader closes the book and says, 'Now I understand.'"

"Well, yes. I hope so. But?" She's going to pounce, I thought.

"But in the first half, how long do you suppose the reader will stick with this, if you'll pardon me, insensitive and womanizing man? To me — to any woman — there are too many instances in this manuscript of his smugness and obtuseness. You need to chop it.

"The major point," she added with certainty, "is that, at least in the beginning, Brick is very interesting, but not very likeable. He seems to make a pass at every woman he sees, and he doesn't hesitate in his letters to let his 'sweetheart' know about it! Why on earth did Dickie" — that's the sweetheart — "put up with it?"

"Well, you *knew* the man," I replied. "You know how charming he could be."

"You wouldn't have been on my short list for marriageable mates if *I'd* received a letter like this one!" She turned right to January 15, 1926, which she'd marked with a Post-It.

"I never wrote one," I reminded her.

She said nothing; she just raised an eyebrow. She is the only woman I have ever known who could actually do that.

Then she said: "We need more stuff in the first few chapters like Brick's remark about his delighted mother not talking much about anything but Dickie." She pointed to it. "It's a very sweet remark; normally he doesn't talk sweet at all; he talks smart, witty and glib. The sweetness is that he is already speaking of Dickie as though she were part of the family."

"Well, first, I can't make stuff up. This book is real; it is not fiction.[1] Second, I've got to show he has a roving eye, so that the upheaval in Chapter Ten — that tragic fall — doesn't come as a big surprise. Third, he's in his journalistic mode, and journalists of that era thought of themselves as hard-boiled and unsentimental."

"Women will not like this book," she enunciated clearly.

"They may not like the man — for a while — but they'll like the book." I felt sure of it. "And men? Well, young men can relate to Brick's early smugness. Middle-aged men can recall the joy they felt at the birth of their first child; the trauma they may have gone through in a divorce" — she looked a little thoughtful at that — "the failure they felt in themselves when the money wasn't there, the feeling that life is passing them by.

"And the oldest men of all, those guys you see on the park bench or shuffling down the sidewalk. In some ways, I like that 'Feeling of Finality' chapter the best. That decay comes to all of us, men *and* women. You know, Shakespeare's Seventh Age."

Vivian riffled the manuscript.

"But this 'Janet' chapter? So many devious things come up beforehand that when the reader reaches the 'Janet' chapter, he or she might shout, 'Enough, already!' and throw the book down. It should be eliminated!"

That one stopped me. I had really been greatly amused at my father's

---

1 Except for this foreword, which is put together from various telephone conversations, e-mails and letters that Vivian and I exchanged over many months. And some poetic license in Part Three involving a daemon and a goddess. And I changed the names of some of the people whom Brick wrote about, did a massive amount of cutting of his letters and some editing I think Brick would have agreed with.

taking such pains to break up the romance of his young woman friend with a man he thought didn't suit her. Still, I did have the feeling that Brick blabbered on much too much about his scheming.

"I'll go through the chapter and see if I can cut or paraphrase."

She seemed somewhat mollified and then read aloud from her notes:

"The book is most strongly the story of Brick's life — from the young man who wants to swallow the world and everything in it in one huge gulp — to the older man who is content with his small piece of the world, something interesting to read and good music playing quietly on the stereo.

"Intertwined with the playing out of Brick's life is his need to be a 'writer.' Sometimes it plays out in a major theme with a full brass section, and sometimes it recedes to a minor theme with piano and violin playing softly in the background. This works.

"Theme three — his struggle to come to terms with a defining incident in his teenage years — this is the weakest. This theme drops in, says 'Hi,' and leaves for a period of time, wandering back ever so often to say 'Hi!' and 'Gotta run now.' "

I looked at her.

"That is really good. Listen, *you* write a book and *I'll* be the editor!"

We both laughed, and then I said: "But I think you're ignoring the very strong theme of *family*. And the Twentieth Century family was not like his Mama and Papa and their five kids. It's more like Brick's and his friends' and his children's families. Oh, gosh, there must be half a dozen divorces in that manuscript. And yet *family* is the theme from the first page to the last."

"Oh, yes." She smiled. "That 'Kids' chapter. That was *so* precious — in the best sense of the word."

"Thanks. I enjoyed writing it." More than enjoyed; I had *relived* those scenes of my childhood, when my brother and I spent the summers with our father, causing him some grief but much joy. Of course I didn't know how *he* felt about it all until I pulled his letters out of the envelopes in which they had lain for so many years and read them — some of them for the first time.

And then I said, "You know, there was a period in my life — oh, just about the time Lisa was a toddler — when I thought Brick was just a big blowhard, and my mind is a blank about a lot of what happened between us. That's why researching and writing this book has been so important for me."

She nodded. In sympathy, I thought with some annoyance. "And that's why you want to call it *Brick's Book?*

"Yeah, well, it has a double meaning. The letters he wrote — they make up his 'Book.' And his life was so much driven, even from the beginning, by his need to *write* a book, *the* Book."

She was gentle but still firm: *"Brick's Book* is *not* going to fly off the shelves. Instead, use that title you have for Chapter Thirteen: 'Usually Lives With a Female.' " Can anybody resist picking the book up and looking inside it with a title like that?"

I guess I made a face. A title like that seemed so, well, *dismissive.* And yet . . . it was certainly true enough. "Hmm. Maybe if it were a complete sentence: *HE Usually LIVED With a Female.* If we go that route at all." And that's where we left it for a few days. I didn't care for Vivian's suggestion. But then I figured I would ask my deceased father himself what I should do. So I imagined this conversation:

"What about that new title, Pop? Give me your honest opinion."

"Will it sell easier that way, son?"

"Vivian says it will."

"I've always said that Vivi has the most brains of any Garrigues I know. And remember, son, the most important thing for a book is . . . to get read!" And he turned back to his typewriter.

I phoned Vivian and told her what Brick had said about the title.

"Good. But there's something else." Uh-oh, I thought.

I had to write an introduction, she said.

"When I'm browsing in a bookstore, if I find a book that entices me by the cover," she explained, "and it isn't a book by an author I've heard of, nor about anybody I'm familiar with, I turn to the introduction to see if this book will hold my interest. The intro will pique my curiosity (or not), and if I am in a buying mood, I'll buy it."

There would be a lot of reasons for a publisher to turn down the manuscript, she said — "ironically, none of them relating to the quality of the book" — so it's imperative to write a preface that would sum up the whole thing.

"So stew for a while, then write a knockout intro and let me see it."

So I did.

Part One
Narcissus

We start out, all of us,
to do magnificent things.

Chapter One
The Mysterious Letter

I held a mystery in my hand: two sheets of aged paper, browned by the passage of some seventy years, bits and pieces flaking off in my fingers, scattering on the carpet. "Star office" was typed and "August 1925" written at the top of the first page; the two sheets were covered with single-spaced lines: *"You were right. I was wrong. I was engaged in the furious pursuit of falling in love." "Let's begin at the apparent beginning — the Oracle trip and the dance."* The width of the paper told me it had been trimmed from the big sheets that in the first half of the past century were stacked in newspaper composing rooms for pulling proofs from the big metal page forms filled with type. The creases in the two typed pages told me that the paper had once been folded inside a very small envelope; the transparent mending tape that kept them from falling apart over the years indicated that this was a very special letter to the person who had received it.

The person who had received it: That was Fanny Strassman. I met her once when I stopped off in Manhattan on my way home from Europe. She was then an effervescent New York literary agent midway through her sixties. But that was some four decades after she had received the mysterious letter.

The person who wrote it: That was my father, or at any rate, the man who would become my father. He signed it: "Your playmate, Brick." That was his nickname; his legal name was Charles Harris Garrigues.

Star office

My dear Fanny,

You told me to write you a letter some time, didn't you? It may be overdoing it a bit to write after I've seen you twice today, but maybe if I do this, I can get you out of my thoughts.

You were right. I was wrong. I was engaged in the furious pursuit of falling in love, and didn't realize it until you caught me. So I plead guilty, and throw myself on the mercy of the court. And if the defendant may be permitted to introduce evidence of extenuating circumstances, I only ask that you take a long look at the business side of a mirror.

I didn't quite realize it even this evening, until I'd sat at my desk and pecked futilely at a typewriter all evening with my mind never off that scene I made yesterday afternoon. Finally what I was doing really hit me, and now it's all right. So I'll only have to thank you for doing what made me so angry, hurt, disappointed, call it what you will, yesterday. And you're a good scout for having done it.

It's a peculiar business, this falling in love. I hadn't done it for five years, and couldn't be expected to realize it. You forget all about your own ego, your own ideas; the whole universe is out of focus. You only want to do that which somebody wants you to do, or thinks she wants you to do, or you think she wants you to do. When all the time you mustn't do that at all. It's a form of youth that man should put off when he becomes of age, and I feel sure tonight that I won't have any inclination to do it again.

Since I'm doing this chiefly to get it out of my system, lets begin at the apparent beginning -- the Oracle trip and the dance.

There can be only three propositions. If the first two are incorrect, the third must be right. (Weininger says women cannot reason. We shall see.)

Proposition 1. -- Conceding that we are "playmates" and there can be no thought of jealousy between us, except insofar as one of us departs from this status and seeks to become something more. That I might do that and become jealous of you is conceivable, but that you might is impossible. We agree on that. Therefore, it could not have been your dislike of the thought of Dickie spending the day with me that caused the trouble. That, I believe, was one of your points, and that is clearly untenable.

Proposition 2. -- Conceding that we are "playmates," and further conceding that Dickie is the only sort of girl I'd go with, and again conceding that I'm perfectly honest with her, as I have been with you, there can be no thought of Dickie feeling badly if you went to Oracle.

Only Proposition 3 remains: The realization that I was falling in love with you with an accelerating velocity. Can you blame me that when I'd been stopped in this process and brought back to earth I was a bit stunned? It took me some time to get used to it -- first to the realization that I had fallen in love, and second to the conviction that I must fall out at once. So I wandered around dazed, and finally came down here to write stories backwards and things like that.

So that's over. Whatever hurt there is -- and love always hurts -- can be patched up overnight, and I'll be as good as ever in the morning. And I feel sure that if I ever find myself loving you again, I'll recognize the symptoms and quit -- cold. That's the only thing to do. Before I knew I mustn't, daren't love you, but I unconsciously wanted to. Now that I don't want to I'd like to come up this afternoon as we'd planned, partly to see you, partly to look at all the bad things there must be about you if I could only have seen them before, and partly to appease my vanity by letting you know that I'm not always so foolish as I have been -- even though I may be utterly inconsequential.

This is a hell of a letter -- typewriter, copy paper, and subject matter. To you, perhaps, who have not been affected by the catacclasm (or however you spell it) of the last two weeks, it probably seems foolish to waste so much time writing on a (to you) inconsequential subject. It was only a short time, and can't seem to matter very much. Yet I had started to rebuild myself -- all unconsciously -- according to your wishes; it was brief, but the most monumental thing that had happened to me in years. If I had a confidante to whom I could talk, I should not have troubled you with this, but I still feel that I can confide in you as I can to no one else, as I can hardly do so with myself. So you'll forgive me if I've taken your time with all this.

I'll see you, if I may, at two? And I can assure you I'll be my own self again, a self that doesn't fall in love, and which, if you don't like, you can lead ungently to the door. May I sign myself

Your playmate

Brick

But oh, lady, lady, how wonderful it would have been if I'd dared to love you as much as I wanted to.

"Oracle"? What was Oracle? Who was Weininger? I looked him up: Otto Weininger was an Austrian philosopher who wrote that all living things combined varying proportions of masculine and feminine elements. The masculine element was positive, productive, and moral, while the feminine was negative, unproductive and amoral. He shot himself to death at the age of twenty-three. That was a damned stupid philosopher to quote in a love letter written by a man who himself was only twenty-three years old.

"The Star office." Simple. Brick was a reporter just starting out on the *Arizona Daily Star,* one of the two daily newspapers published in Tucson, the capital of the thirteen-year-old state of Arizona.

"Dickie"? I knew *her,* all right. She was my mother; or at any rate, the woman who would become my mother.

Yet this letter, and perhaps a hundred others like it, posed some real questions. As I contemplated these brittle pages, I came to realize that I had to find the answers, to find the man behind the words: This man whom I had known for so many years, but had scarcely known at all. This comforter of small children. This wearer of hats and smoker of pipes. This reader and writer of books. This twentieth century man, this flawed man; my father, Charles Harris Garrigues. And so I went looking for him.

I sought him in a hot, dusty farming town just north of the Mexican border, and there I found his ghost. I found it also in the yellowed files of newspapers in old metal filing cases. I found it in the mind of a boy named Bliss Lane. But most of all I found it in the letters he wrote over a period of almost fifty years, back in the days when he wasn't a ghost at all, but was a living, breathing man with the passions and failures common to all of us. Sometimes I think of him as Everyman.

His letters: Fanny Strassman saved them, hundreds of them, including that first one, the mysterious one. My mother saved them. My brother and I saved them. The letters taught me a lot.

My father, Brick Garrigues, was a man who loved music and women and the ideas he discovered in books and the soft, flowing sound of his own voice. He was an opera reviewer and a jazz columnist. He was a grand jury investigator and a newspaper reporter. He was briefly a Communist and he was always a devoted father, but he deserted one wife and quarreled constantly with another. He believed in romantic love, and he believed in marriage, but he felt that the union of two minds could not be maintained within the confines of marriage. He wondered if love could last forever. Yet he was almost always in love, or just out of it. He spent his life searching for his Answer and thought he had found it but later realized he hadn't yet found his Truth.

That first letter to Fanny is as good a starting point as any for this book. Some of the mystery was easily unraveled: If I had been brought up in Arizona, instead of California, I would have known about Oracle. It was a health resort in the foothills of the Santa Clarita Mountains, thirty miles from Tucson, famed all over the nation for its beautiful scenery and moderate climate. Today it is the site of the experimental Biosphere 2.

The woman who would one day marry my father, Beulah May Dickey, was the "Dickie" referred to in that letter. Poorly nourished as a teenager, at age twenty she thought she was underweight (she weighed 105 pounds and stood five feet three), and she seemed to be running a permanent fever. A doctor diagnosed tuberculosis, wrongly, it turned out. She took a month off from her job as a secretary in a Tucson law firm and went to rest and eat and drink and breathe fresh air in one of the many low-priced accommodations that dotted the nearby mountain community. A little packet of letters from Brick, addressed to "Donnee's Tea Room, Oracle, Arizona," was part of my mother's treasures through her entire life.

While Dickie was away in Oracle, Brick was invited to a party. I found this newspaper clipping in an old scrapbook:

> A dinner-dance was given Saturday evening by Miss Dorothy Douglass honoring Mrs. Hugh Tuttle of Salt Lake City who recently came to Tucson to join Mr. Tuttle and make her home here. The Douglass house at 602 North Seventh avenue was attractively arranged for the evening, the tables being spread on the porch and decorated in pink and colored favors.
>
> Following the dinner the guests were taken to the outdoor dancing pavilions where they danced until late. Covers at the dinner tables were laid for Mr. and Mrs. Tuttle . . . Mrs. Gilbert Cosulich, Miss Fanny Strassman, . . . C. H. Garrigues [and twelve others].

That's where Brick met Fanny Strassman, and he asked her along on a drive to Oracle to visit Dickie and escape the summer heat.

                              July 29, 1925
Dear Dickie-girl,

    It's been lonesome up here, too, but not nearly as lonesome as it will be before that month is up. The car is not working well yet, and I may have to spend about fifty dollars on it before I can take it on a long trip.

    We made the trip back Sunday in good time and pulled into town about six o'clock. Then we picked up Bernice[1] and took the girls to the dance. Of course, I tried to neglect Bernice for Fanny, but didn't succeed very well. However, we had a good time. Last night I took Fanny out to the Blue Moon and tried to dance in the mob that was there. We ditched out about ten-thirty and sat in front of the house until two o'clock. I guess we would be sitting there yet if I hadn't insisted that she go in. She bawled me out thoroughly for taking her along to Oracle to play second fiddle to you, and I had a good time laughing at her. However, she is a good scout, and there's no chance of me going astray while you're gone if I stick around her.

---

[1] Bernice was the Mrs. Gilbert Cosulich mentioned above. She was twenty-nine years old and her absent husband was seven years older.

Fanny Strassman had come to Tucson for her health. This thirty-year-old, very attractive New York University graduate had visions of becoming a great dancer or actress on Broadway. She was fascinating to young Brick Garrigues, whose early life on the Kansas prairie and in the Imperial Valley had not prepared him for her big-city sophistication. And — she was Jewish. That fact startled him. He may have never known a Jew before. Her cosmopolitan flair enticed him as he danced with her or sat across from her in a Tucson drug store and shamelessly wooed her with his charm and good looks. She read books; she *owned* books. She lent him a copy of *Jean-Christophe,* by Romain Rolland. And later she gave him another book to keep — *Green Mansions* by W. H. Hudson, the strange love story of Rima, a mysterious creature of the forest, half bird and half human.

You see, Fanny's a pretty square shooter and insists that as long as I'm going with you, I can't play around seriously with anyone else. She likes you quite a bit, I think, although she didn't say so in as many words, and I really think she has an idea she'll sort of take me under her protecting wing and keep me from wandering around until you get back. More power to her.

I also have a date for next Sunday night with a big nurse from Pastime Park. She's a friend of Bernice, and Fanny is putting on an Italian dinner, so I'm supposed to bring the big one. Such is life. Also I saw Sally and Nell at the dance tonight -- the two girls I told you about meeting in Nogales. So you see I'd have plenty to occupy my time if I had any time.

All of them, though, don't keep me from being lonesome for you. I feel perfectly lost in the evening after dinner and sit around puffing on a cigarette wondering what to do with myself.

You see, as I've possibly intimated before, all the other girls (even Fanny) are the bunk as far as I'm concerned, and I simply can't become interested. Just as you said, it's probably better for me to step around a little more, but I don't get any particular kick out of it. Fanny is nice to talk to, not only about art and music and literature, but about life, for she's seen quite a bit of it, but when the evening is over I wish I had you in the car. I prophesy a terrible time for myself until you get back.

July 30, 1925

Dropped in to see Fanny tonight during my dinner hour, and we sat on the front porch and talked (I'm not telling you this to make you jealous, but so you'll know just what I'm doing with myself, and won't imagine I'm doing a lot of things I'm not). Anyway, we talked of love-making and things like that, and Fanny said I did very well for a

young boy -- from what she saw of you and me on Sunday. She
really knows I'm in love with you, and is a good listener
when I need somebody to tell how lonesome I am for a little
blonde who's going to weigh 135 pounds in the next month.
But every time I compare her with you, she seems the bunk
-- except just to talk to.

I think I've got an assignment to cover a fight in
Nogales a week from Sunday. It's to be a finish fight, and
we'll have to have a man there.

With this boxing match, Brick developed an interest in promoting
fights. He and a friend determined to put one on and make their fortune.

August 4, 1925

I put the car in the garage and will dig down into my
savings account to get it out some time this week. I'm
having all the insides taken out of the green bug and new
ones put in, so maybe it will work. At any rate, it should,
as it's setting me back eighty dollars. But that should put
it in good shape.

Ellinwood[2] took me down to Nogales with him Saturday
night, and I proceeded to mix drinks and get my feet
tangled up and everything. But we finally got back, and by
the time I had snatched a few hours' sleep, it was time to
go to Fanny's party. It was a hell of a party, and I felt
like the devil and had a perfectly rotten time, although I
did drink up a lot of fig wine. I was supposed to be with a
nurse from Pastime Park, but some way or another Ralph took
her away from me, and Dorothy Douglass took Bernice's soul-
mate away from her, and Fanny was with somebody else and I
had a hell of a time filling in with Fanny and Bernice and
Jane when they weren't otherwise occupied. Today Bernice
and Bob and Fanny and I had lunch, cleaning up what was
left of the dinner, and thus ended an imperfect weekend.

I've rather formed the habit of dropping in at Fanny's
house when I go home to dinner, and we sit on the front
porch and chat a while. She's a tremendously interesting
girl -- as you've no doubt heard me say before -- but a
peculiar one. The funny part of it is that the more I see
of her, the more I think of you. You have a lot that she
can never have, and I go home at night to hold you in my
arms again. You don't know how wonderful you are, honey; to
tell the truth, I didn't know it myself until I compared
you with other girls like Fanny.

August 5, 1925

I went up to look at the car today and found her
insides strewn all over the floor. They had to put in a lot
of junk and I guess they'll raise the ante on me when it
comes to write the check. It won't be out until Friday, so

---

2 Otherwise unidentified.

I won't know until I try it out whether I'll be able to
come up Sunday, but I'm practically sure I will.

I don't know whether I'll bring Fanny up with me or
not. She'd like to go up, but is afraid you wouldn't like
it, even if I parked her at the Wilson Ranch and got her
only after your bed-time. I told her you weren't inclined
that way, and that you stepped out on me all the time, but
she only shook her head.

But Brick had been wearing a different face for Fanny, one that the
young woman did not care to see on a twenty-three-year old would-be
lothario, no matter how charming. No, no, no, she insisted. You are
Dickie's man, not mine.

August 6, 1925

Fanny is not coming up with me Sunday; she and I had
quite a row this afternoon, and she gave me a decided pain.
She seemed to feel that I'd be cheating on you if I brought
her to Oracle, or cheating on her if I spent the day with
you; I haven't been able to figure out which. Since I've
never attempted to make love to the dear girl, I don't see
how she can figure either way, but I can't drive it into
her head. I don't care a darn whether she goes or not,
although I'd like to have somebody with me on the way there
and back. But if she thinks I'm going to cheat on you,
she's crazy, and if she thinks anything would be cheating
on her, she's crazier yet.

That's all I know that's happened, except that I fell
in love. I don't know just when it happened, but the girl
in question is a little blond who lives in Oracle this
month, and who becomes more adorable every day in the year.

And a wounded, confused Brick retreated to his office to puzzle over
his feelings. He ran a sheet of copy paper into his typewriter and poured
his heart out to Fanny in the mysterious letter that she then saved for
decades. Was he being unfaithful to Dickie, or merely being twenty-
three? I like to think the latter.

Fanny having put him in his place, Brick went back to Dickie with
full aplomb:

August 15, 1925

It doesn't look as though the fight would go over as
well as we expected -- more expenses, and all that sort of
thing. If we break even, I suppose we'll be lucky. But such
is life. And really, that's all I've been thinking about,
you and the fight. Oh, Fanny, of course, but she really
doesn't count. While she's interesting enough, she grows
less so while you grow more so. I still see quite a bit of
her, but you could stay away ten years and she'd never make
me forget you.

August 20, 1925

The car seems to be working all right again, and except for two eventualities, I'll be up there Sunday. If I lose more than fifty dollars on the fight, I'll have to hock my car to pay it. If I win more than a hundred and fifty, I may cut everything and spend a week on the Coast.

We really can't tell a thing about how it is going to come out until we get the people inside the gate. Sometimes I think we'll make good, and then again it looks as though we wouldn't have enough people to pay our license. That means I'll have to do something desperate to pay off the bills. It's been one worry after another, with fighters not showing up, and all other kinds of difficulties, but it will all be over in a couple of days now.

I lay down this afternoon and tried to rest a while, but picked up Fitzgerald's "The Great Gatsby" and couldn't put it down until I had finished it.

I saw your sister Mabel last night, and she reproved me severely for chasing around with Fanny. Your friends -- or perhaps my friends -- seem to care more about it than you do. But it will all be over when you come back, as you're worth 1,934 Fannys.

Three carloads of love,

Brick

Soon Dickie returned to Tucson from Oracle, her health improved. Fanny, her health worse, left Arizona for the even more rarefied atmosphere of Colorado, and for all Brick knew he would never see her again.

Chapter Two
Roots

I've never been much for ascribing traits of a living person to the influence of a distant ancestor, whose genes are so mixed with those of others that they lose any meaning, yet in looking for my father — and pondering on his longing to become a writer — I was drawn to the distant past. I caught a glimpse of him in the stubborn race of the French Huguenots. His family name was French, and it comes from *quercus,* the Latin word for *oak.* His family, Les Garrigues, fled religious persecution in southern France; they made their way to Philadelphia and became Quakers.

But I think I found more than a glimmer of him in eighteenth century Philadelphia, in a youth named James Ralph, who was perhaps Benjamin Franklin's best friend. It may have been Ralph who was responsible for a kind of artlessness — and restlessness — that was passed down to my father, and to my father's children, because Ralph was my father's grandfather-preceded-by-five-greats. Ralph and my father were much alike, from a tendency to read poetry to their women to a longing for immortality through their words in print.

The young James Ralph wanted to be a poet, not a merchant as all the important people were then in Philadelphia. I found these words in Franklin's *Autobiography:*

> Ralph was ingenious, genteel in his manners, and extremely eloquent;
> I think I never knew a prettier talker. Ralph was inclin'd to pursue the
> study of poetry, not doubting but he might become eminent in it, and make
> his fortune by it

He married young, too young, and when his friend Ben decided at the age of eighteen to go to London in 1724, James Ralph left behind his wife and little girl and went off with Franklin to England. It didn't take Ralph long to find romance.

> In our house there lodg'd a young woman, a milliner, who, I think, had a shop in the Cloisters. She had been genteelly bred, was sensible and lively, and of most pleasing conversation. Ralph read plays to her in the evenings, they grew intimate, she took another lodging, and he followed her.

The couple lived together for some time, but her sewing didn't earn enough to support them both, and her child by a previous lover, so Ralph went to teach at a boys' school in the country, where, oddly enough, he actually used the name "Benjamin Franklin" instead of his own, explaining to Franklin that when he became a famous poet he would not want anybody to know that he once had to engage in such undignified work as teaching.

> He continued to write frequently, sending me large specimens of an epic poem which he was then composing, and desiring my remarks and corrections. These I gave him from time to time, but endeavor'd rather to discourage his proceeding. All was in vain; sheets of the poem continued to come by every post.

While Ralph was away, Franklin took a new look at the milliner and tried to seduce her. She refused him, and when Ralph came back from the country, he, in effect, told his Pennsylvania chum to go to hell.

> Thus I spent about eighteen months in London. My friend Ralph had kept me poor; he owed me about twenty-seven pounds, which I was now never likely to receive; a great sum out of my small earnings! I lov'd him, notwithstanding, for he had many amiable qualities.

Franklin went home; Ralph stayed in England and in 1728 he published his poem, *Night,* which Alexander Pope ridiculed as mere howling. Decades later, when Franklin was in the Pennsylvania General Assembly, he returned to England and visited Ralph on his death bed. Franklin found that "he was esteem'd one of the best political writers in England" but his reputation was "indeed small as a poet, Pope having damned his poetry in the *Dunciad;* but his prose was thought as good as any man's."

In a library in Philadelphia I found the wife that Ralph left behind with a baby named Mary (she was either Hannah Ogden or her sister, Rebecca Ogden; the records differ). Mary grew up and married Samuel Garrigues, a grocer, who begat William, a carpentry inspector; who begat Samuel, a carpenter and farmer; who begat William, a constable; who begat Samuel Pierce, who was my father's grandfather.

My father remembered Samuel Pierce Garrigues only vaguely because the old man died in 1909 when Charles Harris was just seven, but he had been first a clerk and then a carpenter. He and his family moved to Indiana between 1854 and 1858, to a pretty little farming town called Rockville, which I once visited, and then, following the westward course of America's new empire, moved to Kansas in 1878, where they stopped being Quakers and became Methodists.

The land was there for the taking. But first the family had to dig sod from the prairie and make a lean-to house to shelter them from the bone-chilling winters and miserably hot summers. Afterward Samuel and his older boys built a real wooden house. Samuel became prosperous, and one day he was named a probate judge in Lane County. He was, in the eyes of his small agricultural community, an important man, and he remained that until the day he died, in February 1909.

Samuel and Ellen's third son was Charles Louis Garrigues, who married a German-American girl named Emily Young in 1890. I remember him when he was seventy or so, a tall man with white hair and a white mustache and bony knees (I know, because I sat upon them). In Kansas, Charles Louis was a farmer and Emily was a farmer's wife, and they produced five farmer's children — Samuel C., George William, Eleanor, Charles Harris and Jessie Patricia.

Charles Harris Garrigues, born July 7, 1902, was my father. His last name is pronounced "GAIR-uh-gus," and sometimes he spelled it Garrigus. Though his parents called him Harris, his friends knew him as Brick, for his red hair. And that's why this book, the result of my search, is *Brick's Book.*

Chapter Three
Imperial

While Charles Louis and Emily Garrigues were trying to raise wheat or corn or livestock in the parched fields of Kansas, a thousand miles away in Southern California a wealthy man named George Chaffey was buying up large flat pieces of land and dividing them into smaller flat pieces of land to sell to people from Kansas. He brought in water, too, from the Colorado River, and after tumbling through an aqueduct it gushed forth into the rich, untapped soil of a valley called Imperial. Crops sprang up as if by magic. Decades later my father wrote a book about that land, a novel called

Many a Glorious Morning
"They farm different here," Albert said musingly to Ruth in the hotel room in the little Southern California town where he took them the first night after his family got off the day coach. They'd traveled straight from Kansas to join him in what would be their new home. Ruth had had faith that Albert wouldn't fail them, that he would find a way to double their savings, maybe even triple them, as the land promoters had said. "I could've rented a place, but maybe we'd've lost money on it the first year until I learned California farming," her husband went on. "I thought it'd be better . . ." He stopped. He didn't want to talk more about the deal he had made to manage a ranch owned by somebody else.

It was the first time since they'd been married, some twenty years, that he'd worked for wages, and he felt that maybe he was taking a step

backward instead of forward, even if this was California instead of Kansas. But Ruth, flushed and excited at finally arriving in San Julian, gave his arm a squeeze and said: "I declare, Albert, if you aren't a one to look on the dark side of things! I think you did just splendid."

He was pleased at that, but something made him go on: "It isn't the place I'da picked, maybe, in some ways. I'm afraid they're a godless family, those O'Connells, besides being Roman Catholics. There's five grown boys who don't do a lick of work so they have hired hands do everything. And then I'm supposed to manage that place with . . ."

He looked at the children sprawled in sleep across the mattresses on the floor, Bliss, the youngest, just eight years old; Grace, who was ten, and Cal and Tom, young men they almost were, and he lowered his voice.

"There were beer bottles scattered all along the path! I'm almost afraid to bring up the children in such a place. . . ."

"The Lord will watch over them, Albert, if we trust in Him," she said. And then, as though still unbelieving, "And it's really got an inside . . . bathroom?"

He laughed at that and came over and put his arm around her. And the next day after a good night of rest they rented a livery stable buggy and drove out to the O'Connell ranch.

In some ways it was even worse than Albert Lane had feared. There were quarrels almost from the beginning. Mrs. O'Connell objected when the Lanes used a ranch team to drive to the Methodist Church on Sundays; she objected to their use of fuel from the farm woodpile and to Bliss's playing near the windows of her house; she found fault with the way the work was done and with the way the crops were handled. Albert Lane was almost cowed by the virulence of her tongue and the depth of her profanity, but nevertheless he swallowed hard and faced her down on every point. He was after all the manager, he kept telling himself.

At the end of the year, to his astonishment, she offered him an increase in wages if he would remain for another year, and, to his even greater astonishment, he accepted, though he'd vowed time after time that no power on earth could compel him to remain a single day after the year was up.

"I need a man who'll not let himself be put upon," she declared. "A man that'll stand up for his own self will stand up for his employer, in my way of thinking. So there'll be another ten dollars a month in it for you if you'll take the job for another year."

But hardly had Albert decided to stay when she entered into an even greater fraud, insisting (in the final settlement for the first year's work) that they must pay her twelve dollars a month rent for the house which they occupied and steadfastly refusing to hand out the full sum due them for the last quarter's work.

Albert Lane came back to the house white with anger.

"I wonder she doesn't fear that the Lord will strike her dead," he declared. "I'd fear to tempt God in that way."

He dug into his little box of papers and found the letter fixing the terms of the deal and read it over to see that it did indeed provide that the house should be rent-free and, after dinner, he went over and shook it in the face of Mrs. O'Connell and her eldest son and demanded his money in full. The old lady picked it up and spat upon it and suddenly seized her throat and cried out in a choked voice for a cup of water and fell forward on the carpet and died while her son screamed: "Mother! Mother!" in a hoarse and horrified voice.

That night, at family prayers, Albert read aloud the story of Ananias and Sapphire and asked God to save them from the lying and the cheating. Bliss lay awake for a long time on his cot on the side porch and saw the reflection of the candles burning beside the body of the dead woman in the big house across the yard; he was not old enough for death to be very terrifying, but he was impressed and uncomfortable and even frightened by the solemnity of his own family and the grief of the five O'Connell sons who wept and shouted by the bier.

The next day the eldest son came over and counted out 144 dollars in gold pieces and silver dollars; he counted them out on the table and then hurled them on the floor and ordered Albert Lane to clear out before sundown. Albert picked up the money and counted the coins again and wrote out a receipt, which he put behind the O'Connells' screen door, and then went into Edendale and rented the frame house on Euclid Avenue and moved his family that afternoon. They loaded their belongings into a borrowed lumber wagon and hauled them into town; Bliss and his brothers and sister — Cal and Tom and Grace — piled the things in the weedy yard and then carried them into the house while Mrs. Lane lit the kerosene stove and cooked supper.

Ruth Lane saw the hand of the Lord in it. "I always said He would clear the way if we had faith in Him," she told Grace as they bustled about the new kitchen. "Maybe some people would have lost faith in Him all these years, but I never doubted Him for a minute."

"But, Mama," Grace objected. "Do you think God would strike Mrs. O'Connell dead just to make Papa bring us into Edendale to live?"

"The Lord's ways are His own," Ruth Lane declared firmly. "Mrs. O'Connell was a wicked woman and deserved whatever she got."

For that was the way it had happened.

My father's manuscript was, of course, autobiographical, as first novels are. The Lanes were the Garrigueses; Bliss was Harris; Cal and Tom were George and Sam; and Grace was Eleanor. There was no Jessie Patricia; Harris's little sister, so inseparable from him when they were little children, died of tuberculosis when she was sixteen, leaving a curious hole in his life. Harris Garrigues went through grammar school in San Diego County, where his family lived on a farm named Hillsdale. Bliss Lane's grade school was in a town Brick called Edendale. And there Bliss met Forrest Bingham, whom all the kids called "the Stinker."

Salt Pork Sandwiches

It was the first time Bliss had had a friend, and he thought it was wonderful to have one who knew so much and was always for you and never tried to put you in the wrong. Every day after school they went up to Forrest's house or sometimes sneaked down to the railroad tracks and watched the trains go by. They put little bits of wire on the tracks and then ran to see how the wheels had flattened them after the freight cars had passed. There were not many things to do in town like there had been in the country, but when he was with Forrest, even the dull things seemed interesting.

One day, instead of going up to the Binghams', Bliss took the Stinker home with him. There weren't any cookies, but Mama gave them each a sandwich of homemade bread with slices of fried salt pork in between, and they went into the woody backyard and sat with their backs against the wooden fence. Forrest said with the relish he seemed to feel for every experience: "Gee, I never knew anybody that was poor before. I guess it would be tough, huh, to live in a shack like yours."

It took a minute for the words to sink in. Bliss had never thought of himself — had never thought of the Lanes — as being poor. They were neither poor nor rich; they were just the Lanes. They were the people over whose heads the sun shone and around whom the horizon was drawn and to whom all other people were, if not subordinate, then at least secondary. And now, suddenly, he knew.

"We're not poor," he declared after a minute. "Dad's got lots and lots of money. I guess we could live in a house as big as yours if we wanted to."

"Why don't you, then?" the Stinker demanded. "What you live in a shack for, huh? Whyn't you live in a regular house with a lawn and trees outside and carpets inside? Whyn't you, huh?"

"'Cause," Bliss said stubbornly. "'Cause we don't want to." And then inspiration came to him. "We're saving our money to buy a great big ranch with orange trees and a big house and a windmill and a fence around it and a gate so nobody can come in unless we want them to. What do we care what sort of old house we live in until Pop gets around to buying this place, huh?"

The Stinker looked at him with the look one has just before he says,

"Bushwah." But he didn't say "Bushwah." He didn't say anything. He closed his mouth and looked away, and a minute later started talking about something else.

Bliss Lane enrolled in El Jardin High School at the age of thirteen in 1914, and Harris Garrigues, brought with his family from the soft, temperate hills of San Diego to the desert-like climate of the Imperial Valley, enrolled in Imperial High School at the age of twelve the same year.

Ivanhoe Was Beautiful

English and History were even better than friendship. Here was the real world he'd always known about, and if his teachers weren't quite in it (sometimes he thought they were, and sometimes he was not sure), they at least knew about it and could help him find his way into it. He could go into the school library and pull out books and take them home or even go into the Carnegie Public Library downtown and take books out on a card. So that, with so much to read and so much to learn, there was scarcely even time to do his chores at home, let alone explore the mysteries of the town itself or to go to football games on a Saturday afternoon.

There were lots of girls, and they would smile friendly at him from across the aisle. Sometimes instead of studying, he'd sit and watch Maxine Ames, who sat across from him; he would look at the fine down on her arms and wonder what it was that made some girls so pretty and what was the thing he liked best about a girl, whether it was her hair or her eyes or the way she smiled, or even the shape of her arms or hands.

The Ames girls lived over in Fireside, and their father gave them a horse and buggy to drive to school. Bliss thought that Maxine, who was tall and had dark hair and dark eyes, was the prettiest girl he had ever seen. When Christmas time came he was surprised to get a card from her; it was the first Christmas card he had ever got from anybody, and he went about for a week in an agony of embarrassment because he had not thought to send her one. When school took up again he hardly dared to look at her, but when they came face to face coming out of class, he managed to blurt out, "Thank you for the Christmas card," and she gave him a big smile.

That night when he and his friend Ebert were walking home from school, scuffing up the dusty road with their shoes, the Ames girls came along in their buggy, and Maxine said, not bold or challenging like some girls would be, but sweet and friendly, "Want a lift?" So he and Ebert climbed up and stood on the rear of the buggy, and first thing you knew they were talking like all get-out. Maxine was interested in writing, too; she thought Ivanhoe *was beautiful and so was* Idylls of the King, *even though there were some parts in it she didn't understand. When they got to his crossroads and Bliss dropped off the buggy, she turned around and smiled and said, "See you here in the morning, Bliss."*

I looked up from the manuscript. Had this sort of life really existed? If bringing my father to life meant more than paging through his papers, then . . . I found a map of California, unfolded it and stared at a dot labeled "Imperial," in the middle of what had once been called the Mohave Desert. The next morning, I got up about five and drove the two hundred miles from Los Angeles to Imperial, to what was almost another world, a hot, singularly unattractive agricultural town with just a few old buildings on a deserted main road. But on a side street I saw a solid, squat building of that turn-of-the-century style associated with the libraries founded by industrialist Andrew Carnegie.

Imperial High School wasn't hard to find. I parked on the street in front of the low-lying, rambling structure of indeterminate, generic, school-campus architecture. There I met Gerardo G. Roman, the assistant principal, who showed me the vault that housed the school yearbooks of my father's time. I sat down to examine them, and as the students hastened by outside the office, hurrying forward toward their lives in the twenty-first century, I looked at the black-and-white images in the yearbooks of a Wilsonian age and saw ghosts.

My father, a farmer's son in a farm community, joined the Hog Club and helped raise a sow; then he wrote about it for the yearbook, in what may have been his first published article. But he was also the grandson of a justice of the peace: He was in the Iolian Literary Society, acted in a school play, was on the debate squad. In his junior year, fall 1916, he played football.

In casual conversation when I was a child, I had learned that he later quit the football squad because one of his best friends had been killed in a game (it was a rough sport then, with little in the way of protective gear). I forgot about it until I saw an ancient plaque at Imperial High School that paid tribute to "Ephraim Grant Angell," who had died in a football game on November 21, 1916. It was almost a physical shock when I realized that a distant, shadowy, casually mentioned event had suddenly become real in the form of a name etched in metal on a high school wall. And I knew, too, that my father had paid his respects to his friend and teammate, young Angell, by using him as a character in his novel, not as a football player but as a runner.

Dick Angell's Victory

Dick was a little guy with blond hair and blue eyes and a baby face. They called him Angel, not Angell, because he looked like one. He went out for everything and didn't make any teams except the track team, where Coach Clark let him run the mile because they needed some milers. The mile was the last event, and El Jardin was behind Bostonia, so that if Angel could win five points for first it meant victory in the meet. They were ten points ahead of Hillside. If Hillside's miler took first place and

El Jardin second and Bostonia third, it still meant victory. But everybody knew that Dick Angell couldn't possibly place better than third, and by the time the race started everybody was getting ready to go home because it didn't seem worthwhile to stay and watch the slaughter.

But then somebody let out a yell, and those who were leaving turned to look. Bostonia's lone entry had pulled a tendon on the first turn and dropped out. His coach yelled at him to stay in and hobble around because he might get the one point which they'd need to win, but once you're out of the lanes you can't go back; the El Jardin rooters took heart and started yelling, "Go it, Dick! Go it, kid!" and Dick Angell looked around, saw what happened and tried to stretch out his short legs into the miler's stride.

Near the end of the half he threw a shoe. They weren't running on cinders; they were running on dirt, and his spiked shoe caught in a lump of clay and went sailing over his head into the infield. He hesitated a second as though to retrieve it, then realized he couldn't and kept on running with just one shoe. The kids knew what it was to try to walk across a field with bare tender feet; they knew how it was when you started out barefoot in summer after a winter of wearing shoes. They started to yell and the noise grew; Dick dug in and kept going — by the time he came around in front of the bleachers again, his sock was torn off, and his foot was raw and bleeding, and Coach Clark sent in Neil Wiley, the track captain, to pull him out.

Neil ran alongside him for a while and then dropped out and shook his head at the coach, and Clark dashed across the infield and tried to stop Angell; he started to move right in and pick him up and carry him off the track, but at the look on Dick's face the coach, too, stopped and he called to Wiley, "Pace him in, kid."

So Wiley dropped in beside Angel, running in the infield but close enough so Angel could watch his feet and guide his own pace with them and know that he was not alone but that all he had to do was keep putting one foot in front of another and he would get there. Wiley said afterward that he could hardly stand it; Dick's foot was like a big chunk of raw hamburger that left a gob of blood every time he put it down.

The crowd was screaming; half, mostly the girls, were calling for the coach to go out and stop it, and the other half, mostly the boys, were yelling for Dick to win. And the strange part was that he was winning, not first, of course, because the Hillside man came in with first place, but second, which was what El Jardin had to have to win the meet. Somehow he kept ahead of the man from San Benito, who was the only other one left in the race, and when little Dick Angell ran across the finish line and into Coach Clark's arms, El Jardin had won another championship.

Nobody had cried when they lost the football championship to Bostonia. But most of the girls, and, yes, even some of the boys, were crying when they carried Dick Angell off the track and down to the hospital. They followed the car in which Coach Clark was holding Angel on his lap, and they cheered and let the tears run down their faces unashamed.

Nobody saw Bliss Lane start for home, still wearing his track shorts, and turn off the road and go over behind the big Bull Durham sign and throw himself down in the dried weeds. He lay there for a long time, with his shoulders shaking and the tears running off his face and into the caked dirt.

After a long time the sun was setting and he felt cold; he got up and went home. Nobody noticed the marks of tears on his face, and he never told anybody about that, not even his best friend in high school, Bob Reynolds. The nearest he ever came to it was once, when he said to Bob, "Sure, kid, did you ever notice how it's the big shots that let the school down, and a little squirt like Angel comes along and really measures up?"

That was the way his athletic career ended.

Naturally, it didn't happen just the way my father wrote it, anyway not to "Dick Angell." The hero was actually another student. I found him in the Imperial High School yearbook, *The Oasis,* for 1916: "The 'grittiest' race of the day was run by Marion Osburn in the mile. He ran nearly three laps after losing one shoe and 'downed' third place; his foot was torn and bleeding when he finished."

I left the high school and drove past the ornate old library to the Pioneers' Museum of Imperial Valley, a surprisingly imposing structure, quite modern, where the farmers of the Valley had placed their memories, and there in the bound volumes of the weekly newspaper, the *Imperial Enterprise,* I read about the political strife that had roiled the surface of this little agricultural community in 1918. That was when the 38-year-old principal, Myron B. Hockenberry, left Imperial High School behind him and moved on to a different job elsewhere. A newly elected school board then appointed one J. J. Morgan to take his place. (I discovered that the men of that era preferred to use their initials in place of their full names.) But, wait! Some of the town's parents thought the school was run better under the old regime; they wanted Hockenberry back at the helm. Nothing doing, retorted one correspondent in the letters column:

Imperial Enterprise, May 7, 1918. **MR. EDITOR:** Rumor is current that a sly move is to be made to reinstate Mr. Hockenberry in the schools of Imperial. It is to be hoped there is no foundation for the rumor.

Mr. Hockenberry served a sufficiently long term among us, and changes in the school board had to be made at election time by conservative citizens who had had enough of him who allowed the moral level of our high school to lower several notches from the condition in which he found it.

At the election resulting in the discharge of Mr. Hockenberry, everyone knew the issue, it having been freely discussed previously, and the results expressed the desire of the people. To bring him back at this time will only result in injury to the schools.

The writer saw him in action many times. One time in particular at a ball game, Mr. Hockenberry bawled out a command to the ball players, seven different times, and each time was very insolently disregarded. Many other incidents are known to his discredit, among them his system of credit markings, his way of getting state attendance credits and his marked failure in discipline. *Respectfully, W. A. Edgar*

When he read the letter, Harris Garrigues, who was only fifteen at the time, was aghast. So the next week the *Imperial Enterprise* letters column carried a retort:

May 15, 1918. **MR. EDITOR:** The *Enterprise* for May 7 contained an article by W. A. Edgar. It is almost unbelievable that an Imperial business man could be so ignorant or so let his prejudices blind him to facts as to be responsible for so base an attack upon one who by reason of his absence cannot meet the attack.

Mr. Hockenberry left Imperial High School more loved and respected by the students than any man in Imperial. It is for this reason that the students who went to school under Mr. Hockenberry wish to set right the false impression given by Mr. Edgar.

One of the false impressions is the reference to the "discharge" of Mr. Hockenberry. Contrary to Mr. Edgar's statement, Mr. Hockenberry was offered the school for another year. He declined because he could get more money elsewhere.

Mr. Edgar states that Hockenberry left the moral standard of the school lower than when he came. If this statement had been true, it would have been no reflection on Mr. Hockenberry. When Mr. Hockenberry came, the town was dry; when he left, he left a wet town. Naturally it is harder to keep a high moral standard in a wet town than it is in a dry one.

But the standard of the school under Mr. Hockenberry was fully as high as it was before Mr. Hockenberry came or after he left. Under Mr. Hockenberry, a rule was in effect that no one could participate in any interscholastic contest who had not first signed a pledge to abstain from the use of alcohol and tobacco. Under Mr. Morgan this rule has not been enforced, and there have been cases this year when players were late because they wanted to have a smoke before they came to the game. Does this look as though the moral tone of the school was so low under Mr. Hockenberry?

Mr. Edgar mentions several vague "incidents," which he says are to Mr. Hockenberry's discredit and which can be proved. Mr. Edgar is at fault in not bringing them up. But the people of the district want some proofs. They are not willing to accept these statements upon Mr. Edgar's or anyone else's say-so.

Mr. Edgar has shown nothing to the discredit of Mr. Hockenberry. Why, then, is he so opposed to him? At any rate, the people of Imperial will do well to condemn no man with Mr. Hockenberry's record without more proof than the vague statements made by Mr. Edgar. *Respectfully, C. H. Garrigues*

Two days later, the School Board met, and —

MINUTES

Imperial, California, May 15, 1918

The Board of Trustees of the Imperial Valley Union High School District especially convened at the office of the clerk, Mr. J. Roy Adams, at 7:30 P.M. on the day and date first above written, with all members present.

A notice of the suspension of Mr. C. H. Garrigues and signed by the entire faculty was taken under consideration. The reasons given for the suspension of Mr. Garrigues were: Continued insubordination, culminating in certain improper criticisms made over his signature through the columns of the Imperial Evening Enterprise.

The faculty recommended the expulsion of Mr. Garrigues for the balance of the school year.

After a careful consideration of the facts presented, the following resolutions were adopted and a copy ordered handed to Principal J. J. Morgan:

"Whereas, C. H. Garrigues has been suspended by the Faculty of Imperial High School and

"Whereas, the matter of expulsion or re-instatement has come before the Board of Trustees for action, therefore, Be It Resolved: that, after said C. H. Garrigues has made a public apology to the faculty before the student body, he shall be re-instated, and be it

"Further Resolved: that said C. H. Garrigues shall be reprimanded by the Board of Trustees.

"Moved by I. J. Harris, Seconded by D. D. Hairn, and carried unanimously."

But Harris Garrigues discovered that he had made some real friends at Imperial:

May 21, 1918. WALK-OUT OF HIGH SCHOOL STUDENTS: The high school students, with the exception of some fifteen or twenty, walked out of the assembly room at 1:30 this afternoon and paraded the streets to demonstrate their dissatisfaction at the refusal of the faculty to reinstate C. H. Garrigues of the senior class, who had been suspended after a communication from him on school matters, which appeared May 13.

The Board of Education at a meeting last night voted to request that Garrigues, after meeting certain conditions, be allowed to graduate, but it seems that Garrigues failed to meet the conditions. He was given an opportunity this morning to make apology before the assembly. The apology, however, was not satisfactory to the faculty and Garrigues was not reinstated.

The students sent a committee to one of the trustees, who advised them to return to school. Prof. J. J. Morgan, the principal, had also sent word by John Robinson, president of the student body, for the boys and girls to return at once. The advice and invitation was acted upon immediately, and the students were admitted to the assembly room for the afternoon period, no classes being called.

It was reported late this afternoon that a meeting would be held tonight between the Board of Education, the faculty and a committee of the students.

May 21, 1918. EDITORIAL COMMENT: Imperial has the best high school in the Valley and has always had the best behaved student body. And whoever is to blame for the unseemly row now going on in school should be ashamed of themselves. If this sort of thing is to continue, the town had better go back to the saloon in order that the irreconcilables who live here can have something to fight. Better have saloons to fight than wreck our school system for lack of something better to do.

MINUTES

Imperial, California, May 21, 1918

A special meeting of the Board of Trustees and the Faculty of the Imperial Valley High School was called at 8 P.M. at the place and on the date first above written, with all members of both bodies present.

Principal Morgan stated that, following the resolution placed in its hands by Mr. J. Roy Adams, clerk of the Board, he immediately went over to the High School and found that Mr. Garrigues, without waiting for any directions from the office and with only such members of the faculty present as happened to be in the Assembly Room at the opening of the morning session, had come before the student body and made a semi apology for his action, stating that he was sorry the faculty were unable to understand his intentions in writing the article.

Mr. Morgan stated that he further questioned the young man as to his attitude towards school matters, and received the emphatic reply that it was absolutely unchanged.

This being the case, the matter was referred to the Board with the suggestion that, if the Board desired to reinstate Mr. Garrigues without an apology, he would be taken back and given his diploma, provided he completed his work in a satisfactory manner.

On motion of Mr. C. W. Watts, seconded by Mr. I. J. Harris, the resolution passed by the Board at the meeting of May 20, 1918, was rescinded, and it was ordered that Mr. Garrigues be expelled from the High School. The motion carried unanimously.

On motion, it was ordered that the Board adjourn until 1 P.M. May 22, 1918.

May 21, 1918. To MEMBERS OF THE ALUMNI: I agree that it were better if Mr. Hockenberry were here to speak for himself, and had it not been for a suggestion that he would be considered for return, I would have said nothing. I am willing to drop the matter unless the alumni or the people wish to know some more about matters, when I may feel called upon to answer. *Yours respectfully, W. A. Edgar*

Mr. Edgar may have recanted, but C. H. Garrigues remained out of school, and he was barred from graduating with his class. He had to repeat his senior year, but his nemesis, Principal Morgan, had already resigned, and the new principal, C. B. Collins, called young Harris in one day and said he didn't really have to come back to school because he had already passed his courses, but he would have to wait until the next spring to get his diploma. In the meantime, Harris was befriended by the editor of the *Enterprise,* who gave him a job as a reporter, taught him the newspaper business and left the sixteen-year-old lad in charge of the paper when he wanted to go out of town. It was an apprenticeship of the old stripe.

I read on in the bound volumes that had been so lovingly tended, and I discovered:

How My Uncle Died

July 9, 1918. LETTERS FROM OUR BOYS. Dear Mrs. Garrigues: Some few days ago I wrote you about your son, Samuel C. Garrigues, and told you that he was ill in the hospital here. Today I must write and tell you that he has died, and that we buried him in City Cemetery this morning.

I know that you will be saddened by this news, and yet, for his sake, I am sure it is better. He had tuberculosis and was so far advanced that nothing could be done for him, so it was better for him to go without having to suffer so long, as many do with that disease.

I am sure if you could see where he lies — beside the graves of a number of his companions — you would be satisfied. I do not know what disposition will be made of these bodies after the war is over, but I do know this, that if they are left here, the good women of Winchester have already started a movement to decorate their graves on our Decoration Day. The grass will have the best of care. I am sure that this will be comforting for you to know. *Yours in sympathy, J. W. Barnett, American YMCA., Winchester, England.*

What My Father and His Friends Did for Kicks

July 18, 1918. IMPERIAL YOUNG PEOPLE VISITORS AT PLUNGE IN HOLTVILLE. A dozen Imperial young people motored to Holtville last night to enjoy the plunge. On their way home, they became thirsty and stopped at Mr. Seeley's store near the Jacobson ranch for refreshments, which consisted of home-made pop and ginger cookies. It was near midnight when Mr. Seeley was aroused from his slumbers to wait on his thirsty customers.

"Mr. Seeley used to be in the pop business," one of the party reported this morning, "and surely has concocted a peculiar brand, which has all the other makes backed off the map."

The party consisted of Messrs. C. H. Garrigues, W. A. McCall, J. B. Cheatham, Oran Cosand, Benjamin Westmoreland and Thomas and Homer McClannahan; and the Misses Dorothy and Carrie Osburn, Jessie Cox, Willa Mae and Ola Drake.

When My Grandpa Fell Upon Hard Times

July 18, 1918. MESQUITE LAKE RANCHER IS THROUGH FARMING FOR A WHILE: "I'm through farming for this year," declared C. L. Garrigues, Mesquite Lake rancher, while trading here this morning. "I've got about everything in that I am going to plant. So I've decided to lay off and give the horses a rest, as they have been working continually since last September.

"Of course," Mr. Garrigues added, "I'm not going on a vacation or anything like that. I expect to work for the county."

Why the Glee Club Sang in the Dark

May 29, 1919. COMMENCEMENT ORATOR: State Board of Education member Stanley B. Wilson last night probably had an experience which he has not had before and never will have again. Just as Mr. Waite, after presenting the diplomas, had introduced Mr. Wilson as the speaker of the evening, the electric lights winked, warning that they were about to take a vacation, and before Mr. Wilson could get to his feet, they were gone. The large audience had suddenly disappeared from his vision.

By the aid of a flashlight, the Boys' Glee Club, nine in number, sang Longfellow's "Excelsior," set to music by Nevin. The opening line just fitted the occasion, for it announced that "The shades of night were falling fast."

When the singers had responded to the encore with a delightful number and while the audience was applauding, the lights sprang on with full force.

Professor Collins re-introduced Mr. Wilson, who delivered an eloquent address on "Lessons from the War." He declared that the war had pounded sense of various kinds into our heads, in fact, having served as a great school in which we were taught a number of lessons. These he enumerated as a lesson in history, a lesson in democracy and a lesson in brotherhood. Throughout his discourse, Mr. Wilson told many humorous stories, some of which, especially the Scotch dialect, were inimitable, and quoted dramatically from a number of inspirational poems.

"The object of this commencement," he declared in his peroration, "is to waken these young people up to the great purpose of life."

Chapter Four
Westward

Camp County, Texas. 1879. A dying woman lies on the floor. A four-year-old girl, tiny for her age, brings the woman a drink of water. She drinks it carefully, with one side of her mouth. "Go to sleep," a man's gruff voice tells the little girl.

"No, I don't want to."

"Go to sleep."

"Don't spank my baby," the dying woman says.

Ghosts, now. Real, then.

The little girl, left orphaned, was my mother's mother, Ella Gertrude Eskridge. She told her life story, all she could recall, to my mother when Ella was seventy-eight years old.

"That is all I can remember about my mother," Ella said to her middle daughter, Beulah, who took the words down in shorthand.

"After she died, there was just a half-uncle and his wife. She didn't like me. Just because I was better than her, or so she thought. She would tell me she was going to give me away to niggers."

Another family, the Burgesses, took her. Kept her until she finished the eighth grade.

"I worked in the field, I got up at four in the morning. Made a fire in the cook stove, helped get breakfast. I fed the hogs. It was a small farm but enough to have a hired hand. I would stay out of school to help with the washing."

She didn't go to high school but "worked out" for two families as a mother's helper. That lasted two years. "I had to wash, help cook, but I did not work in the field. And I helped the woman take care of the baby."

Hardly any boys asked her to parties or buggy rides or to see a show.

"You wasn't very well thought of if you was 'working out,' no way."

But everybody was welcomed at the square dances, so Ella didn't need a boy to escort her.

"Mister Dickey was the fiddler at one of them. He asked me to dance. And good-looking! I didn't know whether I fell in love with him then. I did know that he had nine kids!"

My grandmother was nineteen at the time, dainty, only five feet tall. My grandfather, William Bascomb Dickey, was thirty-four years old. His wife had recently died.

"We went together about six months. He would take me to dances and house parties. He asked me to marry him. He told me he wanted a housekeeper. I was just a young girl and wanted a home of my own and somebody to take care of me. In fact, I think I never did love that fellow.

"We just went to a justice of the peace and got married. For the honeymoon we went to his house where there was nine children. There was two big rooms, two side rooms, and he built on a new room. We lived there a year."

Three of the boys soon left home. So there were only six kids remaining for little Ella to take care of.

"My own children was first Florence, then a miscarriage, then Eaph. After Eaph we traveled in a covered wagon for a year or two."

My grandfather didn't have a regular job at that time.

"He would get a day's work," Ella said. "It didn't take much those days. Just bacon and eggs on a day's road." Sometimes she used the expressions of her girlhood as she thought about the past.

"We crossed the Arkansas River one time, drove the wagon and team across that river into Arkansas. We stayed all night and drove back, and that bridge could have went down any old time. We just taken a chance. Back and forth, and all in one day. And he did it just to be a daredevil!"

Next came Jesse Bryan, born in 1899, three years after William Jennings Bryan made his "Cross of Gold" speech and ran for president. Mabel was born in 1902.

Ella loved to play with her children.

"We would play set-the-table. We would take broken glass, put them on a board and play setting the table."

Soon William Bascomb Dickey began buying and selling land. He had some property in Guymon, Oklahoma, and made a dugout for shelter.

"Kitchen, dining room, sleeping room, all in one. Built-in bunks. Used raw lumber. Still had bark and was full of chinches that would get you at night. The biggest day's work was shaking the bedclothes to get rid of the chinches."[1]

On April 27, 1905, Beulah May Dickey was born in the dugout in Guymon.

"There was a buggy for you; we was prosperous then," the tiny, white-haired, blue-veined Ella told Beulah almost half a century later. "It cost twelve dollars. I bought some yarn, nice yarn, and hired somebody to make sweaters; she crocheted them. I would push the buggy, walk with the buggy with you in it, and I was very proud. You was skinny and pretty and had blonde hair."

In 1908 the family moved to Willcox, Arizona. They lived in an old church-and-schoolhouse, with blackboards in some of the rooms, even the kitchen. The air stank from the outhouse. Flies swarmed. Two more boys were born, Harold and Hubert.

In the winter of 1911 Ella's husband went to prison.

"Swindled the government. He wrote us letters with cartoons, lots of funny faces."

After he was released, two more children came, Vesta Vae (1912) and Woodrow Wilson (1916). Then, in 1920, Ella obtained the first divorce ever to be entered in the records of the Dickey family all the way back to Ireland and beyond. William Bascomb Dickey then married a younger woman and fathered even more children.

[From Beulah to her
sister;February 1967]

Dear Florence:

I enjoyed your letter, and yes, I do remember Merrill Windsor. He lived diagonally from us at the old schoolhouse (I guess we were never so poor as when we lived in that shack, were we?) That is the place you escaped from by marrying.

The reason I remember Merrill was the fact that he had books -- BOOKS! which we didn't -- and I would borrow from him. He was a pale-faced, squared-jawed youngster with dark hair. He wore suits! Knee pants with jacket. And was truly the minister's son. I was seven, possibly eight.

I borrowed "Pilgrim's Progress," couldn't understand a word of it, but read it avidly and even out loud to you. I mispronounced the word "fatigue," called it "fatty gew," and you really laughed at me. I was chagrined because I thought I read very well at the age of seven, but ever since then I have been very careful to know the pronunciation of words.

When I was seventeen, we lived at Gadsden, Arizona, which was a few miles from Yuma, where I went to school.

---

[1] Bedbugs, from the Spanish.

One morning I missed the bus, so I decided to go visit the
grammar school, where Vesta and the little boys, Woody,
Harold and Hubert went. I visited Vesta's class -- she was
about ten -- she was called upon to read, and she stood up
and read beautifully, only mispronouncing the word
"epidermis." I was so proud of her -- her little, round,
freckled face. I can still remember she had forgotten to
button the tail of the little chemise to her home-made
dress, so it was dangling merrily. I got her to button it
at recess.

I saw my two little brothers in overalls -- with more
snot and filth wiped down the bibs than you can ever
conceive of. At that age I knew everything was wrong -- but
then there were a lot of other poor people in that town,
too, and I couldn't do anything about being poor.

My health was not nearly what it should have been. On
this particular visit I tried to play basketball with the
eighth-graders and became puffed and pained in my chest.
It's not good for children to be without food! The flour
gravy and fried potatoes tasted pretty good when we had
dinner at night, but going without breakfast and lunch --
and trying to enter into sports along with studies -- was
just too much for a young growing body.

I said above that the "church" building we lived in
was about the poorest we ever were, but I'll take that back
and say that the shack we lived in at Gadsden was about the
worst, and I guess Eaph figured that things had to get
better, and that's when he loaded a truck up with our few
belongings early one evening, and we took off and hid out a
few miles from Yuma, until the manager of the grocery store
where we owed money alerted the cops, who found us.

I had told my boyfriend, Bryan, of our plans, and we
spent the evening in the soft light and warmth of the
campfire, kissing and declaring our "love." That's when the
process servers or deputy sheriffs or whatever found us --
I was too inexperienced at age seventeen to know which or
to care, except I knew Eaph was in trouble -- but he parted
with most of his money to pay the grocery bill, and we
started off, California bound!

We started out the next morning -- I had begun to
menstruate and was suffering, so I spent most of the time
in the truck bed on a mattress. Everybody had to push to
get the truck started, but I was excused -- made me feel
guilty, too, with poor Mama out there doing her damnedest.

We crossed the Colorado River, and now we were in California. In the evening we came to the old board road through
the desert. A terrific sandstorm came up. The sand was so
thick we couldn't see anything, and it was worse on driver
Eaph, as the road was only a little over a car's width. He
managed to creep to a siding and pull over and stop.

There we spent the night, trying not to inhale too
much sand. The tarpaulin of the truck was tucked over us
like a covered wagon, keeping most of the sand out. We were
all huddled together -- and we slept, as we were young, but
I can't say how Mom fared, though she seemed to me like the
Rock of Gibraltar.

When we woke, the storm had died, the sun was out, and
I have never seen before or since such a beautiful sight!
On that lovely desert I had the most wonderful sense of
well being that I have every experienced. The white,
rolling hills rippled with the bright sunshine on the crest
of the mounds and the faint shadows in the hollows.

I had spent my whole life in Arizona, among barren
land, mesquite and cactus, so I had another sight for my
young eyes. The little old Ford truck puffed and puffed up
inclines and hills, but when we got to the top and looked
down, what wonders to eyes that had never seen trees,
foliage, flowers! We stopped the truck and took in the
beautiful sight! The kids whooped and hollered and ran
around in circles. All I could do was look! Greenery for
miles and miles. Gee, we all felt good. Even our stern,
eldest brother, who was head of the caravan, was impressed.
Our little mom knew that better days were ahead.

We coasted down the winding road, trees on one side
and frightening cliffs on the other but carpeted with the
tops of green trees, until we came to a stream. A stream? A
brook! Such as we had read about in our poetry books at
school but had never seen. Oh, what bliss! We made camp,
right beside the water, and with the campfire and the
trilling of the stream, it was a night to be remembered.

Eaph went ahead to rent a house in San Jacinto, a little town some
twenty-five miles southeast of Riverside. It was the nicest home they had
ever lived in:

We'd never seen a peach or an apricot tree in bloom,
or a cherry tree, and the blossoms were profuse. The lawn,
although grown over, was worth scampering on, and even I
"rassled" with the little ones and wallowed in the grass.
We explored each room. We had never before been in a
furnished house and looked with awe on the platform rocker,
real dining room chairs and table instead of benches and a
refectory, china dishes instead of tin and even glasses
instead of mugs. Carpets, not bare floors, even in the two
bedrooms and the living room. Such luxury we had never
known! The dinner that night, while simple, was a real
feast -- with the electric globe glowing in the center of
the room instead of a coal-oil lamp and a real tablecloth
left on the table, not the oil cloth we were used to.

We settled into the place as if we had been there
forever. All the children enrolled in their schools, and

good schools they were, too. Tough, as I found out. I slid
by as a senior in high school, and I thought I had been
doing OK in chemistry until the teacher gave me a 3, which
was pretty low (1 was the highest), and Spanish -- which I
thought I knew something about -- was so advanced I could
hardly keep up. I graduated, though, And only seven seniors
in the class, the class of 1923!

The junior-and-senior banquet went off very well, as
there were many juniors; the population of the school was
creeping up, you see. I had never been to a so-called
banquet before -- don't know how we arranged the money for
it, but there must have been all of twenty or twenty-five
kids seated around tables with brilliantly white table-
cloths, little favors and printed programs.

All that at San Jacinto High School took place within
a space of six weeks; I would have graduated from Yuma High
if my brother and family hadn't stolen away in the night to
make a break for greener pastures.

After graduation, now what? I was eighteen, with no
chance of going to college. I had been pretty good at
shorthand and typing in high school, so I decided the best
thing for me was to be a stenographer. But in the meantime,
in this lush country of California, I worked in a cannery
to earn the money to get away to business school.

And as I packed apricots, with my hands deep in the
slush and water, I said to you, Florence, laboring beside
me there, "Believe me, I am going to WORK on my shorthand!"

And I did. I left San Jacinto, left my mother, little
sister and little brothers behind, one of the hardest things
I ever did in my life. I had flown the coop. I would never
again know them as I had to this time. There would be a
separation, not only in years, but in viewpoints, in growing
up. All of us growing up, and our little mom growing older.

[Unsigned carbon copy]

Chapter Five
Waiting

The Great War was over. Sixteen servicemen from Imperial County, including Brick's brother, had died of disease. Twenty-nine were killed or died of wounds received in action. The rest had come home, or most of them had. But many had stayed away. *How're you going to keep 'em down on the farm, after they've seen Paree?* the song had asked. Brick Garrigues, his diploma finally in hand, also wondered how to begin his life, how to break away from the little newspaper job which had brought him in contact with so many important people in his small town.

Imperial Enterprise, June 16, 1919: NEW BUSINESS ENTERPRISE LAUNCHED: Imperial Valley's youngest business was launched in Imperial today by a firm composed, probably, of the Valley's youngest business men.

The business is a sort of brokerage which proposes to put the man who wants to buy something in touch with the man who has it to sell, and the man who wants to sell something, no matter what it may be, in touch with the man who wants to buy it.

The young men are C. H. Garrigues and Houston Smith, both under 20 years of age, who graduated from the high school this year. Their office will be located with Ed Royce, the transfer man, at 121 South Imperial avenue. Mr. Smith will be at work at the office end, while Mr. Garrigues will be the field or outside man.

The boys have great hopes of succeeding with their venture, because they believe the idea meets one of the needs of the community.

But, no. Apparently the community's match-up needs were not as pressing as the boys had hoped. *How're you going to keep 'em . . . ?*

C. H. Garrigues had no intention of going to Paris; his eye was set on Los Angeles, the big city over the forbidding range of mountains just to the west.[1] *You can do anything in the world if you want to,* a favorite high school teacher had taught him. And so it was on to college, specifically the University of Southern California, that big Methodist school that was then almost forty years old. The tuition was a problem, though. He worked as a laborer before he could enroll, and as a student he had to wait on the tables in the dining rooms to earn his keep. Often, when he was more broke than usual, he was fed and pampered by a fellow Kansan, a student named Marguerite, whom everyone called Peggy.

He dropped out of college to become a reporter with the *Hemet News,* a paper in a little agricultural town on the west slope of Mount San Jacinto, just a few miles from where Dickie was attending high school. In time, he got a better job: editor of the *Vanguard,* a daily some fifteen miles from Los Angeles in Venice, a thriving resort town on the beach. Just a few years earlier an enterprising developer named Abbot Kinney had built his vision of a European community there, complete with canals dug through the soft Southern California soil. Venice was a separate city then, with a big salt-water indoor swimming center called a plunge, an amusement pier jutting into the ocean and thousands of beach-seeking visitors each weekend who took the interurban railway — the Pacific Electric Red Cars — from all over Los Angeles County.

In Venice he worked with a reporter named Elizabeth Perkins, and he fell in love with her sister, Louise. He saved up enough money to purchase a small weekly paper, the *Call,* in the independent municipality of Culver City, which had been laid out on the vast stretches of Rancho La Ballona with the idea of luring the teen-age motion-picture industry from its childhood home in Hollywood. Soon carpenters, painters, grips, electricians, cowpokes and second- and third-rate actors crowded the little town, which enticed them with wide-open taverns even in the midst of Prohibition, as local lawmen looked the other way.

By mid-decade, though, Brick's Culver City venture had failed, and the young newspaperman made his way to Tucson, Arizona, where he became a sports and general-assignment reporter for the *Arizona Daily Star.* Working with him was one Frank Scully, a very funny young man who had come to Tucson and its clear desert air because of his wretched health. "It was still a town where people came for their health or were waiting for the sheriff to die back home," Scully wrote years later when he had become a widely read humorist.

---

1 The road over the Tecate Divide and the Laguna Mountains to the west of Imperial Valley was almost impassable in the early part of the century; in 1903, for example, the trip to San Diego took several days. But on April 9, 1913, a paved road was opened, and three years later an arched bridge was built across Meyer's Creek to speed the journey. (Nancy Hall article from the Imperial County Historical Society.)

It was also the town where Beulah had come two years before to study shorthand. This is what she wrote about it many years later:

I can still remember my mother's sweet face, and the sad expression as she kissed me goodbye. How I hated to leave her!

I hated to say goodbye to many things in San Jacinto. My boyfriend, Bryan, had spent the summer in our town, also working in the cannery. When it came time for us to part, I knew I would never see him again. He was my first love, and my heart ached. The ache was real, there was pain, real pain in my chest. The old saying, "Dying of a broken heart," I know from experience, could be true. I have felt pain similar more than once, but this was the worst.

I left home with Eaph and two younger brothers. To finance the journey we planned to stop and pick cotton on the various farms in the Imperial Valley. I had never before had to really get my hands dirty, or to do hard labor. My mother wouldn't even let me scrub clothes too long at a time, because bending over the washboard would "hurt your back." My hands were white and beautiful.

We would stop and ask for jobs. Sometimes we would get shelter, a cabin of sorts, but mostly we would camp out near the fields. In our sleeping bags we would cough and spit from colds, after working in the hot sun in the daytime and sleeping on the chilly ground at night.

I was only eighteen, but never had much acne to speak of, and now I developed boils. A beautiful one, I remember, right in the center of my forehead. Another on my cheek. They pained me, but the worst pain of all was to see the swelling of my young face, which, although it had never been exactly beautiful, had had the prettiness of youth.

I got dirtier and dirtier, although I fought it as best I could. Me, who would never use a towel that someone else had used! When we reached Phoenix, where my half-sister Maude lived, I had my first full bath in about six weeks. I luxuriated in the warm water, leaving a nice ring around the tub, which I used Old Dutch cleanser on and left as clean as I found it.

My sister was beautiful, and here I was, weather-beaten, ten years younger than she, but so, so ugly! I felt low, low, low. And I was yearning for my love. Misery, misery, misery.

Maude, I asked, is it all right if I buy a bottle of -- some sort of patent medicine -- forgotten what kind now that was popular at the time. It did me good, and with the correct diet that she provided, I eventually came forth with a fairly decent complexion. And then with her help with clothes, hair dressing, etc., I started to look almost like a normal teen-ager.

Eaph had given me ten dollars from the cotton-picking money, and I thought I was rich! I took the train for Tucson.

Beulah was outstanding in her business school courses, and she was able to get a job with a firm of attorneys. With the money she earned she bought her little sister Vesta an eighth-grade graduation dress.

She lived in a staid and proper boarding house, and there she met Brick Garrigues. Beulah, curious about the handsome man whose flirtations she enjoyed, wandered down the hall toward his room one morning hoping to run into him "accidentally," but she turned back shyly before reaching his door. The landlady, seeing her walking away from his room so early in the day, put two and two together to make five and evicted her on the spot. Brick moved out, too, furious at the slur toward a woman he admired. From then on, they saw each other often, and Brick began to call her "Dickie," a pet name that became permanent.

That was 1925, and that was the year she read books by Victor Hugo, Freud, Sinclair Lewis, Dreiser, Lew Wallace, H. G. Wells, Joseph Conrad and F. Scott Fitzgerald, and *The Picture of Dorian Gray,* by Oscar Wilde. With Brick or some other young man, she saw as much theater as Tucson could offer, a surprisingly wide variety: *A Doll's House* and *The Master Builder* by Ibsen, *The Devil's Disciple* and *The Miraculous Revenge* by Shaw, and works by Balzac and Voltaire, as well as a staged version of *Carmen* by Mérimée.

And that was the summer that Brick encountered Fanny, who left him to Dickie. He thought about his next move. He wanted to get away, and he wanted a better job. Southern California was calling him again.[2] He kissed Dickie goodbye and drove to the Imperial Valley to see his parents and some high school chums before going on to the coast.

[To Dickie]
January 3, 1926

Sweetheart,

Today I borrowed a typewriter down here at the Imperial Enterprise, where I used to work. I haven't seen anything yet, as most of my time has been spent visiting friends. They had an alumni gathering at the high school here last night, and I attended with bells on, but I'm pulling out tomorrow for San Diego, where I hardly think there's a chance to find a job. Then I'll go into Los Angeles, and will arrive there about Wednesday.

I've been lonely without you. Mother doesn't talk much about anything but you. I gave her the picture I had of you sitting on the wall with me, and she's tickled pink.

---

2 During the 1920s, Southern California experienced what Carey McWilliams called "the largest internal migration in the history of the American people." McWilliams (1905-1980) wrote extensively on California topics. He was editor of the *Nation* magazine for twenty years beginning in 1955.

Imperial Enterprise, January 7, 1926. ALUMNI ASSN. MEETS AT HIGH SCHOOL: Institution of a drive for funds for the erection of a memorial to Ephraim Angell, killed while playing football at Imperial High School several years ago, was the principal business of the semiannual meeting of the Imperial High School Alumni Association held Saturday night. It is understood that the association is planning a bronze tablet.

Many of the old graduates were making their first visit home since the return of Principal Hockenberry to Imperial High.

The alumni spent nearly three hours visiting. Every member introduced himself, giving his class number and present occupation.

Graduates returned to the old songs they had sung ten to fifteen years before and successfully recalled most of the methods by which they had disturbed the equanimity of their teacher.

Brick returned to the beach area west of Los Angeles.

> [Venice Evening Vanguard]
> Venice, Calif.
> January 9, 1926

This typewriter is the first one I used on the Vanguard four years ago, and it hasn't been repaired since.

So far the extent of my dissipation has been two movie shows and one stage play. Saw "White Collars" at the Egan -- in its 103rd week -- and "Hands Up" and "The Merry Widow" at Grauman's houses.[3] All three were darned good. I haven't been to the Venice pier yet, nor to a dance. Anyway, all I want to do is to get in practice so I can dance with you.

> January 10, 1926

If I don't get a letter from you pretty soon, I'm afraid I'll have to come back to Tucson and find out what it's all about. This business of being in love with a girl a million miles away is the bunk.

While missing you, though, I've managed to find a job -- of sorts. I'm now business manager, news editor, editorial writer and advertising salesman of an alleged newspaper known as the Barnes City News, located in thriving Barnes City, California, which isn't a city at all but a crossroads where the Barnes Circus is located. Anyway, they're trying to make a city out of it, and that's one of the jobs of the newspaper.[4]

---

3 *White Collars,* a comedy by Edith Ellis, had opened in Los Angeles in 1924 and moved to Broadway the next year. It was the story of a wealthy young man who married into a middle-class, white-collar family. *Hands Up,* directed by Clarence Badger, was a parody of Civil War movies; it had D. W. Griffith in a lead role. Erich von Stroheim's *The Merry Widow* starred John Gilbert and Mae Murray

4 The A.G. Barnes Circus had its winter headquarters on Washington Boulevard near Sawtelle Avenue. It featured "Tusko, Largest Elephant in the World," and "Lotta, Largest Hippopotamus in the World." Barnes City became a three-square-mile municipality but was later absorbed by Culver City.

January 13, 1926

The temporary job has been quit. It was like this -- the job paid on commission, and after tackling the advertising game for two days I decided there wouldn't be any commission.

The paper that I used to work for in Riverside has been sold, and the new owners want me to come back and work -- for less money than you are drawing. Of course, I didn't take it. I have friends on almost every paper in Southern California, and all of them are watching for openings for me.

Venice is terribly dead -- not at all like the old town it used to was. The old crowd, of course, is gone, but worse than that, it has been settled apparently by a bunch of middle-western farmers who are considerably worse than Arizonans.

January 15, 1926

I wouldn't tell you this if I didn't think for sure that by this time you knew that I really loved you, because you might think I was wandering away, or would wander, or something. Remember the woman I told you about who blacked a couple of my sweet brown eyes one night? She came down to see me yesterday, and kept insisting that I was her own sweet man and a lot of junk like that. In fact, she was quite vehement about it. Wanted me to take her out tonight, but I stalled her off, and didn't make any date. But there'll never be anybody but you. I've never gone with one girl as long as I have you, and -- to be frank -- I sometimes wondered if it was partly because we were away off in the desert. Now I know that no matter where we are, it will always be just you, and nobody else. There is, for example, a girl here whom I've wanted to go with for years -- ever since she was in high school. Now I could; in fact, she'd be delighted, I'm sure. She's a beauty, too, and cute. But I haven't the slightest desire to even play around with her.

January 22, 1926

Once again I have a job -- and once again it's only temporary, although how temporary I don't know as yet. I'm back at work on the old Culver City Call, the paper I used to own. The work isn't hard, and they pay me forty dollars a week, with a privilege of working on advertising and drawing down a commission. It only comes out twice a week. But for some reason or another, nobody has ever been able to stand the boss more than a couple of weeks.

Honey mine, I don't see how I could ever have even possibly dreamed that I could ever give a damn about any of these girls over here after knowing you. I just sit and think about you all the time -- even when I'm looking at another girl, and last night I was so lonesome I could almost cry. I just want you to come over and lead me off to a license clerk and get yourself so tightly married to me that you never can get away again.

I went broke yesterday, so instead of sleeping in the street, I strolled up to Mary's house, where the whole damn family, consisting of Mary and her mother, greeted me with open arms, gave me a spare bedroom and told me to put my feet under the table. I did. Mary is an awfully good scout, noisy as the dickens, but pretty and cute. I used to think she was the classiest job in the state -- but last night I looked at her and would have given anything if I could have just put my arms around you again for a minute and held you close to me. One thing I like about Mary, though, a fellow doesn't have to make love to her or any of that sort of thing. You know how most girls are -- to be friends, they want you to pet a little bit and then -- oh, well, you know. But Mary, in spite of the fact, or possibly because of the fact, that she's played around a lot, is just like another fellow. So don't get any wrong conceptions into your sweet little head.

It sure seems funny to be back here. Especially working on the Call, which I thought I'd never see again after the sheriff turned me out about two years ago. But I have my application in for a copy desk job on the Express, and if I get that, I'll be able to shift over to the Examiner or the Times, where they pay fifty or sixty per week. That's what I'm working for, as I'd hate to have to keep a wife on less.

February 1, 1926

Once more I'm out of a job -- thank God! I got fired off the Call Saturday night when I insisted on having my pay in full, and that was all right as I had intended quitting next Saturday, anyway.

[Handwritten]
February 9, 1926

I have a job -- and one which I hope will last. I'm on the copy desk of the L. A. Express, draw thirty-five a week and have to get up at 4:30 in the morning to get to work on time.

February 9, 1926

I don't know how well I'm going to like this job, but I'm going to keep it if I can. I have to be in bed by eight o'clock every night, in order to get on the job at six in the morning, so there'll be no parties -- except on Saturday night, maybe.

February 14, 1926

The Express is not so bad except for the small pay and

the ungodly hour of the night I have to get up. Remember
one night after I'd worked all week we went down to the
two-bit show and saw "The White Monkey?"[5] Well, last night,
after working all week, Mary and I went down to a two-bit
show and saw "The White Monkey." That's been the limit of
my dissipation, so you can see that Los Angeles without you
is ten thousand times worse than Tucson with you.

[February 1926]

I went down tonight and rented myself a typewriter
-- principally because I couldn't write you the kind of
letters I wanted to in the office. And the way things look
I'm going to keep my job until I can find a better one. I
think I'm a good enough judge of work to know that I'm a
better copyreader than anybody on the paper.

I get up at 5 in the morning, eat breakfast, catch the
5:45 car, get to work at 6:05, wait until 6:20 to start in,
read copy until 11, rush out to eat, back at 11:30, loaf
until the boss comes back from lunch and then read copy
until 2:50. Then I do some errands, come home and pedal the
player piano until 5:30, eat dinner, read until 8 o'clock
and then go to bed.

About 10:30 Mary comes in from work to say good-night
and sits on the foot of my bed while we tell all the dirt
we know. Then I go to sleep again until 5 o'clock.

When do you think you can come to Los Angeles? I don't
know how jobs are here, but I'm sure you could get
something good if you had somebody to take care of you
until you landed, and that's where I come in. But if I keep
this job, it will be a cinch that neither one of us will
starve until something better comes up. And just as soon as
you find out whether you'll really love me in Los Angeles
as much as you did in Tucson, I want to drag you away and
tie you down so you can't ever leave me -- with a little
gold band which I used to swear I'd never give any girl.
That is, if you're willing to take a chance on a thirty-
five-dollar-a-week copy editor.

And then I don't know whether you're going to like
Los Angeles or not. I don't think you can imagine the
mobs of people you have to crowd your way through any
time of the day or night, and when I think of the way you
used to hate a crowd down in Tucson, I wonder. Of course,
it's great when you get used to it, but I don't want you
to be disappointed when you get here. And just as there

---

5 *The White Monkey,* adapted from the novel by John Galsworthy, was released in 1925 and
starred Barbara La Marr. Just a few years earlier, she had been a runaway teen-age burlesque
dancer whose beauty so impressed a municipal court judge that he told her, "You are too beautiful
to be in the big city alone and unprotected." Hearst writer Adela Rogers St. John overheard the
remark, took charge of the young woman and introduced her to the right people in Hollywood. Her
acting career skyrocketed. But she died in 1926 of a combination of drugs and tuberculosis. Her
funeral was attended by 40,000 mourners. Later, studio owner Louis B. Mayer would rename
another beautiful actress, Hedy Kristler, in her honor — Hedy Lamarr.

are lots of material things we didn't have in Tucson,
so there are lots of immaterial things we had in Tucson
that we don't have in L.A.

In the meantime, Dickie was making the most of what was going on
in Tucson. After working all day at the law firm of Matthews and Bixby,
she found time to go to the Rialto Theatre on January 11 with a friend,
Johnny Lowthian, to see the "farewell tour" of Frank Bacon's long-
running masterpiece, *Lightnin'*. On February 10 she went with a Mr.
Giles to hear excerpts from operas by Verdi, Puccini, Gounod and
Donizetti in the high school auditorium.

[From Dickie to Brick]
February 14, 1926

Darling kid,

Received your long letter yesterday and have been
doing some tall thinking ever since.

However, I'm coming over. I think I will have a little
money ahead and hope that I can get a job before it runs
out. I'd take a chance on anything just to have my arms
around your sweet neck again. I love you so much.

I hope Mary takes good care of you for me, but not
such good care that you would forget me. I would like to
meet Mary. I imagine I would like her.

[From Brick to Dickie]
February 15, 1926

You darling, darling kid,

Living here where I am, I pay ten dollars a week for
board and room, and have to get my lunches up-town. With
carfare, laundry and things, the least I can get away for
is twenty dollars a week --which doesn't leave a lot. I
figure that until you come over I will put away ten dollars
a week and that will help us to get started.

Had a lot of fun at the office today. Verne Buck --
he's a comedian and jazz band leader -- came up to the
office to make some pictures to advertise his show, and
that helped to break up the monotony. Then, just before
press time, I had a chance to write one of those masterpiece headlines that never get in the paper. It appears
that Jane Novak,[6] while on a train, gave up her compartment
to a woman about to have a baby, and that the baby arrived
in Jane's section. So I wrote the head

STAR GIVES BERTH TO WOMAN; WOMAN GIVES BIRTH TO BABY.

Even though the boss wouldn't use it, it helped to
lighten up the atmosphere considerably.

---

6 Actress Jane Novak was in sixty-two movies, the first in 1914 and the last in 1950. She was
born in 1896 and died in 1990.

February 18, 1926

I don't know what you've done to me, sweetheart, but you surely changed me a lot from what I was when I first met you -- for better or worse, I don't know.

I'm afraid I'll be terribly stupid about running around, as I haven't really got in the habit of it, but of course if I can run around with somebody I love, it will be different. The principal reason I've stayed so close to home is because I haven't had anybody that I care to go out with -- and the fact that I'm broke.

[From Dickie to Brick]
February 19, 1926

Dearest, dearest kid,

Well, darling, the doctor said I didn't have to stay in Arizona.

I didn't tell you this because you had planned, and I had planned, that I work a while until we could afford my lying around, and I wasn't going to disappoint you by just coming over there and not doing a thing, and I knew you would probably think it was your duty to see that I didn't work, and as I have told you before, I don't want to be a duty.

I just know that we are going to be happy over there.

[From Brick to Dickie]
February 22, 1926

Sweetheart mine,

Went down to Venice yesterday and bummed around a while. Didn't see anybody I knew, so went swimming in the plunge and felt a lot better. It's the first time I've been in since coming back. Then I went downtown and saw a show and came back to dream about you the whole night long. Mary says she's more than anxious to see the girl that could inspire such utter devotion in any man.

Dickie's plan was to stop in Calipatria in Imperial County where her family had moved. Brick's impatience was beginning to show.

February 23, 1926

I'm still hoping you'll decide to come on through and then go back to see your folks later. If you loved me as much as I do you, you'd take the midnight train out of Tucson Friday night and get here Saturday afternoon.

When you come over, if you should get here while I'm working -- which is before 2:50 in the afternoon, take a cab and come out to the house. Or, if you don't want to do that, call the Express, ask for the news room and get me on the phone. Or call Beacon 8182 and ask for Mrs. Munson -- my landlady. Tell her who you are and she'll tell you where

I am. Anyway, do something so I can see you at the earliest
possible moment.

Really, sweetheart, I can't understand why I'm so
anxious to see you. Love, in the ordinary course of events,
doesn't affect me so profoundly. Possibly I'm the victim of
a cruel infatuation. And maybe it's because I've seen most
of the girls in Los Angeles without seeing any that
interested me as long as I have -- or think I have -- you.

On February 26, Dickie went with Mr. Giles to hear composer-pianist Homer Gunn present a concert of Indian tribal music, at which Evalyn Bentley gave a lecture on "Characterization of the Hopi Indians as I Found Them" (illustrated with lantern slides and sponsored by the Saturday Morning Musical Club). There were, I imagine, no real Indians present in the high school auditorium.

March 1, 1926

I'll confess I was terribly disappointed when I
couldn't persuade you to ditch the folks for a few weeks
and come on over.

Anyway, Saturday night I kept from being lonesome by
going on a party -- stagged, of course. Almost took another
guy's girl away from him -- he was bigger than I am -- and
dimly remember that I have a date with her for some time
this week, but I can't remember where, nor when, nor what
the lady's name is, nor anything. Except for the fact that
I got one drink of bad liquor which has persuaded me to go
extensively on the wagon, for quite some time. It was a
completely successful party and interesting, though
intensely moral -- probably on account of the notable
absence of more women.

I had an offer to go to Riverside at $42.50 a week
Saturday, but turned it down, as I didn't know whether
you'd like Riverside or not. I thought I'd risk it for
$45.00, but though they started at $35.00 and kept coming
up until they reached $42.50, they wouldn't go any higher,
and I wouldn't come down a cent. The Western Union got fat
on our telegrams, though.

I guess we can live on the thirty-five, although we're
going to be considerably poorer than church mouses. Anyway,
we'll eat, and you'll get plenty of chance to rest, which
is what I want to see you do most of all.

Lots of love and kisses,

Brick

On a Saturday night, Dickie again went with the available Mr. Giles, this time to see *The Merry Widow,* then left Tucson on the 12:20 a.m. train for Calipatria. The next Wednesday she drove from there to Imperial to finally meet Brick's father and mother — her putative in-laws. On Thursday she went to a dance in Calipatria, and the next morning, March 5, she took the 10:10 a.m. train to arrive in Los Angeles at 5:20 p.m. Brick had arranged for rooms for each of them in a downtown boarding house.

Then began a round of Los Angeles activity — movies such as *Devil's Circus* with Norma Shearer and *The Princess* with Betty Bronson and *For Heaven's Sake* with Harold Lloyd — vaudeville at the Million Dollar Theater or Loew's State — and Mendelssohn, Brahms, Wagner and Mozart with the Los Angeles Philharmonic in an afternoon concert at the new Coliseum in Exposition Park. One weekend they visited the County Art Museum in the same park. On the way home, Dickie wrote in her datebook: Brick cracked a joke — "Napoleon married Josephine for a son and heir; she didn't give him any son, so he gave her the air." Later, she told Brick how good-looking he was, and with his hand to his chin and his eyes upturned, he replied, "Just *The Picture of Dorian Gray.*" They went through the crazy house at the Venice Pier and swam in the plunge. They tried to see a baseball game at Wrigley Field, way down on Central Avenue near Fifty-Fourth Street, but it was called off because of rain.

For the two impatient lovers, there was only a brief wait. Dickie would turn twenty-one in April.

Chapter Six
Los Angeles

This is how I imagine Fanny in her room in a Colorado sanitarium:

She looked out the window at the melting snow and thought about the previous summer, out on the desert with Brick and his friends. That wind-up Victrola. The records. She sang softly to herself "Oh, that kiss in the dark was to him just a lark . . . " They had it on a record that summer, that Victor Herbert-Buddy DeSylva song from *Orange Blossoms*. Galli-Curci sang it.

Brick. An intriguing man, she reflected; perhaps he was a little raw, certainly conceited, but funny — and someone who *listened* to her, those brown eyes fastened on her, those eyes flecked with green and filled with curiosity. She thought about his eager attentiveness, his undoubted inclination to melodrama. She turned away from the window, back to her writing table and unfolded his letter again: "I was engaged in the furious pursuit of falling in love, and didn't realize it until you caught me." She smiled at that; maybe *she* had been caught. Was he still with Dickie? Why hadn't he answered her letter? What the hell; try again. She reached for her stationery.

Perhaps she wrote this: She was feeling a little better, but she still needed more rest before she could go home to New York. There were intriguing people to meet in Colorado and no shortage of books, but she yearned to see the magic of Manhattan as the first breath of spring approached. And: Be sure to write me; tell me everything. This time, a reply came, postmarked Los Angeles.

2016 Arapahoe Street
Los Angeles, Calif.
March 18, 1926

My dear Fanny,

Your letter finally reached me -- the second one, I
mean -- after being carried around in the pockets of half a
dozen newspapermen until it looked like my never-to-be-
forgotten fingernails -- if you'll remember, and you can't
forget. I'm afraid the first one is lost forever.

Venice and I were both changed when I came back. I
hardly know which was changed the most, and every time I
went to the beach I put on figurative mourning for my lost
home and my lost youth. (Please don't laugh.) For I doubt
if I could enjoy the present Venice even if I were nineteen
again, and I hardly think the Venice of five years ago
would attract me as it attracted me then. The things that
seemed so big to me then -- more particularly in Los
Angeles -- seem unimportant now, and I'm busy trying to
strike a balance between the self which developed in
Arizona and the realities of life in Los Angeles as I see
it today. I'm still trying, as I told you once, to find the
right path, and the attempt is still unsuccessful, but I at
least hope -- and fear -- that the pressure of the crowd
will at last start me on one way or the other, even though
it doesn't happen to be the right one.

I'm afraid that I shall turn at last to the refuge of
pragmatism, the philosophy of the Saturday night pay check,
the humble bungalow and loving wife, expending my dreams on
the possibilities of next year's suit or a new tire for the
family Ford. The prospect is not attractive, but is at
least better than milling aimlessly the rest of a lifetime.

I've always been a dreamer, but my dreams have been,
mostly, allowed to flit across the scene and die, leaving
nothing behind them. That is the way to live, but it
doesn't make for creation. And now I've become so used to
dissecting the dreams of others in my search for reality
that I cry "Hokum" whenever one of mine comes upon the
horizon, thus scaring the poor little thing away for keeps.

Just now, the pull of the practical life happens to be
stronger than anything else. (I'm on the L.A. Express copy
desk.) I do my daily stint, go to bed early and crawl out
early to do the daily stint once more. Much like the mules
I used to pilot on the farm, in fact. And while I've met
some marvelously interesting characters, this newly
developed practicality doesn't let me see as much of them
as I should like.

There's Joe O'Carroll, for example, a man whom you'd
adore -- if you didn't faint when you first saw him. Born
in Dublin, educated at Trinity, unkempt, his hair never
combed, his suit ages old and never pressed, he writes the

most beautiful poetry I've ever read. Makes his thirty dollars every week and spends twenty-five of it for Hollywood Boulevard gin and books. A splendid example of how not to live -- yet he's leaving something to live when he's gone, while the rest of us live model lives and leave BROADWAY STAR / DIES FOR LOVE and such gems for the generations to remember us by.

I think of Jean-Christophe a good deal. I like him more and more as time paints out the poor spots in the book, and leaves only what the author was trying to do. He's one of the few friends I've made in books that I'll always want to keep with me.[1]

Incidentally, do you know "An American Bible," compiled by Alice Hubbard? I found it just the other day. The Roycrofters did it. It is a book done to give us the same volume in America that the old Bible gave the Jews, with poetry, maxims, views -- well, I can't explain it, but the compiler has done something extraordinary. There's a great deal that we wouldn't find otherwise in a lifetime. The compilation is from the worlds of Benjamin Franklin, Thomas Jefferson, Thomas Paine, Lincoln, Whitman, Emerson, Ingersoll, and Elbert Hubbard, and after reading it, I was glad for the first time that I was an American. If you don't know it, you should.

I hope you're really chasing a cure in earnest this time, as I often felt like spanking you when you stepped out instead of staying in bed. And you know I'll always be hoping you're getting better so you can go back to your beloved New York -- even though I have spent the entire letter talking about myself. In fact, I should be punished by not hearing from you again, although I hope I won't be, because I'm going to value your letters more than you imagine, if you do write me.

As ever,

Brick

"As ever, Brick." That was the way he normally signed his letters to her, hundreds of them. And Fanny Strassman kept them, for decades. The two, Fanny and Brick, exchanged lengthy letters, almost always typewritten, for almost fifty years, sometimes monthly, sometimes more often, and they were filled with revelations of the most personal kind — love affairs and disappointments and happinesses in a job or in life.

---

1 Romain Rolland's monumental novel, *Jean-Christophe,* was published in ten volumes in French beginning in 1904 and in three volumes in English translation soon thereafter. It is the story of a young musician of pure soul who attempts to break down the barriers between nations and between people with his sense of lofty idealism. In the foreword to the American edition, Gilbert Cannan called it "the first great book of the twentieth century." "The truth about anything," wrote Cannan, "is universal truth, and the experiences of Jean-Christophe, the adventures of his soul (there are no other adventures), are in a greater or less degree those of every human being who passes through this life from the tyranny of the past to the service of the future."

April 5, 1926

I'm glad you're being a good patient because I'm looking forward to the time when you will again be able to dance, frolic or do whatever your heart desires. I can imagine how maddening it must be to lie in bed always waiting for the cure which never comes. You feel, I suppose, as useless as I do, but my uselessness is one of the mind while yours is of the body. When it's all over, you will know that you've done the best you could, and I'll always know that I might have done something -- and didn't. Cheerful, isn't it?

I can understand the undergraduate being interested in you, and approve of your insistence upon having youth about you. You're so eternally youthful yourself. As for the Chinaman -- well, you might learn from him. His people are the wisest on earth. At any rate, if the men there can keep you interested, you can ask no more of the angels them- selves. Unfortunately, I found few interesting people since I've been here. But perhaps I will.

In the meantime, please consider the promptness of this reply, and remember that there's no loneliness like that of a great city.

April 18, 1926

Your letters really do me a lot of good; when I get one I feel like writing to thank Bernice again for that memorable party in the middle of the Tucson summer.

I'm glad you liked "The Genius," for Dreiser is one of the chief among my Lares et Penates. Without having read it, I can endorse all you feel in it. It may be true that the last three hundred pages could have been condensed to one hundred, but then, F. Scott Fitzgerald would have taken "Jean-Christophe" and condensed him into a thin volume. Damn condensation! Condensed milk, evaporated peaches, dessicated literature! Let us have more men who will wander hither and thither and yon in place of those who attempt to slice everything into six episodes and a climax.

I've formed the habit of walking home from work -- it's about two miles. There's little to see on the way except man and the handiwork of man, but it's easier to think -- to dream -- when walking than when sitting still. So you see I have changed -- for I wouldn't have walked across the street in Tucson if I could call a car.

Heard Beethoven's Ninth symphony the other night.[2] Just before I'd been to hear "Rube" Wolf's jazz band. Saturday night saw "Desire Under the Elms"[3] and today heard Reuben H.

---

2 At the Shrine Auditorium.

3 By Eugene O'Neill, first performed on Broadway in 1924. It was harshly decadent, dealing with sex and avarice in a New England rural family. In Los Angeles it played for more than eleven weeks at Wilkes' Orange Grove, a theater at 730 S. Grand Avenue.

Wolf's concert orchestra.[4] Sounds variegated, doesn't it? But it started me thinking about one thing I've been glad of, that I can think and feel in the languages of Wagner, Beethoven, Verdi, Ponchielli, and Irving Berlin without being conscious that one language is better than the other to express thought and emotion. I'm glad of that, very glad.

My first attraction for music was toward the Italians. Gradually I came to like Wagner, and then found the Italians unpleasant. But lately, it seems, they all talk to me in a language I understand. It's like having a lot of friends who demand nothing of you except to enjoy their company. It's like being able to sit in a company and speak half a dozen tongues without being conscious that you are changing from one to another. That's the outstanding thing that has happened to me in the last year.

About "Desire." I'm in favor of a law suppressing all audiences. Putting them in jail if necessary until their minds cease to pollute the channel of human thought. They sit, bored, through the most poignant tragedy, see a wonderful actress without understanding because she's dramatic instead of theatrical, and laugh uproariously at something perfectly natural which tickles the risibilities of their sex-bound selves.

"Desire" is not by any means a masterpiece, but it's a well-written human document which deserves much better than it's received from the people who have seen it. There's not a line in the play that's "off-color", and there isn't a line left out because it might be off-color. Its characters talk exactly as they would talk on the farm, which isn't pretty, but certainly isn't uproariously funny.

April 29, 1926

It is with something approaching trepidation that I take my typewriter in lap this time, for I'm going to do something of which you won't approve. In short, I'm going to commit matrimony. In shorter, I'm going to commit it tomorrow, and -- since you won't approve -- I'm hoping that you'll at least condone.

You know, of course, that it's Dickie, and I think I know her well enough to realize that she's just about the background I'll need. It won't be ideal. Any marriage that's ideal is probably so complete as to crowd other considerations into the background -- and that's just what I don't want to happen; a desire which a woman may or may not be able to understand.

You can see that I'm not madly in love with her, and it's a relief to have a friend with whom one can exchange views on one's own marriage without indulging in the ordinary bromides which one does exchange under such circumstances.

_____

4 This appears to be the same musician waving different batons.

I suppose the world is privileged to assume the ordinary assumptions of a young fool who hasn't better sense than to be married on a newspaperman's pay, but such assumptions bore me, and I'm especially happy that I've a friend to whom I can explain the reasons for an apparently foolish act. It's an experiment. Perhaps it will deaden me, imprison me. But I'm perfectly contented in the belief that it will not.

Dickie turned twenty-one on Tuesday, April 27, Brick bought a ring and a marriage license in Los Angeles on April 29, and they were married the next day in Santa Monica by a justice of the peace. They had a wedding dinner in Culver City with their two witnesses, Brick's colleague (Mr.) Beverly (Bevo) Means and his foot-of-the-bed pal, Mary L. Munson, and then, my mother noted in her diary, "Home early."

Imperial Enterprise, May 6, 1926. WELL KNOWN VALLEY COUPLE WED IN CULVER CITY. Announcement was received in Imperial today of the marriage of C. H. Garrigus and Miss Beulah Dickey at Culver City last Friday. Following the ceremony, Mr. and Mrs. Garrigus left for Honolulu, where they will spend their honeymoon.

After graduating from the Imperial High School, "Brick," as he is better known here, took up journalism, "cubbing" on the *Enterprise.* Since leaving Imperial he has been associated with some of the larger Metropolitan newspapers of Southern California and Arizona. His bride is also well known in the Valley, her parents living near Calipatria.[5]

Like so many other struggling young Los Angeles couples, Brick and Dickie lived in a small apartment on Bunker Hill, just a few blocks from Brick's job on Hill Street between Second and Third streets. Ross B. Wills, a screenwriter, wrote of Bunker Hill in the 1920s that it had at one time been "the city's swank hilltop apartment district but now perched on the metropolis' shoulder like an old incurable carbuncle, swarming with involuntarily retired orange pickers from the East, bus boys, the frowzier streetwalker, and poor and old and defeated people from all over the world."[6]

Not quite. It also housed a young newspaperman[7] who wanted to be a writer and his bride, a bobbed-hair business-school graduate who would clatter down the hill in her high heels and short skirt and race across Pershing Square to her job as a secretary in the Board of Trade on the Sixth Street side, at one hundred dollars a month to start. There were intellectuals on Bunker Hill, too, who were drawn to the big new public library that had just opened at Fifth and Grand Streets.[8] And on Sixth

---

5 Actually, Dickie, having grown up in Texas and Arizona, was scarcely known in the Imperial Valley at all, and the trip to Hawaii must have been somebody's idea of a good joke.

6 In John Fante, *Selected Letters: 1932-1981,* p. 332.

7 Brick didn't use the word *journalist,* quoting approvingly H. L. Mencken's dictum that "A journalist is a newspaperman in spats."

8 Designed by Lodwrick M. Cook, the building, with its distinctive, pyramid-shaped tower, suffered a serious arson fire in 1986, but was repaired and reopened in 1993.

Street, a block away, a string of both new- and used-book shops vied with each other for funkiness and charm.

Two small cable railways, Angels Flight at Third Street and Court Flight between Temple and First Streets, each of them only one block long, ran up the steep slope of Bunker Hill for many decades. In 1969 the top of the hill was sliced off and redeveloped with enormous high-rise office buildings. Angels Flight was reinstalled in mid-1996, as a kind of time-warp for tourists. Court Flight had been destroyed by fire in 1943.

Broadway, then as now, was vibrant and full of life. But whereas today the life force flows from Latin American immigrants, in 1926 it stemmed from the many immigrants from the Midwest, the South and "Back East." Downtown, served by streetcar lines from all over the city coursing down Broadway, had its fine shops, its restaurants and, not least, its movie theaters.

With a population of about 800,000, Los Angeles and Hollywood together were served by thirty-three motion picture theaters. Gloria Swanson was in *The Untamed Lady* at the Iris in Hollywood, and King Vidor's *The Big Parade,* an enormously successful film about the Great War, had recently finished its run. Norma Talmadge and Ronald Colman were in *Kiki* at Sid Grauman's Million Dollar Theater, which had been built, as Carey McWilliams put it, "as part of a grandiose scheme to make Broadway 'the Great White Way of Los Angeles.' And for a few brief years it was." Marion Davies, the sweetheart of newspaper magnate William Randolph Hearst, starred with Antonio Moreno in *Beverly of Graustark* at the Alhambra. At the Forum the audiences were transfixed by the realistic death scene of Lillian Gish, who acted opposite John Gilbert in Vidor's *La Boheme:* The rumor was that, to achieve verisimilitude, Gish had drunk no liquids for three days before filming it.

The movies were silent, of course, often being accompanied by a full orchestra or by a single pianist. Only on the stage could an Angelino actually hear an actor speak. At the Majestic, for example, Marjorie Rambeau was in *They Knew What They Wanted,* the play by Leslie Howard that had opened on Broadway in 1924, a mellow story of an aging Italian immigrant in California and his mail-order bride. It had won the Pulitzer Prize in 1925 and thirty years later was the basis of the Frank Loesser musical *The Most Happy Fella.*

```
                          344 South Grand Avenue
                          June 1, 1926

    This being the wife's night out (notice how
naturally I say "the wife"), I've been on a regular spree
this evening, haunting bookshops and feeling all the
ecstasies of Tantalus as I walked from one to another
without buying. Fortunately, I left my money at home, so
```

escaped with nothing but Walter Pater's "Marius the Epicurean" and Voltaire's "The White Ball." After an afternoon or evening in a bookshop, I feel all unstrung and regret the ones I've had to leave almost as much as I enjoy the ones I bought.

There were a million others I wanted, from old Pepys' "Diary" to "An American Tragedy" -- but you know! Perhaps Schopenhauer drew me more than the others. Because, in spite of myself, I can never quite be delivered from the sincere conviction that the philosophy of Pessimism approximates the truth more nearly than any other philosophy. Old Schop is so damnably logical and so infernally inclusive.

Perhaps you were right about marriage. It does take an infernally lot of time. We've an apartment uptown so I'm near the office, and Dickie is working, so I don't have to worry about family finances, but I've hardly had time to touch a typewriter for weeks. We're getting settled, though, and I'll soon be back at the old schedule. But even the most self-effacing of wives cannot help but obtrude herself upon the notice of friend husband (just think, I'm one of those things!) occasionally.

What I want not to do more than anything else is to settle down into the life of a white-collar wage-slave. And my greatest danger right now is not in the fact that I'm married, but that I don't believe in anything, least of all in skepticism. If I could be a propagandist for some damn thing or another, it wouldn't be so difficult, but what's the use of getting excited about something that doesn't matter in the least. I sometimes even envy a Methodist preacher!

Incidentally, have you seen "The Big Parade"? Drag yourself to the theater to see the greatest picture ever produced. I saw it when it finished a six months' run and will always regret I didn't get to see it again. It's the most flawless production ever made -- or perhaps I should say the most nearly flawless -- and while you don't feel like sobbing, you can't help but be carried away by the perfect technique of the bigger moments. I also saw the picture "La Boheme," which manages to do much better than the opera, despite Lillian Gish.

"The Big Parade," "They Knew What They Wanted" and "La Boheme" have really been my biggest moments in the last month -- except for a sentimental adventure a couple of weeks ago when I met my very, very first sweetheart on the street.

Funny, life is. I was a junior in high school, and she was a sophomore in another high school. I was quite mad about her, and poured out fervent love-letters by the score -- for three or four weeks. Then I gradually forgot about her until a few months later when I met her at an auction sale on Harold Bell Wright's Imperial Valley Ranch.[9]

Business of writing more fervent letters for a few weeks. Another six months and I met her in some other unsuspected place, and ditto ditto ditto.

Then I came to college and discovered that my "best girl" was her closest chum, and that she was a sophomore in another college. After college, I was leaving a railroad station and met her going in -- going to New York to study voice. Then, the other day, I was riding to work on the little cable car we have, when I noticed a pretty woman in the front end. When we got off, the chap with me made some remark, as chaps will, about this woman, but I didn't bother to turn around. We crossed the street and waited for the traffic to turn. Then somebody said, "Why, I know you!" and I turned around to find that the woman was Floy Lee.

I didn't know her at first, and she didn't remember my last name, and I needed a shave, and had a wife, and she, so she told me, had a husband and a five-months-old baby and was going on a trip to San Francisco -- but at that, I think it was prudence on my part that I didn't learn her last name, and on hers that she didn't tell me. Life IS funny, isn't it? But it made me feel abominably old. Floy Lee; pretty name, isn't it?

We DO grow old, don't we? And while age doesn't bring wisdom, experience does bring age. I wonder if I would be different today if I had been content to live more slowly instead of trying to cram the experiences of a lifetime into two or three years. Of course, there's lots that's new, but even that is likely to be seen with a jaundiced eye.

I was thinking this evening of one moonlight night a few years ago when I was much wiser than I am now. "That moon," I told myself, "will be full just thirteen times each year for the next eight years. At the end of eight years, it will have lost most of its glamour, so I'd best absorb it all while I can." Well, I've enjoyed it. Now I say, "Pretty, ain't it?" and go to bed. Is this age?

1747-1/2 West 20th Street
September 5, 1926

Me and my ball-and-chain -- the diminutive for I and my wife -- have just moved again, this time into the duckiest little bungalow I've seen for months. One of these "we have a one-room home" affairs with a breakfast nook, kitchen, dressing room and all the other accesso-

---

9 Harold Bell Wright was one of the most prominent American writers in the first quarter of the twentieth century. His 1911 novel, *The Winning of Barbara Worth,* was based on the building of a dam on the Colorado River to irrigate the Imperial Valley and reclaim it from the desert. In 1926 it was made into a film starring Ronald Colman and Vilma Banky and introducing Gary Cooper. The spectacular ending, with its collapsing dam and a flood, made it one of the most popular movies of the year.

ries tacked on so you feel you're living in a doll's house. But the best of all, there are two little alcoves built into one end of the room -- just big enough to set my portable Victrola in. By closing down the lid, the sound strikes the wall as a sounding board, echoes back and forth in the alcove three or four times, and comes out with all the richness of an expensive orthophonic. I'm so delighted over the discovery that I haven't been able to do anything but play the Vic while Dickie arranges the house and unpacks the stuff.

I came very near going to New York this fall. If I weren't married, I should be there now. One of the chaps at the office -- the most talented human I've ever met -- almost talked me into going with him, but since neither of us could raise a dime, we decided to postpone it until we sold our next novels.

This chap -- Gully Foster is his name -- is twenty-one, writes, paints, has been called the second most promising of the young poets in America by the Lit Dig, doesn't know one note of music from another and improvises the most beautiful piano music -- generally speaking he's so interesting he bores you to tears. He roomed down at the house for a while until we had a fight over a novel he's writing and then he moved out -- went on a three weeks' drunk and only started back to work when I threatened to knock his block off if he didn't.

Gully Foster's real name was Michael. His first novel, *Forgive Adam,* was finally published in 1935 by W. Morrow and Co., to critical acclaim.

Anyway, instead of working this summer as I'd promised, I've been spending most of my afternoons playing golf and my evenings going to concerts. The Hollywood Bowl seats 20,000 and while it's out of doors, the acoustics are almost perfect. The size of the crowds they get permit a pretty good orchestra, and we've had Hoogstraten, Wood, Oberhoffer (terrible), Goossens (same), and ending up with two glorious weeks with Papa Hertz of San Francisco.[10] Really and truly, I never went out without wishing you could be there too, particularly the last two weeks.

The last concert I heard featured the "New World" symphony, and I've been boring all my friends ever since by trying to sing it or wave my arms and show how it's done, or something of the sort. You'd have enjoyed it -- to sit 'way out in the hills, people not too close to you and the moon just rising behind the mountains while that marvelous largo floated up to you. It isn't good musicianship, I believe, (although the last movement is) but it's profoundly beautiful anyway.

Except for that, I've done nothing except write a

---

10 Willem van Hoogstraten, Henry Wood, Emil Oberhoffer, Eugene Goossens and Alfred Hertz.

couple of short stories which wouldn't sell and a couple of
magazine articles which came back even quicker. However,
Dickie's quit her job and is going to cook for a while, and
I'm going to lure the muse between seven and nine every
night except Sundays. If that doesn't work, I'm going to
take a furnished room someplace by myself and let my
profound discontent goad me into something.

Did you ever watch a goldfish? I've been musing over
a pair all afternoon. Imagine spending your life floating
around the inside of a bowl which you can't even see. No
hope -- nothing to hope for. Or even if some imaginative
goldfish did dream that some day he'd break through that
invisible nothing which kept him confined and swim out
into the world -- well, suppose he did. Probably the cat
would get him.

But, after all, aren't we just like that? We can swim
farther, of course, but when we get there, there's no place
to swim but back. And always around us there's that
invisible bowl, the Unknowable -- Fate, God -- its
dimensions guessed at but never known. Suppose somebody
dumped us out of our bowl into a lake of Eternity or rather
the Infinite. Wouldn't we still remain a goldfish, and like
Donander of Evre go back to our little chapel to pray for
the return of Dom Manuel?[11] I don't know why I'm writing
all this junk except that it just occurred to me after
watching a goldfish at lunch (I mean I was at lunch).

Brick soon discovered he could get free entertainment by reviewing
opera performances. He had no musical training but he had a talent for
voicing his opinion on just about everything. He was strong-minded and
he wrote with authority and the conviction that whatever he wrote was
worth reading.

October 9, 1926

I just got back from "Rigoletto" and found your letter.
It seemed frightfully good to hear from you again. It's been
perfectly ages. Why the last time, it was a Chinese student,
and now it's a Russian nobleman. Next time -- !

Anyway, I wish you could have heard the San Francisco
Opera here tonight, although I was a wee bit disappointed.
Schipa[12] sang the Duke, and a new soprano from La Scala
named Melius -- at least she's new to me -- sang Gilda, or
rather tried to. Richard Bonelli sang Rigoletto after the
first scene, a substitution being made in the middle of the
first act, for some reason or another. Altogether it wasn't
bad, but Melius did more jumping around than singing and
had a helluva time getting through "Caro Nome." But the

---

11 The references are to characters in books by James Branch Cabell (1879-1958), who
became enormously popular in the 1920s with his imaginative medieval novels. In 1926 he had just
published *The Silver Stallion,* which later would be charged in court with obscenity.

12 The tenor Tito Schipa, 37, was then in the San Francisco and Chicago opera companies.

crowd applauded, not knowing the difference, so I suppose
it was all right, unless you have a prejudice in favor of
singing rather than physical gymnastics.

Monday night is "Traviata," and Tuesday "The Barber."
Schipa wasn't bad -- but why extend yourself for a flock of
Iowans that don't know the difference. I'll be glad when
the San Carlo comes back and we can go into the balcony
with garlic on our breaths and hear wops sing wopera for
wops. And the Philharmonic Auditorium season opens in a
couple of weeks and we really have a splendid orchestra if
I do say it.

That's about all I've been doing the last month --
working, reading and waiting for the winter music season.
I've read quite a bit that I wanted to read, and pounded my
typewriter religiously but without much zeal every evening
and expect to keep up the same program for the next twenty
years when I'll either be managing editor of the <u>Herald</u> or
retire on a pension. That's about all there is in life when
you're married and forbidden the pleasure of falling in
love all the time.

There are two books I wish you would read. Not because
you should, but because you'll adore them, I think. Or
perhaps you know them already. One is Cabell's "Beyond
Life," and the other is Ernest Dowson's poems. Both are in
the Modern Library.

"Beyond Life," I think, sums up more than any other
book the viewpoint of life which I happen to hold -- that
life is a meaningless sort of trick, unworthy of a self-
respecting Deity, played on subjects who couldn't be
expected to know any better, but that since we're here,
there are a lot of interesting things to fool ourselves
with and thus rob the Deity of his little joke by entering
thoroughly into the damn thing.

I'll never understand how I've managed to live twenty-
four years without becoming acquainted with Ernest Dowson.
You must know his works, but I hope you don't, so you can
have the pleasure of meeting him. I never really knew what
poetry was before Gully Foster brought his copy of "The
Poems and Prose" around one day. Since then I've hardly had
the book out of my possession.[13]

Of course, if you know the man, I needn't tell you
anything about him, and if you don't, I can't find words,
so I'll have to let you find it for yourself. If I could
write like that, I'd be ready to die at twenty-nine -- or
I'd be willing to be dead now if I could have written just
three of the things that he did write.

---

13 Ernest Dowson (1867-1900) was one of the most gifted of the circle of English poets of the
1890s known as the Decadents. In 1891 he published this, his best-known poem, popularly known from
its refrain as "I Have Been Faithful to Thee, Cynara, in My Fashion." The other lines quoted by Brick
are from Dowson's *Extreme Unction.*

> They are not long, the weeping and the laughter,
> Love and desire and hate:
> I think they have no portion in us after
>   we pass the gate.
> They are not long, the days of wine and roses:
> Out of a misty dream
> Our path emerges for a while, then closes
> Within a dream.

And again:

> The fire is out, and spent the warmth thereof
> (This is the end of every song man sings!)
> The golden wine is drunk, the dregs remain
> Bitter as wormwood and as salt as pain:
> And health and hope have gone the way of love
> Into the drear oblivion of lost things.
> Ghosts go along with us until the end;
> This was a mistress, this, perhaps, a friend.
> With pale, indifferent eyes we sit and wait
> For the dropped curtain and the closing gate:
> This is the end of all the songs man sings.

You know, Fanny, when I read that sort of thing, I don't want ever to write -- to clutter up the Earth with more printed words. There's more beauty, more truth in a stanza of that than in all that any novelist has ever produced. I'd much rather sit in the shade and let that sort of beauty seep through me than write the greatest piece of prose ever. Dowson, it seems to me, is the culmination of all that great cycle from the primitive into the romantic, the realist and finally the perfect polished decadent. We have too many decadents attempting to write poetry in America today, but they succeed about as well as Bellows would have succeeded in miniatures. (Hope he never made any.)[14]

Newspaper work, especially copy-reading, plays plain and simple hell with your use of the English language, and while I used to pride myself on writing cadenced prose, I realize that most of my stuff now sounds like a series of headlines stuck together in a sentence. But I do believe this -- that somewhere down in my innards is the ability to write a paragraph that will make you say -- "That's beautiful." And I'm going to write it if I need another thirty years.

December 21, 1926

Here's a picture of my mind, as judged by my library: Anatole France, Ben Hecht, France, Flaubert, France, Pater, France, Cabell, Erskine, Morley, Cabell, Swinburne, Shakespeare, Yahweh (as typified in his book the Holy

---

14 George Wesley Bellows (1882-1925) was known for his lithographs, including *Billy Sunday* and *Dempsey and Firpo*.

Bible), Dowson, Ingersoll, Laurence Hope and the first
volume complete of the Two Worlds monthly.

My choice seems to include principally books which
treat life as though it were of no serious import, yet
treat it subtly and cleverly enough to enable you to forget
the end in the method. All of my favorites take you along a
delightful road and usually leave you no nearer where you
were going than you were when you started. You stop with
France to enjoy the essence of a flower or with Hecht to
catch the soul of a city street -- yet you recognize that
neither is of any particular importance as long as there is
another flower ahead. And neither is the flower ahead of
any importance until the one you have has lost its
fragrance.

I've been working on a play -- solely for my own
amusement. It's the first one I've tried and the first
thing I've ever written because I enjoy putting the words
down on paper. The first act is complete but not finished,
and I'm stuck in the middle of a prayer in the middle of
the second act. Some night when I feel sonorous enough I'll
finish it.

The play is untitled but it deals with Eve immediately
after the banishment from the Garden of Eden. You are
familiar with the legend of Lilith, who was Adam's wife
before Eve. The play reveals that Cain was really Lilith's
son, unknown to Eve -- through a rather subtle bit of work
of which I am quite proud -- and that all the while that
Adam was playing the part of the first husband and
husbandman, he was carryin' on with that blonde hussy. The
devil conceives the idea of corrupting the human race
through Eve, and a daughter is born to him and to her. Cain
marries the daughter, and we are descendants of the devil
and of Lilith -- which explains considerable of the failure
of Jehovah to lure us into his heaven.

However, the theme of the play (or rather the story of
the play) is not so much the devil's seduction of Eve as
the attempts of Eve and Adam to get back into the garden of
Eden. I have tried to picture Eve as the eternal Wife and
Mother -- the wife of the first member of the Great
Unwashed, always waiting "for something to turn up," always
with a boundless faith that some day Adam's "luck" will
change, never admitting to herself that her husband is a
weakling who is only paying for his own weakness, and
always sacrificing -- almost uncomplainingly -- in order
that Adam may "make good."

I haven't succeeded, and if I did, the play would
never be produced because it isn't that sort of a play. But
I have a whole life-time to work on it and others which may
please me as well, and except for reading, I expect to get
most of my pleasure out of doing just that sort of thing.

The wife announces that she's just finished a
particularly pornographic article in Two Worlds and that
it's time to turn out our one light, otherwise I'd probably
be here until morning -- because I do like to write you.
Incidentally, Dickie has become a real enthusiast over that
sort of thing and won't let me have an expurgated book in
the house. She wants a copy of Powys Mathers' "Arabian
Nights" translation for Christmas! At sixty dollars! Coats
are cheaper.

Brick was using *pornographic* not as we would today, but in an older
sense: writing that caused amatory feelings. Samuel Roth's publication
Two Worlds, subtitled *A Literary Quarterly Devoted to the Increase of
the Gaiety of All Nations,* published elevated prose and poetry by such
authors as John M. Synge, John Galsworthy and Alphonse Daudet. Se-
lections from *The Book of the Thousand Nights and One Night* by Edward Powys Mathers (1892-1939) were published in the December 1926
issue; they are gentle, romantic poems with just a whiff of eroticism.

The next summer, Fanny left the sanitarium and went to stay briefly
in Santa Fe, New Mexico.

1101 South Oxford
July 29, 1927

I'm delighted to hear that you are better and have
left the hospital. In a way I'm glad you didn't come to
California, although I'd like to see you more than almost
anything. But I doubt if there's a place in the world as
ugly and cheap and squalid as this city of the angels. It
used to seem lovely to me, but it depresses me terribly
now. I can't think how I could have ever imagined it
beautiful. Especially since my last trip to Arizona I've
felt that Los Angeles is just somebody's mistake. In a way,
it's the sort of city that Yahweh would build after five or
six thousand years of successful warfare against everything
beautiful in the world.

It's different in the spring, for the new gas mains
and real estate signs can't quite cover up everything. But
then it's a city -- without mountains, without a single
building tall enough to be impressive and without even
enough noise to be disturbing. However, the change is
probably in me, and I'm looking forward to seeing you this
fall -- without fail.

I'm actually worried. I've wondered how it would be to
have a son -- and then awakened to realize that such a
thought revealed that unconsciously I had lost all my
desire to write or think fine sentences or high thoughts,
and was already thinking of passing my ambitions on to
someone else.

A number of things have contributed to such a condition. In the first place, the purse strings have been drawn so closely that most of my inspiration has been drawn from four bare walls, the dishpan and the radio -- when we can keep the battery charged. Then, when I came back all the old gang were either gone or intent upon saving enough money to provide a decent accouchement -- most of the gang were married about the same time as I, you know, and young intellectuals quickly become staid fathers under the influence of a forty-dollar-per-week job. In the fourth place, they made me make-up editor, and I'm neither of the copy desk nor of the bosses. I wander around in the darkness of the composing room, and when I'm through, the old feet are too tired to drag me anywhere but home.

Marriage is the principal cause of it, but then I don't blame marriage so much and would probably do it again. It goes perfectly with mediocrity in that it reduces the mediocre to its own mediocrity, whereas romance -- synonymous with unmarriedness -- tends to uplift mediocrity into something false but often beautiful. If one were dissatisfied with his or her wife or husband, things would be different, but where your marital life is perfectly satisfactory, it leaves life in a decidedly unsatisfactory state of satisfaction. And I'm finally coming to discover that I'm so hopelessly mediocre -- that I should have become a banker or traveling salesman.

However, I sometimes have the satisfaction of remembering that Cabell was able to write after having been married and living quite decently enough for a number of years with a probably very satisfactory sort of wife. And so perhaps I may -- after all.

As ever,

Brick

Chapter Seven
Why Herbert Hoover Beat Al Smith

Los Angeles in the Jazz Age, city of dreams, city of romance. Sunshine every day. In every back yard, a swimming pool. Warm, sandy beaches. The women were all beautiful and the men handsome. The waitress who served your morning coffee knew someone who had a friend who was going to get her in the movies. Ah, the motion picture, that illusionist of fantasy. Say, wasn't that Ramon Novarro speeding down Sunset Boulevard in his white roadster? Didn't you just see Gloria Swanson float into the Garden of Eden hotel with her entourage? That was the image.

The reality: Jobs. Lots of them. A six-day week, pay every Saturday morning. Construction. Hard work. Roads being laid, houses built. Myron Hunt, famed for his design of the Rose Bowl in Pasadena, showing off his balloon-shaped seating area of the Hollywood Bowl, rising from the stage to embrace the warm hillside. A new City Hall breaking the twelve-story earthquake limit and soaring to twenty-six floors.[1] Oil wells being drilled. Tough, dirty work. Orange groves, lemon groves, walnut orchards, olives being planted or harvested. Jobs. Money. Leave where you are and come to L. A. Gloria Swanson? Just an image on a glass-beaded screen on a Saturday night.

During the Twenties, L. A.'s population climbed from half a million to more than 1.2 million. Hardly anybody was a native — to be "born here" was a badge of distinction. In number of people, it came just behind New York, Chicago, Philadelphia and Detroit. And it was gaining on Detroit.

---

1 The "earthquake-proof" City Hall was heavily damaged in the Northridge quake of January 1995.

By area, it was the largest: its politicians controlled an enormous swath of territory, from the vast agricultural fields and orchards of the San Fernando Valley on the north, where the water poured in through the aqueduct from the Owens Valley, to the bustling ports of San Pedro and Wilmington, where the booze poured in from Mexico and Canada.

And the people kept coming. Dickie's siblings — Mabel, Vesta, Hubert, Harold and Woody — made the move to L. A. County from the Imperial Valley, with their little mom, leaving the hardscrabble farming life behind them. Eaph went to Kennewick, Washington. Florence stayed in Arizona.

People from all over the country still wanted to go to California, to cash in on the westward dream. One of them had been a young Arizona woman named Rena Vale, who, like Brick, had left the desert for a dream world. On March 13, 1928, she was announced as the winner of a screenplay "idea" contest run jointly by the fan magazine *Photoplay* and Paramount Pictures. She won $3,000 for her story, "Swag," which was supposed to be turned into a film starring George Bancroft.[2] It was never made, but she did not let her dream of fame fade away.

The newcomers found a city laced with streetcar lines and interurban electric railroads, but one that still had miles upon miles of open fields and unpaved drainage ditches. The business core was that stretch of seven or eight blocks running south on Broadway from First Street.

The place to look for a job was in the classified columns of the *Los Angeles Times,* a paper filled with publisher Harry Chandler's scorn for labor unions and other "disruptive" social forces. There were other dailies, too — the *Herald* and the *Express* (both owned by William Randolph Hearst), the *Hollywood Citizen-News* (Harlan Palmer's paper), the *Santa Monica Outlook, Pasadena Star-News, Beverly Hills Citizen, Inglewood Daily News,* and on and on. Every little town seemed to have one.

The brash kid in a new building at Pico and Los Angeles Street was the *Illustrated Daily News,* a tabloid run by tall, aristocratic Manchester Boddy. He had been an enterprising salesman who, using hastily borrowed money, bought the bankrupt paper from young Cornelius Vanderbilt Jr. in 1926. Gradually, he turned it into a success — by adopting progressive causes and fighting against what seemed to be L. A. County's pervasive graft and vice. Brick Garrigues, eleven years Boddy's junior, had left the *Express* copy desk to become one of the *Daily News'* star reporters. His specialty was reporting on local politics — and bashing the city's power structure. There was plenty to bash.

After two years of marriage, Brick and Dickie were doing well enough so that Dickie could quit her job from time to time when she didn't feel like working. She took business law classes at night at Poly High School

---

2 George Bancroft (1882-1956) was a tough-looking actor who had just been successful in his first starring role, in Josef von Sternberg's 1927 film *Underworld.*

(now the site of L.A. Trade-Tech College). She was, in truth, Sense to Brick's Sensibility.

August 25, 1927

Dear Fanny,

I've been doing another interesting thing the last couple of weeks -- studying Greek! I found my old college Greek book the other day, and since then I have gone over a lesson every day. It's really interesting to go back six years, learn paradigms and write out exercises as though you were just a kid again. I rather suspect I'm going to get a lot of fun out of it, and I've always had a desire to read a number of the classics. I may get that far yet.

Last night I heard Dvorak's "New World" and the Strauss "Death and Transfiguration." The first, of course, is nothing, but its pedantic development of some rather interesting themes and its meticulous contrapuntal devices prepare you to go into ecstasies over the tone poem. I'd never appreciated Strauss before.

And another thing. If Strauss can do the things he did in "The Hero's Life" and still be forgiven, surely there is hope for George Gershwin and Homer Simmons. Not that these two compare with Strauss, of course, but that "Rhapsody in Blue" is certainly more conventional than the fourth movement of "Helden Lieben."[3]

Dvorak's program of his symphony is interesting to anyone who can recognize the basis of his themes. Those parts which he says were written under Indian influence turn out to be plantation melodies, while the Southern themes show New English origin. I counted eleven American folk songs in the work besides a few Old English ones.

There was "Oh, Susannah!" of course, the principal part of the first movement, and "Goin' Home," which was a Negro spiritual long before Dvorak made it his largo almost note for note. Then there was "Old Dan Tucker," with which Dad used to sing me to sleep out in the plains of Kansas. The Virginia Reel was present, and a couple of Arkansas "breakdowns." Also he stole a large slice of "The Last Rose of Summer."

In these bucolic years, though, a disaster was looming for Los Angeles.

The city is arid. Water for its populace must be brought from hundreds of miles away. In 1913 the Los Angeles water department, led by its celebrated chief engineer, William Mulholland, completed its famed aqueduct to channel water from the distant Owens Valley. But the farm-

---

3 Gershwin's *Rhapsody in Blue* was first performed in 1924 by Paul Whiteman in an arrangement by Ferde Grofé for jazz piano and orchestra. *Ein Heldenleben* was the fourth tone poem of Richard Strauss (1864-1949), composed in 1898. Indiana-born Homer Simmons, a student of Jan Paderewski, came to California in 1910, wrote songs, spirituals, jazz and atonal music and occasionally played at the Hollywood Bowl.

ers of that valley resisted, going so far as to dynamite the aqueduct in 1924 and interrupt the city's water supply for several weeks. Besides, what if the aqueduct were severed by an earthquake? Mulholland determined to build a 180-foot-high, 600-foot-long dam in San Francisquito Canyon near Saugus, to store a year's supply of water.

But three minutes before midnight on March 12, 1928, the dam gave way, and a 78-foot wall of water tumbled toward the Pacific Ocean 54 miles away, bringing ranches, automobiles, animals, trees, boulders, houses — and people — with it. Within an hour or so, more than 500 men, women and children were dead, and the little town of Santa Paula lay crumpled beneath twenty-five feet of mud and filth. Brick had been in Ventura County a few hours before the dam broke, and ten years later he recalled that visit in a little pamphlet he published, *Why Didn't Somebody Tell Somebody?*

Santa Paula

A curious, graceful peace seemed to hang over the narrow, verdant valley as the season hovered halfway through the spring. Hay wagons were loading in the fields, peaches ripening on the trees. And people, as though they didn't know that all humanity is supposed to rush frantically from task to task, were sitting in the shade in the little towns, gossiping, or chatting, or just sitting.

Usually we don't go on jaunts in such a gentle mood. Usually we boast that we made it to Santa Barbara in two hours or to San Diego in two and a half or to San Francisco between eight and six. But today — because it was spring and because we were tired of the whish-whish of crowded highways, we had chosen the longest way around and were prepared to boast that we had made it to Ventura in not a minute less than eight hours.

You have known, perhaps, a friend, chatting, laughing, making plans — unconscious that he was doomed to die within a few hours? Perhaps he has left your side and started to cross the street and was run over by a truck. Or perhaps a building fell. And you read the next morning that such-and-such has happened and that the funeral will be held at such-and-such a time.

But did you ever take leave of a whole city, a whole population, laying aside, regretfully, a sudden new friendship for a people, while your new friend went on about its manifold tasks unconscious that it, too, had been doomed to sudden death in the night?

None of us knew of — or thought about — Saint Francis Dam, a narrow wall of concrete, bracing itself against billions of gallons, millions of tons, of water back somewhere in the hills. City people don't know about such things. A lake is such a placid thing; one forgets that it can become in a moment a raging carrier of death.

The last place we stopped in Ventura was at a roadside stand where a tawny-haired, smiling girl served us with steaks and French fried potatoes between whispered, laughing conferences with a blue-shirted boy at another table. Afterwards, we sat in the gathering dusk, and after a little while she turned out the lights in the place, and they sat with us for a while and we talked of crops and the weather and the price of gasoline and other things that people talk about when it doesn't matter whether they talk or not.

When he had gone away, she said, unnecessarily: "Isn't he swell! We're going to be married next month." There was pride and challenge in her voice — a challenge to the whole world to try to take away their happiness. And then we swung away into the darkness and saw the man we had to see in Ventura, and by midnight were back in our bed in our smelly, narrow city apartment.

It must have been three hours later that the telephone began to whirr. The voice of the city editor grated through the instrument: "Get on your clothes and get up to Ventura. There's been a big dam break up there and plenty hell to pay. Get going."

At dawn we were on top of a narrow hill from which we could look up the narrow valley — a valley filled from brim to brim with a raging yellow flood down which came tumbling houses and trees and the bodies of animals and people.

They found the girl wedged in the crotch of an uprooted tree — her tawny hair caked with mud, the laughing teeth set in a grimace of terror. Just one of 400 who died because "somebody didn't tell somebody." And what didn't they tell? Listen:

The story begins with two aging men — one a great engineer with a violent temper, the other a one-eyed millionaire with a genius for selling to agencies of government — at his own price — things they could buy from no one but him.

The engineer was William Mulholland — father of the Los Angeles Aqueduct. The other shall here be nameless — because he had no way of knowing that the plan he had so carefully worked out many years before would drive Mulholland into a rage which would result in the deaths of nearly 500 people. . . .

But in 1928 Brick Garrigues did not know exactly what had caused the Saint Francis Dam to collapse; nor did anyone else.[4] Yet this stunning tragedy was a momentary blip in Southern California life near the end of a joyous decade. People across the country were pretty well satisfied with the way things were going, and if some of them were getting rich from building faulty dams, it didn't affect the pocketbooks of most Angelinos.

It doesn't rain much in Southern California, but when it does, normally in January and February, the torrents can be deadly. That's why flood-control barriers are built in the steep canyons above the plains.

In 1928, reporters were beginning to hear rumors that Los Angeles County had made a foolish mistake in attempting to build a huge dam on the San Gabriel River — a debacle that would have been funny had it not been so expensive to the taxpayers. Voters had agreed to a $25 million bond issue for the dam, and work was well under way before it was

---

4 Carey McWilliams wrote later that Los Angeles city officials knew in advance of the dam's weakness, yet nothing was done. "For this folly, the city paid a heavy indemnity, but retained, and continued to honor, its chief engineer." But more recent research has demonstrated that, based upon the scientific knowledge of the time, the dam had been built as safely as possible.

discovered that there wasn't any bedrock on which to rest its foundations. Editors were hearing of fee-splitting and other graft. Eventually, the county wasted $4.3 million on a dam that was physically impossible to build.

In the meantime, Brick and Fanny continued their flood of letters. Fanny returned to New York, and she began to move in an artistic crowd. She was wooed by many men, some eligible, most not. One of them was Frank Harris, a controversial figure in both his life and his writings, whose autobiography, *My Life and Loves,* had been published in three volumes between 1923 and 1927. In 1928 he was seventy-two years old.

                                  2315 S. Flower Street
                                  October 4, 1928

My dear girl, when Frank Harris leered at you, why didn't you flash your most engaging smile? Then your great-grandchildren might have boasted of an affair their beloved ancestor had with the man who wrote those three naughty books. Such a chance doesn't come often, even in New York!

More seriously, though, I've seldom been as bowled over by any book as I was his "Life." I was so utterly amazed that I did something I suppose I'll always be ashamed of -- I sat down and wrote him a letter! But I remembered that you once did the same thing to some female novelist and I let my evil temptation engulf me. I was surprised to get an answer a few days ago.

Strange that everybody who has known Harris speaks of him as having a rather hateful, venomous personality. No doubt he has, toward those he considers his inferiors -- and everybody except Jesus and Shakespeare he considers his inferiors in these aging days. But in his books and in his letter he seems to me to be the kindliest of men. There's a real warmth of cordiality in his letter which I'm sure I should never waste upon an unknown correspondent.

But the "Life" -- ah, the "Life"! The Frank Harris he pictures, that he writes about, the literary character, I mean, who has nothing to do with the author, is a character as great as any in literature. I'm sure Harris -- the character -- is as great as Goethe's Faust or as Don Quixote and much greater than Hamlet. Of course, Harris -- the author -- never realized that he was writing fiction, that is, that he was creating a character. He thought he was depicting one. Perhaps he was. But we can't be interested in a nasty old man sitting alone in Nice, moaning because the world cannot appreciate him. We can be interested, however, in the man who took what he considered the sacred flame from the torch of Emerson, of Whitman, of Carlyle, who used it to light the pathway of Wilde and Dowson and a dozen others, and who now offers it to youth to carry on, only to have it refused because the torch is in the image of Priapos!

I remember your telling me of a friend of yours who died. Young, brilliant with life before him, he died. But that is not tragedy. To live, to fret out existence grasping at futile bubbles -- and seizing them -- to push forward toward the bunch of hay tied in front of the donkey's nose, carrying, transporting the load the gods want carried somewhere else -- and then to find at the end of the journey that the hay is only excelsior -- that's tragedy. Your friend fooled the gods. He did not wear out his existence pulling their chestnuts out of the fire under the illusion that they were to be his.

Of course you wouldn't like Harris. That's probably why I'm devoting an entire letter to him. You couldn't stand him. I can just imagine you trying to wade through the first volume! (Time out while I burst into laughter. You who were shocked at "Fanny Hill"!) Yet after the first ten pages I find it utterly impossible to consider it pornographic, or even daring. He discusses his affairs in the same spirit in which he discusses his stomach-pump. Oh, well.

> Frank Harris
> c/o The American Express
> 2 rue du Congres
> Nice, A.M., France
> 18/9/1928

Dear Mr. Garrigus:-

I am glad, indeed, that you like "My Life". You know, I suppose, that it has nearly ruined me. Till it appeared I used to get 12 - 15,000 Dollars a year from my other books in America, after it appeared this income simply ceased. The Americans don't want to have anything to do with me as a naughty boy.

So I intend to go to New York in October to lecture them again. If I get as far as Los Angeles, I hope that you will come to see me.

To begin at 72 is rather hard lines, but I am not frightened; one can only do one's best.

> Yours sincerely,
>
> *Frank Harris*

Fanny scoffed at Brick's admiration of Harris. She didn't like the man or his work. Brick replied:

> October 23, 1928

Dear Fanny:

You see, I'm still talking about Frank Harris. Disgusting! Rotten! And vile and slimy, too, no doubt. Strange, isn't it, how the element of sex-morality is so strong with women. Women have done a lot to emasculate our arts. In fact, I sometimes think the decline of the arts is due almost entirely to the fact that women have become, in the last analysis, the ultimate critics. And, frankly, I see no hope of improvement until some stronger race who keep their women in the kitchens and boudoirs comes along to wipe us out.

Anyway, the fact that good clean smut is utterly beyond women is something that has often engaged my attention. Even the most utterly emancipated women don't seem to quite understand it. Of course, Harris is not smutty. But open discussion of something that woman seems to realize is vitally important to her place in the social scheme seems as hateful to her as plain dirt. You used to reproach me for my taste in pornography, and I tell you frankly that pornography holds almost no appeal for me. But in his most outspoken moments, Harris is never pornographic.

Of course, I didn't expect you to like him when I mentioned him. And I'm rather glad you don't. It makes even smaller the little circle of us who have sufficient perspicacity to see him now instead of waiting a few hundred years for some critic to "discover" him.

Changing the subject now, do you know Sadakichi Hartmann? He's supposed to be an undiscovered genius or something of the sort. He's written an authoritative work on Confucius. I met him the other night. I didn't get a chance to talk to him much since, when he discovered that I didn't bring him a quart of wine, he disappeared into the bedroom and didn't come back. I believe a quart of wine is supposed to be the tribute paid by all the lesser mortals who desire to hear him talk.

Anyway, I'm supposed to go tomorrow night to a garden party at which he is to demonstrate the primitive steps of the Hawaiian dances. It should be delightful, since he looks like a cross between Nietzsche and a Pershing Square philosopher and is at least fifty years old.[5]

In November, the dour Republican Quaker, Herbert Hoover, was elected president of the United States over the Roman Catholic "Happy Warrior," Democrat Al Smith, 21,392,190 votes to 15,016,443.

January 24, 1929

Dear Fanny,

Did you here about Gil Cosulich marrying Bernice's assistant? Anyway, he did. Can you beat it? She got fired the same day and now Gil has to support both of them -- him

---

5 Of German-Japanese parentage, Hartmann (1869-1944) was an art critic, novelist, poet and man of letters. He was 59 years old at this time. Pershing Square, in the heart of a thriving downtown, was a center for speech-makers and haranguers of all religious and political persuasions.

and her, I mean. I think I'll write a story about a copyreader doing a stunt like that. I'm going down to see "The Front Page" Saturday night and learn some new cuss words to put in.[6]

I've been studying witchcraft -- not the craft but the witch cult. It's strangely interesting. I'd always believed like almost everybody else that witch-hunting was some strange form of hysteria like still-hunting or adulteress-stoning. Imagine my surprise when I found that something, either the old fairy religion of the aborigines or the devil-worship of the Manichees actually existed as a general religion down to a couple of hundred years ago. I've had a lot of fun with it, but think I've read everything available on the subject so I'll have to take up some new hobby.

I haven't been to but two concerts this winter. But one of them was Stokowski, directing the L. A. orchestra. Our orchestra is not bad, even though the director is terrible, and when Stokowski got through with two Bach chorales and his "Passacaglia" the audience was ready to tear the seats up and use them to make loud and tumultuous noises with.

Anyway, he got excited about the noise and the orchestra banging their instruments and proceeded to dash through the orchestra, shaking hands with everybody. I thought one old German, the leader of the basses, was going to kiss him smack flush square upon the mouth. There is a rumor, well-founded, I hope, that Los Angeles is going to hire him away from Philadelphia. Anyway, he's bought a big home here. They'll have to do something because the attendance at Schneevoigt's concerts has dropped to about three old women with season passes.[7]

I've just finished reading the "Golden Ass" of Apuleius and Ben Hecht's "Kingdom of Evil." You know, although I never read a book until it's been out at least five years, I really think that there never has been a period in history when so much great literature has been produced as during the last thirty years. Take the period with, roughly, the ending of the Victorian age. Dowson, Cabell, France, Machen![8] Where can you find anybody to compare with them in their own departments? Even Dreiser, I think, is greater than Balzac, Hugo or

---

6 This was the silent film version of Ben Hecht's raucous newspaper comedy, playing at the Belasco, and the event was a midnight press screening. "It has knocked the town coo-coo," read an ad on the *Herald* entertainment page. Hecht's Chicago City Hall reporter-protagonist, Hildy Johnson, provided an impossibly romantic, hard-drinking role model for a generation or more of young reporters to emulate, even if they had a wife and children parked somewhere in the suburbs.

7 Georg Schneevoigt was music director of the Los Angeles Symphony from 1927 to 1929. He was succeeded by Artur Rodzinski, not by Stokowski.

8 Arthur Machen (1863-1947), Welsh novelist and essayist, a forerunner of twentieth-century Gothic science fiction; Anatole France (1844-1924), considered the ideal French man of letters, awarded the Nobel Prize for Literature in 1921; James Branch Cabell (1879-1958), best known for the controversy over his *Jurgen* in the early 1920s.

Dickens. Hecht, faulty as he is, has hardly been exceeded --
and I'm anything but a Hecht fan. And a host of modern poets
who compare favorably with everybody from Shakespeare to
Dowson.

Oh, yes, I've just found a guide to good literature:
Find a book that you object to and then read it. Speaking,
at the present time, of Norman Douglas's "In the Beginning."[9] Of course, it was thrown together like a restaurant
stew, but then some morsels were exceedingly juicy. The
epidemic of goodness, of course had nothing to do with the
first of the book, and the whole thing was as loose-jointed
as Charlotte Greenwood.[10] But it contained pity and -- if
not terror -- at least some damn good laughter.

2011 1/2 Echo Park Ave.
February 20, 1929

Yesterday I went up to the top of a high hill right
here in the middle of the city -- and dawdled. Did you ever
dawdle? I'd forgotten that it could be done -- that one
could actually sit for three hours watching foolish little
man buzzing back and forth in his funny little cars or
shunting long freight trains from one track to another. I
think it was really the first time I'd been alone since I
came back from Tucson.

The trains that Brick watched that day were probably those in the
Taylor Yard, built by the Southern Pacific Railroad along the east bank
of the Los Angeles River in 1925. He could see this busy terminal from
the brim of what was known as "Red Hill" in the Echo Park district of
the city, given that name for the colony of free-thinkers and liberals who
lived in the area at the time, close by Brick and Dickie's little flat.[11] Just
two years before, the charismatic revivalist preacher Aimee Semple
McPherson (1890-1944) had finished the massive Angelus Temple by
Echo Park itself. Her passionate, Hollywood-style sermons and radio
messages had brought her nationwide fame.[12]

We've found the most bucolic place to live. It's up in
the hills north of Aimee's temple. A narrow little valley

---

9 Published in 1928 by the John Day Co., *In the Beginning* was a story set in the days, as the
author put it, "when Immortals sought pleasure where they found it—not only in their own Celes-
tial Halls but among the sons and daughters of earth; days when mankind thereabouts walked
naked without shame, and the thing called Sin had not been invented." Douglas (1868-1952) was a
Scottish author known for his travel writing as well as his novels.

10 The first movie of actress-comedian Charlotte Greenwood (1893-1978) was *So Long Letty*
in 1929; the last was *Glory* in 1956.

11 As this book is published, the city has plans of turning the abandoned 174-acre Taylor
switching yards into a park and to renovate the nearby Los Angeles River.

12 In 1926, "Sister Aimee" had disappeared while swimming in the ocean in front of her
Venice hotel. Airplanes and deep-sea divers were called into the search, during which a lifeguard
drowned. A month later she reappeared, telling a story of kidnapping and torture and how she
escaped across the Mexican desert. When evidence surfaced that she had spent the time with a
church radio technician, charges were filed against her, but they were later dropped.

between the greenest hills you could imagine. The other side of the valley is studded with houses but there are wide places between, several blocks in width, and trees out of which I'm sure hamadryads would creep if you sat very silently. You never could see my nymphs, could you? Sadakichi Hartmann's most frequent Los Angeles stopping place is just at the top of the hill.

I wish you could hear Sadakichi lecture on the dance. When I heard him he was recovering from one of his epileptic spells and was even more unintelligible than usual. But his gestures are enough to hypnotize you as he sways back and forth, illustrating what he has to say. He claims to have taught Isadora Duncan the things that really made her the dancer she was. After watching him for half an hour I haven't the slightest doubt of it. Incidentally, Marjorie[13] says that, aged and sick and dissipated as he is, he'll sometimes literally dance for hours for his own pleasure much as less strenuous persons would read a book.

July 9, 1929

I must have told you that I've left the Herald and am working on the Daily News. I don't know whether you remember it or not, but it's tab in form and amateur in content. It pays a little better money than the Herald, and I'm reporting, which isn't nearly so stultifying as telegraph rewrite or copy-reading.

Besides that, I've appointed myself music critic, which doesn't pay anything except by-lines and a chance to hear considerable music for nothing. Also I get an opportunity to pan some of my particular abominations such as Percy Grainger and Goossens.[14] The latter is to conduct three weeks at the Bowl this summer, and I'm saving a whole dictionary full of vitriolic adjectives for his particular benefit.

I'm also the paper's only sob sister. Whenever a mother burns her baby to death or has some such pleasant aberration, I get myself another by-line. And really, I'm getting quite enthusiastic over those things since I tired of the anonymity of the copydesk.

Also, I've been studying music, philosophy and history in order not to be too abysmally ignorant.

By September 1929, Dickie's older sisters Florence and Mabel both had children. At the age of twenty-four, Dickie felt it was also family time for her. When straightforward talk with Brick failed, Dickie wept, he yielded, and soon they conceived a child.

---

13 Otherwise unidentified.

14 Percy Grainger was the Australian-born composer, pianist and conductor, then 47, who had written *Country Gardens* and *Molly on the Shore*. Eugene Goossens (later knighted), 36, was conductor of the Rochester Symphony Orchestra.

336 West 82nd Street
September 19, 1929

Back to normal, after a rather disturbed two months. I remember you urged me once not to become domesticated. I'm afraid the process is complete -- so thoroughly that we've bought ourselves a lot of furniture and will probably buy a house when we get the furniture paid for. Wasn't there a story about a poet who had become a pawnbroker? But then O. Henry had a story about a poet with a voice like a crow. Qu'importe?

The process has been gradual, subjective and unconscious. Until we were really established here with the furniture all dusted off, I didn't realize how far it had gone. And now I sometimes suspect that the sands of time will be just as attractive unmarked by my rather large pedal extremities.

October 6, 1929

I had a run-in with a chap named Zorrada the other day. He's Caruso's old secretary, is very close to Otto Kahn[15] and signs the releases for all the Metropolitan singers that the Los Angeles Opera Association uses. Also he's the husband of Nina Morgana, a third-rate soprano whom he manages to keep working at the Metropolitan with enough concerts and special tours to keep him in clothes.

Well, I put Morgana on the grease and gently panned the opera association for hiring her as leading soprano -- not knowing as I should have, that such a rotten singer must be somebody's wife or girl friend. The results were really surprising. He threatened to cut the Los Angeles company off the Metropolitan list and it took three days to cool him down. Now I'll have to write a puff about Morgana tonight when she sings Gilda -- which she can't sing any better than I can. But it's quite flattering to know that at least somebody in town reads your stuff.

Now, have you ever noticed that in retrospection life often attains that very orderliness which is denied it in the present? Somewhat like a rondo, its haphazard incidents, seen from a distance, arrange themselves in a false appearance of organization and form. Or, to change the metaphor, like a group of aimlessly scattered hills, when seen from a valley, fall into ranges and chains and peaks. The moments of happiness live in our memory, and even the moments of sorrow or just plain boredom gain a lustre which half-consciously makes us regret that those somehow-bolder days are ended.

A thing which has always hampered and cramped me was the realization that the long hours of preparation and

---

15 Bruno Zirato (the correct spelling) was an important figure in American music for decades. Otto Kahn was the Metropolitan Opera's president from 1918 to 1931.

working-out were largely sterile. Because life, each moment, seemed so valuable, I have been unwilling to waste a thousand moments of labor in preparation for one moment of production. I would rather have been a hen who lays an egg every day than to have taken 270 times that long to give birth to a Hercules. Only I wanted each egg to be a Hercules.

But enough of philosophy (so-called). It's time to hasten back to the recounting of what Eunice Pringle thinks about Mr. Pantages, and of how a Beverly Hills heiress stole the love of Santa Monica's handsomest policeman.

Alex Pantages, the theater magnate, was on trial for statutory rape of Eunice Pringle, a seventeen-year-old showgirl. The prosecution was brought by Buron Fitts, a former state American Legion commander and California lieutenant governor who had been elected Los Angeles County district attorney with the aid of the conservative Hearst and Chandler newspapers (the *Examiner* and the *Times)*. Pantages was convicted later in the month, but the State Court of Appeal threw out the case on the grounds of what one observer, writer Guy Finney, called Fitts' "theatrically intemperate conduct." That was an appeal that was to make the reputation of Pantages' young attorney, Jerry Giesler, whose high-profile Hollywood cases later made him famous as the "attorney to the stars." On retrial, Pantages was acquitted. Years later, on her deathbed, the story goes, Pringle admitted she had been paid to frame him.

In New York, Fanny joined the newly revived Provincetown Players, the theatrical company that first introduced the plays of Eugene O'Neill and presented works by Edna St. Vincent Millay and Djuna Barnes. It was supposed to present its season not in its traditional Greenwich Village haunts but in the Garrick Theater uptown. On October 28, "Black Friday," the stock market crashed. Investors were wiped out to the tune of $28 billion.

November 7, 1929

I hope the star you are understudying breaks a leg, or even a neck. You've enough of that "elan vital" (whatever that may be) so I'm sure you're going to succeed in something. And it might as well be the theater as the dance. A great dancer and a great actress are made by the same thing, physical handicaps such as a cork leg, aside. Of course, you still have some handicaps, such as your unconquerable puritanism, and, I might add, Victorian romanticism, but you may yet outgrow them.

By the way, my drunken Irish poet, Joe O'Carroll, tells me he once had a very violent affair with the secretary of the Provincetown Players. I've forgotten her name, but I wondered if she were still there. Of course, you couldn't go about asking all the ladies of the organization if they had lived in sin (I love that succulent old expression) with a drunken Irish poet, but I'm sure she wouldn't have forgotten him. Women never do, men like Joe.

We have here all the material for a fair-sized echo of the Stokowski row now going on in the East.[16] Our new conductor, Artur Rodzinski, is a pocket-sized edition of Stokowski. He plays the same things in the same general style, and goes over quite well with the crowd -- even without the blond hair. Our audience, being somewhat unsophisticated, shuddered almost as much at "Festa Romana" as New York's did at the Schoenberg variations. And they received the Bach Toccata and Fugue as enthusiastically as New York and Philadelphia received the Bach "Passacaglia." Now both Stokowski and Rodzinski do those things exceedingly well. But their Mozart and Schubert and Beethoven leave a lot to be desired. So we have all the material for an excellent three-way scrap here, and I can't really take part in it.

Also there's the fact that Rodzinski is under a five-year contract and will undoubtedly make good with the audience enough so they'll keep him. But the prospect of hearing, once a week for five years, the identical dramatizations of each, the inevitable interpretations of some horrific moderns and the weekly massacre of the classics is a prospect none too enticing. Maybe I'll take up gardening or chess as a hobby instead of music.

If some rich uncle would only die, I'd chuck it and start for New York. But I haven't any, and the business of married life precludes any such attempt.

December 8, 1929

I've been busy since I wrote last. A week in a hospital. A new novel which expired on the first page. But a DAMN good first page. I may finish it. A newspaper fight -- the most bitter Los Angeles has ever known -- and I'm doing the leading with bylines half an inch high. And best of all, three weeks of the most enjoyable grand opera I can imagine. I suspect I'm infatuated with the prima donna.

The newspaper fight you wouldn't be interested in. Our little two-penny paper is fighting the two Hearst papers and the Times, with a combined circulation of 750,000. We licked 'em in the first round, and it looks like we might whip them in the next. They're raging, raving, absolutely gone mad. And we pump it into them every morning with an absolutely fiendish delight at twisting the knife.

But the opera! It's a new company formed by a Los Angeles man who thinks you can put on opera in America without a lot of big names, charge reasonable prices and make a financial success. I don't know the financial

---

[16] Leopold Stokowski was in the midst of a furor caused by his performance of "modern" music with the Philadelphia Orchestra.

outcome, but he's certainly succeeded in putting on opera as it should be.

He's apparently scoured South America, Europe and the United States for singers who are good looking, who can sing, and who can be hired for almost nothing. Bright, fresh costumes, a cast under thirty years and 150 pounds (with two exceptions), a chorus of fifty, a large orchestra, and the best seats at three dollars. Modernistic scenery, which seems somewhat out of place, and the efforts of a flock of young singers, singing their heads off, makes opera for the first time something other than a thing you must attend if you would be Cultured.

The coloratura, Tina Paggi, a sister of Ada Paggi of the Chicago company, can't do better than high C and sometimes not that. But just below the top of her range she has the most beautiful limpid tones which would turn Galli-Curci green with envy, and her middle register is clear as a bell.

The dramatic tenor, Nino Piccaiuga, looks like Francis X. Bushman and sings as well as any tenor I've heard. There is a little harshness in his voice -- otherwise, Gigli and Lauri-Volpi would be looking for a job.[17] They have two good baritones, one only twenty-four, and a good basso, who is also a little too young. Genaro Barra, a good dramatic tenor for such things as Zaza, and a youngster named Barsotti fill in the gaps. Patricia Robazza, whoever she may be, turned in a marvelous performance as Zaza last night, and they were actually throwing flowers on the stage.

But the idol, the one I'm half infatuated with, is our new Carmen. Her name is Louise Caselotti, a local girl, nineteen years old, and a daughter of Maria Caselotti, prima donna of the Royal Opera House at Rome.[18] Or maybe it's the mother I'm infatuated with.

The girl, slim and graceful, an excellent dancer, looks like a combination of Clara Bow[19] and the Holy Virgin. Her voice is young yet. For dramatic effect, she creates her tones rather far back, making them a little dark and obscure. Vocally, there have been much better Carmens than she is today, but I seriously doubt if dramatically and in all those other things which Carmen demands more than voice, there has ever been a greater Carmen than she is right now.

17 Francis X. Bushman (1883-1966) was the silent film idol of the 1920s. Beniamino Gigli (1890-1957) had been with the New York Metropolitan since 1927; he was regarded as Enrico Caruso's successor.

18 Louise Caselotti studied with her father, the voice teacher Guido Caselotti, She made her debut with the San Carlo Opera Company in Los Angeles in 1927. She became particularly known for her Carmen, which she sang more than 400 times. She was also memorable as the gypsy Azucena in *Il Trovatore*. As a voice teacher, her most famous pupil was Maria Callas, whom she coached in the 1940s. She died in July 1999 in Malibu. Her sister was Adriana Caselotti, who in 1937 became the voice of Snow White in the Disney movie.

19 Known as the "It" girl after appearing in a movie of that name in 1927, film sensation Clara Bow was seen as the vivacious, emancipated flapper of the 1920s.

In the first place, her Carmen, utterly different from the usual voluptuous (pardon me) hussy, is a fiery little flapper of the year of Our Lord 1929. In appearance, acting and dancing, she actually creates this new character as though Carmen had never been done before. There is nothing wild or unrestrained about her -- in fact she shows considerably more restraint than is usual, yet there's a blazing, suppressed fire about her which makes you want to hiss as you hissed the dirty villain in the ten-twent'-thirt'.

With a flapper Carmen, a Don Jose who looks like F.X.B., a Micaela who can sing and an Escamillo who can sing and is still under twenty-five -- well, the opera has a raison d'etre.

Then, too, the operas are being given in the Biltmore Theater, which is small enough so that you can sit in the top gallery and toss an egg with unerring accuracy on the stage. There is a sort of Italian atmosphere -- I'm not speaking of garlic. But if somebody wants to shout a brava during an aria, he does it, and if he wants to hiss, he hisses. The Cultured Iowans are in a minority, and the theater between acts has the atmosphere of the green room on first nights.

Except for Caselotti, I'm not discovering any new stars. It's the atmosphere and the ensemble. But now I must tell you of someone I have helped to discover.

He's a 'cellist, named Gregor Piatigorsky, comparatively unknown in this country, I think. They call him the Russian Casals, but he's the Russian Piatigorsky. There's only one.[20]

Did you ever attend an orchestral rehearsal? As soon as the conductor lays down his baton, the musicians dash for the door and their lunch. Tuesday I happened to stop in just as rehearsal closed. Imagine my surprise when the conductor laid down his baton and the orchestra turned loose a flock of bravos and dashed, not for the door, but for the 'cellist. It looked like the gang on the bench surrounding the fullback after he had run ninety-five yards to the winning touchdown. So I stuck around. They wouldn't let that Bolshevik out of there until 2 o'clock, and there wasn't a musician left the stage while he sat and played and played and played as Orpheus never played.

The next day I snuck in the stage door and hid for another rehearsal, and the next day the musicians demanded and got another free recital. So you can imagine he's good, regardless of what I might say. Remember the name and hear him when he goes to New York.

As ever,

Brick

---

20 Piatigorsky, actually a Ukrainian, had just left as first cellist of the Berlin Philharmonic to devote his time to solo work. He was then only 26.

Chapter Eight
Janet

By 1930 the Southern California boom was over. Many Angelinos were literally being starved by the Depression. Sad-faced men and women sold apples on street corners. Sometimes entire families would line up for food baskets marked "Americans," "Colored" or "Mexican" given out by a city employees' Food Relief Fund or some other charitable agency. The new Central Library on Fifth Street, just west of the ornate Biltmore Hotel (at that time the symbol of conspicuous consumption in downtown L.A.), was jammed with the jobless, some of them looking for work in the *Times* ads, others merely out of the house on the pretense that they had jobs to go to during the day.

In New York, the crash had put Fanny out of work when financial backers deserted the new Provincetown Players.

```
                                    January 14, 1930

Dear Fanny,

     It's too bad the Players had to fold up. Seems almost
like a tragedy even to me, who am, are, or is not the
slightest bit interested in the drahma, or even the drama.
But even the fact that you're out of a job cannot keep me
from being one of those happy persons whom you'd gladly
choke. Because -- I can't imagine why -- I'm still
fascinated by life. Maybe I've had a glandular renaissance.
```

Yet in Los Angeles, if you had work, it was easy to forget the bread lines and the Hoovervilles springing up in the empty lots. The people with money were able to maintain the roseate glow of the Twenties and to Charleston and fox-trot with the rest of the Jazz Age kids. The motion-picture industry was still the county's biggest money maker (with the possible exception of agriculture), and of course Hollywood had developed its own kind of wacky, Prohibition-era culture.

I've got in with a rather interesting bunch lately. There's a little wop named Phil Pizza whose father makes 100 gallons of wine at a time; and his room-mate, a young artist; and Mary Fabian, the former Chicago Opera Co. singer who has a perfectly golden voice; and Lisa Roma, of whom you may possibly know through her association with Ravel; and Ken Duncan, the actor whom I've discovered I used to room with under the name of Ken McLaughlin; and Alice Gentle is coming over next week if she's in town by that time.[1] There are a few others, motion picture people, and radio persons and that sort of thing. Pizza and I went to college together and since then he's lived in Italy and Germany and France. Seems to know every body from Caruso on down, but doesn't boast about it.

Oh, yes, there's also a little girl with whom I was in love for a week or two. Maybe I am yet, I'm not sure. She's a damnably beautiful little thing, but I haven't been able to find out whether she's just terribly stupid or damned interesting. I think its the third time I've been in love in the last two months. So I must be regaining my lost youth. I suppose I'll be bored with them all in another week, though.

Since August, the News has been engaged in a newspaper fight with the two Hearst papers. We are fairly new and only have a circulation of 100,000, while they have 400,000. Yet last week we beat them hands down, clean, slick as a whistle. I'm the little boy that did it -- or at least, I get the credit, while the boss did it. So he gives me a nice raise and all the newspapermen in town look on me as a "big shot" and I just bask in glory.

417 W. 52nd St.
March 29, 1930

I hope you'll pardon the lengthy delay. It's not that I haven't been thinking of you, but rather that I've been thinking so constantly of another certain person that every time I've tried to write to you I found I was writing of nothing but her.

It's nothing serious. I should say that it's all over now, or practically so. but it was extremely delightful for

---

[1] Lisa Roma (b. 1893) had toured with Maurice Ravel in 1928, was teaching music at USC and had been prima donna of the Berlin Staatsoper. His other friends also had that cosmopolitan air that fascinated the young man from the Imperial Valley: Kenne Duncan (1902-1972) was a Hollywood regular who, over his lifetime, was a henchman in more than 400 B Westerns and numerous talkie serials. Alice True Gentle (1889-1958) was a Metropolitan Opera singer.

a while and for a while not a damn bit delightful. And now -- I don't know whether I'm glad or sorry that the damn thing occurred, if it ever did really "occur."

I did one wise thing -- which changed the outcome of the affair materially, I suppose. Realizing that I was playing with dynamite and that I probably would make a damn fool of myself, I introduced the lady to my wife. Dickie was wise enough to make a close friend of her, and the girl was sensible or honorable enough not to permit the affair to work out to its logical conclusion.

She is an unusual person. You know that it seldom takes me three months or three weeks to attain a mental contact with any man or woman if I'm interested in them. I think I usually inspire a sort of confidence which begets a mental intimacy. Yet, after acting as father confessor to this girl for three months, and after probably knowing her better than any other person knows her, I have come no nearer to "contacting" that mind and spirit than I had the first evening I met her. Yet, whenever I come to the conclusion that there's nothing behind that extremely pretty face, I suddenly discover an intricate mind and a fine spirit -- for just a flash.

She has beauty and that undefinable thing called charm. She has, in a great instance, that elusiveness so fatal to any man, plus the damnedest indifference you could imagine. But, worst of all, there is some indescribable thing about her which is just the opposite of the "clinging vine" and yet which makes every man want to do any thing in the world to help her or make her happy. It's like the feeling one would have for a very likable little kid who is carelessly hammering dynamite caps with a rock. And who turns away from you rather contemptuously -- or indifferently -- when you try to explain that dynamite caps aren't meant to be pounded. And then, when she gets a couple of fingers blown off, instead of running for help she hides behind the house to keep from being scolded.

I find I'm still writing of nothing but her. So bear with me, because my head is clearing a bit, and I think I'll be back to normal again in a few days. I was even able to think of my work for several hours yesterday, and I noticed when Dickie bought a new dress. So I seem to be recovering, and I think with Virgil "Forsan et haec olim meminisse iuvabit."[2]

In the meantime, I've managed to hold my job and bluff the publisher into thinking I was pretty good. I've been detached from the local staff for six weeks and working directly out of the publisher's office for the most part. He is a gem. Frequently I go in to report on what I've been doing and we'll start talking philosophy or art or religion

---

2 "Perhaps someday it will be pleasant to remember even this."

and spend the rest of the day arguing. He has the keenest mind I've ever known, and we hit it off perfectly.

Phil Pizza, who owns the apartment at which our crowd used to get together, has been producing a play for the last six weeks, and his "at homes" have been discontinued. It's a farce called "Slapstick," which was to have opened Friday night. But the leading man went on a two weeks' drunk, and he couldn't afford an understudy, so the opening was postponed until next week.

I'll never get to New York. My work is cut out for me, apparently: pushing politicians about from day to day. We're the smallest paper in the city, but we've captured the City Hall from the basement to the 26th story (how proud we are of that enormous building!) Next week we're going to move in on the county buildings and attempt to capture the Board of Supervisors. So I'll probably be doing this until I dry up and blow away.

Also there's the fact -- hitherto unmentioned, I believe -- that an increase in the Garrigues family is expected within a couple of months. Another hostage to fortune.

April 7, 1930

It's funny how the thing finally ended. I had a friend at the office, a fellow much like myself in many ways. I introduced him to her three weeks ago. Last night they became engaged -- and while a wife may not be a bar to association with another woman, a fiance seems a definite one to association with another man. It's funny.

I sacrifice a part of the happiness of a wife that I think the world of for the sake of her friendship, yet she cannot risk the displeasure of a man she's known only three weeks for the sake of mine. Out of the welter of the hurts and delights, that is the only thing that really hurts, now.

I'm no longer a callow youth, and most of my affairs have dropped conveniently into one or another pigeonhole. But I've never been able to find a place to pigeonhole this one. I've never been untrue to Dickie even in thought, as far as Janet was concerned. There was nothing of that sweet madness which burns white-hot and welds together two persons who, perhaps, should not be together. In that sense, it was not a love affair.

Yet, now that it's all over, and I face the definite certainty of a morrow with the realization that she will not be calling me or seeing me, there comes the realization that the morrow holds little or nothing worth while. For three months I've awakened each morning with my eyes on the clock, counting the hours until I see her. Tomorrow the hands of the clock might as well run backwards. For three months I've started each time a telephone rang in the office, hoping that it might be her. For three months I've

treasured each coup I've pulled in the office until I could
tell her -- and tomorrow I must score the regulation number
of coups with nobody to tell about them.

And tomorrow, and Wednesday and Thursday and Friday
and an endless succession of Wednesdays and Thursdays and
Fridays, will be merely days on which one rises at the
appointed time, stays under the shower for the usual
number of minutes, and eats the appointed quantity of
food before crawling back into the sheets for the
prescribed amount of sleep.

And yet, -- I swear it -- I was never in love with the
person. I would never have given up Dickie for her nor even
have done anything which would hurt Dickie seriously. I
have never felt romantically about the lady nor indited an
ode to her eyebrow. Can you imagine the power of a woman
whose mere presence and friendship -- without any hope or
desire of anything else -- can arouse such emotions in a
usually insusceptible man?

She's always called me her guardian -- she's seven
years younger than I. I've tried to help her through a lot
of scrapes that she's got herself in and I have the
satisfaction of knowing that I've probably been really
closer to her than any other person will ever be.

One thing about it keeps me from marking the thing
definitely closed. She was swinging back from the effect of
a disastrous experience at the other end of the pendulum
when she met this chap. She's told me -- and I don't think
it's vanity which makes me believe it -- that she thinks
she can find in him the things which she likes in me, but
may take them without stealing from another woman.

As I told you, there are many things about Steve which
are like me. But he's shifty and mean and brutal -- things
which I am not. I suspect that his designs are not
altogether what our forefathers would call honorable. I'm
terribly afraid he's going to hurt her. Janet has been hurt
terribly by another man just the opposite of this one, and
I'm afraid if this one hurts her in the same way, the poor
little devil will just about be broken.

I feel that it ended perfectly. There was just enough
fatherly advice, and then a heart-to-heart talk about
ourselves which I'll always treasure. This afternoon we sat
on the hills east of Santa Monica -- and watched the clouds
of fog roll in and obscure the sun while we traced together
her feelings during the last three months. I was amazed to
learn that she had felt exactly of me as I had felt of her.
She had always thought I was in love with her. It took all
the sting out of the ending to have it end in that way.

And then, at the close, I became again the poseur and
made the perfect curtain speech. It was the usual thing,
but well done and after I said "goodbye" she sat for just a

moment before she whispered "adios" and went into the
house. I drove away with the knowledge that something beautiful had ended -- as beautifully as it had begun.

But Toni wasn't buying that line. You're in love with the girl, or
infatuated in some other way, she told him, because obviously you didn't
end it as you said you would. No, no, it's something else, he responded.

May 11, 1930

It seems an experience, a condition, which defies all
attempts to catalogue it. Unfortunately, we have really
only two words to express a personal relationship between a
man and a woman; and by force of custom we are compelled to
force the most fragile human relationships into the molds
of those two words.

"Infatuation" presupposes a blindness to the shallow-
ness, dishonesty and general worthlessness of the object of
the infatuation. "Love" denotes selfishness, a desire to
possess, besides all the other romantic folderol the poets
have written into it.

Neither applies. I am fully aware that Janet is a dumb
little liar, without background, education or sex appeal.
Yet my awareness does not mitigate or increase the
affection I have for her. It only astonishes me that she
can be so damned appealing in spite of these things. Nor
have I ever desired to possess her physically. I do,
however, desire to possess her mentally, to stimulate and
mold a little brain that is keen as hell at times, and this
desire has become more or less an obsession with me.

But, whatever it is, it's an experience without
parallel in my life. From the evening I met her the world
seemed suddenly alive again for the first time in years --
fearfully and vividly alive. That feeling has lasted for
nearly five months, and today I seem to be able to look
past the surface of any person and read the very writing on
his soul. What I mean is this:

Years ago, people and things interested me because they
were strange and provoked my curiosity. Then they became
commonplace; I filed them away in pigeonholes. Since this has
come up, every man, woman and child seems to have become
blood brother to me. I see them blundering and muddling
along, not with scorn and not with compassion, but as though
I could look straight into them and count every scar on their
souls as clearly as though their bodies were of glass.

Of course, the thing didn't end when it was supposed
to. I've become too damned arrogant to let it, and I've
plotted like Machiavelli to restore it to as near my desire
as I can manage.

The trouble was this. The existence of Dickie, and the
fact that Dickie and the girl were friends, forced Janet to

keep at a figurative arm's length. I didn't know that I was NOT in love with her in the usual way, and Janet had no way of knowing it either. We both saw that we needed a fourth to make up a foursome. We selected a rather good friend of mine. That was Steve.

Unfortunately, he went over too well, and immediately insisted that the girl should not see me again. He convinced her that I was madly in love with her (am I?) and that Dickie was weeping her eyes out about it, making Janet so ashamed she didn't want to see either one of us.

Not being able to see the girl, and realizing that her mitt was so full of Steve by this time that she couldn't even hear me if I told her I was not in love with her and that we should all be good friends, I had to plot.

As a result, Janet and Steve broke up in a grand battle which I started, behind the scenes, last week. And she came running back to Dickie and me for comfort and to defy her boyfriend. This was the opportunity I had been waiting for. I rushed her to Dickie and to all her friends that Steve had not let her see for a month. I put her through five days of careful, brotherly, coaching on her duty to Steve and to herself, and I had her committed to a program which would eventually have ended with Steve a very mere fiance, if it had worked out.

Janet was coached by me to work for one thing -- to permit Steve to come back only with the assurance that she was no longer a slave to his whims and that she would continue to be the best of friends to Dickie and me. From the fact that she hasn't called, I suspect that she lost -- and was forced to take him back on his own terms. Which is an utter and downright defeat for me. What's the use of such extremely cunning plotting when you can't depend upon your forces in the field!

Joe O'Carroll suggests that this little chit has caused more plottings and counterplottings than Helen of Troy. And really, it strikes me that there is something Homeric in the story. The Achaians, though, went not to bring back fair Helen, but to avenge the dishonor that had been done to Menelaus. I hope it doesn't take ten years, but if it does, I'll still be on the job, regardless of how old and ugly the girl may be by that time.

(Interval of twelve hours)

I'm satisfied. I just called her and I think the ten-year Trojan war is ended.

It seems that the expected reconciliation did not go through. Steve, instead of being eager to make up, struck the high, mighty and lofty note of a man who had loved a girl madly and who had been grossly and vilely deceived by her. (All she did was to come over to Dickie's and my place).

At first she flatly refused to talk with me. I finally persuaded her to give me an outline of what had happened and how she felt; my revenge on Steve is complete. They may go back together, but I won't mind that. I won't even mind so much losing Janet's friendship, although I'm going to make an effort to retain it for both of us. She blames Dickie and me, although she doesn't suspect all the plotting and connivery that's been going on. And, blaming us, she hates us. I don't want her to hate us, and while I'm well satisfied, I should much prefer that she should hate Steve. If there's any way I can manage that, I'm going to do it.

I really feel quite proud of my dirty tricks.

May 19, 1930

Here I am again, with the threatened continuation of the sacking of Troy.

In our last installment, I had just learned from the little girl that her boyfriend had walked out on her because she had gone out with me. She sounded over the phone as though the world had come to an end, and the moment had arrived to strike the last telling blow by calling up Steve and telling him:

"You can come back and get your girl now; I don't want her any more."

But the civilization of 2,000 years had softened your modern Achilles. I went to the phone to deliver the last, dirty dig at him and instead I found myself assuring him:

That it was all a mistake. That he had no reason to be jealous of me because his girl and I had never been interested in each other. That he could go back to her with the definite assurance that she would never deceive him with me again. That Dickie and I missed her a lot, but that we felt her happiness should come first.

And he came back, on the run. I met Janet by accident the next evening and she thanked me perfunctorily adding "but of course he would probably have come back anyway."

Otherwise, I've been living about the same as I did before I met her -- working and reading and sleeping; a little bored and a little lonely. I've never felt quite so alone as I have recently -- not lonely for her, but just without friends. Of course, there is Dickie, but then a wife is really a part of you and doesn't keep you from being lonely. And a girl I take to dinner occasionally; one who is a splendid pal and lots of fun in a way.

With Janet out of the way, Brick turned to thoughts of another woman. You don't have to look very hard to find a great deal of preening and clucking going on here, with not a lot of serious intent.

Once I might have thrilled at an affair with an opera singer -- even one not particularly attractive, although said to be quite accomplished. Perhaps it might be a tale to tell my grandchildren -- of how I had gone to bed with one of the greatest sopranos of my generation. But it doesn't really seem worthwhile.

She, Mary Fabian, really seems to have taken quite a fancy to me and has asked me to her apartment for dinner several times, but I've alway delayed naming the definite evening. And she really has one of the most perfect voices on the stage today. In view of the fact that I consider a great singer "something above royalty and not below the saints," I suppose I should be thrilled. Anyway, she's going to try to sing "Traviata" this fall with the L.A. Opera Company. She's a lyrico-spinto,[3] who can sing mezzo, and how she's going to manage Violetta, I can't imagine. So I'll probably have to pan her, and it's against my principles to pan anyone with whom I've slept.

But we've been having quite a bit of fun. We've had two grand opera nights at the Press Club with lots of beer and Puccini in the last two weeks. Lisa Roma and Mary Fabian provided the Puccini and our excellent brewmaster provided the beer. Do you like Gloria Swanson's voice in the talkies? I just heard last night that Mary is doubling for her in her singing parts.

Yet, after all, I'd like to be in New York, particularly since you seem obdurate about coming back to California. Or I'd like to be in Santa Fe -- or perhaps herding sheep in the Taos country. I've just finished "Death Comes for the Archbishop,"[4] and feel homesick for the wide open spaces. When music, books, beer and women bore me, I think it's time to start mowing the lawn again and become a respectable householder.

Fanny wrote that she thought so highly of his letters that she was saving them all for posterity, or in case some day he would like to make a novel of them.

June 1, 1930

I hate to think of a long series of my letters in existence. They must be entirely too revealing -- of something. The inconstancy of man, I suppose. I flatter myself that there should be good material in there somewhere for a novel. Not that the character is particularly interesting, but that he is at least comic enough to be human. I do think, though, that if I ever write a novel it will be about you. I have one half-sketched out, but it probably never will come to anything.

---

3 A singing voice having both lyric and dramatic qualities.

4 Willa Cather's novel of French Catholic missionaries in the American Southwest.

I was surprised, though, astonished, flabbergasted and what have you when I learned that my letters about Janet were so desperate as to hint of the possibility of a murder and a suicide. Probably because, in the recesses of my mind, I was having a good laugh at myself all the time for the way things affected me. I wouldn't say that I was ever, for one moment, faking an emotion, or theatricalizing the affair, but from the very start there was always a large part of me watching myself with huge quantities of amusement. And I think that was true even at the worst part. So that, bad as it was, I attained katharsis in rattling my broken heart in front of a sympathetic listener.

Now that it has faded, I'm really happier than while it was going on. Life is not so hectic, for one thing, and it's more pleasant to be oneself than to be a shadow for some insignificant girl. I haven't called Janet for two weeks -- just quit suddenly on the best of terms and with no explanation. And as far as Dickie and I are concerned, she has simply ceased to exist until she comes around and begs forgiveness -- in actions as well as words. Then we may accept her again as a friend -- after plenty of probation.

Saturday night Mary Fabian gave a little dinner for half a dozen or so of us. I took Lisa Roma and we had lots of fun. Mary sang beautifully. Except for Rethberg,[5] I don't know a female anywhere who has the gorgeous golden quality in her voice that Mary has. And Lisa sang, as did a new baritone from San Francisco -- Mario Fiorella. Altogether it was a thoroughly successful evening. Thursday evening, Lisa is singing Elijah with Schuman-Heinck and Tibbett at the USC festival. We're going to the Press Club to drink beer and vocalize afterward -- if a sudden call from the stork doesn't interrupt.

The great event is due Sunday. But I don't know how you expect me to get excited about it in advance. It's utterly impossible for me to anticipate the pangs of fatherhood, although I confess I look at other people's brats with considerably more curiosity than in the past.

But the baby carriage, the clothes and the modern equivalent of a cradle are all ready, there's money enough in the bank to pay the doctor, and all there is to do is wait. And I'm sure Dickie can do that. So I'm not going to advertise the cutest child in the world in advance.

My brother was born on June 6, 1930. He was named Charles Samuel Garrigues, the middle name that of Brick's older brother who had died in England, — the one who had adored little Harris and had passed on to him his love for books.

---

5 Toscanini said that Elisabeth Rethberg had the most beautiful soprano voice he had ever heard.

July 24, 1930

The delay was not voluntary. We've been engaged in the most hectic of political campaigns, one which seems destined to either make me or break the boss. And I've been doing about eighteen hours work a day for the last month. Add that to the necessary care of parenthood and there is little time for sleep. And I always put sleep before even my best friends; although the mayor of San Diego used to say to the mayor of Seattle: "Sleep -- next to a pretty girl -- is the greatest of God's blessings."

As you know, I've been trying to blast the county administration out of office. We uncovered what we thought was a big excavation graft amounting to more than a million dollars and broke an exclusive on it. The story was based on a survey made by a surveyor whom we had hired. After we had broke the story, we discovered that the surveyor had made a mistake. We couldn't retract what we had said. We were faced with several million dollars in libel suits if our story was proved untrue. And we had prevailed upon the grand jury to order an independent survey to prove that we were right! So we had to face the thing out.

At that moment, the boss's father became very ill, and he had to rush to Portland, leaving me in charge of the whole campaign. The only thing I could see to do was to get the libeled persons in jail on something else before the mistake was discovered. And it looks as though we would be able to do it. So I'm taking time out from my arduous duties to dash off a few lines.

The arrival of the infant has more or less dropped the fair Janet into the background. We have lots of fun with the little devil. He has learned to recognize us, and he yells for Dickie when he's hungry and for me when he wants to be carried, as Dickie won't carry him. He's learned to coo a bit, and that gives a little variety to the constant campaign of yelling. However, the poor little guy looks exactly like me, so I can't blame him for crying. I will, however, spare you a detailed account of all the things he does.

As ever,

Brick

Chapter Nine
The Devil Considerably Less Black

From Oasis, *the 1919 student yearbook of Imperial High School.* CLASS PROPHECY FOR THE YEAR **1931:** Harris Garrigus is a speaker on national affairs. He is one of a committee of six who have been sent out by the government to tour the United States and speak on national problems.

January 24, 1931

My dear Fanny,

It's really been so many years since I've heard from you that I've begun to suspect that you may be dead or married or something of the sort. Or did I say something in my last letter which made you angry?

You are really, you know, about the only friend I have left from my youth. With my increasing gray hairs (and I really have quite a lot of them), I can't afford to depend entirely upon the people I meet in my old age.

I'm no longer a newspaperman. It's quite amusing, because neither am I any of the other things which I often thought I should like to be when I quit working for newspapers. Instead I'm a -- a-ah -- detective, believe it or not. Or anyway, I'm being paid to be a detective. Considering that I'm one of the few youths who have never even read more than half a dozen detective stories, you can hardly call it the culmination of a life's ambition.

About a year ago, as you may remember, we started an investigation of the county government which disclosed that there were two or three chaps doing a lot of grafting. We

got almost enough evidence to indict them but couldn't seem
to get quite the goods. The district attorney wanted to
drop the investigation, and when we insisted that he go
ahead, finally consented if I would quit the News and do
the investigating. There was a raise of $10 per week in it,
and we were more or less in the position of being forced to
accept the proposition or quit shouting, so I accepted.
When we get the convictions or find we cannot get them, I
am supposed to return to the News.

However, the district attorney privately asked me to
stay on with him, study law and become one of his deputies
when I pass the bar. On this job I get half Saturdays and
all Sundays off and work seven hours a day at the maximum.
On the other job, I worked Sundays, took Saturdays off, and
worked eight hours a day with no holidays. I know I'd make
a damn good lawyer and probably make pretty good money
after I'm admitted to the bar, but after all, lawyering is
hardly any more a life's ambition than detectiving.

District Attorney Buron Fitts had been elected as a reformer, and one
of his first acts was to prosecute his predecessor, Asa Keyes, for taking a
bribe to, in effect, torpedo the prosecution of two men who had brought
about one of the most egregious stock swindles in U.S. history, the Julian
Petroleum fraud of 1927. [1] Keyes wasn't alone. In the early 1930s, certain elements of the Los Angeles patriciate were awash in speculation and
get-rich-quick schemes. One of them was Board of Supervisors chairman
Sidney T. Graves. Later, it was alleged that Fitts himself wasn't immune
to the temptations swirling around him.

It seems strange not to be a newspaperman. I was one
almost as long as most girls remain virgins, and there is a
peculiar pride about being a newspaperman which only the
old-fashioned girl felt about being a virgin. There is, of
course, a sense of relief in it, too.

I miss the concerts, since I have got free tickets too
long to start paying for them at this age. But I've got
myself a dandy phonograph pickup for my radio and am
starting a library of records which will supply all the
music I can stand. I've only bought so far the Mozart
Symphony in G Major and Bloch's Concerto Grosso, in
addition to a few operatic arias, but hope to pile up a
record library which will include everything I want to
hear. Then, too, I was getting rather tired of being a
music critic -- hearing a lot of indifferent performers
every week and being forced to write the same platitudes
about them. I suppose I'll be quite ready to go back by the
time we get these chaps in jail, but now even the avoidance
of the concerts is a sort of a relief.

---

1 The best account of the fraud is in Remi Nadeau, *Los Angeles: From Mission to Modern City* (New York: Longmans, 1960), pp. 102-106.

As a matter of fact, I've been slipping back into the unsocial person I was until about a year ago. You may possibly remember my surprise when I discovered that I could have a hell of a good time running around nights instead of staying home and listening to the radio. I never was able to explain it. Nor can I explain why the process is being reversed and I am increasingly unwilling to go out at night. Perhaps it's paternity. As a matter of fact, I spend so much of my time at home playing with the baby that I'm all tired out when it's time for him to go to bed. He's a big husky chap, not quite eight months old, trying to walk already and the somewhat puzzled possessor of five teeth.

There was a sort of mental stimulus about working for Boddy which is lacking on this job, and I've felt mentally lazier during the last couple of weeks than I had for a long time. It's surprising how much self-expression one finds in writing an ordinary news story, and with this possibility for expression gone, I may be forced to do some real writing.

We had a gang at the house last night, including a young chap who has just published his second novel. I've forgotten his name, but he's just come here from New York, where -- say his friends -- he is supposed to be good. His first novel was "The Nude Anthony," but whether it deals with the saint, Anthony Wayne or Tony the Wop I cannot say. The soiree was arranged in order to give him a chance to talk about his book, I suppose. If so, it must have been a terrible failure, since the women in the crowd made so much noise that he never had a chance.[2]

Phil Pizza, the chap who brought him over, has also just published his first book -- even if he did have to publish it himself. It's a rather sophomoric imitation of "Songs of Bilitis"[3] and deals with the affair of Apollo and Hyacinthus. But he did such a beautiful job on the printing and binding that it's almost worth the twenty-five dollars per copy he gets for it. Special handmade paper, of course, and type especially imported from Germany and all that sort of thing, but he's done it so well that one catches the mood of the particular book more from the book-work than from the text.[4]

By the way, do you know Ludwig Lewisohn's stuff? I've just finished reading "A Roman Summer" and "Island Within," and I'm inclined to consider him one of the finest modern

---

2 The book was *Anthony in the Nude,* by Myron Brinig. (New York: Farrar & Rinehart, 1930). Brinig, who later moved to New Mexico, was a prolific author; his first book was published in 1929 and his last in 1950.

3 A book by Pierre Louÿs, published in 1894, purporting to be translations from Greek poems dealing with lesbian love.

4 Phil Pizza became a script writer, but in 1932 his vision began to fail, and he moved to Hawaii. When the war began he formed road shows for the entertainment of the military. By 1948 he was totally blind and had returned to Los Angeles. In a feature, the *Los Angeles Examiner* said on May 29 of that year, "Now he lives alone, cooks his own meals, cleans the house and washes his clothes, with the companionship of his guide dog, Bingo."

writers I know. With men like Lewisohn[5] daring to write of
his own people as carefully, thoughtfully and sincerely as
Dreiser writes of his, and with composers like Bloch daring
to write music which is frankly Jewish and yet as finely
done as Bach, my respect for the Jewish race is beginning
to equal my liking for certain members of it.

That sounds like a rather rotten thing to say -- a
purely Gentile thing -- but as a matter of fact, I have
become anti-Semite in direct proportion as I have known
more and more Jews whom I liked. There is a peculiar twist
to Jew-Gentile relations which makes even that apology
sound like an insult. But I've been so filled with Lewisohn
the last few weeks that I'm more or less using his
phraseology. If you haven't read "A Roman Summer," read it.
When you get to the place where she says, "Je suis juive,"
recall a certain afternoon at one of the tables in a Tucson
drug store. Then tell me why either he or I should have
stammered and felt embarrassed, since neither of us had
ever consciously considered a Jew as different from a
Gentile. Then read "Island Within."

(Interruption: Lisa Roma just called up and invited herself to dinner, so I'll have to go and get her. But I'd like
to argue this thing out with you. Write me soon, won't you?)

Brick's new job took him sniffing after a trail of money left by Supervisor Graves. About a year before, February 7, 1930, Graves, in a San Francisco
hotel room, was handed an envelope filled with $57,000 for his vote on
behalf of the contractors who had been building the abandoned flood-control
dam on the San Gabriel River. As a crook, Graves turned out to be a true
amateur. As Brick told it later in his book, *You're Paying for It!*, Graves had

found himself one day in San Francisco with fifty-seven one-thousand-
dollar bills in his pocket which he had received a few minutes before as the
price of a vote upon a public contract. He apparently was nervous at the
thought of carrying so much money. He didn't think the bills were marked,
but he could not be sure. He didn't believe there was great danger of being
robbed, but again he wasn't sure. At any rate he didn't want to drive the
car back to Los Angeles carrying the currency with him.

So he went across the street, entered a bank and bought a $40,000
cashier's check payable to his aunt, signing the application with a false
name. He then went a block down Market Street, entered another bank,
and bought a $17,000 cashier's check payable to his sister-in-law. By that
time he was practically on his way to the penitentiary, for the bank records
of those two cashier's checks started a chain of records which established
a complete trail of Graves' efforts to transmute his receipts into income. It
took the district attorney a full year to find that trail. But at the end of that
time he was able to demonstrate, almost entirely by these financial records,
that Graves had been bribed, and to send him to state's prison.

---

5 Ludwig Lewisohn (1883-1955) was a novelist and short-story writer of Jewish heritage. He
was also a distinguished literature and drama critic. Dreiser's background was German Catholic.

[Handwritten]
Palace, San Francisco
February 13, 1931

I've been in San Francisco the last week, working on some angles of the case up here, but expect to return to Los Angeles tonight.

I've been rather lonely here -- don't know a soul -- but the change has been good for me, I think. It's a lovely city, and I think you'd like it almost as well as New York. I spent all day yesterday wandering around Golden Gate park, visiting the aquarium and feeding the squirrels and getting acquainted with the DeYoung Museum. Dropped in at the concert the other night and heard Horowitz with the symphony orchestra. He was excellent, but the orchestra is all shot to hell since Hertz left. They've been using guest conductors, and the one they have now is worse than Goossens. He played the allegro con grazia of the Pathetique as though it were a fox trot and the last movement as though it were a streetcar coming down Market Street.[6]

The most amazing thing about San Francisco is that I have not seen a single woman who realizes that her clothes have any possible relation to her body. They wear them as though clothes were designed to keep out the fog rather than to make a woman attractive to the male of the species in order that she may get someone to support her the rest of her life. Nor have I seen any evidence that powder and rouge are sold in San Francisco. It is a strange thing, but indicates, I believe, a difference in the thoroughly civilized San Franciscan and the Angelino just out of Iowa. People here are happier, more cerebral and better adjusted to the problem of living in cities.

Lisa Roma, who has been literally starving in Los Angeles ever since the Ravel tour, got a great break last week. She signed with What's-his-name, manager of the German opera company, to create his new opera "Mona Lisa" in Berlin next season. Of course, she has sung there before, in the Staatsoper, but I think she's on her way. She deserves it, poor kid. There isn't a better soprano on the stage with the exception of Ponselle and Rethberg and even these two can't touch her for technique.[7]

Well, the sun has come out, so I'm going to go sit for

6 Vladimir Horowitz (1903-1989) was the pianist. The conductor that drew Brick's scorn was Issay Dobrowen (1891-1953), who had been preceded by Alfred Hertz (1872-1942); and Eugene Goossens (1893-1962). Alexander Fried, the longtime music critic of the *San Francisco Chronicle*, had a more favorable opinion of Dobrowen's conducting. "The lilt of the five-fourths time movement and the peremptory step of the march were carried off at swifter than usual pace. Nevertheless, in brilliance and color Dobrowen made his conception of them thrilling."

7 The opera *Mona Lisa* by Max von Schillings (1868-1933), had actually been in the German repertoire since 1915; he cast his new version in 1931, the same year he completed his second American tour, but he was not able to perform it until 1933, with Inge Borkh as the prima donna. Rosa Ponselle (1897-1981) sang with the Met from 1918 to 1937; Elisabeth Rethberg was with the Met between 1922 and 1942.

a while at the foot of the Stevenson statue[8] and see if I
can re-create the old San Francisco.

March 9, 1931

You know, when I look back, I've really got a hell of
a lot to thank you for. I might almost say you made me what
I am today. I'm probably more satisfied with the job than
you are. But anyway, if there's anything good in the job,
I'm afraid you're mostly responsible for it.

I don't know why I got off on that trail. But I got to
thinking of my purely animal (not quite that, but almost
illiterate) existence before those Tucson days. Remember
the book you gave me the night I went away -- the end of a
bookless existence. Well, anyway.

What I started out to say was that your illness is
caused, first, by a species of frustration, biological in
the larger sense, deepened because of inability of your
people to take vital root in strange soil -- particularly
in the second or third generation. The second part I'll let
Lewisohn develop, but of the first I have first-hand
knowledge. It was in such a state you found me -- a less
serious state because I was young. You gave me at least the
first boost out of it, and the path since then has been
pretty indistinct, at times, but it's been a path.

We start out, all of us, to do magnificent things. We
fail, of course, but we hold on to the dream until it
becomes all tarnished. We hold on to it because to let it
go means to admit, not only failure, but literally
spiritual death. At last, if we're lucky, we let go and
find ourselves in a meadow fairer than the dream. To lose
that dream DOES mean spiritual death, and yet Jesus was not
guilty of hyperbole when he said we must die and be born
again in order to be saved.

We can only get one thing out of life -- and that is
ourselves. We must live with ourselves, eat ourselves, drink
ourselves, feel ourselves pulsating in the throb of a great
orchestra, and see ourselves swinging in great circles with
the stars. You have been unable to do this because the "yourself" which you tried to eat and drink was not the "yourself"
with a noisy Jewish family living in Brooklyn; and I failed
because the "myself" upon which I depended for sustenance was
not the "myself" who was a farmer boy with holes in the tops
as well as the bottoms of his shoes.

You are now, of course, a totally different person
than when you went out to do magnificent things; just as I
am different from the boy who started out to fame by way of
a hod-carrier's job in Los Angeles. You are a person of
deep and heady bouquet and when you have learned to sip of
yourself, to take great dizzy draughts of yourself, to be

---

8 Robert Louis Stevenson, in Portsmouth Square.

drunken with yourself, you will be doing the most magnificent thing that man can do -- living.

For the last few days I've just been bubbling over with happiness. Nothing material, of course. I'm still as undecided and unsettled as ever as far as work is concerned. And of course it frightens me a bit, for the gods won't let it last. (I see I used the word "happiness" above. It isn't that. You can't quite name it. But a sort of positive, dynamic content, where all life seems to fall into perfect order.)

Yesterday was one of those marvelous times of early summer which even your eastern springs can't equal. Played with the boy in the back yard, stretched under a tree. Came into the house and put Mozart's D Major Symphony on the phonograph. Actually, I wanted to turn handsprings to that first movement.

I find, of course, that I can't begin to relate it, because I seem to be describing an action or emotion when I'm really trying to put into words the essence of beauty itself. I don't know what's back of it. Parenthood, partly, I suppose. Because parenthood DOES give life a continuity which it couldn't otherwise possess. I can't really say I'm GLAD because of the boy, or that he makes me happy, because the little beggar is a terrible nuisance, and when I'm not trying to entertain him I'm trying to figure out some way to send him to college fifteen years from now. But his existence sinks roots into the universe which I never before realized that I didn't possess.

Partly, too, it is a reaction to having Dickie back again after her vacation -- although I can't say that there is any more affection between us now than before, nor any more particular pleasure in her society. Of course, it's the first time we've been alone together in a year, and that is something in itself. It's rather a sense of belonging, not only to a family, but to music, and books and every emotion set forth on paper or canvas.

I don't think there's any danger that I'll become a detective or a lawyer. In my present mood I couldn't even think of it. When this job is over, I expect to go back on the News. But I hope that this business of getting away from the paper has freed me from my devotion to newspaper work. I hope to do some writing evenings while I'm on this job, and I may have enough to start to keep it up when I go back.

Nothing is ever as stupid as another person's child, but Dickie sends these two pictures of the boy. The old gentleman feeding him a cigarette is his father. In the other picture his mother has just told him the joke about the traveling salesman.

As for going to New York -- of course I will. But I'd hate to have to wait that long to see you. I can't seem to see myself working for a newspaper in New York. But I'll come to see you and the towers of the East. Only by that time you'll probably be married and have a husband who is jealous. Our regret at losing the World was inspired, I'm afraid, by fear of a horde of hungry newspapermen descending on Los Angeles. Every paper in town except the News has laid off half its staff. The Express, the oldest paper here, folded up and died, the corpse being invaded the same day by the spirit of William Randolph Hearst so that it has been resurrected. But everybody and his brother is out of a job. Still, the longer I stay away from newspapers, the more enthusiastically I'm in favor of a monument to Munsey, who could make one newspaper grow where six grew before.[9]

May 8, 1931

I'm back on the News, working as political editor during the present municipal election. The News is the most powerful paper politically in town, but there is serious doubt as to whether or not we can re-elect the administration next month. So I've been working like the devil.

I don't really know whether or not I like the work. In a way it's the best job I've had, but most of my time seems to be wasted. And I'm not getting any younger.

In fact, your letter found me slightly discouraged about the whole mess of living. The trouble, I suppose, is that life is too easy right now. I work when I please and quit when I please and make enough money to live in extremely modest circumstances. But none of the things I do touch me very deeply.

The old nose, however, is pretty much to the grindstone. I don't like to leave Dickie and the kid alone in the evenings, and so I don't go out much any more. And all my friends seem to have an equal ability to bore me. I've even sworn off falling in love again. If I could become sufficiently impressed by the tragedy or injustice or beauty of anything, I think I should write a novel.

Myron Brinig joins in the chorus of those shouting I should go to New York. He's kind enough to say I should do music reviews there -- even though he seems to know little about music. But I'm afraid I'm hopelessly here. Somehow, I'm oppressed by the thought that in New York I should find six times as many people of exactly the same kind as I find in Los Angeles.

I sometimes wonder if the trouble with all of us is that they've succeeded in taking God away from us -- the good, old-fashioned, hell-fire-and-damnation god that

---

9 The Pulitzer family's *New York World* was sold to the Scripps-Howard chain in 1931, which combined it with the *New York Evening Telegram.* The *Los Angeles Herald* was combined with Hearst's *Express* and continued as the *Herald-Express.* Publisher Frank Andrew Munsey (1854-1925) was sometimes called "The Executioner of Newspapers" because of his practice of buying newspapers to shut down or consolidate with another.

burned little children. As long as God existed, we amounted
to something. No matter how cruel he might be, we had a
personal contract with him which made us his heirs if we
would only consent to a little sprinkling of water or a
minor surgical operation. Now that we've effectively
destroyed Him, we haven't anything left but a Life Force or
a Primal Urge or something of the sort. And you can't have
a personal compact with a Life Force!

The truth is that we are, all of us, utterly homeless
and unable to take root in any soil. There isn't in fact, any
soil. We just drift along like a dried-up tumbleweed on the
Kansas prairie. The urge to live, to procreate, has worn
thin. Our ancestors could live because they would some day be
rewarded with a swell golden crown, a harp, a harem, a street
of gold or a chance to bust some other ancestor over the head
with a mace. Being far down the scale of human comfort, they
could reproduce without the fear that their children might
have less of the world's comforts than they. There might be
winters of famine, but they knew that in the spring they
would always have as much to eat as they had the year before.
There was security in their misery -- with always the
absolute certainty that when the misery was all over they
would suddenly find themselves twanging a glissando with the
princess or at least the leman of the local duke.

When Bliss Became a Rebel

*The Stinker — his name was Forrest Bingham and he lived in a big house
with a lawn and an iron fence around it across Whitfield Avenue — was
waiting for him after school, and they spent a joyous half hour fishing for
debris with a bent pin let down on a string through a gutter grating. Later
they went up the hill to Forrest's house and mooched cookies from the colored girl who worked for them. On succeeding days, they climbed trees in
Forrest's yard and explored the unused stable in back of his house, sitting on
piles of ancient straw in the hay mow, or curled up in an old manger, smelling the faint, bright smell of horses and watching the millions of motes of dust
dance through the golden oars of sunlight slicing through the dark.*

*The Stinker knew everything. He'd put his hands in back of his head
and lean back on the hay and rattle away like a house afire on any subject
that came into his head. They'd go on like that for hours, and the Stinker
would never get smartalecky about knowing things that Bliss didn't but
would say, "Aw, that's a lot of bushwah, kiddo; this is the way it is ..."*

It was the Stinker who explained about God and the Devil.

*"How can it be a bottomless pit, huh?" Bliss wanted to know. "If it
don't have any bottom what's to keep the coals from falling right out and
the sinners on top of them and just keep falling and falling as fast as God
shovels them in?"*

*"Oh, that!" the Stinker said, his condescension directed not against
Bliss but against the world of preachers and teachers and Sunday-school*

superintendents. "They don't mean that. That's just exaggeration. They don't mean it don't have any bottom. They mean it don't have any top. So that there's always room for more of them no matter how many God shovels in. Millions and millions and millions of them."

He leaned back in the haymow and closed his eyes and his voice rattled on. "The very first ones — all those that died a long time ago are down at the very bottom because it don't matter about them because they don't have any families in Heaven. But the new ones are near the top and they can look up and see their folks up in Heaven having a good time and not caring about them frying down there in hell. They can look up and see their folks maybe eating watermelon or ice cream and listening to the preaching and singing, while they're down there frying on the hot coals…"

"Not my Mama and Papa. They wouldn't go off and leave me like that!"

"What could they do?" the Stinker demanded scornfully. "When they die they gotta go off to Heaven whether they want to or not because they're saved but you're not saved and God will shovel you into hell."

"And besides," he added, "your mama won't want to see you because you'll look horrible. You'll be all eaten up by worms and flies and you'll stink and pretty soon you'll get to look like just another devil so that your mama will hate the very thought of you. You'll fry on one side all night and in the morning the devil will come along with his pitchfork and turn you over so you can fry on the other side all day."

"Say," he interrupted himself. "I'll bet he's a pretty busy old devil. I'll bet he needs a lot of help to get all those souls turned over every day. Maybe after you've been down there for millions and millions of years he turns you into a devil yourself so you can help turn over the newcomers. Say, I'll bet that's what he does! I'll bet I'll be one that he'll pick to be a devil. Then I can go 'round every morning and turn over the sinners with a pitchfork…."

But Bliss wasn't listening. This was too much. The flames, the stink, the everlastingness of it, the shouts and groans and howls… all these he could stand to think of because there was some justice in it. Even the picture of Mama eating ice cream while he roasted in hell, though dreadful, was tolerable. But not this other: not this business of the devil turning you over with a pitchfork, like a piece of dirt, like a turd. Suddenly he knew that it could not be that way. It was not that he doubted; it was just that he withdrew; he refused to be a party to it, to accept, to serve. He knew then that he could not worship that sort of devil.

"Oh, Bushwah! To hell with your old devil." And his voice for the first time was scornful. "He ain't going to turn me over with his ol' pitchfork ." He stood up, half expecting a bolt of lightning to blast through the old stable and shiver him into nothingness in punishment for his blasphemy. When nothing happened he grew bolder. "He's just an old Presbyterian devil. I don't believe he's even got a pitchfork!"

But now -- ! The best we can look for is a rented flat, a husband or wife as the case may be to whom we gradually become accustomed and indifferent, and perhaps a brat or two whom we know will be condemned to the same sort of pointless existence as we. The wife may be very dear at times and the brat the cutest little devil in the world, but they hardly seem to make existence less pointless nor to supply that unnameable want which we carry as youngsters and which most of us keep in the back of our minds, somewhere.

That's one side of the picture. How we, as a human race, are going to get our roots back in a nonexistent soil, I don't know! It seems that we must possess, as thoroughly as we can, those things which are left for us to possess. That's why I said that you must eat, live, sleep, think, dream with yourself. I don't mean to think of yourself all the time. But rather to so sensitize yourself to the world-as-is that each contact with the world brings a corresponding reaction or emotion in yourself. And then, in the words of Elbert Hubbard (on whom be peace), make motion and emotion equal.[10]

Because, after all, thought can only heighten the pleasure of action. It can never take its place. Man is a mobile animal, and "motion," action, creation, are the only pleasures we are capable of having. Whatever strange disease we are afflicted with -- neurasthenia or schizophrenia -- is caused by our inability to act, move or create. We are often deterred from action by our recognition of the futility of all action. We are only unhappy when we are at rest. We are at rest most of the time because we are intelligent enough to recognize the inutility of the object of motion. Whereas, as you know, the pleasure comes from the action itself and not from attaining its object.

Suppose, for example, I were obsessed with the idea that to write a novel would be a grand and glorious thing. I should labor over a novel and work and cudgel my brains as countless others have done. I would write a lousy novel. But I would really live while doing it. As it is, I realize that it would be a rotten novel and that the money, if I got any, would probably not be worth the effort. So I don't write a novel. Instead I sit and sit and sit and think and think and think (like the bawdy old song) and am thoroughly unhappy.

That devotion to sitting and thinking, too intelligent to do anything, causes all of the 'thenias and 'phrenias. If you were to stroll down Broadway and criminally assault the first good-looking man you saw in the street, they might put you in jail. But you'd go with your head up and a sense of accomplishment. Instead, you're in a jail formed of your own inhibitions, social, mental, financial, reli-

---

10 Elbert Hubbard (1856-1915) wrote *A Message to Garcia* in 1899, a lesson in duty and efficiency. He was an ardent believer in rugged individualism.

gious, but your head is hanging down and you don't have any sense of achievement.

So, I say, live with yourself. Recognize in yourself the possibilities of pleasure -- and take advantage of them. Take advantage particularly of those possibilities of pleasure which are peculiar to yourself. Don't, as Rockwell Kent suggests, forget yourself and live in something else.[11] Recognize and practice those virtues which set you apart from the rest of the mob -- whether the virtue in question is the ability to make a surgical dressing, drink a pint of whisky without taking a breath, or carry on fifteen love affairs simultaneously.

You don't do these things, of course -- for the same reason I don't do them. We are so obsessed by small comforts and small slaveries that we do none of these things. But if we did them, we might approach nearer to the happiness we crave.

I recognize now, as I didn't when I started, the reason for that low, dispirited feeling. Except for my Jewish collaborator,[12] I've hardly seen anybody for a month or more, except at work. Too many politicians give me a profound distaste for anybody. My collaborator and I are still working on the second chapter of a mystery thriller. Every time he does a chapter I send it back to him rewritten. But it's good practice for him.

The first story came back from Liberty, although they kept it more than a month. That used to be unusual for Liberty. Redbook has it now. Perhaps, through his influence, I may get up enough energy to tackle something good. God knows I must be as competent as Brinig or some of the other younger novelists I've met recently.

P.S. My individualism reveals itself in two things: an insistence that ribald should rhyme with piebald and a stronger insistence that only very dear friends should be addressed as "My dear Fanny" or Gretchen or Agnes, as the case may be.

June 28, 1931

I'll soon be an old man and I haven't written anything yet. But it's so marvelously pleasant to lie on the beach during the morning or to lie in the porch swing under the moon and play the phonograph during the evening that the business of writing doesn't seem at all important -- until I come down to the office to work.

And how is it back in the sticks? I suppose eventually you'll marry some person, a Jew, by preference, who'll be kind to you and interfere as little as possible with what

---

11 Rockwell Kent (1881-1971), the artist and author, in 1930 had just published his autobiographical *This Is My Own.*

12 Unidentified. Possibly Myron Brinig.

goes on in your head. Most of us eventually consent to take what life has to offer us -- because she has the annoying habit of not raising her price in response to our demands. We compromise, and compromise and compromise until we've compromised everything away. And then we hate ourselves for doing it -- but it doesn't really matter, because it would be gone anyway.

And so it goes. I'm going to compromise by going down to the corner for a sundae and then going back to work.

August 9, 1931

We have a summer opera company now, performing in the new Greek Theater in Griffith Park. The theater is, in a sense, a miniature of the Hollywood Bowl, and really much more lovely. They give an opera about twice a month, with resident talent. The shows have been fair in a way, but of course, so utterly different than we've been accustomed to hearing. They use a loud speaking system, which makes the bad voices sound good and the good ones bad.

I should like very much to see you, but as I get older, New York seems less and less desirable, either as a place to see or to stay. In fact, all places seem less desirable. The most significant thing the American people are doing is taking root in a soil which, though it may not be new in the sense our earlier patriotic critics insist, is still, nevertheless, the only soil in which they can take root. Perhaps I shall take root here.

I haven't, so far, of course; partly because I hadn't felt the necessity, and partly because every Iowan in Los Angeles is trying to keep from taking root here. They fancy a sort of airy existence which begins in Reel One and ends in Reel Five, and so they are rushing about from cheap stucco to cheap stucco, asserting their individuality and their freedom from the mores of the nation.

I've been reading snatches of Dreiser intermingled with Pater. You may not believe it; nobody before has ever done it, but I've been doing it. I think it has cured me of reading Dreiser. It's not only his horribly ugly style, but his heavy, clumsy, romantically realistic approach to life. But that stuff isn't realism, and I should like to indite a passionate essay against those who dare to call it realism.[13]

Also I've been reading Rolland's "Beethoven," and Rolland is almost as bad. His style is better, but he, too, approaches his subject with that fuzzy, woozy attitude. Of course, "Jean-Christophe" was something else. But where did Rolland get his reputation as a music critic? Wasn't he,

---

13 Walter Horatio Pater (1839-94) believed that the ideal life consisted of cultivating an appreciation for the beautiful and the profound. His masterpiece was *Marius the Epicurean* (1895). His style was noted for its precision, subtlety and refinement. Theodore Dreiser (1871-1945), on the other hand, wrote what was called "naturalistic" works that painted man as the victim of unmanageable, impersonal forces. Virtuous behavior had little to do with happiness, he wrote.

after all, purely a propagandist for the now-discredited
Wagnerian literary school? Did music, as music, mean any
more to him than to that popular writer who once wrote
"Seated on the deck at night, he would often play the
magnificent symphonies of Beethoven on his beloved 'cello"?

But how different with Pater! He transmutes with calm
but certain pen the "sweetness and strength, pleasure with
surprise," in which the ancients worked, and as he traces the
outlines of old works, not forgotten but lost in the shadow
of years, he uncovers for us a new world in which men lived
not as the puny individuals of today, but as men who walk
with the gods in the shadows of the evening. He reminds one
of Brahms, whom Rolland abhorred, but a classic Brahms,
refined by a lifetime in the "sweet shadows" of Oxford.

I read too damned much, anyway. I average about two
books a week, and I couldn't tell you half a dozen books
I've read in the last six months. So I think I'll invest in
a vest-pocket edition of Pater, a Bible and a checkbook and
leave all the other books in the library.

You know, Collier's still has that story of mine. It's
been there several months now, and they're still "considering" it. If by any chance they should accept it, I've half
a notion to rent a room somewhere and spend at least three
hours a day there at the typewriter. It's impossible to work
at home with a fourteen-months-old infant trying to climb up
into my lap every time he hears the typewriter clicking.

He's a cute little devil. Talks a bit and cries when I
go to work, runs around and plays with a puppy I got him.
Lots of fun to be a proud papa.

> 2083 W. 20th Street
> September 14, 1931

As you can see, we've moved again. We have seven
rooms, including a big attic where I sleep and which I've
reserved to myself for purposes of writing when the mood
strikes me.

You spoke of my going to seed. Perhaps that is what I
have already done. But I suspect that a blade of grass,
having put forth a stem and seeing a baby blade beside it,
must feel somewhat as I feel about my baby. Of course, the
original blade started out to be an oak tree, and while it
regrets that it has remained merely grass, it is not
entirely discontent, particularly when it realizes that the
offspring may turn into the oak that it, the original
blade, failed to be.

There is literally not enough room in a man's life for
the existence of both a family and that other something
which one must have to be an artist. At least not in mine.
It is of infinitely more importance to me that a warm, soft
little bundle of flesh learns to say "I love my mama" than

it is that there exists a totally different kind of
importance -- I am speaking now of authorship -- which I
once worshipped but to which I now devote only fleeting
half holidays or a week of an annual vacation.

Do you remember my telling you a year or so ago about a
most marvelously beautiful little Italian girl who made her
debut here in "Carmen"? I quite lost my reason over her -- or
would have if her father hadn't given me such a doubtful look
and if Dickie hadn't proceeded to make good friends of her at
first meeting. I understand she is in New York doing
television songs for the Columbia network. Her name is Louise
Caselotti. If you mingle with the radio crowd this winter and
happen to see her, you'll know what makes music critics wild
-- although she was putting on a little fat the last time I
saw her -- which was some time ago.[14]

2083 W. 30th Street
January 5, 1932

I've really become quite a serious young man. We aim
our popgun at a star and reach half way to a sparrow
sitting on a telephone wire. I've definitely abandoned the
"manana" idea and for several months have been conscientiously working -- at trying to hit the pulps!

Not that I've got anything to show for it, except
possibly a different attitude toward writing. There's one
fifteen-thousand-word yarn which I didn't even bother to
re-type, another of twenty thousand which Dickie is typing
for me now and another of eight thousand which is three-
fourths done. But I've quite definitely set myself the
hours of nine to eleven in the morning to peck at the
typewriter. I usually miss about three mornings a week, but
I've actually come to the place where it's more difficult
to keep away from the typewriter than to go to it.

Myron Brinig is a good influence in my sweet young
life. His new novel is coming off in the spring. While he
is unusually reluctant to talk about his work, the long
arguments we have on writing in general give me a more
professional slant than I could get otherwise. I've only
read one of his books, "Singermann." He is not so hot in
this, but his later stuff seems to have made quite a hit in
Hollywood. The new one is "That Man Is My Brother," or some
such thing, and is written to make Brinig's point that the
Jew should become a Gentile or hide in some way in the
modern social fabric.

3119 West 77th Street
June 16, 1932

Recently there have been interruptions. One of them --
a mere incident -- the arrival of a second son. He's two

---

[14] Commercial television didn't begin in New York until 1939, so in this earlier period TV
was in its experimental phase.

months old and screaming at the top of his voice at the present instant. But second sons, unlike the first, seem to be of little importance.[15]

Life has not been entirely beer and skittles at the News. For economy's sake I was shoved back on the rewrite board last year. Then came two pay cuts, totaling twenty-five percent, and there was some doubt for a while as to whether the sheet would survive.

Of more moment right now is the purchase of a house. It was a brave deed, this planking down of my last dime at a time when nobody knows whether I'll have a job in another week. It's away out of town, near Inglewood, in a new tract.

It was one of the worst years of the Depression, and William Z. Foster, 51, was running for the third and last time as the Communist Party's candidate for President of the United States. He had started his radical career as a militant labor organizer in 1894, and his platform envisioned the ultimate demise of capitalism and the establishment of a workers' republic; but it also painted a hopeful picture of an America free of racial oppression, labor strife, hunger and poverty.

Los Angeles Illustrated Daily News, June 29, 1932. RED PRESIDENT CANDIDATE ARRESTED AS SYNDICALIST. William Z. Foster, Communist candidate for president, and nearly a score of persons seeking to hear him speak, were arrested yesterday by the police Red Squad as the leader attempted to address a political meeting at the Plaza.

Foster was booked on suspicion of criminal syndicalism.

Later in the day, Superior Judge Elliot Craig signed a writ of habeas corpus for Foster's release. Bond was fixed at $10,000 on the writ, which was made returnable today at 3:30 p.m.

Although Foster's sympathizers milled about the city for several hours, demonstrating against the arrested, violence was confined to the throwing of a few gas bombs by the police squad.

Local Communist leaders had announced that they would hold a meeting at the Plaza in defiance of police orders, after a similar meeting in a hall on Broadway had been broken up by police. In addition to its political significance, the meeting was to protest the recent shooting of a member of the Unemployed Council in a police raid on an open meeting in a private home.

Nearly 1,000 sympathizers immediately started shouting, "We want Foster," continuing until the officers dispersed them with tear bombs.

Minor outbreaks took place throughout the city for the rest of the afternoon as Communists gathered on street corners to throw "red" literature on the sidewalks.

Los Angeles Illustrated Daily News, June 30, 1932. FOSTER, OUT OF JAIL, IS PROPHET OF DICTATORSHIP. *By C. H. Garrigues.* The politico-economic warfare which has engulfed the western world is already in America

---

15 That was me, George Louis Garrigues, born on April 8, 1932, and named after Brick's other brother and given the middle name of their father. So Brick had succeeded in using both his father's first and middle names for his own two sons.

taking its final form — a battle to the death between communism and fascism, in the opinion of William Z. Foster, Communist candidate for president, who got out of jail early enough yesterday to give a brief interview before flying to Phoenix for a speaking engagement.

Neither socialism nor democracy, he declared, exists today as a living force; each constitutes only a moribund body of doctrine from which the rival forces are seeking to draw recruits. Each has lost, not numbers of lip-servers, but the once firm faith of its adherents that through one or the other doctrine lies salvation.

Socialism, he intimated, has been captured bodily by industrial leaders, now advancing theories half-socialist, half-fascist. Democracy is being attacked from without by communism, while its own leaders bore from within, seeking to undermine its walls and capture the citadel in the name of fascism.

The wave of contumely, contempt and ridicule directed at Congress during recent months is a deliberate attempt to destroy the confidence of the American people in representative government, clearing the way for a dictatorship, he says.

Even to one accustomed to finding the devil considerably less black than he is painted, the Communist leader proves a figure of disturbing contrasts. The blue eyes are mild, gentle, almost dreamy. He smiles quizzically as he talks, so that little laugh wrinkles appear about the corners. The lean, rugged fighter's jaw is in startling contrast.

One looks in vain for a sign of the zealot, the fanatic, the bigot. Foster, it seems, approaches the religion of communism not in the spirit of a missionary or a Savonarola, but as a priest celebrating its rites before the altar. When the time is ripe, the worshipers will come. Meanwhile, it is his duty to keep the font filled and the altar swept.

He disagrees with many non-Communists that the police departments' policy of suppression is helping the Communist cause.

"It changes the direction; that's all," he says. "Makes the workers more determined; induces the fallen ones to answer force with force. But it doesn't help us, nor hurt us.

"Tear bombs can't unmake Communists because you can't fill a man's stomach with tear gas. Nor would it help the capitalists to let our leaders talk because campaign oratory can't fill a man's stomach either. The capitalists are damned if they do and damned if they don't. They know it and are afraid. That's why they hire policemen to beat us up."

Brick recommended to his friend Bill Golden that he see Fanny when he went to New York. Golden did so, and was charmed by the knowledgeable New Yorker, who by this time was working as a reader for Viking Press.

August 1, 1932

A letter from Bill Golden recalled the glamorous Slavic princess I met one night in Tucson, she whom I had almost forgotten in a further acquaintance with a somewhat dissatisfied, neurotic girl who became one of my best friends until she had been freed of both the neurosis and the dissatisfaction. It is, however, a peculiarity, of my own -- shared, probably, with some hundred million others -- that my interest in my friends arises rather from their faults than from their virtues.

I had completely forgotten that seductive, Oriental person who glowed all over a Tucson landscape.

I have, from pure lack of energy, cut myself off from each of the interests I used to have. I have enough to do in trying to keep my own life unentangled without involving myself in the lives of others. I suppose my retirement is temporary, induced by the stringent financial situation in which I find myself. At forty-five dollars a week I am a morbid, nervous, irritable person who beats his wife and sulks most of the time. At fifty dollars I am a fairly normal person. At sixty dollars I begin to expand and am really quite genial and easy to get along with. I suspect that the sort of person I am now bores my friends and so I manage to keep away from them as much as possible.

And then, damn it, the realization of what a lousy writer I actually am makes me even more irritable. I can't even write the sort of rot I'm trying to sell to the pulps, while to actually write a decent book would be as impossible for me as to become an advertising salesman.

If I had actually any brains I would settle down and decide to become a successful newspaperman -- the kind who becomes publicity man for some politician, eventually his secretary, collects a little here and a little there and finally settles down on a country estate. I was out to such an estate last week. A whole canyon, oak trees, landscaped gardens and what have you. The owner used to work on the Express at thirty-five dollars a week. But instead, having this writing mania I keep pecking away at a typewriter. I can't turn out a good formula yarn for the pulps; I can't write for the slicks and even if I could write a decent paragraph -- which I can't -- I'll be damned if I'll struggle along for a year polishing phrases for the rewards of a decent writer. To all of which, being a sensible person, you shrug: "Who cares?"

March 16, 1933

I'm still on the News, holding a somewhat precarious position on a somewhat precarious newspaper, but still receiving as large a salary as the managing editor. You may remember a graft investigation I worked on a couple of years ago? We cleaned it up last month with an indictment. I was a nine days' wonder in the newspaper world here, with aged and decrepit (can one never be decrepit without being aged?) newspapermen pausing to shake my hand on every street corner. The paper entered my story for a Pulitzer Prize (I don't know the particular classification) and my boss wrote an editorial praising my work. As a result, if

the News should go under, I'm going out in the hills and
raise goats, since I refuse to work for the salaries the
other papers are paying. Meanwhile, our cub managing editor
keeps shoving me about from desk to desk, apparently
unwilling to let me do the sort of work I've been doing.
For a while they called me picture editor, and right now
I'm assistant city editor, and next week God knows what
I'll be doing.

On March 31, 1933, ex-Supervisor Sidney T. Graves was convicted
in Superior Judge Fletcher Bowron's court of accepting a bribe. He served
three years on that charge, was released in 1937 but had to serve more
time in a federal prison for evading taxes on the bribe.

> *Editorial from the Long Beach, Calif., Spokesman, September 29,
> 1934.* **C. H. GARRIGUES:** You may pronounce that name to suit yourself.
> But I call the man one of the best citizens of Los Angeles County, or even
> the state of California.
>
> "The Spotlight" is a feature editorial article appearing almost daily in
> the *Los Angeles Illustrated Daily News,* and the days that it does not appear
> there is experienced a lonesomeness and "vacant chair" feeling that does
> not wear off until the next morning, when Mr. Garrigues reappears with
> more light on some spot where crooks would rather find darkness.
>
> It was the work of Mr. Garrigues that played an important part in bring-
> ing former Supervisor Sidney Graves to justice by landing him in prison.
>
> It was largely the work of Mr. Garrigues that brought final indictment
> against the California Reserve Company officials in spite of a marriage
> relationship with the office of the district attorney. Such is the work of
> patriotic journalism. And the honest readers of such comments will be
> molded into a better citizen, which is the real objective of true journalism.

Sometimes Brick's columns took a less serious turn. As, for example,
when a Senate committee chaired by Henry F. Ashurst of Arizona came
to Los Angeles to investigate how bankruptcy cases were being handled.
The examiner in these hearings was William Neblett, law partner to Senator
William G. McAdoo of California.

> *Los Angeles Illustrated Daily News, November 15, 1933,* THE SPOTLIGHT,
> By C. H. Garrigues: The Senate receivership hearing will probably go down
> as setting some kind of record for inept unfairness in the handling of wit-
> nesses. The inquisitors remind a veteran police reporter of six not-very-intel-
> ligent detectives giving a suspect the third degree.
>
> Transfer the subject of the investigation into a phrase that everybody
> understands, and a typical examination would go something like this:
>
> Neblett: Now, Mr. Witness, tell us about this tragedy.
>
> Witness: Well, Colonel (they all call Neblett "Colonel"), my
> grandmother's cat was crossing the street when it was run over by a car. It
> was so badly hurt that my grandmother asked me to kill it. So I did.
>
> Neblett: Now, Mr. Witness, after you killed your Grandmother Catt,
> where did you hide the body?

Witness: You didn't understand me. I didn't say I killed —

Neblett (roughly): We're not interested in what you didn't say. What did you do with the body?

Witness: If you mean the cat —

Neblett: Exactly. Did you bury her?

Witness: I didn't kill my Grandmother Catt. I killed her —

Neblett: That's it. You killed her. Did you bury the body?

Chairman Ashurst: Answer "yes" or "no," please.

Witness: No.

Ashurst: Now, Mr. Witness, do you seriously want to go on record as stating to this committee that you left the body of your poor old grandmother lying in the gutter for the street sweeper to carry away? .

Witness (with infinite patience): I have a grandmother. Her name isn't Catt. She had a cat — a feline — the sort of thing that has fur and kittens. The cat ran —

Five senators (simultaneously): We heard all about that.

We're not interested in that.

You told us that before.

You're cumbering up the record.

Please answer the question.

Ashurst: Now see here, Mr. Witness. This committee regrets that, being a lawyer, you are constitutionally incapable of answering a simple question. We would like to find out what you did with the body of your poor old grandmother whom you have testified you brutally murdered after stealing her jar of pennies. But our appropriation is limited. It will require practically all of it to pay for printing the long and evasive explanations you have made. Now tell us, did you bury the body? Answer "yes" or "no."

Witness: No.

Ashurst: I have never seen such utter callousness in a witness. The committee will consider legislation to make it illegal for a murderer to leave his victim's body lying in the street where cats can run over it.

December 4, 1933

I have a rather decent assignment now as the senior member of what is loosely termed the Daily News brain trust. The other members are one Duncan Aikman, whom you may possibly know as a contributor to the Mercury and a few other magazines, author of two or three books (I think his best-known is "The Small-Town Mind" or something of the sort), and another chap named Edwin Bates, former government economist and the best writer of the trio.[16]

We have an office to ourselves where we gather daily to chart the fate of the nation during the next twenty-four

---

16 Aikman's book, *Home Town Mind,* was published in 1926. He was named executive editorial manager of the *Illustrated Daily News* in 1934. He was also for some years the West Coast correspondent of the *Baltimore Sun.* Bates had been a special agent of the U.S. Bureau of Foreign and Domestic Commerce. He later became an aide to Democratic Senator Sheridan Downey, and in 1950 was appointed manager of the Los Angeles field office of the U.S. Department of Commerce.

hours. I specialize in local political economy, with an occasional foray into sociology and the ethics of bribery. Aikman does wisecracking interviews with the nation's leading lights as they appear on the scene locally, and Bates interprets economics in words none of us can understand.

The opportunity to do that sort of thing has given me more confidence than I've had before, and I feel less like a hack than I ever did. If the boss wants me to write something in a style which I think would stultify my reputation, I simply tell him "no" and that's the end of it. So, there are even some sections of the dear public which follow me more closely than even the boss (who is the leading publicist of the West, at present), and I have a lot of fun with it.

Tomorrow, for example, I'm holding a council of war with the grand council of the AAR, which is a semi-revolutionary, semi-fascist organization with more than two hundred thousand members in Los Angeles. Next week I'm to lecture before the school of revolutionary journalism of the Young Communist League. Stalin only knows what the Communists want, but the AAR wants me to be the fourth quadrumvir.[17]

The trouble is that it doesn't seem a bit important. When I get tired I go home and read -- D. H. Lawrence is the latest obsession. I feel that I should be tremendously excited about that AAR crowd. They have the most perfect machinery for a peaceful but organized revolution that you could imagine, and I have a perfect program for them to initiate. But I'll probably give them an outline of the program and go back to sleep while they put it over.

The American Army of Rehabilitation was one of the many organizations attempting to find some way out of the mire of the Depression. Brick's scheme to end the effects of the economic calamity in Los Angeles County involved the same kind of "production for use" later adopted in 1936 by the radical Upton Sinclair in his campaign for governor.

Los Angeles Post-Record, undated. RELIEF PLAN WOULD SAVE 31 MILLIONS. Here is the outline of the program as drawn up by C. H. Garrigues, *Daily News* writer:

Under the Los Angeles plan, the entire body of able-bodied unemployed would be put to work producing their own necessities of life and would receive their wages in commodities produced by themselves and their fellow-workers.

In addition, a program of public works would be undertaken by the unemployed.

In effect, the program would unify and co-ordinate the efforts of the various self-help co-operative relief associations, which, before their recent breakdown, supported one hundred thousand persons for more than a year at an average cost of less than a dollar a month.

---

17 A reference to the four columns of Fascists who descended upon Rome in 1924, led by four party members later to be known as the Quadrumviri.

The machinery for putting into effect this program is simply the established machinery of the old County Farm, modernized, enlarged, and made sufficient to carry its load. The sole difference will be that the disemployed will no longer be "on the county." They will be, as they want to be, "on themselves."

Brick was a bylined writer on politics, but on the small *Daily News* staff he covered his share of breaking news stories. On the first day of January 1934 he was out wading through the dramatic flooding in the San Gabriel Mountain foothills above Glendale. As he recalled four years later in his pamphlet *Why Didn't Somebody Tell Somebody?*

Montrose

The strangest thing about the Montrose disaster was that nobody would believe it even after it happened.

Look back through the old files of your favorite newspaper for the first week of January of 1934 and you'll see that for three days not a paper carried a story which gave any inkling of the disaster which had struck on the morning of January 1.

The *Times,* the morning after the historic flood, carried a story, "Damage Slight in Southern California Rain." The *Daily News* on the following day carried a colorful account of citizens boating on South Figueroa Street but only a few paragraphs about the major disaster of the day. Not until January 4 did even the newspapers discover that the community had gone through a major disaster — with forty-three dead and five million dollars' worth of homes destroyed — three days before.

The reason, of course, is obvious. Newspapers are manned by newspapermen, and newspapermen are human. On New Year's Eve, newspapermen went out for the evening. When they woke up in the morning they could remember only three things — that they'd had a blinger of a party the night before, that they'd had a devil of a time getting home through the rain and that they had to squeeze some kind of story about the Tournament of Roses out of aching heads.

A few of us knew — a few reporters who had been assigned to cover flood damage in the northern area.

We had driven out Foothill Boulevard, over streets full of running water, had climbed through canyons cut fifty feet deep across the highway, seen houses crushed beneath rolling boulders weighing hundreds of tons. Sticking up through the same we had seen the chimneys of houses and had been told there was a family buried beneath the gravel. In an abandoned car, filled to the top with sand, we had found the body of a baby girl, one tiny hand sticking out of its grave. Where there had been a street lined with rows of houses, there was now a boulder-strewn wash. At the lower end there leaned drunkenly a red and white traffic sign, still commanding impudently and futilely:

STOP!

We knew these things but when we went back to our offices and tried to tell, or write, what we had seen, our city editors would not believe us — because our city editors had never seen — or heard of — anything like we had attempted to describe.

After the flood, the survivors asked: "Why didn't somebody do something about it?" But the wiser ones asked instead, "Why didn't somebody tell somebody?" The flood control engineers knew, of course, and they did their best to make it known, in advance, what would happen some day to these "plateaus" beneath the mouth of canyons. But they might as well have talked into an empty rain barrel. A dreadful conspiracy of silence buried all they had to say. Why? And again the answer — Greed!

Unless you've worked on a Los Angeles newspaper, you can have no conception of the care with which these newspapers must guard any information which might indicate that some spot in Southern California is anything other than an ideal place to buy real estate.

Strange as it may seem, no Los Angeles newspaperman dares, in advance, write a story that disaster is on its way — if that disaster would affect the price of real estate in the area affected. And no newspaper dares to print such a story.

And the strangest thing about the above excerpt is that nothing in the first three paragraphs is true. All the newspapers, of course, did cover the awful calamity in Montrose thoroughly, from the first day. The *Daily News* used a banner headline in inch-high type on January 2, 1934: "32 Killed, Score Missing in Great Storm Disaster; $5,000,000 Damage as 3,000 Homes Inundated." By 1938, though, when Brick published his thirty-eight-page *Why Didn't Somebody Tell Somebody?,* he had abandoned the idea of writing as a journalistic craft representing the "facts"; instead, he seemed to feel that it had become a more creative art representing the "truth." Perhaps his investigations with both the 1931 and 1934 grand juries were important in this shift. And in 1934 he was also working on behalf of the Mexican- and Filipino-American farm laborers in the Imperial Valley whose strikes were being violently broken up by vigilantes and sheriff's deputies.

Still, with all that, he found time for a new enthusiasm.

                              May 25, 1934

I'm holding down two jobs in addition to my job on the News and in my spare time have written two movie yarns, both of which have got to the point of interesting a director at Universal, while promoting at least the beginnings of a fairly promising political machine of my own. In addition, my boss is ready to run for governor with at least a fifty-fifty chance of election. If he makes it, I and two other chaps from the paper will constitute his brain trust and, bless his little heart, he'll need one. He knows about as much about being governor as I do about writing a novel.

It all started when George Yohalem (did you see "Topaze"? He did the screen story) got the job of story editor at Universal. He picked my collaborator, a writer named Rena now working as a steno, as his assistant, and she saw a good chance to sell stuff under somebody else's name, so she picked me. The story we wrote was all ready to produce when Yohalem was carefully picked up and tossed in the ashcan for writing an anti-munitions-makers story on the day that the Duponts took over the movie industry.

That left us with a story but no market. However, his successor on the story that caused the row called in Rena for an unofficial collaboration and that gave us a new opening. But Rena made the mistake of submitting the new yarn through her friend, his secretary. The secretary had also been a writer, and she wanted to ditch Rena and get collaborator's credit. So I wrote a new yarn for Rena and a new yarn for Vera, the secretary, and shot them both at the director from different angles. I can't tell yet how they will come out, but if they don't sell I'm going to take Rena's story and fictionalize it. It's really too good for the movies.

However, that suggests another possibility. It seems that this clash of the girls for collaborator's credit is not an isolated instance but a sort of a disease in the studios. Practically all stenos in the movies are former free-lance writers. Movie yarns are one type of writing on which two heads are better than one; consequently, the girls get $210 per week for writing half of a story for which the writer gets $1,000 per week.

Being in the studio, a steno cannot even attempt to sell her own stuff without being blacklisted, but she has a chance to sell stuff under other names. So every girl in the studio is looking for a name under which she can sell a yarn. She can then get collaborator's credit, half the check, and reestablish herself as a writer.

Do you remember Van Vechten's "Spider Boy"?[18] It was a fairly accurate story (not a burlesque) so far as it went. I'm tinkering with a similar, though different, idea: Fade in on a chap taking a stroll through the Hollywood hills, carrying a book, not realizing that he is near a studio. Camera pans up and reveals, behind every bush on the hillside, a girl with a notebook, carefully stalking him because, since he carries a book, he must be an embryo writer. "Spider Monkey" (Charlotte Greenwood-type) gets there first by climbing a tree beneath which he is sitting and drags him off to her apartment after rescuing him from the other girls. The story is started, adventures, encounters, male-Cinderella stuff, and a happy ending with our hero brightening the lives of some forty girls by

---

18 *Spider Boy: A Scenario for a Motion Picture,* a humorous novel by Carl Van Vechten, was published by Knopf in 1928. A satire, it told of a writer's misadventures in Hollywood. Bess Taffel, one of the few women screenwriters working in the industry in the late 1930s, recalled in the book *Tender Comrades,* by Patrick McGilligan and Paul Buhle, that some men at Paramount refused to work with her "because they couldn't feel free to curse around a woman."

lounging in the center of a vast hall and permitting them to write stories for him. It would have made a good movie burlesque in the days when movies used to burlesque themselves, but they don't do it any more.

After all, this movie stuff is excellent training in building a story through (my greatest weakness), but if I ever show signs of taking it seriously, please come out here and shoot me. I've seen half a dozen good friends ruined by getting on a movie payroll for twelve weeks.

As ever,

Brick

Chapter Ten
Passions

In a man's life there may come a point of crisis, a kind of watershed of emotion, a violent stripping away of the past and a preparation for an uncertain future. It's no accident that this point often coincides with the early thirties, and marks the end of youth. In these mid-Depression years my father lost a job, a wife, his children and whatever dreams he might have had that his life would be an endless procession of success and applause. Like the book he finally completed in this turbulent time, this storm of passion marked "the end of a phase, rather than a beginning." Of course there was a woman involved.

November 17, 1934

Dear Fanny,

It's always with a sense of gratitude for the fact of your existence that I turn to you on those occasions when I find myself no longer the self-sufficient person I would like to believe, but rather a not-too-sensible kid who has been really only playing at being grown up.

When I wrote last spring I was doing all kinds of things: electing a governor, instituting a reformation of our economic system, becoming a writer on politico-economic subjects, writing scenarios and indicting a district attorney. I didn't know it at the time but I was falling in love, too.

The whole thing grew into a wild, hectic, impossible summer in which I averaged some fourteen or fifteen hours

of work a day and seemed to occupy the other hours in love-
making of some sort or another. Now the whole business has
gone smash; there is nobody to make love to and no more
work to be done on the graft investigation.

You remember I was hired, part time, by the grand
jury to run certain investigations. We soon ran into the
district attorney, and it was necessary to indict and
convict him before we could go after anyone else.

District Attorney Buron Fitts had accommodated nicely to Los Angeles County's breakdown of government, a stew of crime that had led
concerned civic leaders to form the Minuteers, or the Minute Men. Moving cautiously, sometimes secretly, the group attempted to gather information that would result in indictments of the politicians who ruled the
city and the county. They were helped by an honest man, Judge Fletcher
Bowron. (He was to be elected mayor of Los Angeles four years later as
a reformer.)

Bowron took the jury out of the dirty corridors of the D.A.'s office
and handed it over to a special prosecutor, Clyde C. Shoemaker. The
new man began to look into Fitts' favorable treatment of the well-con-
nected Dave Allen, who had been head of the motion picture industry's
Central Casting Bureau. Allen was facing a morals charge, which Fitts
should have been prosecuting. But, as the *Daily News* political writer,
Brick had reported in his column on July 11, 1934, that

> Rightly or wrongly, some of the jurors seem to be convinced that there is
> somebody in the district attorney's office who is more interested in freeing
> Allen than is Allen's own lawyer. At least some members are looking
> longingly at that part of the penal code which deals with conspiracies to
> obstruct justice.

This leak enraged Fitts and his gang: A judge friendly to the D.A.
hauled Brick into court to find out just who had squealed, but Brick was
sent out of the courtroom without having to reveal his source.

That summer, Brick was released from his newspaper duties by Manchester Boddy, who was friendly to the Minute Men, to once again work
as a special grand jury investigator, paid not by the county (for the corrupt Board of Supervisors stubbornly refused to appropriate money for
anybody to assist the jury), but by private donations.

The head of our group was the presiding judge of the
superior court, and the angel was the foreman of the grand
jury, a millionaire who was willing to spend his own money
for the cleanup. The millionaire had a heart attack and had
to take a trip around the world. The only man with brains
in the crowd was running for governor and couldn't even
give us his advice and attention. And I, the only other
person who was squarely out in front as a target, couldn't
run away.

A target of the jurors was George Gregory, who was the brother of Buron Fitts' wife, as well as other financial promoters connected with a failed mortgage company called California Reserve.

A decade later, Guy Finney, a newspaperman who was active in the Minuteers, wrote in his book *Angel City in Turmoil* that

> The gouging and swindling practices revealed to the county grand jury followed the familiar pattern of get-rich-quick promotions, with defensive deceits and political knaveries that made the case outstanding in California criminal annals. Officers dipped into the corporation's funds to pay themselves enormous commissions and salaries, and at Gregory's direction more than $200,000 went from the same source into District Attorney Fitts' political campaigns.

The home of Lyndon Foster, another grand jury investigator, was bombed, Finney wrote. And Brick also met with the D.A.'s thuggery.

```
        It was an exciting experience, I was set upon in a
vacant courtroom one day and beaten up by a gang of the
district attorney's plug-uglies (without coloring the facts
to fit a theory, it is true that the district attorney here
is a member of a real, old-time pre-Repeal gang of
racketeers).

        I went out in the last day before election and whipped
the judge back into line. I fought the attorney general of
the state and forced him to appoint a special prosecutor to
conduct the investigation and provide a payroll after our
angel went away. The prosecutor is a civil lawyer who
doesn't know anything about criminal law, and since then
I've run the case (even to drawing the tremendously
technical perjury indictments) for $12.50 per day while he
drew $125 per day for examining witnesses.

        But I couldn't quit because if we don't succeed in
finishing our job with the district attorney he'll finish
us as soon as this grand jury is discharged the first of
the year.
```

The case that brought about the indictment of Buron Fitts was a curious echo of the Pantages affair of 1929, which Fitts, ironically, had prosecuted. A millionaire real estate promoter, John P. Mills, had been accused in 1931 of having sex with a minor, a call girl, really. It was a sensational case involving a group of teen-age prostitutes, which the newspapers dubbed the "Hollywood Love Mart."

Fitts did bring a prosecution against Mills but dragged out the case, and when it finally came to trial, he failed to produce any witnesses: The judge then had to discharge Mills and the other defendants. The 1931 grand jury investigated but, after the D.A. denied any wrongdoing, it failed to issue any indictments. But did Fitts lie under oath to that jury?

Three years later that question was beginning to smell very ripe, like a fallen orange rotting in a grove. As Finney wrote, when the 1934 grand jury

decided that there were enough peculiar features about the long-submerged Mills case to warrant its reopening, C. H. Garrigues of the staff of the *Los Angeles Daily News* was engaged to do the investigating; one of several able fellows who worked tirelessly, day and night, for several hazard-filled months digging into the heart of this dramatic story.

Brick discovered that, while the Mills case had dragged on, the millionaire had hired one Lucien C. Wheeler to assist in "arranging things" with the D.A. for a fee of $10,000. It appeared that Wheeler paid the Fitts family an inflated price to buy a family orange grove, the suspicion being that the fat profit to the Fittses was payoff money supplied by Mills, through Wheeler, for a quick end to the morals trial. Brick found that Buron Fitts had invested $45,000 in real estate in the previous 18 months (where did he get it?), but Fitts denied the charge, testifying that he had only $10 in the bank and $7,500 worth of equity in an orange grove.

The grand jury was deeply split, with five of the seventeen jurors adamantly backing Fitts. John P. Buckley, a Hollywood dentist, was the jury foreman. He was, Brick wrote, "an average man, somewhat fussy, yet, as it turned out, the bravest of the brave." Shouting could be heard from within the jury room. But on November 1, the jurors indicted both Fitts and his sister, Berthal Gregory, for lying about their financial transactions to that other jury in 1931. As Brick described it later in a self-published pamphlet, *So They Indicted Buron Fitts:*

It was late at night when Shoemaker went into the grand jury room with the completed document. Two floors above, our little group of accountants and stenographers held their breath lest the twelfth juror should seek to change his vote and invalidate the indictment. Then came word that the jury was coming into court. One by one Fitts' investigators filed into the room. Grief for their chief, black hatred for the grand jury, were written on their faces. Solemnly, quietly they sat, strong men, brutal men, some of them, men hardened to the seamiest side of life.

Fitts came in. Shoemaker and the jury came in, and Dr. Buckley handed the indictment to the clerk. As though moved by a common will the horde of detectives and deputies surged forward, beyond the rail, and Fitts stood up for the arraignment. That was all.

Almost every reform juror had received threats — mysterious warnings of death or kidnapping which would follow if Fitts were indicted. From the things we had seen, the evidence we had heard or gathered, we knew that Fitts, backed by the most powerful political machine in California, held a power of life and death over his enemies such as no citizen could suspect.

And as we waited for the elevator, the lights went out and the hall was wrapped in darkness, punctuated by the screams of women. The darkness was filled with hatred — a lust for murder. We did not know, frankly, what was about to happen. And then — nothing happened. The lights went on, the elevators dropped swiftly. We went to our homes.

We finally succeeded in indicting the district attorney for perjury, and we have a bribery indictment to be voted upon Monday. My work is done. I'm still on the payroll and have to show up and give the boss moral support. But the case is out of my hands now, and I've gone into such a state of nervous reaction that, in the last two weeks, I've lost eight pounds.

And then there's the other affair.

I first saw Marianne at a concert several years ago. She looked as a devout painter would have wanted his Madonna to look. The face of an absolute nun -- not remarkable except for that. I met her a few days later at another concert when, sitting with a friend of mine, I saw her brush past the usher, who, quite unreasonably, insisted upon her having a ticket. Then she turned and blacked his eye, calling him two kinds of bastards and three kinds of sons-of-bitches in an indignant tone of voice. To my surprise I found when Marianne reached where we were sitting, that she was my friend's sweetheart or quondam wife or something of the sort.

When I started this job last spring, I needed a stenographer, so I put Marianne to work. My mistake -- perhaps.

She was a member of an old French anarchist family. Her father died in an American prison during the war.[1] She grew up without any attempt at discipline. Her first love affair at the age of fourteen occurred, not under the usual bush on the high school grounds, but when she and another kid about her age went away and lived together in a sort of Daphnis and Chloe existence, taking a week before they found out for themselves what it is you do under those circumstances.

She is intelligent, cultured, without a trace of intellectualism, yet, essentially, her mind, or rather her spirit, has never grown up. Her kindnesses are utterly sweet and her cruelties entirely unconscious. She has a strong maternal instinct which forces her to enslave herself for a while to the man she may be interested in. But she remains, despite such enslavement, strangely untouched, almost hysterically jealous of her individuality. When the enslavement threatens to become a habit -- pouf! It's gone! And the entire affair with it.

From the beginning, she threw herself into the work because it was mine. And I loved the work because she was

---

[1] Marianne later told Brick a different story about the death of her father. See footnote 10 in Chapter Fourteen.

part of it. Yet it was an affair which was bound to be sterile and fruitless. It could never have been enough to either of us to have caused me to leave Dickie and the kids. She realized as well as I that it was temporary -- an interlude. Such infatuation usually culminates with physical contact. Yet that was, also, merely an interlude in the greater business of love-making of a different sort.

As the work became a nightmare, I leaned more and more upon her. She came to fill the horizon so completely that I liked my kids better because they liked her and would play games with her when I took her home for dinner. Everything she touched at my home, even Dickie's things, became hers and important because of her.

And what did Dickie think about this?

Curiously, Dickie didn't more than half mind what little she saw. There was about the whole thing something so innocent that I might almost have gone to bed with her in Dickie's presence without Dickie really sensing the situation. Wives are curious things: They fear what threatens their economic stability and can be jealous about the other things without being deeply harmed. It probably wasn't pleasant for her, but since the time I spent with the girl would have been spent at work anyway, and since the extra work brought in more money, Dickie didn't mind, so much.

Of course, things like that have to end some time, and it was unfortunate that this ended at the most nightmarish period in the investigation. Since then I've been clawing the air, trying to find something to cling to. There was almost a week that I didn't average three hours sleep a night. Yet it wasn't just lovesickness, nor concern over the girl, but rather a complete collapse of everything I had been living in for months.

To make things worse, we've had to go on working in the same office, with really nothing left to do. So I stare at her and wonder if, by any chance, the thing can be revived, and she feels my stare and wonders if this impossible creature is about to make love to her again.

December 10, 1934

I'm in a literal nervous collapse, Marianne has been in bed for two weeks from a nervous breakdown; Dickie would be just as bad if she didn't have to take care of the kids and, I've no doubt, there are probably several other people who would gladly shoot the three of us.

I really feel sorrier for Dickie than for anybody else. She doesn't know what's been going on, but the fact that I've seen so much of Marianne has suggested limitless possibilities to her. I've been able to pour out -- most unwisely -- most of my troubles to Marianne, and Marianne to me, but Dickie, utterly in the dark, has had no means of escape whatsoever.

It is strange to realize that, even at our age, we can lose ourselves so whole-heartedly in a love affair. I had always thought that that sort of thing was worse at sixteen or seventeen, but apparently it only seems that way because we are then unused to it. Later, as we grow emotionally, we become capable of loving more broadly and more deeply, we make more contacts with the other because we have developed more nerve endings of the spirit, and the result is much more painful than when it depends (as it does at sixteen or seventeen) upon Vanity and wounded Pride.

Yet Brick's work had to go on. On January 4, he was called into court by Fitts in the D.A.'s fight to quash the perjury indictment. Brick told the judge that he had indeed been in touch with Fitts' enemies — the Minuteers — while working as an investigator and that he had told one of them that "If we fail to sink the district attorney in this investigation, all of us will have to leave town." That was a prospect Brick didn't much relish, but it turned out to be all too true, at least for Brick.

2064 Oak Glen Place
February 15, 1935

From being terrifically tragic, life has suddenly become amusing again.

About six weeks ago, while Marianne was away on a sea trip, it finally dawned upon me that if I was to keep from going insane, I should have to take Dickie into my confidence as far as my feelings were concerned. I did, and she, who had been terrifically concerned over our situation (known about it all the time), took it in excellent spirits and was as much relieved as I was. I didn't, at that time, tell her that we'd really been sweethearts, however.

A couple of weeks later, after thinking the matter over sanely, she decided that we'd best live separately until I got over it in some way or another.

I was only two-and-a-half while all this was going on. My memories are of incidents only: Night. A strange bedroom, perhaps a rented room. A white slip hanging on a hook behind a closed door became a spectre outlined by a light seen dimly through a window. The shape frightened me. Dickie turned on a lamp to assure me there was nothing to fear. It was indeed only a harmless piece of cloth. I fell asleep with her in the same bed. And then there were a few days or maybe a week in a kind of a foster home with a bunch of other kids; that was fun, and we were fed scrambled eggs with little bits of bacon mixed in. I wasn't frightened there; my big brother, Chuck, was with me. And he was four-and-a-half.

So she found herself a nice, tiny home in the country, with a couple of acres of grounds for the kids. While preparing to move, she discovered -- in true movie fashion -- a letter from Marianne which told her the rest of the story. She had all the normal emotions, but I was in such a condition by that time over the whole affair that when she showed me the letter I went into a complete state of hysteria which stopped her from doing the same and, incidentally, enabled me to really explode and saved me from actually going batty.

Well, she moved.

I took a beautiful little place up on the hills near Elysian Park, and she has apparently been as happy as could be expected in her new place.

Naturally, the change was a terrific shock to me. I had not really been living at home much, but it was always a place to sleep and a place to eat. After Dickie and I had had our talk it had also become a pleasant place to live. I didn't want to leave it, but I simply couldn't go on living with Dickie and thinking about Marianne. But the business of going into a bare and empty house, cooking my own meals, sending out my own laundry was almost impossible for me.

I don't know how Dickie really felt about things by that time. She seemed happy, fixing up her place and -- for the first time -- actually owning something of her own. But I suspected that she was pretending to herself a good bit.

As for Marianne -- she was mentally and spiritually ill. We all thought her trip would cure her, and she came back with the intention of resuming her life and at least casual, friendly, normal relations with me. The first evening I saw her she became violently ill, nauseated, and was in bed for two days. (Isn't that flattering?) Occasionally I saw her, and more frequently as time went on. Once again I spent an evening with her, and again she became ill. (I seem to have emetic properties.)

A week ago Monday I started my vacation -- a voyage to British Columbia. It was a splendid vacation. The sea was calm and I stayed in my berth most of the time and read and wrote and slept. I felt tremendously rested and, the last day or so, enjoyed living again. All of the dramatized memories of the last year just fell away as I regained strength.

In Vancouver I spent a day and an evening with Robert Cromie, publisher of the Vancouver Sun, and the only really intelligent newspaperman I ever knew. He offered me a job, temporary or permanent, and I stalled because Vancouver is close to Tacoma, and Marianne is going to spend the summer in Tacoma.

When I got back, Marianne's sister, Astrid, met me with tears in her eyes and a note from Marianne. It was all off -- and she didn't even trouble to be dramatic about it.

I can't tell you yet how it affected me. I was tremendously
hurt at first. Then, later, I realized that Astrid and I
had spent the afternoon and evening laughing and enjoying
ourselves as though my whole existence had not just ended.
I spent the latter part of the evening and the night with
Dickie. I was "myself" again, and Dickie, unfortunately,
got the idea that we would soon be back together. But,
really, I was no more free of Marianne than I had been,
except that I was no longer tragic about it.

Anyway, I had to spend last night with Dickie and
destroy the hopes I had unwittingly raised. We both did a
bit of emoting, but I think everything turned out well.

A few years later, when I was nine or so, I asked my mother why she
and my dad didn't live together any more. That was in 1941, and I didn't
know any other child whose mother lived in one house and whose father
lived in another.

She touched me gently and lied, "Differences . . . money. We argued about money." That was good enough for me: money. I didn't
know about Brick's grand juries, about Brick's passions, about Marianne,
about Astrid, until I was past sixty and read my father's letters.

Today I spent with Astrid. We laughed and talked and
sang much as Marianne and I used to do. And here's the
amazingly insane thing -- in all probability, Astrid will
move in with me as my housekeeper, on a purely platonic
basis, within the next few days. It's so goofy that nobody
else could have thought of it. So I must tell you about
Astrid.

She's not yet twenty-one, an artist's model, rather
Hollywood, with a beautiful body and, probably, a beautiful
face. She has Marianne's sweet, simple nature and something
of her background, but more intelligence.

She's madly, desperately, in love with a chap on the
paper, a weak, selfish, spoiled darling who has all of my
bad qualities and some of my good ones greatly intensified.

We became close friends during the weeks Marianne was
gone when Astrid was doing office work for me. Most of our
work consisted of sitting in a saloon around the corner,
holding hands, weeping, and talking simultaneously -- she
about Sascha, I about Marianne. So --

I really can't live alone while this is working itself
out. I must have company, and yet I must have absolute
freedom from emotional demands. Fond as I am of Dickie, I
can't live with her yet because she unconsciously makes
those demands on me. If anybody had told me a year ago that
any normal man could live in a small house with a beautiful
young girl of whom he is very fond, and live without even
an emotion passing between them, I'd have developed the
same leer anybody else would.

Astrid wants to try it because she's desperately poor, needs a home and, particularly, somebody to whom she can talk for hours about Sascha. It's the craziest idea I ever heard of. I can't live successfully with either of the two women I really care for, so I live with (in one sense) a much more beautiful sister of one, and she, who can't live successfully with the man she's in love with, lives with a really more attractive friend of the man.

I don't know yet how I feel about the other things. When I'm with Dickie I feel most strongly the tremendous hold Marianne has on me, and when I'm with Marianne I can't help but think how much I care for Dickie. The affair has made me realize that Dickie has more sense, intelligence and companionship than I even suspected and, if it weren't for Marianne, I could be happier with her than I have ever been.

Strangely enough, in these days of depression, I haven't given a thought to work. I have the job at the News, but it doesn't pay very much. I have also a chance at a job with the county at almost twice the salary, but I've done nothing about it. Then there's the Vancouver job -- the best paper in North America to work on if you're good -- but the boss at the News is working on a plan to send me to the Gran Chaco for a book, lectures and magazine stuff on the war. (There's a most fascinating story there.) But I've done nothing about any of them.[2]

Meanwhile other eyes, unfriendly eyes in the pro-Fitts camp, were noticing Brick's troubled relationship with his attractive assistant. I found a memo in a metal cabinet in a big University of Southern California warehouse, where the files of the long-deceased *L.A. Examiner* had been stored for decades. In February 1935, an *Examiner* reporter, Ralph "Casey" Shawhan, wrote to his city editor:

memo city desk:

I would like to suggest that the district attorney's office be checked to see whether or not any investigation of Marianne Claire and her associations with C.H. Garrigus, the 1934 grand jury secret investigator, is being made.

There probably is nothing to it, but a Times man asked me today what I had heard about the girl in connection with Garrigus, and I said I did not know her.

Fitts's office might be very interested in what the girl could tell about the operations of Shoemaker, Buckley, possibly Judge Bowron, if she knows anything. I understand the girl was staying with Garrigus in an apartment and she was his sec.

---

2 The Chaco War was a bloody and costly conflict between Bolivia and Paraguay, with 100,000 casualties (1932-35). Progressives were interested because the Bolivian army was led by a German general.

March 21, 1935

The thing has gone beyond the stage of a nice, ordinary, sentimental tragedy and has developed tabloiditis. Which seems a rather facetious preliminary to telling you that Marianne is in a sanitarium after having tried to commit suicide.

She was evidently afraid that she would change her mind for she used two kinds of poisons, gas and cut her wrists. Then, although she won't talk about that part of it, she apparently struck herself on the temple in an effort to knock herself unconscious so she couldn't change her mind.

The *Examiner* city editor sent a reporter to Marianne's room at the French Hospital, possibly in an attempt to pin an assault rap on Brick Garrigues.

> *Los Angeles Examiner, March 6, 1935.* 'SUICIDE GIRL' EX-JURY AIDE. Recovering from what police reported was an attempt to end her own life, Marianne Claire admitted yesterday that she was the same woman who recently served as a special investigator for the 1934 county grand jury.
>
> Miss Claire denied she had been the victim of an assault, declaring that "Anything that happened to me was done by myself."

As soon as she was ready to leave the hospital, I put her under the care of the best local psychiatrist -- Dr. A. J. Rosanoff.[3]

It will be a long time before I've rebuilt my physical and nervous reserve, though. I'm some fifteen pounds underweight and get terribly weary. But I'm able to rest again -- dragging down great copious quantities of sleep, so that it won't be more then a few weeks until I'm back to some kind of a new normal.

Meanwhile, I'm spending what time I can spare doing a more or less satirical study of modern politics to be called "The Politician's Handbook, or, The Guide to Graft," and purports to be the first textbook ever written in a sympathetic vein to teach young grafters the essential elements of their career. It's a serious study of government-as-is, as opposed to government-as-should-be. I haven't any doubts as to its success.

May 7, 1935

The split between Dickie and me appears to be permanent -- and on a friendly basis. We still have a good bit of affection for one another, but apparently neither of us can regard our married life as anything but a series of concealed annoyances. When Dickie really

---

3 Rosanoff was later director of the state's mental institutions under the progressive Governor Culbert Olson. He was at that time roundly criticized by Brick's friend Frank Scully and other moderates for his stewardship of the hospitals. He resigned in 1942 and huffed, "I will never again enter politics of any kind." He then established the Langley Porter mental health clinic in San Francisco.

began to reflect on how many objectionable things there were about our married life, she seemed happier at the termination than I was.

I'm taking care of Marianne at my place. She had a pretty serious mental breakdown (a manic-depressive psychosis of mild grade) but seems to be going through the final convalescence now.

I've turned definitely to writing at last. It is the only work I can do with any sense of satisfaction and, while the magnum opus is not proceeding as rapidly as I hoped, it is going forward steadily and, it seems, in excellent style.

July 5, 1935

The book is finished, except for the last part, "Clinical Notes," which is done but not entirely in a satisfactory manner. Dickie has typed most of it.

As for myself, things are better. It took a psychiatrist to show me that I, as well as Marianne, am a manic-depressive and that it was merely a peculiar circumstance that two manic-depressives should happen to go through a stage of elation together.

The fact suggests numerous lines of thought. For example, having been really in love last summer, I can understand for the first time how literally true it is that love is a madness.

July 29, 1935

I'm sending you the first half of my baby, "A Guide to Graft" -- conceived, most likely, in sin, carried in travail, and brought forth to its present condition with more pleasure than ordinarily attends the earlier preliminaries in such matters. All I ask is that you remember the poor little brat reverses the ordinary procedure in such cases by possessing a father but no mother. As an experienced father by this time, I can assure you that I possess all the ordinary affection for the creature but coupled, too, with a sneaking sensation that the brat is probably not quite mentally bright.

I suppose you've read Richard Aldington's "Death of a Hero" and "All Men Are Enemies." He is also a manic-depressive, as is the hero of "All Men Are Enemies." To me it's very curious that you find in both books samples of "elated" writing which might have come from the clinical notes of any psychiatrist. Much of the first draft of "Guide to Graft" showed the same symptoms, but I think most of that has been eliminated. Some day I'm going to make a collection of manic-depressive writers. Lamb was one, and much of the charm of Elia is due to elated writing.[4]

---

[4] The two books by Aldington (1892-1962), published in 1929 and 1933 respectively were deeply reflective of the disillusion of those who had fought through World War I, the "Lost Generation." Charles Lamb, the English writer (1775-1734), completed his autobiographical essays under the pen name of Elia.

I'm feeling infinitely better. I'm going to have to get away from newspaper work and politics, even though I can't see how just yet.

September 11, 1935

Marianne came out of her depression a few weeks ago and, feeling that both of us needed a break from one another for a few weeks, I helped her get her regular steamer trip north. It's the first time I've been alone for more than a few days for many years. At first it was ideal, having no demands on my time or attention. Then, quite suddenly, the old agitation and depression came back.

In the midst of that attack, Marianne came back to town, unexpectedly, to stay for a few days until the ship sailed again. She had passed definitely out of her depression into a condition of mild elation and was, quite morbidly, having a hell of a good time aboard ship.

Marianne being what Marianne is, an emotional gold-digger, a mental wanton, and her elation expressing itself, as it frequently does, in a sort of psycho-eroticism, she was embroiled by this time in a triangle aboard ship involving the skipper, the chief mate and a sailor.

A ship is somewhat like dear old Boston, for the mate speaks only to the skipper and the skipper speaks only to God. Naturally, the skipper's dignity was hurt whenever Marianne talked with the mate. The mate was jealous when she talked to the skipper. It's an absolute rule that nobody from the bridge may speak to a sailor, so Marianne made them both madly jealous by showing all the attention to the sailor she could get by with.

Monday night, she and I had a very tentative date to meet at her mother's. Since she wasn't sure I would be there, and since a manic always does exactly what he wants no matter what anybody else wants, she brought the mate along, and we had a very pleasant triangular evening which resulted in me going into an elation of my own.

Those mild elations are very peculiar things. They're not pathological or morbid, exactly, but rather like a normal elated feeling except that you know they're not real, not based on anything. I knew it was time to see a psychiatrist, so the next day I went to see Dr. Rosanoff. There I found Marianne, trying to get the doctor to take her last fifty dollars to take care of me until she came back. He refused and I refused and we finally agreed on a case study for me.

Marianne and I had a marvelous time the rest of the day. We just chased around town and did silly things like buying toys, etc., and we spent a very happy evening at the harbor talking in a restaurant until nearly midnight.

When we got to the ship in the evening, it appeared that

Marianne had arranged for precisely the same sort of half
date with the mate she'd arranged with me the night before.
Instead of making the same sort of triangle, however, she and
I slipped away, leaving him to fret in the evil juices of his
own jealousy. When we drove back at midnight we pulled up on
the dock and had chatted about ten minutes when the mate
poured himself down the gangplank, roaring that he was "dom
tired of such ____ ___ ___ _____ _____ _____ _____." (I
didn't know there were so many four-letter words), and
ordering me off the dock and Marianne onto the ship.

Since I had no desire to have either my face or
Marianne's trip spoiled, I went precipitately but not in
confusion, and she spent the next hour listening to a
lecture on how vile it was that she (who has been drunk in
half the waterfront saloons on the coast with either the
skipper or the mate) should "make a dom fool of herself" by
such (more four-letter words) with me.

I spent a couple of hours yesterday with Dr. Rosanoff,
going over my case. Tomorrow he's going to talk with
Dickie, and later I'll have some more sessions. Out of
those, we hope, I'll be able to find some adjustment to
stop this emotional pendulum.

September 27, 1935

I've been going through a couple of weeks that have
been as bad as, although different from, my depression of
last fall. Dr. Rosanoff says the only thing to do is to sit
and wait until I get over it.

The worst thing is the feeling of utter alone-ness. One
feels so completely out of contact with humanity. I sit here
in the apartment, hour dragging after hour, unable to work,
unable to see people, unable to read, unable to think. More
as a sort of game than anything else, something to pass the
hours, I watch for the mailman.[5] I haven't heard from
Marianne since she arrived in Seattle, and when the mailbox
is empty, the depression grips me harder and harder.

Forgive this weeping letter. There are so few people
on whose shoulder I can cry. I wish it were here -- I'd cry
on it literally.

October 10, 1935

I had rather disquieting news from Marianne. She
hadn't written me, and I was getting more and more alarmed.
I had a plane pass, and I finally wrote that I'd fly to see
her if she didn't let me know she was all right. The doctor
got a night letter the next morning to the effect that she
didn't want to have anything to do with me, didn't want to
write to or hear from me, and would either kill herself or
me if I went to see her.

---

5 In that era mail was delivered two or three times a day.

I haven't been able to work, but I've been dabbling with ideas for two books. The first is a "Psychopathology of Love." Written in much the same style as "The Guide to Graft," it would take up the various symptoms of love and consider them in the light of psychiatry as symptoms of insanity. Nothing quite so trite as "love is a madness," but it's a curious thing that there is scarcely a symptom-pattern of a psychosis which is not also a symptom-pattern of love.

(Interruption by the landlady who is a theosophist and who assures me solemnly that Marianne's breakdown was caused by thousands of little devils, or rather the souls of suicides who are feeding off her. Pleasant person to have around, eh?)[6]

October 14, 1935

I've been feeling much better and am beginning to hope that recovery is really in the offing. It's true that Dickie has been a great comfort to me, especially since she's begun to understand what it's really all about. I've been spending most of my spare time with her, but we avoid the house, the kids and the domestic arrangements and concentrate on shows and dances. I try not to lean on her too hard, since I still can't see myself going back to domesticity when I'm well, and I know I will hurt her if I pull away.

As for Marianne, I'm waiting for her to come back with a sort of vague curiosity as to what effect she will have upon me. I'm rather piqued at her walking out without a word after I'd cared for her all summer, but not really hurt about it: Either she's still abnormal or something I wrote hurt her very much, or, probably, both.

One trouble with "The Politician's Handbook," if it's published, is that it doesn't lead anywhere. It's what a first book shouldn't be, an end of a phase rather than a beginning. If it should be accepted, I suppose I should be prepared to turn out a lot of other things on the same subject -- but there aren't any more, for me. Is it better to be a writer whose succeeding books you can buy in perfect confidence that each will be just like the one before, or one who jumps from politics to love to psychiatry without warning or reason?

October 19, 1935

Things have rather come to a crisis for me. It seems vitally necessary for me to leave Los Angeles. Do you think that I could get a job in New York where I could support myself and send Dickie a few dollars a month?

Dickie agrees that I should go and is willing to try

---

6 Theosophy was a worldwide movement based somewhat upon Buddhist teachings. It stressed mysticism and pantheism.

and support herself and the kids until I get established.
It'll be a tough job for her, but things have been pretty
tough for her anyway, and we'd both be better off if I
could get away from things that remind me of Marianne. And,
unfortunately, there's nothing in Los Angeles which doesn't
remind me of her.

The thing goes beyond the affair with Marianne. I used
to work and live enthusiastically; I've always been
interested in my job; I couldn't work if I hadn't been.
Last year, so far as my own line of work is concerned, I
was absolute tops on the coast. It wasn't that my reputation was so great (although it was), but I was doing
something that no other newspaperman could do. I was a
byword among a fairly large percentage of even the ordinary
people: When I walked through a crowd, I'd overhear people
say: "That Garrugos" or "Gerigs" or "Gargus" or something.

That's gone. I'm at the bottom.

The thing which finally precipitated this was
Marianne's complete, absolute, definite departure. She
breezed in earlier in the week with the most studied air of
icy friendliness and announced that she was packing her
things and sending them away. I was burned up at her
attitude. One would have thought that I'd been living off
her for the last year instead of her living off me.

That isn't the real Marianne. She overacted her part.
Sometimes I think that even when she's normal she's bugs.
Her rehearsed explanation, offered at every opportunity,
was: "I won't have you in love with me when I'm not in love
with you." To which I could only reply that I wasn't enough
in love with her for her to get all burned up about.

However, that part of it hurt. We've been through
enough together so that we should have salvaged some
affection out of the thing. Now I feel that all the time,
effort, care, the hurts to Dickie, were utterly useless and
vain in that they only created resentment in her, Marianne.

Her going has left a vacuum. Caring for her has been a
substitute for all the other energies, activities and
ambitions which I used to have. It's an old truism that we
love those whom we help and hate those who help us. Even
you have no conception of how completely she's filled my
life the last year. I think I used to push the sun up every
morning just so it would shine on her, keep the stars
moving around so she could amuse herself with them; I know
damned well I used to ride the streetcars and climb a
quarter of a mile up this hill on foot so she could use the
car, used to go without clothes to buy her food; I deprived
Dickie and the kids of the affection and care they should
have had in order to help her. And yet I can't resent her.
I am too busy feeling sorry for her.

And so I want to go to New York. Perhaps I'm being

romantic about it (in my heart I know I'll hate the cold
and snow and the noise and the crowding; I who can't stand
to sit in the house but must write this out in the yard). I
know it's absurd, but it seems inevitable. Nothing is so
absurd as to keep on trying to live here, the way I feel.
Tell me quite frankly -- how much I'll need to live on and
how much chance there is of getting it.

If it's true that we like those we do things for, then
you should be extremely fond of me.

As ever,

Brick

Chapter Eleven
The Dream Ranch

771 North Hyperion
Apartment 501
October 28, 1935

Dear Fanny,

Important as Marianne was, she is not the essential
element in whatever has happened. Call it manic-depressive
psychosis or temperament or just plain emotional instability, the result is the same. Something is changed in me;
perhaps Marianne is a result, but I don't believe she was
the cause. As I wrote you nearly a year ago, there's a new
phase; perhaps she helped end the old one and, of course,
the memory of the experience will color the new one.

My old self is gone. I'm frightened of the new thing
because I don't know what it is. I know I'm alone as I have
never been alone before; I can cling for a few hours to
Dickie, much as I used to cling to Marianne, but there's no
power that I can really depend upon. I've always thought I
knew pretty well where the world was and where I was in
relationship to it, now I know nothing. I stumble blindly
forward, never knowing when I'm going over a precipice.

I've taken a small apartment in a section I've never
lived in before. The routine of living is reduced to the
minimum. I have eliminated most of the things which could
remind me of what's happened. I look back upon the last two
years as one would look back upon an illness. I regret
what's happened, regret the lost joy I had, but I don't

really wish for it back. So long as I'm not called upon to make certain contacts, particularly in newspaper work, I get along very well.

I'm working nights. I get up at nine and, after breakfast, write until two or three o'clock. Sometimes I see Dickie, and sometimes I look up a few choice old friends I haven't seen for many years. Then, in the evening when there is no work to do at the office, I write again. I think I can write a novel. I wrote "The Politician's Handbook" because I had to. The novel is going the same way. It writes itself, probably badly. I think every word will have to be rewritten at least three times. It's pure autobiography, of course, and I don't like that, but I fancy the background, the real worth of the thing, makes it more than just a sophomoric outpouring. It will be long -- I've finished fifteen thousand words and have hardly made a beginning. I'm in a fever of impatience, not to finish it, but to spend every hour on it I can. I'm really only unhappy when I'm too tired to work on it; then that feeling of being lost and alone comes back.

But I need human contacts -- I'm afraid not to have them. I've made very few, but now I find I can go back ten or fifteen years and re-establish a few of the old friendships. One family, particularly, I enjoy. The father was a newspaperman. The oldest daughter was a magazine writer until she threw it up and started raising prize chickens. The younger daughter (I used to think she was the most beautiful girl in the world) is a vaudeville dancer. They are Basque, and with that environment are the most completely stable of all the intelligent people I know.

The fact is, I really don't know what I need. I could go back to the family if I ever, definitely, once and for all, gave up the idea that I should ever write success-fully. But that would be death. I would have to stop thinking, for I can't think except by writing.

I have just finished re-reading "Jean-Christophe." Remember, you loaned it to me first in Arizona, when I was coming out of an episode similar to this? Strange how big it has grown since.

November 24, 1935

Knowing me as you do, you know I couldn't be in this contented frame of mind if I hadn't a new girlfriend. In this case, it's an old, old one, made over. I looked her up again a month or so ago and found, very surprisingly, that each of us had grown, or changed, in precisely the fashion that would enable us to be the very best of friends. I don't believe there's any danger of anything serious developing.

The woman he sought out was Louise Perkins from his days as a young editor in Venice. She was the Basque vaudeville dancer.

December 30, 1935

Yes, I'm "at it again," but not in the way you mean. For the last month or so, I've been feeling unusually well, filled with that free-flowing energy that I used to have a couple of years ago and which went up in smoke so suddenly.

That was where Louise came in. She provided a comparatively safe outlet; when I was with her it was lots of fun, and when I wasn't, I could relax as I haven't relaxed in years. Altogether it's been one of the most nearly flawless companionships I've ever known -- and I say "it's been" because it's about over. She's going to be married in a week or so; both of us are wise enough to realize that we mustn't confuse interludes with permanent arrangements.

Brick was working on another book idea, a burlesque of *Gabriel Over the White House,* a 1933 movie about a U.S. president who assumes near-dictatorial powers to reduce unemployment and slow the arms race.

This book would sketch rather accurately the political events in the United States during the next six years. It seems to me that an open, fascistic, military dictatorship will be in effect either just before or just after the 1940 election, and that it will come about through certain devices which I can almost foretell one by one. The book would be immensely valuable to the Farmer-Labor Party, which will undoubtedly run up several million votes in 1940 and at least a couple of millions in 1938.[1] As a working title, I'm using "Lucifer Over the Back House," and I believe I could depend on publication and promotion by the radical press if I can't do better.

I'm still staying at Dickie's but have also taken a room downtown -- in the old Casa de Rosas, where Ruth used to stay -- in which to write if the oppression at home grows too much.

Brick's manuscript, the one he had titled *The Politician's Handbook* and sent to Fanny the preceding July, was accepted by Funk & Wagnalls, to be published as *You're Paying for It! A Guide to Graft.*

January 23, 1936

Of course I can't tell you how delighted I am at the news about the book. There's really no feeling like it. With newfound loyalty, I imagine there's nobody I'd rather have publish it than Funk & Wagnalls, though I know I'd feel the same about Viking if they had taken it. And the terms are, really, better than I'd ever expected, particularly the advance.

I rather suspect, though, that if it hadn't been for

---

[1] A minor political party of farmers and urban workers, which supported Robert M. La Follette in the 1924 presidential election and Franklin D. Roosevelt in 1932 and 1936.

you, the manuscript would still be lying around in some fly-by-night agent's desk. I hope I'll really be a credit to you some day.

The Fitts pamphlet fell terrifically flat, partly because the town is cold on pamphlet exposes (which it looks like until you read it) and partly because the price, twenty-five cents, was purposely put a little high in order not to make it look like a political pamphlet. We printed five thousand as a first run and will be lucky if we sell three thousand of them, which would just pay expenses.

The last chapter caused quite a sensation in the political fringe,[2] so I had to debate day before yesterday at the Municipal League forum. It was the first time I'd been on a platform in years, and I was scared to death, but I seemed to do all right, and now all the little discussion clubs and open forums that don't pay anything for speakers want me to speak. It's the only way to advertise the book that doesn't cost anything, so next week my manager and I go from luncheon club to luncheon club. I make the speech about graft, and he sells the books after the meeting is over, and that way we make a few dollars. They're trying to arrange a debate in the Trinity Auditorium (capacity two thousand) against a local radio racketeer, but I'm ducking it as he's big time, and I know when I'm outclassed.

Well, anyway, the boss has been trying to find a good excuse to fire me, so he used the pamphlet as the excuse. I shamed him out of it, and we compromised with an agreement that I would quit when I could find a better job.

Meanwhile, I have a new enterprise. After the Sinclair campaign,[3] several small liberal or left-wing political weeklies sprang up, among them the United Progressive News. My local manager is running it, and he finally managed to get rid of the woozy liberal crowd, and we're trying to run it as a newspaper specializing in news that no other paper will print -- strikes, suits against department stores, covering the radical and fascist movement from a nonpartisan angle. No scandal and no exposes. I'm organizing the staff from behind the scenes and will not appear in it but I'll have a lot of fun.

On February 7, 1936, after a rousing final plea by District Attorney

---

2 In it, Brick stated baldly that, despite his eight years of work as an investigator into the corruption of government, despite the conviction of Asa Keyes in the Julian case, despite the fact that Sidney T. Graves had been sent to jail, despite the indictment of Fitts, "From that eight years of work, not one public benefit has come." He reasoned that graft and corruption were an integral part of the election process because even "honest" politicians had to rely on donations from crooks and gangsters for their campaign expenses. And because of that, Brick wrote in the last sentence of his pamphlet, he was giving up — he was "through with graft investigation."

3 Upton Sinclair, the progressive author, had been drafted by the liberal wing of the Democratic Party to run for governor in 1934. His program to End Poverty in California (EPIC) was ridiculed by the state's ruling establishment and all the major newspapers. But he lost by only the narrowest of margins to the Republican, Frank Merriam.

Buron Fitts' lawyer, Jerry Giesler, the same man who had successfully opposed Fitts in the 1929 Alex Pantages appeal, a jury found Fitts not guilty of the perjury charge laid against him by Brick's grand jury.

March 1, 1936

    Just at the moment I'm the human kaleidoscope. I'm
concentrating right now on: organizing a merger of three
weekly leftwing papers, preparing for a series of radio
talks to last all summer (fifty dollars per week for
fifteen minutes), making speeches (free), finishing the
book, writing another article. Between time I'm still
working (?) on the Daily News. (We just had a baby
earthquake: "None Hurt in Calif. Quake.")

    The most interesting thing right now is the newspaper
merger. The Progressive News, on which I was going to work,
was too small, and I didn't have enough authority to build
it up, so I pulled out and took over the Utopian News
(owned by the Utopian Society, of which you may have heard,
quite moribund but with potentialities). Then there's the
Unemployed Leader, an organ of the Public Works and
Unemployed Union (a Communist outfit). I'm trying to merge
the three under my direction. If I do it, we'll have a paid
circulation to start of twenty thousand a week with a dead
certainty of an increase during the months of the political
election campaign. Meanwhile the radio job will carry me
until September 1. If things are successful by that time, I
may stay and, if not, I'd like to be in a position to get
to New York -- at least for a visit -- shortly after the
book is published.

The Utopian Society was one of the many groups that had arisen in response to the Depression. It was similar to another outfit, Technocracy, which advanced a scheme in which abundance would be brought about by everybody working only four hours a day, four days a week for about a hundred sixty-five days a year between the ages of twenty-five and forty-five, which would be the retirement age. The Utopian Society took Technocracy a step further: It introduced secrecy, symbolism and religious tones. Members could work their way up through five "cycles," become "Hermits" and give up their names for numbers.

Utopian News, March 23, 1936. IN WHICH WE BOW. By C. H. Garrigues. With this issue, the Utopian News is reborn — a new spirit in a new body, but dedicated to the permanent ideals of Utopians and the Utopian Society and determined to carry those ideals into the homes and minds of every family in America.

Until now, the Utopian News has been what we call in newspaper parlance a "house organ" — that is, a periodical published by an institution for its members, carrying articles primarily of interest to members of that institution.

With this issue it becomes a newspaper of general circulation, intended for every reader in Southern California who is interested in the fight to attain that new era of super-abundance in which there will be no more poverty and no more hunger.

Hereafter, the *News* will concentrate on news of the entire liberal movement in California. Next week the *Utopian News* will appear as *The People's Progress.*

People's Progress, May 11, 1936. FUN IN BED.[4] *By C. H. Garrigues.* Every time I woke up the first two days, there was a doctor making annoying little jabs at the back of my throat with a wicked little gadget and remarking that I should have had those tonsils out years ago.

Sometimes I came out of it long enough to think of Frank Scully and *Fun In Bed,* but it didn't seem like fun, and I wondered if it was sumpin I et or if some ouija-worker had put the gypsy curse on me.

The third day there was another doctor, and he shook his head at the little gashes the first doctor made and said:

"You can't cut poison out with a knife. When it gets that bad, just keep sipping hot lemonade and the fluid acts as a poultice, and the first thing you know it draws the poison out and you're well."

So I sipped hot lemonade the third and fourth and the fifth day, and the sixth day was able to sit up and read the *Epic News* and the *People's Progress* and take other forms of spiritual nourishment. Then came the thrill that comes but once in a lifetime.

The End Poverty League (and the *Epic News*) was founded to save some million California people from poverty and starvation by Upton Sinclair's plan for production for use. Yet here, on the eve of its second important election, as the final effort of its great fight, was a copy of the *Epic News,* which gave Sinclair himself a scant three columns of type and devoted not less than five full (count 'em) columns to our own little self. Boy, were we proud.

And such type! Such verbiage! Listen:

"C. H. 'Brick' Garrigues has earned for himself the reputation in the inner circles of the newspaper fraternity and progressive and liberal groups as an unscrupulous, double-crossing, sharpshooting, sniper newspaper pirate who would stop at nothing from 'cutting the throat' of his best friend to resorting to the lowest type of journalistic depravity to accomplish his own greedy, selfish desires.

"If you have any doubt that the reputation of Mr. Garrigues is justified, just ask *any* veteran newspaperman of your acquaintance for his very *private* opinion of 'Sniper' Garrigues. He is, by reputation, the living exemplification of the 'prostitutes of the press' that Upton Sinclair tells you about in his famous book, *The Brass Check.*"

There was something vaguely familiar about the style, and then we thought, finally, of Tom James, second assistant fixer-upper for Chief of Police Davis. There was no mistaking the style; Tom had sent us too much similar tripe in the past.

---

4 The title is the same as a series of books written by Brick's old Arizona friend, Frank Scully, who had capitalized on his notoriously bad health by writing humorous pieces about it. At this time, Scully was writing a regular column for a rival, and much larger, newspaper on the progressive fringe, the *Epic News.*

Was it possible that the underworld crowd which runs Los Angeles had gained such influence in the End Poverty League as to take over the local politics of the organization and make Upton Sinclair's great effort a cheap political machine to perpetuate vice and political corruption in Los Angeles?

A telephone call to Epic Temple brought the answer: Yes, Tom James was "the guy," even though some members of the board of directors were pretty sore about it. Yes, they knew Tom was Chief Davis' official fixer-upper, but then it didn't do any harm to have a friend in the Police Department these days.

Thomas H. James was a brutally colorful cop whom newspaper reporters loved to call a "stormy petrel." In 1930 James had been accused of trying to remove all Catholics from the police force. In 1931 he made scurrilous attacks against Mayor John C. Porter and Police Chief Roy E. Steckel, and he was fired. When Frank Shaw was elected mayor in 1934 and appointed a new Police Commission, James was reinstated, and Police Chief James E. Davis made him his spokesman. He served in the police "red squad" (which Brick had attacked in the pages of the *People's Progress)*. In 1938, after the reform Republican, Fletcher Bowron, was elected mayor, James was demoted to a beat patrolman and sent to distant San Pedro. James retired from the LAPD in 1947 to become editor and publisher of the weekly *American Policeman*. He died of a stroke in 1949.

So that was that. So far as we are concerned, it's all part of the story. The *Epic News* is going to "get" Garrigues — the *Epic News* and Tom James and Jim Davis and Buron Fitts and the rest of the black reactionary movement of Los Angeles which the *Epic News* was launched to fight, and which Garrigues has fought for the past ten years.

If the *Epic News* can "get" Garrigues with the kind of tripe it published last week, he deserves to be "got." We haven't time nor space to engage in a running cat-and-dog fight — nor inclination to engage in an olfactory contest with a skunk.

Read Tom James in the *Epic News* each week, remember that he is the paid agent of Chief Davis and the fascist police department, hired with taxpayers' money to turn the Epic movement against itself.

You won't be able to read about it in our paper. We'll be too busy telling the news of the people's movement in California.

That wasn't the end of it. The May 4, 1936, edition of the *Epic News,* continued the tirade:

"You have all been reading the filthy lies and gross distortions about Mr. and Mrs. Upton Sinclair and the EPIC movement in general in Mr. Boddy's little yellow *Ulcerated Daily Edison News,* and in Mr. Boddy's — Mr. C. H. 'Brick' Garrigues' newly born little scandal rag — we will not dignify it by naming it — which the latter publishes (when he can 'chisel' enough side money, said to be $50 per week, from Senator George W. 'All things to all men' Rochester's much heralded district attorney campaign

slush fund to get an edition off the press) about 5000 copies weekly." And
so forth for several columns.

Meanwhile, in New York Fanny Strassman was on her way to becoming a literary agent. She was still working as a secretary at Viking,
but she changed her name to Toni.

May 14, 1936

My dear Toni:

Thanks for the copy of the Hearst book,[5] which I read
with great pleasure while lying in bed with an attack of
tonsillitis. I think it's swell. Probably as good a
contemporary appraisal of a controversial figure as it
would be possible to do.

I am sure I haven't any intelligent ideas on putting
over the book in Los Angeles. The Hearst boycott has been
fairly extensive, but there is, so far as I know, no
militant organizations or organ which would give a
sufficiently wide sales outlet to justify a paper edition.
I have been wondering if it would not be possible for our
paper to handle an edition of this sort on a premium basis,
but I am afraid our outlet is not sufficiently large. The
American League Against War and Fascism is operating, but
is not sufficiently well organized here to handle an
effective sales campaign.

I've never met Carlson, although we have many mutual
friends. He is well known in the extremely limited
intellectual circles of the city but apparently not known
to the other 224,994 people here.

I've been busy as hell -- nineteen hours a day
except Sunday and twenty hours on Sunday. I've been doing
a radio broadcast and publishing the People's Progress
but very little sleeping or eating. The paper is not
going so well, and I may fold it up within a week or so,
in which case I'll still be thinking about New York early
in the spring -- when Mr. Fitts will probably be re-
elected -- so don't hide the welcome mat where I can't
find it.

P.S. I like the new name. I think it fits.

Alhambra, Calif.
June 11, 1936

Dear Toni,

(It makes you seem a different person.)

I'm still walking on a kind of a tight wire. The radio
job continues, taking more of my time as the campaign gets
hot, but not paying me any more, and it will probably run
out when the campaign ends August 25. If Fitts should be
re-elected, my life wouldn't be worth a hell of a lot here,

---

5 *Hearst, Lord of San Simeon,* by Oliver Carlson, published by Viking in 1936.

so I'd have to pull out -- but with no money and no way to
support the family while I'm gone.

What I really want to do is to go to the ranch of a
Negro friend of mine in Mexico, not far from the border. He
-- a second cousin of Theodore Roosevelt, a Harvard Law
graduate, etc. -- started a colony there twenty years ago,
and it went flooey. He has 8,700 acres with two families on
it.[6] I might possibly rake up a couple of hundred dollars,
buy a .22 to shoot rabbits, load the family into the car
and spend the winter there. It would be the best possible
thing for me -- I'm inconceivably tired, tired physically,
tired of people, tired of confusion, even the confusion of
buying a lamb chop at the corner grocery -- perhaps if I
could shoot my game on the hoof it might get me back to a
sense of reality.

The Responsibility of Boyhood

*After Cal bought him his .22, Bliss decided he would supply meat for
the kitchen. In the early morning or late dusk he would take his rifle and
walk along the edge of the grape vineyards where the rabbits came down
to feed upon the tender vines. He would sight a gray shape in the dusk
and draw a careful bead and press the trigger carefully — not really
pressing it, but squeezing the gun as Cal had taught him — until the rifle
gave its tiny "spat!" And then he'd rush forward and pick up the furry
beast and hold it by the hind feet while he gave it a sharp blow with the
edge of his right hand behind the ears so that its neck was broken and it
died painlessly. He would feel pity and revulsion as he held it but he
would take refuge in his knowledge that the blow was called the "coup de
grace," which was pronounced "coo duh grah" and that when prizefight-
ers used it, they called it a rabbit punch, and it was illegal because you
could kill a man with it.*

*Somehow it eased the pity and revulsion to know these things. He
would pick up the rabbit and take it in and skin it and clean it because
skinning and cleaning game was not woman's work and every hunter
ought to be able to skin his own game; then he would give it to Mama,
who would cook it for the next night's supper, and Bliss, eating it, would
feel proud because a cartridge cost a quarter of a cent and for two car-
tridges you could get enough meat for supper for the whole family. That
was pretty good providing, he would tell himself as he took another piece
of Mama's good broiled rabbit.*

Then there wouldn't be any women there. Or probably
there would. If there were, I'd be a cinch to get into
trouble. Not that I'm in any particular jam at the moment,
but life is much too complicated when I'm tired. I've been

---

6 Asked if Theodore Roosevelt had any Negro relatives, Linda E. Milano of the Theodore
Roosevelt Association told me, "None that we know of. The closest we can come is a relative who
ran a hotel/resort in Haiti and had a Haitian mistress."

unusually constant (that is, within reasonable limits) to the old flame I met again last fall, and I've been too busy to get involved with anybody else, but somehow whenever I look up from my work there's some dame there, and I never learned how to say "no." (This sounds like the sort of boasting that accompanies the approach of impotence, but I think not.)

I think Louise and I make an almost ideal pair. She's obligingly postponed getting married until fall, and I think I've postponed going back to Dickie largely because of her. We get along perfectly. She spends Sunday with her fiance, and I spend Sunday with my wife. I drive her home from work about four evenings a week, and we usually drink and talk until about midnight, since we're both too tired to go anywhere. The other evenings we're usually out with somebody else -- or I'm working and she's out. The delightful thing is that there is such a complete lack of jealousy on either side.

An artist whom I know has gone to the beach for the summer, and I've taken his studio -- a delightful place with a fireplace and lots of windows, stuck on top of a garage on a side hill. It's a real shack, with beaverboard and rafters, and I can even take a bath if I go to the cellar of the house next door. I pay twelve dollars per month. He paints well, unusually well, in a pleasing sort of way, and he's left most of his canvasses here so that I'm surrounded by attractive things, and that makes it nice. It's the most comfortable place I've had, and if I can get over this fatigue, I will certainly do some more writing.

"Hush, now, play quietly," Dickie said. "Daddy's on the radio. I want to hear it."

"Me, too! Me, too!"

I was four years old. The voice poured from the big radio speaker and filled the room. It sounded like Daddy, but it wasn't saying, "Hi ya, big guy!" It was just talking, talking, talking, talking. No fun.

I went back to my toy cars on the bare wooden floor. But I tried to be quiet with them.

People's Progress, July 24, 1936. DEATH IN THE AFTERNOON. The following radio address was given over KRKD last Monday night by C. H. Garrigues, publisher of the *People's Progress.* Listen in again next Monday night for another of these radio revelations.

Good evening: Tonight I'm going to break down, put my feet on the pressroom table and try to give you a very brief picture of the inside of one newspaperman's life for the last six years — what was behind the old "Spotlight," what is behind the *People's Progress,* what's behind these radio broadcasts.

I sometimes think I must have been the most naive newspaperman in the world when I started in on this sort of work six years ago. My first assignment was the San Gabriel Dam case, and I went into that investigation — six years and two weeks ago today — with the sincere, earnest conviction that all we had to do was to prove wrongdoing in connection with that five-million-dollar fiasco and those responsible would automatically be punished.

You all know how that case ended. One supervisor was convicted of bribery and went to prison. The contractors only last week agreed to return $737,000 — every penny of the money obtained by means of the bribe. A new flood control administration was set up and the county flood control district is being capably administered for the first time in many years.

I am glad that I have been to any degree instrumental in getting back for the taxpayers three-quarters of a million dollars which was hopelessly lost to them. But to me that money is of little importance — the thing that stands out about those six years is the fact that in that time I have come into contact with a fact so momentous, so horrible to those who believe in democracy, that even yet I can scarcely believe the evidence of my own senses.

When I started to work on the San Gabriel Dam case, I must have believed that our government was operated very much as we had been taught in high school civics. True, I had heard many stories about graft in office. But I never believed, never suspected, that graft constituted both the fuel of our governmental machinery and the product of the machine. I never suspected politics was a sort of perpetual-motion machine which not only made its own fuel but enriched its operators in the process. I never suspected that graft was the rule, rather than the exception, in government.

Between 1930 and 1936 stand six years of hard work — work down in the sewer of practical politics. In those years I discovered that those peanut politicians up at the Hall of Records were pikers. I discovered that while we had been worrying about the few millions they had stolen, the real politicians had stolen our government itself.

I don't mean that as a mere figure of speech. When the law is perverted to protect the guilty and frame the innocent, the last safeguard of free citizenship is gone. When it becomes possible to send to prison even one man because some official covets his wife or his wealth or his girlfriend — then no man with wealth or a desirable wife is free from the danger of prison. And when it is possible to free one cutthroat, one murderer, because of influence at the district attorney's office, then no man's life is safe.

And that time has come in Los Angeles. In San Quentin Prison is an aging man, in Tehachapi Prison an aging woman, sent there by perjured testimony because a man in a high position coveted a gold mine they owned. In San Quentin Prison is another man, sent there because another man in a high position coveted a movie star with whom he was friendly. Through the streets of Hollywood walks a known murderer, free because his arrest and conviction would cost a certain motion picture studio the services of a high-priced star.

It was when I began to realize those things that I started to do something about it. The old "Spotlight" was born. I took service with the 1934 Grand Jury in the hope that — some way — we could remedy conditions.

And it was then that the problem began to become personal — I learned from actual experience how little one's life was worth when the forces supposed to enforce the law had been taken over by gangsters. That realization came first one morning as I stepped into a courtroom in the Hall of Justice. It was Saturday and the room was empty, but in the inner chambers sat five Superior judges, waiting for certain documents they had asked me to bring them.

As I entered the room, two detectives — investigators from the district attorney's office — leaped upon me. I knew them — and I don't mind saying I was scared — scared to death. One was the official strong-arm man of the office — only a few months earlier he had come within an ace of killing an *Examiner* reporter with his feet.

You think fast when you're scared — and I was scared. I didn't know whether I was to be killed, beaten up or just robbed of the evidence I was carrying. I had no desire to be kicked where the *Examiner* man had been kicked. If I ran, I knew, I'd be shot — and there would be a fantastic story of my attempting to escape arrest. So I stood back and took it — giving a few myself. Fortunately, the strong-arm guy wore a heavy ring which cut my face so that I bled a lot and looked worse off than I was. For that reason, I suppose, the guy with the black-jack didn't use it — and I got off easy.

I guess I scared the five judges to death when I staggered late to their meeting — blood-covered, clothing torn, hair matted. They, too, realized there was nothing the august and dignified judges of the Superior Court could do about it.

And it had dawned on me, too, as I stood by an open window and watched that man circling me with a black-jack, that there was nothing anybody could have done about it if they had laid me cold with the sap and then tossed me out the window. It would have been an accident — pure and simple. I resolved then never to get near an open window while my friends from the D.A.'s office were around.

That decision stood me in good stead five or six months later. Again I was in the Hall of Justice on a Saturday afternoon and again I ran into my friend, the strong-arm man, on the eighth floor. It was that time I found what death looks like in the afternoon.

My friend, it seems, was argumentative, and not quite friendly. He wanted to talk — and he wanted to talk directly beside the stairway leading downward from the eighth floor.

That's a peculiar stairway. For some reason, a space of some four feet has been left between the tiers of steps so that a falling body would drop a full six stories before striking stone or concrete. And my good friend wanted me to talk above that seventy-two-foot hole.

Of course, I didn't. We were alone on the floor and I knew by this time that should I tumble over — accidentally like — my friend could prove by nineteen fellow detectives that he was exactly a mile away at the time.

And then he did a startling thing. He grabbed me and forced me over to the rail, trying to bend me back over the hole. I could have cried out — but I wouldn't have been heard. And as we fought there, silently, an elevator came to the top and he stepped back. We walked away while he whispered in my ear all the ways he was going to take me apart if he ever caught me alone again.

I think you can see why I believe we need a change in the district attorney's office. Perhaps I'm stressing the personal angle a little too much — but I know that it could happen to you — or to anybody who tries to break the hold of gangsterism in Los Angeles.

I had reached this point in preparing tonight's talk this morning when an almost incredible thing happened. A friend of mine, a newspaperman named Herb Stutz, walked into the office. Around his head was a bandage. His eye was blackened. Three broken ribs were taped up.

Stutz also had been active in the campaign against gangsterism in the district attorney's office. And last night he had become careless.

During the day he had attended a picnic in the Verdugo Hills and had passed out copies of the *People's Progress* and other literature telling what was going on in the district attorney's office. Also at the picnic was Mr. Buron Fitts, making a campaign speech.

On the way home, Stutz drove down a dark road. A car swung up beside him and forced him to the curb. Two men leaped out, dragged him from the car, kicked and beat him into unconsciousness. When he woke up they were gone.

Suppose I had gone tumbling over that rail. Suppose the blackjack used on Stutz had been swung just a little harder? What could anybody have done about it? Who would have prosecuted the murderers? The district attorney? Hardly.

There are dozens of other cases — more serious cases — which I could tell you about if I had the time. Men beaten; in some cases, men murdered. Nothing done. Verdicts of suicide. Verdicts of accidental death.

Only you can stop these things. You can stop them August 25 by electing a new district attorney — one who is not gang controlled; one who believes the law was made for the people. You can help to stop them by reading the *People's Progress,* listening to theater talks and then telling your friends about them.

August 25, 1936

Well, here we are, an orther with his book finally published (whether anybody gives a hang or not), broke, out of a job for the first time in twelve years -- and that gives me a chance to sit down and write a letter.

I've really a lot of things to tell you -- nothing important, but just the general results of the mad whirl during which the actual publication of your godchild (though you didn't choose the name) passed, not unnoticed but uncelebrated. I suspect that it isn't a bad book -- for one who likes that sort of book. It seems to have been carefully done, and it is possible that the apparent overstatement is a result of thorough knowledge of the subject. I'm only sorry that Lincoln Steffens couldn't have read it; but even if he were still alive, I'd still believe, after reading it over in print, that I know more about politics than any man in the United States.

The one Californian whom Brick Garrigues most admired was Lincoln Steffens, the leading figure among the early-twentieth century muckrakers. In 1906 he published *The Shame of the Cities,* a work closer to sociology than to an exposé. It's not hard to imagine young Harris Garrigues checking this book out of the Carnegie Library during his high school days. Steffens died in Carmel, California, just two weeks before this letter was written.

> If I may say one thing about my very excellent publishers -- I was more convinced of the quality of the content when I saw the printing job they did on it: They must have figured that something was worth two dollars.

> Anyway, getting down from the auctorial high horse, I can't tell you how grateful I am that you put it in the way of being published. It's really an absolute life-saver to me right now -- to my self-respect, sitting in somebody else's shack and wondering where I eat tomorrow. When I get hungry, I can walk past the book stores and feast my eyes, maybe.

By summer 1936, Brick had quit being a reporter; and he never went back to that job. Like his ancestor James Ralph before him, he became a public relations man for a politician — in Brick's case for George W. Rochester, who was running against District Attorney Fitts and three other candidates. Rochester had been a city fire commissioner, a state assemblyman and a state senator. He was essentially a moderate. The other candidates were Harlan G. Palmer, publisher of the daily *Hollywood Citizen-News,* who was campaigning as a reformer; Assembly member Ralph W. Evans, backed by the Epic organization; and Grover C. Johnson, an attorney with the American Civil Liberties Union who defended farm strikers in the Imperial Valley and elsewhere.

> But here's the situation, or at least the immediate situation: The radio announcer just banged a gong and announced that it was seven o'clock. All over Los Angeles County 4,325 precinct polling places closed, and election officials are now starting the count of ballots in today's election. Buron Fitts will be nominated district attorney. If he gets a majority of all votes cast, he'll be elected, and my life won't be worth the price of the book. If he doesn't get a clear majority, another candidate will be nominated with him. If that candidate is Rochester, I eat. If it's Palmer, I might eat. If it's Evans, I'll die slowly, by starvation, rather than quickly, by a bullet. If it's Johnson, which it won't be, I'll starve in the street for the pleasure of campaigning for a Communist as district attorney.

> Well, anyway, it's been a hectic summer -- not as hectic as 1934, but hectic enough. As you probably know, the People's Progress progressed just like the people and,

after four months of it, I managed to sell it to the Epic
News for thirty dollars -- on condition that I pay
outstanding debts of fifty.

(The first returns are coming in, and it's going to be
close. Fitts is running second on all widely scattered
precincts reported but will lead the ticket without getting
elected at the primaries with the others bunched.

(This is damnably thrilling. They're announcing the
single precincts so far, giving the addresses, and in the
districts where my following is, Rochester is running far
ahead, although the Daily News, strong in the same districts,
supported Palmer. It almost looks as though a large part of
the Daily News political influence went along with me.)

I've been in lots of campaigns, but this is the first
one in which the result meant food or no food, and it's
much too exciting to share it with anybody by going down to
headquarters. (Palmer is pulling up as Rochester slips
back.) But, whatever the result of the vote, I think that
I've pretty well figured out what I should do when this is
all over.

No matter what I do -- politics, newspaper work,
writing or what -- I'm going to need something to fall back
on, economically and otherwise, and that, to me, suggests a
farm in the hills. But a farm can't be self-supporting, and
I couldn't stand to be tied down to a farm, so I've a plan
that may work.

The girlfriend (yes, Louise, the same one I wrote
about last winter) has a sister who used to be a magazine
writer and who has, for the last couple of years, had
really remarkable success in raising fancy breeding
chickens. She has the experience and the chickens but no
ranch; if I can make a down payment on the ranch, she and
her family will keep up the interest payments. When I feel
like staying on the ranch I can do it, when I don't feel
like it, I can be on my way. The mother will take care of
the kids when I want her to and, altogether, it looks like
it might be a swell idea. (Rochester has dropped back to
fourth place, with one-fourth of the total in.)

I don't know where that leaves the girlfriend -- and
it doesn't really matter, I think. Anyway, I don't know to
what extent she's involved in the picture. Theoretically,
she's still supposed to be married next week or next month,
but that's been going on for more than a year, and you'd
think the poor guy would lose hope. If she doesn't, I may
marry her myself, some day. Dickie is going to get a
divorce, and Louise is just sufficiently undependable,
vain, fickle and so forth to be a good match for me.

We've got the ranch picked out. It's about sixteen miles
east of San Diego, on a main highway, but completely in the
wilderness, with one side abutting the base of a long

mountain which runs far into Mexico without a house or a
road. You have to plant tomatoes along the hilly side to feed
the deer so they won't eat up all your garden. There are
three acres of bearing lemons which bring in about twenty
dollars per month net profit, a creek bed, dry, a couple of
oaks, cottonwoods, willows, fruit trees and a little house.

(Here's the way it will end up: Fitts 139,310, Palmer
111,050, Rochester 76,010, Evans 73,990, Johnson 20,160.
One-tenth of the vote is in, and that will be the final
total. That means that I'm out my money. Palmer and Fitts
will run it off, with Palmer being elected in November.
He's a darned good friend of mine, even if I did work for
another guy, and may even offer me a job. If I take it, it
will just be to get enough money to get the ranch going.)

With that, the radio goes off for a while. What I
really want to do is to get away and digest the experiences
of the last couple of years. I think the ranch will give me
that -- and if the girlfriend comes down to the ranch, I
rather suspect that she'll shield me from too many
emotional experiences. Not possessively; she'll be too busy
sparkling for other people, but a little of her goes a long
way, and, curiously, neither now nor when I knew her before
did I have any particular desire to interrupt with other
affairs. Without her -- well, the other evening I was
talking with Dickie about whether or not I need a horse on
the ranch, and Dickie said:

"You'll never have just 'a horse.'"

And I said, "Why not?"

And she said, "Because it'll have to be a mare."

I suppose that's true; I seem to surround myself with
feminine creatures. Perhaps I have a terrific inferiority
complex where women are concerned.

Next morning

What a night! But I may recover. Fitts and Palmer will
run it off. Dropped in at one congressman's headquarters
for whom I made a five-minute radio talk at nine o'clock
election morning. You'd have thought my talk won the
nomination for him. Same thing at Palmer's headquarters;
instead of being angry at the fact that I'd supported
Rochester, all my old friends acted as though I were the
fair-haired boy. But that doesn't put soup in the pot.

Getting back to the book (and I can write much
better than I could last night when I was listening to
the radio with one ear), I was delighted with that Sunday
Times review -- a discerning reviewer, more in what he
hinted at than said. He discerned radical propaganda but
was kind enough not to say so. So did Elmer Davis, for
that matter. Have there been any other reviews that you
know of?

New York Times, August 16, 1936. In so far as it covers the situation in regard to graft in present-day democracy, Mr. Garrigues's cynicism is complete. It is almost, but not quite, hopeless; almost, but not quite, lethal. In an elliptical, not to say cryptic, fashion, he throws in a few positive ideas.

Saturday Review of Literature, August 22, 1936. By Elmer Davis.[7] Mr. Garrigues, a California reporter who seems to be a disciple of Lincoln Steffens (or perhaps has only encountered the same conditions and drawn the same conclusions), has written a valuable handbook of political biology. Written as advice to the young would-be grafter, its irony eventually becomes monotonous; and it is marred by occasional overstatements and generalizations from Los Angeles which would not apply everywhere.

My morning series of radio talks to housewives has been built on the theme of "You're Paying For It!," translated into terms of the table and the ice box and, if one has any audience at all that time of the morning, they should be fairly effective. One thing I'd like to do would be to carry on the radio feature as a sustaining program for a couple of weeks until I can find a sponsor, but I don't suppose there's much chance. Eventually, they'd sell some books -- although I'm constantly amazed at the number of people who don't read books.

It seems nice not to have a job. It's been the first day since 1924 that I haven't been on a payroll. In a couple of weeks, of course, there'll be no food on the table, but you can't imagine the sense of freedom in knowing you don't have to go anywhere or do anything. It's almost worth starving for.

September 15, 1936

I may be able to get some writing done this fall. I've leased a beautiful ranch out in the San Diego Hills and, if I pay the rent, Beth (Louise's sister) will probably be able to make enough from her chickens to feed the kids. If it works out, it will give me a little freedom.

My candidate came in fourth. But I'm working for Palmer in the finals and expect to get paid for it. And I think Palmer will be elected. If he is, I'll be OK. He'll probably want me to be chief investigator -- and I hope I don't take it.

I really wish I could describe "my" ranch -- and that you could see it. It's forty acres with a creek running through it, big oaks and cottonwoods, an old barn, deer, quail, rabbits and lots of space. I can't wait to get there -- but I suppose it will be months before I am really able to get away.

No you're both right and wrong about my paying too much attention to women. I'm surprised at the fact that I

---

7 Elmer Davis (1890-1958) was a reporter and editorial writer for the *New York Times* before he joined the Columbia Broadcasting System in 1939 as a radio newscaster. He soon gained a national following and was appointed to head the Office of War Information in 1942.

can take 'em or leave 'em alone -- that is, individually.
Just think, I've been "true" (at least in a certain sense)
to Louise for nearly a year now. Ain't that sumpin? Yet I
haven't seen her in a couple of weeks -- which is sumpin.

I'm continuing my radio talks as a sustaining feature
and seem to be building up quite a reputation. I received
123 letters from fans one talk, which set a record for the
station so far as "educational" programs are concerned.

Los Angeles Times, Oct. 4, 1936. GRAFT IN POLITICS. YOU'RE PAYING FOR
IT! By Charles Harris Garrigues. Funk & Wagnalls. Grafters' handbook, written with tongue in cheek by one of the cleverest journalists in America.

> 316 Lissner Building
> October 7, 1936

I was rather surprised to hear that the book had been
published in England, especially since I looked up my
contract and discovered that I had apparently sold only the
American and Canadian rights. Not that that matters, if
it's published over there, that's splendid.

Times Literary Supplement, October 17, 1936. YOU'RE PAYING FOR IT!
A GUIDE TO GRAFT. By Charles Harris Garrigues. Funk & Wagnalls Co.
10s. 6d. The author of this important volume is a journalist who has taken
an active part in several exposures of political corruption on the Pacific
Coast. It is doubtful whether there has ever before been produced so elabo-
rate and complete a survey of the bewildering variety of forms which graft
takes in modern America or so acute an analysis of its sources.

Meanwhile, some of our local Communist leaders have
been suggesting that the Soviet government might be
interested in publishing it in Russian.

I've moved again -- taken a fifteen-dollar-a-month
apartment down at the beach, Playa del Rey. It's delightfully quiet here now, no people, and I try to stay here and
work mornings, going to town in the afternoon. Towns drive
me bugs. I haven't got the ranch yet, although I hope to
have it within a few days.

As ever,

Brick

' . . . Just as Good as We Are'

*"Tell you what," Forrest said one day. "When you grow up you'll
have to get a job in the bank where dad works, and then you'll be rich
and you can buy the house across the street from ours and have a place
just like ours. Then we can visit back and forth, and have parties."*

*That would be swell, Bliss thought. He felt warm and good that his
friend wanted to have him live across the street so they could have parties. And then the Stinker added:*

"And then you'll be just as good as we are. Dad says that one man is

just as good as another as long as he has as much money and manages to keep out of jail. I'm going to be richer than that. But I expect you'll have enough if you just get to be as rich as dad, huh?"

It wasn't either the words or the tone. It was the fact that, now, Bliss knew beyond question that the ranch did not exist for the Stinker any more than it existed in reality; it did not exist in reality any more than it existed for the Stinker. There was no ranch; there was nothing in the world except a too-large family which was, mysteriously, "not good enough" to live like other people lived.

"Oh, bushwah!" he said. He was surprised to find that there were no tears crowding up in back of his eyelids; there was nothing he could do, nothing he could say, no further pretense he could make since all his belief had dried up and shivered away in the cool commiserate kindness of his friend's voice.

"Oh, crap!" he tried again. "I wouldn't live in your old shack with other houses crowded up against it . . ."

But it was no good. He found himself walking away, stiff-legged, stepping over little stones and the little mounds made by gophers and finally stepping over the curb itself and walking through the gate without seeing any of them. He heard Forrest calling, "Hey Bliss! Hey, wait up!" without hearing him, just as he saw the stones and the piles of dirt and the curb without seeing them.

And after that he and Forrest were not friends any more. When school was out he'd play in his own yard, building corrals and barns out of sticks, digging irrigation ditches with a piece of broken hoe, leading water from the faucet to the rich fields which he had sowed to alfalfa and in which herds of milk cows grazed and from which they came up at night to be milked. He raised horses, too; from his box of toys he dug up an old sack filled with marbles, and these became the horses which he raised on the prairie and drove into the corrals and broke to ride. There was a huge glass one which was the stallion for the herd: Bliss would put him into a corral with one of the beautiful lovely agates which were the mares, and soon the mare would have trotting at her heels one of the little red or yellow or brown agates which were the colts. What happened in the pen between the stallion and the mare was never quite clear to Bliss, but it was all very exciting and, somehow, obscurely terrifying

It was a beautiful and lovely and satisfactory game, but Bliss knew, too, with that part of him which always kept a fingerhold upon reality that it was a game which could last, at best, for only a few weeks. When school was out for summer vacation, he knew the dream ranch would crumble away, leaving him playing a foolish, childish game in a dusty, barren, littered yard.

Chapter Twelve
Naomi

Father once told me that in 1937 he abandoned the human race. What the heck happened in 1937? — From a letter by Brick's son Chuck, 1962.

It wasn't pleasant being out of work in California in the mid-1930s, in the depths of the Great Depression. In San Diego, for example, some fifty thousand people were on general relief and fifteen thousand were registered as unemployed. Employers reduced wages. Throughout the country, Communists were in the forefront of a battle to organize unemployed workers and to fight such Depression "solutions" as sending the unemployed to rural work camps, far from their families and loved ones, to work at wages barely high enough to cover their room and board. The Communists and some others on the Left also lobbied and wrote against the order by Los Angeles Police Chief James Davis stationing L.A. police at the California-Arizona border to turn back unwanted, mostly poor travelers—often entire families—on their way to Los Angeles to find work; the "bum blockade," it was called. Most American Communists of the 1930s weren't at all interested in revolution. Many of them, in fact, like Rena Vale, Brick's friend and collaborator, were Communists only because the Party was able to scrape together enough — or it received a new infusion of cash from the Soviet Union — to pay its employees a regular wage.

The Party had its interests — mostly organizing unskilled and semi-skilled workers — and supporting the workers' demands for a voice in controlling their lives. Sometimes these interests took on a dramatic color: In late 1936 three union officials, Earl King, Ernest Ramsay and Frank Conner, were on trial for murdering a ship's officer aboard a freighter anchored in the East San Francisco Bay. Though the trial drew little attention outside California, it was a celebrated cause for progressives and radicals.

Earl Warren, Alameda County's energetic district attorney, made the case a personal crusade. Warren was strident in his depiction of the defendants as part of a Communist plot. His tactics, though legal at the time, were outrageously flawed by today's standards. Even as the trial dragged on, the San Francisco law firm of Gladstein, Grossman, Margolis and Sawyer, with Aubrey Grossman as the lead attorney, was desperately seeking evidence to defend the men before a hostile judge and a possibly tainted jury.

                                    1931 Hearst St.
                                    Berkeley, Calif.
                                    December 13, 1936

Dear Toni,

I'm seated in a curiously comfortable chair, full of breakfast, with an old fashioned coal heater heating away and being delightfully lazy. Meanwhile the ranch -- five hundred miles away -- goes on its accustomed way.

Just as I was down to my last dollar about three weeks ago, I got a call from the International Labor Defense attorneys in San Francisco, asking me to come up here and do a little investigation in connection with the King-Ramsay-Conner frame-up (of which you haven't heard, probably, unless you read the Daily Worker). So I've been here, from then until now, but now the defense committee seems to have run out of money so I'm out of a job again.

The worst of it is, I hate to leave -- it's been awfully good to get away from Southern California -- among new people with new habits of life. Someway or another I seem to have fallen among the campus radicals who (believe it or not) are not objectionable as either radicals or intellectuals. The girl of the moment is curled up at the other side of the stove reading a book, and the two other denizens of the flat are cramming for finals and all is peace, quiet, comfort and, possibly, work.

Toni, dear, will I ever learn to keep away from women? It was all right on the ranch but I hadn't been in the Bay Area two days until I was up to my old habits again. She's charming, lovely, sweet -- and apparently much more affected by me than is good for her -- but, Toni, must I spend all my life being involved?

I have one more week to work and then I think I'll go

back to the ranch for Christmas -- and possibly stay. But
it would be much better if I stayed here -- the atmosphere
is precisely what I need and life seems much more enjoyable
and less intense than in the South. If it were not for the
kids I'd start my wandering by staying here for a while --
but I suppose I can't.

I'm completely recovered from the fatigue and the
disgust and disappointment of the political experience in
L.A. I almost feel like beginning that article I've been
promising you -- and I know that if I stay here with Naomi
I will have plenty of writing to do. There's the advantage
of the campus crowd -- they take writing not as a tour de
force, but as something usual in their daily work so it's
easier to do one's work along with them than among
newspapermen or others who suffer from an inferiority sense
whenever they think of writing anything other than a news
story.

This is a curious household. Dorothy is in school and
Hugo, her boyfriend, is in school besides being credit
manager of the largest department store in Oakland (at
about twenty-three) and Naomi is working as secretary to
one of the professors.[1] I seem to have dropped into the
household as definitely and naturally as though I had
belonged here for years. They're all Jewish and all their
friends are Jews but (as we often talked about in the old
days) they seem as curiously unconscious of that fact as
though they had never run up against the fact that there
are Jews and gentiles. What I mean is, I've always
maintained that it was the Jew who set himself apart,
through self-consciousness and that when he ceased to be
conscious of himself as something excluded, others would
soon be unconscious of it. This menage, within its limited
area, proves it. Possibly that sort of thing can only be
achieved on the campus -- and among radicals -- but it's
the first time I've ever been among Jews without being
conscious of the fact that, somewhere, there is a "Jewish
problem."

> [Handwritten]
> Spring Valley, Calif.
> January 4, 1937

The election found me broke, unsafe in L.A.,[2] without
a job or the prospect of getting one and with no assets
except two small children and twenty acres of uncultivated
land near San Diego which was mine by virtue of having paid
twenty dollars down out of a total price of some twenty-
five hundred. But the ranch had a house on it, and the

---

1 Naomi Silver was then twenty-nine years old, almost thirty. Her birth date was December 19, 1906.

2 About this time Buron Fitts was claiming he had evidence of mass murders committed by Communists, and he actually raised a small private army to "fight subversion." These people had guns.

people who were taking care of the kids (Louise's family) needed a house and a place to put their chickens. So we formed a partnership for the purpose of raising chickens and kids.

Honestly, this woman trouble seems to be caused almost entirely by the fact that women seem to need somebody to spoil -- they're always working at it.

You know, my inability to keep out of trouble has been puzzling me as much as it does you. Frankly, I don't know anything I do, or say, but you take a girl out to dinner, and the first thing you know, you're in bed and, then, chances are you discover that you are her affinity and, because you've slept with her one night, you're expected to sleep with her in perpetuum, as it were.

I know that isn't a nice way to talk -- but what's a guy to do? I certainly didn't have any intention, when I went north, of even talking to a girl, and I hadn't been there a week before I had a most delightful home with a charming companion who, it seemed, naturally assumed, as did all her friends, that I was going to continue to live there permanently.

Naomi was -- or is -- good for me, up to a certain point. She spoils me, it's true, but then, not having been spoiled since the early days of Marianne, I think I'm due for a little spoiling. But she's good company, a bit of formal education and makes me work.

Even at the ranch, I noticed before I left, the fat wife of the crossroads store keeper fixing me with a speculative eye while she inquired why I didn't ever go to the dances up at the next corners.

King, Ramsay and Conner were convicted on January 5 by a jury composed of six elderly businessmen and six middle-aged women chosen from a panel from which union members were almost entirely absent. One of the women may have had a sexual relationship with a deputy D.A. The convicted men spent more than five years in prison, but early in 1942 Governor Culbert Olson, a Democrat, commuted their sentences to time served. In the ultimate irony, Governor Earl Warren, who succeeded Olson and as district attorney had been the trio's prosecutor, granted Ramsay a full pardon in 1953, just hours before Warren left for Washington to take up his duties as chief justice of the United States.

[Handwritten]
Berkeley
January 20, 1937

Some time, of course, I'll have to leave here and then Naomi (if she doesn't breathe a sigh of relief) will curse all men for villains. But that's satisfactorily in the future. Meanwhile, Berkeley is less a strain on the nerves

than Los Angeles or even the ranch, and I hope I'll be able
to find a job here within the next few days.

I think there are numerous other things to write, some
political, some not. I think I might even deal with the
love life of Ernest, our patriarchal rooster. Somehow, to a
budding Marxist, the political picture seems vague, and I
doubt if I have any more factual stuff (of any length) to
write. It's as though "You're Paying for It!" summed up
what I had to say; I don't mind doing re-hash for magazines, but I'm afraid that I haven't found the theme on
which to hang another book -- unless I go either fictional
or Marxist. It isn't that I want to be a pamphleteer, but
nobody but a fool could write about 1937 without writing
some sort of propaganda.

Meanwhile, if I can build the job I want, I'll at least
have fresh material. I'm trying to get the left-wing labor
unions here in the Bay Area to create a bureau of investigation for use in criminal cases and put me in charge. There's
plenty doing here -- and a fresh point of view.

The kids are on the ranch, unwashed, unspanked and
much healthier and happier than they've been in a long
time. The Perkinses remain there; I wish I could tell you
about them, but it would take fifty thousand words to do
it. They're almost mythological. And if I can get enough
money, I'm going to build a house there to be occupied by
no one but myself. I certainly can't live in the same house
with that noisy gang. In fact, at the moment, I can't live
in the same house with anybody -- except Naomi, who is a
curiously comforting person to be with.

To Chuck and me, at seven and five, the ranch was heaven. There
was lettuce to peel fresh from a plant in the ground and nibble, just like
rabbits. Steaming hot, sweet corn-on-the-cob. Crates of fresh oranges,
and we could have as many of the juicy fruits as we wanted. Chuck had
the chore of milking Daisy, our goat, and as soon as Louise or Beth
Perkins skimmed off the foam, we drank it warm. Chuck and I hid in the
tool shed in fright as our dad chased a chicken around the yard, caught it
and chopped off its head with a hatchet (Chuck peeked out through the
dirty window, but he told me to stay down until it was all over). Then we
lay on the linoleum in the warm kitchen, and Chuck taught me the words
from his first-grade books. From a creek at the bottom of the hill, our
water was pumped to a rooftop tank by a noisy gasoline motor that Brick
tried his best to keep in repair.

I had a dream on the ranch: My father and I were in the rumble seat
of our Ford; he threw me out, and his car drove off without me. I screamed,
and Brick was quickly by my side, in the quiet bedroom, to wipe away
my tears and hug me.

Sometimes we had campfires and weenie roasts. We had a crank-up

Victrola, and we could listen to novelty singer Frank Crumit do "The Old Arm Chair" or "Abdoul Aboulboul Ameer" to the accompaniment of his bouncy ragtime mandolin. We still had Gypsy, the collie.

> [Handwritten]
> Spring Valley, Calif.
> January 29, 1937

> I couldn't get a job in the north and, with ten dollars left in the world, I heard that the San Diego Sun was looking for me to give me a job. So I came back and took the job. I hope it isn't much of a job because I don't want to work very hard.

> But farm life is not exactly conducive to writing. It's been bitter cold -- the ground has been frozen solid -- and we have only a stove in the kitchen. So the entire family gathers there at dusk, and the Perkinses and the two Garrigues brats practice talking -- or rather, screaming -- all at once until about eight o'clock. By that time my ears are ringing until I haven't the slightest idea what I'm writing about. Now that I have a job, though, I think I'll buy another stove and see if I can get a little seclusion. The chickens, too, are making a little profit, and the garden will soon be producing so that, I think, the economic question will become slowly but steadily less important.

The chicken house was usually off limits to Chuck and me, though I was once allowed through a little door to see and smell a dank interior dimly lit by two small clouded windows high under the eaves. The chickens clucked and shifted nervously on their perches. One afternoon, Chuck and I took turns rolling each other down the hill in a barrel that had been used for chicken manure. We came down with chicken pox soon after, but I was told by a doctor many years later that one event had nothing to do with the other.

> Perhaps the place will produce something other than eggs. Chickens are more interesting than economic theory or political practice, and maybe I'll learn to personalize my stuff. How about a sketch on "The Love Life of Ernest, Our Rooster"? Chickens, you know, are more like humans in their love affairs than are any of the mammals. Each rooster has his own harem, including about four favorite wives and eight concubines. He may do a bit of philandering now and then but never neglects his favorites. And hens -- the Number One favorite (and most of the others, for that matter) remains true to her own lawfully wedded husband in many cases. Even after he has been whipped in a fight (the concubines usually desert) two or three of the favorites usually stay with him. We have one hen who was Number One to an old rooster named Lawrence nearly three years ago. Ernest whipped Lawrence -- so badly that he had to be sold.

But his own hen remains true to her first love; mated, or rather exposed, with three different males, she has remained a faithful widow for more than two years.

[Handwritten]
March 8, 1937

I can't pretend that I wasn't disappointed to get the article back -- I rather thought it was enough better than the other one so it would sell. I have a feeling I'll have to lay it aside for a few weeks; apparently more research and less language is needed. My difficulty is, though, that the technique of tracing such payments is dry stuff -- too much detail is sure to lengthen the yarn and spoil the interest. Perhaps, after a week or so, I'll see the way around it.

I'm sorry you're still a little under the weather. I wish you could come out here and vegetate a while. It's good for one -- not necessarily in productivity but at least in keeping one alive. In spite of the uncertainty and the financial stress, I feel myself again, and if I can just get a few back bills paid up, I'll almost be set to get smug again (I hope not!).

My plans on the place are rather uncertain as yet, but I think I'll keep the ranch; the Perkinses will probably move, and I'll have to get someone to take care of the kids. That'll be better than giving up the ranch and trying to start over again in town.

There's a possibility that Dickie may come down to the ranch for a while and take care of the kids. We haven't seen much of each other for a few months, and I don't think either of us wants to be married again, but we might possibly be good enough friends by this time so that we could maintain a harmonious household.

There's even a chance that the Berkeley girlfriend might come down for a few months. That would be a typical Garrigues situation, wouldn't it?

We ran screaming up the dusty driveway when we heard Daddy's noisy car turn in from the road. Big hugs and big kisses.

"These are my kids. This is Charles and this is Louis."

Tattered overalls. Striped cotton shirts. Shoeless. Dirty faces matching dirty clothes from a hard day of outdoor play. Lots of freckles under the dirt. My blue eyes. Chuck's brown ones. Open, inquiring, eager. Chuck in front. Me hanging back.

A smiling lady, friendly, anxious. Down on her knees to face us.

"Hi, you two. I'm Naomi."

We tried to say it. Couldn't. And that is how I imagine that we met the woman whom we always called "Noma."

She came down for the weekend -- and she is really lovely. I'm not crazy about her, but I think she's really fine and that she's good for me. We got a little cabin near the sea north of San Diego and spent a happy three days. She really helps me to fulfill myself -- I might not write better with her around, but I'd write more. We came out to the ranch Sunday and went for a hike. The kids, usually aloof with strangers, are crazy about her. She'd really make an ideal companion on the ranch -- if only Dickie is enough interested in her new boyfriend so she wouldn't resent it.

As you may suspect, I haven't written a line since I've been back here. It's partly the business of getting adjusted, worry over finances, fighting with the Perkinses, getting acquainted with the kids, breaking in on a new job. I sometimes suspect, too, that the book was a flash in the pan; the style was, in one sense, fresh, clear and vigorous -- I find myself falling into it now as a stereotypical thing, and when I think I have something to say, I find I haven't.

I've tried and sketched numerous things -- begun them, but there was no inner necessity to write them. In "You're Paying for It!" I had to get something off my chest, and that necessity carried it through to some sort of conclusion. I haven't that need about any of these other things; the best I could achieve would be a "sequel," and I'd rather not do that because, in the long run, I'd lose by it.

That doesn't mean I'm "through"; it does mean, I think, that I've got to forget that I once wrote a book on a certain subject and go to work all over again. That isn't, I grant, any way to make money or please publishers.

Then, too, politics is a thrice-told tale to me. Before, the doings of politicians were important in some sense. Now I can't interest myself in them; I'll find myself reducing them to a Marxian formula. I'll have to have either a fresh slant or a fresh subject.

Maybe it'll be fiction -- or a serious novel. I told you once I'd like to reduce "Personal History"[3] to microcosmic proportions -- doing the same story of a personal development but keeping it within a radius of two hundred fifty miles. I think I'll ultimately come back to that. After all, my principal trouble is the fact that my experience has been microcosmic -- I've never been any place or seen anybody that anybody else would be interested in.

That condition may be remedied. The boss on the Sun is

---

3 Vincent Sheean's *Personal History* was published in 1935. As a young man, Sheean was a reporter for the New York *Daily News* but gave it up quickly and became a prolific writer specializing in current events, biography, travel and philosophy.

very enthusiastic about my stuff -- he wants me to do some
series for the Scripps-Howard chain, which, ultimately,
would lead to a good bit of travel in the United States and
elsewhere. I'd rather sit down and honestly try to write a
serious novel.

I'll renew, more definitely, the invitation to visit
the ranch this summer. If the Perkinses leave, I'm going to
hold open house for a very special few of my friends --
interesting people but not in the sense you know. Just kids
who will probably talk too much and have to be chased
across the creek occasionally until they quiet down; fresh,
vigorous, but all of them with a curious sensibility and
each of them with a need for seclusion and privacy.

That'll be a feature of the summer -- we may all have
to chip in three or four dollars a week and eat out of a
common pot, but everyone will have a nook of his own where
nobody else can come.

Los Angeles Times, March 8, 1937. DIST. ATTY. FITTS SHOT BY GANG
OF GUNMEN. Assassins made a cowardly attempt on the life of Dist. Atty.
Fitts at 8:15 o'clock last night, when a volley of shots was fired through
the windshield of his car, one of them shattering a bone in his left forearm.

> [From Naomi Silver,
> handwritten;
> to her parents and sister]
> Berkeley, Calif.
> March 22, 1937

My most dearest ones,

I hardly know just how to begin telling you what I
have to say. But I am going to Spring Valley, which is
eighteen miles from San Diego, and marry a swell guy. His
name, my darlings, is Charles Harris Garrigues -- and the
only reason I said nothing about this before is that I knew
nothing definitely until Sunday night. You see, I've known
"Gary" -- that's what I call him -- since November, when he
came up here to assist in the King-Ramsay case. I met him
through Aubrey Grossman, and I guess it was love at first
sight, or something.

He's thirty-six years old, has beautiful reddish brown
hair, green eyes, dimples and is six feet something high.
You see, I'm slightly giddy about it all -- and since it
is, as Gary puts it, "an event that fills him as full of
fear, anticipation and eagerness as a Victorian bride," you
can well understand how I feel.[4]

I sure am happy.

On May 17, 1937, the defendants in the California Reserve case
were acquitted by Los Angeles Superior Judge Raglan Tuttle, who said

---

[4] Naomi must have been addled with love. Brick at the time was 34 years old, and his eyes
were actually brown, though they were flecked with green.

that the prosecution had "failed utterly even to suggest a motivating cause for this alleged orgy of crime." But whatever outrage Brick might have had for that unwelcome verdict was undoubtedly muted by this time. For Brick had left Los Angeles politics—with all its unhappiness and danger—behind him, and he had a new enthusiasm. He was named editor of the *San Diego Labor Leader,* the official organ of the San Diego County Federated Trades and Labor Council, which was affiliated with the American Federation of Labor, or AFL, then under the presidency of William F. Green.

Several months before, Brick had filed an application to join the Communist Party and, after some hesitation (because they thought this stranger might be a police spy), the Party took him in. That was just at the beginning of the period in which the Communists and others on the Left were waging their furious drive to woo workers to the Committee on Industrial Organization, the CIO. The committee had been formed within the AFL to unite all labor in big industrial unions, not divided by occupations, or "crafts," as was traditional in the old-line, somewhat fusty AFL. Later, the CIO was expelled from the AFL and changed its name to the Congress of Industrial Organizations. Brick was a member of the CIO Newspaper Guild's negotiating team with the San Diego papers. The CIO unions were generally more progressive than the older AFL unions. The veteran Southern California Communist Party leader, Dorothy Healey, reminisced about the era:

> That was the time of our greatest involvement in the class struggle, a time when lasting gains were made. If there was ever a moment when we came close to being what we always said we were, a party of the working class, that was it. The years between 1937 and 1940 were so jam-packed with organizing drives and strikes that I felt like a whirling dervish.[5]

June 23, 1937

Dear Toni,

    The Labor Leader is a weakly weekly of which I'm editor, staff, editorial writer, etc., etc., -- on a salary. I fell into the job through a curious set of circumstances and left the Sun to take it, first, because it's a little more money, second, because I thought I'd have more time to myself, and third, because I'm really interested in the labor movement.

    It was a very lousy little sheet when I took it over and is now the best labor paper in the United States from the viewpoint of readability. It's almost paying its own way now, has a circulation of ten thousand and will soon be able to support an assistant to the editor and pay raise or two -- if all goes well.

---

5 *Dorothy Healey Remembers,* Oxford University Press (1990), p. 69.

It's by way of being a good experience for me, partly because I realized I was washed up on politics and needed some new activity, partly as a way of re-establishing myself, partly because I'm not ready to do any writing as long as I can't support myself by it. It's taken a lot more time than I thought, and the farm has taken the rest.

I've almost settled down to the old routine -- the determining factor being that I seem to be saddled with a couple of kids who are so much better off on the farm than they'd ever be in the city that I can't bring myself to make plans which would take them out of the country, at least until they're older.

The domestic arrangements? The Berkeley girlfriend, Naomi, is running the establishment. She's ideal; as I grow older I grow more irritable, more exacting, but there's a curious sort of harmony at the ranch now -- both kids crazy about her, she apparently very happy, and I as happy as one could expect to be, I suppose. Dickie, who's obtained a divorce, comes down for a weekend occasionally to see the kids, and the rest of the time I alternate between molding the San Diego labor movement by brilliant editorials and raising ninety-seven baby chickens.

It's a peaceful existence for even a vegetable; out in the country you really do feel remote from every sort of modern conflict. But a change is coming -- I feel it in my bones. I don't know what; I'm running a little better paper than they deserve, and the labor movement (which is well financed these days) may pick me up and put me somewhere else. Or maybe I'll get fired. Anyway, it still seems a long way from that next book.

The last one seems twice as remote. I'm so completely disinterested in the subject, and the world seems to have changed so much in the last year that I've almost forgotten it happened. I was astonished this morning to find a letter from Funk and Wagnalls enclosing a little leaflet they use for direct mail advertising of the book. It was as though they had dug up my grandfather's bones and held a funeral for him.

But I'm sorry you're not coming west; I'd like to have you spend the whole summer at the ranch. We're really establishing a place for people who need to unbutton and sit under an oak tree -- and sit and sit and sit. We always intend to make them dig in the garden or something to help earn their board, but we don't have the heart after we see the way they set out to relax. One doesn't have to wash one's face or put on clothes or shave unless one wishes, and it's rather swell.

As ever,

Brick

On the days when he did have to shave and drive in to town to put out the union newspaper, though, Brick was back in his element. As a member of the CIO, he wasted no time in taking on the entrenched San Diego labor fat cats.

San Diego Labor Leader, June 26, 1937. IT SEEMS TO ME. By C. H. Garrigues. It seems to me that I'm probably a bit of a sap. If I'm not, there are a lot of other people around here who are, and I'd rather think I'm the guy. If I'm the sap, the labor movement can easily get rid of me; if it's the rest of the guys, the labor movement is in a bad way.

I pick up the morning paper and try to find out what happened in the last 24 hours. Everywhere union men and women are being shot down, plants are being opened by force and violence, troops act as strikebreakers, steel barons defy the government, known labor phoneys defy their unions. The fate of labor hangs in the balance.

I come into the Labor Temple. "Temple" is right — architecturally it may be remote from a medieval cathedral, but it's equally as remote in spirit from the outside world. Not a whisper of the pitched battle that labor is waging — the outcome of which will determine for perhaps a generation the right of labor to organize, even the right of a worker to quit his job without the permission of an employer-controlled dictator.

I go into the Federated Trades meeting, where the cream and the flower of the labor movement is gathered to determine policies, outline plans, direct labor's battle in San Diego. An hour of bickering over whether Whoozis is a bigger so-and-so than Whatsis. Another hour, and another. The delegates go home tired, filled with second-hand smoke, disgusted. Three hours of work, 300 man-hours wasted.

I'm a sap! But I think I'm the only sap in the labor movement in San Diego who's spent six or seven years in the inner councils of the enemy's camp. And I'm just sap enough to know that if you birds keep on with what you're doing for another two years, you'll have to go on your bended knees to the J. P. Morgans of the world and ask them, please, if it'll be all right if you join the Elks or the Masons or the company union. Because you're headed for the rocks — incorporation of unions, compulsory arbitration by capitalist-controlled agencies, military rule of all industrial plants, open fascism — just as sure as shooting unless you cut it out.

The hell of it is (and the word is used in its strict Biblical sense) that nine-tenths of this quarreling is over "power," "importance," "authority." And the sad part is that there's ten times as much need for men of power, importance and authority as there is supply. It's like a bunch of nuts who went out to pick melons, wandered into a 660-acre field of honeydews, and then started rioting over who would get the melons on the first vine. My youngsters, aged five and seven, do it — but must you?

San Diego Labor Leader, June 26, 1937. NEWSPAPER GUILD EXPELLED FROM COUNCIL. EDITOR IS EJECTED FROM ROOM. Overriding protests from the floor which at times seemed destined to end in a fistic free-for-all, Ed Dowell, district organizer for the American Federation of Labor, last

Wednesday night expelled the San Diego Newspaper Guild from affiliation with the Federated Trades and Labor Council.

The action was taken on orders of William Green, federation president.

During the mix-up, the editor of the *Labor Leader,* who still holds a Guild card despite his membership in the Office Workers' Union, found himself also ejected on personal orders of Dowell.

(Editor's Note: If you don't find any news in the paper this week, don't blame me. I wasn't there.)

Administration forces executed a swift and effective bit of strategy to bring about the expulsion of the Guild.

President Brown took the chair as usual, rapped the meeting to order and turned the chair over to Dowell. Dowell read the telegram from Green and, amid a flock of protests from the floor, ordered Guild delegates Adair and Mayne to leave the chamber. The delegates refused, while several delegates moved to file Green's telegram.

Dowell refused to recognize the motions and ordered Conductor Lee Gregovich to escort the Guild delegates from the chamber. Gregovich stood with folded arms until Dowell had repeated his order three times. Then said:

"I'll take them out when the council orders me to take them out."

Dowell then appointed a squad of three bulky delegates to carry out his orders, and the Guild delegates, after a hurried consultation, left peaceably.

Dowell noticed, to his horror, that the atmosphere was still rendered impure by the presence of the Editor of the *Labor Leader.* Dowell ordered him to leave the room.

Four days later, William F. Green commanded that thirty delegates to the San Diego labor council, all of them CIO supporters, be expelled from the AFL. Brick Garrigues was one of them, and his job as editor of the *Labor Leader* was taken by John Lydick, head of the plasterers' union, who railed in the newspaper against the ousted delegates as being "Reds and disruptors."

The deposed CIO forces then began a paper of their own, with Brick in charge. Lydick sneered at the idea of a rival union newspaper: in one of his editorials he snidely dubbed Brick as "'Bricky Boy' (I've got experience!) Garrigues." Clearly, life was not dull in the San Diego labor movement in 1937.

Chapter Thirteen
Usually Lives With a Female

917 Douglas Street
Los Angeles, Calif.
December 26, 1937

Dear Toni,

It's the day after Christmas and raining; there's no
top on the car (the goat ate it down on the ranch), and
it's the first time in more than eight months that I've had
two successive days off -- one to rest in and the other to
"spend." Hence the letter.

We're back in Los Angeles, Naomi and I. We're being
quite vagabondish, living on jobs which last two weeks or a
month at a time, living in other people's houses, and even,
at the moment, I'm wearing another man's suit. We're also
being quite amusingly poor, although I feel like an
aristocrat today, having received for Christmas a beautiful
blue polo shirt. In a couple of weeks we're going to move
from this lovely old white house with ten rooms and a
balcony on which the rain drips, and we'll probably have to
take an apartment somewhere that smells of cabbage cooking,
but then nothing is really quite worth worrying about
except the peril of permanence.

When the AFL-CIO split reached the coast, my job went
one way, and I went the other. Since then I've managed to
live in one fashion or another by getting on one or another
CIO payroll as an editor, an organizer or something of the
sort. That necessitated leaving the ranch and moving into

San Diego, renting the ranch, meanwhile. After three weeks
in town, I was transferred to Los Angeles for two weeks;
when the three weeks were up, the payroll was slashed, and
out I went. By that time I'd succeeded in establishing
myself as a pretty fair sort of trade union leader, and the
Newspaper Guild here put me on the payroll to help them
complete some work by January 1. But by this time I've
started so much more work and have it all in a condition of
semi-completion that the Guild has been forced to extend
the contract to March 1 in order to salvage their invest-
ment. And of such is the staff of life.

Passage of the U.S. Wagner Act in 1937 frightened employers: at
last workers had a federally guaranteed right to organize into effective
unions. Some, like newspaper writers, editors, salespeople and clerks,
had never thought of grouping together before, but under the leadership
of an articulate and wealthy New York newspaper columnist, Heywood
Broun, they picked up their picket signs and were often successful in
their struggle for unionization. Brick Garrigues and people like him were
in the negotiating trenches for these poorly paid newspaper workers,
who, before the days of union contracts, had no job security at all — a
fearful condition in the middle of a depression.

The labor movement is, however, a very exacting
mistress (and so's Naomi). I've a minimum of five meetings
a week and have been starting the day at the office about
ten. That doesn't leave any time for writing; it doesn't
leave any time for reading; it doesn't even leave time for
worrying because you don't have time to read or to write.
I've honestly forgotten that once I wrote a book; it
strikes me with a feeling of surprise when I come across it
on a bookshelf. But that needn't worry me -- all of its
potential readers have also forgotten it. They even forgot
to buy it. I think my sale now has reached the astonishing
total of seven hundred copies. I can't say that I'm hurt. I
think it was amusing and perhaps instructive.

Most of my present job consists of what is called
"negotiating"; one goes in as head of a Guild committee to
act very tough and convince the boss that he should give a
better contract than he pretends to be willing to give,
knowing all the time that the boss knows about what he will
give and that that figure is usually identical with the
lowest figure the union will accept. But it's fun; you do
have the satisfaction of knowing, when the job is done,
that a lot of poor devils are better off than before.
During the last six months I've negotiated yearly contracts
which have added some hundred thousand dollars per year to
the paychecks of about two hundred newspapermen. And I
think I enjoy it because I never was able to get a raise in
my life for myself.

The domestic arrangement is a partial improvement over the previous regime. Naomi is no help in smoothing away the minor irritations of life; she's about as much help as one of the kids in avoiding interruptions. I shouldn't be surprised if, when I come to write the great American novel, she should insist that I write it with her on my lap. But there's no internal conflict such as there was with Dickie -- we get along with a maximum of three quarrels a day, but they usually end with both of us laughing over some very poor pun, and there is very little after-bitterness. I have a feeling, though, that I can only really work in absolute loneliness and here, far from being lonely, I haven't even a moment's solitude in the big house we are temporarily occupying.

[Handwritten]
2034 Oak Glen Place
March 27, 1938

By some curious chance, I have been peaceful and quiet lately -- at least internally, although the labor movement is twice as hectic as ever, with near-strike, contracts and whatnots.

By some other curious chance, Naomi and I are living on the same hillside where Marianne and I spent that hectic summer -- if not in the same house, at least in the same group of houses, the lower terrace. It was pure coincidence; there was hardly another house to rent in the whole town. But for the last few weeks the hills have been unbelievably lovely -- rich green grass, sprinkled with graceful, nodding purple brodiaeas and golden poppies (bigger this year than I've ever seen) and wide carpets of sweet alyssum, which scent the entire hillside on a warm day. People here have flower gardens, too, but it is the wild flowers, growing just as they did before the city swept around our little promontory, that gives our hills that which I won't try to describe.

Then, too, there are, you know, some places that seem curiously haunted by peace. Remember the river east of the little shrine at the Tucson mission? There's another at the mouth of San Juan Creek near Laguna. And I've discovered a bit about ten yards square in our canyon which, if not in our back yard, is at least the first place one sees when one wakes up in the morning and sees the sunlight pouring over the hill.

I've a hunch that these places were the favorite haunts of fauns or nymphs or hamadryads before Man came into the picture and that the enchantment has lasted here many centuries -- and will last until man has finished destroying himself as he seems to be doing so effectively just now.

So, you see, there is at least the environment for

peace and quiet -- the shell of the ivory tower. I haven't,
it's true, spent much time in the tower. The labor movement
demands too much -- and I'm not sure that I'm the best
organizer in the world. I fret a little too much; when the
fascists drop bombs on Spain or invade Austria, I'm
inclined to forget that the average Guild member is
primarily interested in wages and hours -- and can't
realize that the Chicago cops and Hitler's Nazis are both
just "goons."

In 1938 millions of Americans were out of work. Of those working,
some half million had been involved in sitdown strikes. Four were killed
and eighty-four injured in a strike against Republic Steel in Chicago.

In Europe Hitler was threatening Poland over Danzig. German avia-
tors destroyed Guernica, Spain, on behalf of Franco. Twenty-eight hundred Americans went to Spain as part of the Lincoln Brigade, and nine
hundred of them were killed. Most of these Americans were communists, or thought they were. The Germans had stripped all Jews of their
citizenship and many were fleeing the country.

Then, too, if I'm to be effective, I have to spend a
lot of time in reflection. Agitation, propaganda, dynamic
analysis of a given situation, pregnant with danger, wear
me out unless I can get away and sit for long hours
contemplating my navel.

I've been doing that today -- reading "Birth of a
World" after having, I thought, finished "The Soul
Enchanted" when I read the penultimate volume a couple of
years ago.

I wonder if there are people like Annette? Of course
there are -- one catches glimpses of them everywhere, in
French -- and in some Jewish -- women, or perhaps in other
Europeans. I think I said once that Annette -- the younger
Annette -- reminded me of you. And the older Annette
reminds me of my own mother, who is as broad and helpful as
one could ever imagine an American woman to be. I wonder,
though, if there are enough of them, these fertile
intellectuals, to prevent the world from going the rest of
the way into the Dark Ages of Middle Europe?

Annette Rivière was the protagonist of Romain Rolland's *The Soul
Enchanted,* in seven volumes, of which *Annette and Sylvie* was the first
and *A World in Birth* the last. "You are," a suitor tells twenty-three-year
old Annette, "an amorous rebel. You feel the need of giving yourself,
and you feel the need of withholding yourself."

Well, if something saves us, it will be something
beyond ourselves. And anyway, I'm leaving the labor
movement this week -- or at least ceasing to be a "paid
agitator" -- and may possibly be able to see it better from
the outside.

The job has fallen out from under me -- treasury all shot and a recession on its way. Fortunately, I still know a few politicians and think I can pick up some publicity work during the campaign. If I don't -- ugh! I shudder as a fair section of our population is already eating out of garbage cans again.

I'm going to try to reduce my working hours to a normal quantity and perhaps spend more evenings over the yellow tablet. I have, on the front terrace, the same old wicker chair in which I wrote "You're Paying for It!" -- certainly not a memorable piece of work, but at least something. And I find myself able again -- for the first time in two years -- to sit quietly and write slowly.

I think I have, most surely, a novel maturing -- getting ready for the process of growing. It will be written slowly; more, it will have to be developed away from the clamor of the labor movement -- and the petty details of housekeeping. This place is ideal -- completely cut off on three sides by terraces, dropping sharply off toward the west with the nearest street a good 200 yards away. Nothing near to disturb -- except Naomi.

She's ideal, almost, as a companion except for an annoying habit of interrupting one's excursion into some far-off reflective (or perhaps creative) country with a request to set the table or bring her a drink of water. But perhaps she can yet be trained or (more likely) she'll recede into the background as the characters of the novel start moving so that such interruptions won't count.

She's a curious little person -- we fight like hell over such interruptions, but it never seems to have any effect on curbing the spontaneity of her childlike explosions -- demands for attention. Strange how the possessiveness of women shows itself in different ways. With her it's almost a mania so that whenever she sees -- or senses -- that I am wholly, completely immersed in something -- a plan, a book, a treatise -- she almost invariably interrupts with some trivial request solely to bring attention back to herself. And if one protests, why, then: "Well, I don't see why you shouldn't get me a glass of water. I would, for you." And the hell of it is that she would.

But even such interruptions (if you're working out something, they seem pure vandalism) are less dangerous than the flitting from place to place (from bed to bed) when one is detached. And so I'm, if not ecstatic, at least content. (Though a little chagrined to realize that we've been together a year now and that not yet have I been tempted to stray.)

That temptation presented itself only a few weeks later, when a piqued Naomi moved back to the Bay Area.

[Handwritten]
3220 Larrisa Drive
July 8, 1938

I'm living at the moment in a vast, airy, inconceivably dirty flat, rooming with another newspaperman. Tomorrow -- I think -- I move into a house with two women -- which is even more complicated than it sounds although not in the way you'd suspect.

As you might well know, by this time the Affaire Naomi has ended -- but not, I believe, permanently. In fact, I should not be at all surprised if I tried marriage again, and I rather suspect that this time it might last.

All of which items are just a few little factors in what seems to be an unduly complicated existence. Just for fun, let's see if I can piece it together. During my year in the labor movement, I almost worked myself to death and did, apparently, work out of my system -- for a while -- that regrettable tendency to attempt to change the world. So that, a couple of months ago I quit the Guild job and started a political publicity bureau.

ITEM: I'd always been afraid of getting too closely tied to Naomi; I knew that some day I'd go chasing off after another Marianne, and I didn't want to get too thoroughly tied up. She didn't particularly fear the chasing probabilities, but deeply resented the fact that I kept her to a degree at arm's length.

ITEM: About a month ago, she decided "to hell with it" and went to Oakland. Probably I would have tried to keep her except that her departure coincided with the arrival on the scene of the devastating female whom I had long feared. One would have thought, as I did, that the presence in the picture of this new girl, Miriam, induced Naomi to leave in a fit of jealousy. But apparently it wasn't that -- as Naomi explained it the other day.

"I couldn't have worried about Miriam -- she hasn't sense enough to take and keep what she wants. But if I ever catch you interested in a real girl, I'll cut her throat."

ITEM: The new affair -- after Naomi left -- started out like a house afire and ended up like a January blizzard. She works in the office where I spend nine-tenths of my time. She is very lovely, very possessive, very flirtatious -- and terrifically inhibited -- I suspect -- against a deep emotional disturbance. Also she is a Communist and determined that nothing will interfere with her Party work. And so, gradually, the thing soured for both of us -- we've never got together in any sense -- we've never even been out together alone. Dinners, luncheons, a brief ride home after a meeting. And in the daytime we sit in an office together and want each other -- until we come to hate each other like poison.

Tacitly, each of us has developed the technique of feigning complete indifference -- which she does more successfully than I. But we sit and get on each other's nerves hour after hour until some day one of us is going to hit the other over the head with a blunt instrument.

ITEM: Last weekend, I suddenly got some sense in my head, announced that I was through and grabbed a train to San Francisco to see Naomi. It was a wonderfully successful experiment; I realized definitely that Naomi was exactly the sort of woman I could live with in peace and comfort and that Miriam was not. But it seems necessary for me to stay here until November.

ITEM: Before the trip north, Miriam suggested that I go in with two gal friends of hers who are renting a big house and share household expenses. She herself was to move in about a month. I agreed; the girls took the house. Now I can't get out of it without putting them in the hole -- and there is every probability that Miriam -- who is the especial chum of one of the girls -- will spend about half her time at the house. All of which is not conducive to rational living.

All of which seems to me rather complicated for a guy who only wants peace and quiet -- except when some gal like Miriam shows up.

The experience with the labor movement has done two things: Given me a different view of my "reform" attempts and -- by over-emphasis upon the active life -- prepared me to go back to the intellectual life. I seem to be at another one of those cross-roads but a more pleasant one this time -- even though I am, and expect to be for a few months, very unhappy and dissatisfied.

The labor movement has made me completely sterile mentally; I suppose you can't write of things when you're overwhelmingly busy doing them. Complete lack of social and intellectual contacts, almost complete abstinence from reading, working by formula, has dulled the observing eye and slowed the analytical brain. For months I've wavered between trying to be a writer and trying to be an organizer.

I hope to be able to make enough money in the campaigns this summer so I can quit work for a few months. Then Naomi and I will either go to the ranch or I will go to San Francisco -- where she has a job -- and will spend a few months seeing what I can produce. In the spring I may come down for the municipal campaigns and pick up a few more hundred dollars. But until then I shall probably sit and stare at Miriam and keep both our nerves on edge.

What is it *with* you? Toni asked. Other men don't seem to have the kind of problems with women that you do. Explain yourself, if you can.

138 North Lake Street
July 31, 1938

I can assure you, the problem of why I still get
excited about dames is one that has perplexed me most
frequently. The answer, of course, is: Affairs such as that
provide the excitement without which life would be
extremely monotonous. But if you ask me why that is
particularly true for me and not for others, I couldn't
tell you.

I believe the psychologists say that a sense of social
inferiority is behind such bad habits. I think that is
definitely true in my case. Some men, feeling inferior,
take to liquor, some to writing, and some to women. Liquor
does me very little good; women are plentiful, easy to find
(not so easy now as a couple of years ago) and writing is
difficult, requires time and, in addition, doesn't work
unless I'm so low that the other methods are insufficient
to lift me out of it.

Seriously, though, I've wondered to what extent that
sort of thing has kept me from going ahead with my writing.
When I'm with somebody who is thoroughly satisfactory, I
become logy; a romantic adventure seems to act as a dose of
spiritual calomel and get me all stirred up inside and make
it more nearly impossible for me to do things.

All of us have a sort of "governor" or automatic speed
control (our fatigue sense). When it gets out of kilter, as
it does with me, we disrupt our whole system by top-speed
work for months; the body, anaesthetized to a sense of
fatigue, enjoys it and as its reserve flags, requires new
stimuli until the machine is going around so fast the
flywheel falls off.

Naomi and I are going to settle down somewhere or
other, and I haven't any serious doubt, nor even a slight
doubt, that it will be for life. There will, of course, be
interruptions, but they'll only be interruptions. She's a
very swell person and, after nearly two years, I haven't
any reserves of doubt as I've always had before. Or, in
other words, for the first time in my life, I'm willing to
meet a woman half way.

The only thing that bothers me in the immediate future
is the necessity of earning a living. The publicity
business is shot all to hell; none of the campaigns have
any money, and my hopes of a couple of thousand dollars'
profit for the summer have dwindled to hopes of getting a
few dollars' back pay out of a candidate to buy groceries.

Now about this business of writing. With my usual
enthusiasm, when I went into the labor movement, I went in
over my head. (You can't really go any other way.) For about
fifteen months now, I've averaged at least four nights a week
at meetings. That not only takes time, it dissipates one's

energies. You're so damn busy doing things -- petty things with big results -- that you don't store up any of the reserves which seem to be necessary. In a way it's good. You overcome your tendency to think in terms of what someone else has written, and you think in terms of people. But it also gives you "social consciousness"; being right inside things you can't view them from the detached point of view which was always your particular strength. You tend to become a propagandist. And not wanting to be a propagandist, you struggle against it and you get all tied up.

Some people have written with a fair degree of social consciousness, or at least awareness. On one hand Romain Rolland and on another Leane Zugsmith.[1] But I haven't yet learned to weld social consciousness with detachment. Then, too, when a book or something begins developing, it's invariably interrupted by a crisis in the labor movement. Wasn't it Goethe who was supposed to have run around tearing his hair after every affair with his chambermaid, shouting: "I have lost a book!"? Crises have the same effect.

If I go to San Francisco, I'll keep entirely away from Reds and such things so I'll never have any responsibilities. If I stay here, I'll continue my recent campaign of gradual withdrawal. In either case, one thing is sure: I've had enough organization work to last me a while. It's back to the pen and the old yellow tablet for a while.

You know, reverting to your letter, I'm amazed that anyone can stay in love for four or five years, particularly with someone whom one sees every day. To me it would seem a peculiarly feminine quality, although men seem to do it as much as women. I can't; some women have become a habit that it was difficult to break; others continue to trouble me in one way or another for a long while. (Miriam, for example, will always trouble me a little as long as we're working together.) But the analytical faculty always starts working sooner or later, and the whole thing becomes amusing or something other than romantic.

There are four of us -- two women and two men -- living platonically together en famille in a big white house with a big back yard and, so far, in perfect harmony. We're all more or less communists at heart and, without any plan, the place is set up on a sort of communal basis. If I get home from work first, I cook dinner; if I have a meeting, somebody else washes dishes. There is a lot of privacy and sufficient company to satisfy one's gregarious instincts, and altogether it is very satisfactory. If Naomi comes down, we're going to stay here instead of getting a place of our own.

_1_ Books by Leane Zugsmith (1903-69) included _A Time to Remember_ (Random House, 1936), a sympathetic portrayal of American Communists, and _Home Is Where You Hang Your Childhood and Other Stories_ (Random House, 1937).

Jump forward now, to 1943. It was not yet the McCarthy era, but all over the country, war or no war, anti-Fascist alliance or not, tinpot bullies were busy sniffing out Communists from years gone by, busy assembling data to "prove" that this liberal or that lawyer, this progressive or that producer had either once been a Communist or had "followed the Communist line," and in California it was a radical-turned-reactionary state senator named Jack B. Tenney and his Joint Fact-Finding Committee on Un-American Activities in California who were leading the pack of sniffers. The committee boasted that it had "filed and indexed nearly 14,000 cards listing the activities of as many individuals in California."

In May 1934, Brick had collaborated with Rena M. Vale when she was working at Universal Studios. In 1936 she joined the Communist Party as a paid worker and was assigned to various progressive committees in Los Angeles which, she said later, were more or less under the domination of the Communists. By 1943 she had become an anti-Communist witness for the House Committee on Un-American Activities in Washington and also for the Tenney Committee in Sacramento (where she was on the payroll).

She named names and she gave dates. In a lengthy affidavit for the Tenney Committee, she fingered author John Steinbeck, actress Gale Sondergaard and Carey McWilliams, as well as C. H. Garrigues. She said that in 1938 she had been working with the Federal Writers Project, a New Deal agency, whose members were represented in labor negotiations by the Newspaper Guild local, but because of her growing opposition to Communist policies, she was expelled from the Guild in that year. She said that

> the attitude of the members of the American Newspaper Guild who were likewise Communist Party members was well expressed by Charles H. ("Brick") Garrigues when he stated, "It is not the Guild that is important; it's the Communist Party."
>
> [D]uring the spring of 1938 while I was in the throes of severing my connections with the Communist Party, all manner of inducements were held out to me in order to entice me to remain within it; Charles H. ("Brick") Carrigues [sic], whom I had known for a number of years, took special interest in my case and sought to iron out my grievances and to keep me in the Communist Party; he knew of my interest in local politics and, as a member of the Professional Section Committee, "co-opted" me for work on the Professional Section Political Commission, of which he was chairman; it might be explained here that the word "co-opted" is derived from a Russian word meaning to draft, or to command,[2] and has become accepted in the Communist Party of the United States; I discovered that all important positions are filled in the Communist Party by "co-option" rather than election;

---

2 Not quite. It is from Latin and has been in the English language since 1651.

[M]embership in said Professional Section Political Commission was (besides myself):[3]

Charles H. ("Brick") Garrigues, Chairman;

Naomi Childress,[4] common-law wife of said C. H. Garrigues.

Decades later, I was able to examine the records the Tenney Committee had gathered about my father. The first predated the formation of the committee itself and could have been drawn from the records of any of the law enforcement agencies of 1936 — the District Attorney's Office, or the L.A. Police Department, or the state Attorney-General's Office, all of which had their Red Squads or "Subversives" files. Even the Tenney staff did not know where this item came from; the file is headed "Source is not known, but will give it to you for what it is worth."

```
GARRIGUES, C. H. ("BRICK")
c/o Illustrated Daily News
12th & Figueroa Street
Los Angeles, Calif.
```

Publisher of Utopian News. Broadcasts over KRKD Monday nights at 7:30 for Utopian Society.

Special investigator for 1934 Grand Jury at Los Angeles. He was primarily responsible for indictment of Buron Fitts, District Attorney. Later returned to Daily News as a reporter and has written book on Fitts' indictment.

One of founders of the Utopian movement. Extreme left wing liberal and in talks and his writings has attacked alleged Fascist or Vigilante methods of California farmers in handling labor problems.

3/30/36. Broadcast KRKD, defended Negro Communist McShane, in jail for rioting.

3/31/36. Broken off all connection with Illustrated Daily News.

10/1936. Author of "You're Paying for It: A Lesson in Graft." Book review appeared in Pacific Weekly, 10/5/36, p. 223.

A later memo makes it clear that Brick's signature on an election petition for a Communist candidate had launched a probe of not only C. H. Garrigues but any other person named Garrigues:

```
GARRIGUES, C. H. (SEE C. H. (Brick) Garrigues)
2034 Oak Glen Pl.
Los Angeles, Calif.
(From Secy. of State Office)
```

Occupation: Writer. (Reg. Democrat)

---

3 I am omitting some names here.

4 Perhaps Rena Vale was confusing the name with that of Naomi Childers, a silent-screen actress known in the Vitagraph days as "the girl with the Grecian profile."

Sponsored LEO GALLAGHER (Communist), for Secy. of
State, on Demo. ticket (GALLAGHER) cross-filed on Demo.
ticket, Los Angeles, Aug., 1938. (R. V.)

Claimed to be in San Diego during 1937-38. Had ranch.
Great Register of San Diego County shows that CHARLES L. &
EMILY GARRIGUS lived at 4627 Spring St., La Mesa, in 1937;
came from 366 Sola St., Santa Barbara. Undoubtedly parents
of C. H. Garrigues.

Another memo in the Tenney Committee file was more fervid:

GARRIGUES, C. H. (Brick) 9/6/40
2034 Oak Glen Pl.,
Los Angeles, Calif.

Joined C.P. summer of 1936. Sent by Grover and Gladys
Johnson to S.F. to investigate for C.P. in murder trial of
King, O'Connor [sic] and Ramsay.

From there to S.D. where he operated a Communist
fraction of A. F. of L. Became editor of A. F. of L.
Newspaper in S.D. After Newspaper Guild, to which he
belonged, went CIO, was kicked out of there. Came to L.A.
as paid secretary for the L.A. Newspaper Guild.

Left that job in 1938 to go with Gardner Gregg and
Carl Kegley. Said to have left C.P. and retired from active
political work, although Carl Kegley reported in July 1940
Garrigues was working on Voice of the Federation, Bridges[7]
Maritime Fed. paper in S.F. Did write under name of Vincent
Sutherland for People's World.

Member C.P. fraction Newspaper Guild, whose membership
identical with Unit 140, Professional Section C.P.; served
on Political Committee of this Section. This is man whose
ears were knocked down by Tom Cavett in 1936. Age 30 - 6
ft. 2 in. 195 lbs. Red sandy hair. Unscrupulous writer.
Usually lives with a female. Not active lately.[5]

On August 4, 1938, Rena Vale quit the Communist Party, despite,
she said, Brick Garrigues's impassioned pleas to remain a member. But
Brick Garrigues was just about on the edge of quitting himself.

And on September 2, his father died at Patton State Hospital near San
Bernardino, with a diagnosis of "Psychosis with cerebral arteriosclerosis."

---

5 According to Brick's later testimony to an investigative committee, he did not join the
Communist Party until 1937. Gardner Gregg was Brick's partner in a short-lived political
publicity bureau. Carl Kegley was an attorney who was active in the Minute Men movement.
He was the Democratic candidate for attorney-general in 1938, losing to the Republican Earl
Warren, who was fresh from his victory in the King-Ramsay-Conner case. Harry Bridges was
the head of the International Longshoremen's and Warehousemen's Union, often cited by
conservatives as a Communist-front organization. Thomas L. Cavett is listed in the 1936 Los
Angeles City Directory as a detective with the District Attorney's office, living at 815 Cloverdale
Ave. Between 1941 and 1943 he "did a great deal of work " for the Tenney Committee in
Southern California, its 1943 report said. He later became an attorney and died on November
8, 1958.

[Handwritten]
5318 E. Ocean Blvd.
Long Beach, Calif.
October 29, 1938

From where I'm sitting, I can see nothing but blue ocean, bright and sunny, with Catalina Island away off on the horizon. Occasionally a lumber schooner or tramp steamer slips by, and if I moved to the other end of the sofa I could see San Pedro with a lot of warships and airplane carriers anchored out around the breakwater. It's warm and sunny, and when I finish this I'm going to walk along the beach about two miles to a little inlet from a little bay where I'll lie on the sand and read "Richard Feverel."[6]

I don't know how many years it's been since I've felt both the inclination and the ability to relax. Two or three, I suppose. But the surf thunders at our very door day and night and there's no sign of human beings, graft, corruption, politics or the class struggle.

The occasion is the fact that the political publicity business blew up -- or rather quietly collapsed -- and I started looking for an honest job. A chap who had started a little paper in Long Beach sent for me, and I started dickering with him for a job as editor. It would have been a pretty good job, but it didn't work out, so I agreed to work for him three days a week on a temporary basis until he decided whether he wants to pay me what I want -- and give me a contract -- to take over the paper. That probably won't develop, but it's an excellent chance to get away from Los Angeles for a few weeks, get a rest, try to re-orient myself a little and enjoy at least a bit of solitude.

Naomi is with me -- she isn't the most solitudinous person in the world, but there's a long, wide beach, and the place is really a sort of ivory tower. No radio, no telephone, almost no visitors, and no daily paper. I'm afraid the job won't last very much longer -- it's almost too good to last.

I've been surprised to find how far I've shifted away from my old habits of solitude (occasional, but very important) and my attitude of individualism since I've been in the labor movement. I'm also surprised to find that I've completely ceased to be a "writer" in the years I've been thinking in terms of action rather than words. I can't even write a good news story any more. I envy those chaps who can rush home from a meeting and dash off an article or a story and then dash out to organize another meeting. I can't do it; apparently if I'm going to become a writer again, I shall have to seek to achieve some measure of objectivity -- which means I shall have to cease being a radical.

---

6 *The Ordeal of Richard Feverel* by George Meredith (1828-1909), first published in 1859.

I remember once you gave me good advice: To stop trying to change the world. I've been trying sporadically to follow it ever since. But it's difficult for a meliorist like myself -- particularly when the world seems tipping over into fascism and we seem headed for a new Dark Ages.[7] The walls of one's ivory tower must be pretty thick to keep out the smell of Hitler and Chamberlain. Even from my window I see battleships and suspect that, ultimately, they'll be used on the side of fascism rather than against it.

The next morning

I suppose one trouble is that I've been seeing the world too much through Marxist eyes. It's difficult to become interested in details (such as graft, politics, etc.) when the whole thing over-simplifies itself into a war between two fundamental systems. The colors of one's world disappear and there is nothing but black and white. That's probably why I feel so thoroughly out of touch with the world -- unable to write.

Ruth, you know, is here.[8] She's fundamentally a very nice person but she, like me, has grown a little middle-aged. A little dumpy and complacent and inclined to worry over food, clothing and shelter. Where are all the fine Bohemians of the '20s?

The revolutionaries of today are much too serious. They're collectivized already -- they're not rebels, just serious believers in a new order. They work too hard and bathe and wear nice clothes, when they can afford them. Revolution isn't an adventure, but a business.

I've had too much of them. There's nothing so nice as solitude. Yesterday I walked miles down the beach and found an old stone jetty running away out into the sea near the entrance to a little bay. Down among the rocks, just a few inches from the water there was a natural granite couch on which I curled up and read "Richard Feverel" -- and looked at the breakers thundering in past me into the bay -- or watched a family of seals going out to catch their lunch.

Hecht once wrote a book about a chap who couldn't stand people nor to be alone who built a house and peopled it with strange companions who he thought were phantoms. Maybe I should try that.

I'd better quit and do a little job of work I'm supposed to do for a politician. Free-lance writing is much more profitable than real writing -- when you can get it. I did one ten thousand-word little booklet last summer and got two hundred dollars for it.

---

7 Meliorism is the belief that the world is getting better and that mankind can aid its improvement. The "growing good of the world," wrote George Eliot at the conclusion of *Middlemarch*, "is partly dependent on unhistoric acts . . . [and to the people] who lived faithfully a hidden life and rest in unvisited tombs."

8 A friend of Brick's and Toni's from the early years.

138 North Lake Street
Los Angeles
December 26, 1938

I thought I told you that Naomi and I were finally
married. But maybe I didn't. We're living a rather hand-to-
mouth existence right now; I work two days a week on a
little weekly newspaper, have one political publicity
account and one job managing a prospective candidate for
the Board of Supervisors. Out of the three (all temporary),
I make not quite enough to pay rent and buy groceries, but
then I have about four days a week free and just enough
economic pressure to keep me pretty busy grinding away at
these alleged articles. After the first of the year, I
shall really have to start putting the pressure on to find
a job if we're going to continue to eat. The fact is,
though, that I really don't want a job; it's pure laziness,
or rather reluctance to spend more than a few hours a week
doing politics or reporting or in other ways engaging in
the competitive struggle.

We had a nice Christmas. Rather blew ourselves on
cheap toys for the kids and spent the day at Dickie's playing with the toys. Now I have a full day with no responsibility to go downtown and scare up another publicity
account so I'll get back to work.

My mother needed a job, too, so she took the No. 5 yellow streetcar to a little town some ten miles from Los Angeles, to answer an ad
placed by one of the few attorneys there. He was out of the office, but
as Dickie was waiting, his partner wondered if she could type something for him, and so she did, and when the boss, Victor Sparks,
returned, he found her at the typewriter hard at work, as if she had
been there always. He hired her at once, a good example of her wish
going hand in hand with her deed. It didn't hurt that Dickie had a
youthful spirit and very clear skin.

That's how Chuck and Dickie and I came to live in Inglewood.

We all stuffed ourselves into a little shack on Stepney Street, Chuck
and I in the bedroom and Dickie on a pull-out bed in the living room.
It was just fine; the roof didn't leak too bad, and when it did, we just
put pots and pans around on the floor to catch the drips. We walked
the half mile to school, taking care not to step on the cracks in the
sidewalk, and afterward we'd hurry home to . . . Mrs. Mossbrook, a
plain Iowa woman in a simple housedress, who took care of us and
taught us bad grammar and fixed bad dinner just before Dickie got
home from the office around six o'clock.

Russell Gray was my best friend. He asked me to his seventh
birthday party, and Chuck made sure that my hair was combed, my
new shirt was buttoned at the neck and I was carrying a present as he

sent me down the street to Russell's house. Chuck was only eight himself, and in these years he was about a head taller than me; I know because he'd wrap his arms around me protectively as we watched Dickie work in the kitchen, and he'd dig his sharp chin into my scalp.

December 1938, Monday

Are you still agenting? I'm just finishing an article that I've been working on for a month. Unless I hear to the contrary, I'll be sending it along in a few days. I don't known how it is, yet, because I've just typed the first draft after rewriting it nineteen times, but it seems about as good as I can make it. It's pointed at something like Harper's, I think.

We're back in town, and I'm out of a job and spending all my time writing again. It's fun, rusty as I am. I have another one plotted, all ready to start as soon as I get this one finished and spend about a week in the public library.

January 9, 1939

Another article is about half finished. It's being called "Money Makes the Mayor Go" and describes a political campaign from the very practical inside point of view of the man who makes up the budget and spends the money for everything from billboards to bribery. I think it's going to be pretty good and should be the first in a series of three or four complete articles on the technique of modern politics, which could possibly form the basis for another book -- a somewhat more mature "Politician's Handbook."

January 27, 1939

Not that I want to load you up with unsalable manuscripts, but here's another one. It may possibly be the last one for a while as the family fortune has vanished, and I've got to start really looking for a job.

If I had sufficient income, I'd be all set for a serious attempt at the Great American Novel. The thing is really beginning to get shaped, and I'd like six months in a hermitage. But by the time I get enough reserve built up again, it will probably have vanished. Meanwhile, I'm trying to line up enough candidates for the spring election to keep the wolf out of the Frigidaire and, simultaneously, trying to land newspaper jobs in San Diego and San Francisco.

March 14, 1939

I'm afflicted with a very delightful form of spring fever. Saturday we drove away down into the desert and spent the night in a little desert auto camp. Sunday we drove back over a new and little-used highway through the mountains. The sun was hot, but there were fields and fields of snow and few people. I found it difficult not to keep on going until we came to that little adobe shack that Bernice used to have out east of Tucson.

Naomi is working -- thank God! That keeps the wolf from the door and also serves to give me just a little more privacy. She's an extremely pleasant creature to have around, but just attentive enough so that I miss the opportunity to enjoy my own quiet company as much as I should like.

I spent the morning reading over the first nineteen drafts of a novel I started a couple of years ago. As usual, I was pleasantly surprised. It's thoroughly disorganized and very badly overwritten but shows definite possibilities, and I think I can possibly reorganize it and write it before long.

I'm still wondering which is worse: to have a steady job and no energy left to write, or to free-lance and have periods of extreme activity (with income) sandwiched in between periods of no work, lots of time and lots of worry about the next two meals. At the moment I should prefer the steady job.

I'm enclosing a couple of snapshots taken at the ranch which seem to include the whole damn family. The collie was killed a few months ago, but the rest of us are in good health.

As ever,

Brick

Part Two
Amaryllis

Life renews itself.

Chapter Fourteen
San Francisco

In 1939, a new chapter began for the newlywed couple. Naomi struggled to merge her life with her husband's. And Brick's struggle was no longer on behalf of newspaper workers or against corrupt politicians. Instead, his fight was an interior one: against that "refuge of pragmatism, the philosophy of the Saturday night pay check, the humble bungalow and loving wife, expending my dreams on the possibilities of next year's suit or a new tire for the family Ford," as he had put it thirteen years before. It is hard to say if Brick in 1926 had been uncannily predicting the course of his life or, once having expressed the words, they became a self-fulfilling prophecy; that is, written down they provided a kind of charter for his life, or maybe a strait-jacket.

2223 Roosevelt Avenue
Berkeley, Calif.
May 24, 1939

Dear Toni,

The publicity business ran out after the city election this month so Naomi and I took the thirty dollars we had managed to save and came north where we are camping with her cousins while we look for jobs. That is one nice thing about Jewish people -- they come in such large families.

Anyway, it's swell up here, even if you're broke. I think we, or one of us, will get jobs or a job before the thirty bucks runs out, and in the meantime it's a lovely place to live and I feel that I'm enjoying a vacation.

Naomi ran into Anna Louise Strong ("Remaking an American," "I Change Worlds," etc.) last week while I was down south and she wanted to hire us both as a kind of commbined secretary. While Anna was up here, Naomi was to do stenographic work; while she was in L.A. I was to act as her social secretary.

Anna Louise Strong was then fifty-four, an admirer of the Soviet Union who had already traveled extensively there and in China. The few days Brick spent with her were part of a tour suggested by Eleanor Roosevelt to find out how the New Deal had helped the country.[1]

I'd frequently wondered what it would be like to be a guard in a bughouse, but I wonder no longer. I had two of the wildest days of leaping from place to place one could ever expect before I dashed feverishly northward to get away from her.

She had a bad habit of making appointments for her-self, writing them on a slip of paper and sticking them into the huge pockets of her huge coat, the huge purse or the tiny briefcase she carried. She'd always remember the time of the appointment but never the place, the telephone number or the name of the person she was going to see. Then for hours we'd drive frantically about town trying to get someplace we were supposed to be until finally I'd call up enough people to find out who so-and-so was and where, then we'd get there.

One of the girls here drove with her down to Sacramento (one hundred miles away). She had no appointment, merely wanted to see the town, but planned to arrive at three. For various reasons they were an hour late in arriving. As they got into the outskirts of the town, Anna realized it was four o'clock. Raving that she'd spent more time on this trip than it was worth, she compelled Helen[2] to turn around and drive back, without even entering the town she had come a hundred miles to see.

The next day they drove to Fresno. Helen had made reservations at a hotel, but on their way down somebody wrote down the name of an auto court that was supposed to be good. Anna stuck the name in her pocket. When they got to Fresno, she made Helen cancel the hotel reservations and then they started looking for the auto court. But Anna had lost the paper. So, after two hours, they went back to the hotel and went to bed.

In the morning when Helen woke up, Anna was gone. Several hours later she came back, explaining that she had found the address of the auto court in her pocket, had

---

[1] The tour is described on pages 184-188 of *Right in Her Soul*, by Strong's daughter, Tracy B. Strong, and Helene Keyssar, published in 1983 by Random House.

[2] "Helen" was Helen Hosmer of the Simon J. Lubin Society, "investigator of California's farms," as Strong put it in the book she wrote about her transcontinental trip. The Central Valley portion of this journey is described in Chapter VI of her *My Native Land*, published in 1940 by Viking.

dressed, taken a cab five miles out of town at three in the morning and spent the rest of the night there.

So if you think you have troubles, pray that your path never crosses that of Anna Louise Strong.

Berkeley may be the environment I have been looking for. There's a sort of cloistered air about the whole town; one's friends are in the habit of studying, reading, writing, etc., and when they do come over, one may either engage in intellectual concord (how's that?) or go off in one's own room and work. There is just enough removal from hectic rushing around to permit one to cogitate not too idly. Also, it seems, I've finally got Naomi trained not to demand too much in the way of constant companionship. Or rather she, too, seems to have developed work of her own which gives me more time for work and thought and study.

June 22, 1939

Curiously enough, I have, I think, every letter you've ever written me, NOT tied up in a pink ribbon, but I have them, nevertheless. And they're the only letters I've ever kept. Don't ask me why, but I suspect that they probably represent some kind of a left-handed diary of my own -- and don't ask me why about that either.[3]

In New York, Viking Press had a hit with *The Grapes of Wrath*. The author, John Steinbeck, had been brought to Viking by an energetic senior editor named Pascal "Pat" Covici.

I can assure you that everybody in California is discussing "Grapes of Wrath." Down in Hollywood the screen colony has become completely and wholly migratory-worker-conscious, and in San Francisco wherever two or three are gathered together, John Steinbeck's name is first among them. I haven't had a chance to read it yet because I can't even afford a daily paper, and the lines are apparently blocks long in front of the circulating libraries. But I'm anxious to; those hot central valleys are my country, you know. We had migratory workers, too; we called them Texans instead of Okies and didn't sentimentalize over them, although, as I recall, conditions were almost as bad for them then as they are now. No, not quite as bad because they did have a chance at sharecropping, which they don't now.

We have some friends who are in charge of a federal migratory camp in Imperial Valley, and it's a little like the American consulate at Tientsin, China, I should imagine. You're safe as long as you're inside the camp limits, but outside almost anything can happen.[4] You know, I suppose,

---

3 Brick later disposed of these letters, as he did most of his other personal papers.

4 The Japanese invaded China in 1937 and occupied Tientsin. In 1939 they blockaded the British and French concessions there in response to anti-Japanese demonstrations by the Chinese residents.

that the Imperial Valley vigilantes do not hesitate to run federal agents out of the county at the point of a gun. The thing makes fascism a much more immediate problem than it would appear in the larger cities.

I'm at least temporarily out of politics, uplift, reform and all attempts to change the world or prevent its changing. Somewhere or other, I've got off on the wrong track in the last couple of years, and I've got to spend a little time in trying to find out where and why and how to get back on the right one. Part of that realization comes from the fact that I've pretty thoroughly eliminated myself from a chance to make a living and part from the fact that the contribution I've made to the labor movement appears to have been infinitesimal.

Of course, I've sworn repentance before, and it didn't click. I seem to be about equally moved by the desire, when I confront an interesting situation, to do something about it and to write about it and, since, it's easier to do than to write, I do -- and then promise myself I won't again. At the moment, I'm lost in a fog and so I just sit and, perhaps, re-read something I read years ago or practice a little penmanship under the delusion that I'm writing something.

I suppose you read Sheean's "Personal History."[5] I just finished re-reading it and (without sentimentalizing over myself) was struck by the curious similarity in the way Sheean got out of adjustment and the way I did. I mean that development of a reporter who finally ceases to be a reporter and becomes a partisan and finds that he's neither a good reporter nor a good partisan or, if he doesn't find it out, his employers do.

Berkeley isn't a bad place for contemplation. I usually manage to get up by nine o'clock and start writing immediately after breakfast, usually continuing until the middle of the afternoon. That goes on about four days a week, and I usually put in another hour in the evening. I wish I could say I'm producing something, but I'm not. It's almost literally practice -- attempting this or that approach to a (or the) novel, thinking I have it and then deciding it's wrong. It's true that I don't work very hard at it; after so long a time away from work with words, I find that they've lost weight and color and it's largely a process of getting acquainted with them again, I suppose. It's also a matter of disassociating myself from the cliches of the Left with which I have been so much in contact during the last couple of years and, I hope, will ultimately be a process of beginning to look at people as people instead of political units.

Naomi is doing some temporary work, and we live on the small amount of money she makes while Dickie takes care of

---

5 Journalist Vincent Sheean's best-selling memoir was published in 1935 by Doubleday.

the kids down in L.A. without benefit of alimony. I managed
to get four days' work on the Examiner last week reading
copy; I used to be a damned good copy reader, but either I
wasn't fast enough or something and got fired. That was the
first time in my life I'd ever been fired for "incompe-
tence" (oh, horrid word!) and it was a bit of a shock.

It would be fun to live up here if one had an income;
San Franciscans go places and do things and know nice
places for lunch, etc.

San Francisco was tiny, compared with Los Angeles. The entire city
converged on Market Street, where four sets of streetcar tracks competed
for space with the few autos that people owned in those days. But it had
hustle, and it thought of itself as the metropolis of the West Coast. The
San Francisco-Oakland Bay Bridge, one of the preeminent engineering
feats of the twentieth century, had been open for just a few years, and
another bridge, a graceful span across the Golden Gate, attracted San
Franciscans out for a stroll above turbulent waters. For the first time,
America had two World's Fairs running at the same time — one in New
York on Flushing Meadow and one in the San Francisco Bay on man-
made Treasure Island, before it was commissioned as a naval base.

Yes, we have a World's Fair here, too, but I understand we're not particularly proud of it. They stuck it out
in the middle of the bay, almost under our magnificent
bridge, and its lighted tower looks like a toy from the top
of the bridge. The whole damn thing looks like a very
cheaply constructed Hollywood movie set; it costs you forty
cents for bridge tolls, fifty cents for parking, fifty
cents apiece to get in and twenty-five cents for most of
the exhibits. So I haven't been yet -- although we probably
will.

Instead, when we think we can afford it, we take a
ferry across the bay and then another across the Golden
Gate (a very swell ride lasting more than an hour) and end
up at Mill Valley, which is a lovely old village in the
redwood forests. We hike across a couple of young mountains
and come down in Muir Woods, which is another redwood
forest of trees incredibly high and incredibly old and
where there are almost never any people and it's dark and
cool and almost scary. Then we ride back and go to a
Finnish bath in Berkeley and steam the fatigue out of our
muscles and end up at a Finnish restaurant where the
proletariat eats and where you can get amazingly good food
in enormous quantities for fifty cents. (Notice that I
translate everything into terms of the right-hand side of
the menu, these days.)

In a recent letter, Toni told of meeting the great singer Paul Robeson.

I'm glad, for some reason or another, that you know
Robeson. He happens to be one of my pet heroes although

I've never met him. I used to have a very close friend --
Rena Vale -- who knew him very well.

   I'm really going to send you that pamphlet one of
these days. And I'd like you to do something for me. Read
it. And then see if you think that there is any material in
it which would possibly constitute the basis for anything
that would be saleable. My very charming and admiring
little Naomi insists that the material is saleable and I
think it isn't. But maybe what I want is just encouragement, somebody to say: "Ah, that's fine. A real genius!
It's an amazingly moving style; I wept when I read it."
Then I can say to myself: "Good old Brick. You really can
write, can't you? Now you can afford to take a day off and
sit in the park, or a week off to start a dahlia garden or
a year off to do some labor organizing."

"That pamphlet" was *Why Didn't Somebody Tell Somebody?*, privately printed by Brick in May 1938, with a second printing in January
1939. In it he told the story of four man-caused natural disasters of epic
proportions, the collapse of the Saint Francis Dam in 1928, the severe
Long Beach earthquake of March 1933, the destruction of Venice Beach
by the building of a breakwater in 1933 and the devastation in 1931
caused by the flood in Montrose. The pamphlet linked the disasters with
political payoffs and graft. On the cover was a drawing of the new City
Hall, which had been opened in 1928, an earthquake toppling its tower
into three chunks.

   At first men cowered in caves when floods came, drowning like rats if
waters reached their hiding places. Volcanoes, earthquakes wiped out whole
tribes, forest fires penned them in, drought burned their pastures, bliz-
zards froze them.

   The first magician was an angry, bedraggled, hungry caveman who,
after forty days and forty nights of rain, lifted his face from the rock where
he had been marooned, shook his fist at the sky and shouted imprecations
at the rain clouds. The clouds vanished, a warm sun came out, and an awe-
struck people fell down and worshiped the man who could command the
storm. During the next rainy season, unfortunately, the magician tried it
again without waiting forty days, and the rain, having just begun, continued to fall — indifferent to his curses. So the people knocked him in the
head with a stone club and found another magician who knew when, as
well as how, to make magic.

   Then, on the banks of the Nile, the first priest was born. He studied
the angle of the sun as it crossed the river, gauged the ebb and flow of the
seasons and learned to tell the villagers exactly when to plant their wheat
and barley so that the river, spreading over the fertile delta, would bring
fulsome harvests. And so knowledge was added to magic, and the priests
came to rule over great empires.

   Later came the scientist. Slowly, haltingly, knowledge moved forward, was organized, specialized, harnessed. But fire, flood and earth-

quake remained "acts of God"; one could pray for deliverance from such evils but it was considered blasphemous to attempt to prevent them. Year after year, thousands died until at last came the cry of the survivors: "Why didn't somebody tell somebody?"

But the hand of Greed stayed the hand of Science. In our modern day, when the scientist rules, dishonest contractors build dams of sand instead of cement. Instead of employing steel and concrete, dishonest officials built schools of bricks, manufactured and sold by their friends. Dishonest subdividers sell homes lying in the certain path of the next flood. And so men and women die by the hundreds while the cry went up from the survivors, "Why didn't somebody tell somebody?"

A hundred years ago our fathers swept in a confident horde across the "Great American Desert," which spread from Montana to the Mississippi. They tore at its sod with plows and harrows, transformed it into the bread basket of the world and sent its millions of gleaming bushels to the cities to be chips for the gamblers on the Exchange. Then, silently, drought slipped into the realm. Robbed of its fertility, denuded of its protecting sod, the soil began drifting across fences, piling into drifts, burying houses. And it was only then that the American people, seeking desperately to halt disaster, cried again: "Why didn't somebody tell somebody?"

> 1530 Leavenworth
> San Francisco, Calif.
> September 11, 1939

I suspect the thing which keeps one awake nights is anger. I can recall (I suppose I probably wrote you about a dame a year or so ago who worked in the office with me)[6] waking up regularly at two o'clock every morning for weeks and writhing with impotent rage. I didn't recognize it as rage at the time, but it was.

We've moved in to San Francisco. The war has brought a bit of additional work, and I'm hopeful that the job may even last for the duration.[7] So we've taken a place on Russian Hill --quiet and high and civilized and only a few minutes by cable car from the office. It's the first time I've every really lived in a city. In Los Angeles we were in the suburbs even if only a dozen blocks from downtown, but even if you lived a dozen miles out it was noisy and gasoline-y and crowded.

This is an old district (all of San Francisco is old except a few horrible white stucco flats out by Twin Peaks), but the apartments, which look like slums on the outside, are bright and fresh and roomy inside, and from the kitchen window (by standing tiptoe) you can see the ships coming in the Golden Gate. There is practically no automobile traffic. One comes home by cable car, which is just like going up the roller coaster (although they put on

---

6 Miriam.

7 The job — as a copy editor on the *San Francisco Examiner* — lasted for thirty more years.

the brakes coming down), and every block has its little neighborhood shops in which the same people have been buying their groceries or liquor or curios or books for a couple of generations. It's the most peaceful place I've found -- peaceful without being enervating. One loses a lot of one's dislike for people and doesn't mind the thought of looking out of one's window into a dozen kitchen windows across the way.

But it's much too soon to say that I'm finding myself. Life is a lot more bearable, at the moment. After five years of doing subjectively exciting things -- being a columnist, running newspapers, radio commentating, speech-making, having love affairs, etc. -- it's nice to relax into the comparative routine of a well-paid job, even though it only lasts from week to week.

Looking back over fifteen or twenty years, I find that for the first time I am not concerned over (1) the comparative artistic merits of Hemingway and Joyce, (2) the tendency toward dissonance in modern music, (3) the inability of the managing editor to produce as good a paper as I could produce, (4) the possibility of a Republican victory in 1940 and (5) the condition of the toiling masses.

I hope this period will last for a while. I don't want to be promoted or to save a certain sum of money each month or visit a swanky night club or be able to discuss intelligently the sociological value of Dos Passos. I don't want to buy a house or move out to the country and raise chickens or to make radio or after-dinner speeches or help elect the next governor of the state.

I really think, Toni, dear, that a lot of your and my trouble comes from the fact that we let ourselves believe that by throwing our willpower at an objective we can achieve it by sheer force of determination. Our old high school principal used to say, "You can do anything in the world if you want to badly enough." Somehow we seem to think we can -- and so we lie awake and grind our teeth in helpless rage or hurl our willpower at some desired objective until we turn green. And get nowhere.

You Can Do Anything

Everybody in school knew that the principal, whose desk nameplate read "C. W. Bottoms," was on the up-and-up and didn't have any use for anybody that wasn't; they called him Old Buttocks or Old Pratt or Old Rear-end but they knew he was for them. Bliss began listening now more attentively to the two regular speeches which the principal made on every possible occasion.

One came almost weekly when, at meetings of the Associated Students, he would sit silently, watching and listening with approval to the surge of debate back and forth. By rule or custom, each action of the student body required approval of the faculty: theoretically the approval was to be in writing, indicated by the principal's signature on the minutes. But not with Old Bottoms: He would sit, listening until the motion was adopted and then, if it were doubtful or controversial, he would rise and his glass eye would go shooting away at the ceiling and he would say. "You have now reached the age when you must learn to be responsible for your own acts. I can only adjure you: in all matters where the honor of El Jardin is at stake, do the right thing!"

That was one speech, and when Old Bottoms had made it the leaders would confer to decide whether they had, in fact done the right thing and, sometimes, somebody would move to rescind the action or expunge the minutes and, whatever they did, the principal would sign the minutes.

The other speech came once a year, a month or so before the end of the term. Bottoms would suspend classes an hour early and come in and talk to the students as a whole but particularly to the graduates-to-be. He would try to tell them what they would find waiting for them in the great world outside the classroom. And always he would finish: ". . . and remember this: you can do anything in the world if you want to badly enough. Anything!"

To Bliss, it was wonderful. Anything you wanted. Anything. He went home, not talking to the others about it because he knew they would spoil it. But he knew it was true. It just had to be.

He asked Tom about it on Saturday; Tom was home now, and they were playing catch on the driveway after supper. Bliss's shoulder hadn't healed yet so he could throw, but he wore a catcher's mitt and sat back and let Tom pitch to him and then rolled the ball back over the hard ground. Bliss told him what Old Bottoms had to say, and Tom wound up and lobbed over a knuckle ball and said, "Anything?"

"Anything," Bliss said. "If you want to bad enough."

"Do you suppose," Tom said, "you could throw a baseball as fast as Walter Johnson? [8] No matter how bad you wanted to?"

"If I practiced and practiced and kept on practicing?" Bliss asked.

Tom let go a hot one; it was going so fast you could hardly see it, and it stung clear through the catcher's mitt. "Not if you practiced 'til you was too old to pick up a glove," he said.

"You oughta be able to," Bliss insisted.

Tom shagged the rolling baseball and wiped off the dirt.

"That's the trouble with going to school," he said. "You, kid, you're going to get more education than any of us except maybe Grace. But you gotta remember; teachers and preachers and college professors are all alike in one thing. They teach you what you oughta be instead of what is.

---

8 Walter Johnson pitched for the Washington Senators for 21 seasons. He had 416 victories and held the shutout record at 110 games. He pitched 56 consecutive scoreless innings in 1913.

Then after you get outa school you spend half your life trying to untangle the oughts and the is." He grinned and threw a wide outcurve that Bliss had to reach for, and Bliss let it drop.

But just the same, he thought, you oughta be able to. And maybe, if you tried real hard, you could.

Later, on the screen porch, he thought about it some more. Of course, you wouldn't want to do impossible things like being Walter Johnson. But the things you could do . . .

Like making a go of the ranch, for example. All you had to do was really want it — to take thought, to hurl your will against the universe and demand that the universe comply. All you had to do was find out what you really wanted . . . what you wanted to do, what you wanted to be . . .

He began to puzzle over it at night before he went to sleep; he'd lie on the screen porch, looking at his wishing star, no longer wishing (nor waiting in terror for it to melt and run down the sky) but trying to find out what he really wanted . . . what sort of person he really was. It was no longer a question of wanting a bike or skates, or even a ranch. It was a question of finding out who you were, what you really were . . . in order that you might know what you wanted to be. He remembered how, when he was in grammar school he used to write in the flyleaf of his book:

> *Bliss Lane*
> *Descanso*
> *Box 173, RFD No. 1*
> *El Jardin*
> *California*
> *U.S.A.*
> *The Earth*
> *The Solar System*
> *The Universe*

But he knew now you couldn't do it that way; you couldn't locate yourself with just a map and an RFD address. You had to know who you were in order to know what to be so you would not make a mistake and be somebody else instead of yourself.

It all sounded mixed up when he tried to say it to himself, but inside it was very clear. He began to take stock of himself; he began to measure himself physically and mentally, against the others. He studied to learn his aptitudes and his weaknesses, not for purposes of self-improvement, but in order to be (in strength and weaknesses) the sort of person that he was. He studied to cast his own shadow, and he took great pains to be sure that the shadow would be his own. He went about asking himself not "What is true?" but "What do I believe?" because the important thing was not to discover Truth but to discover Bliss Lane.

Oct. 18, 1939

This is my night off. I'm working nights now; go to work at eleven and quit at seven. So when I have a night off (since Naomi works days and can't go out late), I have a whole night to kill -- with nowhere to go. . . . The fact is that we're both extremely anti-social these days and never see anybody. When it happens that we get a day off together, we go out in the hills -- all by ourselves. You'd really never suspect that we're married; we don't do anything -- socially, I mean -- that married people do.

Curiously, except for the difference in hours and women, life is astonishingly like it was twelve years ago. Eight hours a day on the copydesk, a small apartment, a very infrequent movie -- and that's life. The only difference in the job is that a dozen years ago newspaper work had dignity and importance (to me) and now it's just drudgery.

But I like it. San Francisco is -- well, San Francisco. All the junk that's been written about it hasn't succeeded in spoiling it, in spite of the Fair and the bridges and an apparent determination to emulate Los Angeles. I wish I could really write you about it. The old Barbary Coast had declined to a couple of honkytonks before the Fair, so they spruced it up, put in a half a dozen synthetic joints for the Fair and made a showplace out of it.

They've put up a fancy memorial tower at the top of Telegraph Hill,[9] cement-gunned the exteriors of the shacks on the side that was once a rabbit-burrow of would-be artists, put in showers and tripled the rents. You can now be both Bohemian and odorless for fifty dollars a month -- if you have the fifty. They've cut a six-lane auto highway through the town and messed the bay up with bridges.

But the bums who mooch you along Market Street are still authentic; you can get a plate of fried chicken, mashed potatoes and sauerkraut a foot high at Breen's for thirty-five cents -- and the place smells as bad as it did in 1906.[10] There are still places stuck around behind closed doors where the menu, the waiters and the patrons haven't changed in fifty years. You still ride up to our place on one of three or four cable car lines with the gripman shouting wisecracks at the girls or singing at the top of his voice, and the foghorns still bellow through the night.

You never see anybody with that drawn, tired look that everybody wears in L.A. Even the reliefers -- old women with shopping bags -- sit on the curb outside the relief office, and nod and smile and gossip quite contentedly. There's something 19th century -- very definitely 19th

---

9 Coit Tower was constructed in 1933 with $118,000 bequeathed by Lillie Hitchcock Coit to honor San Francisco's firemen. Its tower is reminiscent of the shape of the nozzle of a fire hose.

10 Breen's was a workingman's bar and delicatessen just across the alley from the *Examiner* building. It smelled of pickles, herring and tobacco and lasted at least into the mid-1950s.

century -- about it. The small business man hasn't heard of
the chain stores; and -- the real marvel -- you can find an
independent bakery in every block. I hadn't eaten non-
bakery-trust bread or cake since I was a kid.

I'd almost forgotten that the world had changed. So
I'm a fifty-five-dollar-a-week newspaperman? So what? So
there's just as much dignity and importance in being a
newspaperman as in being a plumber or a snob on Nob Hill.
One doesn't go to the opera because the opera is for Nob
Hill folks and you don't pretend to live on Nob Hill when
you don't. You probably don't even go to the movies; you
stop in at the corner saloon for a beer and then come home
to read a book or go tramping over the hills.

It's authentic -- even though it isn't real. For
they've built acres and acres of subdivisions of shiny
white stucco houses out beyond Twin Peaks where nobody but
a few eccentric millionaires would have lived a few years
ago and it won't be long until this'll be just another
American city. Meanwhile, it's a swell place for a
regressive mood.

The experience with -- or rather without -- Miriam was
a sort of culmination of a lot of events which carried out
a progressive deflation of the self-esteem that I'd carried
around with me most of my life. I don't know why -- she
really wasn't important -- but she just happened to come
along at a time when I needed a boost to the morale. So I
got a kick in the face, instead. That's how I happen to
recall what a situation like that can do to one -- when
you're thrown into daily contact with the other person. It
raises hell with the self-esteem and makes a lot bigger
scar than you know at the time. That's why I particularly
need San Francisco and a routine job, for a while. Maybe
I'll start building it up again.

You and I very early formed the habit of barking at
the moon. It might be only a street lamp but even if it
was, we wanted it -- because we'd made up our minds it was
the moon, and the moon it had to be. Not until we decide
(quite without sour grapes) that a street lamp really casts
a lovely light do we quit making ourselves unhappy.

I just finished "American Dream" by Michael Foster. (I
roomed with him years ago.) It's a swell book -- maybe one of
the best. But he suffers from the same complaint. He can't
look at people. He looks at them through the very fine
literary eye of Michael Foster. And that eye has nothing to
do with the actual Mike Foster (I don't actually believe
there is such a person) but is a separate organism compounded
from a long line of celebrities beginning with Hecht and
working both ways. You no longer see Hecht in Mike's stuff;
you see Foster -- but it's a Foster who has been trying to
see his boyhood and manhood (all his life) through a novel.
So there's no Mike Foster. And the book shows it.

Michael Foster's book was published in 1937 by the Literary Guild. In it, a disillusioned newspaperman discovers through old family letters what America meant to the writers and what America should mean to him. Several scenes are reminiscent of the tawdry political atmosphere rendered in Ben Hecht's and Charles MacArthur's 1928 play, *The Front Page*. Hecht soon went to Hollywood to become one of the industry's most influential writers.

Oh, well. I've at least refrained for nearly three pages from giving you a literary review of "Grapes of Wrath." I've just finished it -- and it left me rather a -- well, I don't exactly know how to describe it. Despite the fact that he has -- Oh, hell. I guess all I'd better say is that Viking has done the most important piece of publishing since "Uncle Tom's Cabin." And even that sounds like something I read in a blurb.

I have a curious feeling about it because it was one of those farm strikes -- in Imperial Valley in 1934 -- that first got me started in this labor business. It happened to be in my own home town where the vigilantes were people I'd gone to high school with. I've been living more or less in that world ever since -- and even before -- since it was one of my jobs on the News during the worst days of the Depression to meet the starving people who came in and give them a word of encouragement.

I think it was that sort of thing, as much as anything else, which pried me out of the comfortably safe existence I was in and made me a crusading columnist, a labor agitator, etc., et seq. Marianne was an important element since she'd been a labor agitator all her life (her father was lynched in Washington during the war).[11] And now here I am again -- working on the old routine job and determined to do nothing more than stick to it as long as I can. I don't even go to union meetings any more.

But it didn't produce a novel. Steinbeck could get anger in his heart, vision in his eyes and go to work. I either rushed out to organize a union or stood back to protect my job and standing -- or tried to do both at once.

Lately I sold a couple of articles to the Hollywood Tribune. They pay -- strangely enough -- but went broke the following issue. They were the best things I'd done since the book. More in the old style. But when I read them, they

---

[11] This was the second version of Marianne's parentage, the first being a tale that her father, of an old French anarchist family, had died in an American prison during the war. I have not been able to find records of any anarchists who died under those circumstances. It is true, though, that scores of conscientious objectors were sent to Leavenworth Prison during the First World War for opposing the draft. As for the second tale, the only lynching in Washington around the war years was that of Nathan Wesley Everest, an IWW organizer, on November 11, 1919, the first anniversary of the Armistice, in a logging town called Centralia. His violent death at the hands of a mob was graphically described in John Dos Passos' *Nineteen Nineteen,* published in 1932 by Houghton Mifflin. I could find no record of Everest's having had a daughter.

stank. No zip; no umph. Chromium-steel satire like a
breadknife that grows dull after the first whack. So that's
that. I've got to learn to write about people -- not about
social forces. In a sense that means starting over again.
From being away from them so long, I've lost the sense of
the weight and color of words. The copydesk helps on that,
to a degree. I hope there'll be no more articles.

For the last few weeks I've been writing a story and
sketching a novel. The story is slanted at Ladies Home
Journal -- piffling stuff even if it were good, and it
isn't. It's a practice exercise; the only thing to be said
for it is that I can bring myself to work on it. The novel
may not be the one I'll write; it's also a practice
exercise. But I want to get the feel of this old guy under
my fingers. He's an ex-newspaperman, turned reform
politician, turned chamber of commerce secretary, fat,
fifty, with a family of five unprepossessing kids, a swell
house on a hill that it takes all his salary to keep paying
for. They're moral, old-fashioned people -- say grace every
meal and the oldest son is a preacher who turns Communist,
loses his rural church, comes home to live. But that isn't
the story -- the conflict is, generally, the usual conflict
between the modes of thought of the children -- all
different -- and those of the parents. But it's a novel of
acquiescence, for the most part, rather than revolt.

The family, in the original, belongs to a gal I used
to run around with in college. Their social background was
much like ours, and the old man, twenty years earlier,
actually did almost exactly the same things in politics
that I did. But he acquiesced and I didn't. Thus I avoid
writing an autobiographical novel yet project a locale
which is my own and get rid of some of the venom in my own
system. It will be fun to work at even though it isn't at
all the novel I want to do. But the stuff is under my
fingertips -- I'll have to learn how to select and build.
And how to write again.

I think one reason, Toni darling, that I write you
four-page letters is that I always more or less half
suspect that you just "take a peek" at them and then file
them away for the archives. Thus I am assured a sympathetic
audience without infringing upon anybody's time. But never
mind, when I do die famous I'll will you the job of editing
them with explanatory interpolations. And then you'll have
to read every line.

As ever,

Brick

No, that task went — many years later — to Brick's younger son.

Chapter Fifteen
Extra-Specials

My grandmother Emily — Brick's mother — was one of those round, wrinkled people little kids just think of as *old*. There was a kind of odd smell to her house; I guess now that it was her lavender-scented soap. She still used a real icebox, not a refrigerator. And she once did a strange thing in my presence; she took her teeth out. Never knew that could be done.

She taught Chuck and me rummy (not gin, which I have never been able to understand, but pure rummy), hearts, canasta and a few forms of solitaire. That was in Santa Barbara, where she lived with our aunt Eleanor in a solid Craftsman house in a neighborhood shaded with trees. There were plenty of good holiday meals served there, all prepared by Eleanor, who had married in the 1920s and divorced quickly, the first Garrigues, I suppose, to go through that procedure all the way back to France and beyond. Eleanor, like Grace Lane, had gone to Normal School and become a teacher. Dickie was a frequent guest with her two boys in the comfortable old house.

Grandma Emily took us to Santa Barbara's Oak Park once, and we watched her dance in rounds and squares with other old people. She was good, too; when she insisted that a man step out with her, he never protested. She had her favorites, her boy*friends,* as she said, with the accent on the last syllable. She joked that she was outliving them all.

January 3, 1940

Dear Toni,

I think of my mother, who is well past seventy. She lived a miserably hard life, beginning in a sod house in the early West, twelve miles from the nearest store, raising a family of boys and girls, two of whom died, spending the last ten or twelve years with my father, whose mind was failing from day to day from old age, finally burying him when she herself was past seventy -- and starting out on a little pension of forty-five dollars per month to do all the things she'd wanted to do when she was fifteen. I saw her a few weeks ago -- she's a leader in the Townsend Club,[1] goes to teas, dinners and dances every day in the week, enjoys life with the gusto of a young girl and, so far as one can tell, has stepped untouched out of nearly fifty years of living to pick up her life where it stopped when she was married.

It reminds me of Masters' "Lucinda Matlock."[2] Remember, the one that runs:

> . . . We were married and lived together for seventy
> years
> Enjoying, working, raising the twelve children,
> Eight of whom we lost
> Ere I had reached the age of sixty.

> I spun, I wove, I kept the house, I nursed the sick,
> I made the garden and for holiday
> Rambled over the fields where sang the larks, . . .
> Shouting to the wooded hills, singing to the green
> valleys.

> At ninety-six I had lived enough, that is all,
> And passed to a sweet repose.
> What is this I hear of sorrow and weariness,
> Anger, discontent and drooping hopes?

> Degenerate sons and daughters,
> Life is too strong for you --
> It takes life to love Life.

Does that mean anything? I can't express my vague feeling -- perhaps it's only that Lucinda never had any date with Destiny, but only childbearing and work and wooded hills and valleys. With Life, I mean.

How Mama Got Her Way

After supper they all turned around as usual and got on their knees and stuck their faces in their hands, cupped over their chairs, and Bliss's father said the evening prayers. When he had finished and said "Amen,"

---

1 The clubs were part of a movement founded by Francis Everett Townsend, who proposed regular government pensions for everybody, funded by a national sales tax. It was the first national organization of the elderly, those folks who later became known as senior citizens.

2 From *Spoon River Anthology* by Edgar Lee Masters (1869-1950), published in book form by Macmillan in 1916.

they all started to rise, but stopped when they heard Mama clear her throat as she sometimes did when she had something special to say to God that she wanted all of them to hear.

"Our blessed Heavenly father," she said rapidly as though to get all the words out before anybody dared stand, "we thank Thee especially that Thou has seen fit to guide us and lead us into this new home, and we pray that Thou wilt never send us to new wanderings but will let us serve Thee here until Thou shalt choose to call us to Thee. In His name do we ask it, if it be Thy plan, Amen."

There was a long silence, and Bliss knelt tense beside his chair while he waited for his father to repeat the "Amen" which would end — and signify his approval of — the prayer. And after a while Mama got up, and then Papa and then everybody went about doing whatever he had to do, but Bliss felt funny because he knew that Mama had wanted Papa to say "Amen," and Papa must have known it too, and hadn't done it.

That was the way, Mama said, she so often got what she wanted. She just asked God for it and God gave it to her. Not always, and not often just at first, but almost always — sooner or later. Like coming to California from Kansas.

"I always say that if a man works from daylight until dark to make a living for his family, the least his wife can do is not interfere," she told Aunt Dora once. "Every man wants to feel he is the head of the house and if he provides the living it's a mighty poor sort of woman who'd keep trying to tell him how to manage things. So I just keep my hands off and let him make the decisions."

"But, Ruth," Aunt Dora asked, "How is it you get your own way so many times?" This was on a long, hot summer afternoon in Kansas and Mama was bending over the ironing board and the air was full of the smell of hot beeswax and the sound of locusts singing outdoors, and Bliss never quite forgot either the sound or the smell. Or the words.

"I just pray," she said firmly. "I just get down on my knees and ask the Lord for what I want."

"Silently?" Dora asked, and Bliss looked up and saw she was smiling to herself in a funny sort of way.

"No, siree! Right out before Albert. If the Lord does not see fit to provide the first time I ask, I keep right on asking. And if I don't get it, well, I just don't give the Lord any peace until I do."

And that, Bliss understood, was the way they got to come to California and it was the way — he understood now — they had got to come to live in Greenstone where there were sidewalks and water out of a faucet and where you didn't even have to hitch up the trap to go to the store, but drummers came around every morning and wrote down what you wanted and delivered it in the afternoon.

I'm philosophizing in this way partly because I seem
to know so many girls who are looking for what Marianne
used to call the "extra-special." I think it's something
that affects Jewish girls, particularly. And you find them
here, near the campus, more than you do elsewhere. One of
three things seem to happen to them. They may drift dully
between incipient or actual love affairs -- or marriages --
never quite finding the extra-special. Or they may, a few
of them, marry and succeed in convincing themselves
permanently that their marriage is the extra-special thing.
Or they may actually have the ability to embrace life --
considering the man in the case an unavoidable necessity
for living but in himself neither remarkable nor, as a
specific individual, essential. The first group I feel
sorry for. The second gives me the jitters. For the third I
have an admiration that amounts almost to reverence.

For my own part, I think I've had more than my share
of the "extra-specials." Destiny, as though to give quality
as well as quantity, has, from time to time, added a few
little quirks of a purely individual nature. None of these
quirks seemed more individual to me than the experience of
these last few years with Naomi. She's been a delightful
companion, the only person I've ever known who never seemed
for a fleeting moment to lose her extra-special quality. I
don't mean that every moment was the acme of high romantic
sentiment, but there wasn't a moment that it wasn't more
fun doing something with her than, even, doing it alone.

Yet there was something wrong: Fate — or the struggle for social justice
— had brought together a couple whose backgrounds were, in many respects, completely alien to the other's. Naomi was a strong-willed older
sister, the darling of her father and mother; Brick was a younger brother who
had to vie for attention from his mother and father and, later, from the people
around him. But as a younger child, he had subconsciously learned to give
way: To get along, you go along, as I learned myself. Yet I think he always
resented that lesson, and fought against it.

But she IS a pervasive person. She knows more ways of
getting her own way than any other dozen women in the world.
She never insists, she never argues, weeps, calls you a brute
or does the other usual feminine things. But somehow --
I don't know how -- she manages to succeed in making all
alternatives to her wishes completely impossible. A few
months ago I gradually began to realize that my role had been
completely rewritten for me without my knowledge and that
I was reading lines I had never thought of reading. The life
we had had was vanished somewhere, and I'd become merely a
minor partner in the firm of Silver, Silver, Silver and
Silver. I was trapped in a (presumably) steady job, turning
over my paycheck on paydays, making weekly calls upon the
relatives -- leading a normal, simple, suburban domestic

existence. We had to live in Oakland (with me spending two
hours a day commuting) so she could be near her sister.
Office work was too hard for her[3] and, since it was lots of
fun to do things together, we did the housework together
after I got home. It was, in brief, a much worse existence
than that with Dickie against which I rebelled -- the only
advantages being that she is fun to be with and I get a lot
of enjoyment out of living with her.

Worst of all, she'd been the only woman I'd ever lived
with that I could talk with as I write to you. But it became
impossible for us to talk with one another. Quarrels. Swell
quarrels -- but they didn't end in a pun and a laugh and a
special supper of toast and coffee as they used to.

The situation had fairly started when it was consoli-
dated by the death of her father.[4] More than ever it became
necessary that I become amalgamated with her family. And I
was resenting it more and more. I think that among Jewish
people there is a great tendency for sons-in-law to become
members of the family, whereas among Gentiles the daughter
becomes a member of the husband's family. She's a very
subconscious sort of gal and was resenting very much my
failure to become a good Jewish son-in-law. And I was
suddenly realizing that this was a hell of a lot different
sort of existence than I'd bargained for when she and I went
adventuring and ranching and labor-agitating and whatnot.

Strangely, I realize that she is entirely right from
her point of view, and yet I wouldn't feel any sense of
wrongdoing in making a decision to leave her. I'd be very
reluctant to make it. Before, I always felt that there
might be another woman around the corner just a little more
exciting and possibly even better for me than the one who
was just then giving me up as a bad job. Even when the
split came with Marianne, it was the reluctance to admit
that I hadn't been smacked by Destiny which was probably
the worst thing. But now I just feel: "Well, if I can't get
along with Naomi, I'll never get along with anybody."

In lots of ways that would be good for me. I enjoy my
solitude -- I've never really felt emotionally alone since
the Tucson days. And I'm going to enjoy it these next two
months while she's away at her mother's.[5] The place she
induced me to take is up in the hills, hidden beneath huge
pine trees but with a view across the bay and the Golden
Gate -- a lovely spot where I can be more than contented
for a while. The kids have been up here during Christmas
vacation, but they'll be leaving in a couple of days, and

---

3 Naomi, unlike Dickie, was brought up to believe that a woman's place was in the home, not
sitting behind a typewriter.

4 I never knew Noma's father, Jesse, a portly Russian immigrant in a vested suit, staring
stolidly from a photograph. He had a beautiful voice, she told me, and had been a cantor in a
synagogue. He died of cancer.

5 Naomi's mother, Lottie, was living in Prescott, Arizona, where she owned property.

I'll settle down, I hope, into quiet, solitude and
meditation. It seems years since I've had it.

Now I'm going to make some New Year's wishes for you.

First, that you'll learn what you used to tell me --
that life is meant to be lived, not judged -- that it is good
to be made love to, that love-making itself is good and that
the man (or woman) involved is merely a necessary adjunct to
a highly enjoyable practice -- that Beethoven wrote greater
symphonies than Tschaikowsky, but that when the orchestra
plays Tschaikowsky, you shouldn't stay away from the concert
because you feel that you deserve only the best.

Second, failing the first, that you'll find a guy with
whom you can be as happy as Naomi and I were happy for a
couple of years. "It takes life to love Life."

Toni's next letter continued the conversation about "extra-specials,"
particularly as they relate to love affairs, and Brick replied:

February 3, 1940

We don't actually want these extra-specials for
themselves. They constitute a symbol of the personal
relationship between ourselves and Providence -- God, Fate,
Destiny, the Cosmos -- call it what you will.

We reason like this: "If I am more than a lump of dull,
insensate clay, the gods have some extra-special experience
picked out and reserved for me. If there isn't such an
experience, then it proves I'm just a lump of clay -- a
foundling wandering in the universe -- one of the gods'
stepchildren. But I can't be that -- I mustn't be that -- I
cannot stand the thought of just being ignored by the leshy[6]
-- Where is my extra-special? There he is (or she). No, that
wasn't it. This one must be it. No, wrong again. It'll be
terrible if there isn't any. That must be the one. No? Well."

It isn't that we need go through life without our cake.
In order to validate our special relationship with the Fates,
we insist on having frosting on it. So we lose our cake.

I can't help but remember the letters I wrote you
almost exactly five years ago when I was sure I'd lost not
only all cake but all reason for existence. It had seemed
to me that the Fates had dangled the symbolic brass ring
before my eyes,[7] made my whole justification for existence
dependent upon it, upon its validity -- and then snatched
it away. And yet, now, I realize that the real, actual,
honest-to-goodness extra-special was the one that came a
little later. Extra-special in the sense that the individual involved[8] didn't have to be permanently possessed in

---

6 In Slavic mythology, a forest spirit who enjoys playing tricks on people, though when
angered he can be treacherous. He is seldom seen, but his voice can be heard in the forest laughing, whistling, or singing.

7 Marianne.

8 Louise.

order for the experience to be valid. It is, after all, the experience which is possessed -- not the individual.

That doesn't mean just sleeping with somebody or anybody or some few. It merely means undergoing some experience of which we are able to say: "This is beautiful; I don't deserve this!"

Let me illustrate:

1. The most minor sort of extra-special --

Years ago, before I went to Tucson, I lived with five other newspapermen in Venice, California. The oldest, the most sophisticated, the one we all rather looked up to had a little gal friend who was unquestionably the loveliest little thing that any of us had seen at the time. You can imagine the sort of cheap little trollop that a bunch of twenty-year-old would-be sophisticates in the middle of the Jazz Age, in the Coney Island of the West, would admire.

Well, Mary and Verne split up. Mary went more or less from bad to worse, lost her looks and her freshness (she was sixteen at the time). During the months or years I suppose that each of the six (excluding myself) had had an affair with her -- more or less by turn. But she and I became excellent friends. I suppose in a way I never ceased to admire her because she'd been Verne's girl. And I helped her out of various scrapes, and she used to come and sit on my lap and weep a bit when things weren't going so well. Then she married, and I didn't see her for years.

During the interlude of bachelorhood, I ran into her one night on the street, bought her a drink, discussed old times and put her on a streetcar. The next morning, very early, the phone rang, and Mary said: "What are you doing?" I said: "Nothing." She said: "I'll be right over." In an hour or so she knocked at the door of the apartment. I opened the door. She looked at the pulldown bed, said: "Pull it down" and proceeded to undress. Afterwards she said: "There! I've been wanting to do that for fifteen years," put on her clothes and went out.

I recall this (physically minor) incident as a real "extra-special," not because it was an "affair," but because it was an experience and, furthermore, because it was an experience that by all the laws of normally asymmetrical life I didn't deserve to have.

2. A less minor sort of extra-special.

When I was married to Dickie, I knew another girl (about eighteen) of whom we both became very fond. Janet, this girl, had the unusual ability of having men be just forty-nine percent in love with her and still actually keeping the friendship of their wives. I was forty-nine percent.

She also was a sort of street gamin -- a very lovely elvan one. Her people were very poor. She was worried --

thought she'd probably become a regular little bum if she didn't get straightened out. She wanted to be a grande dame. I introduced her to a fellow on the paper who happened to be a very good friend of mine -- and we were rivals for a promotion which would have meant Success (with a CAPITAL) to the one that got it. He got it. And he also got the little gamin. (Remember that I was forty-nine percent.)

He had the not uncommon masculine desire to take a pretty, intelligent young girl and make out of her exactly the sort of wife he wanted to have. And the sort of wife he wanted was exactly the sort of woman she wanted to be. He set her up in an apartment where (I more than half suspect) she slept alone. He sent her to a finishing school to acquire polish and (one might almost say) learn to read and write. Eventually, when she was sufficiently polished, he married her.

In the meantime, I'd had to step in several times and help her save the situation. He was certain that I was much more than forty-nine percent and had forbidden her to see Dickie or me. She disobeyed, and I had a hell of a time to straighten things out for her. Before he consented to marry her, he was extremely cautious and inquisitive about her technical (and long since forgotten) virginity. She had to slip away and find out whether the thing she was going to tell him was the right thing to tell him (because, despite her ability to handle a situation, she possessed a curious schoolgirl lack of faith in herself).

But finally he consented to marry her. He prospered. They have a fine home, a fine income. I saw them last summer; we became quite close friends again, and I must say that of all the people I've ever known, she is the most complete, utter, absolute success. Janet is exactly the sort of person she has always wanted to be, living exactly the sort of life, presiding at precisely the same sort of intellectual soirees; she is lovely to look at, lovely to talk with, lovely to watch as she keeps a party going.

Of course, it doesn't matter a damn that she's actually a silly, vapid little fool or that the life she leads is precisely the sort of life that would drive an intelligent person nuts.

The point is, I think, that I've had a hand in creating one of the few perfect things I've ever seen. For she is perfect -- of her kind. But the situation is not static. Past thirty now, she is beginning to realize that she and her life are vapid. She's beginning to reach back to the gamin days. I'm the only person who remembers when she used to burn the furniture in order to have a fire to pop corn in the fireplace. And she's trying to find something -- way back there -- to tie to, a signpost or landmark to give validity to her success. I more than half suspect that within the next few months I'm going to have the responsibility of saving, destroying or transforming that really perfect thing that she's spent years in creating.

Why is that an extra-special? Because it's the sort of thing that doesn't happen in a chaotic universe. Men's lives are not normally molded into the first, second and third acts of a play.

3. I'm sure I must have told you of Louise and the experience of knowing her and of being romantically in love with her (and her with me) more than fifteen years after I'd been in love with her as a youngster. That's much more usual; I'm sure that life plagiarizes not only art but also the very cheapest sort of fiction. Yet it's the sort of thing that one doesn't deserve to have happen to one.

To me, these are the extra-special things -- rather than the mere experience of having been in love with one or another woman. As the Chinaman says in the advertisements, upon refusing to go see a horse race: "It has long been established that one horse can run faster than another." It has long been established that men and women can live together. We want the extra-special things as a symbol, rather than for themselves.

You'll note a couple of things about my little incidents: first, that they possess a certain "literary quality" (ranging from the milieu of True Stories to that of Ladies Home Journal), and, second, that each symbolizes the carrying-over and fulfillment of an unfulfilled youthful wish.

When the Marianne affair ended, I was completely and utterly indifferent as to whether I pleased another girl or not, because there was no girl anywhere that I found even remotely pleasing. And then I re-met Louise -- all the barriers which had been between us when we were kids collapsed and (without really losing the sense of the importance of Marianne) life began again.

I think I know a little about the business of being in love. But I know very little about matrimony. And I don't know yet how my own affair is going to turn out. But I think it will be favorably. It would take such a small adjustment to move into precisely the only sort of married life that would be possible for me. But it's an adjustment that I can't make; if it's done, Naomi'll have to do it.

This last year has been for me a rather difficult one. For six years I've been intensely active in public affairs. There were union meetings, political meetings, radio programs, newspapers taking up my whole time and more daily energy than I now put out in a week. I won't say I became disillusioned but, at any rate, I became tired. When I started, it was going to be easy for me to earn a nice living and still do the things I was interested in. I found, however, that in the labor movement and in politics -- labor, liberal or reform -- you had to think constantly of your own advantage if you were going to keep your nose above water. And that was what I refused to do.

Ultimately I had to give in and start earning a living. Naturally, I found that it didn't help to find a job (when there were no jobs) to have a reputation as a labor agitator. I found, in brief, that when I'd finally decided to sell my soul, I was going to have a hell of a time in peddling it. And finally selling it has brought me back into about the same general relationship toward life that I had in 1927. Except that I no longer believe that my special form of prostitution, newspaper work, is particularly sacred.

But I had to make almost as drastic an adjustment in 1939 as I had made (in the other direction) between 1933 and 1938. And it was all very confusing. After I'd quit going to meetings in order that I might work on that novel, I found that the novel didn't exist. I tried various tacks, and nothing worked out, because what I was trying to write kept sliding back and forth between the viewpoint I was getting away from and the one I was just getting into.

February 21, 1940

Dear Dickie:

Saw Steve and Janet O'Cochran a couple of times recently. Steve is smug, fat and prosperous, and Janet is just beginning to turn middle-aged. It seems funny because when she's in a crowd she still clowns very much as she used to, but when she stops clowning she shows her age a bit.

Kiss the brats for me, and assign Charles to plant a chaste and ex-husbandly kiss upon your cheek for me, will you? I don't know whether I ever remarked upon the fact or not, but you're unquestionably a very swell person.

March 24, 1940

Toni, my dear

Speaking of extra-specials, remember Janet, the gal I wrote you about who was going to come up here and ask my advice on what to do with the husband I'd helped marry her to? Well, she's here as our house guest. It's rather amusing because my impulse a few years ago would have been to play Iago and assist the fates in wrecking things. But instead, because she'd obviously made a serious mistake in giving up the good meal ticket, I've been trying my best to patch up things between her and her husband. And -- she's determined to get herself a divorce and, perhaps, acquire herself another chap who already has a wife and child and who's really a swell guy but who won't be nearly as good to, or for, her as her present husband. It's all what you might call rather messy, in a way, but I find myself with a ringside seat which is more enjoyable through sheer inability to interfere with the plot at all.

That's the chief thing I do these days -- sit back and watch things go to hell. And it's not the most unpleasant way to live, even though I haven't learned entirely how to do it yet. There's only one thing I fret about: the necessity of accepting, completely and in full, Naomi's precise prescription for living. I'm constantly amazed at myself because I've always insisted upon having my own way. Now I'm compelled to realize that I haven't won an argument in three years and that I will probably never win one again. At the moment it isn't unpleasant (here, too, I have a ringside seat at an interesting show), but sometimes I wake up in the middle of the night boiling with helpless rage. And ultimately, I think, I shall just have to pack a toothbrush and go away permanently and silently.

Naomi is really a lovely person to live with. And I know damn well she'll be very unhappy when I finally walk out. But there's no way in the world I can make her see that she's just writing herself a prescription for divorce by her refusal to adjust in any degree to the situation arising when two people live together. For example, when we were first together, it was very easy for me to work with her in the room. Then she got the habit of interrupting with some inane remark at ten-minute intervals so that I'd just get thoroughly back into what I was doing when I'd be interrupted again. I remonstrated with her. I explained that if she persisted she'd soon develop in me an inability to work at all when she was around. I explained that I was already beginning to work with only half a mind while the other was lifted up defensively against interruptions. And she took it all very seriously to heart -- and ten minutes later would brightly raise her head and say: "Isn't it terrible what they're doing in Spain?"

As a result, it's very difficult to work at all when she's in the house. I know that in ten minutes or so she'll slip quietly into the room and start dusting the furniture or plop herself down on my lap and suggest we go for a walk or do something else equally silly. It isn't that she's indifferent; she's merely drifting through her own lovely dreams, timeless and spaceless, until they call for my participation. And then, of course, I must participate.

May 2, 1940

In Los Angeles, you know, spring plays around with some April showers, and then, in May, goes behind a blanket of high fog. You never see the sun until the end of May -- and then it's summer. But here in Oakland it's marvelous. Our little place is on a wooded hillside with huge pines around us and with big eucalyptus reaching up from the canyon below so that we look into their tops. The hill below us is covered with natural undergrowth, and our own yard is filled with mountain shrubs of a dozen kinds with shining leaves on which the sun dances as it shines down between the pines. There are masses of yellow broom and shaded corners filled with azaleas and rhododendrons. The house is a rustic redwood, and there's a sundeck where, at eleven o'clock each morning, the sun and we go out together, all three of us unclad, and stay until one, when the sun goes behind a pine tree and the other two of us go into the house.

In a way it's better than if one were only twenty-one or so because when you're twenty-one you feel that you must DO something about it, but when you're damn near forty, the verb "be" seems to have infinitely more validity than the verb "do."

One of my few real regrets has been the fact that I could never sing nor play anything more complicated than the radio. But I do find again (after being largely immune to it for several years) that listening to music, even on the radio, becomes a rare treat. I ration it out to myself in small doses since there are two or three stations playing excellent records practically all the time. I loathe crowds, concert crowds, and so we never go (Monteux and the S.F. Symphony are pretty bad),[9] but the radio does well enough.

Meanwhile, in Inglewood, I was beginning to learn about the world. Six days a week, rain or shine, a boy on a bike would throw the *Inglewood Daily News* with a thump onto our front porch. On weekdays I would come home from Russell Gray's house about five o'clock, bring the paper in, lie on the floor with my rump stuck in the air and read the entire paper — from back to front, because the funnies were on the inside back page, and I wanted to start with them. The *Inglewood Daily News* told me about the invasion of Poland and the start of World War II.

I shouldn't worry too much about the war -- it begins to seem quite likely that the human race will finally succeed in committing suicide. Sometimes one is inclined to accuse Jehovah of vacillation in having tipped off his hand to Noah in time to permit the construction of the Ark. I'm sure that the world will be no less beautiful in a hundred years if the human race, by that time, has been suffi- ciently stupid to have completed its own destruction, and it shouldn't matter too much to us that we, as humans, will not be able to enjoy it.

There's going to be an almost incalculable amount of suffering and hunger and bloodshed in the next couple of dozen years -- but when since the cornerstone of the first Pyramid was laid has there not been an incalculable amount of suffering and hunger and bloodshed? And I think it not impossible that out of it may come a more rational,

---

9 The Paris-born Pierre Monteux took over the newly reorganized San Francisco Symphony in 1936 and was music director until 1952; he was widely praised for his elegant and refined interpretations. He died in 1964 at age 89.

pleasanter world in which some of the things we have
imagined to exist will actually come to pass. That, of
course, is mere wishful thinking since there's no real
evidence that the very evident desire of the great majority
of humanity for peace, justice and the end of human
exploitation can be transformed into effective and
intelligent action.

Yet the mere fact that desire does exist, plus the
fact that the Chamberlains and the Hitlers and the Dala-
diers[10] seem to be doing a thorough job of hanging
themselves on their own gallows, indicates a remote
possibility that we are headed toward better things.

Meanwhile, the novel progresses. I don't know how
well. I've accomplished a solution to the difficulty of
working around Naomi. It happened one Sunday: Naomi was
chattering, the radio downstairs was shouting the baseball
scores, the man-of-all-work was hammering in the yard, and
I was huddled in a corner trying to write. So I said: To
hell with it. And I dragged my tablet out into the front
room, parked across from Naomi, turned on our own radio and
went to work behind the complete barrier of noise. It went
swell; since then I've not been disturbed and I've even
begun to write directly to the typewriter.

Just after school I liked to read the front page of the newspapers
displayed on the rack at the corner drug store (the pharmacist was the
same man who made the cherry phosphates behind the soda fountain).
One June afternoon as I looked at the headlines of the *Los Angeles Daily
News* I was struck by the imagery of Italy stabbing France "in the back."
It sounded gory and awful.

In the next few days France collapsed; the British evacuated three
hundred forty thousand men and a few women from Dunkirk. The Germans entered Paris on June 14, and Marshal Pétain, the new head of the
French government, concluded an armistice with Hitler. Stalin attacked
Finland. American Communists left the party in droves, and those who
stayed had to rationalize the war as a battle between two sets of imperial-
ists. Brick had already quit the Communist Party, though he kept up his
membership in the International Workers' Order — said by some to be
linked to the party — at least during the first few months of 1940. His
reaction to the war mirrored the anti-British and anti-French feelings of
his former labor comrades, although he was disheartened by the possibility of a Nazi victory.

June 28, 1940

I'm not as remote from the war as I might have
sounded. As a matter of fact, about four times a day during

---

10 Edouard Daladier had resigned as French premier on March 21; the hapless Neville
Chamberlain hung on as prime minister of Britain until May 10.

the four hours I'm home I wander over and turn on the
radio. Then we sit in silence for a while and talk a little
about it. Then we sit rather restlessly and wait for the
next news broadcast. Most of it is almost unconscious -- or
anyway, unspoken -- but I find that we no longer listen to
concerts on the radio. Turning a dial has come to be too
closely associated with horrible things. Nor have I been
able to do much writing lately. The novel seems so trivial
and unimportant; I can't concentrate on it.

The only thing is that I've discounted a good bit of
it in advance. That is, from the time of the invasion of
Spain in 1937, I've realized that this phase was inevitable. I went through most of my emotional reaction at that
time; it wasn't only the bombing of Madrid and Barcelona
but the necessity to accept (far in advance of the
actuality) the fact that Britain and France would sell out
Spain and that then France would be overrun or Nazified.
Now that it's actually come about, the edge is taken off of
it. But in some ways, it's worse. You can't do anything
about it, like you could if you could hold the illusion
that a British victory would end it. You just have to sit
and wait for the next radio broadcast.

But aside from the purely emotional reaction, I think
it should help intelligent people if they can realize that
it's an inevitable crisis and that the prognosis (despite
the apparent condition of the patient) is generally
favorable. I think we must accept one fact; that the world
we've known is ended -- all smashed to hell like Humpty
Dumpty. Regardless of the outcome of the current phase of
the war, neither America nor Britain can compete with
totalitarianism, militarily or economically. We don't like
it but we have to accept it.

But then, the world as we've known it was only a
pleasant myth anyway. We had the right to freedom of
speech, freedom of culture, only so long as our opinions
and our tastes were unimportant. The right of the American
people to choose their own rulers was a right which existed
only so long as they chose rulers who would rule as the
economically powerful classes desired. (That isn't a
quotation but the result of experience.)

And so, in the United States, we permitted ourselves
the luxury of choosing between Tweedledum and Tweedledee
only so long as they remained Tweedledum and Tweedledee.
But very shortly that right is going to be abolished -- not
because our real rulers are "bad" but because our old-
fashioned, pseudo-democratic capitalism can no longer
compete with Hitler's streamlined super-capitalism.

And capitalism is already destroying itself. The
process will go on. That doesn't mean that we will be
magically transported into a Utopia -- nor that the
resultant civilization will be one which you or I, liberals

and intellectuals, will find ideal. I think I would much
rather live under a benevolent plutocracy than under the
rule of the proletariat. Many, if not most, of the things
which we consider finest will be lost -- at least temporarily. But so will the really evil things: race hatred,
mass misery, mass insecurity, etc. Certainly, for most of
us, the change will be worthwhile.

But for all of that, I still can't get away from the
war, except for my best days -- those two days each week
spent on my favorite mountain, Mount Diablo, about twenty
miles east of Oakland.

It's impossible to convey the feeling one gets from such
a perch in the sky. Early Tuesday mornings, without listening
to the radio, we drive to the place we camp -- under a huge
live oak with branches spreading a hundred feet or more. A
few feet away, the hillside drops almost straight down for
nearly 3,000 feet; it isn't a precipice, but a soft hillside
on which are fields of wild grass (gray and yellow, now) and
little oak or pine groves, but which is so steep that you
feel you'd slide all the way to the bottom if you slid down.
Some thirty miles away are the lights of San Francisco;
beneath you are big valleys, miles and miles of farms, three
or four towns, the mouth of the broad Sacramento River; you
can see a hundred miles to the north and to the south. Yet
there is no identifiable sign of human life except an
occasional airliner beneath you and, at night, a faint string
of moving lights on a highway.

We stay there until Thursday morning. Sometimes a deer
will wander by the camp; hawks come over and try to catch
the squirrels which live on the hillside above us; blue
jays scream in the juniper bushes nearby, little flocks of
tiny, noisy birds come by on regular foraging expeditions,
searching the oak bark for bugs; winds come up and die
down. And we sit. The world is below us, yet we cannot
identify it; we're out of it; it might go on and on and
leave us there. Yet it's before our eyes all the time. And
then on Thursday we come back, listen to the radio, the war
starts again, everything is as it was before.

It's my temporary method of escape -- mountains, too,
are the opiate of the people. It's been difficult for me to
learn to become an ivory towerist after those years of
activity. Sometimes I think I will rush back into the thick
of things; life seems terribly dull as I'm living it now.

122 Alpine Terrace
September 27, 1940

The big excitement in our lives has been the vacation.
I think it was the first real vacation I ever spent; I can
recall others vaguely, but I don't believe I've ever got
the feeling of re-creation that I did this time. We went
out into the Sierra (not very high because it was late in

the season), got stuck on innumerable hills, carried
hundreds of pounds of camping equipment up steep trails
that the car wouldn't make loaded, found ideal camping
spots, swam in deep mountain pools miles from the nearest
human and finally finished up with four restful days in
Hollywood.

I came back to San Francisco, and Naomi continued her
vacation in Prescott while I looked for a flat. When I was
finally in despair, I discovered this place -- the lower
part of an old house, really a charming old place,
completely modernized as to floors, etc. And all for $27.50
a month. Five big rooms. Ten minutes from the office. So
I'm really feeling quite exuberant. And now I'm sitting on
our only chair in a five-room flat furnished only with a
camp bed and electric plate.

I hope I can hold this feeling of relaxation for a
while. I don't even worry about the war any more (for ten
days we never saw a newspaper or heard a radio). I do as
little work at the office as I can get by with and worry
about it as little as possible. And this last two weeks
here alone has been good, too; it's given me a little time
to collect my thoughts, etc.

Sometimes I kick myself because just when I was
getting a start as a political reporter and so forth, I
seemed to dump it all over, and anything I attempted to do
in that direction afterward was merely beating a dead
horse. It seemed that I should have gone forward instead of
back.

So I'm engaged in dissecting the novel I was working
on early in the summer and preparing to junk most of the
slants I had. Maybe it's just that I'm tired of social
content, but I think we go into those things backward. You
begin with a Depression novel such as I started and you end
up with a lot of fictionalized statistics which prove to
the author (and nobody else) that there was a Depression
and that life under capitalism is a vain and fruitless
business even to the members of the middle class.

In a recent letter, Toni had written of the death of her father.

October 28, 1940

There's no experience, Toni, which can be quite the
same as the loss of one's father or mother. My own father's
death came after several years of illness, and we all
welcomed it as a release for him; all of us were honestly
and frankly glad that it had come, for his sake. But it
took something out of me; it represented a loss which was
more than a personal loss, more than the loss of a
personality. We lose, also, to a degree, our childhood, our
youth; we become another person and have a different
relationship to the world. I've never been quite the same,

never had precisely the same incentive to live and do things. I think it's that way with most people, yet we must learn to accept it -- even when it happens to us. There's nothing anybody can say which will help; there's no anodyne. We must just learn to accept.

For most of us, there is a sense of personal continuity ("How late it is! You stop in for a couple of beers, and the first thing you know you're forty!") which keeps things going. The death of my own father broke it for me; I've been literally a different person since. [11] And the same has been true of Naomi.

I don't want to enlarge upon it. But I think one turns then somewhat from the task of trying to live happily, intensely, and begins to try to grow old -- gracefully and perhaps fruitfully.

I know that I'm intensely dissatisfied with the way I've been living since I've been on the Examiner (I'm still reading copy and swinging in as makeup editor two days a week -- a routine job lacking in pleasure or satisfaction), [12] and like the traditional old war horse, I sometimes dream of the bugle calling to battle -- the thrill of excitement at doing things, addressing meetings, feeling important.

Living in San Francisco helps. It's a most remarkable city. Of course, there's the tourist aspect -- the beauty, the sense of comparative antiquity, the huge bronze statues stuck around on the main streets, the hills and big green parks and, above all, the civic inferiority complex which keeps San Franciscans insisting that their city is the cultural capital of America because Tetrazzini sang in front of the Lotta Crabtree fountain in 1902 [13] and the gastronomic center of America because in 1880 it was the only town west of Kansas City where you could get a decent steak. But that's all false front.

He worked in the twelve-story Hearst Building at Third and Market streets, with its white terra cotta face and polychrome ornamentation and its marble staircase with gilded railings. The *Examiner* was the first in the chain of dailies owned by William Randolph Hearst, whose papers under his irascible command were in the forefront of mean-spirited red-baiting and anti-communist witch-hunting, not to mention incendiary picture pages against vivisection. It is no wonder that Brick did not like his

---

11 It was around this time that Brick left the labor movement and the Communist Party.

12 The makeup man — or makeup editor — was the interface between the editorial department and the print shop. In his white shirt and tie, he stood by the blue-collared printer and watched as the latter placed the type and metal engravings in the forms. It was the makeup man's task to indicate where stories could be trimmed and to find small items to fill the holes at the bottoms of the columns.

13 This Market Street landmark was donated to the city by an enormously popular actress, Lotta Crabtree (1847-1924), who became one of the city's wealthiest women. The Italian Luisa Tetrazzini (1871-1940) was seen as one of the finest coloratura sopranos of her time.

job, though he did have a beautiful building to work in. It was in the heart of town, across from the cast-iron shaft of Lotta's Fountain and the colorful blossoms of an outdoor flower stand and a block from the magnificent Beaux Arts structure of the Palace Hotel. The sidewalks hummed with pedestrians. The Greyhound depot was two blocks away and the Southern Pacific station was a short bus ride down Third Street. The streets were just beginning to fill up with sailors in blue or white and soldiers in khaki.

The real thing about San Francisco is something different. In Los Angeles, you feel expansive, out-of-doorsish, socialistic. The stars belong to everyone; so do the beaches, the mountains, the highways. You have no boundaries; you're in a state of flux, and you flow all over the landscape. You crowd other people and they crowd you. Your lives merge with theirs.

But in San Francisco you live in a little set of cubicles, set within larger cubicles. Your house or apartment constitutes the boundaries of your life and, if you overflow, you flow into the district: Mission, Richmond, Sunset, Rincon, etc., in which you were probably born and will spend your life. The final cubicle is the city itself.

It's a shock to get adjusted to such an environment after living so long in Los Angeles. But it's good for writing; you become an individual, you take refuge within your ivory tower and observe -- or imagine.

January 11, 1941

You'll be interested to know that I ran into my old galfriend, Marianne, the other night. It was the first time I'd seen her since those dim months in my distant youth when the world was falling down about my ears (although we'd sent each other courtesy messages through mutual friends). Anyway, I was standing in front of the office during dinner hour when here she comes with her new husband, lugging a couple of suitcases from the bus depot en route from L.A. to Seattle. It was quite a pleasant shock; we stopped and talked for a few minutes about this and that; it's funny, but I've always known I'd run into her on a San Francisco street some day. She's a very lovely person; I'm glad to have know her.

And today, as though by pre-arrangement, spring arrived. (Really, I mean.) It will be gone tomorrow, but today it was spring -- lovely, misty, sunny spring, warm and delicious and scented as the remembrance of the days of one's youth. I'm glad to have known that too.

As ever,

Brick

Chapter Sixteen
The Kids

You know, George, most of the psychological talk is about early experiences (one-to-six, and all that), but I would propose that now it's time to take a look at what happens between ten and thirteen. I'm sure your experience was different than mine, but, well, anyway, I think that all and all I was luckier than most with my early experiences. I mean, I really dug the Old Man, felt secure and all that — really worshipped him. I guess you didn't have it so good.
— *From a letter by Chuck, 1962*

It was Christmas season in 1939 when Chuck and I made the first of many trips from Los Angeles to the Bay Area to visit "Dad and Noma." Dickie would give Chuck an enormous sum of money, maybe fifteen dollars, drive us downtown to the teeming, Spanish-modern Union Station, kiss us goodbye and put us on the Southern Pacific train for the trip through Santa Barbara, San Luis Obispo, Salinas and on to Oakland. Chuck would spend some of the money on lunch for us in the dining car or on buying a box of fruity candies called Aplets and Cotlets.

At the end of the trip Dad would be waiting at the station with Noma, and we would jump into his arms and just about ignore her. The shoulder of my father's tweed jacket was rough against my cheek, and it smelled of pipe tobacco or cigarettes, but his arms seemed strong, though he would say things like, "Ooof!" and "What a couple of elephants!" Then a little later Chuck would divide between us what was left of the money, and we had a lot to spend, for a while.

Brick and Naomi lived on Merriewood Drive in the Oakland Hills.

Chuck was nine in 1939, and I was seven. In the winter it rained a lot, but we played outside under the trees as often as we could; we knew about war because of the kids' shows on the radio and our comic books and movies like *Wings,* so we pulled on our fake aviator's headgear with the flaps that covered our ears and snapped shut under the chin, and with our arms outstretched, we were airplanes in battle. Up the road lived Noma's younger sister, just a wisp of a woman named Corinne Sussman, with her husband, Irving, and when Noma was not around and Brick was at work, Corinne would sometimes watch over Chuck and me.

We made that trip at least once, maybe twice, a year, for many years. Sometimes we took the Greyhound bus or Santa Fe's Burlington Trailways. Once in a while, Brick would show up at our little home in Inglewood, and he liked to take us for car rides or go out to Venice and walk up and down the pier. Once he sang a little ditty:

> *It ain't gonna rain no mo', no mo' —*
> *It ain't gonna rain no mo'!*
> *Now, how in the hell*
> *Can Roosevelt tell*
> *It ain't gonna rain no mo' ?*

When he was away from us, though, there were the letters. Chuck and I would talk out our letters and Dickie would sit at a manual typewriter and transcribe the words almost as fast as we could speak them. Brick's letters to Chuck (to whom Dad was to give the nickname of Slats) were on a much more adult plane than his to me. And vice versa. Chuck was a brilliant boy, the first born, the apple of his father's eye.

The country was at peace but war was in the air. Boys played with guns and metal toy tanks. In the fall, Chuck was playing soldier with an army of boys in the city park just a block from our home, and Brick wrote him his objections in a five-page, single-spaced letter, of which this is only a part, explaining just what war *was* anyway.

                              Apartment 12
                              1530 Leavenworth Street
                              [November 1939]

Dear Charles,

    Since you're so busy being a soldier, I suppose you
need some equipment or something. I don't know exactly what
branch of the service you belong to, but I'm sending Mother
an extra dollar -- one for you and one for Louis -- and if
you want to spend it for a tin helmet or a copy of infantry
drill regulations or something else you need as a soldier,
it'll be OK. The same with Louis. Maybe if you can get a
canteen to carry water in, that would be good equipment.

    However, before you do, I think you and I ought to go

into this war question and see exactly what it's all about.
There are two kinds of people in the world, you know --
those who get their heads blown off to make somebody else
rich and those who get rich by having other people get
their heads blown off by beating drums, waving flags and so
forth.

Brick explained the history of World War I.

All in all, ten million people were killed in the war.
And none of them had anything, really, against any of the
others -- nor did any of them get anything out of it except
the merchants and the bankers who stayed at home.

If you went out to rob a bank for a guy, you'd expect
him to give you part of the loot, wouldn't you? In fact, if
you did all the work and took all the risks, you'd have a
right to expect all the loot. But these soldiers who went
over to rob the German banks and stores and farms and
factories didn't get any of the loot for themselves. The
bankers and merchants and factory owners took it all.

That's what war is all about. So while you're being a
soldier, be sure you're not being just a sucker.

Got it? It's something like having an earache. There's
nothing grand and glorious about it -- it's just too darned
bad if you have it, but if you do have it, you've got to
have it lanced. Being a soldier is a necessary evil like
being a garbage collector or sewer cleaner, only it's such
a dirty job that they have to dress you up in fancy
uniforms and medals and surround you with fancy words and
flags and everything in order to get you to do it.

Don't get the idea, either, that there is any one
country that is a very fine country and another country
that is a very bad country that ought to be destroyed. The
Germans are a good people and so are the Poles and the
Russians and the Italians and the French and the Americans
and the Mexicans. And the English. But the common people in
each of these countries are prevented from finding out that
they haven't any quarrels with the common people of every
other country and are persuaded to do foolish things.

We feel that England is doing a fine thing in fighting
for Poland. But England has been the worst of all the
countries in robbing other countries. For years she kept an
army in India which is (and always has been) engaged in
nothing except systematically robbing the Indian people of
their money and jewels and even food and cotton for the
benefit of the few rich companies which own England. We all
felt sorry for Belgium during the last war, but Belgium has
been one of the worst countries; it has hundreds of
thousands of negro slaves in Africa working night and day
in the sun to enrich the few owners of Belgium.

It won't be very long now until you'll be a Boy Scout.

The Scouts are very fine, and you'll have a lot of fun and learn a lot of things. But the Scouts have frequently been used to train youngsters to act without thinking so that when they grow up they can be persuaded to go over and shoot some other ex-Boy Scout from some other country in order to enrich the wealthy people who put up the money to keep the Boy Scouts going. So when you do become a Scout, I hope you remember to take the good things and just grin at the bad things they may try to teach you.

All of this is summed up in the word "patriotism." It should be a very good emotion but it is frequently a very bad one. It should mean: "We have a very fine country and a very fine flag, but unfortunately our country has done and is still doing dishonorable things. That's because my dad and the dads of my friends and the other ordinary people in our country aren't smart enough to make the flag represent what they think but let it represent the selfish acts of a few rich and powerful people.

When I pledge allegiance to my flag, I mean that I'll try to make it represent the best that is in America, instead of the worst. That means not robbing other people in other countries and not using the flag to permit the robbing of Americans at home." That's what patriotism should mean and, if it does mean that to you, you'll be a very fine American and, if necessary, a very fine soldier.

Do you get it? I think you do because you're quicker to see things like that than most grownups. If you do get it, tell Mother what you want to buy with that dollar in the way of military equipment, and I'm sure she'll buy it for you. Because the only string on this particular present is the fact that you should understand what it's all about before you buy it.

[From Chuck, handwritten;
late 1939]

Dear Dad,

After I got your letter I sez to myself, "I think I will quit the army," so I tells that to the General, and he sez "an army without you would be no good" so we starts a newspaper. Thanks for the buck. We are going to use it to buy a printing press ($1.50). We are having a lot of fun.

We have a job printer who is going to print us some letterheads. Of course, I know what letterheads are, but the other kids don't.

[Early 1940]

Dear Charles,

Sometimes I think you are a very intelligent guy.

I think the newspaper will be a lot of fun -- and I guess I ought to know. On a big newspaper, you know, they

have it organized very much like an army. There's the
Publisher in place of the General; he usually owns the
paper and draws the big pay but doesn't do any work except
go to luncheons and tell people how important he is.

By the way, what sort of guy are you, anyway, who is so
important that they can't have an army without you? Of
course, I've always said that if the soldiers would just say
to the General, "We're going to resign; we don't have anything against those guys," there wouldn't be any war. That's
what the Russians did after the last world war. They finally
figured it out that they were just fighting for somebody
else's profits, so they went to the Generals and the big-shot
politicians and said, "We're not going to fight any more."

The big shots looked around and saw that there were
several millions of soldiers and only a few thousand big
shots, and they all started running. Some of them haven't
stopped yet, but others went over to England and got a lot
of money and came back and hired a lot of other soldiers
and made war on the Russians, who didn't want to fight. But
the Russians found out there was a difference between
fighting for somebody else's profits and fighting for their
own land (which by this time they had taken when the big
shots ran away). They didn't have any cannon nor any tanks
and not many rifles, practically no food nor clothing but
they fought the ex-big-shots off and established their own
country with no millionaires. That's what I mean about it
being necessary, sometimes, to have an army.

In one of my letters, I had pulled a seven-year-old's joke on my father,
just to see what his reaction would be. I wrote "P.S." at the bottom of the last
page, but didn't put anything after it. He jumped to the bait.

[Early 1940]

Dear Louis, my boy,

I suppose that "P.S." on your letter was put there so
I could fill in whatever I wanted to. Anyway, I didn't see
any writing under it. It's like the Chinese plays; instead
of having scenery, they just move chairs around the stage
with signs on them: "This is a mountain" or "This is a
river." They say: "Well, if we painted a picture of a
mountain, it might not be as good a mountain as you can
imagine, so you imagine your own mountain and that way
everybody will be happy." Is that what I'm supposed to do
with your letters?

This year nine-year-old Chuck discovered science fiction of the Buck
Rogers–*Amazing Stories* variety. He wrote Brick about an idea he had
for a heat ray to be used in warfare, which he called an E ray, very much
like the laser finally developed in 1960. Perhaps he got the idea from
frying ants with a magnifying glass.

5763 Merriewood Drive
Oakland
[Early 1940]

Dear Charles:

First of all, will you give Mother this check because
if you don't you may not have anything to eat on the rest
of the week. And don't try to blackmail her out of any of
it, either, or I'll come down there and larrup you.

I've been trying to figure out your heat ray proposition, and I don't know for sure what you're going to do
with it when you get it. I hope you're not going to ride it
out to the stars, are you? I'll admit you've got something
there, but I don't know just what.

What you say about the magnifying glass is correct.
The glass simply bends the sun's rays so that they all come
together in a point, and, naturally, that point, "C,"
(called the focus, where they come together) gets all the
heat which would normally be spread over a much larger
area. (See Figure 1) But you'll notice that when they pass
that point they keep right on going and separate again so
that when you get out to "D" you haven't got any more heat
than you had at "B." Now it ought to be possible to put
another glass at "C," which would make them bend out
straight (see Figure 2). Then "E" would be your heat ray.

But I think there are two difficulties. First, your
glass would absorb a large part of the heat. Then, too, it
seems impossible to send a ray of light in a perfect beam.

Well, that's about all for tonight. Give my love to
Mom and Louis. And a kick in the pants to yourself.

[From Chuck, dictated]
April 3, 1940

Dear Dad,

April Fool's Day me and Johnny were in my room waiting
for Brandstetter (that's Charles Brandstetter) when he
comes rushing up to the house and after he is inside he
says, "It's in all the newspapers, haven't you heard?" And
I says, "Heard what?" He replies: "It's about the end of
the world," and I says to him, "Say, are you trying to
April Fool's me?" and he says, "No, honest, it's in all the
newspapers. My dad told me." And then Johnny pipes up, "Why
don't we go down to the drugstore and find out?" And I
says, "Sure, let's go," and Brandstetter says, "Come on";
so we goes to the drugstore, and sure enough there it was.

It said as follows "PHILADELPHIA SCARE END OF THE
WORLD" and then it goes on to say something about a
Martian invasion and that the information bureau in
Philadelphia had nearly 4,000 calls, and I reads on until
I gets down to the bottom, and then drat the luck it was

continued on Page 6, and the drugstore man wouldn't let
me open up the newspaper.[1]

After that happened, Brandstetter started to get
interested in astronomy and the Buck Rogers Club is
beginning to come up better. They elected me Boss as usual,
partly because I was in the Buck Rogers Club anyway, and
partly because I was the Boss anyway. Now, I'll bet you are
saying right now, "Weren't the other guys in the Buck
Rogers Club, too?" Well, they were after I dubbed 'em in.
This is how I went about it: First, it was Brandstetter
that asked me. He says, "Couldn't you swear me in to be a
deputy, eh?" And I says, "Why, sure." Then he says,
"Thanks." Then Johnny pipes up again (Johnny's always
piping up). He says, "Could you swear me in, too?" And I
says, "Sure," and then I says to Brandstetter, "Kneel," and
then I put my hand on his head (I wouldn't have done it
unless he had told me that was the way to do it), and then
I says, "I dub you deputy under my command to serve for
three years" (although it probably wouldn't have lasted
three minutes), but it lasted about a day, then my army
began to revolt, and I was fuming (and I still am).

Isn't this a short letter? You're a swell dad, and
it's been nice having a letter-side chat with you, even if
it does make Mother tired.

[From Brick; May 1940]

Dear Mom, Chas and Lou:

In preparation for the arrival of you kids, we just
traded in the old Ford on a 1938 Willys, and Naomi is
learning to drive so she can chauffeur the kids around.
(Better start climbing a tree, Louis.) I expect she'll be
driving by the time you kids get here.

It really is a swell little car -- I hope. It looks
brand new and seems just as comfortable as a big car. We
should really get about twenty-five miles to the gallon as
compared with less than fifteen in the Ford. Really, it
cost so much to run the Ford that we never used it except
to go to work.

[Early summer, 1940]

Dear Dickie:

Well, as you know by this time, we got 'em and are
having quite a time. They haven't got adjusted yet and are
really homesick for you and their gang of kids, but we're
hoping they'll snap out of it before summer is over.

Louis, I think, has matured remarkably since I saw
them last. You can see the difference in his attitude

---

[1] The scare was caused by a zealous publicity agent for the Franklin Institute in Philadelphia,
who on April Fool's Day sent out a press release stating that "Scientists predict that the world will
end at 3 p.m. E.S.T. tomorrow" to arouse interest in the opening of a planetarium show.

toward Charles. It used to be that anything Charles did was perfect, and Louis' great hope was to be able to equal or exceed him in some one thing. Now he seems not only to be able to resent Charles' position but to understand exactly why he resents it and to propose to do something about it. He no longer wants to emulate Charles but wants to have his own activity. The only trouble is that Charles is so dynamic, so quick and insistent mentally and vocally that Louis' interests just get crowded into the background. While he's trying to formulate a thought, Charles will have formulated and expressed a dozen, and poor Louis relapses from a stammering attempt to get out what he wants to say into screams of rage.

I felt so sorry for him the first few days they were here. He kept saying, "It's murder. Oh, Daddy, it's murder!" Eventually I got him off to one side and we had a talk and it developed that, as he himself phrased it, "Charles makes so much noise I can't hear myself think!" I think I appreciate his position; I'm sure Charles' mouth didn't stop once in the first three days they were here. And I got to thinking what it would be like to have lived eight years in the shadow of a vocal boiler factory.

Louis said, one of those times: "Oh, Daddy, when you do get interested in me, I can't talk to you because I don't know anything to talk about." Poor devil; it seems to me that he's been crowded so far into the intellectual background that he hasn't really developed to any degree the technique of self-expression. I find that when you get him by himself and prompt him with questions, more or less as is done in school, he's very brilliant but (especially when Charles is around) he can't organize or articulate his thoughts at all. So I've been spending most of my time with him trying to develop conversations.

They didn't want to come up here and in their boyish way they've made up their minds not to enjoy a thing. Sometimes they forget themselves; Charles had a very good time on our camping trip, but whenever they remember, they act very doleful about it all. Whenever we start out with a now-we'll-go-out-and-show-the-kids-a-good-time look in our eye, they get twice as doleful and succeed not only in spoiling their fun but also our own. This afternoon we took them down to a swimming pool nearby where they could really have a good time, but they knew what was expected of them and got very doleful. So we took Charles home (he was the ring-leader) and dumped him out and finally agreed to take Louis down to inspect another park. Then Charles wanted to go and finally decided that he would forgive us and that we would then take him along. He was quite surprised when he found that it was up to US to forgive HIM. Since then he's been amazingly good.

But it's all very interesting. Their Dad has been, for

so long, a sort of holiday phenomenon that they've forgotten that he's also a parent. And it's time they learned -- Charles is actually growing up, and if I don't succeed in re-establishing connections with them pretty soon, I won't have any little boys at all.

[From George Louis,
dictated; summer 1940]

Dear Mom:

We went to a little swimming pool, and Charles wouldn't get out. Neither would I. I almost had to stay home like Dad made Charles do. But I got to go. We went down to a re-e-e-e-al big swimmin' pool. After that we went to a market, and Naomi bought three-e-e strawberry ice cream cones, one for Naomi and one for Daddy and one for me. In other words, one for each. Kiss! Kiss!!

I WANTA GO HOOOOME! PDQ. How are you. I am fine.

[Summer 1940]

Dear Dickie:

Just a few lines before I dash off to work. Don't forget to write the brats as they sure are homesick for you. Charles spends every morning out at the mailbox waiting for a letter. And Louis, after he goes to bed at night, will lie there and say: "Gee, I can hear Mom calling. She says: 'Boyees, Time to get u-up.' Gee, I wish I was home."

They've been awfully good kids after the first few days, but they don't feel like making new friends here, and it's very lonesome for them. I think it's good for Charles, especially, to be away from his gang and perhaps get a little more adult attention.

Louis seems to be getting over his inferiority complex to a great extent, and it's Charles' turn to be jealous because Louis gets the most attention. But neither of them does; it's only that Charles can't understand how anybody could pay any attention to anybody else when HE is around.

[From Chuck, dictated]
July 5, 1940

Dear Mom,

Poor Dad! he hadn't slept for about twenty-four hours. See, it was this way: At 9 o'clock Monday morning Dad got out of bed; he had to go to work at 4, so we sat around all day until he had to go. Then at 8 o'clock or so, Louis and I went to bed, and the first thing I know, there's Dad -- it's 2 o'clock Tuesday morning, and he had just got home from work (remember, he hadn't been in bed since 9 of the previous morning). Well, we got up, Louis and me, and got dressed, and Dad started to get ready and we rode until we got to Angel's Camp.

I guess it was about 10 o'clock by the time we got to our camp, and it's a sw--e--1--11 place.

We did see a porcupine. (Or rather Dad did.) You see, it was this way: in the night -- way in the night -- Naomi was lying awake, she said later, and she heard a scratch, scratch, scratch, unkwunk, unkwunk, unkwunk. This time she was scared. She thought it might be a bear.

Dad was sleeping in the same bed with her, and she reached over to him and she says: "Dad, hey, Dad! Wake up! Hey, honey, wake up!" Dad just went z-z-z-z-z-z-z. Then Naomi said, "Hey, wake up, Dad, it's a bear -- I think!" And Dad went z-z-z-z-zz -- umph, whatisit?" Naomi says: "Wake up, it's a be-a-ar!" And Naomi says: "It's over by the car, I think it's in the trunk!" And Dad says: "I-I-I'll get me a club!" And Naomi says, "Oh, Daddy, sa-a-ave me, sa-a-a-ave me!" Then Daddy gets very brave, and he yells out, "I will save you; do not fear, my darling!" (Editor's Note: You let this guy listen to the wrong kind of radio program.)

And he marches forward determinedly. After he got about fourteen feet away, he began to wish he hadn't've said that, but he marched on anyway. He picks up his club and -- wham! It was the most beautiful sound-resorting sock I ever heard. (Editor's Note: He was asleep all the time!). The curve was beautiful, the speed terrific -- but he missed. Well, he tried again and again -- and he kept missing. Finally, the gallant hero broke his club (I think). Then he resorted to stones.

Finally, the porcupine was gone, and Dad tore over to the bed, whipped off his pants and climbed under the covers. I am sure he will be written of in many history books in the future. He shall be in Ripley's Believe It or Not auditorium.[2] Imagine, a man scaring away a porcupine without even hitting him!

July 13, 1940

Well, I don't have much to tell, but we went up to Mt. Diablo again but there wasn't much there except one thing. You know I'm always trying to play jokes on Dad, and this time I finally got Louis to go with me. Louis was supposed to be chasing me, and we chased around the camp and around the camp, and I'd be screamin' and yellin' and yappin' and Louis'd be cussing and cursing and cussin' and then we ran outside the camp, a little ways off and then we both stopped and we counted to fifty and then I began to run. After I'd run a little way with Louis behind me, I began to scream as loud as I could

---

2 At the San Francisco World's Fair.

and Louis began to yell as loud as he could and we tore
through the camp like a house afire.

Well, we got just a little ways out of camp and up
comes Dad. He's a runnin' real fast to save me. Well, he
catches Louis by the arm (or sumpin') and then we both
stopped and Louis says: "Hah! I guess you fell for it!" And
Dad let's go of him and steps back and stares dumbfounded.
And then we all began to laugh -- us most. It was the first
trick that ever worked on Dad.

[From Brick]
July 29, 1940

Dear Dickie,

Things have been going very smoothly; the kids have got
adjusted to being here, and we all have a very swell time.

I expect you'll have a swell place when you get all
the work done on it, and I think the idea of a bunkhouse
for the kids is a splendid one. I wish it were possible for
them to have a little workshop where Charles, particularly,
can carry on his scientific experiments. He and I spend a
lot of our time talking about chemistry and electricity and
so forth but it all remains academic to him because he
can't actually see any of it happen.

Naomi spends a lot of time encouraging Louis to
develop little hobbies of his own. He has a big scrapbook
and spends hours cutting pictures out of magazines and
pasting them in. It seems rather childish, but it's a real
project for him, and he gets a lot of satisfaction out of
completing a real job.

He also got a lot of satisfaction when I matched him
and Charles in a formal wrestling match and he succeeded in
pinning Slats -- that's what we call him now -- to the mat.
So far as he's concerned, he's no longer No. 2 Boy in the
family and he gets along all right. Louis is so cute that
Naomi and I have a great temptation to treat him as a baby,
particularly in conversation, but as he learns to do more
things with his hands that will be overcome, I hope.

It seems to me right now that Charles is the one that
needs the most attention. I know he's worse when he's
around me because he has a tendency to regress into
babyhood; he seems to want to spend all of his time sitting
on my lap and acting, to a great degree, as he did when he
was two years old. (For heaven's sake, make sure he never
sees this; he does read other people's mail, you know.) But
aside from that tendency to regress, he seems much less
sure of himself than he did a year or so ago; he seems
secretly worried, and he doesn't have the stamina he should
have. He's very nervous and quickly wears out just from the
strain of playing or reading.

I think that all of us have been inclined to overemphasize Louis' brilliance in Charles' presence so that the shoe now begins to be on the other foot. But since Charles isn't as aggressively competitive as Louis, his tendency is to say: "Well, so I'm not as smart as Louis, so what? So I'm just not and there's nothing I can do about it." As a matter of fact, I still think that Slats has a more brilliant mind than Louis, though not necessarily a deeper nor more stable one. He grasps things very quickly and insists on knowing everything about a subject when he starts on it, even though he doesn't have the staying power.

While Charles' present tendencies are toward scientific things, I think his real interest is ultimately going to lie in the artistic field; he never seems to be so completely fulfilling himself as when he is showing off, acting a little skit or reading poetry aloud or dancing.

He'll take a bit of poetry (Shakespeare, perhaps, although he doesn't like Shakespeare) and study it over for an hour or so and finally come back and give a performance like a finished actor. And he says that nobody's taught him; that's just the way it should be read.

Furthermore, give him a book and he'll instinctively pick out the most famous and most readable sections (if he can understand them) and work them out for a performance. I can't help but believe that, ultimately, his interest is going to turn in that direction. His apparent interest in science really deals more with imaginative things, rocket ships and so forth, than with the accumulation of fact, and I think he'll outgrow that very definitely.

But while I feel much more at home with Slats than with Louis, I think he does much better with you than with me. I have too much of a tendency to baby him and to do things for him instead of making him do things for himself. We get along swell together -- but I think he progresses a little better with you.

Naomi and I were planning to spend our vacation in the mountains, but I think now we'll drive to Los Angeles and that maybe I'll look around and see what chance there is for a job down there. In some ways I like this part of the country very well, but I don't seem to get anywhere.

When the summer was over, Chuck and I returned to Los Angeles on the train, very happily because that's where all our friends were.

122 Alpine Terrace
San Francisco
[September 1940]

Dear Dickie,

Do you mind very much if I skip the check this week? This business of moving is rather expensive, and I'm short.

Naomi isn't back yet, but I've rented a place,

unfurnished (I'm sitting on an apple box typing on a card
table) and rather on a hill but without any views. It's one
of those old-fashioned places with high ceilings, five big
rooms, but modernized with a nice bathroom, oak floors,
etc. And the rent is only $27.50 a month.

By the way, have you written to Mother recently? We
drove to see her before I came north, and she wanted very
much to go down to Inglewood, rent a room near your place
and spend a month or so near the kids. I think I know where
I got my restlessness; Mother can't seem to be in one place
more than a month or so before she wants to go somewhere
else.

I'm going to miss the kids a lot. I guess I'm
growing old; I find I like to be among kids, even in
droves. I've even made friends with the neighbors' kids.
Guess I'm getting mellow. I don't know how it will be
when Naomi gets back -- I rather half think that I get
along much better in complete solitude. But she says
she's gong to get a job, and this house is big enough so
one can crawl off into a corner when necessary. If we
ever get it furnished. I hope that after we get settled I
can dig into the writing again. Apparently that's my only
chance to get off the Examiner copy desk.

In the park near our Inglewood home, workers found some dinosaur
fossils, and Chuck and his friends decided to dig there, too.

November 11, 1940

Dear Sourdough Slim, Hermit of Swinetooth Gulch,

So you've taken up prospecting, huh? And have you
found any dinosaur teeth yet? Remember when we used to go
down to the museum in Los Angeles and look at the dinosaur
bones? I never thought then that you'd ever go out digging
for them. Also, I always wondered how a guy got to be a
paleontologist; I supposed he was driven by a keen
scientific interest to cross deserts, endure burning
thirst, risk his life among wild animals and savages, etc.
But I suppose it's only because he hopes to be able to sell
a sack of elephant teeth, right?

Naomi says that maybe you'll be a scientist and maybe
an actor when you grow up (which won't be long now) but
that she thinks you'll be a writer because you can write
pages and pages and make every word of it interesting. I
think she's got something there, and it just struck me that
you should sit down and write a little article and try to
sell it to some kids' magazine. I don't know much about
that market, but there must be thousands of kids who would
be very much interested in those prehistoric bones. And the
fact that you are actually on the spot is really something
to write about.

If you want, I'll collaborate on it with you; send it up to me, and I will go over it and see how it can be, as we say, "boiled down or fattened up."

[From Chuck, dictated]
November 14, 1940

Dear Dad,

I have a complaint to make. When I was in kindergarten, my kindergarten teacher used to say, "You're big people now," and when I was in first and second grades, Teacher would say, "You're big people now," and when I was in the third grade, she would say, "You're grown up now," and when I was in the fourth and fifth grades, she would say, "You're not babies any more," and here you go in your letter and say, "It won't be long until you're grown up." And I'm getting tired of being talked to like that by people, and furthermore teachers are ninety-nine percent bluff. Every year since I've been in the fourth grade they have threatened and fumed and threatened to write home to our mothers, or when our mothers came to visit us, they would tell what bad boys we'd been, and my mom came and the teacher said, "Sometimes he is a little bad," and that was all there was to it. And furthermore the teachers and the principal like to give fancy names to things to scare the pupils. They have a so-called Council of Seven, which consists of every teacher from the sixth grade down to the kindergarten, and not one kid that I know, and I know some of the worst, has ever been near this Council of Seven. They say if you get your name down three times in a book that's when you got to go, and Norman Quit said he got his name down about eight times, and I know I got mine down more than three, but still no Council of Seven.

I'm back in the army now, but it's really in the blueprint stage.

I don't see why Naomi thinks I'll be an actor. I might be a writer, and I might be a scientist, as that's what I want to be -- but not an actor.

Jeemeny Christmas, oh mighty oh jeemeny. I don't know what to say next (Mom hopes I've run down). So, love.

With his letter Chuck also enclosed a diagram of a battle plan he had drawn for his little army of boys, since he was once again playing at being a soldier.

[From Brick]
November 25, 1940

Dear Slats,

From the diagram and the order of battle, I think you must be quite a military strategist. It looks all right to me, except that I think the modern plan is to have the tanks go over before the men because otherwise the men will

get themselves mowed down by machine guns. Of course, I
confess that I still feel very much about it like I did a
year ago -- that you gotta have something more to fight for
than a few square feet of ground that won't belong to you
even if you capture it.

The French and the Italians proved that pretty well.
The French soldiers (they'd had most of their liberties
taken away from them by their own government) simply said
to themselves: "Heck, let's get out of here. This is no
place for us; if we get shot we're dead, and if we don't
get shot we don't win anything even if we win." And so they
scrammed. And the same thing with the Italians; the
government took everything they had, cut their wages until
they could barely live (in civilian life, I mean) and then
dressed them up in uniforms and sent them out to fight.
They were perfectly willing to yell "Doochay! Doochay!"
because it didn't cost anything and the guy that yelled the
loudest might get a better job. But when they went up
against the Greeks they figured out, quite sensibly, "Nuts!
What are we doing here, anyway?" And they scrammed.

The reason the Greeks proved such good fighters was
the fact that they had -- or thought they had -- something
to fight for. And the same thing has always been true of
the Americans in the past. When we invaded Mexico a hundred
years ago and took Texas and California and New Mexico and
Arizona away from her, the men figured that they'd be back
as soon as the war was over with ploughs and horses and
have some swell farms. And when the Americans fought the
British, they did a good job of it because they owned the
country and they didn't want the British running it. Even
in the Civil War the men from the North fought because they
owned the whole country (or thought they did) and the men
from the South thought they owned the South. And it was a
question of who was going to own it and run it and get the
profit from it.

So if your army was fighting for the bone deposits and
if the soldiers, and not the International Bone Digging
Co., Inc., were going to own them if they won, I'd gamble
that your chances of winning would be a whole lot better.

Your complaint is duly received and filed. If I may
venture another philosophical observation, I think one
trouble with grown-ups is that we can never be quite sure
that children are people. Maybe we remember too well when
we used to stretch you out on the drainboard and rub you
down with olive oil. So we keep on talking down to you --
and you'll probably find when you're thirty years old that
we're still doing it.

But you've discovered one thing for yourself that most
people never find out: that teachers are ninety-nine percent
bluff who think up fancy names to scare people with. You'll
find that's one of the oldest gags in the world -- and that

it still works. In fact, the surest way to get people to do what you want them to is to give them fancy words which actually mean something else than they are supposed to mean, and to keep repeating those words over and over until anybody who doesn't shout it with them begins to feel strange and out of place. That's the way people in authority manage to run things, and I guess teachers are no exception. You could pick up a newspaper tonight and find at least a dozen of those "words of power" which are being thrown at the people today from every angle.

Naomi has written you a letter which I'm enclosing. I think she was a little worried because she thought you felt insulted at the idea that you might turn into an actor.

[From Naomi]
November 19, 1940

Dear Charles:

This is just going to be a note. I started to write to you while I was stuffing potatoes for dinner, and I dropped a beautiful gob of butter right in the middle of a perfectly good letter. That goes to prove that I can only do one thing at a time. So, I'm writing you another one.

I see you have decided most definitely not to be an actor. Before I begin on that I might mention that Daddy and I had a merry time through dinner, he shouting that HE said you might be an actor and I, shouting a little louder, that I said you MIGHT be an actor. Sometimes you're a bit of a nuisance.

We sure do hope you'll spend Christmas with us -- in fact, there will be a very disappointed parent and step-parent if you boys don't show up.

[From Brick]
November 25, 1940

Dear Lou,

Did I ever tell you what it was like when I went to school? Well, after I'd get through cleaning out the chicken house, I got my lunch and walked to school. It was about half a mile. Some of the kids rode horses and one rode on a burro. There were only about fifteen kids in the whole school, and we all studied in the same room. The class that was reciting would go up in front on a bench while the rest studied.

At 10:15 we'd have our first recess, and we'd usually play some kind of game like pump-pump-pullaway or blind man's bluff. Then the bell would ring and we'd go back in and study until noon. At noon, sometimes we'd take our lunches and go back up in the brush and eat under a sumach bush, or sometimes we'd try to dig a cave in the side of the hill. But the thing I remember most was sticking our

lunch under our arms and running as fast as we could about
a half mile over the hills to a place where there was a
reservoir. Then we'd pull off our clothes and jump in --
that's where I learned to swim. Then we'd stay as long as
we could, and finally we'd jump out and start to run back
to school -- trying to put our clothes on and eat our lunch
and run at the same time.

It was a lot of fun. Sometimes after a rain we'd find
a spot of wet clay and make mudballs, which we'd mold on
the end of a swishy stick, like a willow branch. Then we'd
haul them back and s-swish-h-h them through the air, and
the mud would fly off and go farther than a baseball. We'd
have wars with them or throw them at the school house until
the teacher ran out and raised heck and made us stop.

After school was out at three o'clock we'd all start
home together, and I'd get into a fight with a guy named
Harold and always get licked because I was the smallest in
the bunch. Then I'd swear that some day I'd grow up and
beat the tar out of him or get rich and buy an automobile
and run over him.

[From George Louis,
dictated]
November 28, 1940

Dear Dad and Naomi,

Some day I'm going to grow up and beat the tar out
of Charles, or get rich and get an automobile and run
over him.

When Grandma and Aunt Eleanor were here, I put on a
play all by myself, and I was all ten characters -- not
including the announcer. I am going to do it for you when I
come up there. I just want to be eight characters, though,
because ten characters get me out of breath.

I think I'm going to be a proof-reader on the
Examiner, or a fireman, or a policeman, or a doctor, or
maybe all of them, and then I'll get my picture in "Believe
It or Not Ripley."

[From Charles, dictated]
November 28, 1940

Dear Dad,

Every time I give you a simple diagram you take it as
though I am enthused with war. Well, the only thing that is
good about my military strategy is the way I do it -- well,
I can't exactly explain it, but what I mean is the
sleekness of it -- like you see these field guns and tank
operations that make you feel sort of good and makes you
think you want to be in the army, but the real killing or
the taking of other people's land I'm not interested in at
all. And so don't give me any more of this grown-up

philosophical observations, because you spend half of the letter saying something to me that I already know, and besides even if I didn't know, I would still think it was a good idea about all this military strategy and everything.

Say, Dad, doesn't it seem sort of fishy that the Greeks should be winning like that when by all the experts' opinion they should be losing like the Polish did. I don't think this is possible -- but maybe it was just like France surrendering to Germany because I am sure that France could have beaten Germany if the big bosses hadn't given up. When you receive this letter don't go telling me the same things you've been telling me about your philosophical observance; but at least put a few lines in about what I'm talking about and tell me what you think.

Say, do you know anybody by the name of Mr. Lewis? One day I was walking down the aisle in the school room, and my teacher says to me, "Is your Dad known as Brick Garrigues," and I says Yes. And she said, "My husband knows your father," and I says Oh. Do you know Mr. Lewis? Mom says that Mrs. Lewis told her that Mr. Lewis submitted an article or did some work on the People's Progress when you had it. He is a schoolteacher too.

Our school has a newspaper, and the second edition came out just about four days ago. I was writing a story and I put it in the newspaper. It might sound corny, because they hacked it, but I guess you know about that, as you have probably done plenty of it when you were an editor, and you've had plenty of stories hacked, too.

> [From Brick; December
> 1940]
> Wednesday

Dear Slats,

Yeah, I see exactly what you mean about "the sleekness of it." Forgive my obtuseness, and don't mind too many philosophical observations. Fact is, I feel exactly about it as you do, though not exactly in regard to war. (I think I did, at your age. I remember studying the formations of the Greek and Persian armies in our history books.)

Do you remember one time, coming back from a ride, we got to talking about radio programs and music and you asked me what the heck I liked in symphony programs, and I couldn't tell you? Well, it was the "sleekness" of it. Each section of the orchestra has a particular job to do at a particular time, and it's much more complicated than a battle, and a great composer makes them all do precisely the thing at the time which they should do. And he has to make it all up out of his head and nobody knows until it's on paper what they should do, and even then nobody's sure that he's done it until it's been played.

For example, there's one piece of music in which the orchestra stops playing and the violin goes along by itself. Now, there are regular paths in music, and one step just follows another, but this violin wanders off the path and runs up hills and down valleys and turns handsprings and you know the composer will never get him back in time to start with the orchestra. And then, all of a sudden, the whole thing falls into a pattern, the violin moves up a path, the orchestra starts -- and there he is, marching along with them.

I used to get the same kick out of watching football. It's the same thing again, with a really great team playing strategy. But I guess you have to know more about the subject than I really know about war to appreciate it.

When I was ten years old or so, my job on the ranch was to clean out the chicken house every morning. I'd clean 'em all right, but we were studying ancient history (or I was reading it), and the hills around there were just jammed full with Greek and Persian armies, marching and countermarching and charging up hills, etc., etc. I don't think I was as good a strategist as you are, though; anyway, I never worked it out on paper and really got things down right. But then, my Greeks and Persians never had anything except swords and shields and spears to fight with.

Bliss and the Chickens

He hated chickens. He walked around the farmyard in his bare feet, trying to avoid the squishy chicken droppings but always getting the icky stuff between his toes. When he went to gather the eggs and when he made the rounds of the nests, there was always a broody hen on one of them, and she would cluck furiously at him and, when he sidled up close to her and tried to force her off, she would shoot out her sharp beak and make him jump and almost drop the egg pail.

It wasn't that he was afraid of a hen. He wasn't scared. He was just afraid of the sudden start, the jump he would give every time she shot out her sharp beak. Every single time she would do it, and every time he would jump until he was furious with embarrassment.

And, the worst of it was, there was nobody he could tell. He couldn't tell Mama or Grace or even Cal — and least of all Tom or Papa. They would have laughed at him and maybe larruped him, to boot.

Once, he did rebel, though — and did get larruped. He told Mama he was too old to be doing girl's work and Grace could gather the eggs after this. And Mama took him by the seat of the pants and the shirt collar and shoved him into a chicken house and locked the door and kept him there until Papa came in from the fields. Papa larruped him, turning him over

his knee and walloping him with the flat of his hand, and sent him out to
gather eggs by lantern light.
    He hated chickens.

[December 1940]

Dear Louis,

    Today it was so foggy I thought I was in Inglewood.
But the fog-horns kept howling -- you could hear them on
three sides of you. They were hooting last night, too; they
go HOO-oop! and br-r-AW! Each one has a different sound.
Pretty soon I heard one that sounded like a girl fog-horn;
it went br-r-e-eeep! br-rreep! And then I listened again
and it was Naomi snoring! (Naomi says she has something to
tell on me, too.)

[From Chuck;
January 17, 1941]

Dear Dad,

    I've got a lot to say but I wish I didn't have to be
my own secratary.

    First is about school, I'm getting to like it. At
first I told you I liked school because of a few pleasant things that happened now I'm getting to like even
the bad ones!

    For instance, school is like a club or a lodge,
because you meet your freinds there and discuss things with
them. And another instance, school is like a miniture
civilization the kids have there sweetharts (insa-dent-ly.
I've got my I on Joan Taylor) and they carry on their
affairs just like anybody. Tonight I just sat down and
thought that out.

    Louis is working just as less as ever.

    I haven't used my Chemistry set yet but the kids have
started a Chemistry Club; We call it "The California Ass.
of Chemistry," Complete Details in my next letter.

January 21, 1941

Dear Slats:

    I like what you said about school, and if you hadn't
told me otherwise, I'd have said that somebody else thought
it up for you. That's what a school is supposed to be, you
know: a miniature civilization. And I suppose that the best
thing a really good school can do for you is to get you
acquainted with the outside world by seeing it reflected
right within the school. Of course, they never get it quite
right because when you get out of school there's no teacher
to ring the bells and keep somebody from sticking a pin in
your seat while you're studying.

Also I see where you're getting yourself a lot of work by being so smart. Just like your old man. Every time I go to a meeting, I think up a plan for a committee. They like the idea so well they make me chairman of the committee. Then I have to do most of the work. That's what happened the other night, and today I've been running all over town being chairman of a committee. But such is life.

I wouldn't worry about Lou doing less than ever. The fact is that Lou has, in one way, a kind of tough time simply because he's the kid brother. (Remember how I said I was still Uncle George's kid brother? Well, it kind of puts a mark on you.) That isn't because your older brother doesn't treat you right, either, but just simply because, since he's a couple of years older, he's been through all the things you are just going through, and naturally he's very grown up and superior about it. And you try to keep ahead, and you can't (no matter how smart you are), and you get mad because he acts superior and because he naturally thinks he has the right to be boss, and so it makes you very unhappy -- even when you've got a very swell big brother.

You just don't worry about Lou's reaction too much, but give him a hand now and then and remember to praise what he does when he does something particularly clever or wise, and you'll find that things move along a lot smoother -- and that it will be a lot of help to Lou. Of course, there aren't many youngsters that a guy could write to like this with the hope of having them savvy it. But you've got a lot of savvy.

February 19, 1941

Dear Slats,

I'm beginning to start counting the days until you fellows will be up here next summer, although it's a long time away yet, and I remember my promise that you won't have to spend all of your summer here again. But you'd have a lot better time here in San Francisco than you would in Oakland.

Have you written any of those stories we were talking about? And how goes the army? Maybe the next time a plane flies over and wobbles its wings it'll be a Japanese bombing plane, huh? And that won't be so much fun.

In 1941 the peacetime draft was in effect, but Brick, at age 39, didn't have to worry about being called up. The Lend-Lease Act had put American industry to the service of the British, and later the Russians started to get some munitions from America as well. Roosevelt and Churchill met on a warship in the North Atlantic and signed a charter of war aims. The Navy leased a portion of Treasure Island, where the fair had been, to use as a transit base.

In Inglewood, Dickie's career as a secretary was paying off. She was able to borrow enough money to build a garage with a big attached room for Chuck and me. At night we watched a searchlight swing through the sky from a newly installed anti-aircraft battery in the city park just half a block away. The big gun pointed mutely toward the clouds, waiting.

In San Francisco, Brick and Naomi moved diagonally across Alpine Terrace, to a top-floor flat with a magnificent view of the Bay, and they had finally bought enough furniture so their home no longer looked as though they were either just moving in or just moving out.

When school was out, Chuck and I were back in San Francisco for the summer.

[From Chuck, dictated]
June 18, 1941

Dear Mom,

I can ride a bicycle swell now, but I can't stand up on the pedals and I can't start off. We went to a place where you could rent bikes, and Dad and Naomi and Louis and the neighbor kid Joe and I rode around in a big parking space.[3] We got some pictures.

I've been having a lot of fun with the kids, but around here they don't have no imagination. Back home you could see a log and pretend like it was a torpedo or something, but here it's just a log. There is a big rocky cliff here, and they don't pretend like they're mountain climbing or anything. We made some swings of ropes that we hung on by our hands, but we didn't even play like we was Tarzan; we just swung on the ropes. What a place!

July 13, 1941

Dear Mom,

Gee, Dad and Noma are sure nice people. You know how much trouble I had getting to sleep? Well, at first I was sleeping on an old camp bed that creaked and groaned and creaked like anything. So I couldn't get to sleep. Well, I got lemon-and-honey-ade at all hours of the night and everything, and so they moved me to Louis' bed, which was a little bit softer and didn't creak. And so I slept all right for a couple of nights. Then they got the idea to leave a lamp there so whenever I couldn't sleep I could turn on the lamp and read some boring book which they had furnished.

In the past few nights Dad has been getting up and laying beside me when I couldn't get to sleep. A couple of nights ago, I got to sleep and about one-thirty Dad got up to get a drink, and he slammed the door, and that woke me up. Well, I kept going to sleep and getting awake again until about three o'clock, then I heard Dad coughing and decided he was awake, so I called him.

Immediately there was a lot of hustle and bustle in the house, and Dad came in and talked, and I got some warm

---

3 Near the old Kezar Stadium in Golden Gate Park.

water and he laid down on my bed with me for about fifteen minutes. And so after that I got to sleep. My main reason for keeping awake was usually because Dad was using the typewriter, but he said he'd quit that, and now he can't even write on his own typewriter!

They make you work a little harder up here, like washing the dishes and bothering about the table manners all the time, but I think it's worth it.

[From Brick; early August 1941]

Dear Dickie,

Unless you have other plans, I think I'll send the kids back Monday. Tentatively, they'll arrive about 7:30 by Santa Fe bus. They are both well -- and swell -- (Louis is looking over my shoulder and grinning) but are anxious to get home. Besides, their clothes are all dirty, and I'll have to turn laundryman if I don't get rid of them pretty soon.

But they're swell guys; they cleaned up the front room this morning and swept it like grownups.

151 Alpine Terrace
November 13, 1941

Dear Slats,

For the first time, this war begins to look something like the last one -- only on a tremendously bigger scale. When I was just a little older than you, I can remember how the armies were dug in in close order and would attack and counterattack, gaining a big victory if they advanced more than a couple of hundred yards. Now they seem to be doing the same thing except that they expect to gain five or ten miles. It's like seeing the same movie twice, only bigger.

November 25, 1941

Dear Slats and Lou,

It's turned cold and the days are short. I don't do much outside. The old tennis courts are deserted almost all day, and every time I pass them I wish you guys were here with your rackets.

I've been trying again to line up a job in Los Angeles in the hope that the draft would take enough reporters and copy readers so there would be some jobs down there. But I haven't had any luck as yet. However, I'll keep on trying as I'm determined to get back to L.A., where I can see you guys once in a while.

Are you fellows having a nice Thanksgiving? Is there enough to eat in Inglewood? Food is pretty short up here, but we manage to get by with substitutes. I'm learning to drink tea instead of coffee, and we're using margarine

instead of butter (which there isn't any of), but it's fun
to go to the store and see what you can find for dinner.

You've got talent and some good sound sense, and
you'll have your troubles, but you'll get along all right.
It's a funny thing; several of my friends have kids about
seventeen or eighteen, and it seems that when kids get to
be that age, they always drive their dads crazy by getting
into jams. Then I tell the dads that there's no use trying
to teach a kid not to get into a jam; the only thing you
can do is to try to teach him not to get into the same jam
twice -- and not to get into one that's so tough he can't
get out of it. So when you guys get to be seventeen or
eighteen, and I start hounding you, remind me of this bit
of philosophizing, will you?

What Bliss's Father Told the School Board

*They already knew the strike was going to be lost when they came to
the school board meeting in Harker's book store after supper and none of
the grownups were there.*

*All the kids were there, practically all the kids in town and several
from the country. They hung around a while, waiting. Bliss came along,
walking with his old man. Bliss didn't say anything, and the kids were too
bashful to give him a yell like they would on the football field. After a
while Editor Rankin came in, stuffing a wad of copy paper in his hip
pocket and pausing at the door to knock the ashes out of his pipe. And
Mr. Atterbury came, shouldering his way through the kids and followed
by Mr. Walker. And the other teachers came, one at a time. Mote Salisbury
said, "Whyn't we go in?" and Ray McKay said, "We better keep out of
it." Dub McLain said, "Why? It's a public meeting, ain't it? There ain't
nobody going to keep me out of a public meeting." But nobody went in.
The kids hung around the door, twenty-five or thirty of them, but nobody
went in.*

*And none of the adults came. They'd thought that there'd be a crowd,
all rooting for Bliss, with the grownups going inside and telling the school
board that free speech was free speech. Because, after all, this was something that affected the whole town, the whole country, really, because
Valley Forge and Gettysburg and Thomas Jefferson belonged to everybody. But nobody came. And Bob decided the other kids' folks let them
strike not because they believed in free speech, but because the other
kids' folks were like his folks.*

*After a long while Bliss came out and closed the door behind him.
Somebody said, "How's it going, kid?" and he said, with a frozen smile,
"Oh, swell." The sass had gone out of him.*

*Somebody asked, "What are they going to do with you?" and Bliss
said, "They wanted to talk to my dad first, so they asked me to come out*

here and wait." Then he added, not exactly as though for information or for advice, but as though talking to himself: "Mr. Harker said that if I'd publicly apologize to Mr. Atterbury I'd be allowed to graduate with the class. I guess that's what they're talking to Dad about."

One of the kids said, "Oh," and the word fell without emphasis into the warm night. Everybody knew what everybody was thinking about: if Bliss would apologize they could all go back and graduate. But they couldn't say anything: they couldn't even say "Attaboy, Bliss!" or "Give 'em hell, kid!" because the decision had to be his. If he stuck it out, they would, but they weren't going to encourage him in it. Everybody was glad when Mr. Harker finally put his head out of the door and called Bliss inside.

After a while they both came out; Bliss and his old man. They started walking down the street, not saying anything to anybody, not even looking at the kids, but planting their feet and picking them up again as though walking on and on without progression. Everybody knew then what had happened, without waiting for Mr. Rankin to emerge, stuffing his copy paper in his pocket and cussing under his breath.

Chuck and I spent Christmas with Brick and Naomi. The war had come to America and, as the Japanese bombed the open city of Manila and laid siege to Corregidor, the lights gleamed on our Christmas tree in San Francisco before we headed back to Los Angeles aboard the Southern Pacific Daylight.

Former District Attorney Buron Fitts, whom Los Angeles County voters had finally removed from office in 1940, joined the Army Air Corps in 1942 with the rank of major.

February 13, 1942

Dear Dickie:

I've been trying to get down for a visit. But there are expenses. I finally bought the suit I was going to buy last spring and will have it paid for in a couple of months.

From the window you can see planes and a blimp patrolling up and down the bay, all day, looking for subs. And an occasional convoy going out. But it doesn't really look as though there were a war on. Existence in San Francisco is much too peaceful. The apple tree in the yard below is kind of bare.

I don't know what the war is going to do to the newspaper business. Advertising is falling off and papers are getting smaller. That'll mean layoffs before very long -- some pretty harsh cutting, I imagine. But there should be jobs of some sort; it won't be like the Depression when there were no jobs. Maybe I can learn to make airplanes or ships.

[From Chuck, dictated]
February 17, 1942

Dear Pop,

Our room is finished, and boy is it neat. It's white on the outside and knotty pine on the inside. We have a rug that will go with anything. It is all colors. Every night Louis and I trade beds. We call one bed, the one facing the door, the getting up bed, and the other the dozing bed. Every morning at the crack of dawn, when you can't see your hand in front of your face, the one sleeping in the getting up bed jumps up, turns on the lights, slams on the heater, lifts the Venetian blinds, and closes the window. We need that heater. It's so cold in there that you can see your breath, and I don't mean sometime, I mean every morning.

Johnny and I have joined the Junior Army. It is run by the Herald & Express paper, and you get your orders of the day and things like that printed right in the paper. We know it is an advertising stunt, but we're learning a lot anyway. There is one order telling how to handle incendiary bombs and what to do in an air raid, and they have another article telling all about gardens (and we're supposed to plant Victory gardens for defense). Johnny and I have got most of our vegetables up now, and we're very proud.

About three weeks ago when my little brother was riding my bike, I discovered that the front wheel was flatter than a pancake. So Johnny and I decided to fix it. Well, we started out all right, but you know me: I decided to put it off until another day. Well, last Saturday when I went out to fix it I discovered that some long-eared, yellow-livered, blue-nosed, baboon-faced, son-of-a-donkey had swiped my good tire, and they cost the dough, bo.

The other day Johnny and I got our guns and decided we would play soldier (we can't play in the park, I'll tell you why in the next paragraph) so we went off in a wild spot of town and killed nineteen Japs. Yesterday we played cowboys and killed nine lawmen (we was outlaws) and today we was goldminers and killed about ten or twelve Indians. Period. Paragraph. MOTHER, DON'T YOU TYPE THAT, STOP.

Now I'll tell you why we can't play in the park. It's government property now, and the Army is occupying it. Mother told me that you said it didn't seem like there was war going on in S.F. Not down here. We have P-38's flying about 500 feet above the ground all day long and sometimes they fly in squadrons of six. Then the soldiers have practice air raids in the middle of the night. You can't sleep for the sirens. The other day a sentry was shot at by someone. We hear rifle shots, too, but I don't think it's anything. We don't need alarm clocks in this neighborhood. They have the darned bugle hooked up with a loudspeaker system and you can hear it everywhere.

I am president or vice president of almost every committee in the whole darn'd school. On top of that, I am on the best basketball team in school. Ain't you proud?

[From Brick]
March 15, 1942

Dear Dickie,

In a way it's a relief to have the war here at last. It hasn't been pleasant to sit and watch it come; anybody who had half an eye open must have known that it was on its way since at least 1936. The United States could have stopped it in Ethiopia and we could have stopped it in Spain because the Fascists had to begin little in order to grow big. But we didn't. Lots of us used to go out and organize meetings and make speeches and try to make people see it. But Spain was such a long way off. And we used to go down and picket the docks as a futile gesture of protest at selling scrap to Japs when we knew damned well it was going to be shot back at us.

I get such a tremendous kick out of Charles's letters. He's really a remarkable kid -- but I think he's more like you than like me. Even though he does seem to have my gift of gab. I wonder whatever will become of him? Louis is more like me; I can sit with him and read half of the secret little thoughts in his funny little brain. But the other half I don't think he can read himself. I'm still hoping to be able to get down to see you all, and possibly I will when I get the new suit paid for and buy an extra pair of shoes.

[Spring 1942]

Dear Slats:

Nothing much happens here. I work a little on my book most every day and hope to have it finished in another month or so. Sundays Naomi and I usually go out to the beach and walk a couple of miles, stopping every couple of feet to play catch. She's the only dame I ever saw that could throw and catch a ball. Once every couple of months we go to a movie and occasionally go out to the zoo.

May 29, 1942

Dear Slats and Lou,

We went up to Yosemite Sunday, but instead of going to the Valley where the falls are, we camped about thirty miles south of there at Wawona. The first night was swell; the second morning it started to rain, and I rushed around and gathered dry wood and stowed it away in the tent and under the car. The rain kept putting the fire out, and we didn't have any paper, and I knew that if it ever went completely out, we'd never get it started again. So I lay down in the rain and blew on it to keep it going. Boy, was it cold! But the next morning the fire was out, but the rain had stopped and I hunted around until I found some huge logs that were

rotted so I could dig into them with the axe. On the under
side the tinder was dry, and I finally got a fire started and
we had breakfast and spread our clothes on the line over the
fire to dry. Then the sun came out and it was swell!

Once again Chuck and I made our annual trip up the coast to San
Francisco. But this summer the train was filled with servicemen, and
when it passed through Camp Roberts near San Luis Obispo, very close
to the Pacific Ocean where Japanese submarines sometimes lurked, the
window shades were drawn, and we were forbidden to look out at the
soldiers in training as we could do in the days before the war.

June 1942

Dear Dickie,

The kids arrived; sound in wind and limb. Lots of fun.
It sure is good to have them around, and we're going to
have lots of fun together this summer.

Charles is going to try and write some science fiction
and send it to the magazines -- in the understanding that
he probably can't sell anything for several years but that
there's no time like the present to start. He's pretty
smart. Tonight he came around and said: "Pop, I was looking
at your manuscript today, and I don' think you write very
well. You have a good subject, and you seem to have it well
organized, but the writing isn't so good." Encouraging,
isn't he! But he's probably right.

Chuck and Brick spent hours talking about science, about writing,
about economics, about history, and the room would get darker and darker
because Brick never liked to turn on the lights, and I would sit near them
on the bare, carpetless floor (because there was no money to buy a carpet), listening to Brick's soft, quiet voice and Chuck's higher, more intense one, not understanding a thing they were talking about. It was a
continuation of their long conversation, which lasted through their lives.
I was ten and Chuck was twelve. On July 7 Brick turned forty.

July 15, 1942

Dear Toni,

Lately I find myself just sittig, mind a blank,
perfectly content, gazing out over the bay. It drives Naomi
batty; but then I had my fortieth birthday the other day
and she's still a youngster. Don't ever marry; any woman
that does so is doomed to an unpleasant existence. There's
nothing in it; for myself I get along well enough. But if a
man's contented, his wife wants to pull his hair and if he
isn't, he goes batting around here and there and then she
does pull his hair. It all seems confusion.

As ever,

Brick

Chapter Seventeen
Sunrise Over the Next Hill

Even though the Bay Bridge was open for travel in the early forties, the Key System electric trains still unloaded their passengers in front of the Oakland Ferry Building in the morning and sat waiting in the evening to take them back to their houses and apartments all over the East Bay. The morning ferries were jammed with men and women who read the newspapers or just gazed at the choppy waters before the short trip was over and they caught a streetcar — or walked — to their jobs in downtown San Francisco. During those months when he commuted from Oakland, Brick could have used this quiet time, morning and evening, to think about what was really important to him — his writing. And after he moved into San Francisco and had gotten used to the numbing routine of the *Examiner* copy desk, he thought about it even more. But he wanted somebody to tell him, "Go ahead; write that book."

December 2, 1940

Dear Toni,

    I need some professional advice. Or maybe only encouragement. Or maybe discouragement. And I think I shall have to depend upon you to give it to me.

    First, about three weeks ago I laid aside the would-be novel and started writing a bit of nonfiction I've had germinating unwillingly for some time.

    The working title is "The Immediate Future of Men" (lifted from an H. G. Wells lecture series) and it's an analysis of the present plight of the world from a standpoint of Marxist theory -- done entirely in words of one syllable and completely without Marxist terminology. It attempts to take the things which the ordinary person sees about him and put them together in such a light that what is happening in the world becomes comprehensible to him. It's objective as hell, expository and only occasionally argumentative to any degree.

There's a short introduction called "In Peril of Change" in which we start with the assumption that the world as we've known it is ended and that everybody is worried as hell about What Next? We promise to tell 'em -- not what WILL be, but the two or three things that CAN be. So we say: "Let's take a look at the pleasant little valley where we are and see what it's like, then go up into a high mountain and see how we got there -- and the paths that lead out."

Then the first section (about twenty-five thousand) is titled "The American Way." It takes up four or five things which everybody knows, and, entirely on the basis of the daily life of the reader, lines them up in such a way that you have a very good picture of the economic organization of society -- still without terminology. No philosophy nor sociology but straight Marxist economics -- yet designed so that the reader finds nothing strange or unfamiliar, nor provocative, but of which he can say, "Why, yes, of course."

But "The American Way" means more than just a way of getting our food, we tell 'em. It means freedom, liberty, democracy, etc., etc. And these are living, changing things. So we must go back and see how we got 'em -- see what they're really like.

That's the second section: "The Way of the World." In about twenty to thirty thousand words it will trace the development of The American Way from the earliest days of feudalism, down through the development of capitalism, probably as far as the World War. Or even as far as Munich. The emphasis will be upon the class nature of society -- still being very objective.

The point of the whole thing is that society tends to organize itself at any given time in the method which is best fitted for its immediate needs. We show why feudalism, with its denial of liberty, with its monopoly ownership, was better at its given time than pre-feudal tribal organization, with its freedom, liberty and communal ownership. We show why capitalism, with its denial of feudal security and its increase in liberty, was a better way than feudalism -- and why it could not come into existence until a certain time. We show that just as feudalism brought about (or made possible) technological

and economic advances which resulted in capitalism, so
capitalism also has changed and has completed its cycle by
accomplishing its task.

The second section shows the development of the middle
class and its steadily widening division into two classes:
owners and non-owners of means of production.

The third section takes up the sharpening of the
conflict between these two groups. It shows the present
world conflict (not merely the war, but the preparations
for war in America) as essentially a part of this conflict
and as, politically, a conflict between the two possible
"ways" which lie before humanity.

The final section outlines the two possible paths
which humanity may take. Understanding that the accumulation of capital and consequent monopolization is an
inherent part of the profit system, we show that this must
necessarily continue until either (1) a complete world
monopoly, international in character, is established,
ownership resting in a small group of world capitalists who
exist independently of national boundaries, or (2) private
ownership is abolished and world revolution establishes a
world communist society.

Time has proved Brick correct. Today's world is organized almost
exactly on the first principle (although multinational conglomerates are
really oligopolies and not monopolies). Brick seemed to be predicting
what would today be called globalization. His second option, world revolution, collapsed years before the Soviet Union did.

I've described the thing at length because I want you
to tell me, quite frankly, whether you think there would be
a market for such a book under the conditions existing in
1941. Nothing of the sort has ever been written. John
Strachey's "Theory and Practice of Socialism" comes the
nearest to it, but Strachey wrote as propagandist for
socialism and not in words of one syllable.[1] I think my own
forte, if I have one, is the ability to explain apparently
complicated things in a fashion which is as easy to read as
the average comic page.

Then, too, this is, in a sense, a book of inspiration.
It is written on the theory that most of mankind is
floundering around, getting nervous indigestion from
wondering what the world is coming to. And, quite demagogi-
cally, it says, over and over: "Courage, my friends. Let us
take heart and go forward bravely. The way ahead is not
easy but it is not impossible, and there will be a sunrise
over the next hill."

Toni did more than just give Brick encouragement. She told Pat Covici

---

[1] Strachey (1901-1963), was a British writer and labor leader, who, like Brick, had broken
with the Communists in 1939.

at Viking about this talented author in the West, and probably she even showed Brick's letter to him.

Pascal "Pat" Covici was one of the leading editors in America. He had discovered John Steinbeck and was always looking for new writers. In 1922, Covici owned a book store in Chicago when he published Ben Hecht's *1,001 Afternoons in Chicago*.[2] Covici also printed Radclyffe Hall's lesbian landmark *The Well of Loneliness* (for which he was convicted of obscenity), Hecht's *The Front Page* and works by Francois Mauriac, Gene Fowler, Clifford Odets, Richard Aldington and, of course, Steinbeck, whom Covici brought to Viking afer his own publishing house went bankrupt in 1938. It didn't hurt for Brick to have compared himself with Strachey: Covici was the one who had published Strachey's *The Coming Struggle for Power* in 1936. Covici was known as a good-natured, caring man who brought out the best in his authors. To be taken under the wing of Pat Covici was like being blessed personally by the Pope.

[February 1941]

Dear Dickie,

    Things go on much the same here with me spending every available spare minute on the book and not finding enough time at that. Pat Covici, who is one of the big shots at Viking Press, was in town today and he called me up and invited me to lunch. The upshot is that he is interested in the new book and wants to see it by the middle of June.

Covici, who was then fifty-two, was making one of his periodic trips to the West Coast to see his authors and to check out new talent. At that time, Brick was being represented in his literary life by the Curtis Brown agency in New York. In the six months ended on February 28, 1941, the agency reported, Funk & Wagnalls had sold two copies of *You're Paying for It!*, at two dollars a copy, and there were still one hundred twenty-seven copies in stock. Brick's royalty for those six months was forty cents.

February 24, 1941

Dear Toni,

    It was swell of you to tell Pat Covici about me; he did call me up and we spent three hours over lunch, although I'm afraid we did more arguing over world affairs than constructive discussion of the new achievement I'm about to inflict upon the world.

    As you say, he is a swell guy; aside from the practical aspects of the matter, it was a real pleasure to

---

2 Hecht wrote in his *A Child of the Century:* "The deft and endearing secret of my friend Covici's charm was that he opened a book — the shabbiest and dreariest of them — as if he were looking into a ruby." Covici, Hecht wrote, "rushed manuscripts into print as if they were a new issue of greenbacks," and as a result his Chicago publishing house went bankrupt.

talk with him. I'm afraid, though, that I fell into my
usual habit of talking too much and listening not enough.

He was definitely receptive to the idea I'm working on;
I detected a personal curiosity as to how I could do the
things I told him I was doing. So, when it's ready, I think
it will at least get an interested reading. That's a lot.

Toni, in this period of the Hitler-Stalin pact, felt a chill in her heart.
She and other Jewish progressives were rapidly abandoning the old-line
Popular Front groups they'd been supporting for many years. The Communists leading these groups, which had brought liberals of all stripes
together to work for social justice, made a quick about-face when the
Soviet Molotov and the German Ribbentrop sat down together to carve
up Poland, delivering hundreds of thousands of Jews into Hitler's hands.
Stay out of the imperialist war, these Communists and their allies told all
who would listen. Toni wasn't listening anymore.

I'm sorry you quit the Magazine Guild because,
apparently, it was following the Party line. Naturally, it
was inevitable that there would be a great dropping away
among liberals from organizations that have radical leadership, particularly when these same liberals were attracted to
such organizations by reason of anti-Nazi activities.

It's a problem here at home; Naomi and I no longer see
within a million miles of one another on political matters,
and it hasn't helped the domestic situation a bit. In fact,
I could take you and Naomi and half a dozen of the most
intelligent people I know and shake them together in a big
sack and whichever came out first would express the
identical views of each of the others.

But all of that is wishful thinking, plus unwillingness to face the facts in the world situation. If we're
destined to go through a period of fascism (thirty years?
three hundred years?), it will be largely because of that
inability of the average intelligent, imaginative person to
face those facts frankly and fearlessly and to meet the
needs of this world as they are instead of shutting his
eyes and hoping for the best while recognizing the worst.
The ideal of democracy is not an "inherent right of man";
it is one of the things which must be earned; it is a
domain which must be conquered.

May 14, 1941

Dear Toni,

When I talked with Covici, I got so enthusiastic about
the idea of writing a book that I've been reluctant even to
give myself time to sleep. The job was done, in fact, ten
minutes ago by the clock. There's no possible question that
it's a much better book than "You're Paying for It!," but
if I'd suspected it was going to be as much work as it was,

I doubt if I'd ever have started it. I've really worked on the damn thing, and I feel like a mountain that labored. Yet I had a job to do which, simple as it was, was almost beyond me -- to wrap up the whole of the Marxist concept of history, and of the present, and of the future into a single volume without including a single phrase, or a single concept which would alienate the average American with the average American prejudices and ideas.

The weakness, from a publisher's standpoint, may be the fact that it's written for people who read Sunday supplements. Anybody who has finished the eighth grade can understand it and, I think, the follower of Mickey Mouse can follow it with interest. But, as Covici said, the follower of Mickey Mouse doesn't buy books.

I hope I haven't bored you with these details, but the fact is that I know nothing else, and I'm excited at having written after seven months of work, and you're my literary inciter anyway. I remember once, a million years or so ago, you asked me if I'd ever read a book or something, and I said, "No," and you gave me one. I suppose I must have owned books before that, since I did have a year in college, but I still insist that was the first book I ever owned.

After another week to be spent on the finishing touches, I'm going to take the most intensive vacation anybody ever had in their lives. I'm going to take long walks in the park (we have the most beautiful park in the world here) and go on camping trips and see movies and plays and just generally raise hell. And the good old world can keep rolling right along and they can declare war and raise taxes and kill everybody between the ages of twenty-one and thirty-five and occupy Dakar -- and I won't even notice it. Unfortunately, I still have to work for Mr. Hearst -- or somebody. But the eight hours I put in at the job is just a time-killer; I'll actually have sixteen hours a day left for myself.

Don't let my enthusiasm over having finished the job infect you at such a distance. Anybody can write a manuscript if he keeps at it long enough; it's a different thing to write one that will be published. So I'm not either really over-confident or under-confident. I'm just through -- thank God!

Brick's manuscript, which he had retitled *This Grim New World,* was sent to Curtis Brown, which sent it at once to Pat Covici at Viking. Apparently nobody at Curtis Brown bothered to read it at that time.

May 17, 1941

Dear Dickie,

Now that the book is finished, I'm going to have to start thinking about what I'm going to do next. One reason

I've hesitated to come to any conclusion was that San
Francisco is such a good place to work that I really wanted
to try another book before I broke away. Also, I needed to
kind of live down some of the tough times I had down south
before I went back and tried to get a job again. Now that
the book's finished, I don't like to face the prospect of
settling down here on a steady routine job with the kids
five hundred miles away. It just doesn't work out well that
way. There isn't anything in it.

[From Dickie]
May 27, 1941

My dear Brick,

Well, Brick, about your getting a job down here -- of
course, it would be nice for you to be near the kids, but I
certainly dread the possibility of your being out of a job.
From my standpoint I am just now beginning to get my head
above water. I want to buy the kids some good mattresses,
and that is going to take a little dough. They are getting
big enough now to complain of their beds, and I can't say
that I blame them. Louis' cot is atrocious, but Charles
does the complaining.

If perhaps you could hold out up there a year or two
more, both of us would be better off financially. The kids
say when you make your million dollars on your book they
are going to have a house with a bathroom for each bedroom,
like my boss does. That's too much house for me, but it's
nice to think about the successful selling of the book.

At Viking Press, Toni was keeping track of the progress of the book.
"A couple of our Leftists have read your manuscript with tremendous
interest and excitement. (One of them is neglecting his work this moment
because he can't tear himself away from it.)" She added: "When the boys
found out I knew you, they besieged me with questions, and they're sure
you have a great future. " And, she wrote, Pat Covici was enthusiastic
about the work and was trying to figure out a way to present it to "the
boss" — Harold Guinzburg, who had formed the company with B. W.
Huebsch and George Oppenheimer — so that Viking would actually publish it. "What is in store for it here," Toni wrote, "will depend on Covici
and God. So, here you go, Brick. It will be nice to say, 'I knew him when
he was a young man looking for the truth.' "

On Sunday, June 22, Germany broke its nonagression pact and invaded Russia.

July 21, 1941

Dear Toni,

The kids are up here, and I can't write or do much of
anything while they're here. But I'm getting a little

impatient -- it always leaves me slightly jittery with
nothing to do except my extremely monotonous work at the
office. I'll be glad when September comes. I'll make at
least a couple of false starts and find out which of two
books I'm going to do. One I have in mind is a personal
history sort of thing -- fictionalized autobiography. The
other is somewhat similar to the one just finished -- but
on a definitely higher plane, for the educated reader who
can read words of more than one syllable. "The Eclipse of
Democracy" is a working title.

On July 28 Toni had to inform Brick that, despite the report by one
of the Viking readers that "Mr. Garrigues may well have written what
may well be a classic in its field" and by another who wrote, "Of the
hundreds of mss. received by us dealing with 'economics for the layman,' this is the most well-written and intelligent," despite the friendly
intervention of Pat Covici, despite all that, Guinzberg, the president of
Viking, didn't want to publish it. "Not for us," he decided, and that was
that, so far as Viking was concerned, because even the Pope has to answer to a higher authority. The manuscript was sent back to Curtis Brown.

August 10, 1941

Dear Toni,

Your letter -- announcing the bad news -- arrived just
before I started for the Sierra. So I set out in the serene
confidence at least that I needn't watch for the mailman
for a few weeks. That, at any rate, was a real comfort;
between keeping one eye covertly cocked in the direction of
the mailbox and one ear tuned in for war bulletins I was
going slightly daffy without realizing it.

It was a swell vacation trip. We took a sleeping bag
and a few utensils and a little food. When night came we'd
find a quiet place a few miles off the road and cook our
dinner beside a brook, then curl up and go to sleep. Always
we were above five thousand feet and three nights above
seven thousand. One night, up eight thousand, we got caught
in a terrific thunderstorm and had to take a cabin at a
little resort. But it was magnificent. Imagine yourself up
eight thousand feet on the mountain edge of the desert, in
a cul-de-sac surrounded by peaks from eleven thousand to
thirteen thousand feet high and the loop of the peaks
enclosing terrace of lake after lake -- melting snow
pouring over the cliffs in waterfalls and cascades, forming
an intensely blue lake miles around and then plunging down
the next terrace to the next lake -- all surrounded by dark
firs and pines with deep red bark.

Behind the peaks, huge, dark thunderclouds with
lightning shooting from peak to peak --

Coming back we decided to try and take the little

Willys across Sonora Pass, which is the worst of the passes over the Sierra.

From the valley floor at six thousand you climb to seven thousand up the bank of a tumbling river which pours down from the glaciers. Then the road sign says: Steep grade ahead, and you shove it into low and give it the gun, winding up and up the bare side of a huge glacial moraine. The storm is still thundering; you climb fifteen hundred feet almost straight up, and the rain gets heavier and heavier. You come out in the pass itself, stunted, wind-whipped trees, gnarled rocks and the river gnashing itself against the fantastic stones. Two huge peaks on either side: the lightning smashes at one and then the other, and the rain beats down so heavily on the tin top of your car that you can scarcely tell the sound from the thunder. The car digs in and pulls as you go up and up, swinging around curves, until finally she straightens out and you seem to be pointing the nose of the car straight at the sky for the last two hundred yards. The car groans -- and starts to take it and finally -- just a dozen feet from the summit -- she dies.

There's a terrific clap of thunder and the rain changes to hail -- and there you are -- a dozen feet from the top in one direction and two hundred miles from any other pass. You try again and she moves forward six inches; you try it again and get a foot; you try it again and again, and in a dozen tries you're over. But the rain is coming down so you can't see the road; the lightning is still crackling around your head and you'd give anything to get out of there.

You put her into low gear and creep down with your foot jammed on the brake. The rain has loosened some stones, and they rattle down on top of your car. You'd give anything to be able to go down at more than five miles an hour. As you round a turn, you see that the rainwater is pouring in a cataract five hundred feet high into the top of a small snow field on the perpendicular mountain and you wonder if the flow will loosen the hundred acres of snow and start an avalanche. You try to keep from going any faster, and finally you get down below the rain, and people are having a picnic in a meadow, and you realize for the first time how scared you really were.

It probably wasn't actually dangerous; I'll never know. But for sheer dramatics (especially the thunderclap and the hail just as the engine died), it was quite enough for me.

There! I have written about something other than the book. I knew that some day I would. We got home tonight to find a letter from Curtis Brown saying merely that Viking had rejected it and that they (Curtis Brown) were now reading it.

The official reason for the rejection is that "it
falls between two stools -- it is not technical enough for
experts and too technical for the casual reader."

Personally, I think that a good love affair is
infinitely more important than a book but (maybe it's the
effect of Naomi) I've developed in the last few years the
idea that a book -- even an unsuccessful manuscript -- is
infinitely less dangerous to one's piece of mind. And,
besides, I'm getting along in years.

In September somebody at Curtis Brown finally got around to reading Brick's manuscript. "I think Covici put his finger on the difficulty of
this book," Alan P. Collins, one of the agents, wrote. "Added to that, I
am not at all sure that the average person, confused as he is by the state
in which he finds himself, is interested just now in having that state
analyzed." Brick withdrew the book and Curtis Brown sent the manuscript back to him on September 30 for extensive rewriting.

February 13, 1942

Dear Dickie:

I'm working on the book and hope to have it finished
in a month or so. You know, maybe I'm kidding myself, but I
sometimes think that I have something there -- something
really important. It's a much stronger book than it was
before, and if it turns out the way it's intended, it may
be one of those things that people will be quarreling about
and quoting twenty-five or fifty years from now.

April 28, 1942

Dear Toni,

How long since I've heard from you? A long time, I
think. But spring is here, and the apple tree in the back
yard is in full blossom and I always seem to come up out of
my daze in the springtime. Soon the summer fogs will begin,
and then it will be cold until September -- a strange town,
this.

But the magnum opus is nearly finished -- again. The
last half dozen chapters have to be pointed up a bit, but
the first dozen are finished, and Naomi is about to start
typing them. They've reached the place where I can't
honestly improve them except by throwing them in the
fireplace.

How's the man problem? Sometimes I suspect that the
Almighty made a serious error in adopting the mammalian
method of reproduction after having devised the much more
painless method of the fish. Only, I think, our chief
troubles are not really romantic. They arise from our
insistence on hurling our will at the world and attempting
to make it conform to our wishes by sheer force of

willpower. They arise from our inability to distinguish between the Me and the Not-Me. We will our hand to move, and it moves; we will some man to move in such-and-such a fashion, and he does not move.

A baby lies in its crib and sees its hand move. Then, to its delight, it learns that it can direct the hand's movement. The discovery is fatal; it attempts in the same way to make the face of its mother appear before it. The effort fails, and in indignation the brat lets out a bellow. The mother's face appears -- and speech, incantation, magic is born.

Pat Covici made another visit to San Francisco and insisted Brick have a drink with him and talk about writing.

October 26, 1942

I had a very interesting, instructive and valuable meeting with Covici last night.

I can't honestly -- speaking for either of us -- say it was enjoyable, particularly. We talked in the St. Francis bar from eight-thirty at night to one-thirty in the morning; the joint was jammed to the doors with ensigns and second looies who fell all over themselves; I was tired, having just come back from a ten-mile hike in the hills; Covici was obviously tired. So we nagged at each other, arguing economics hour after hour. Like a couple of old women.

The only time we agreed was when I asked him about you. His face lit up with a sparkle and we spent ten minutes telling each other what a swell gal you are. I gather that you're as charming as you were years ago. In fact, my recollection of how charming you really are was more than confirmed. So, at least, on one thing we agreed.

As for the book, Covici confirms the haunting fear that's been in the front of my mind since I began the enterprise: I had written a book perfectly designed to appeal to precisely the people who never read books.

Aside from that, life has become singularly even tenor. Is it middle age? I suppose so, because I find myself more and more able to relax and enjoy things with a certain tolerance.

As ever,

Brick

Chapter Eighteen
The Role to Which She Was Assigned

They were gone, those days of wine and roses; they were gone, those days of the radio broadcasts, the picture at the top of the newspaper column, the sound of people murmuring his name as he passed in a hallway. They had not been long. Somehow he had fled them, or perhaps they had been wrenched from him. Their loss rankled. Publishing a book, some say, can give immortality to a man. But, say others, so can children. Brick had one book behind him, and two sons. He sought another book. Another child? No. And yet —

November 17, 1942

Dear Dickie,

Naomi, whether by accident or design, has got herself pregnant. Or, to be perfectly fair, Naomi is pregnant. And I'm stuck. It was the one thing that wasn't ever going to happen. But it did. I can imagine almost nothing, outside a death in the family, that would have hit me quite so hard.

And I rather suspect I've been unconsciously sending you telepathic messages ever since we found out about it. I wanted at least to hear you say, "Well, what the hell did you expect? Serves you right!" But since I couldn't get down there to hear you say it, I just imagined you saying it, and that helped me to buck up. Though I still can't adjust to the situation.

There are a lot of different angles. There's the fact that I can't stand to be tied down to family routine.

That's one. Then there's the fact that I've never got over considering you and the kids my "family"; according to my philosophy, Naomi should have kept the role to which she was assigned.

There's the financial angle, too. Partly the fact that I've condemned myself to a life of poverty. Three kids in one family would be bad enough. But three kids in two families is expensive as hell. Naomi is working and should earn enough to take care of the first expenses. But it'll be close figuring. With no relief in sight -- ever.

There's also the fact that I can't see myself going through the trials and tribulations of fatherhood again. With you it was different; we were young, it was fun, it was exciting. But now it's a chore, a burden to which I can bring no enthusiasm.

It seems just as though a big door has closed in front of me. I can't see through it, and I can't see around it. And about all there is to do is to sit and stare at it and wonder what's going to happen.

But I think that I can "take it" better than I've been able to do in a long time. I mean there comes a time when you quit struggling, when you no longer try to figure out how to get what you want, when you stop demanding those things as your right. Then life becomes somewhat more placid. And, in consequence, I haven't had any great emotional upsets about it. Oh, I wake up sometimes in a towering rage at the whole situation, but then I can hear you say, "Well, what did you expect?" and I am eventually able to laugh at myself, quite honestly, for having expected anything else.

Now don't say you feel sorry for Naomi. In a way, I feel sorry for her myself. After all, it's no minor thing to have a first child at her age, and she's been horribly spoiled and pampered by her family until she's just horribly scared of pain. And it's no bargain for a woman to go through that sort of thing with a husband who is completely out of sympathy with the whole process. So I do feel sorry for her, and I try not to be too damnably resentful. But I'm sorrier for myself -- though it's my own fault.

Should you tell the kids about this? Somebody'll have to, some time. The great event comes off in May, I think. I haven't even been interested enough to start counting on my fingers.[1]

> [From Dickie]
> November 20, 1942

Dear Brick:

So there is life in the old boy yet! Needless to say your news struck me like a bolt of lightning.

---

[1] It was Naomi who broke the news, in one of her rare letters to us. Chuck and I were amazed and excited by this change in our lives.

I can't understand how one man can expect so much sympathy. I'm really the long-suffering one in the family. Well, Brick, there is nothing much for me to say. Our kids are puny and come from a long ancestry of non-money-makers. So trust that your next family does better by you. Of course, you know that I am always concerned about you (too damned much).

November 25, 1942

Dear Dickie:

The fact is that our divorce never "took" for me. But I've been so thoroughly -- shall I say -- humiliated, or remorseful? over the way I booted our own marriage that I really tried to play this one with Naomi out without, as you once said, trying to eat one's cake and still have it. So I've walked the straight and narrow without even allowing myself regrets. Yet I realize now that I was doing the same old thing: trying to keep Naomi as a gal friend and you and the kids as my family.

With you I swaggered around and was so god damned perfect and high-and-mighty that when I fell and bumped my head I couldn't get up again. I couldn't swagger any more; I couldn't be high-and-mighty. And there wasn't anything either of us could do about it. I really felt that your interest was in me -- not in some picture you carried around. (But with Naomi, on the other hand, all I really needed to do was to walk through the motions of conforming; she was married to a picture which she made up -- not to me.)

I suppose this is unfair to Naomi. She's a sweet, lovable, irresponsible, fun-loving, grasping, selfish, self-centered, chiseling, angling girl. I'm very fond of her. Lots of ways we get along fine. But I don't really "belong." I guess it won't do any harm for me to say it once.

Don't let me make any demands on you for sympathy. But don't dislike me, either. I've got no sense. I know it.

Naomi was happy. Years later, she wrote: "I was so thrilled when I became pregnant — I never felt better in my life. I can still remember how I felt, that curiously mingled feeling of great elation and some alarm, and then that wonderfully good feeling that this is what we want, and should have." And that was the role Naomi assigned to herself.

Brick, though, was filled with discontent. He was trying to birth a book, but Naomi had rewritten his life's script by preparing to birth a baby instead. He rewrote the book. But he couldn't rewrite the life script.

December 7, 1942

Dear Toni,

I sometimes wonder what happened to that former ability of mine to write simply and unsentimentally and somewhat satirically. I spent last evening keeping warm by burning hundreds and hundreds of pages I'd written and thrown away. (Remember the scene in "Boheme"? I'd never realized how much warmth was in a manuscript.)[2] And I glanced at some of it, and it was horrible; much worse than I'd ever written before.

January 25, 1943

All is quiet on the domestic front. Perhaps in one way you're right: that the necessity for more money will drive me to greater efforts.

It's a relief to get the book off my hands, though. For two years I've done nothing but write and re-write -- and for two years before that I was busy recovering from the strain of an active life. Now, for the first time, I feel relaxed among people, and it becomes possible to see them again.

In one way, I'm having a little fun: They're filling the office up with copygirls, and I've become a sort of father-confessor to the brood. They're sweet kids -- or my protegees are -- and very young and filled with troubles: boyfriends in the Army, husbands in the Navy, etc., etc. We're developing the habit of having a bevy of them and their boyfriends to the house once a week. Everybody brings food and drink; we play phonograph records, and somebody reads poetry or something. So far I haven't fallen for any of them yet; wisdom, I hope, has come with years. But it does give a freshness and vividness which one is likely to lose as middle age comes along. The kids love it.

I'm always surprised at the number of lonely women there are in the world. I think the trouble must be with the women; there are certainly as many men as women, and I haven't noticed that most men show any particular aversion to feminine company. But somehow women seem to build up their own obstacles. It puzzles me.

I feel sorry for these particular kids. When a woman is twenty-five or thirty, she should have developed some resources within herself which (however poor a substitute) give her a philosophy or something to enable her to solve her problem. But these youngsters (one is eighteen, one nineteen, two are twenty) are dumped on the world at the exact time they should be having fun -- and nobody to have fun with, except 4Fs.[3] Maybe it's a good thing I've reached the years of discretion, if not wisdom.

And that's enough philosophy for tonight. Isn't the news swell from Russia? Leningrad! Kamensk? Rostov next?[4]

---

2 Act I of the Puccini opera, in which the poet Rodolfo burns his play to keep warm. "So the fruits of brilliance achieve fulfillment," a friend tells him.

3 The draft classification 4F was given to men who were physically unfit to serve.

4 The references are to cities in Russia. The Battle of Leningrad had just ended. Total Axis losses (Germans, Romanians, Italians, and Hungarians) were about 800,000 dead. Some historians estimate that 1.1 million Soviet soldiers died in the campaign. The retreating German forces still held Kamensk and Rostov.

February 15, 1943

Naomi says she will not be satisfied until you come out here on a visit. I think she wants to keep me away from the little girls. But when I point out that you're much more dangerous than a whole flock of little girls, she collapses. But she still thinks you're so swell she could trust you.

March 23, 1943

I have been paying too much attention to the youngsters at the office and have fallen upon evil ways, drinking iced bourbon and staying out until all hours and using the time in chattering that I should be using in working. However, the scripts are completed and Naomi is mailing them to you this afternoon.

Association with these kids is doing me a lot of good. None of them have ever heard of politics or economics. The boys go off to war very reluctantly, but nobody wonders very much what it's all about, although they resent it. We seldom talk about any of the things I've been interested in for the last ten years -- and I think it's good for me.

You go along and the world becomes grayer and life shorter; the path before is, at best, a weak reflection of the path behind, and vigor and delight have gone out of the world. People are old, and the world is old, and even spring awakens but a dim remembrance of other springs. And then you look behind you and here comes a whole host of rushing, laughing, wondering, enthusiastic, vigorous kids. And you realize that life isn't gray and dull; it's only that you've been among gray and dull people.

Life renews itself; spontaneously they come, wave after wave of kids, as hopeful and youthful and beautiful as we were twenty years ago. It would be a mistake, I suppose to become too interested in the new generation. But it's splendid to know that they are there and, in a measure, to live with them. I think that, subconsciously, I always resented the youngsters who were twenty when I was thirty. But those who are twenty when I'm forty are marvelous.

I have, of course, a favorite among my youngsters. I must always have a favorite girl around somewhere. But it isn't serious.

May 16, 1943

Dear Dickie:

I've been wondering precisely what Emily Post advises on the matter of informing one's ex-wife that one is a father again?

Anyway, it's a girl, born last night, and everything seems to be perfectly all right. She's a healthy brat with a healthy squall, and Naomi seems to be accomplishing her part of it without too much difficulty. I've refused to have anything to do with it.

When the baby was born on May 15 she was called Patricia Jesse, the first name for Brick's sister who died when she was only sixteen, and the second for Naomi's father.

I suppose my attitude on the thing hasn't been all it should be. I've been very much opposed to it, and even the last couple of days hasn't got me more than reasonably interested. But it did take me back to the days when our kids were born; I think I thought more of that than I did of what was going on in the hospital. I sometimes think that history does more than repeat itself; sometimes it burlesques itself.

I'm really ashamed at the way I feel about it. I no longer resent it actively, but I'm surprised to find in myself so complete an indifference. Once more a phase of my life seems to have ended. But this time I don't look forward to the succeeding phase with any particular enthusiasm. Possibly that feeling won't last.

The fact is, I don't like myself very well. In that circumstance, life goes on none too satisfactorily.

Of course, there is also the fact that the book hasn't sold, and I'm beginning to believe that it won't. And I buried myself for a year and a half getting ready to write it and for two years in writing it. No friends and not much fun. And I can feel a novel welling up inside of me and demanding to be written. But I'm afraid I can't write it; afraid to tackle it because a book like that is written out of the pains and disappointments of the past, and I don't want to go through that again, even on paper. But I think I shall have to write it or explode. Maybe when the kids come up I can take refuge in having fun with them.

May 20, 1943

Dear Toni:

I have a little daughter. I'm rather glad it's a girl, in a way. Makes for variety. But there's something ironic in the fact that I just reach the age when girls cease to trouble me, and then I find myself saddled with one for life. Anyway, the fact of another infant in the family doesn't thrill me with the sense of possession. (It's strange that my brother, who is crazy about kids, has none, while I have three.)

I'm really glad for Naomi's sake. She's as happy as can be and as proud as a little queen. She orders all her relatives around as though she were the first woman who ever had a baby; she's had a phone installed by her hospital bed so she can call and give orders to her sister

and to me. And she's being very sweet. But the whole
business seems one in which I'm purely an onlooker; it's
almost as though she had invited a cousin to come and spend
her life with us.

But she's a cute brat. The hospital is so busy I've
only succeeded in getting one look at her,[5] but she looks
as though she'll be all right. I hope she has Naomi's hair
and eyes and my face. And I'm eager to see how it really
seems to have a baby in the house again.

Trouble is that Naomi's affection is so all-pervading
and possessive. More than that: She insists upon identify-
ing the two of us into one person -- and that person, of
course, is she.

As ever,

Brick

---

5 The war had taken military-age doctors, nurses and attendants. In addition, these were the
days when mothers and their newborns were often kept for a week before being sent home.

Chapter Nineteen
Love's Old Sweet Song

It was after I started working on this book but before I had asked Vivian to do the editing on the manuscript. She and I had finished a light refreshment at a cappuccino *boîte* in El Cerrito and were following it up with some idle shelf-shopping at the various upward-striving stores on Fairmount Avenue. We were in Wonderland, an aptly named used-book shop, and I headed straight for the "California History" section to see if I could find anything useful in my research.

Jackpot.

There was a hardbound orange volume bearing on its cover the California state seal (the Goddess of Wisdom holding her spear, with the motto "Eureka," which means "I Have Found It,") and the words *Un-American Activities in California; Report of the Joint Fact-Finding Committee to the Fifty-Fifth California Legislature; Sacramento, 1943*. I turned to the index and called Vivian over.

"Look," I said, pointing to a name. It was my father's. GARRIGUES, C. H.

"And look here." I flipped over several pages. There was her mother's name as well. PRAGER, MOLLIE.

I bought the book and it will be our grandchildren's treasured heirloom some day.

The story of the various state and federal legislative investigative committees during the McCarthy era has been told many times, so I won't go into it now. Just let me say: The listing of names — not any kind of legislation or uncovering of treason — was the important product of

these morally deficient politicians. They prepared and published black-
lists of the worst kind, disseminated widely through the mail and at John
Birch Society bookstores like the one open for many years at the corner
of Solano and San Pablo avenues in Albany. Employers would refer to
them when making decisions on whom to hire and whom to fire. Once
you got on a list, you couldn't get off.

At ages twelve and ten, though, Chuck and I knew nothing of these
matters early in that war year of 1943. Our letters kept flowing, some of
them rather silly (not including an interesting exchange between Chuck
and Brick about Einstein's theory of relativity and the nature of time and
space), with Chuck spinning off parodies on some of the science fiction
he and Brick had been reading. Brick told him he should try his hand at
a burlesque of a good biography for a change.

> [From Chuck to Brick,
> handwritten;
> April 1942]
>
> Re: Your remark that "There is nothing more left than
> to burlesque a good biography." Nothing more! Why, I am in
> the bud of life! My career! To write a b. on a g. b. would
> ruin me! But I'll tell you what. When I'm on my deathbed,
> the wife and fifteen kids and all the rest gathered around
> me, I'll struggle feebly upward, write a b. on a g. b., and
> then take it with me to show to you in that strange heaven
> where Garrigueses go!

But Brick at this time had more on his mind than responding to the
idolatrous japes of his talented son — or to the scurrilous rants of legislative
committees. He was teaching Naomi how to mother a baby; he was getting
up at daybreak to bring Patty into their bed and cushion her between them; he
was insisting that his wife not wait the then-fashionable three hours between
feedings but instead give the little girl her bottle whenever she was hungry.
Like many men of his day, he felt unable to really talk with anyone about his
conflicted feelings; and so he turned to his old friend, the typewriter.

> [May or June 1943]
>
> Dear Dickie,
>
> Things are rather busy at the house right now. The
> youngster is coming along fine, and she's really a very
> good baby. She cries very little. But since I'm the only
> experienced parent in the house, I have to do all the
> experting, and that means mixing formula, sterilizing
> bottles, deciding whether a cry means colic or hunger or
> sleepiness. And it keeps me more than busy. I haven't had
> more than about five hours' sleep a night for at least a
> couple of weeks and feel that I'm going to blow my topper
> some of these times. So your letters give me a much-needed
> touch of sanity.

What you said about the kids being a lot of bother to you gave me the idea -- or the courage, rather -- to wonder if you might not be willing to let me take them for a year or so. I've hesitated to suggest it because, since you've raised them, you're certainly entitled to them when they become more fun and less trouble. But if they're reaching the age when they're more trouble and less fun, maybe you'd like to get rid of them for a while.

But as a matter of fact, I'm sufficiently depressed so that I don't even know whether having the kids up here will lift me out of it or not. I hope it will, but I'm not counting on it. The uncertainty about the book keeps me down. I charge it off as a nonseller, and I don't feel that I can tackle another one.

You seem to be the only person I know to whom I can weep at the moment. Naomi is filled with the problems of motherhood, which are exactly as boring to me as the problems of writing picture captions. I don't seem to have any particular friends up here, and it isn't as easy to talk to people as it used to be.

May 31, 1943

Dear Toni,

I'm still very low. I think it's the present sterility of life: making formula, washing diapers, going shopping, and holding down the dullest, most monotonous job I've ever had.

I'm glad you think I should seriously try a novel again. I think so too. I've worked long enough on the last manuscript so I've lost some of the fear of tackling a two-year job. I feel sufficiently superior to character and situation so I can dig around in it. And I'm filled with ideas. I'm also far enough away for the first time from politics and economics so I won't be tempted to write propaganda. (That's been a grave difficulty with me in recent years.)

June 30, 1943

I'm writing again, but still not fiction. It's another book in the same field, expounding the "theory of industrial feudalism" which was developed in some degree in "This Grim New World."

My own kids are up here now, but I'm glad to find that they don't interfere too much with my own work. On the contrary, we use the same study and work without interfering with one another. Charles is devising short stories for the science fiction pulps and has written one that, for the field, is not half bad. Louis has dedicated his life to the writing of animal fantasies in the style of Hugh Lofting[1] and has been working on a book-length yarn with which he hopes to carry on the tradition of Doctor Dolittle when

---

[1] Hugh Lofting, author of the Doctor Dolittle books, was born in 1886 and died in 1947.

Lofting passes to his reward. The funny thing is that the
kids curl up after dinner or after breakfast and really
write without bothering the adults.

                              August 11, 1943
     The new script, "The Imaginary Revolution," is coming
along splendidly. I've got into the habit of writing so that
nothing can interrupt it very seriously; every morning after
breakfast I sit at the typewriter by 8:30, and the session
lasts from an hour to an hour-and-a-half before I get up. I
manage to spend half an hour or an hour with the boys in the
morning and ten or fifteen minutes with them after I come
home from work. The rest of the time I'm doing little chores
or feeding Patricia or changing her pants or working.

The brief amount of time we spent with our father that summer was
just about right. Chuck and I were beginning to have our own friends in
San Francisco, and we both had either paper routes or a corner to sell
papers on. Mine was at Haight and Ashbury in a neighborhood shopping
district that was then merely a collection of Italian businesses in a time
when "hippy" meant somebody who was fat. Later, it would be the colorful but seedy district where the flower children lived in the 1960s.

                              August 28, 1943
Dear Dickie:
     Charles says he would like to come up next year and
enter high school, if it's still all right with you.
     They are the best kids I ever saw, and it seems like
I've hardly had a chance to see them this summer. I'm sorry
they took the paper jobs since it prevented us from going
anywhere on my days off. But today we took a drive into the
hills across the bay, and the three of us went for a long
walk among the redwoods and then out into a prairie, where
we found an old apple orchard with some apples that we
started to pick. But we were attacked by a swarm of bees
(Louis had started back by that time), and you should have
seen us run -- tearing off our clothes to get at the bees,
which had already got at us. But I was stung only three
times and Charles once, and -- as Charles says -- it's an
experience he'll never forget.
     Louis has become the great explorer. He starts out
with one streetcar token to see if he can find a method of
transferring that will take him all over the city and back
in a circle to where he started from. So far, he's always
made it, but I suspect that some day he'll have to walk
about five miles home.
     The baby is fine; I'll let Charles tell you about her,
as he is her chief admirer. Boy, is he proud when he's
allowed to hold her for a minute!

October 30, 1943

Naomi and Pat have gone away to Prescott for a long visit, and now I'm preparing to settle down to a winter of idleness.

Little Pat is just as cute as can be, and we became pretty good friends, although I never came to feel about her as I did about our kids. Fact is, I think Charles is fonder of her than I am. She's really been a perfect baby for health and behavior. But I honestly can't say I miss her.

I'm hoping that I'll be able to save up a few dollars this winter. Things have been so damned tight; we've always had enough to eat, but it's been a continual battle to keep from running into debt -- carrying a lunch and making the old suit do another year and shining your own shoes. I hoped I'd never be this broke again. Or rather, I hoped that when I skimped on a minor necessity to have a minor luxury, I'd have it. Instead -- although Naomi has really tried to learn how to handle money -- the more I skimp, the less I have. It isn't that she doesn't try; it's only that she doesn't know the difference between a dime and a dollar. And never will, I suppose.

The European war should be definitely over by spring; perhaps even by Christmas. And the five-hundred-dollar severance pay I have coming will do a lot to protect my job and make certain the kids will eat when the crash comes.[2] We were pretty lucky in the last depression, and this time there'll be a lot of safety nets under us: severance pay, unemployment insurance, etc., but I remember the last one well enough so I don't want to take a chance of having them pulled out from under me. I'm off the picture desk and back on the copy desk, and I like it infinitely better.

I think that, if I have time this winter, I'll look up San Francisco's bohemian crowd just as an experiment to see if I could stand now the sort of people we used to gang up with in the old days. I'm fairly certain I couldn't; they're too callow, and the spark of real intelligence is lacking. But it will be an interesting experiment. I haven't mixed with enough people in the last few years.

I often wonder what I'm doing up here, anyway. The town never seems like home; I neither know anybody nor want to know anybody. I should have been much better off, I suppose, if I'd been content to lead a normal, bourgeois life, making installment payments and raising the kids and finally growing old and dying with the normal dissatisfactions of existence. I really haven't written anything, although I've used up countless reams of paper. I've read and studied and philosophized to myself until it seems that I'm infinitely more ignorant than I was twenty years ago.

---

2 He was a year or more off on the end of the war; it ended in May 1945. There was no crash, either. In fact, there was a postwar boom; times had changed since the 1930s.

November 4, 1943

Dear Toni:

I wish I weren't so stubborn about things. I keep on rewriting "The Imaginary Revolution" and seem determined to put it into saleable shape if it takes a lifetime. And it isn't worth the effort. I have about a third of the new draft done, and now I've been rewriting the introductory chapter and changing the angle and, at this moment, I like it.

What I should do is to fall in love this winter. It would be nice to have that feeling of delight and excitement and anticipation. It seems years since I've had it. But perhaps I'm too old or something. Or maybe the rather unpleasant development of the second marriage has developed a big caution signal. Anyway, all the gals I know are the kids at the office who are much, much too young.

Besides, I'm an old man with family responsibilities.

Naomi stayed away for a long time; it was a real separation; she had gone back to her mother. Brick sought advice from Toni.

January 11, 1944

I have a secret fear that if Naomi and I finally break up, I shall be just as big a fool again, even at my advanced age. What makes my present situation of singleness rather gray is that, while I've always valued my individuality, my self-sufficiency and my privacy, most (or maybe all) of my playtime has been spent with women. But Naomi has been such a completely "feminine" sort of person, and I have been so badly disappointed in the entire relationship, that any other feminine associations immediately affect me like a danger signal.

When I first met Naomi I was in considerable need of feminine sympathy and understanding. That is, I suppose, a weakness -- but it's one I'm much afflicted with. So we used to spend countless hours talking -- about me. And she was the most intelligent, sympathetic, understanding person in the world; there was nothing in my hopes, aims, aspirations, which she didn't understand perfectly. Our whole relationship was based upon that agreement, sympathy and understanding.

Then, gradually, over a period of years, it began to dawn upon me that she hadn't heard a word I said. Nothing, literally nothing, penetrated into her consciousness; she lived entirely in a world of her own -- an entirely subconscious world in which she went her own sweet way with complete indifference to everybody else: literally, complete unconsciousness of the fact that anybody else existed. Gradually, I came to see that there was "no use talking to her"; she didn't hear me.

But I can't help suspect that maybe I've been wrong

from the beginning. I can see quite a bit of Naomi's point of view, enough so that I'm completely confused. Naomi can't tell me her side because there has been so much emotional conflict between us. And because all her logic is unconscious, sub-visceral, affective logic. Maybe you could. I'm terribly confused.

February 17, 1944

You misunderstood my problem. It isn't a question of a dame being compelled to spend her lifetime listening to a man's brilliance in return for her share of a paycheck. It was more a question of whether or not a woman could understand a simple statement like "We have no money in the bank; don't write any more checks" or "We can't afford a ten-dollar telephone bill every month for you to gossip with your sister," or "I don't want to settle down and raise a family." Some simple statement of fact like that which, one would suppose, a woman -- should I say "even a woman"? -- would understand.

I can think of nothing worse than a woman earning her living by listening to a man's brilliance, or his antique stories; it would be even worse, I suppose, than the usual procedure of earning a living by sleeping with him. Much more stultifying. But I had supposed -- naively, as I see now -- that some such statement as "We can't pay any bill at the Emporium next month" would be comprehensible. I was trying to discover whether women didn't hear such statements, or didn't understand them, or were moved by some form of logic which a man cannot follow.

Your answer convinced me that the latter was the case and since that time I've been engaged in trying to find the secret of that peculiar feminine logic which men would call illogic. It's a fascinating occupation; for the first time in my life I'm beginning to understand that I never knew -- was never even remotely acquainted with -- any woman. Something like the old story which ends with the indignant demand: "Since when has sexual intercourse been a justification for social acquaintance!"

I've been an incurable romanticist about women; an incurable illusionist. As a Marxist, I have fallen into the common belief that because women are men's equals (or so the Marxists say) they are entitled to be treated and considered as rationally and logically as men are considered. But that is patent absurdity; I don't see how I could have been a victim of it for so many years. Just another case of confusing the Not-is with the Is.

Don't misunderstand me; I'm not being chauvinistic. On the contrary, I think their logic is a fascinating one; I hope some day to be able to understand it -- or if not, to be able to annotate it to some degree. And it undoubtedly will be an interesting occupation. But why, merely because we make it an article of faith that women and men are equal, should we assume that they are identical?

Before I fell under the influence of the Marxists, I got along well enough. Women were women and one went one's own sweet way, fell in love and out, jilted and was jilted. Then I began to look upon women as human beings -- common members of humanity, blood brothers, etc.-- and to treat them and regard them as I should want to be treated or regarded. It was a most embarrassing course of conduct, leading, as it did, to matrimony and paternity and a hell of a lot of difficulties. All of which I supposed could be cured by masculine logic.

But masculine logic isn't worth a damn. The more I play around with Aristotle and Bertrand Russell ("there are classes of classes of classes") and others the more I'm convinced that masculine logic is simply a game men invent to amuse themselves with. Feminine logic is the thing. I don't know how it works, but it does work. When I find out, I'll really write that novel.

Yes, you're right in another thing. It would really be nice to go to New York and to ruin a lifelong friendship. And ruin it we would; I have a genius for it.

Seriously, though, I think maybe Naomi and I will get back together. I'm beginning to believe that love is a fact -- an illogical fact, but nevertheless a fact. We quarrel and fight, we frustrate one another in every possible way except physically. We do everything that rational people shouldn't. Neither of us can have anything we want out of life when we're together. And yet I think we're happier together than apart. And that -- I suspect -- is maybe my first venture in feminine logic.

June 4, 1944

Dear Toni,

At long last "The Imaginary Revolution" is finished; the last line is written, re-written, edited and re-edited and there remains only to stick in a couple of footnotes and half a dozen references and then persuade Naomi to type it.

It's a good book. Or, at least, if "This Grim New World" was almost a good book -- almost a book -- this new one is excellent. It's the first time I've ever written a manuscript with which I was thoroughly satisfied as to content, organization, style and everything. I thought "This Grim New World" might be good enough to get by. I think this one, if it gets published might very well put me up among them -- you know, the place where you start being a footnote reference yourself.

Don't think I'm too enthusiastic about its chance for publication. I realize the difficulties of introducing a book of this sort by a new author. And it's reasonably long

-- about 20,000 words, I think. But it definitely has permanent value; it'll be as important ten years from now as it will next year, yet it's geared to next year. I think it's definitely a book which a great many publishers would turn down only with extreme reluctance. I don't know how long it will take to get it typed, but by the middle of the summer it should be on its way to you.

I suppose "This Grim New World" has knocked at its last door and been tossed out on its ear. If you think it's had its last chance, don't hesitate to send it back. I know you don't have room to store all the decaying manuscripts your friends produce. And I have a nice little graveyard where I bury them.

Naomi is back and we quarrel somewhat less frequently than before. At least, we've both apparently made up our minds that there's no use in resenting things so that if a quarrel flares up it doesn't last long. We move along from day to day. The youngster is cute. With a Jewish mother and a French-German father, she looks as Irish as Paddy's pig. I like her, but I don't have the feeling about her that I had for the boys. In other words, I'm willing to let Naomi raise her, and when I take care of her for an afternoon or an evening it's just another not-unpleasant chore.

The boys will be practically grown up now; Charles is already taking girls to school dances. Just now I find myself resenting even that a little bit -- unconsciously. I suspect I've reached the age where one wants to cling to what little's left of youth. (Does this all sound horribly banal? I suspect that it does.)

On Moonlight Bay

In the evening Tom would sometimes hitch up the mare to the buggy and Bliss and Tom would drive to some neighbors' — where Bliss would sit, quiet in a corner, and listen to the wisdom of the twenty-year-olds. Ivor Thorberg had a clear tenor voice and Tom a rich baritone, and the others would fake a second tenor and bass, so they would make up a barber-shop quartet, singing until the dark shadows in the orange groves rang with sound and the mockingbird would stop to listen. The war was on in Europe then, but "Tipperary" had reached only as far as the high school in El Jardin. They sang this and other war songs in the high school, but in Edendale it was:

> *We were sailing along on Moonlight Bay;*
> *You could hear our voices ringing; they seemed to say,*
> *You have stolen my heart, now don't go 'way . . .*
> *Just as we sang love's old sweet song*
> *On Moonlight Bay . . . 3*

---

3 *Moonlight Bay*, lyrics by Edward Madden, around 1910.

And:

> *Down upon the levee,*
> *Though she's fat and heavy,*
> *None can dance like she . . . * [4]

They liked these best, when the boys sang together on Ivor Thorberg's verandah. But sometimes they would take their sisters along — sometimes there were even dances, arranged by their parents, and the girls would want to sing:

> *A Spanish cavalier,*
> *Stood in his retreat,*
> *And on his guitar played a tune, dear;*
> *The music so sweet.*
> *Would ofttimes repeat*
> *The blessing of his country and you, dear.* [5]

It was all very mysterious and very beautiful to Bliss, sitting in his corner of the verandah and watching the moonlight against the hillsides. He thought he was at the very threshold of some magic experience, that his hand could reach out and open some enchanted doorway which — if only he could find it — would open into undreamed vistas of beauty and magic and loveliness.

You said something in a recent letter which I think was incorrect: to the effect that what I wanted was a woman with a youthful body and a mature mind. That is what the comrades would call an over-simplification. I think the real burden of maturity is the discovery that nobody -- least of all your wife -- is really interested in you except yourself. Why should they be? You're not interested in anybody except yourself, either. So why should you expect anything different? Yet the result is a deepening loneliness. A love affair, or even a semi-platonic association, relieves you from it for a while; for a time it becomes possible to imagine that you and the other person are really interested in one another. And thus one gets temporary relief from the burden of existence. But only temporary.

I suspect it's different with you -- and with most women. Women are much more sensible; if nothing else, they can always build themselves private worlds in which to live. But even so, I think you're fortunate not to have been married; people of sensitivity shouldn't be.

But write me, won't you, and tell me about yourself. I'm afraid my semi-annual report on the condition of my emotions must become a little monotonous. But when, in the future, wise men will praise the clear, level, objective

---

4 Origin unknown.

5 *The Spanish Cavalier,* lyrics by W. D. Hendrickson.

thinking of the author of "The Imaginary Revolution," you
can say, "Oh, but he really wasn't like that, at all. He
was really very thus-and-so and this-and-that."

Once again, Chuck and I made our yearly visit to San Francisco. We
were now fourteen and twelve. But this summer was different. On this
trip we were supposed to stay for at least a year with Brick, Naomi and
Patty; Brick's hunger for his boys had overcome Dickie's anxiety about
separating from them.

[Summer 1944]

Dear Dickie:

I've never seen two finer kids. They get along swell
and do their chores every day (if reminded) and Charles
takes his typing lesson every day (if reminded). Both are
healthy; Charles seems to be putting on at least a little
weight and goes around trying to stick out what he calls
his "typical globe-like Garrigues belly." But it still
seems more like a washboard to me.

Louis can beat Charles playing tennis and does it
quite regularly. He can also beat all of us playing rummy,
but the main evening feature now is Louis' readings of the
adventures of Doctor Dolittle. He reads well and sure
enjoys it, and we all sit around and listen avidly --
especially Charles.

Charles dabbled a bit with soap sculpture, but he's
lost interest in it. He has a real talent, I think --
flashy, perhaps, but authentic. When he goes to the art
galleries he's always interested in technique. I think he
has even more talent for art than for writing. Louis is
steady and thorough, but he keeps us laughing with his puns
and quirks. Sometimes he'll go out and sit on the limb of a
tree in the park and chatter and chirp to himself like a
bird for an hour or two. There's nothing quite like him. In
many ways, he seems to be the leader of the two of them.

July 14, 1944

Charles is particularly good: mature, understanding
and helpful. He and Naomi get along fine -- much better
than I and Naomi. He is very wise and tolerant. Louis is a
little more of a problem. He and I get along splendidly,
but he has learned how to work Naomi by sulking, and he
overdoes it a little. I would like to keep him under my
wing if possible and put a lot of time on him because I
think that I could do things with him. But he's just in a
certain stage; he's so much like me at that age that it
isn't even funny. And he'll grow out of it, just as Charles
did.

August 28, 1944

Naomi left yesterday, and this time the split-up is

really meant to be final. So I suppose it will be. I am constantly being astonished at the good, practical sense of the most erratic of women. When Naomi finally reached the conclusion that she couldn't drive me into providing the sort of life she wanted, she just ups and leaves with very little hesitation or regret or indecision. Whereas, I, who had reached the same conclusion nearly five years ago, was unable to do anything of the sort.

As for the situation of the kids, we'll get along all right until school starts. They pitch in and help out, with a certain amount of nagging, and we manage to keep things going even with my unusual hours.

Putting meat back on the ration list has hurt a bit because most of the things I know how to cook are now rationed. The big thing that troubles me -- in prospect -- is the ironing of their shirts (which I don't know how to do) and getting them to comb their hair when they get up to go to school before I am up. But I guess these things can be worked out.

Did you ever think of moving up to San Francisco? How about coming up and visiting for a couple of months and looking the situation over? You could loaf (in the intervals of taking care of the kids) and look around and relax, which you haven't done in a long time. You could take over the flat and spend your days looking over the city and your nights brawling in bars. I don't know exactly what Emily Post says about entertaining one's ex-wife; maybe I'd have to get a room somewhere. I'm earning a good salary so long as the six-day week keeps up.[6]

I don't want to press the point -- partly because it isn't solely for your sake or that of the kids that I think it would be a good idea. I feel myself so rather disoriented, so much not-my-former-self, that I feel I could find out where I was if you were around.

I suppose my greatest trouble to Naomi was that I was always comparing her with you -- her housekeeping, her sense about money, her general interest in her husband and the things he was doing. The comparison was always to her disadvantage and she knew it and resented it, and there wasn't anything I could do about it.

That's all for today. Now I take a two-hour nap (2 p.m. to 4), then get up and cook dinner, then go to work at 7 and come home at 5 a.m. Tomorrow I get up at 11 and go to work at 7. Then the next day I get up at 1 p.m. and go to work at 2:30, meaning the kids will have to fix their own dinner. But I think it will all work out all right. Let's hear from you, huh?

---

6 Many offices and factories had switched to a forty-eight-hour week for the duration of the war, with time-and-a-half paid for overtime.

August 29, 1944

Dear Toni:

Life here has been a mad rush of necessities, climaxed Sunday by the final (I think) separation of the Garrigueses. This time it wasn't a sudden flare-up but rather a studied decision made by Naomi herself and adhered to over a period of weeks. She and Pat are in Pasadena, and the whole thing is over -- except for the business of paying for it at so much per week from now on.

It's something we should have done -- I should have done -- years ago. Now that it's done, my chief reaction is one of fear -- almost horrified fear -- at the thought of the entire feminine half of the human race. I feel that I was trapped and, further, that I don't resent it but rather realize for the first time that I was damned lucky to have escaped so many times in the past. And so the thought of women -- gal friends, even feminine acquaintances -- horrifies me. (Yet the habits of a lifetime are not easily broken.)

Aside from that, I feel a considerable concern for Naomi's welfare. I've spent so many millions of minutes taking care of her that it seems as though she couldn't possibly get along by herself -- although I should certainly know by this time that she's very well equipped to look out for her own interests.

Meanwhile, to complicate matters, Dickie has a flare-up in her own personal life; she quits her job and, for a while at least I have the boys on my hands. They're fun, and it isn't impossible to "batch" with two teen-age boys. But it's still far from the restful life I very much need right now. And I can't plan any changes until Dickie gets settled.

You can't imagine how hectic the summer has been. I work a night shift, ending some time between midnight and 5 a.m. Usually I've been able to get only four hours' sleep on my late nights -- filling in with an hour's nap in the afternoon. And every other minute has been spent in doing laundry or shopping or doing other household tasks. Working a six-day week, I have one night off. And the final blowup came when Naomi started to complain that I didn't take her to a movie on that one night. Or, rather, continued to complain and insisted that if I didn't think enough of her to give her one evening a week, why, then, to hell with me!

From her point of view there is a very great deal to be said on her side. Her own mistake was in not marrying a typical bourgeois of Jewish background (for, say what you will, the traditional, cultural spirit in Jewish families is different from my own cultural background).

I'm just beginning to become acquainted with some of the more obvious facts of life. As, for example, love. I suppose I've always been a romantic; I was never willing to let myself be convinced that love is primarily an economic emotion, even though it was possible to demonstrate the fact logically and sociologically.

I had a curious experience on my vacation which I hope I can tell you about as vividly as it affected me.

Do you remember, about ten years ago, a terrific upset I had about a girl named Janet? I was married to Dickie; she was a youngster; I took her about quite a bit -- or, rather, Dickie and I sort of adopted her for a while. It was a curious sort of an attachment which I didn't understand and can't fully analyze yet. I wasn't really conscious of being in love with the gal; yet she gave me a terrific "lift," a terrific sense of well-being, which I missed a lot when I didn't see her.

Well, anyway, she eventually married the guy I introduced her to. He was doing very well and eventually was made technically my boss. For a while they had quite a bit of dough; she was playing the social hostess and doing it well and, apparently, living exactly the sort of life she was designed to lead.

Some years later Steve and I were both doing political publicity in Los Angeles, and we had a business deal to talk over, so I spent a week-end at their place at the beach, and Janet and I instantly fell into the old relationship of kid protegee and elder guide -- with all due regard to Steve. We became great friends without seeing a great deal of one another, but -- in some fashion or other -- we began to depend on each other, it seems to me, as confidants.

So, a couple of years later (this was after Naomi and I were married), Janet spent a month with us up here while debating whether or not to divorce Steve. She got her divorce, and we remained good friends at a distance. Then she shows up with a new boy friend who happens to be a very good friend of mine; they teamed up for a year or so, and we spent our vacations together. I was very fond of the gal; I honestly think that each of us depends a great deal upon the fact of the other's existence. When the new boy friend came back from the Army, they decided to make it legal. So they were married and lived happily together for a couple of months and then split up.

Naturally, when I went south on my vacation, I dropped in to see Janet and talked over my trouble with Naomi and hers with Nick. I told her I was planning to move south for good, whereupon she turned around and said: "Better not do that, or I'll marry you myself." So I said, somewhat truthfully: "I was afraid of that" -- and then we stood and looked at one another for a while and went out to dinner.

I should say that she is a very distinguished-looking, cool, self-possessed dame -- lovely and nice to look upon but very unfeminine. Then we talked about what we'd really been thinking of each other all these years -- curiously, objectively, as though it were two other people. There really wasn't a word said about being in love with one another; both of us were more curious, I think, than emotional.

The next day we went to her boss's house (a woman), and before the evening was over the boss had offered me the advertising account for her business -- a net $3,000 a year for myself if I could swing an agency. And a chance at her husband's business, good for another $6,000 per year.

By the next night, Janet had the whole proposition arranged. She was determined to get into the big money. She couldn't do it on her own. She needed a man to front for her, and together we could make a terrific income. She laid it all out as coldly and logically as any business proposition could be. It would be a shame, she said, to spoil our friendship by experimenting with romance. Yet, being a curious soul, she knew she'd have to find out what it would be like. So we'd just as well plan it all out in advance and have the pleasure of both satisfying our curiosity and teaming up in an excellent business deal.

I can't quite describe the effect of the whole thing. I was frightened -- not merely at the thought of walking into another trap, but by the feeling that I was confronting a monstrosity: a woman who made no pretenses, used no feminine lure. A woman who would shoot you for your life insurance if it was big enough -- and who would even warn you about it in advance. Yet this was my same old friend -- I'm really fond of her, and I think she honestly depends upon me.

Well, nothing has come of it -- because I've stayed up here. Yet if I went to L.A., something might.

But the point is that for the first time I've found a woman who lives coolly and logically and intellectually; who plans her moves and weighs possibilities. And yet she -- in this curious world -- has to depend upon a man to front for her own peculiar abilities in publicity and in public relations. And she'll ruin a beautiful friendship, even sleep with a guy, to do it.

I'm afraid I haven't made much of this story. It sounds trite or something. But it has added to my sense of panic when confronted by a woman.

As ever,

Brick

So far as I know, Brick never saw Janet again. But I could be wrong.

Chapter Twenty
The Hearts of Women and Men

Now it is time to take stock of Brick Garrigues' life as the weather cools in San Francisco in the fall of 1944.

Number of women who had reminded him of the Virgin Mary: three (he mentioned only Louise Caselotti and Marianne LeClerc, but to those I add Naomi, who possessed a fine, Semitic beauty).

Number of wives: two.

Number of children: three.

Kinds of cars he drove: two (Ford and Willys).

Nervous breakdowns: one major, perhaps other minor.

Number of times in these letters he mentioned *money:* fifty.

Number of times he mentioned *love:* ninety-one.

Number of times he mentioned *women:* too numerous to count.

Number of times he mentioned his *job:* a hundred and two.

Number of times he mentioned *suit:* five. (As a symbol of banal pragmatism, 1926; Joe O'Carroll's unpressed, 1926; wearing another man's, 1937, bought on time, 1942, and making the old one do, 1944.)

Number of times he used the word *complicated:* three, with more to come.

November 3, 1944

Dear Toni,

Life is more complicated than I suspected. And this will probably amaze you and, I suppose, annoy you. The fact

is that Dickie is back, occupying a corner in the Garrigues
menage -- or perhaps, I'm occupying a corner in her menage.
It's an equivocal sort of an arrangement: theoretically
temporary. Or rather, transient.

It started like this. She, it seems, has been having
an affair of some years' standing in Inglewood. Quite
serious, I suppose, and apparently reasonably satisfactory
even though the guy, who is an Inglewood big shot, has a
wife and flock of kids. So after about seven years of this,
the affair blows up.

Well, her situation in relation to the kids has been
bad enough, in a way. She's had to hold a job, take care of
a house and the kids, live her own life, etc., all out of
twenty-four hours a day. Last spring she insisted that I
take the kids for the summer and winter -- which, of
course, I was delighted to do. So, when Naomi left, I had
to tell her she'd have to take them back. Then, a couple of
days later, she called up and wanted me to keep them a few
weeks more. The affair had blown up and she was pretty well
broken up about it. She was going to leave Inglewood or, at
least, get a job in Los Angeles. That would mean at least
two hours a day commuting -- which added to her emotional
upset, would just have made a hell of a life for her and
the kids. It was impossible to find household help.

So I told her that I'd keep the kids for a while. But
I couldn't see how I could possibly send them back to her
at all under existing conditions. And I couldn't see how I
could take care of them myself. I even went so far as to
suggest to Naomi that we call off the split-up and try it
again, with me making still more concessions as a matter of
necessity. But, anyway, I was left with the kids.

Well, Dickie came up for a week's visit while she was
preparing to look for another job. We talked over the
economic situation, and she finally decided she'd get a job
here, take over one half the house, and we'd share the
business of taking care of the boys. So she did that and,
so far, it has worked out as well as any rational arrangement could possibly work out. Both of us are out from under
an intense strain which was really raising hell with our
digestions; both are gradually becoming fairly sane and
normal people again. And so far no untoward emotional
situation whatever has developed.

She works in the daytime and I work at night. I help
with the housework and she helps with the finances. She's
off on Sundays and I'm off on Thursdays. Sometimes we sit
around and talk when we happen to be home at the same time.
Sometimes she goes to bed early or I go out. She goes and
comes when she pleases: she's developed a great liking for
night clubs and bars. I come and go when I please. Yet --
it isn't an existence in which there is a great deal of
fun, excitement or pleasure. I mean, I'm living the life of

a bachelor without, in reality, the freedom of the
bachelor. Or, in another way, it's like living at home,
with your own family. So it isn't too much fun.

Then there's also the fear that, out of boredom or
propinquity or habit, we'll begin to fall into an emotional
domestic relationship. It shouldn't develop that way. But
people aren't very sensible. We don't, really, have a damn
thing in common -- and both of us understand that ad-
equately now. But we like each other very well, and we get
along very well in relation to such matters as cooking,
laundry, washing the kids' ears, etc. And it's really a
comfortable sort of an existence -- comfortable enough so
it would really be a relief to be in love with one another
and settle down.

But, as I say, it's on a temporary basis. With the
general understanding that it will last at least until the
boys' school term ends in the spring. Yet each is at
liberty to leave anytime we wish -- and anytime we are able
to carry on the financial agreement we originally had. So
it isn't as though I had nothing to look forward to, except
more drab years like this. I have, instead, the chance to
look forward to more drab years like something else.

But it has been good for me. I didn't realize what a
strain I'd been under. For years. Now I'm getting plenty of
sleep. I'm putting a few dollars in the bank. I'm doing
somewhat as I please.

Furthermore, I think it was highly necessary that I go
back to some of the previous conditions of my existence
and, as civil engineers do, take a back-sight upon a known
position in order to know better where I am now. I mean
I've really been lost. I'd wandered out into a wilderness
some nine or ten years ago and I just didn't know where I
was. Nothing I decided remained decided; nothing I was sure
of possessed any validity. I didn't know how I felt about
Dickie, or the kids, or the business of making money, or
whatever goal of attainment there might be. I was much too
much in an ivory tower and the world pressed around me too
closely. I didn't have any place in it -- and that was
partly because nobody who lives with Naomi can have a place
of his own. Her life is too all-inclusively Naomi.

Well, a lot of that is cleared up. I'm very much
alone, but I am myself again to some degree. I don't know
exactly where I'm going or what I'm going to do. But I am
learning again to make decisions. And I can visualize
myself making them as easily as I used to do.

Not that I really know yet what I want to do in the
future. If I'm going to do any writing after "The Imaginary
Revolution" is finished, I'll have to find different
domestic arrangements which will give me more time and more
privacy. There's nothing, yet, I want to do very much. But

meanwhile, until there is something I want to do, I'm building up a little reserve of cash and nervous energy so that, later, I can do it. Meanwhile, I drift.

[From Dickie]
October 12, 1944

Dear Victor:

Thanks, darling, for your nice letter. I don't know what it is, Victor, but when I don't get a letter from you I am unhappy and when I do I am just like water, so it is just one vicious circle. It must be because I am still not yet out of love with you, and I don't suppose I will ever be.

This really is such a damned lonesome place. I haven't made any friends yet, although last night I telephoned the secretary of the Legal Secretaries Association, and she is taking me to the next meeting. All I do is go to work, come straight home, have a drink all by myself and cook dinner. After dinner I do a little cleaning or ironing and then go to bed and read. At first I couldn't even read for thinking, but I am gradually getting better.

I am settling into a married-life routine, which isn't what I want to do at all. But I am being forced into it because the men friends I know or am apt to meet look askance at showering their affections on a woman who has a husband at home.

Brick is very easy to get along with now under the present setup. We make no demands on each other but try to be sweet and kind. Each is filled more or less with his own personal problems. He is still handsome and charming, but has become somewhat stodgy and anti-social. On his nights off we sit at home, drink highballs and talk. Thursday before last he played the records for me; the week before we took a drive up to Twin Peaks and looked over the city. It was such a clear night; the moon was shining and the lights from the city were beautiful. Last Thursday we drank a little and read poetry to each other.

His relaxation, besides doing things like the above, is to work on that damned book -- which doesn't bother me because he types during the day while I am at work. He loves to get out in the hills or mountains, so last Sunday we took a picnic lunch and went to Mount Diablo. From the summit you can see for miles around.

The boys are fine and definitely love and enjoy their father. They can discuss things "man to man," but on the other hand, they jump on him, hold him down and almost thoroughly beat the tar out of him. It pleases me to see such a fine understanding between them.

Louis' little friend, Donald Fell, said, "Louis, you are a lucky boy. You have a handsome father and a beautiful mother." Brick had to have Louis repeat this so he could

hear the compliment again, but of course I believe the
child is half-blind.

This being Thursday and Brick's day off, he is amusing
himself by writing. I can hear his typewriter from the
other room as I sit by our big bay window with the sun
streaming in on me.

Brick stopped me at this point and asked if I wanted
to go to Golden Gate Park. I did, so we had quite a tramp;
fed the squirrels and saw the fishes. I had forgotten that
there were so many simple things in life to do to have
pleasure. Brick is really teaching me that there are. He
acts like a "contented cow" and even admits being one.

I hope I am not boring you with all this, but a habit
of seven-and-a-half years is hard to break. Even if our
affair had to end like it did, dear, all those years were
worth it.

At age twelve, I didn't know why my father and mother were together again. I only knew that life seemed more complete. That was the
year that Chuck and I really became San Franciscans, not for just a summer but for an entire year. For a while Brick put me in a drama class at
the California Labor School, where I acted in skits about such certifiably
progressive activities as the Dumbarton Oaks Conference, which laid the
groundwork for the founding of the United Nations. (Some of us were
German spies intent on killing Soviet and American negotiators; and we
got to crawl around on the stage with pretend rifles and speak in guttural
Teutonic accents.) Later, the school would be named in a Tenney Committee report as a Communist-front organization.

In the fall, Chuck enrolled in the academically oriented Lowell High
School, which Brick said was like a "public Stanford prep school," and I
went into the eighth grade at Dudley Stone Grammar School on Haight
Street. That school year I had a paper route, a crush on a girl, scarlet
fever and mastoiditis.

Brick sent Toni the manuscript of his *The Imaginary Revolution*.

December 7, 1944

Dear Toni,

I'm not too optimistic about selling it right off the
bat, if the paper shortage is as bad as I hear it is. But
I'm really very well pleased with it as a whole and think
that it should ultimately sell, even though it may have to
wait until after the war. It is infinitely more solid,
mature and basic than "This Grim New World." There isn't a
chapter I'm dissatisfied with.

For once my own life seems comparatively uncompli-
cated. "Seems," I said, and "comparatively." One would
think that sharing a flat with one's ex-wife with a legal

wife off in the background waiting to sue for divorce, and
with a couple of kids to take care of, and a job, and at
least the necessity to do some writing, would be sufficiently complicated. But by comparison it's ideal and
peaceful bliss.

So far the arrangement has worked out reasonably well.
Better than that, really. It's a good financial arrangement;
I'm able to save some getaway money. It relieves me from a
sense of dodging responsibility in connection with the boys.
And it has completely released me from a sense of doubt as to
whether I was wise in splitting with Dickie in the first
place. One is inclined, in troublous presents, to sentimentalize about the past, and I suppose I did more than my
share. It has taken this arrangement to convince me fully
that I should have split with Dickie when I did. Much as I
like her and respect her and admire her, there were never two
people who had less justification for a permanent attachment.
We're just -- and have always been -- strangers.

The lack of complications comes from the fact that
there are, at present, just simply no women on the edges of
my life. Not that there haven't been candidates; this
manpower shortage is simply terrific. But so far I've been
safe. Is it too much to hope that I may continue to be?

The only dark cloud on the horizon is a brunette from
New York who is much more my sort of people than any I've
met in San Francisco: a dramatic school product who thinks
she can write a play and wants me to collaborate. On a
play, I mean. She has a bit of talent in handling dialogue
and knows a bit about the theater and is ignorant enough
about writing so that she's full of confidence. I think it
would be a good idea because my dialogue is lousy, and I
suspect I could learn something. I know I would if I had a
bit of confidence that the collaboration would be confined
to the typewriter. But I'm too damn susceptible, and I've
encountered that collaboration gag before.

January 9, 1945

I think a great deal of my dissatisfaction with life
(and it is still profound) is due to the fact that I
haven't sold anything. I think I've crowded the feeling
into the background. But so long as my stuff remains
unsold, I can't convince myself that what I've been doing
for the last five years is important. And I needed to feel
it was important because I was using it as an excuse for
trying to live the way I wanted to live.

I'm trying to work on two things: an article on
postwar inflation, and a play, in collaboration. I think I
told you about the collaborative idea. It would work out
very well if we had more time. Frankly, I don't like plays;
I don't like to read them and don't care to see them. But
it is excellent for me: I'm developing through the force of

necessity an unexpected ability to construct the skeleton
of a piece of work. I am learning things I should have
learned years ago -- under the compulsion of a collaborator
who really insists on me working. I'm getting almost
interested in the project.

February 8, 1945

Sooner or later I've got to get out of this damned
town and have set the date for June, when the kids will be
out of school. I don't know where I'll go, probably to Los
Angeles or possibly to New York, which might be good for a
little while. Yet I suspect it's a little too much like San
Francisco. Just at the moment I feel I need the freedom and
lack of channelization which one finds in Los Angeles. But
perhaps by the time I'm ready to go, the labor draft will
have frozen me here permanently.

Don't mind my moaning. I have to have somebody to moan
to. As for my personal affairs -- well, I don't have any.
Much to my surprise, I still find myself backing up with a
cautious look in my eye whenever I observe a female in the
distance. A strange performance for me. Sometimes I think
that at some time in the future I shall again make
overtures in the direction of Naomi. Strangely, I really
like the gal, and in spite of our disagreements we had a
much better life together than I'd ever have had with
anybody else. I don't honestly think I'm sentimentalizing
over the past -- although I confess I do have that
tendency. But we really did have a closeness which -- in
retrospect -- was extremely compelling. I do think that
Jewish people do have that much more than Gentiles; at
least it seems so among our friends.

As you know, I've carried a torch plenty of times in
my young life; there have been periods of complete and
utter vacuum elsewhere. This isn't like that. It's just
that something is missing which I didn't entirely value
fully because most of it was subconscious -- buried between
disagreements which, now, look very silly.

March 21, 1945

My own life is uneventful, except that my younger boy
is in the hospital with mastoiditis, and they may have to
operate on him today. It has sort of taken most of the
starch out of me -- if there was any left.

Aside from that, nothing. No gals, no particular
troubles, no particular ideas.

April 1, 1945

Spring has come to California; the robins are here;
the trees are in full bloom -- and I wonder if I'm going
to get through without involvement. I think I will; so
far the season has done no more than to lift me from

utter indifference to casual indifference in regard to
life.

Dickie and the kids are going back south this summer.
I'm rather looking forward to it; it would be nice to have
the flat to myself again, for a while at least.

A few months ago I wanted never to think about another
manuscript, but now I want to get back in the groove. Do
you know anything about the pulp field? Particularly
science fiction. My older son, Charles, is a terrific
science-fiction fan; in fact, he's a collector of such
magazines and makes a fair bit of change out of it.[1] And
he's written a couple of yarns which are almost salable.
But, anyway, I think I would enjoy writing that sort of
thing and may take a whirl at it. I'll have to hurry or
he'll beat me to it.

The other youngster is recovering from his operation
and should be home from the hospital tomorrow or the next
day. Which is one bit of light in the week's existence.

April 12, 1945

I don't think there is anything in "The Imaginary
Revolution" which need be changed as the result of
Roosevelt's death today. Honestly, I shouldn't be amazed if
the thing sold. For one thing, it seems that the death of
Roosevelt has thrown things into a turmoil out of which will
come a revival of popular interest in many questions which
have been tucked away during the last couple of years.

I suppose that if either you or I ever make a dime out
of my writing, I'm going to have to start to learn to write
for a market which exists, rather than trying to create a
market. I can't, at the present time, write the sort of
nonfiction which is wanted -- personality stuff and such.

I've just finished a first draft of an article on
spiritualism -- which at least has the sole advantage of
getting away from economics. Now I'm going to re-handle it
in a more chatty, popular vein, attempting to point it
toward a definite market. Then I'll decide whether to send
it to you or not. Probably not.

Also, I have in mind a swell anti-union article which
should sell -- making certain that I will be damned to hell
by all my friends.

I'm really interested in science-fiction. Astounding,
the magazine, is running some really remarkable fiction;
their formula is very broad and includes a lot of precisely
the sort of sociological stuff which is my meat. It is,
incidentally, the only magazine field in which a writer
can, apparently, retain any sense of integrity. So I may
have a whirl at it.

---

[1] Chuck, who was fourteen, bought and sold the magazines, some dating back to the early
1920s, mostly through the mail.

June 8, 1945

A friend of mine named Paul Meagher may call you soon.
Or he may not. He's a youngster who roomed with me winter
before last and is now going to NYU or some such place. I
suggested he call you because I think you might find him
interesting. He has one of the most brilliant minds I've
ever come in contact with; we used to spend night after
night juggling abstractions. But he's lost in the company
of women -- or was. He was raised a very devout Catholic
and then quit the church; meanwhile, I think his soul had
been put in immortal peril by having been seduced by an
older woman. And he just couldn't disentangle the things
the priest had taught him from the things he had learned
and observed and experienced.

July 6, 1945

I'm working on the yarn for Astounding and am having
fun with it. Also learning a lot about tempo and stuff.

Almost got a good job today. The man said "no"; if
he'd said "yes," I'd have had it. Assistant editor of
Sunset magazine. (Do you know it? A Pacific Coast garden
and barbecue pit mag.)

Dickie and Brick broke up their household in the summer. She and
Chuck and I crammed into her 1939 Ford coupe (it had only one bench
seat) and took two days to drive down the Pacific Coast Highway back to
Inglewood. We sang Les Brown's "Sentimental Journey" many times
during that trip. Brick was left alone.

July 23, 1945

I'm still working on a serial for Astounding, chiefly
as a valuable exercise in learning how to overcome the
difficulties of story-building. It is difficult to realize
how hard it is to shift from straight analysis into
fiction. And I've been doing analysis now for painfully
near to twenty years. One has to start at the very
beginning -- as an aging cello player would have to start
if he decided to learn the piano. Yet I think I progress.

I'm glad you liked Paul. And I'm flattered by his
impression that you were "young." Because of course I told
him that I knew you in our youth -- which was so terribly
long ago. Yet I don't mind -- shall we say -- maturity?
It's rather fun. Even to avoid many of the complications
into which one would have leaped so joyously a few
centuries ago.

I suspect I'm growing mellow, and I don't know whether
it is age, or the release from the immediacy of domestic
problems, or simply the amazing sight of seeing the sun
shine in San Francisco in July. Something will probably
happen to spoil it soon.

On August 6, the United States dropped an atomic bomb on Hiroshima. On August 9, it dropped one on Nagasaki. That wasn't science-fiction, either.

August 11, 1945

I'm still struggling with two things: the flu and the possibility of improving "The Imaginary Revolution" with a bit of rewriting. The flu will take care of itself, but I may have to do something about the second problem.

Brick took his flu to work with him. It seemed to be settling into his chest. I see him rubbing his shoulder, trying to breathe. He looks up from the headline he is writing, drops his pencil and squints at the editor in the center of the horseshoe-shaped desk. Brick's usually ruddy complexion is paper-white. The editor stares, concerned: "You OK?" Sweat stands out on Brick's forehead. "Sick. Feel rotten." He slumps in his chair. A copygirl rushes to his side. Commotion. "Call an ambulance." "Emergency room."

The next day or the day after, August 14: I was playing tennis with a friend in the park. Car horns blared on the road above us. Joyful toots. Without being told, we knew. "It's V-J Day!" I ran home, dumped my racket, got some money, ran back to the main road and took the No. 5 yellow streetcar to downtown Los Angeles. At the center of the city, streetcars and automobiles were stalled on Broadway by throngs of revelers filling the streets. Reams of paper rained from office buildings onto the crowds below and piled up in the gutters and on the sidewalks. Soldiers and sailors grinned like fools and kissed the women and drank as much booze as strangers would buy them. The shops were closed, their employees given the day off; but one or two dime-store managers stood in front to sell noisemakers and confetti.

[Postcard; handwritten]
August 15, 1945

This will cancel all plans, arrangements, intentions, etc. I am stretched out on a cot in St. Luke's Hospital after a heart attack and will be here for some weeks or months yet.

Apparently I'm going to recuperate, but in the meantime I'm not going to worry about it. Since I am forbidden to read, write, think or smoke, I dictated this to let you know. Write me when you have time.

As ever,

Brick

Part Three
Foxglove

A would-be writer lives . . .
almost wholly in the delusion
that life can be grasped through words.

Chapter Twenty-One
Full Stop

So after years of fretting and smoking, sitting at a desk writing or editing, and fighting with one wife, and separating from two, exercising very little or not at all, and eating French toast and scrambled eggs for breakfast and maybe a potato with a gob of butter for dinner, Brick was in the hospital, where he couldn't do any of those things — except eat scrambled eggs, for the doctors hadn't yet figured out the relationship between high cholesterol and heart attacks. His children were hundreds of miles away, Chuck and I in Inglewood with one ex-wife and Patty in Prescott with an estranged one.

By that time Dickie and her kids no longer lived in a shack. Over the years she had earned enough as Victor Sparks' secretary to pay for new siding and paint and additions of one sort or another, including a garage and an attached large room paneled in knotty pine, where Chuck and I slept and kept our books and our clothes, our radio and our stamp collection (me) and soap carvings and science-fiction magazines (Chuck). Now back in Inglewood after her year in San Francisco, Dickie was quickly able to find a job with another attorney.

[Postcard; handwritten]
August 27, 1945

Dear Toni,

Not permitted to write letters yet, but am expected to recover. May be sitting up in two weeks.

[Handwritten]
St. Luke's Hospital
San Francisco, Calif.
September 20, 1945

I hope you can read my scrawl because I feel in a mood to write a long letter this morning -- being full of rest, bacon, eggs, toast, gruel, orange juice, coffee and contentment.

I continue to improve slowly. Yesterday I was in a wheel chair for forty-five minutes. I wouldn't be averse to settling down here for the rest of my life. The food is good, the beds comfortable, the nurses pretty and one's worrying is done for one. I can be conscious that the world is in a hell of a shape but it doesn't seem worth worrying about. Almost certainly an atomic bomb will blow us all to hell within a generation or so. And just as I reach that conclusion, I also reach the place where I can't commit any of my favorite sins. So what the hell?

This is a very valuable experience for me. On three levels.

(1) I am in constant contact with the mass mind via (a) my ward-mates, (b) my nurses, (c) the little radio I use to drown out the stupid conversations that go on in the ward.

(2) This period of rest provides a needed "full stop" to all my previous life -- after which I can begin again. And such things as "The Imaginary Revolution" no longer seem quite as important as they did.

(3) I am being cultivated by what one of the more abominable poets of the nineteenth century referred to as "an accomplished female friend" who appears to be the only intellectual woman I have yet encountered. (Sounds of Toni laughing, "My god! He's doing it again!" But I don't think so. I certainly hope I have not yet reached the point where I could fall in love with a woman's brains.)

She and I have been carrying on by letter an investigation into some of the more abstruse aspects of sociology, for example: "Work: Its Nature and Necessity," and, as a result, I'm learning to think in very tight spirals. Being unable to write very much, or to think very hard, I have to boil everything down to a few symbols -- a sort of mental shorthand, and it's very good exercise -- I've never before encountered a little girl that I could play that sort of game with. I'm developing a lot of practice in "functional" (non-Aristotelian) logic.[1]

---

[1] Brick was introduced to non-Aristotelian logic, as were many others at this time, by a novelette, *The World of Null-A*, by the science-fiction writer A. E. Van Vogt (1912-2000) in the August and September 1945 issues of *Astounding Science Fiction*. It was based on a work by semanticist Alfred Korzybski, *Science and Sanity*. The theory teaches that words themselves can limit the ability to think.

Also, this dame -- Anne -- is doing a novel on the
days of the Pony Express -- than which I can imagine
nothing more horrible. But she really is a brain (why does
God seldom give beauty and brains to the same woman?), and
the novel may turn out.

Also, I've another near-discovery. A guy named John
Clayton -- who has written one unpublished novel and is
working on another. I read the script of the first and --
in spite of the fact that it's an abominably bad novel -- I
hardly slept for the two nights between days I was reading.
Because he created a couple of characters that -- for my
money -- outlived anything that Steinbeck or Farrell ever
did.[2] He hasn't learned to carpenter a story or to burnish
it up -- but if he does -- I'll try to snag him for you.

John Bell Clayton was five years younger than Brick. For a time he
ran a lending library and quite often he was employed as a temporary
editor on the *Examiner*. His boyhood in the South formed the backdrop
for his short stories and novels, the first of which, *Six Angels at My
Back,* was published by Macmillan in 1952. It was a sharply outlined,
exciting adventure story. Then in 1953 came *Wait, Son, October Is Near,*
the story of a ten-year-old farm boy with a passionate desire to remain
with his philandering father. And finally, in 1954 came *Walk Toward the
Rainbow,* about a Virginia writer whose first marriage fails and who
flees to San Francisco to make a new start.

John's eventual success in writing came in great measure from the
support of his wife, Martha, who was Hoagy Carmichael's sister. She
was well aware of her husband's tendencies toward defeat and pessimism. But she liked to give an example of the long wait between the
passion of creation and its acceptance by the public: Her brother's *Stardust*
had lain on a music publisher's shelf "three solid years" before it was
finally printed.

Also, I've caught up on several things I've missed
during the last fifteen years, for example: (1) I've learned
to like "Barnaby"; (2) ditto "Dick Tracy"; (3) I'm exploring
the minds (via Dorothy Baker's "Young Man With a Horn") of
that curious breed of young intellectual who decided during
the thirties that jazz was to be taken seriously.[3]

I guess what this long scrawl all amounts to is that I
am having a lot of fun and doing absolutely nothing
constructive. When I leave here, I will go back to the flat

---

2 Steinbeck's novels since *The Grapes of Wrath* were *The Moon Is Down (1942)* and *Cannery
Row* (1945). James T. Farrell had published the Studs Lonigan trilogy in the early 1930s and
completed other works about the lower middle-class Irish in Chicago as well.

3 "Barnaby" was a comic strip by Crockett Johnson that featured a little boy, a fairy godfa-
ther that no one besides the boy could see, and a talking dog. It appealed to intellectuals and
children alike. "Dick Tracy," the strip about a square-jawed detective, was in its fourteenth year
of being drawn by Chester Gould. Dorothy Baker's 1938 novel *Young Man With a Horn* was the
tragedy of a young jazz artist unable to reconcile his art with the acceptance of the world at large.

(the old address) which has been sublet to my accomplished female friend, but in which I have reserved a room.

After a few more weeks, I may be strong enough to decide what I'm going to do about Naomi and my very lovely little daughter. Possibly I will go visit them. I hope to loaf until the first of the year. Then I suppose I'll drag myself back to the job.

[Handwritten]
September 25, 1945

I'm leaving the hospital today. Doctor said I was doing so well there was no use in staying longer. Privately, I suspect it was because I've been eating up all the profits since I made friends with the pretty little dietitian.

Toni wrote Brick that the *American Scholar* magazine might be interested in an article he had sent her months before — a piece on general semantics. She suggested a general rewrite.

[Handwritten]
151 Alpine Terrace
October 2, 1945

The nibble from the American Scholar is the most exciting news I've had since the doctor told me I'd probably live. I seem to have a psychological need to invade that academic field -- maybe I have a scholastic inferiority complex. At any rate, I'll rush the revisions on the carbon, retype the ms. and send it along. Or rather Anne will do these things as I am as yet incapable of doing much of anything.

Yes, I did write "my lovely daughter." And you did tell me so. So, just as a forfeit, I'm going to send you one of the three really good snaps I have of her -- and you'll see that I do not exaggerate unduly, even though I may confess to a slight parental prejudice. If you want to know who she looks like, it is her maternal grandfather and her Aunt Corinne (Naomi's sister), who is a beautiful woman. She, my daughter Patty, is a lovely blonde with blue eyes.

UNITED NATIONS CONFERENCE COMMITTEE
133 Montgomery Street • San Francisco 4, California
Telephone SUtter 8158

[From Anne Hawkins]
October 20, 1945

Dear Miss Strassman:

You don't know me, so don't search your memory.

I had charge of your author Charles H. Garrigues for three weeks after the hospital discharged him, and saw him safely off to the South yesterday. I have sent a brief report to his wife, and it occurs to me that you should have one, too.

First: the kind of heart attack he had will not shorten his life. He will be a semi-invalid for another three months and will thereafter have to be careful for a while. With smoking, heavy coffee-drinking, and climbing long, steep hills, he is through for good. To all this he has made adjustment already -- knocked off coffee and cigarettes without a falter, though not without a good deal of noise.

Second: your request for a revise on that semantics article not only did him no harm, it did him good. He was then still pretty weak, but beginning to come back to life and in need of something to focus on. He worked in bed, long-hand, about forty minutes at a time; I found he was to be trusted to knock off before overtiring himself, except on one day when he felt exceptionally good; however, the ill effects even then were only trivial. What did upset his pulse for a couple of hours at the start was what proved to be an emotional unwillingness to look again at his own ms. for purposes of mayhem.

We got around that by the following trick: Without re-reading, he handed the script over to me, and I made a rough cut to a little less than your proposed length and typed a clean copy. He worked then entirely from that. This prevented his being reminded of his own amputated felicities; also, since I had supplied a few transition sentences, he could blame me for anything which offended him. This perfectly eliminated emotional block.

Third, his physician, Dr. Walter Beckh, is emphatic that he is making a complete and excellent recovery, but sees in him the makings of a very fine hypochondriac.

Yours very truly,

Anne Hawkins

After Brick left the hospital, he determined to go by train and bus to recuperate with his brother in El Centro, but first he stopped in Inglewood.

Dickie drove him from Union Station. His appearance startled me, no longer the strong arms, the ability to pick up a small child. He was drawn, haggard, his suit hanging on his weakened frame. For a week or two he slept in our knotty-pine bedroom attached to the garage, and he and fifteen-year-old Chuck carried on their conversation when the lights were off, while I fell asleep to the drone of their voices.

720 Stepney Street
Inglewood, Calif.
November 6, 1945

Dear Toni,

Just a few lines from Southern California before I get even farther south to El Centro. Naomi is going to join me

-- and we'll see how we get along. Probably we will go back to San Francisco together in January.

Southern California is marvelous. I had forgotten that skies could be so blue, air so balmy, clouds so white. Yesterday we finished two days of what the San Francisco weatherman calls "Fair and warm; high fog over ocean," but which is known in the South as "Rain." And today is the most marvelous spring day you've ever seen.

Has it been only a little less than a year since you were sunning yourself on your Florida island? How much I wanted to stretch out in the sun with you! And now, I at least am getting a sunburn on the back of my neck.

As I guess you suspect, I am feeling fairly well. In fact, I feel swell. Except, of course, that I can't do anything except eat and sleep, read and write letters. I sometimes think I could do a litle more, but I prefer to err on the side of caution. Even so, it is rather dull here; there are few books and the conversation is not particularly stimulating.

I've been keeping a notebook filled with exercises in symbolic logic as a preliminary to a really adequate study on the relationship of logic and semantics. But it is kept purely for my own amusement and with no expectation that it will turn into a book. Anne helps a lot since we exchange notes and the exchange provides the katharsis of publication without the annoyance of publishers.

In that connection, I ran across this yesterday in "The Way of All Flesh":[4]

"He was kept back by the nature of the subjects he chose -- which were generally metaphysical. In vain I tried to get him away from those matters. When I begged him to try his hand at some pretty, graceful little story which would be full of whatever people would like best, he would immediately set to work upon a treatise to show the grounds upon which all belief rested.

"'You are stirring mud,' said I, 'or poking at a sleeping dog. You are trying to make people resume consciousness about things which, with sensible men, have already passed into the subconscious.'

"He could not see it."

So I keep such matters, now, for my private amusement. So far, fiction is a little too difficult even to attempt. I tried to start a little short story the other day and immediately found the blood pressure going up.

---

4 *The Way of All Flesh,* by the English essayist Samuel Butler, was published in 1903, the year after Butler's death. Brick may have found a kindred spirit in this largely autobiographical novel telling of Butler's escape from the suffocating religious atmosphere of his home. In the excerpt, a character based on Butler as a mature man ("I") is giving advice about writing to a younger Butler representation ("he").

A little more than a year later, Toni received what Brick considered to be the definitive rejection of his manuscript on *The Imaginary Revolution*.

HARCOURT, BRACE AND COMPANY, INC.
Publishers
383 Madison Avenue, New York 17, N.Y.

November 14, 1946

Miss Toni Strassman
24 East 51st Street
New York

Dear Miss Strassman:

    In the final analysis, I am afraid that Mr. Garrigues leaves me cold. There is a kind of hardboiled brilliance in the writing, but when you come to a close analysis of THE IMAGINARY REVOLUTION, you are bound to feel its extraordinary thinness compared with the four or five writers on whom he draws most copiously.

    Naturally one doesn't expect to wait until one has found a Marx or Spengler before publishing work in this field, but one does expect a writer of this day dealing with such a subject matter to make more use of modern knowledge. I am thinking particularly of such a fact as, while modern Marxists are eagerly exploring anthropology and psychiatry to repair the admitted crudities of Marx's own psychology, Mr. Garrigues can find nothing better than the hypothesis of the connection between ideas and action. This is implicit throughout the book, and rather explicitly stated in the concluding chapter.

    I am not asking that any writer should conform to my pattern of thought; but I do think it is fair to ask that he show awareness of some of the significant trends in modern thought. With all its points of sharp awareness, it seems to me that THE IMAGINARY REVOLUTION nevertheless fails to embrace the opportunities offered it.

    Let's hope for better luck the next time. The manuscripts you send are interesting, even when my rejections are as sharply worded as this one.

Sincerely yours,

Lambert Davis

151 Alpine Terrace
San Francisco, Calif.
November 6, 1946

Dear Toni,

    It isn't that I am discouraged by the "near and yet so far" achievement of "The Imaginary Revolution." I'm convinced that it's an excellent piece of work, in its own particular way. Only that way isn't the way of the market.

In the semantics article (which, too, "almost" sold),
I pointed out that the word "book" has a different meaning
for a publisher, a reader, a writer. When I say, "I have
written a book," I mean that I have set down a certain
number of connected words on a certain subject in such a
way that, if they were published, I would be proud of the
achievement, since it sets forth what I believe to be true
and what (I believe) millions of other people would see to
be true in coming years. When a publisher says, "I wish we
could see some way to make a book out of it," he has an
entirely different meaning for the word "book."

The vacation was marvelous. We stayed only two days in
Cathedral City, then went to El Centro. On the way we found
a little desert road leading to the Salton Sea and drove
down there for a picnic lunch. Imagine a desert beach in a
vast area without fresh water, beside a huge lake as blue
as blue, miles from the nearest hut, the sun beating down,
in the distance the marks of the ancient tideline clearly
visible against mountains some twenty miles away.

One night in El Centro; dinner across the border in
Mexicali. A brief tour of spots made sacred by the boyhood of
C. H. Garrigues. The next day over the mountains to San Diego
in a desert sandstorm, remembering that HERE was the senior
class picnic in 1918, THERE my first overnight trip with a
girl (we camped out by a mountain stream beneath a pine tree)
-- and so to Coronado, which we found ruined by the war.

The next day to Inglewood to see the boys again, but
on the way we stopped at Laguna for lunch -- another picnic
on the beach. You have never seen anything like Laguna on
such a day. The east wind had brought over a mass of desert
air so that San Clemente Island, thirty miles away, was
clearly visible; the sea is an intense blue which is almost
purple, and so clear that you can stand on a rock and see
fish swimming far beneath the surface.

In Laguna it was difficult to believe that people
actually live in San Francisco and are content. Now,
looking out upon a dirty street on a dull, gray day (the
sort the weatherman describes as "partly cloudy"), it is
still difficult to believe it. I have, as you see, achieved
a point of view. And it hasn't a hell of a lot to do with
revolutions, imaginary or otherwise.

I haven't seen the Claytons yet. We'll probably call
them this evening. As you say, it has been very good for
me to know John; he, also, helps one get a point of view.
And he's a guy that can really write. If he succeeds in
lifting the whole of his novel to the level of the best
parts (and I think he will), its publication will be a
major literary event.

                    As ever,

                    Brick

Chapter Twenty-Two
The Family Divided

> But when we got into our teens, we ran into those problems that Father couldn't handle himself — sex, society, values, friendships, creativity-outside-of-kindergarten, love, and the actual implementation of all those things in the world. — *From a letter by Chuck, 1962*

I came home from high school to find Chuck sprawled almost motionless on the couch. He slept through the afternoon and the night. He didn't go back to school for almost a year. Distraught because of the illness of his father, Chuck had finally collapsed. I was recently asked how I *felt* as a child about the illnesses of my father and brother: I was numb; a thirteen-year-old has so many fears and doubts about his own young life that he doesn't have much uncertainty left over for the older people he has come to rely on. I believe now that I must have left such serious thoughts to Chuck. A doctor recommended a long rest for my brother, who was then fifteen, and out parents agreed to send him to El Centro, where Brick was being tended by *his* sibling, George.

[From Dickie]
November 19, 1945

Dear Brick,

Charles seems somewhat better today, although he has been terribly discouraged and says he has the feeling he is dying, which doesn't make me feel any too good. I talked him out of that, though, and left him feeling quite cheerful this morning, and at noon he didn't have a temperature and had taken a nap and felt much refreshed. He can talk of nothing now but getting to Arizona. He seems to think that is the only thing that will save him.

Meanwhile, an old friend, Janet, had come to visit Dickie. Janet took me off Dickie's hands for a while, to an air show in Long Beach. She was an animated woman. Like my mother, she was pretty and youthful and listened to what I had to say, and — this was important to a child — she bought me a hot dog.

Louis and Janet apparently had a wonderful time together at the air show. Janet had acquired a stiff neck, though, and Al, my boyfriend, who likes to massage, offered to rub her neck. If I were crazy about Al, I might not have taken what ensued as graciously as I did, but, knowing Janet, I sat back and was amused by her technique -- which was:

After becoming acquainted with the guy only a short half hour, she strips for action. All the cushions are removed from the couch and chair and placed on the floor, and Janet lies down half naked and gets her chiropractic treatment. She has a wonderful time the rest of the evening with my boyfriend -- all to my amusement.

Al Baldwin was a handsome, devil-may-care butcher with an Errol Flynn mustache and a roguish air. He worked behind the glass counter of an Inglewood meat market on Manchester Boulevard just east of Market Street, where he joked with the women as he sliced off a steak or cut up a chicken for them. He had some missing finger joints, the result of either inattention or hangover in earlier years. During the war he kept our table well supplied with meat, for which Dickie otherwise would have had to hand out our little red ration coupons.

Two hundred miles to the southeast, Naomi and Patty came to El Centro from Prescott, and Brick's *other* family was together again.

                              [Handwritten]
                              1249 State Street
                              El Centro, Calif.
                              November 29, 1945

Dear Toni,

Imperial Valley is marvelous at this time of the year; the offspring is adorable, and Naomi and I are getting along splendidly.

I confess I'm getting a little bored with illness since I do not yet have strength enough to enjoy myself -- even to walk downtown. And there is practically no radio nor conversation.

My chief amusement is writing long letters to Anne -- the gal who took over my flat. She is really a remarkable woman. Our letters consist, largely, of long discussions

upon abstractions -- everything from the nature of the
Aristotelian katharsis to influences leading to the
development of baroque art. From my point of view, I'm
getting a lot of stuff out of my system which will serve as
permanently kept notes if I decide to try nonfiction again.

I confess I was a little pleased by what Davis said
about The Imaginary Revolution. I don't know why; I think
perhaps because even if it failed, it seemed to fail upon a
somewhat higher level than the paper shortage. But I was
honestly rather puzzled about his reference to modern
trends of thought because I did not know that there were
any.

You speak of talking contract on "Cornelia's" book —
as if I should know who Cornelia is. Could it be my little
sister-in-law whose real name is Corinne, although she uses
another name? I'm afraid to ask Naomi; apparently she
doesn't know. I hope it's true; as I've always maintained
that she, Corinne, and not her husband, Irving, is the
writer in the family. (The only reason I think it might be
her is because you speak of being grateful.)

Corinne's birth name was actually Cornelia Silver, but like many
women she had renamed herself as a teen to suit her peers: A friend had
told her she would never get any boyfriends with a name like Cornelia,
so she became Corinne. She chose *Cornelia Jessey* as her nom de plume.

December 1945

This is a very bad habit you have, and I can only hope
that the letter to me which Mrs. Postel got did not include
a discussion of your recent love life. I may add that the
fear of switched envelopes has long haunted me; I make it a
point never to begin one letter until the previous one is
safely enclosed and sealed. But some day, I suspect, I'll
pull a terrific one.

(To date the worst I've done is this: Having an
unexpected afternoon off once, when I was married to
Dickie, I thought I'd take the gal friend to the show.
Carelessly, I called my own number and got Dickie.
Fortunately, I woke up at the sound of her voice but
couldn't think of a good reason I should have called her
so, in desperation, I took HER to the show. Nothing lost
but an afternoon.)

Damn it! I'm still struggling to keep my mind and
attention on fiction instead of economics. I'm getting well
enough again to start working a little and find myself
waking up at night thinking "Well, THIS topic of The
Imaginary Revolution could be handled thus-and-so," and
then, "Get thee behind me, Satan" But I'll get over it.
Meanwhile, I'm plotting a detective-adventure novel and
quietly reflecting upon my sins.

January 15, 1946

Naomi is not going back with me. Possibly later, when the housing shortage has cleared up somewhat. But probably not, she thinks. Seems like I just simply can't live with that woman; or, more accurately that she just can't live with me. I view the situation with mixed feelings. It seems rather ironic that when -- after nine years -- I finally decided it was time to quit kicking and give her an approximation of the bourgeois existence she wanted, she should simultaneously decide that THAT wasn't what she wanted after all. What she does want, God only knows. But I have the feeling that this time we came much closer to making it than before and that, this time, there was nothing I could have done -- no extremity to which I could have gone -- which would have altered the outcome. (Don't ever marry a Gentile.)

I was sorry the semantics article didn't go. Not surprised, particularly; it was a good article and should have been precisely what the PhDs wanted. Particularly after my friend Anne (an intimate and associate of PhDs and Phi Beta Kappas and things, and a genius at avoiding offense) had very carefully helped me take out anything that might offend an academician. But perhaps it's just as well; I don't want to get mixed up in writing-for-fun again.

Corinne-Cornelia was in to see us the other day -- terribly excited about "These Too Are Americans" (God, what a title!) She and her husband are sweet kids, as naive and delightful as anybody could ever want. I say: Good for her! It tends to restore one's faith in Santa Claus.[1]

Brick returned to the chill winds and fog of San Francisco. Chuck remained in El Centro the rest of the school year, resting, reading, working in the yard and not attending any classes. But he did find the energy to get into a spat with Naomi.

Saturday

Dear Chuck:

The answer to your question is:

"Yes, you are too young to expect from adults the same courtesy which they expect from, and give to, other adults."

Note that I don't say you're too young to be entitled to it -- only that you shouldn't expect it, because unfortunately you will probably not get it. And it is not generally a good idea to expect something that we are unlikely to get.

I'm not so sure that that situation is, really, as unjust as it seems. For the fact is that, in lieu of

---

[1] The title of Corinne's first book was changed by her editor to *The Growing Roots* before publication. The Sussmans were then living in Cathedral City, near Palm Springs, where Irving was teaching high school.

courtesy, adults extend to children other advantageous, beneficial modes of regard which they do not extend to other adults.

As you get older you will find that you get more courtesy -- but you will also find that you will get a great deal less consideration. Until a guy is 21 or 22 he will find that older men will give him a boost, lead him into the right way to do things on the job, etc. etc. -- but sometimes give him scant courtesy. Later they will be inclined to cut his throat or knife him in the back at every opportunity.

If I say -- and I do say -- that you cannot expect to be treated with courtesy until you have learned to use courtesy in treatment of other people, it is not that I desire in any way to take Naomi's side in that particular argument.

I have had puh-lenty of arguments with Naomi in the last nine years and I would say that your letter was an almost word-for-word transcript of at least 90 percent of those arguments.

You reacted almost exactly as I have always reacted -- even to that slight sense of bewilderment with which you asked yourself (and me): "Was I entirely wrong?"

All I can say is: "Move over, Rover, I've spent enough time in the doghouse so I guess there's room for Chuck, too."

Sure, Naomi shouldn't act in that particular way. But she does. It would be different if she were malicious or hateful about it. But she's not; she's tremendously fond of us all and we are really tremendously fond of her and, the way I figure it, why should we let our lives be spoiled in any degree because there are certain ways in which our gears just don't mesh?

You will find that you will be able to achieve the status of an adult only when and if you begin to act like an adult while still enjoying the status of a child. Some people have lived to middle age without ever having learned to act like an adult, and yet they expect to receive the courtesy due an adult and fly into a rage when they don't get it. Let such people be a horrible example to you -- so you may remember that you cannot expect adult status until you have carved it out for yourself and placed it upon your own shoulders.

At the present time you are right smack in the middle between adulthood and childhood and it is only natural that you should sometimes act half your age and sometimes twice your age. But, in either status, you are often discourteous (I say this from my own observation) in the manner in which a child is discourteous (in children we call it impudence).

You yourself have the job of providing yourself with adulthood; nobody else can do it for you. Part of that is the job of learning courtesy -- which, after all, is simply the social device by which we avoid such scenes as you described.

I think you will agree wholeheartedly that you were neither courteous nor considerate in the matters which led to the quarrel.

In my opinion, so far as the substance behind the quarrel was concerned, you were perfectly right -- but it isn't really, essentially, important because nothing that happened during the quarrel, and nothing that could happen to you as a result of it need injure you in any way. (And whatever can't hurt us -- can't hurt us, can it? Not even our dignity.)

But in the events leading up to the quarrel you were wrong at every point. That wrongness apparently arose from ignorance -- and ignorance is something that DOES hurt you -- and hurts everybody else. And so may I suggest that you set about to cure your ignorance on those particular points?

You admit that you acted with grave discourtesy. Now, ideally, life might go something like this: Having erred, you might have come home and said to Noma with proper humility, bowing gravely: "Mea culpa, ora pro me" (whatever is the proper case of "me")![2] And Noma might have waved her wand over you and said "Benedite! Pax vobiscum!" But it doesn't work that way and you as a writer should begin to see how it did work. It worked something like this:

You decided to go to the library at least partly to be by yourself and escape family ties a little while. Noma, with the curious blindness which almost every woman has toward masculine needs, wanted you to do an errand for her, partly out of practical need and partly out of the feminine instinct to keep the men of her family more or less under her thumb even when at a distance.

You fussed a little bit -- just enough so that Noma, who really wanted to avoid a row, lost her temper (because her offer of lunch money was really better than you were entitled to). You left her with the idea that you were coming home to lunch. And then Naomi, as we so often do with those we are very fond of, had a reaction against her own temper and decided that she would fix you an especially fine lunch to show how much she really likes you. So she did. And waited. And waited. And got mad. And madder. And madder. And after that anything could happen.

Now there are two things about that summary which are deserving of attention. First: your own ignorance and stupidity leading to inconsiderateness and discourtesy are deserving of censure and should be remedied. Second, sooner

---

2 Chuck, who had begun Latin in high school, was continuing to study it with the help of books from the El Centro Library.

or later you are going to have to follow the motivation of a scene like that if you are going to write it. And I think you're darned lucky to be able to start now instead of waiting 20 years.

You are right in saying that quarrels such as that always occur when both parties are arguing about different things. It is that sense of bewilderment and perplexity and being lost which has so frequently driven me into violent rages when arguing with Naomi -- the sense that we couldn't possibly agree because we weren't talking about the same things; and that no words could bridge the gap.

But on that point I most earnestly entreat: Don't let it worry you. Understand that it happens that way. And relax. Otherwise you, too, may have a worn-out ticker at 43. Life becomes comparatively simply when one does nothing about it.[3]

Only one more thing:

I naturally watch the relationships between you and Noma with deep personal interest. I hope you do not at any time doubt Noma's very real affection for you. It is sometimes difficult for you and me to understand some of the curious little recesses and bulges of Naomi's nature because of the difference in our backgrounds. (Remember, she had no brothers, and no close masculine friends when she was a little girl.) But there are little things that you and I do which shock her sense of affection very deeply and there are little things which she does out of affection which we do not notice and rebuff. I think we should keep that in mind.

151 Alpine Terrace
February 7, 1946

Dear Toni:

I'm back at the old stand, on the job and not liking it a bit. The energy level is very low; by the time I've done my eight hours of work, I'm a complete wreck, even though the work consists chiefly of sitting still and doing nothing. Then I crawl into bed and stay there religiously for ten hours. In the morning I feel better, but I know that I have to take it easy if I'm going to get through the day, so I write a letter or two and perhaps read a bit and listen to the phonograph and then crawl back on the bed for another hour of rest before I go to work.

It seems strange to come back here to the old flat where I spent (for me) a lot of years. I feel that I'm walking around in a sort of limbo; my things are here, but the place isn't mine; I look out over the same view, see the amazing display of lights, etc., but it is almost as though I were not here. I don't actually have any emotional

---

3 In a parenthesis, Brick credits Sylvia Townsend Warner for having written this in her 1926 book *Lolly Willowes*.

response -- not even an unpleasant one -- to them.

Naomi will be up whenever I can find a place to live.
(Anne, I think I told you, is still occupying the flat.) I
think that Naomi and I have at last come to an understanding of one another; perhaps I'm too optimistic, but that is
one really bright spot in the grayness. I could never get
over the idea that there was, somewhere, a magic word
which, if I could find it, would solve all our difficulties. Strangely, I think I found it -- and I will be very
much surprised if this attempt is not a success. The
housing shortage, however, is terrific, and we do not hope
for a place to live for several months at least.

Why did Naomi keep returning to Brick? Corinne remembers: "Patty
was on a porch swing in Prescott and saw Brick coming up the hill, and she
let out a great cry, 'Daddy!' and went running, *flying,* into his arms." Naomi
told her: "I couldn't deprive her of a father like Brick. He loved her. He
loved his kids. And he was loving with them." Naomi couldn't deprive
herself of a husband like Brick, either, the good with the bad. Besides, he
still had those exciting brown eyes flecked with green.

Meanwhile -- well, I should not complain. My quarters
here are comfortable. Anne has an amazing library, a
Capehart with hundreds of records. I learn something about
writing, and I do have a little time to work.

However, one of the most important things I have
learned is that I can sit back in an easy chair and type
with the little portable on my lap. That is amazing for me;
I have never been comfortable sitting at a desk; never
really able to think at a typewriter. Now half the strain
is gone. Furthermore, I have discovered that I can do the
same thing in the car -- drive out to some point overlooking the Golden Gate and work until I get tired -- with
neither the view nor the work interfering with the other.

Toni kept sending Brick's book manuscript to one publishing house
after another, but —

February 19, 1946

Naturally, I was disappointed, but not surprised, to
find that the opinion of publishers on "The Imaginary
Revolution" is approaching disgustingly close to unanimity.
Yet they are right; it is not a book upon which a publisher
might hope to make any money.

I really have learned a lot in the last five years
that I've been working on "The Imaginary Revolution" and
its predecessor, though. Not so much about writing as about
the idiocy of writing without regard for publishability. I
think I blame Covici a little for not having set me wise
when I first talked with him; if I were an editor, I should
certainly be able to explain to a new writer that there

were some things which worked against publishability to
such a degree that a guy was practically wasting his time
working in that direction.

Nevertheless, you will probably receive from me,
within two or three weeks, another non-fiction manuscript.
Here's the story:

While I was down south, Anne and I corresponded on
this and that, and the correspondence covered about 239
subjects, among which were semantics, and Aristotelian
tragedy and a few others. When I got back here, we started
checking over them, and finally Anne copied out that
section of the correspondence dealing with Tragedy and I
did a little cutting and brought it down to about twenty-
five thousand words (imagine! that made up only about a
tenth of the correspondence!), and the thing proved to have
a lot of interest and dramatic form. So after I'd done a
little bridgework where the cutting had been too deep, Anne
undertook to type it out -- on the remote possibility that
some publisher might be interested. The idea is that it is
a written discussion, not essays but letters, very
informal. The form is enough off the beaten path so there
is just an outside chance --

Naomi is coming up for a visit early next month, and
we may possibly be able to find a place to live while she's
here. And I do think we are going to get along after this;
some curious thing has happened which seems to have cured
the major misunderstandings. Gosh, I hope so; I've
certainly had enough troubles in the last ten years or so.

It is pleasant here with Anne; a curious brother-
sister relationship which (I suppose) is possible because
coronary thrombosis removed one from certain very pleasurable activities. But I'll be glad when Naomi gets here.

March 7, 1946

Naomi and Patty are here and we are having a grand
time. So far (a week) things have been marvelous, and I
have the conviction that they will continue to run along on
an even keel. I do find I can relax better with Naomi and
the baby around. I'm sitting here with the door open while
she plays the "Eroica" variations on the phonograph and the
baby races up and down the hall and neither bothers me.
That was something I couldn't have done a year or so ago. I
still do have a little of the residue of the sense of
responsibility which used to keep me from relaxing. But I
catharize it by doing some simple household task immediately after breakfast -- like carrying an empty water glass
from my room into the kitchen. Then my conscience is clear,
and I can settle down to rest or work.

Brick and Naomi bought a big, floor-model Silvertone radio-phono-
graph from Sears with an "electronic eye," an illuminated circle that
helped tune in the stations. They used cactus needles; Brick would buy

them in little packets and sharpen them by placing them in a device to twirl them over circular disks of fine sandpaper. Then he'd patiently insert a sharpened needle into the tone arm and listen to two or three singles or an entire symphony, which took perhaps four to six records.

W. W. NORTON & CO. INC.
Seventy Fifth Avenue • New York

March 18, 1946

Miss Toni Strassman
24 East Sixty-first Street
New York 21, New York
Dear Miss Strassman:

We have had an opportunity to consider THE IMAGINARY REVOLUTION by Charles Harris Garrigues. Now I have to write you that we have decided not to offer publication.

I am especially sorry because I believe the manuscript possesses much merit. It is well written and the author knows his economics. I suppose that our decision is based primarily on the fact that the book falls somewhat between two fields; that is, it is somewhat too much of a text for the trade field and at the same time it is not suitable for ordinary text use.

Sincerely,

Addison Burnham

March 28, 1946

Dear Toni,

The reason the book falls between two fields is that it falls between two points of view -- or rather it doesn't achieve a point of view at all. Essentially, I conceived of it as an essay for posterity; one by which future generations would learn that in 1944 one C. H. Garrigues was able to outline the future course of civilization and to develop a process whereby such predictions could be made. I didn't intend it either as a book for the trade, or as a text -- although I didn't realize it at that time. Such a book should, of course, by its very nature, be published at the expense of the author and, perhaps, put in a "time capsule."

It's true that Anne is a marvelous correspondent. And, for the most part, a very swell gal. And it's true that the CHG-AH correspondence is a fearful and marvelous thing; it is almost incredible that we should have produced so many thousands of words upon so very many different subjects. But it isn't true, as you say, that I found in Anne the sort of correspondent I didn't find in you.

I think that I have wept many salt and bitter tears upon your shoulder, even from three thousand miles away, during the last many years, and I rather suspect that I shall continue to do so. True, I've sometimes felt that you were too busy to be bothered with matters which I should have outgrown long ago. But it has never ceased to be a matter of great comfort to me that you were there -- as definitely there in recent years as long ago. So don't say what you said.

[To George Louis]
April 5, 1946

Hiyuh, chum,

About algebra, it's too darned bad that they can't teach mathematics for what it is: a branch of Logic. The reason they can't (I suspect) is that the average teacher isn't capable of understanding, much less teaching, Logic. It was years after I finished high school before I began to understand that any problem in algebra is in reality an argument in logic, in which you use sheer reasoning to prove -- and to discover -- something you didn't know before. Instead of being just a lot of senseless symbols to memorize, it really is the most marvelous instrument ever invented.

April 12, 1946

Dear Dickie,

Letters from you are like vitamins; one needs at least a certain minimum in order to keep bright and shining -- otherwise the hair falls out, the teeth look dingy and the fingernails break off easily. I do always feel much better after hearing from you.

I'm really feeling good these days. I don't know whether it is a gradual recovery of health, or just this spring weather, or what, but these last few days -- since I've recovered from my vaccination -- I've felt just fine. Like a thirty-year-old! I had a day off yesterday, and one day away from the office always takes ten years off my age, so maybe that has something to do with it.

But what burns me up a little is the fact that I am smart enough to be earning good money now -- if I'd been smart enough to want to. Now, when I'm smart enough to want to, it's rather late to start doing it. In other words, I'm sort of kicking myself for not having spent the last twelve years in chasing the dollar so that now I could have a surplus big enough so I could sort of do things -- you know, provide nice presents for the kids, send them to college, etc. etc.

[From George Louis]
April 28, 1946

Dear Dad,

A funny thing happened the other day. My friend Russ was over here. I have one of your columns from the

Illustrated Daily News stapled up on the walls about Chuck
and me. He read it, and then I pointed up to the wall on
which I have a poster saying stuff about "Read C. H.
Garrigues every day," etc.[4] I said, "Yep, my dad used to be
a full-fledged columnist."

"Huhh?" Russ said and looked at me kind of queer like,
"Your dad?"

"Yeah," said I, "from way back."

And Russ is still looking at me as though I were
poison. "Your dad," says he, "your dad, A COMMUNIST!"

Well, I hastened to inform him that you were nothing
worse than a Democrat, and what I meant was columnist.

P.S. Mother is forty-one years old yesterday.

                                        [To George Louis]
                                        May 1, 1946

Hiyah, fellah,

I never knew very many politicians, Democratic or
Republican, I'd want to have around the house unless the
silver was in a vault. No columnists, either. Tell Russ for
me that most communists are much preferable to most
columnists.

Patty is swell and so is Noma and they are both
looking forward to you visiting us for a while this summer.
Pat goes through the snapshot album and says, "That's Patty
when she was a lee-eetle, teeeny baby, and that's her
brother Loou. And that's Chuckie. And that's Uncle George
and Patty." She spends more time looking at pictures of
herself than most kids do looking at Mother Goose. I guess
she's her own pinup girl. But she is a very good little
girl and, I think, more like you than anybody else in the
family.

                                        May 6, 1946

Dear Dickie,

I always enjoy your letters too much and started to
answer at once, but things have been moderately hectic
around here. Besides, I had to wait until I got some money
in the bank to send you a check.

It sure is terrible the way money goes. Ultimately, I
suppose, we'll settle down to realizing that the dollar is
worth only fifty cents and that on seventy-five dollars a
week you can live just about as well as you used to on
thirty-five. But it takes a little readjustment, especially
when -- like me -- you've had the idea that your income was
going up all the time as you get older.

I'm certainly delighted the boys are doing so well.

---

[4] It was a news-rack card publicizing Brick's column of the early Thirties, "The Spotlight."

From Lou's letters, he is surely getting better adjusted, and I think Charles must be feeling much better now that he's back home where he can go to dances and things. Chuck will put on more weight from now on; the exercises and the dances seem to be doing him a lot of good.

A week or so ago I caught cold in my left shoulder and since then I've never been quite sure that the slight pain I feel is a muscular pain or is in my heart. Tried to see my doctor, but he's been sick, so I saw his partner, who is an old guy who, apparently, doesn't believe in doctors. He fussed around and finally said he didn't know anything about it but he didn't think it was my heart and gave me some high-power vitamin pills with the statement, "I don't know that these will do you any good, but I gave some to my wife and she stopped complaining!" He didn't say whether she had stopped complaining permanently or not.

Yes, I frequently get letters from Lou -- and very fine letters they are. The last one ended with a P.S. "Mom is forty-one years old today." A cheerful little cuss, isn't he? But, gosh, it sure took me back and made me realize how long we've both lived. And had a lot of fun and a lot of trouble, I guess. I got quite sentimental over it.

May 24, 1946

Dear Toni:

It seems rather silly to write a letter with a rail strike under way, but I seem to need an excuse to get away from my attempts at fictioneering this morning. And as a matter of fact, I had intended to write you a couple of weeks ago to congratulate you on the big sale that Corinne-Cornelia told us about.[5]

No, I'll definitely not do anything more on "The Imaginary Revolution" -- unless somebody is interested. To abstain from even thinking about it has become an act of contrition; I abstain and thereby pile up credits in Heaven.

And as a matter of fact, there are two books that I want very much to do. One is the book "Beyond The Imaginary Revolution." "The I.R." told what must happen and why, based upon theoretical considerations; this next one would take what has happened (since 1934, say) and relate it in considerable detail -- a research job, in other words -- showing the process step by step, causation by causation, and out of these causal chains showing the theory which must develop.

Meanwhile, as I say, I've been trying to find some way to get around the psychological block which keeps me from writing fiction.

---

5 Toni had placed *The Growing Roots* with Crown. It became a Jewish Book Guild selection.

Brick kept up his conversation with Chuck. Often a fat envelope would arrive in our mailbox, and inside would be a long letter for Chuck and a shorter one for me. Sometimes the two of them talked about books.

[From Chuck; mid-1946]

```
Dear Pop,
     I was mowing the lawn yesterday, when all of a sudden
I realized why grownups like "Alice in Wonderland" while
most kids dislike it intensely.
     Kids have the ability to adapt themselves to new
conditions without being particularly impressed by them.
So, in Alice it is explained to the reader that time works
backwards, and the queen first cries out, and then pricks
her finger with a pin. The adult is delighted by this, but
the child says, "All right, those conditions are taken into
consideration, proceed with your anecdote."
     What do I think of the kind of people who enjoy
"Alice"?
     They are fascinated by situation -- much as a child
likes a bright colored object. Therefore, they aren't very
imaginative; something has got to be really unusual to make
them react. Parenthetically, I liked "Sylvie and Bruno"
better than "Alice."6
```

It is a very curious thing how much effect Chuck and Brick had upon each other. One expects the father to influence the son, but in our family the opposite was also true. Chuck's teen-age enthusiasm for science-fiction had sparked a similar curiosity in Brick. In one letter Brick tried to persuade Chuck that space travel would be impossible because "there would be no air" for a rocket's jets to push against. Brick had apparently forgotten Newton's third law of physics, or the way a shotgun kicked his shoulder when he was a kid.

Chuck was, at the time, writing science-fiction short stories and plots, and to help him do it, he had subscribed to the magazine *Writer's Digest*. Brick had never studied writing in a formal way, and he reacted eagerly when Chuck suggested a book on writing by the caustic Jack Woodford,[7] who had written several books on authorship. Brick found a copy of Woodford's *How to Write and Sell a Novel* (1943) in the Mechanics Institute in downtown San Francisco, which boasted a private library with a moderate fee and an excellent and varied collection in floor upon floor of open stacks.

---

6 *Sylvie and Bruno* and *Sylvie and Bruno Concluded* were published in 1889 and 1893 by Lewis Carroll. Adult in nature, they featured chapters alternating between discussions of nineteenth-century ethical problems in England and the serio-comic adventures of a good monarch and his children in a mystic fairy-tale kingdom.

7 His real name was Jack Woolfolk (1894-1971).

[To Chuck]
June 10, 1946

Hi,

Having got the Jack Woodford book out of the library, and having read part of it, I am now sufficiently discouraged with the story I was writing, so I guess I can take a morning off and write letters.

It was good to hear from you -- at long last. I was really beginning to miss you on your birthday; and, as a matter of fact, I almost called up your Mom to congratulate her on the very splendid event.[8] I guess it was because you're sixteen; after that a fellow is more or less on his own -- while his old man retires into innocuous decrepitude.

Still, I do think that by application of due diligence and fortitude you can manage to finish a letter occasionally. And if they are not enough, let me give you some Woodfordish suggestions on: "How to Get a Letter Finished in Six Easy Steps."

1. Address an envelope before you start to write.
2. Put a stamp on it.
3. Start the letter.
4. When interrupted, write "more" and put the letter in the envelope.
5. Take five steps to a mantel, desk-top or other place where it can be noticeably propped.
6. Keep reminding Mom to mail it for you each day until she does it.

By following the Garrigues technique you cannot fail to succeed.

The Jack Woodford book is a find -- whether disastrous or not, I don't know. My present feeling, after getting halfway through, is one of discouragement and distaste -- much as I am amused and delighted with the book. And I'm inclined to think that his description of the process of writing -- even to feeding the canary -- is exactly accurate.

His book raises a point which every writer attempts to dodge but which, nevertheless, must be answered. Let me expand in a Socratic dialogue:

SOCRATES: So, you want to write, eh? But why?

PLUTO: Well, ah -- you know -- well, I think I want to be a writer.

SOCRATES: But why?

PLUTO: Well, writers get talked about, and everybody knows about them and they make a lot of money, if they're

---

8 Brick had a horror of long-distance telephone calls, principally because of the cost. It was a constant sore point between him and Naomi, solved only when they agreed that Naomi would pay for her calls herself and that he would not have to look at the bills.

good. And they are able to put over their ideas, and some
of them, if they are good enough, gain lasting fame so
that, hundreds of years from now, little children will be
tortured by being compelled to read what they have written
and write book reports upon it.

SOCRATES: In other words, you expect writing to
bring you wealth, and notoriety and -- perhaps -- fame;
is that right?

PLUTO: I suppose so.

SOCRATES: Very well, then; are you aware that writing
may bring you one of these three things, that it might
bring you two, but that it can hardly, under any circumstances, bring you all three.

PLUTO: No, I was not aware of that. That is, I had
noticed that something of the sort did seem to occur but I
did not know that it must occur.

SOCRATES: It is something that all mature writers are
aware of. Therefore, you must decide, and tell me now,
which of these three things you want. And when you have
decided, you must determine to be satisfied with the one
you have chosen. If you choose fame or notoriety you must
not complain if you and your children do not have enough to
eat. If you choose money, you must not complain that your
mind comes to smell like a pigpen and that you are
unwilling to look at yourself in the mirror when you go to
shave.

So, then, which do you choose?

PLUTO: Before I answer that, Socrates, tell me why it
is that I must choose either-or -- Why cannot I choose to
have both.

SOCRATES: It is because publishing has become a mass
production industry in precisely the same way as the
production of bread or soap is a mass production industry.
That means that only the most profitable enterprises can
survive. That means not the best goods but the lowest
quantity of goods that can be made acceptable to the
largest number of people -- the lowest common denominator.
The publishing houses, in order to survive, must find
writers who appeal to the broadest -- that is, the lowest
-- tastes; precisely to the people who read the advertisements.

For I think you will agree with me, Pluto, that no man
or woman of taste or intelligence could read the advertising columns of any modern "slick" without being compelled
to regurgitate at intervals.

PLUTO: But isn't it true, Socrates, that some writers
do achieve notoriety, and fame and money, all together?

SOCRATES: Perhaps one in a million does. Or, rather,

one in about seventy-five million. But even for those, the principle still holds; they must still choose, at every step, whether they are writing for fame or for money. For it goes without saying that Hemingway would make more money if he would (as he could) write as badly as Taylor Caldwell and would make even more money if he would (as he couldn't) write like Lloyd C. Douglas.[9] Every writer must always turn himself in one direction or another. So now tell me, Pluto, which do you choose?

PLUTO: Well, now, Socrates, I think you will agree that this has turned out to be a hell of a Socratic dialogue. In the Socratic dialogue (as you will agree if you have read your Plato), Socrates is supposed to ask all the questions and trick his young pupil into giving silly answers. But here I have been asking the questions and you have been giving the silly answers.

                                        June 17, 1946

What I'm sort of wondering about is how greatly your future education is going to interfere with your future writing. You'll get acquainted with the classics. You'll read great writing. You may even pick up an idea or two. And do you, thereafter, become increasingly handicapped as a money-writer? (That is at least half facetious.)

As for myself, my first trouble was that I began to come into contact with writing and writers at just about the time when the United States was becoming literarily self-conscious. There was Dreiser and Hemingway and Hecht and Cabell and Dos Passos -- all geniuses. And it was, as my friend John Clayton says, a question of either being a genius or nothing. If I'd stuck to my Western Story and Argosy, I'd have probably been a money-writer twenty years ago. It's only now that I'm getting over the effects.

I think one thing that has startled me since I've gone back to thinking in terms of fiction is the fact that, after having done reams and reams of reading in the last twenty years, having become acquainted with the best in all literature, I suddenly discovered that I have added not one thing to my ability to write fiction.

That discovery startled me. Woodford's book drove it home. I should be able to learn more quickly now than I could have learned at twenty-five. But the learning process has to be done all over.

I'm sitting in the car on the beach, and Naomi and Pat are playing out in the sand. We've had two weeks of the most beautiful warm summer weather. It seems inconceivable that in a day or two fog will come in -- to stay.

I'm glad you're going to come up this summer. I've

---

9 Lloyd C. Douglas published *Magnificent Obsession* in 1929 and the best-selling *The Robe* in 1942. Taylor Caldwell, a prolific novelist, was best known for *This Side of Innocence*.

been wondering if you were going to get a job. Assuming
that it wouldn't be bad for your health, I think it would
be a good idea if you were able to earn enough money to buy
you some clothes this fall.

August 3, 1946

Dear Dickie:

Patty is growing like a little weed and is as cute as
can be. At the moment Naomi is playing nursery rhyme records
to her and she's singing at the top of her voice. She's got
so that in this nice weather she plays on the sidewalk with
the other kids and has a very good time. Some day I hope she
can have a yard to play in, but I don't see how.[10]

Lou writes me that he and Chuck are planning on coming
up about September 1. That will be swell; I only wish they
could have got here to spend more time. I know both of them
will be crazy about Pat, and it's too bad they won't have
time to get more fully acquainted with her. She shares
Lou's liking for dogs but is scared to death of them when
they get too close to her. She looked out of the window and
saw a dog and said: "There's a cute little doggie. His name
is Get Away, Little Doggie!"

How is your job going? I hope you make enough to help
take up the excess expenses as it seems the world is nearer
starvation than I've seen it. This part of it, anyway.
We've been going in the hole about thirty-five dollars a
month, even before the OPA[11] went out, and with the new
prices, God knows what we'll do. Besides, July used up the
last of the savings, so from now on it's a case of going
into debt. Which doesn't bother Naomi because to her debt
seems to be the natural state of man. Fortunately, this
last month she got some typing work to do at home.

September 30, 1946

Dear Toni,

I can't say I'm surprised that Holt turned down "The
Imaginary Revolution" -- nor, I confess, particularly
disappointed. The fact is that I hadn't any business writing
on that particular topic -- not that I don't know enough, but
economics is a much more institutionalized endeavor than I
had supposed. And I'm not a member of the club.

Whenever I look back at the last seven years or so and
see how my interests were centered -- up until a year or so
ago -- I wonder how I ever got that way. Or how I got out
of it. It's curious to reflect upon how uninterested I was
in the things that interest most people -- making money,

10 Brick and Naomi were still living on the second floor of their walk-up flat on Alpine
Terrace, a very quiet street only two blocks long on the east side of Buena Vista Hill. Anne had
moved out.

11 The wartime Office of Price Administration.

making even a normal living, even a normal emotional life, as usually considered. At that time to have published "The Imaginary Revolution" would have been the most important thing conceivable to me because there is much in it that is new and that would be valuable to future students of social science. But now! Pfft! Or, anyway, half-pfft!

The pfft! would be complete if I had developed any flair for fiction. I haven't -- but I struggle away at the science fiction story as a matter of self-discipline.

Being around the Claytons helps a bit. (They are our only social contacts now.) All these fiction possibilities were rigorously suppressed in me; now they begin to open up just a little bit. And I have a plan about doing a novel called "Neither Five Nor Three." (Or, maybe, "The Fact That Two and Two.") You know, Housman's "The fact that two and two makes four, and neither five nor three, The heart of man has long made sore; and long 'tis like to be."

A. E. Housman (1859-1936) included this untitled poem, No. xxxv, in Last Poems, published in 1922 by Henry Holt and Co. I can understand it now as a metaphor for Brick's feeling about his own life.

> When first my way to fair I took
> Few pence in purse had I,
> And long I used to stand and look
> At things I could not buy.
>
> Now times are altered: if I care
> To buy a thing, I can;
> The pence are here and here's the fair,
> But where's the lost young man?
>
> To think that two and two are four
> And neither five nor three
> The heart of man has long been sore
> And long 'tis like to be.

The fact is that I'm a hell of a lot more relaxed than I've been for years. It has been a good summer; beautiful weather, which is rare here, and a home life that is not too troublesome, and a job at the office which is not too trying -- and no immediate necessity to set the world on fire. I have toasted myself in the sun until I am a reddish chocolate down to a rather forty-four-ish middle; I have lain in the sun longer and oftener this year than ever before. And while my non-fictional mind is incapable of explaining why it should be good to lie in the sun since (1) nobody admires a coat of tan strung around a middle-aged balloon, and (2) you can get Vitamin D out of pills, my fictional mind tells me that lying in the sun is excellent.

Not too many weeks earlier, Brick had sent a number of John Clayton's short stories to Toni; she was entranced by them and sent them on to *Harper's*. One, "My Apples," resonated powerfully, but the editors suggested a rewrite of the conclusion.

Clayton showed me your letter about "My Apples." He's going to re-handle the ending and try again. I really think John is the most promising writer I've known. I think his characters are better than anybody else's now writing. And he improves.

In a way, it's very discouraging. I go over his stuff with him and think: "Jesus Christ, I'll never be able to write like that." Oh, well, I learn.

A few weeks later, the sale was made. It was Toni's first for John Bell Clayton.

Cathedral City, Calif.
October 30, 1946

Just a few lines for no particular purpose except to make you envious. We are vacationing -- spending a couple of days at Corinne's -- what's her pen name? -- Cornelia's place. And wishing you were here. It's a great deal like Arizona at Arizona's best. Perfect colors, perfect weather, inconceivably beautiful mountains.

Both Corinne and her husband have been mightily improved by their escape to the desert. They have the most delightful little two-room house I've ever seen, beautifully furnished, with gimcracks and knickeries that are just right. They seem to be people of importance in the little community and are just settling in to what -- I suspect -- is the fulfillment of a largely unconscious dream. So it's very pleasant to be here.

I was delighted that you were able to sell Clayton's story and feel pretty confident that he'll have a steady sale as time goes on. Martha, his wife, is just terrifically excited. I hate to give a woman credit for anything, but I do think that Martha pulled John out of a very tough mental situation; she drove him and carried him and encouraged him -- and will either make him a writer or herself a widow.

I can't remember if I told you that I finally think I'm ready to write fiction. I have a short story about half done -- and it's the first time in my life I've ever felt I "had" a story. I enjoy working on it -- and when I don't, I work on something else I have. So maybe, if all goes well, I'll start producing some of these days.[12]

---

12 Toni to John Clayton on November 5, 1946: "Brick writes me that he is now writing his first short story. If you can inspire him, and I can sell something for him, I'll be happy. So far he has sent me two clients, and I have sold for both, and not for Brick, which makes me unhappy. Except that all editors agree that he is brilliant and has something to say. If he were hale, I'd insist on his going on with the same kind of book, but I'm a little afraid to burden him with that kind of heavy writing."

I may have to get a part-time job to make ends meet
financially. The situation has been the cause of great
discord in the Garrigues household. I don't think I should
work more than five days a week. And Naomi doesn't think
she should work. But she does think I should earn enough
money so she can stay home and be an ideal mother. And she
may be right. But in that case, I shall have to find two
extra days of work a week.

I know that some people live a life of dodging bill
collectors and hounding grocery stores for credit. But I
can't quite imagine myself doing that. In fact, I can't
imagine myself doing anything, either positively or
negatively.

In a way, I'm more or less resigned to many of the
things which were driving me crazy a year or so ago.
Particularly, I'm amused at my complete inability to make
Naomi understand that you cannot possibly spend a hundred
dollars a week on an income of seventy-five. I used to
think she was willfully perverse or indifferent. Now I
understand it's simply a different way of thinking -- a way
I'm not familiar with. To her it seems that if you mention
an unpleasant fact you are creating that fact. If
you refuse to recognize it, then it doesn't exist. If you
make plans to meet some situation, you thereby create that
situation.

What the hell does one do under those circumstances?
Damn if I know. I only know that such a point of view isn't
nearly as rare as it would seem to be. (Incidentally, I
wonder if it is in some degree a Jewish trait? I've known
plenty of non-Jews who had it: my own mother among them.
And many Jews who didn't. But I could understand it better
among Jews who have lived under so much insecurity -- in
conditions in which they could not plan for security --
that they might fear even to mention disaster, lest they
bring it upon themselves.)

As ever,

Brick

Mama's Method of Dealing With Money

*That would have been the worst summer ever if it hadn't been for the
.22 and the rabbits. Except for the rabbits there wasn't any meat, and
Papa went around with a worried look, and Mama kept singing "Trust in
Jesus" louder and louder. They did manage to make the last payment on
Grace's piano before the money ran out, and Grace sat in the parlor,
practicing hour after hour while Bliss stood outside, hating the thought of
not enough money.*

*When the hens had not begun to lay in September, Papa went into El
Jardin and talked to the county farm agent who came out and looked over*

the flock and said they needed more green fodder in their feed. But there wasn't any more green fodder. The little alfalfa patch had been big enough for a few hens and a cow, but Papa hadn't enlarged it as he increased his flock. That was what was called being a poor manager, Bliss guessed, and he knew that if the time ever came he wouldn't make a mistake like that. But he knew he had to make it up to Papa in some way.

The farm agent recommended a certain patented chicken feed which he said was "balanced mix," but Papa told Mama, pshaw, if you had to buy your greens and maybe your milk-stuff too, as well as grain, there wouldn't be any money in the chicken business at all, the way prices were this year.

Mama said maybe he ought to go down to F. L. E. Skinner and borrow fifty dollars to buy the feed that would get the chickens laying again, and Papa wanted to know how in tarnation he was going to pay it back. Mama said the Good Lord would provide, and Papa said he wished the Good Lord would provide the fifty dollars without waiting for him to owe F. L. E. Skinner four dollars' interest on it, to boot. Bliss was sitting at the supper table, grasping his fork with the tines sticking up, sitting there with his mouth and ears open, taking it all in because he'd never heard Papa and Mama talking like that before. Mama looked at Bliss and gave Papa a look, but Papa kept right on talking.

"As a matter of fact," Papa said, "Maybe if I'd been smart enough to get a promissory note from the Good Lord for the fifty dollars we sent them evangelists . . . ."

Mama said, "Albert!" and Papa broke off talking, with his mouth still half open and looked down at his plate and didn't say anything until Mama said, "You can go out and play now, Bliss." Bliss could see Papa's face getting red as he sat there without making a sound, and Bliss hurried out because he felt embarrassed. That night after Papa had read the Bible and they all turned over on their knees to pray, Papa said a long prayer asking forgiveness for those who would find levity in Thy name and pointing out that he and all the Lanes had always been people who would never fail to trust completely in Thy promises. When Papa finished and said "Amen," Bliss started to get up but was startled to hear Mama repeat the "Amen" in a loud and determined tone of voice.

The next day Papa went down to El Jardin again and saw F. L. E. Skinner and borrowed fifty dollars and bought balanced mix and after awhile the hens began laying again. But it seemed that, afterwards, the Lanes stopped trying to get ahead because it was all they could do to catch up.

Chapter Twenty-Three
To Dig Furiously in the Earth

[December 1946]

Dear Toni,

I've been working the last six weeks on what may turn out to be a novel. At any rate, I'm reasonably certain of this: that either this is the novel or there is no Garrigues novel.

I've been working joyously, with gusto. I've done about forty thousand words. I have overcome my first grave difficulty: how to see life through the eyes of a college boy without making it seem college boyish.

It is, of course, autobiographical (when has Garrigues ever been interested in anything but himself), but what is wrong with an autobiographical novel? And anyway, who the hell cares? I am having fun.

Today I feel really good. Patty is in nursery school. We got more presents than we sent. Maybe Naomi is going to get a part-time job after the first of the year. Then maybe we will have enough money to eat on.

Yesterday was not so good. It has been ten years that Naomi and I have been more or less teamed up; Christmas is some sort of an anniversary or other. And they haven't been particularly good years. One can expect to go downhill after forty-five. But between thirty-five and forty-five one should not. And it's been downhill all the way. But today is a nice day. And now I must shave and go to work.

January 26, 1947

The more I see of women, the more I am convinced that the Almighty might well have thought up a less troublesome way of propagating the species.

A story: When I was in the hospital, I met a gal. One of the most beautiful, charmingly beautiful, beautifully charming women I've ever seen. Married to a big-shot gambler who used her as a gem-tray to display evidence of his standing: To wear diamonds and clothes -- and to be home (in a fine house in Seattle's most expensive district) to cook dinner, just on the possible chance that he might be home, was her sole duty. Otherwise, her time was her own and her behavior was her own business.

So she falls in love with an Army officer and, for some months, commutes by plane between Seattle and San Francisco. They are swell kids and we have them around quite a bit. Then she leaves her husband and disappears in L.A. and, after nobody hears from her for a while, reappears in Seattle visiting friend hubby and inquiring what the hell she's going to do with the baby she's going to have by the Army officer.

He, the gambler, being a good guy, says, "Stick around until it's born and it'll be legitimate; you can get your divorce later." But she answers: "No, my sweetie and I will be true to each other in name as well as in fact." So, since a divorce will take too long, she finally decides on an abortion, which hubby pays for. So she almost dies, lies in the hospital for months -- husband paying all the bills -- and finally, during that time, discovers that the husband is running around with a teen-ager. She screams: "No sonofabitch is going to do that to me!" and sues him for divorce, slaps an attachment on the house and all his ready capital and drives him into bankruptcy because, hitting a losing streak in his gambling, he cannot call on his reserves -- and also because he's lost his nerve, his morale and his social standing.

Well, I don't mean this as a fiction story; it is too corny. The trouble is that it happens; it is too common; it is just true to life. Can I say it is "just like a woman"? No, that just about fifty percent of the women I know would do it -- with variations.

No matter what the price one may pay for not marrying, it is less than the price one pays for marriage.

Do I sound unusually cynical? I mean, compared with my usual naive self? I honestly think that the trouble is not with women but with the fact that we let them out of the harem. And by that I don't mean an Oriental enclosure, but a whole half of a universe in which they actually seem to be much more at home.

I am, in other words, being a grumpy old man.

Anne is back, proudly wearing her new husband, who is a very fine guy. She has finished her novel. It's about the Pony Express and represents a hell of a lot of research. She wants you to handle it for her.

Clayton tells me he has sent you the first eight chapters of "The Unwanted." I really think the guy is marvelous. On an impulse I showed him a few pages of "Neither Five Nor Three" the other evening. He was exceedingly (it seemed to me at the time) critical of my "style," as "flat," "full of cliches," etc. I confess I was a little shocked at first; then I began to realize the real value in the sort of discussions John and I have been having. It does sharpen that which is individual in you by holding it up against that which you admire but cannot achieve.

But more, the experience demonstrated that, for the first time, I am ready to write fiction in that (after accepting thankfully the technical criticism, but not too gracefully) it didn't matter to me whether John likes it or not, or whether you like it or not, or whether anybody likes it or not. The problem is to get it so that I like it.[1]

February 17, 1947

Almost all men are basically ambivalent in love. That is because in the sort of deep, lasting affection which we are talking about, the woman must inevitably become in a large degree a substitute for the mother; for the mother-refuge, for home, security, nirvana. But at the same time, almost all men are under the same basic necessity to escape from home and mother and security, etc.: the necessity to go out into the world, to strut their stuff, to assert their individuality, their superiority.

So comes marriage. Almost all men enter into this reluctantly -- but determinedly. They attempt to project the mother-image upon the wife, yet they are restrained from doing so because this girl who has now become the mother-surrogate is the identical girl before whom they used to strut, the girl for whom they demonstrated their masculinity and individuality. So, in either way they are almost certain to be frustrated unless by some miracle the woman succeeds in being two different women, so that the man can project himself alternately as the little boy seeking refuge and then the dominant male.

Now consider the situation of the woman.

First, woman seems to be largely univalent (or is it

---

1 John Clayton to Toni: "Saw Brick a night or so ago and he read me parts of the novel he is working on. I believe that when he gets it finished and edited he could very well have something. It seems alive and fresh." And later: "So Brick is really getting somewhere with his novel? I'm pleased as hell about that, because he needs all the encouragement you can give him, and I'm sure that is what has him at work. He has been – is being – a great help to me. I honestly think he is a good editor and adviser."

monovalent?) She wants more than one thing out of love, but those things are not (as with men) mutually exclusive. The woman cannot say whether she marries for love or money because she marries for love and money -- not as separate things, but as things which are not even two aspects of the same thing, nor even two sides of the same coin, nor even two figures in the same design -- but as things which are one thing.

Second, most women's ideas of love are formed almost exclusively by the comparatively recent literary concepts of romantic love, even though her practice is based upon much more fundamental necessities.

Take for example the question of polygamy. Most women believe that they would be very unhappy sharing a man with another woman or two. Yet in fact, most modern women find themselves sharing a man with other women; the wife shares him with one or more gal friends, and knows she does, and usually considers that no irreparable harm so long as she doesn't lose face by admitting that she knows it; the sweetheart shares him with the wife, and knows it and admits it -- because she doesn't lose face in the sharing -- and is not too happy about it. But each is willing enough to make the best of it if her basic needs are met.

Women will tell you that love is a woman's career, etc., but very few women ever take as long to learn their business as they take to learn shorthand. I don't think a woman can get or keep a man by making him unhappy -- intentionally, that is. But, by god, it seems they do it by instinct.

I shudder to think what my life has become; the narrow limits of activity and hope and effort within which it is now contained. Yet I more than half suspect that I have myself created the net in which I am entangled; at any rate, I have been unwilling (and grow daily more unwilling) to escape from it.

I am not quite forty-five, and yet I find myself looking upon life with the viewpoint of a man of sixty; as though the game was finished and the score in and the count about completed -- and only some last-minute discovery of a hidden error could save it from being a lopsided defeat.

Partly that is due to reasons of health. Until now I could always jump into the car and escape my sense of frustration; or go back into the hills and hike, or camp, or something. Or even fly into a rage. Now I do not dare to do any of these things.

And partly it is due to economic reasons. Just as there is no margin of energy, so there is no margin of money for even the slightest kind of freedom -- such as a trip to L.A. to see the kids, or even a couple of nights spent in a bar. Nor will there ever be, I realize, such a margin: with Naomi's complete indifference to money she will always succeed in spending every cent before it's earned.

And partly it is due to -- what shall I call it? -- poverty of illusions. I no longer believe it is particularly important whether the Newspaper Guild, for example, adopts a progressive program, or whether the British continue to misrule Greece and Palestine or whether the Negroes vote in Atlanta.

Nor am I very seriously deluded into the belief that I shall ever be a successful writer; that illusion, too, has quite faded. I think I might successfully have taught; at the moment it seems to me that the only useful thing I've done in recent years was the help I've given Clayton. I feel quite honestly that I've whipped him into being a better writer than he could otherwise have become. (Without in any sense making him write my way; my god! I wish it were my way.)

And partly it is due to my final acceptance of the fact that my relationship with Naomi will never be better than it is now, so that my own life, my personal life, will be frustrated. But the result is not so much a frustration as a negation, a diminution, a whittling down, an impoverishment which I cannot fight against.

Does all that seem gloomy enough? It has been a long while since I have got so much off my chest in a single morning. So now I feel quite cheerful about it all. I think this has been a morning more usefully spent than it would have been had I written on the novel. Because some of the things I've said have helped to clarify some of the things which the novel was supposed to be about -- and which I had forgotten.

I was a little amused by Clayton's attitude about it. I read him a couple of paragraphs to make a point we were arguing about, then on impulse, read a couple of scenes. He was astonished, apparently, at how poor it was -- and said so, quite definitely. Later, apparently, Martha (who is a very swell gal; I'm very fond of her) gave him hell, and he called up several days in a row to assure me that it was fine writing, etc., etc. which, unfortunately, it is not. I'm utterly astonished at what a poor writer I am; I go over a scene time after time, trying to make it smooth, trying to make it live, and each time it gets worse than before.[2]

---

2 John Clayton to Toni: "I was out to see Brick the other night. He seems reasonably cheerful and is enjoying his writing. I somehow have the very strong wish that he would divorce himself from the Hearst organization; I just feel that the psychic energy he uses in defending his alliance with Hearst could well be released and utilized in other directions. But maybe I'm wrong; I find it hard enough to regulate my own life, much less prescribe for anybody else. Anyway, he is a very fine guy."

My novel is, basically, formula: the middle-aged man who finds that life, circumstances have tended to diminish him, to whittle him down, to surround and circumscribe him. Autobiographical, you see. An opening of some three thousand words done as high comedy on a low level, in which this Caspar Milquetoast (who is physically big and was a football star) socks a cop. A good opening; at least one I'm well satisfied with.

Then a cutback to childhood, youth, young manhood, designed to show, scene by scene, why it is so important to him that "a man should be able to stand up and cast a shadow" and why the symbolic loss of his shadow has driven him to sock the cop, get hell beaten out of him, get thrown in jail, etc. Then the final working out to a happy ending on the level of high comedy; that is, one which is obviously and satisfactorily contrived so that the reader will say: "Of course it doesn't work out that way in real life, but it's nice to think it does."

The body of the story was really intended to deal with newspaper work, city politics, graft, etc., and it was on the level of political power that the protagonist loses and regains his "shadow."

So -- I start the cutback to childhood and find myself involved, not in writing a novel, but in re-living boyhood and youth. I cannot stop. Words pile up, scene after scene, and now I've written enough words for a novel and have just got him graduated from high school.

I suppose I shall cut the whole thing down to a chapter. But I don't regret the lost wordage; it was actually necessary for me, both for reasons of katharsis and to enable me to know my character. And to clear the rubbish out of my system.

The Most Beautiful Night of Their Lives

It was Bob Reynolds who brought the news. He had picked it up at the breakfast table, and he ducked out to get to school early so he could tell everybody. He ran into Ned Rayborn and Ray McKay and Pink Stephenson walking together as they always did and demanded, "Know what?"

Pink said, "No, what? Your kid brother wet his pants again?" Bob just said, "They fired Old Buttocks."

Everybody looked at Ray McKay because his old man was cashier of the bank and he knew everything before anybody else did. But Ray just said, "Aw, shut up, kid; you're full of crap."

Just the same Bob knew it was true, and before noon everybody else knew it was true, and Ray McKay was telling everybody it was because the school board thought that no principal with a name like C. W. Bottoms could enforce discipline.

The kids were pretty sore. Even the tough kids like Mote Salisbury and Tim Healy and Dub McLain, who were always in hot water with the principal, were pretty sore because, when you came right down to it, there was nobody like Old Buttocks. Some of them talked about staging a protest parade downtown. But nothing ever came of it; the first thing anybody knew they were right in the middle of Commencement Week and then they were having Commencement itself and nothing had been done.

Only, seeing Old Bottoms on the stage, they realized they were seeing him maybe for the last time. Afterwards, they all slipped around to Mr. Bottoms's house and gave him a songfest. He came out pretty quick and stood on the porch, and after the first song he started to make a speech but before he got halfway through he broke down and began to cry and the first thing anybody knew, all of them were sniffling, or at least rubbing their eyes. After a little bit, Mr. Bottoms got his voice working again and finished his speech; he told them he would always remember 1918 as the happiest year of his life, just as they would remember it as the greatest year El Jardin had ever had.

Then over in the shadows near the front porch Isabelle Heard began to sing "El Jardin Forever"; she had a clear warm voice that went up and up, and all the kids cleared the tears from their throats and joined in, just as they would if El Jardin had lost a football game and the other side was tearing down the goal posts. Their voices rose in the warm moonlit night, and Isabelle's above them all until it seemed she touched the stars and they all could feel shivers — warm and quavery shivers run up their backs when everything seemed to melt together: the song and the moonlight and the sad sight of Old Bottoms, standing on the porch with his coat off and his collar off and his collar button showing and his face all twisted up. If they'd seen any other grown-up standing there crying like that it would have made them sick, but with Bottoms it was different: he was FOR them and FOR El Jardin, and El Jardin was for HIM, and this was the saddest and most beautiful night of their lives.

February 27, 1947

Dear Dickie:

    I don't see how you get by with two hungry kids. I know I should be sending you twice as much as I do, but it seems that I can't even scrape together enough for a pair of shoes.

    Well, I did wish I could give the boys a better break, but, to be honest, I think they are darned fortunate to have the sort of home they have. I suppose everybody hopes in their youth that they are not going to be poor folks when their kids are growing up. If I'd had enough sense not to get tangled up in new responsibilities, I suppose I

might have made the grade. But then I was awfully naive,
wasn't I?

I do, think, though, that if the boys are strong and
well enough, they should be getting some work outside of
school hours. Not merely for their spending money, but
because they'll have to realize sooner or later that
they're poor folks. Or should they? I don't know; sometimes
I think that a youngster does better if he doesn't discover
which side of the fence he's on.

March 24, 1947

Dear Toni:

I only reflect that the troubles of love seem to be
identical with the troubles of trying to write a first
novel. You're up; you're down; you're through; you're off
again and you resolve to say to hell with it. And don't.
And can't.

I have been in the depths for the last week. Not
merely depression but vacuum. Completely empty. A bad cold,
plus my first experience of hay fever, plus a period of
waiting while Clayton took the completed draft of the first
part of "Neither Five Nor Three" and went over it. Last
night I was beginning to recover when he came over and
dumped the script in my lap, holding it gently at arm's
length in a pair of tongs -- and what the hell do I do now?

Generally speaking, I wouldn't go much for the idea of
letting somebody else go over a partly finished manuscript
nor be too much impressed by what he said. But in this case
I knew that I had myself in an impossible situation that I
couldn't get myself out of. And I knew also that I was
violating some technical requirements as to point-of-view,
but hoped I was writing well enough so I could get by with
it; I hoped in fact that I was using an unorthodox method
that was going to be very effective. To all these things
John says "No." So I'm low.

It's the matter of letting the narrator, Bob Reynolds,
(who is himself an interesting character, a boyhood friend
of the protagonist, now a police surgeon who wanted to be a
psychoanalyst), come into the story in the early part to
comment on and sum up and outline the supposed effect of
this or that situation upon the development of the boy's
character.

I myself like that sort of thing when it is well done;
Butler did it in "The Way of All Flesh," and Wells used to
do it. I'll have to puzzle it all out. Meanwhile, about
fifty percent of what I've written will be saved.[3]

---

3 And the curious thing is that John Clayton did the same thing in a short story he called
"Laws of the Universe," a technique he defended in a letter to Toni as a method "successfully used
by Joyce, Faulkner, Wolfe and others." But when the point of view became a bar to a sale to
Harper's, he hitched up his pants, rewrote the piece with a single point of view and sent it back to
Toni for marketing.

On the fifth of April, Anne Hawkins sent her manuscript about the Pony Express to Toni. And Anne wrote: "I bootlegged a half-hour glance through Brick's unfinished script while I was in San Francisco a month ago. Part of what I saw was terrific, part was fairly good, none stunk."

Meanwhile, Toni was trying to recover from a serious, unhappy love affair.

April 16, 1947

I do hope you are coming out of it. There is nothing worse than the feeling of having been blind and then having your sight and losing it again. And don't I know! How accurately you have expressed it -- if I remember about Marianne, my anarchist girl friend of twelve or thirteen years ago. And how long it can last!

How long can it last? Well, in a way I was lucky. When the thing was finally over and done with (after about a year and a half) I met a gal with whom I'd been in love when we were kids,[4] and we had a very lovely few months and all the sense of pain and loss was taken away. Only, it wasn't until years later -- until recently, perhaps -- that I've fully realized to what an extent my life has been dominated by that brief period in which, having been blind, I could see.

May 19, 1947

I'm not sure whether I've written you about Anne's book. I think you were much too kind about it. It stinks. Curiously, it stinks in precisely the same way that the thing called "Neither Five Nor Three" stinks. In some ways, Anne and I must be very much alike because we set about doing the thing in the same wrong way. Both Anne and I have been trying to write theses entitled "What kind of a guy was her hero, Dave Wagent (my hero, Bliss Lane), and how did he get that way?" That ain't fiction.

The O. Henry Award was a terrific boost for Clayton.[5] He needed it at the moment, partly because he was just then finding out that he was not yet mature enough to write a novel. Right now, I think, he's going through a considerable period of change -- a masculine crisis which seems to take place about forty -- in which he doesn't know what he thinks or believes in.

I had bad news this week. My brother had a stroke. We can't find out how bad it is, but pretty bad, I guess. It really is a shock when things like that happen. He and I were never very close, but he's a guy with a terrifically big heart and was always bobbing up doing things for people -- me, or Mother -- and was such a competent sort of guy. It doesn't seem possible he's laid up.

---

4 Louise.

5 He had won the O. Henry Memorial Award first prize in 1947 for his story "The White Circle," published in *Harper's*.

Corinne Sussman's first novel, *The Growing Roots,* was published in Crown's spring list.

[Handwritten]
May 26, 1947

Dear Corinne,

I expected a good novel, but certainly nothing like this. It comes very near being in the class of great novels. What is most remarkable to me is the even quality of the work. There isn't a bad scene, or paragraph, or sentence in the whole book.

I envy your deft characterization, especially in dialogue. Each character emerges as distinct and individual by a simple twist of phrase -- almost of dialect. I don't know any writer who does this so well.

I always hesitate to discuss "the Jewish problem," but I'd like to say that it is your line of reasoning which has made me (as a goy) into a pro-Zionist. It seems to me that any people who decide they want to be a nation have the moral right to a place on the earth where they can be a nation. For those who want to be Jews, there should be a place to be Jews and those who don't want to be Jews should be content to such assimilation for themselves and their descendants.

I am certainly aware of the difficulties of assimilation. But to some degree those difficulties exist because most Jews seek only pseudo-assimilation; they seek to remain an island within, even while they make every effort to become "Americans." Religion is free only when it is individual; nationalistic religion is not, and should not be, free. It is not that the Jews "killed Christ"; it is that the Jews persist in being "an island within" -- and furthermore, one which clings to an innate belief in its own superiority as the chosen people. I have no way of knowing what I'd be if I were a Jew, but I think -- no, I don't know.

Well, anyway, it's a fine book. It's nice to be related to a great writer. I knew her when.

May 20, 1947

Charlie, my boy:

Did you know you owed me a letter? Oh, yes? You started one but couldn't find an envelope? Oh, I see.

Well, how are you? And are you thinking of coming up here this summer? I wrote Lou and your Mom, extending an invitation to either or both of you and asking for an inkling but haven't received any reply. I'd enjoy a nice argument this summer -- and I don't mean the kind I lose to Naomi. (I haven't lost one to Pat yet.)

I was thinking I might try to get you on the Examiner
as a copyboy for the summer if you liked. It does pay
pretty well and you could get the jump on the rest of your
generation if you want to get into newspaper work after
you're out of college.

We seem very much unchanged. Patty is very insistent
that at age four she's a big girl now, especially since
she's got skates and a scooter, and I'll be darned if I
don't think she's right. She knows a lot of tricks like the
big girls do. And I gotta admit she's a real Garrigues.

I am still engaged in learning to write a novel. It's
more difficult than learning to roller skate. I suppose I
thought that if you watched enough people roller skate long
enough you could finally put on a pair of skates and go
zipping away. But, nay! It isn't what you know; it's what
you know how to do.

But Chuck didn't succumb to Brick's entreaty; he was at an age when
his school chums were more important than his father. I got the job
instead, and so began a new, more adult phase of my life with Brick
Garrigues.

The *Examiner* was predominantly a male world; somewhere in the
building women answered telephones and took classified advertising. In
the city room, the heart of the paper's editorial coverage, cigar smoke
and cigarettes were everywhere. A spittoon squatted on the floor. The
reporters used old-fashioned, stand-up telephones, or they wore telephone
headsets; they banged out their copy on manual typewriters, some of
them poking rapidly with two fingers. An ancient telegraph operator listened to the clacking of Morse code, his sounding board covered with an
empty Prince Albert pipe tobacco can to make the chatter even louder.
The teletype machines were separated from the city room by a sound-
proof door, but the noise when deadlines approached was still overarching
and, to me, exciting. Some of the sports reporters got to calling me
"Young Brick." At fifteen, I was the youngest in the room.

In those days the *Examiner* was a morning newspaper that went through
several editions beginning with the afternoon the day before. The copy
editors were seated around a horseshoe-shaped desk facing the chief copy
editor, or "dealer," in the center. As deadlines approached during the
cycle, they would speed up their work, marking up the typed copy, scrib-
bling headlines on short sheets of paper and sticking them on a spike in
front of the copy chief. He would glance at the work, occasionally make
a few corrections, then pass them to a copyboy who put them in a pneu-
matic tube for delivery to the battery of noisy, clanking Linotype machines one floor up in the composing room.

One of the two ex-copygirls who remained after the war was the boss of
the messenger staff and the other was her assistant. They were pleasant young

women, and sometimes, after a deadline had passed, my father went out to the reception area where one of them would sit receiving visitors and talked with her, listening, nodding in agreement, and he seemed content just to be engaged in some kind of communication with a pretty woman and away from his duties on the copydesk. I could tell that they liked him.

But when the deadline rush was over, the editors would sit back and relax; sometimes they would banter and make wry jokes, and often Brick would take out a Mechanics Institute library book and bury himself in it. He had written Toni that he hated his job, but I honestly don't see how any other job than night man in a mortuary would have given him more time to read.

This was the summer Brick and Naomi finally bought a house. Using a down payment borrowed from Naomi's mother, they moved to a ticky-tacky subdivision in Richmond, at the end of a long bus ride across the Bay.

```
                      983 South 47th Street
                      Richmond, Calif.
                      August 26, 1947
```

Dear Toni:

    I am once again a homeowner, a thing I swore I'd never be. (I also swore I would never again be a father, a husband or polish a car. I have just finished spending a week polishing a car.)

I was living for the summer with Brick and Naomi in their new wood-frame house with the weedy garden in the back, bored alone at home and sick of looking at the grimy gray 1941 Willys they used as transportation when they didn't take the bus. I bought some car polish, determined to make it shine. I had never polished a car before — or seen one polished — and, without bothering to wash off the dirty old thing, I applied the potion liberally all over its hot, sun-baked surface. The polish and dirt caked to a mud, and I rubbed it frantically with a soiled cloth in a vain attempt to get it off before my father got home. He broke into a grin when he saw the smears and dirt, but after he changed his clothes we both manfully strove to lift off the grime. Eventually we got a faded gray Willys with a sheen to it.

    I have relapsed, temporarily at least, into the habits of a suburbanite. Until now I have not touched a typewriter for a couple of months, instead spending my time in delving and digging and putting and pottering. The crackerbox in which we live -- named Nabisco Acres -- is a 1947 replica of the white stucco with the false front in which I lived in the early '30s with Dickie. Consequently everything is -- or has been -- a ghostly repetition of things that have gone before.

Occasionally Brick and I would share a bus to or from the *Examiner*.

Once he tried to explain Engels' Iron Law of Wages to me; that is, the theory that under capitalism employers pay their workers only enough money to live on and reproduce enough little workers to slave through the next generation. I couldn't quite equate that theory with record collections and college educations, and so mostly we didn't talk about anything very serious; I enjoyed my dad but was somewhat suspicious of his philosophy, what little of it I could understand. And we certainly didn't talk about life as we ourselves were actually experiencing it.

As for Naomi and Patty, I put up with both of them as best I could. Patty I could play with and push on the swing and take on the slides and read to, but I sometimes tired of a little girl of four who had such boundless energy and self-determination. Naomi was difficult; I thought she was snappish, and one night when Brick was at work, we quarreled and I shouted "Drop dead!" and stormed out of the house. Chagrined and remorseful, I waited at the bus stop for my father, and I told him what had happened and asked him to smooth things over for me. He disappeared into their room, and though it was about midnight, Naomi was still awake — she never went to sleep before Brick came home — and I guess he did the best he could on my behalf, because I never heard any more about it. I soon escaped that tension-ridden house and returned to the security of the knotty-pine room in Inglewood.

September 9, 1947

Dear Dickie:

I suppose Lou arrived home all in one piece. He really is a swell fellow. I got a good chance to know him this summer, and I don't think I've ever seen a finer boy. I got a lot of work out of him, and he proved a swell worker at the office. The other kids all liked him, and so did his straw bosses, and I believe he had a very good time.

He didn't have quite such a good time at home, I think. Naomi never had any brothers and has never been around any kids of that age, and I'm afraid they made it a little difficult for one another. She used to be the same way with Chuck, and I thought it was because she didn't like Chuck, but it's just that she doesn't like -- or doesn't understand -- boys of that age. But then who can stand them unless they happen to be your own?

Patty and Lou got along fine -- squabbling constantly. Just like brothers and sisters are supposed to do. Of course, she wasn't going to stand for anybody cutting in on the attention she's accustomed to. And already she's learned the little-girl trick of starting a fight, knowing that they'll both get bawled out, but figuring it will be worth it since Lou will get bawled out, too. But Lou took it all very stoically except sometimes when he would lose

his temper and then get descended upon like the wrath of
God. Altogether it was a very interesting summer.

I think I work in the garden to keep from doing
something more useful. I ought to get out and get a part-
time job somewhere because I'm not making enough on the
Examiner to meet even our minimum of expenses. I do know
that I don't drive myself the way I used to, and that's the
reason I continue to feel better even in this tumultuous
and vituperative hangout.

That, incidentally, is why the check is for only $85
instead of $87.50 this month. I don't want to cut down on
the boys but I do, honestly, think they could take a cut in
their spending money since they are both old enough to earn
something for themselves. If you don't agree, I'll try to
restore the $87.50 next month. I want them to have a lot of
fun in life but they are both -- and Chuck particularly --
old enough to lend a hand now, I think.

They're both so darned sweet, but then in a way we're
spoiling them financially just as we didn't ever spoil them
in behavior. I don't think either of them has ever been on
the giving end of anything in their lives. I know I feel
reluctant to try and set them right in that regard because
I don't want them to think I'm a tightwad. But, gosh,
they're going to have to learn.

Well, anyway, it's hell to be poor.

Dickie had left her job as a secretary and set herself up as the owner
of a secretarial service, the beginning of a long career as a business-
woman in our little town. She helped organize the Legal Secretaries Association and later was a charter member of the Soroptimist Club. For a
while she was studying law through a correspondence course, but she
gave that up.

How's your business going? I have a hunch it will go
fine, and that you'll be in the money before long. In your
letter to Lou you were wondering whether to hire help or
try to do it all by yourself. Well, I hope you don't mind a
person of my undoubted financial brilliance giving you
advice, but the only people who get rich are the people who
hire other people to do the work and who do the managing
themselves. Nobody yet ever got rich by working -- only by
working the other fellow. And that means paying somebody
else five dollars for work that you get paid ten for.

September 22, 1947

Dear Toni,

Honestly, Toni, I'm surprised that you still have faith
in "The Imaginary Revolution." I'm grateful for the faith.
But, Jesus, it must be covered with curses by this time. It
has come so near clicking so often -- Maybe, some day --

I think I wrote you that we'd moved to Richmond, which is a little suburb about fifteen miles out of town. We have a cute little crackerbox, white and shining, with roses around the door, plus a couple of mortgages, plus a lawn, plus a vegetable garden, etc., etc.

The first few weeks here I worked feverishly at getting settled and getting the garden in shape, and something in the process set off a long-buried associational pattern so that since that time I've been hurling dirt and planting and digging weeds and spraying bugs like mad. I mean like mad; it is a process as senseless as that of the schizophrenic picking his bits of straw apart in his corner.

I enjoy it, yes. But I'm only now coming to realize that I don't do it out of any sense of enjoyment but for other reasons which I don't entirely fathom. I did the same thing when I had the ranch in San Diego and, for that matter, when we had the house in Los Angeles. I understand something about it, and you will, I think, if I ever get that novel finished.

When Albert Lane Felt the Soil in His Fingers

And then spring moved quietly across the hills and valleys. Human beings, who had been too busy with their own affairs to observe the coming of California's soft winter, scarcely raised their eyes to see the new miracle. But it set a thousand meadow larks in a thousand fields to shouting their bubbling "Peter-peter-rainy-kew"; it set quail calling across soft valleys and filled the trees with the song of mockingbirds and covered the waste spaces along the railroad's right-of-way with golden poppies and blue lupin.

Albert watched the coming of the spring; he heard the bubbling of the meadow larks and the call of the quail and saw the wasteland turn blue and gold and saw the fields become green and then golden with California's early summer harvest. The stink of road oil was in his nostrils but the sight and sound of California's spring, which is at once spring and summer and early fall planting and growth and harvest — the sight and sound of spring was in his eyes and ears. And he went one day to Mr. Flynn, who was the superintendent of the yard and announced that he was drawing his time on Saturday night.

The superintendent considered Lane a good workman even in an era when men took pride in being good workmen.

"It's not the money, is it?" he suggested cautiously. "Because if it is, I had plans for makin' you a gang foreman this fall . . . "

"It's not the money," Albert said. "I'll be buying a ranch."

"A ranch!" The super was scornful. "You work your fingers to the bone and what you get for it, I'd like to know . . . "

"You got the ranch, " Lane said quietly. "And when you walk over it, you know it's yours. Nobody can take it away from you. Not the President of the United States nor anybody in the world . . . "

"Except the bank, " Flynn interrupted. "Seen ranches without houses and some without barns but never seen a ranch without a mortgage. And the commission merchants take your crops and pay you what they please for them . . . don't talk to me, I know!"

"And besides, " he went on after a moment. "The days of one-horse farming are over. They'll soon have automobiles running right out in the fields on special wheels to do your plowing and harrowing. And that'll take money — too much money for men like you and me. Believe me, the money's going to be in the oil business — selling gasoline for automobiles, building roads for them to run over — why, I bet you in ten years we'll be hauling gasoline right out to the farms. "

But Lane shook his head. "People will always have to eat, " he said. "And the farmers will have to grow the food. . . . "

He came home that night and told Ruth he was quitting his job on Saturday and going to take the train down to the Imperial Valley on Monday to look at a ranch he'd seen advertised — and then maybe go on to the coast, if he had time. He was surprised to find that he was telling it defensively, as though he expected his wife to object; surprised because it had always been understood in the Lane family that the women never interfered with business; surprised because he had not known until this moment — and did not, perhaps, know now — that the last eight months had been a time of pulling and hauling, of hidden, tacit, unrecognized conflict.

"If it suits, " he added, "I intend to buy, and we'll move in as soon as we can. " He said it flatly, finally, as though to cut off some expected protest but Ruth Lane was wise enough to say simply: "Why, Albert, I think that will be just fine!"

But later, lying beside her husband and listening with inner pride to the sound of the tap dripping in the kitchen — listening to the silence punctuated by the sharp tap-tap of the water, and later, interrupted by the sudden rush and cough and gurgle as one of the children rose and went to the toilet and used it and flushed it — listening and remembering the long way they had come since their first winter in the sod-built hut on the Kansas prairie, she remembered that God does answer silent prayers as well as those spoken in the presence of your husband. And she resolved that the battle was not yet lost.

Albert Lane drove out from San Julian in the real estate man's buggy, and his heart ran far ahead of the plodding horse; it ran swiftly along the dusty road and past the thin line of eucalyptus which fringed the range of barren hills; it ran across the hills and slowed momentarily in a valley, kissed with sunlight, ringed with sage, fragrant with sage and orange, warm with the pressure of sunlight and cool with the relief of shadow; his heart ran ahead and brooded in quiet delight upon a white house upon its knoll, surrounded with the peace of groves and vineyards and the quiet of a kitchen garden.

The real estate man sat beside him in quiet silence unbroken except by his clucking at the horse. He watched his prospect from the side of one eye and decided it was no good to oversell him. He looked like the kind of man who would sell himself. There was something about the way he looked at the hills, at the fields about him, which told the agent that here was a man who had come to buy.

Albert Lane sat quiet. Beside him on either side were rectangular fields of rich bottom land — land on which in a few years one could use those automobile tractors Mr. Flynn had been talking about: tractors which could plow and harrow and rake forty acres in a day. But Albert Lane did not see them: neither the fields between which he rode nor the ghosts of the tractors coming down to make factories of the fields.

Instead his heart saw a white house, he saw a home where one could raise what one wanted to eat, together with the few things one needed to sell, in order to buy what was needed to wear. He saw room for a family which would soon be grown; he saw grandchildren — a fresh crop of children to replace those about to go away. He saw, and was surprised to see it, on a vacant, silent hillside, warm in the afternoon sun, room for a quiet grave.

He was tired. Not with the day's fatigue, not even with the pressure of years, but with the pressure of moments: the pressure of a constantly succeeding, mounting flow of moments, moment after moment, each of which must be seized and mastered and turned to good account to speed him along toward the goal which had for forty years eluded him.

In twenty years he had scarcely paused. There was the rush to get seed into the ground, to get water to growing crops, to fight the onrush of weeds, to get the harvest into the barn before the threat of gathering storm, to get the cow bred to the bull and the calf safely born and then butchered; the rush to get to town on Saturday afternoon and the rush on Sunday morning to get the chores done and the team hitched up for the drive to church. Even after Sunday dinner there was the rush to stretch out for an hour or two and desperately attempt to seize a measure of rest before time to start, once more, the evening chores which would lead, seemingly without pause, to the rush to get to bed in order to get up before dawn and start the morning chores in time to be in the field by seven o'clock.

Even in Greenstone the pressure had not slackened; even during the comparative inactivity of a ten-hour day, even as he sat in his chair and attempted to read, or lay in bed at night knowing he need not awake until six o'clock — even then the moments would rise up, one by one, and confront him and fade away, each moment lost irredeemably so that he could not rest in the thought that each moment brought him closer to death without bringing him closer to his goal.

Now, for this brief moment, there was peace and he knew he was tired. Even while his heart ran ahead of the plodding horse, it ran to seek a place to rest. He was ready, now, not to quit but to make the last desperate lunge to put his goal within his grasp. Deep in his heart he knew that — afterward — there would be no strength left beyond the strength necessary to survive.

The buggy passed through a thin line of eucalyptus and through the sparse sumach and rounded a hill, and Albert Lane knew that this was the place.

A white house sat upon the top of a knoll, surrounded with orange trees: orange trees which gave way to a farm garden — bordered by guavas and blackberries on one side and a family orchard of peaches, apricots, nectarines, quinces, plums and pears upon the other. Beyond, grapes which ran to the hillside and beyond that, wasteland of sage and chaparral; below, level bottom land for corn and beans and melons. A tall windmill whirled merrily in the brisk noon breeze and a mockingbird leaped and sang in ecstasy from its fan.

And the warm sun upon his back, sending little trickles of sweat beneath his shirt, warming his toes; bright cool air which he drew into his lungs slowly so that he tasted at one and the same time the fragrance of the sage and the sweet cloying smell of the orange blossoms and the strange, salt smell of the sea a dozen miles away.

"Diversified farming, that's the ticket," the real estate man was saying. "Everything you could want for your own use except, maybe, bread. And good money crops: oranges and raisins — they'll bring you in cash money in September and January. I'd put in a flock of chickens to provide early summer income. A man could live like a king on a place like this."

This, Albert Lane knew, was it. If there was a faint bell of warning somewhere in the back of his mind, he turned resolutely away.

"School's down at the other end of the valley," the real estate man said. "Less than half a mile away. Edendale district, they call it, and for once it's well named. Ever see anything more like Eden in your life?"

But he did not wait for an answer.

"Same with El Jardin," he went on. "Means 'The garden.' That'll be your shopping place. Only three miles away. Make it in thirty minutes in

the buggy. Hell, your boy could even walk to town for groceries if the team's busy. Good neighbors; three churches, not counting the Catholic church that the spicks and the Irish go to . . ."

They were passing beneath a faded and weatherbeaten wood arch on which the word DESCANSO had been painted.

"Good name," the agent said. "Means 'rest.' You'll have the rest of your life here. Air like wine, sleep like a baby . . ."

But Albert Lane, drowning in the flood of words, impatient for the crunch of the soft, dry, rough, rust-red, sun-warmed soil beneath his feet, had vaulted over the wheel of the buggy and was scooping up clods and crushing them beneath his fingers, feeling their warmth flow into his muscles and nerves and veins until it became a part of him.

"Good soil," the agent called after him. "Soft, friable; mulches up well and holds the moisture. Not too rich; don't want it too rich for grapes — but you'd have to buy fertilizer anyway for the oranges. And if you put in chickens and give them straw scratch you'll find you get exactly the right formula for oranges in this country."

There, thought Lane, will be the chicken house, protected from an occasional northwest wind by that barricade of huge boulders. He'd let them run at first, building only a few pens for trap-nesting and for special stock. And there he'd put in hay for the horses; there in that flat place below the well he'd have an acre of alfalfa for the cow, and to provide extra greens for the chickens. On an embankment a ground squirrel sat up and chirped his sudden, birdlike note. Yes, he could cut down that huge eucalyptus and get enough firewood to last for three years. And when he'd cut a second, and a third, the first would be grown again to a towering height.

A vast and arching pepper tree reached above a wooden water tank near the houses. Albert Lane clambered up the stanchion which held it and felt the cool, mossy touch of the damp wood against his cheek. Below, the clanking windmill sent its pulse of fresh, cool water through the artery of buried iron pipe, spurting at last into the tank.

"Running water in the house, and you could put in a cesspool and have an inside privy if you wanted," the agent was saying. "Right now the water from the sink and bathtub runs out into the berry garden in the back. One thing about this soil, it never waterlogs . . ."

There are times when a man knows; there are times when a man stands and watches and sees his fate sealed, times when he knows that this thing, this decision — a job, a task, a sacrifice, a woman — is something from which there is no escape; now and henceforward, now and forever, the decision is made; the inviolable fate is sealed; it is this or nothing.

"Wait," he said, almost roughly — this man whose quiet, grave courtesy forbade him ever to raise a word of criticism against a fellow man. "Wait, Mr. Skinner. You talk too much. I'm going over there — I want to look around . . . to see that barley field."

He walked down the driveway and through the barnyard, past the pile of huge boulders, each as big as a house, which sheltered the apiary, along a path which wound through the scant sagebrush; his feet felt the crunch of rough soil through their thick-soled-shoes; his lungs felt the tang of rich, sun-warmed sage, his ears sang with the crisp dry lovesong of cicadas singing in the dry tufts of grass. And all this, all these, were blessed silence after the clatter of the agent's voice, after the clamor of the towns and the ranches on which he'd worked, after the clamor of his own fears and doubts and hesitations.

Back in the yard, the real estate agent eased the horse into the shadow of a huge mulberry tree and stretched out to be comfortable while keeping one eye on the progress of his prospect. He knew when he had his fish hooked. And not merely hooked but impaled and netted and — practically — gutted. F. L. E. Skinner, his business card read, and the folks in El Jardin said he was rightly named: "He'd skin a flea for its hide and tallow." He mentally decided to hold to his price of ten thousand dollars for the ranch called Descanso. Everything he got above eighty-five hundred was to be his; he had been prepared to drop to ninety-five or even — if absolutely necessary — to nine thousand.

He wouldn't, now. He'd seen the expression on this farmer's face.

Needless to say, the novel is lying untouched. Or, at any rate, unworked on. I dug it out a couple of weeks ago and sent it to Anne because Anne is a smart girl and I wanted some advice from her on what I could do with it. I didn't get the advice -- not yet, anyway. What I wanted was Anne to tell me how I could make one or two or three novels out of the stuff I have. Because, you see, it's all mixed up. But she just grinned and said, "You are the goddamnedest fool ever; you are writing three novels, but since you seem to prefer to do them simultaneously, go ahead and do them." So that's no help.

Anyway, I hope to get back to it when the weather gets cold. We have been having beautiful Indian summer, and warm days are rare enough. So I hope I may be forgiven for working in the yard for a while.

As ever,

Brick

Chapter Twenty-Four
To Think That Two and Two

How can you relate to a teen-age boy and never talk about how to make it with a girl? How can you continue to share human emotions when certain emotions are taboo subjects, such as the meaning of love, or the pains of group rejection? But of course poor Father couldn't talk because he couldn't figure it out himself.   — *From a letter by Chuck, 1962*

January 2, 1948

Dear Toni,

Things have been hectic here over the holidays. A good friend whom I found on the streets, down and out; he'd been in the money in Hollywood and it had gone to his head and he'd got his personal life all tangled up and was really on the rocks. He spent three weeks here, sitting in a sort of daze, muttering to himself, "Ah, me!" and then telling his story over and over again.

Chuck (my older boy) came up for the holidays and he and Naomi have been quarreling -- or on bad terms -- most of the time for the last week or so. And yesterday my brother (who has been quite ill for the last eight or nine months) came up to spend his convalescence. George is a bright spot in the picture as Naomi likes him, and he is a very nice guy and makes things pleasant around his part of the house.

March 24, 1948

Night before last I dreamed about you: I had gone to New York, to your office to see you (you were either a senior member of a very large and important firm; either book publishers or a really tremendous agency) and you were out at lunch, so I sat by your desk and was then pushed around from chair to chair by busy executives until finally a lovely young girl -- even prettier than you were in Arizona -- came in and sat down, and I didn't know if it was you or not -- and I never did know, I guess.

Homer said somewhere that there are dreams which come through the gates of ivory and some which come through the gates of horn; those which come through the gates of horn are true, and those which come through the gates of ivory are false, and (I think he added) though we may be mistaken about those which come through the gates of ivory, but we always know those which come through the gates of horn.[1]

All of which does not mean that I am going to visit you in New York. It only means that I am in a curious psychic state which (though I do not believe in such things) enables me to reach across distances and be in touch with people.

In November I worked for a politician during my vacation and made enough to meet the household deficit until January 15. On January 15 I became an Income Tax Consultant and (by working about sixty hours per week in addition to my regular job) made enough to meet the deficit until May 15.

I have not seen John since before Christmas. Their new place is just across the straits from us, and there is a ferry which goes across -- the only ferry left on San Francisco Bay, and we love to ride on it, but there has been no time.

Returning after a half hour's interruption, I wonder how in hell anybody can ever hope to do anything in such a screaming-meemie domestic situation as I have. I am well enough aware that it is a neurotic compulsion which keeps me here, and the worst of it is that no matter how many million times the thing blows up, I am always ready to attempt, once again, to relax in peace and quiet. On the average of three times a week, I get ready to pull out -- and yet I know I won't -- and then have a couple of days of something resembling an idyll (a most distant resemblance, I admit) and then go through one of these wild scenes again. The day started off very nicely, and it is now 11 a.m., and I'm saying to hell with it and getting ready to go to work.

If I had the money, I should go and get psyched and see if anything could be done about this compulsion which keeps me here.

---

1 In Samuel Butler's translation of *The Odyssey*, ". . . dreams are very curious and unaccountable things, and they do not by any means invariably come true. There are two gates through which these unsubstantial fancies proceed; the one is of horn, and the other ivory. Those that come through the gate of ivory are fatuous, but those from the gate of horn mean something to those that see them."

April 12, 1948

Did you ever realize the difference between desperation and despair? Before, I have been filled with
desperation, but for the last few days I have known
despair. It's the exact opposite of desperate; it is simply
that you know there is no effort which can be successful
and, even though you know that some effort is necessary to
save you from annihilation, you know that you'd rather face
annihilation than try, once again, to turn a hand when you
know that no hand can be turned.

Today I feel better and, in a sense, almost hopeful of
things. Naomi, after weeks of delay -- the most picayunish,
niggling sort of delay -- has finally gone out today,
apparently in good earnest, to get herself a job.

The financial grind has been terrific; financially and
in every other way my life seemed to rise in a parabola
until the time I met Naomi and then to decline, just as
implacably as hell so that each day has been a little worse
than the day before: each day there have been new obliga-
tions unmet, and each day has been a little further from
meeting the old until I have forgotten that I once
expected, not merely to be able, some day, to stand up and
shake myself free to do some single, simple, sensible thing
just because I wanted to do it.

There was a time immediately after I got my job on the
Examiner when Naomi was working and I was working, and it
seemed in six months or so we might have achieved some
liberty of action. And then Naomi announced (since we were
married by that time) she wasn't going to work any more.
And there was a time when we had split up once and I had
saved up almost a thousand dollars in a few months; then
one of the boys had to have a mastoid operation, and I was
back where I started from. And again, a couple of weeks
ago, when we had hired a housekeeper and she was ready to
start work, I thought that, perhaps it would be now. And
then the same old pattern of evasion and excuses until I
was in complete and utter despair.

Don't think it strange that all this revolves about
finances because, after all, it is finances which takes my
life and controls it -- and when your life is taken, what
do you have left?

But it is much more than that. It is the arrogance of
the woman -- in the correct, technical sense of the word,
which means to arrogate to oneself power, or privileges which
one does not possess. I have never admitted that any woman
has the right to expect a man to give up his life simply to
her whim and whimsy because (as near as I can understand her
inexpressible view) she is a woman and he is a man.

What you have written about me and the novel has
turned my attention back toward it for the first time since

we've been out here in the country. I am beginning to feel, again, that something should be done with it, but I still do not see exactly what. I have not been able, in any degree, to cut the cloth to the pattern.

Part One (which as a working title I call "Narcissus") carries the protagonist through boyhood and high school and, I think, is in part damn well done. Because, you see, every frustration is more than a mere passive disillusionment; each time he discovers that Two and Two doesn't make what he wanted it to make, he conscientiously corrects his addition and, of course, makes a completely different mistake later. (Anne has most of "Narcissus" and refuses to send it back lest I spoil it by rewriting it.)

Part Two has the working title of "Amaryllis." An amaryllis, you know, is a rather harsh, unpleasant pink, and Amaryllis must deal, I think, with his life as a young married man in the twenties -- his and the century's. But not a line of this has been written, except the title.

I'm not ready for a professional editor to look at it yet. Most of the problems are psychological within the writer. True, there are technical problems: a professional editor might be able to look at it and say, "This problem of shifting points of view between Bob and Bliss need not worry you any longer; simply do it this way." Or, again, he might say, "Look bub, you are a fine headline writer and income tax consultant. But your stuff falls flat; you get pathos instead of tragedy and bathos instead of pathos. Go back to cutting lawns." In that way he'd save me a lot of time. But I've got to write that second part before he could do even that.

April 21, 1948

Monday morning I said the time has come when I must get back to work on the novel, and I sat down reluctantly and began fumbling through my notebooks. I knew precisely where "Amaryllis" must begin and how the scene must be written and what it must contain, but I was unable to bring myself to start it. And I picked up a chapter which I had written in December 1946 and I immediately saw that THAT, which had been written as the first chapter of "Amaryllis" and found completely unsuitable, was precisely the chapter I needed. So I am again in the novel.

I have the same feeling of being lost, submerged, as I had when I was writing my most enthusiastically on "Narcissus." The situation is that one doesn't give a damn, really, whether it is any good; it is only important to get through breakfast and start living in it again -- to get to a typewriter and let it flow. I can even -- so far -- write and babysit at the same time; Patty comes charging through, riding her scooter or dressed up in her mother's best dress, and I say, "Yes, Sugar, run along now," without being interrupted.

That is the miracle: that of finding yourself so
deeply in a story that you know it cannot fail to be
written so long as you stay alive.

May 16, 1948

Corinne's book made me understand Naomi a lot better
because, it would seem, quarreling and rowing and shouting
at one another seems to have been part of the girls'
background. So much so that she, Corinne, reports it almost
as though there were nothing about it quite worth noticing.

This morning I feel swell. The garden is beginning to
come into shape with most of the weeds out and the blue and
yellow violas and the delphinium and bachelor buttons and
coreopsis coming into bloom.

Saw Clayton Sunday for a while and was pleased to find
that he is feeling better than for some time.

In the summer Chuck and I returned to San Francisco, and this time
we both worked on the *Examiner*. With one of his first checks, Chuck
bought Brick a present that would eventually lead to solace and even a
measure of happiness in the years to come — jazz records. Chuck had
learned to dance to the popular swing music of the Dorseys, Goodman,
Miller and Krupa, and for Brick's birthday he went to a record store and
bought enough ten- and twelve-inch swing and jazz music to fill an album. They were good records, too — already classics or pieces that
would become classics: records like "I Can't Get Started" with Bunny
Berigan, and Tommy Dorsey's version of Carmichael's "Stardust," and
Benny Goodman's "Swing, Swing, Swing." This was the summer their
conversation turned to swing music and jazz.

July 16, 1948

Honestly, I think I should take -- or should have
taken -- a course in short-story writing somewhere. Maybe
it's just fatigue or rustiness, but I wouldn't have the
slightest idea how to write a story.

Anne and I have discovered the most important single
clue about the matter of content; that is, about the
relationship of experience and fiction. The problem is to
transmute experience (literal truth) into art (fictional
truth). Every story which is at all serious in intent must
stand or fall, both for popular interest and artistic
quality on how well, how COMPLETELY, that transmutation is
accomplished.

But how? Anne and I have decided that the fictional
process is performed by the daemon.[2] Or, to use another
figure, it is like playing in the band upon a transposing

---

2 A supernatural being of Greek mythology intermediate between gods and men. Rudyard
Kipling wrote, in *Something of Myself for My Friends, Known and Unknown* (1937), "When your
Daemon is in charge, do not try to think consciously. Drift, wait, and obey."

instrument: you blow B-flat and it comes out F or something.

About "Five Nor Three" -- I find the transposing
instrument is not working. I am simply in the doldrums. I
pick it up and blow, and nothing comes out.

A curious thing happened the other night. As a
preliminary, I should say that Naomi and I have been having
the usual trouble about the boys being here -- or rather, the
usual trouble has transformed itself into resentment over the
boys. But for the last five or six days she has been just
remarkably sweet to both of the kids; it has been very
pleasant and -- as always -- I've been inclined to forget
anything except this little interlude of pleasantness.

Brick experienced chest pains and went to the hospital for an electro-
cardiogram; and the reading was that of a virtually normal heart.

Naomi took the new reading to mean that my heart was
perfectly normal now and that I need no longer observe the
precautions. After that, I could tell that something was up
-- though not exactly what. She continued very sweet and
pleasant -- until last night.

Last night I picked her up as usual after work, and we
were starting home when the battle began. I don't know yet
what it was over, but after the first flareup I decided to
ignore her anger and be as nice as I could and see how long
it lasted. Since that time, all night long and all morning,
she has been getting furiouser and furiouser, and I have
been treating her with calm and indifferent politeness.

It was Chuck's night off, too, and she marched off
into her room while I was doing the dishes, so Chuck and I
spent the evening in the living room listening to the radio
and records and she was able to take refuge in the belief
that I was neglecting her and spending all my time with
Chuck.

Up until now, whenever she looked up to discover that
her life wasn't going the way she thought it should, she
could take refuge in the fantasy that even though I was a
bastard, she was being a noble soul and sacrificing herself
for a man who had a weak heart and could be kept alive only
through her sacrifice. But now that the new EKG has given
her the idea that I am completely normal, she has nothing
to fall back on, and her fury is just boiling up and up
within her.

It's a curious result of what should be a happy
discovery, but I have a very strong feeling that this
blowup may well be final. If the boys weren't here, I would
really just slip away quietly this morning while she's
downtown and avoid a big blowup.

Incompatibility: Two sets of configurations that do

not match and cannot be made to match.

Toni suggested that Brick once again make a date with Pat Covici of Viking to talk about his new book.

August 8, 1948

On first and second and third thought, I'm not going to try and see Covici. There are a lot of reasons --

In the first place, while I know that a great many writers swear by Covici, I just simply don't have any faith in his judgment -- nor, particularly, in his good faith. That feeling goes back to our earlier meeting when (as you may recall) I went to see him to ask him just one question: whether or not a book like "This Grim New World" would, if it were reasonably well written by an unknown, have a fair chance of selling. That was the one thing I wanted to know, and I wanted to know it before I spent a couple of years sweating out a script, and he was the one guy who could tell me. Now the fact is that "This Grim New World" was a fairly good script; you may remember that a number of publishers turned it down with regrets and that a few praised it rather highly but that everybody was unanimous in agreeing that it could not possibly have a sale -- largely because the author was utterly unknown and had no following.

Okay. Covici either knew that when I talked to him, or he just didn't give a damn and was just giving soft answers. I wouldn't want to have my writing influenced by anything he might say about it because I just simply don't trust his judgment as an editor, a publisher or a critic.

I know them's harsh words about a good friend of yours, but in this particular case that feeling I have about Covici is so much at the core of all the other reasons that I'd just as well get it out of my system.

Apparently this particular novel has to be written the way I'm doing it and later it has to be taken apart and put together. It remains, as yet, simply a mass of anecdotes out of which a story is later to be carved.

[Fall 1948]

When the boys left a week or so ago, I moved back into my own room and started trying to build myself a little corner in which I could live for a while until it was possible to do something else. I slept, for a change. I rested. And the more I slept and rested, the more ill I became. I developed a head cold, sinusitis, burning, smarting eyes, which I knew were none of these things but a desire to weep out of sheer despair.

It lasted for a week; it was like hay fever; I was a wreck. Yesterday I sat down and wrote it out -- the relationships between the hay fever and the desire to weep

-- and gradually it vanished, until today, for the first time, it is gone.

So you can see I am a mess. There is no telling what comes up next. I leave on my vacation September 26.

November 8, 1948

You are right in warning me not to let fiction try to imitate life. Life can provide the gimmicks of fiction, but nobody would want it to provide more. Because we read, whether we know it or not, in the hope of finding a life which has organization and rhythm and meaning and purpose as our own life does not. Fiction must symbolize, not represent, life.

The vacation -- on which I saw so many old friends -- made things worse because it brought into such sharp relief the respect and affection and consideration which I always knew elsewhere, and which is so utterly lacking here. But I suppose these things are the things which happen to people who make mistakes and who are unwilling or unable to correct them.

The domestic situation is no better, basically, although not quite intolerable. I have reached the point, now, where I know I'd pull out, finally and definitely and without rancor, if it were not for Patty. But I'm very fond of Patty and she's very fond of me, and I keep delaying final action.

Patricia was five years old at this time, and she was a bit more than a quarter of the way through her time living in the household of a dysfunctional family. I didn't see the whole picture of Brick's and Naomi's relationship, as she did, because for the most part the atmosphere was quiet among us all when I came to visit. My relations with Naomi were sometimes rocky, but we both tried to get along.

But Pat was there twelve months of the year, except for the many visits to Prescott she and Naomi took to visit Naomi's mother — an escape for both of them. Years later Patty recalled:

"Even as a young child, I could see the kind of game they played with each other, not having any real concern for what this was doing to me. Basically, Dad was obsessed with never having enough money, and he would arrive home to find Naomi had spent money on clothes for me, or a big phone bill, or whatever, and he would scream, yell, cry and go off — lovely! I would stay in my bed and shudder. Only a few times do I remember anything physical, and it would be like throwing a hairbrush, and one time he knocked over the Christmas tree.[3] He never raged at me, or anything I was doing. I raged, however, as a young kid, and he always thought that was very funny and would put me in front of the mirror to see how funny I looked all scrunched up and crying."

---

3 Naomi once told Corinne of a smashed water glass.

Brick was trying to understand the situation himself. In a letter to Toni, undated, which was written around this time, he tells of a conversation he had with John Clayton just after Corinne's *The Growing Roots* was published.

First, the usual polite praises for what a relative has done. Then, John takes me aside to talk about Cornelia's book:

JOHN: Well, to tell the truth, after reading THAT I began to think Faulkner's characters were sane, and normal and well adjusted.

ME: Yeah? (Silence.)

JOHN: Say, tell me, do you think she realized that there isn't a character in the book that isn't the most damnably neurotic, confused, self-deluded mucked-up hopeless, lost -- For Christ sake, do you suppose she thinks there ARE characters like that?

ME: For Christ sake, I've been living among them for the last ten years.

JOHN: (Wonderingly.) For Christ sake.

In the same letter:

Sometimes there seems to be a failure of communication between people so very complete that never at any time do either of the people see or hear or understand the other. The basic trouble is that words are not used in the same way by one person as by the other. Let me give you an example:

I am stretched out in my own room, taking my prescribed afternoon rest, fiddling with the radio. Naomi comes in and picks up the typewriter and starts writing a letter.

NAOMI: Oh, does it bother you to have me type in here?

ME: We-e-ell --

NAOMI: I can go in the other room just as well if it bothers you.

ME (not wanting to seem inhospitable): Well, if you WANT to stay here --

NAOMI: Oh, no; I can just as well go into the other room. I don't know why you should object to me coming into your room. I wouldn't disturb you for the world. Just say the word and I'll get out.

ME: Well, if you're more comfortable here --

NAOMI (very pleasantly): Oh, of course not. I know you want to listen to the concert. (Silence. Then decisively.) I'll take the typewriter in my own room. (She begins to write, clattering away a mile a minute for perhaps a full sixty seconds.)

ME: When?

NAOMI: What? Oh, you don't want me in here. Very well, I'll get out. But I don't act that way when you come into my room.

ME (curious about the lapse between her announced intention and her course of action, more interested in that than in whether she gets out or not): Tell, me, sugar, why did you say, "I'll take the typewriter in my own room" just as you settled down to finish your letter in this room?

NAOMI: For God's sake, what's the matter with you? Stop trying to pin me down! I'm not a machine! Etc. etc.

I am completely convinced that she was perfectly honest and sincere in everything she said and did. But what did it mean?

I suppose the situation between me and Naomi is an extreme one in that these misunderstandings occur almost hourly. But most other people may be almost as bad and some may -- God forbid! -- be worse. Take, for example, the people in Cornelia's book; there is scarcely one of them whose major difficulty in life is not caused by some failure of communication: simply, two and two makes four does not mean what it means to any other person in the world. I talk, not to Naomi, but to an entity existing in my own head and nowhere else, while she listens, not to me, but to an entity which exists only within her head.

In 1948-49 Chuck was student body president at Inglewood High School. Because of his sickness the year before (and the fact that I had skipped the first grade), he and I were in the same senior class though we were almost two years apart in age.

[Early? 1949]

Dear Dickie,

I rather wish Lou were here because, while he's difficult, we do find it possible to do a lot of fussing without quarreling (I suspect he's so extraordinarily fond of you that he just blows up every time you try to tell him anything). As a matter of fact, Dickie, the guy is only really happy when he's around you -- if he knows you approve of him. On the other hand, he doesn't much care whether I approve of him or not; he's more interested in whether he approves of me.

March 28, 1949

Dear Toni,

I was running my income tax preparation business again this year, and I'm only beginning to recover from the effort. I didn't make much money -- just enough to get my nose temporarily above the water.

Just before the season started, I followed your suggestion and sent a carbon of "Without Capitals"[4] to Anne. She agrees that it is unsalable -- but goes further and suggests that I drop quickly the idea of writing commercial fiction. I'm afraid I'll have to agree.

I thought Anne's book was swell.[5] It was amazing how much improvement she made in it; I took the original draft and the published copy and went over it line by line. Actually, the changes were not so great, but the improvement was terrific. It gives me the idea that something could be done with "Neither Five Nor Three."

Anne wrote to Toni about Brick and his problem of getting down to work: "That man can think up the most ingenious ways of defeating himself. The longer I think of it the more heartily I agree with your diagnosis of male menopause."

[Spring 1949]

The income tax business this year revealed to me unsuspected qualifications for huckstering. I lived for a couple of months as a business man -- avidly pursuing the dollar and enjoying the pursuit. I have never done anything like that before, and it left me a little shocked at myself. Since the season ended I have been trying to rearrange my ideas of what I want to do in the light of my new knowledge.

Basically, as you may remember, my split with Dickie was a split with a way of life: I firmly and definitely decided that I did not want to pursue the dollar as a career.

On the other hand, life with Naomi has developed into the same pursuit -- with Naomi standing behind me with a pitchfork and with me pursuing the dollar very reluctantly.

April 6, 1949

Dear Dickie,

I suddenly woke up this morning to realize that Lou has another birthday on tap this week, and I decided I'd have to sit down and write you a letter congratulating you. Gawd, it seems incredible, doesn't it, that it has been seventeen years!

In fact, the realization adds to the general condition of spring-fever despondency in which I have been groping for the last few days. Certainly there never has been so much time wasted as that last dozen years or so. Boy, am I burned up at me!

I guess it's mostly spring fever. Such a nice spring

---

4 A potboiler "slick" romance he had been working on.

5 *To the Swift*, a 296-page novel published by Harper.

after such a horrible winter, and I've been wandering about
in a daze, wondering where the last twenty years have gone
and what I'm going to do with the next -- well, the next
five or six anyway. And I guess I've been very homesick for
the scenes of my youth -- so much so that I came darned
near just walking out of the whole business and going back
to L.A. The only trouble is that I'm just intelligent
enough to realize that it's my youth and not the scenes
thereof that I want. Gosh, do I need a vacation!

Partly, it was the damn income tax business, which
made me a few dollars but got me into the habit of chasing
dollars again so that I stand here stymied, not knowing
whether to turn this way or that. Besides, I'm coming to
realize that I'm not a fiction writer. But I'm still
unwilling to give up the idea.

There isn't as much battling as there used to be. It was
really grim while the boys were here and for a long time
after they went back. But in the last few months it has
changed greatly. Not that we don't have an occasional row,
but I think she knows that I don't give a damn enough about
it to worry about it and her attitude has changed a lot.

Fact is, I'm still burned up at the way she treated
the kids last year. I still walk around with a chip on my
shoulder most of the time.

                    April 19, 1949

Dear Toni,

Chuck was here for a visit last week. (He's the
oldest: nineteen soon.) It does me a great deal of good to
have him around, and I realize how great a part in my
general dissatisfaction is played by my separation from the
youngsters. But, conversely, to have them -- or either of
them -- about drives Naomi mad. Part of it is a normal
unwillingness to have big, hulking strangers in her house.
Part of it is simple jealousy.

She has served notice that she'll not have them in her
house. (That was last fall.) I have served notice that I'll
not support a home in which my own children are not
welcome. Anyway, he's coming to spend the summer here, and
this winter he's to go to college here, though probably he
will stay in town with some other kids.

The last week I've been using what time I have to
attempt to do an analysis of "Neither Five Nor Three" on
the basis of the Uzzell principles of plotting.[6] I find it
all fascinating because it tends to throw into relief all
the faults which obscurely puzzled me in the manuscript and

---

6 *The Techniques of the Novel,* by Thomas H. Uzzell, was published by Lippincott in 1947.
Uzzell was trenchantly critical of what he called the "true to life" fallacy, which results from "a
writer's transferring to his pages an action which actually did occur to a character in real life but
which couldn't have occurred to the character in the story."

which caused me to lay it aside. Ultimately, I think, it
will teach me to be ruthless in chopping off and digging
out those things which do not belong. I have wished so many
times that I had actually started the study of fiction many
years ago. Yet it was necessary to spend enough years
coming croppers to understand what I was doing wrong. If I
can hold on another ten years, maybe you can collect some
commissions from me.

Naomi would often take Patty and sweep off to Prescott. But when
the wife was separated from the husband, there was nevertheless a kind
of communication there anyway. Patty remembers the many thick letters
that came from Brick in the Bay Area to Naomi in Prescott; perhaps he
wooed her by mail, as he had once tried to woo Fanny Strassman. But
Toni was still the sounding board for Brick's confusion.

April 29, 1949

No, I don't think that my difficulties with Naomi are
because she is Jewish. Differences in background are not
just Jewish-Gentile. They are much more likely to be
economic or family-cultural. Rightly or wrongly, I am one
of those who holds to the idea that there isn't really such
a thing as a Jew -- except insofar as he or she regards
himself as a Jew.

There is much more difference in background between
(say) a kid from the Midwest or the prairies and a Gentile
bourgeois raised in New York or San Francisco than there is
between the same Gentile bourgeois from New York and a
Jewish bourgeois from New York.

And the fact is that each of us, when we do start to
build our own domestic partnerships, do attempt to re-
create the home of our childhood. If our "partner" comes
from a different sort of domestic environment, then our
partner is very likely to become our antagonist because
she, too, is under the necessity of creating a new home in
the image of her childhood home -- so that each partner
frustrates and destroys the other.

Brick scrounged up some money somewhere, and when Chuck and I
marched with our graduating class of four hundred seniors on the Inglewood High School football field in June 1949, Brick was there, probably
attending a high school graduation for the first time since 1919. He gave
Chuck and me our first wristwatches.

I was beginning to be less and less interested in my father and more
and more interested in myself, but Chuck was different. He fled for San
Francisco after graduation and never looked back. Chuck wanted to be
where his father was. He returned to Inglewood only for infrequent visits
or, years later, to take care of occasional family problems when our
mother grew elderly.

I, on the other hand, was perfectly content to stay on with Dickie, bunking in the little room with the knotty-pine walls and going on to a student's life at UCLA, where I studied international relations and had dreams of going into the Foreign Service.

June 30, 1949

About the novel -- I've got the script back from Anne and have spent a couple of weeks going over what's been done and have come to conclude that the thing has gone sufficiently far that it could be looked at by an expert.

In any case, if anybody ever wanted to read this novel, he'd have to want to read it because he enjoys living in the company of a certain small boy who has various adventures -- emotional and psychological -- for about sixty or seventy thousand words until he is graduated from high school.

Me, I find it interesting because it shifts around the things in my own life just enough to make the memory of them tolerable.

The Preacher Couple

The first winter they were on the ranch Grace was in high school and wanted to take music lessons, and Papa went into San Julian and bought a piano on time. It was the first time the Lanes had ever bought anything on time, and Bliss knew that Papa went around with a guilty feeling about it because only shiftless people bought things they couldn't afford to pay cash for. But Mama said, "Oh, Albert, you fuss and worry too much. I always say that God will open up the way if we trust in him."

The second winter they were on the ranch the orange crop was very good. They had nearly a thousand hens now and the ranch was beginning to pay for itself, and Papa took fifty dollars from the orange money and wrote to a team of traveling evangelists and asked them to come to Edendale and hold meetings in the schoolhouse. The fifty dollars was to be their guarantee, and whatever they took in at the meetings was to be theirs, too. In addition, they were to stay with the Lanes for the two weeks they were in Edendale, so it would not cost them anything for room and board. There were not many sinners to save in Edendale, but Papa and Mama talked it over between themselves and with some of the neighbors who were Methodists, too, and everybody hoped that a really successful revival meeting might make it possible to organize a church in Edendale.

After Papa sent the fifty dollars, he started going around with that worried look again — Bliss thought it was a sort of sick look, a sort of now-I've-gone-and-done-it look — but Mama said, "Now, Albert, the Good Book says to cast your bread upon the waters and it will be returned to you a hundredfold." That night when Papa read the Scriptures it was the part which said, "In my father's house are many mansions; ye

*believe in Him, believe also in me," and Bliss wondered if God would
really give them back a hundred dollars for every one they sent to the
evangelists. He got a paper and pencil and figured out that that would be
five thousand dollars, and the next day he spent the money on a shiny new
automobile and a bicycle with a New Departure coaster brake and a pony
with a silver saddle and bridle. But when evening came he knew it wasn't
true; he remembered how God had avoided the deadline on the ranch,
and he knew now that God was under no compulsion to keep a promise
merely because it was written down in a book.*

*But when the Gustafsons arrived, Bliss found that they had an auto-
mobile. Bliss stood in front of it, parked in the barnyard, and spelled out
the name O V E R L A N D and wondered how it got that name and why
when you looked in the shiny headlights you saw yourself upside down.
Afterwards all the other kids, even Harold, came over to look at it, and
Bliss told them what a swell car it was until Harold said, "Aw, bushwah;
you don't know an Overland from a Hupmobile," which was true, and
Bliss shut up.*

*He kept away from the Gustafsons as much as he could, though. It
wasn't only that they were preachers and that he had a vague reluctance
to get mixed up again with God. He knew by this time that he just naturally didn't like preachers. The men preachers smelled like women and
they had soft hands and touched you or patted you on the shoulders or the
bottom and asked you to come to Jesus. It was all very holy but Bliss did
not like it.*

*He kept out of the house as much as he could while the Gustafsons
were there. They had been given Grace's room, and when the door was
closed he would walk by, half guiltily, thinking of these strangers in the
house, people who were not Lanes, and would hasten out into the yard to
do his chores or sit under a tree and read.*

There was something about it which was fascinating to Harold, too.

*"I'll bet they do it right in your sister's bed," he declared, nudging
Bliss excitedly. "Preachers do it just the same as anybody else. I'll bet
they do. Notice the way her butt jiggles. That's a sign that she's a hot one
and they do it all the time."*

*But it was not this thought of sex which fascinated and repelled Bliss
when he thought of the evangelists' occupying his sister's room. It was
rather the smells which drifted from the window and through the opened
door — the smells of toilet water and perfumed soap and sachet, and the
foreign smells of bodies, the smells of bodies which were not Lanes. And
it was the thought of thick, white grubby bodies in their thick, white
grubby gentility, hidden in the darkness of his sister's room which made
him feel squirmy and uncomfortable.*

The revival meetings lasted one day less than two weeks, and in that

*time everybody in Edendale beyond the age of eight was converted except
Bliss. Old Mr. Barnes found the Lord once and threw his pipe out the
schoolhouse window, and then he went down to El Jardin and bought a
new pipe and came back and got converted again.*

*Grace was converted and went around for nearly two weeks with her
nose stuck up in the air like everybody stunk. Cal and Tom were away,
working on a ranch on the other side of El Jardin so they weren't in
danger. When Mama called Bliss into the house after school, he knew
they were going to try the same thing on him. He thought he couldn't
stand it. Mr. Gustafson came over and put his soft, smelly hands on his
shoulders and started talking to him about coming to Jesus, and pretty
soon Mrs. Gustafson came over and knelt down beside him on the other
side, and every time Mr. Gustafson stopped to draw a breath Mrs. Gustafson would say, "Yes, Bliss, that's true," and Mama sat back in the big
chair not saying anything but waiting.*

*Just the same, he held out. He had got accustomed to hearing about
hellfire; when he'd been little he'd been scared to death, but he was ten
now and he could sit in church and close his mind to the terror, the
horror, the weeping and wailing and gnashing of teeth as though the
preacher were talking to somebody else besides him.*

*So he stood there now, stubborn, knowing he could hold out, know-
ing he wasn't going to give in, until Mr. Gustafson began talking about
Mama and how lonely she'd be up in heaven with her three boys turning
into ugly devils down in hell, and suddenly he remembered what the
Stinker had told him about Mama sitting up in heaven eating ice cream
and looking down upon him while he roasted on the hot coals, so the
sharp bitter panic of desolation swept over him and he knew that he was
lost: he knew that in just a minute he'd flop down on his knees and begin
to cry, and then nothing could save him from being converted.*

*He shut his eyes to keep the tears back and to shut out the sight of
Mama eating ice cream while he fried. He could still hear the preacher's
voice and feel Mrs. Gustafson's arms about his shoulder; he could smell
her perfume and when he opened his eyes again he could see her cheek
and he knew that what some of the people said was true: she did use
powder on her face, even if she didn't paint. And before he could shut out
the thought he remembered what Harold had said about them 'Doing It'
right in his sister's bed; he remembered how her butt jiggled when she
walked and what Harold said and he smelled the perfume and the powder
and felt her soft arm and breast pressed against him and he was suddenly
filled with disgust and revulsion so that he flopped down on his knees and
put his face in his hands over a chair just to get away from them.*

*He knew that Mr. Gustafson thought he had won, and Mrs. Gustafson
kept saying "Bless God!" and Mama joined in and everybody prayed but*

Bliss. They kept asking him to pray but he kept his mouth shut, and finally Mr. Gustafson got tired and said a final prayer thanking God that He had at last put this innocent lamb under Conviction of Sin and asking Him to lead him to repentance and salvation at the altar call; he was sure the boy would find salvation if only he would open up his heart.

When he got out into the open air he still couldn't think. He knew they thought they had him under Conviction of Sin — which was when you were scared to death of hellfire and damnation — and they'd work on him at the service. He wasn't so scared, really; he'd been a lot scareder when he'd been just a little kid and had gone to services three times a Sunday in Greenstone and had come home waiting for the moon to turn to blood and the stars to melt and run down out of the sky. Just the same, he couldn't think; he couldn't see what business Mrs. Gustafson had to rub up against him and make him smell her perfume and he couldn't see why Mama couldn't leave him alone. He wished there was some way he could keep from going to the meeting; he thought wildly of running away, or of just going out in the hills and hiding until it was all over, but he knew he wouldn't because that would cause even more attention than going down to that altar rail.

When suppertime came, he couldn't eat. He wanted to get up and go outside or maybe go to his room and lie down where he could just spend all his time dreading what was going to happen that night. But he knew if he did Mama would think he was under Conviction of Sin and would follow him into his room and start praying again. So he sat in his chair and stuffed food in his mouth and washed it down with his milk until supper was over.

As soon as he got up, though, he knew he was going to puke. He ran out the side door and tried to get out of sight, and he began to heave, and all his dinner came up and he kept on heaving and couldn't stop. Mama came out and held his head and still he couldn't stop. He'd never been so sick; after a long time Mama managed to get him to bed with a big bucket beside it, and he lay there and felt miserable and heard everybody get ready to go to meeting.

He dozed. When he woke up the house was dark, and for a minute the sharp terror came back, the sharp and bitter desolation that they had abandoned him, even when he was sick, to go off and shout and sing and pray. He could feel his stomach give a sharp jerk as though he were going to heave again, and the terror suddenly became panic at the sound of breathing in the dark: breathing in the dark and the sense of an unseen presence so that he knew the Devil was standing at the head of his bed ready to grab him and carry him off to hell. He lay frozen with terror, feeling his heart ready to burst in his throat and knowing his life would go out with it in his final breath before the Devil whisked him away . . . and then a rough hand — a rough, gentle hand — brushed his cheek as it smoothed the blanket around his throat and Papa's voice said in the dark, "Feeling better, young'un?"

He was surprised that his voice could say, "Yes, Papa," as though he had just woke up and as though the Devil had not been there; he could feel himself wiggle under the blanket in a warm eagerness which was not merely release from panic, but delight that Papa had stayed, that he had sent the others on to shout and pray and he had sat in the dark, waiting for Bliss, waiting to make sure that he would not be frightened or desolate or alone when he awoke. It was delight and confusion, and yet the confusion won so that he wriggled under the blanket unable to say anything. After a minute Papa's hand came over again and smoothed his forehead and Papa said, almost experimentally, "Sometimes I guess womenfolks make too much of things. Womenfolks and preachers." He said it in a funny tone so that Bliss got the sudden, sharp feeling that Papa was FOR him and against the Gustafsons and everybody else. He tried to say, "Yes, Papa"; he wanted to say a lot more, but no words came. After a while he reached up and took Papa's hand in his own and sort of tucked it under his cheek and stretched out as though he were going back to sleep. He lay there for a long while, feeling good, and then he slept.

The Gustafsons left right after breakfast. They didn't pay any more attention to him and seemed anxious to get away now that their two weeks' work was done and the last collection had been taken. He went down to the chicken houses and started scraping out the manure from under the roosts and didn't turn around until the shiny Overland was gone over the hill. It was a bright and sunny morning, and after a while the sun seemed to pour down and bake the two weeks' tension and excitement and fear out of him, and when he went in at noon Mama had aired out Grace's room and Grace had moved her things back in. At dinner Grace acted like she'd got over being converted and everybody was happy again. It was almost as though the evangelists hadn't come at all.

July 24, 1949

I am so deeply engrossed in "Neither Five Nor Three" that I can scarcely take a moment for a note or letter. It is strange: three hours each morning of scarcely interruptable work and then a complete mental blank during the rest of the day. At the office, I can scarcely write even a caption for a picture. At home, the writing is fun; the rest of the day is simple boredom in which I find it difficult to read, or write or talk.

I have performed a major surgical operation. I am in the position of a man who has killed his firstborn to provide food for his second. I have slaughtered my lovely first two chapters and have solved, thus, my major problem and need now only to write the novel.

(Somebody once said -- maybe it was Wylie[7] -- that the way to write a novel was to take an opening chapter and write it and work it over, lovingly and carefully, time after time, as you write the rest of the book, going back to it each time you are stuck and writing it again and trying to bring the rest of the book up to it. Then, when you've finished, throw it away, mark Chapter 2 as "1," etc., and your work is completed.)

August 11, 1949

I'm surprised to find that you are still trying with "The Imaginary Revolution"; surprised and still a little pleased by the pleasant tone of all the rejections I'm piling up. It has seemed to me for quite a while now that events have passed by "The I.R." and that many of its predictions would come, by this time, to seem rather quaint -- simply because they have now occurred and have come to be accepted.

I think Scribner's is right in suggesting the university presses, though I don't know whether it has sufficient academic acceptability. I'll be glad to put up the cost of shipment. I'd very much like to get some academic reactions from it.

As for "Five Nor Three," there is no experience quite like it. After a while, the characters begin to live and move; you can sense them dimly coming to life within yourself, and you struggle, over and over, trying to put that life on paper, and you never know how well or how badly you are doing it, but you know it is never well enough.

The first part of the novel takes the protagonist as a boy and the second part as a young man, and the third part will take him as a mature man, and in each part the problems are different; so completely different that when you have learned to do the first part as well as you can, you haven't even begun to learn how to do the second part because the thoughts of a boy are utterly different from the thoughts of a man.

I would not be surprised if it were true that the Sussmans had become Catholics. On the other hand, they have been accused for a good many years (by their religious friends) of having become Catholics, and in the past it wasn't true, though it may very well be now.[8] The basis of the accusation seemed to be their perfectly normal (for them) custom of surrounding themselves with what they assumed to be objets d'art:

---

7 Probably Philip Wylie (1902-71), author of *Generation of Vipers,* whose *Opus 21* had just been published.

8 It was true. Naomi's sister and brother-in-law developed a deep attachment to Thomas Merton, Roman Catholic monk, poet, and prolific writer on spiritual and social themes. They became active in the Catholic Worker movement and wrote articles for Catholic publications.

crucifixes and junk like that, from Mexico or Arizona and which they insist that they prize for their artistic value.

Irving is precisely the sort of character who does turn Catholic -- and Corinne, of course, would follow. He is the most fear-ridden man I have ever known: afraid, chiefly, of death but afraid of life, too, and of being a Jew and of not being a Jew. From that fear rises his peculiar tendency toward Christian mysticism. However, there is no religion which can give you so much assurance as Catholicism; the priest says positively, absolutely: he's the guy that has the keys to heaven, and there need be no doubt in your mind that you're okay -- if you just do as he says.

Did you, by the way, read a book by Norman Katkov called "Eagle at My Eye," or something of the sort?[9] It treats of the problem of Jewish-Gentile marriage from the standpoint of the son of Orthodox parents who marries a Gentile girl. It is powerfully done, so much so that I cannot help but believe that Katkov must be a very shrewd and bitter Gentile anti-semite. So much so that I haven't shown the book to Naomi.

As ever,

Brick

---

9 *Eagle at My Eyes,* by Norman Katkov (Doubleday, 1947). Katkov, a prolific writer of stories and screenplays, was actually born in Russia into a Jewish family named Kotikofsky.

Chapter Twenty-Five
The Characters Begin to Live and Move

September 16, 1949

Dear Toni,

    I have become engrossed again in the idea that I can write a novel and have been pouring it out. It's the second volume of "Neither Five Nor Three," of course.

    It is a very fine feeling when the scenes begin to flow again. It is difficult to quit; this morning I started at nine and stopped at eleven thirty and then started again at one and wrote until three thirty. That's the longest day I've put in. You don't, at times such as this, worry very much about whether it's going to turn out or not because to you, as you write them, the scenes feel right.

As ever,

Brick

The words poured forth, and it was all there, Brick's life as he had lived it, Brick's women as he had known them, twenty, thirty years before. The words told how the young Bliss Lane arrived almost penniless in Los Angeles and stood staring at the twelve-story skyscrapers and jumping at the clatter of a streetcar or a newsboy's whistle. He stared also at the job listings posted in a shop window, went inside and was hired to fill out a crew mixing mortar, carrying hod and learning how to set tile.

As they went from one job to another, he sometimes saw motion picture people strolling, and sometimes there was a movie company shoot-

ing a scene at some intersection, the cameraman with his cap turned backward, grinding away at his crank. After work when the downtown offices closed, the streets would be suddenly filled with a surging flood of pretty girls — beautifully dressed, carefully made-up girls, with marcelled hair and French heels — and Bliss would take refuge against the side of a building and wonder that there was so much loveliness in the world.

At night he often went to a movie show or to the Orpheum or Pantages (or at rarer intervals to the Morosco), to see a play or a comedy. He tried to get in the thick of the theater crowd so he could smell the perfume the women used, could accidentally feel the touch of their furs or their dresses.

And on Sundays he would take the Pacific Electric train and ride out to the beach at Venice and go swimming in the cold water and look at the girls in their shapeless, skirted bathing suits and wonder how they could bring themselves to walk around so nearly naked in front of all the men and boys. He wondered what would happen if he were to speak to one and invite her to have a soda with him or join him on the Race Through the Clouds or share a seat in the boats that ran through the Tunnel of Love. But he would never speak: Every day men called "mashers" were arrested for speaking to women on the street or at the beach.

The daemon may have given Brick a kick in the backside, but it was Brick's memories that flew through his rapidly typing fingers and struck the keys of his little portable typewriter, making the words describe how Bliss Lane, now a college student, met a young woman named Marj (just as Brick had once met a woman named Marguerite), who invited him to her family's home to feed him (just as Marguerite had done). Sometimes on Wednesday evenings Marj and Bliss would go to Westlake Park, which nowadays is called MacArthur Park and at night seems dangerous and deserted, but in 1921 was one of the most romantic places in the romantic city of Los Angeles. Bliss and Marj would take a canoe slowly to the middle of the lake.

He would paddle and she would trail a finger through the warm water until the lights on the other canoes began to go out all around them. Each canoe carried a candle stuck in a Japanese lantern, and there was a city ordinance which said that you had to keep the candle lit in the interest of morality, but the candles would go out, one by one, all over the lake, and the canoes would begin to drift, unguided. Soon their candle flame, too, sputtered and vanished, and they found themselves close together, lying out of sight. Afterward, she would straighten her hair and fix her face in the dark and he, feeling weak and trembly, would paddle slowly back to the landing place.

It was Marj who said to him when she learned he planned to drop out of college after only a year,

"You're spoiled, darling. You've always been used to being the center of things. Now you find life a little dull, don't you?"

And, when he had stalked away from her angrily after a quarrel in a city park,

"Darling, I do adore you and I'll always be there, whenever you want me, but don't expect me to chase after you, don't ever!"

And, most pointedly,

"I want to marry you, and I mean to, some day."

Just as the real Marguerite had once told Brick. Or at least she had thought it.

Marianne flew forth from his fingers, too, and Miriam, and Janet, and Dickie. But they were all mixed together, some of Marianne Claire or Janet in with Dorothy, some of Dickie mixed with Marguerite, and the young women in his book, his *Amaryllis,* had names like Marj and Nelia and Paula, and one of them was actually named Claire. Nelia ushered at the Philharmonic — the old building at the northeast corner of Fifth and Grand, opposite Pershing Square — and introduced Bliss to the love of opera. During that first performance, he had to retreat to the men's lounge and pore over the libretto so he would know what was going on; later, Bliss would routinely sneak down from the upper-balcony cheap seats to sit with Nelia at the rear of the orchestra level. Nelia herself was like a character out of *La Boheme;* to Bliss's astonishment he found she lived with a man named Tim in Santa Monica.

"Well, gosh, how do you go about living with someone. I mean . . . how does it start? Who says what to who? I wouldn't know how to go about asking a girl to live with me . . ."

"Oh, it just happens," she said.

"But, how?"

"Oh, sometimes one way, sometimes another. Sometimes you say to him, 'Gosh, it's too late to get up and go home now; better stay for breakfast.' Or, 'Better bring an extra toothbrush over here,' or sometimes you just show up at his place with your suitcase."

He said, "Gosh!" feeling embarrassed and countrified but still excited by the idea.

Now that he knew about it, Nelia began inviting him to the parties out at the cottage, two or three times a week, and everybody brought food: pickles and olives and celery and stuff or sandwiches and sometimes eggs to boil and sometimes sour red wine. The house would be filled with fellows and girls, all of them artists of one sort or another, painters or poets or musicians or dancers. During the day some of them would sell ribbons or books or shoes or punch a typewriter or sling hash, but at night they'd take dancing lessons or practice the violin or come out to Nelia's and talk about the things they were going to do and the triumphs they were going to have when they got around to it.

When Nelia tired of Tim a few weeks later, Bliss, infatuated, went in his turn to live with this exciting woman. By then, Brick's words tell us, Bliss had dropped out of school to work as a newspaper reporter.

There wasn't any doubt that he was good. He had the knack of always being where things happened and of taking the dramatic aspect of a story and playing it up and, above all, the knack of knowing names and how to use them, and he knew how to make news and how to make friends. He was proud of being a newspaperman. At times, when Nelia was studying and he was sitting by the fire — just sitting and listening and thinking — he'd find himself hugging his knees and pondering how so many wonderful things could have happened to him. But it just went to show, he told himself, that you could have anything in the world if you really wanted it. That is, if you were really good. If, in other words, you were Bliss Lane.

But Nelia was not like Bliss; she was Nelia, and when she met a new man, "a longshoreman or something," she told Bliss their affair was over. Brick began fairly hammering at the keyboard.

At first he thought she was joking or that it was a crazy idea she'd get over in a day or so. He went to bed and expected that soon she'd be there, too, and he'd be able to love her out of that strange, awful idea. But after a while he heard her stirring in the living room, saw the light go out and realized that she had made herself a bed on the couch. He knew it was real then; he lay there feeling the anger rise up his legs, into his body and out his arms until his very fingers were stiff with rage and jealousy. He lay in a very catalepsy of rage until he thought the veins of his head would give way and his chest would burst. He heard her regular breathing and he got up and went into the other room where he stood looking down upon her and wondered if he could get out of the room without taking her throat in his fingers and choking until the breathing stopped. The next thing he knew he was walking down the street; he was fully dressed, it was dawn and the great, curling breakers were rolling over and smashing onto the sand, and he was staring at them and wondering if he had killed her.

He was a long way from the house now, walking past the Venice pier, and he remembered the night he had kissed her there for the first time. He hailed the little tram that plied the beach walk and rode back to their corner, then stood in a doorway until he saw her come out, calm and smiling, pull the door shut and walk down to where the big red train picked her up and she was gone. Then he went inside and lay down on their bed and tried to cry and couldn't.

A week later Marj found Bliss in a cheap hotel room in the same kind of anguished, melancholic stupor that Brick had undergone in the days of Marianne. She nursed him back to health, and he realized she was *for* him, and so he married her.

One day he went out to the beach, where, even on a Monday, there were throngs of people as the concessionaires opened up their booths.

He normally liked to walk down the beach and see the girls, some in short, one-piece bathing suits which didn't even come to their knees; he liked to watch their legs and their pert faces and the way they carried themselves. He usually looked at them as they passed, half unconsciously waiting or expecting some sort of answering glance or smile, or even a dropping of their eyelids to show they knew he was there and was a man. Now he found that he didn't look. His eyes slid past them without seeing — carefully without seeing — and concentrated instead on the kewpie dolls and the cheap lamps and machine-embroidered cushions. He looked at the white froth of the breakers near the shore and the green rollers farther out and the fishermen on the pier. After a few minutes he sat on a bench and took off his hat and let the sun fall on his face; he closed his eyes and let the sun beat on him and felt that something had gone out of him. He was a married man now, and his life would be different from now on, and if he missed the fun he'd had — the fun and the sense of expectation, the excitement and intensity even when he was being intolerably miserable — if he missed all these, why, being married to Marj and having your own place and your own life and somebody who was for you were more than enough to make up for it.

Brick might have paused at this point and thought about his two marriages, and maybe he got a drink of water to refresh himself. Then he sat down at the typewriter again and allowed Bliss the luxury of walking down Hill Street in Los Angeles at the end of the Roaring Twenties before the chill of the Great Depression and the terror of World War II had fallen upon the nation,

not hurrying but striding along, looking at the people and feeling the cement pavement under his feet and listening to the hiss of trolleys against the wire and the clatter of car wheels on crossings, and it seemed to him that the whole town, the whole great and fantastic, glorious town — cement and bricks and plate glass and people and trolleys and winking electric signals — belonged to him. They belonged to him and he to them; he'd found a niche — his place — and now he was a part of it all. The good feeling rose through him from the hot July pavement, and he wanted to take it and hug it and then turn it over and examine it. The hotel elevator took him to his floor, and halting just outside the door — his and

Marj's door — he decided to put the feeling away, wrapping it up care-fully to take out and hold and examine and analyze some other time when he was alone.

Then Brick might have thought of the many times he had moved into a new place on Bunker Hill or on Red Hill or in Venice, or helped a friend do so, and he decided to move Bliss and Marj into one of these places, and the remembered image flowed from the tips of his fingers through the typewriter keys to the yellow manuscript paper in the little Remington.

It had a tile kitchen and a modern high-oven stove, all white enamel and chrome faucets in the bathroom and a separate stall shower. The bed pulled down and filled the whole living room, but there were tiny re-cessed bookcases on either side at the head of the bed, and you could reach over and get a book without getting up. It was this — this and the shower — that sold Bliss on it, and he paid the whole thirty-five dollars for a month and they went to the hotel and got their things, came back to the two-room apartment and went to bed.

Brick made this room a happy place for Bliss and Marj; they were young and they were in love. But one day, Marj told Bliss she might be pregnant; Brick used the word he knew from the days of his own youth, "caught."

Even while she was telling him, he couldn't help thinking about how they did it in the movies; the man would come in and find his wife knitting tiny garments and look at her inquiringly, and finally she would blush and nod her head, and he would cry out, "Darling!" walk over and put his arms around her, and she'd breathe, "Darling!"

That was the way it was supposed to be, only that wasn't the way it was. He cried, "Good God!" when she told him and he sat down. He wondered how you could raise a kid on thirty-seven fifty a week. He said, "Good God!" again after a minute and then "What do we do now?"

They just couldn't possibly do it. Not on a newspaperman's salary. Marj didn't argue one way or the other. She listened and made sugges-tions but mostly let him talk. After dinner he went down to the drugstore and bought some pills he knew about, and she took them for three days but nothing happened.

Finally she said what they both were thinking. "You knew a girl once who got caught. What did she do?"

"I don't know."

"Well, gosh, there must be somebody at the office who knows — Maybe if you'd ask somebody . . ."

He didn't know how to bring up the subject. He told her he'd ask, but he didn't. When he got home the next night, he lied: "I asked a couple of the fellows on the quiet and nobody knew anybody." She just looked at him, and he was sorry inside, but there was something that kept him from doing it, and he knew he wouldn't ask the next day either.

When he got home the next night, she was gone. He made a sandwich and ate it silently. He was worried about her, but soon the door opened and she came in. She dropped her handbag on the chair and looked at him.

"Darling, do we have a hundred and fifty dollars?"

"No, why?"

"Because we're going to need it. I got the name of a doctor."

"You did!"

She said, "Sure. I got to thinking this morning, 'What's the use of belonging to a sorority if you can't use your sisters in case of emergency?' So I got busy this afternoon, and wham! just like that!"

That was the way she was. As long as there was a chance he'd do something, she kept her hands off. But when she saw he wasn't going to do anything, she stepped in and took charge.

They had to figure about money, though. He had almost enough in the bank, and he decided he'd have to go downtown before work and sign up with a loan shark. He'd almost rather have the kid, he thought, than go into debt. But he'd do it.

He could see she was almost ready to cry, and he sat on the couch and put his arms around her for a long time. Finally, he said, "You don't need to, you know, honey. Gosh! We could go on and have it." He said it experimentally, but as soon as the words were out he knew he meant it. They could get by some way. Even if it meant nothing but debts and scrambling to get by, scraping the barrel every month like everybody else did and not being Bliss Lane . . . not being anybody —

But she was shaking her head and smiling. "This one's on me," she said. "Every man has a right to be rescued from fatherhood at least once."

She was going to the doctor's the next day; she'd meet Bliss at noon to get the cash. You didn't need any appointment, she said; all you did was go in and pay your money and take your turn. "And your chances," she added.

They went to bed and he put his arm around her and tried to sleep, but he couldn't. He lay there a long time, hating himself —

He opened his eyes and the light was streaming in his face from the open bathroom door; Marj was leaning over him. She was laughing and crying at once. She kissed him and said, "It's all right; everything is all right."

He said, "Darling!" and put his arm around her, and she said, "Dar-

ling!" and held him close and rested against his shoulder, and they sat on the edge of the bed for a long time, being glad and feeling good and happy again that they were together.

It was just like the scene in the movies. Only, of course, in reverse.

All these words, to be sure, were not written in one day. Brick would have to go to the *Examiner* to put in his eight hours on the copy desk. He would also work in the garden, or help make dinner and trade stories with Naomi about their day, or shower and shave, buy gas for the car, play with Patty, kiss her knee when she fell down, write to his sons. Sometimes the daemon would be forced to get tough with Brick, and she (for Brick, of course, the daemon was female) would insist that he spread his old manuscripts upon the table, would pry open his fingers and have him pick up a pen to mark out huge passages of typescript and scribble in a sentence or two of replacement. The daemon whispered, "Music, music . . ." And Brick remembered. He went to the typewriter and brought Bliss back to the Philharmonic as a young reporter, and there Bliss was

standing outside the auditorium doors, when somebody said: "Well, if it isn't the boy genius of the copy desk!" He looked around and saw Ted Neilsen, the telegraph editor. Ted said, "Christ's sake, fancy seeing you here. Are you a cultural snob or do you like this stuff?"

Bliss didn't know what to say. There wasn't any use trying to explain to a fellow like Neilsen, who was the most cynical guy in the office and never had a good word to say about anybody or anything. He'd sit hour after hour mumbling over his scissors and paste pot, making wisecracks about the copy that came in or about the people in the world and the screwy things they did. He was absolutely impartial; he'd be just as bitter and cynical about Al Smith as about Herbert Hoover.

Brick walked with Bliss and Ted to the restaurant next door, and Ted held up two fingers to the waiter, who

took a flat bottle out of his pants and sloshed two shots of moon into the thick coffee cups. Ted went right on talking.

"But the whole thing about music is that it is meant to be listened to — played and listened to — instead of being written about. It was all right before Beethoven; they didn't have music critics in those days; they had performers — *and audiences. But when Beethoven went out in the woods and came back with the "Eroica" variations in his pocket, he'd discovered something . . ."*

Bliss interrupted. "Jesus, Ted, you should have been a music critic yourself!"

Ted set down his cup and laughed. It was a belly laugh that brought the waiter over with a warning shake of his head. Ted said, "Christ, kid,

I am one. Didn't you know I'm Alexander Borisoff?"

Bliss said, "Jesus, no!" Alexander Borisoff was the Express *music critic.*

"Hell, yes," Ted said. "I get five bucks a week and two passes for doing this stuff. That's better than what Julius Schmid at the Herald *gets, though. He has to buy his own tickets or rewrite what Jacques Milliard says in the morning* Times. *He gets a half hour to do it between writing obits for the first edition."*

"Well, I'll be damned," Bliss said.

"Not will be," Ted said. "Are. Have been. Ever since you got into this goddamn racket."

That was what made Bliss uncomfortable about Neilsen. Of course, newspapermen were always running down the newspaper game, but then Bliss had the feeling that Ted meant it. And it made him uneasy; he had the feeling that in another twenty years, when he was as old as Ted, he'd be as bitter and as hopeless about his work as Ted.

Brick might have stopped there and leaned back to gaze absently past the cautiously expectant daemon at a framed picture of little Chuck and Louis in their sailor suits. And he could have rolled a fresh sheet of paper into the typewriter.

When Marj told him for the second time, he said, "My God!" and went to sit on the big chair just as he had done before. But it wasn't like the other time. It was as though some decision had been made without his knowledge or consent so that all he had to do was acquiesce.

The next day he went into Jim Larch's office and asked him for a raise. It hadn't been six months since he got the last one, but Larch said he'd see what he could do and, sure enough, they brought his paycheck up to forty dollars a week. Marj put the extra two and a half into the bank every week so they'd have enough money to pay for the baby when it came. They decided to give up Marj's piano; they had the radio for the music, and they'd save the ten dollars a month the piano had cost.

A few weeks later Ted Nielsen just stood up and shoved all the piles of papers and the two spikes, the telephone, a wire basket, the paste pot and an ashtray from his desk onto the floor and walked out of the office for keeps, and Larch gave Bliss Ted's old job as telegraph editor. Three months after that, Marj gave birth to a girl. The next day Bliss's managing editor called him into his office and fired him. And Brick experienced Bliss's rage.

It was anger Bliss could feel coming up in him now, anger and not panic, and he held it down because he didn't dare let himself lose his temper. He fished for a smile and stretched his face to fit it and said, "Look, Mr. Larch, let's be reasonable about this. I know how it works as well as you do. You fire me and take some punk off the copy desk and make him telegraph editor at thirty-five a week and keep him until he's worked his way up to forty-five and then fire him and do it all over again. And I go back on the copy desk at another paper and spend a couple of years working my way up to thirty-five and everybody loses. So why don't we just get sensible and I'll take the thirty-five with you and you'll have a real telegraph editor and everybody will be better off."

Brick had the managing editor consider the suggestion and reject it, and after Bliss had bought some cigars and passed them around the office, Brick made the managing editor call Bliss back behind the glass door and say he'd changed his mind and Bliss could stay on with a five-dollar-a-week pay cut.

Bliss opened his mouth to say, "Thank you, Mr. Larch; I really appreciate it," but the words didn't come out. The words which came out were "— you, you cheap, chiseling bastard! — you and all the Express, *too, and every bastard that would work for it!" He heard the words fall, sharp and distinct in the quiet office, and he saw Jim Larch's mouth drop open, and then he was walking down the street; he was halfway to the corner and he didn't know if he'd taken the elevator or gone down the stairs or whether he'd socked Jim Larch or maybe smashed up his office. All he knew was that he was fired and Marj and the baby were in the hospital and he had to have another job by Monday.*

Brick would have exhaled deeply then and got up from his chair, and he might have stood staring at the page he ripped out of the typewriter and perhaps he wondered if he should have used the dashes after all, but that's the kind of man he was; he never used really vulgar language and he certainly didn't want to see it written down in his own house. He would have stacked the pages carefully and put everything away; he would have made his lunch, put on his topcoat and hat and walked to the bus stop.

In the succeeding few days or weeks, he might have wondered what would happen to Bliss; but inwardly, he already knew: He remembered how he himself had been hired at Manchester Boddy's *Illustrated Daily News* two decades earlier. And when he finally had a chance to sit at the typewriter again, the house quiet with Naomi at work and Patty in first grade, he sat down with Bliss to eat dinner and then moved with him down the crowded sidewalks of 1929 and glanced with him up at the massive structure of the *Los Angeles Times* (on the northeast corner of West First Street and Broadway, before Harry Chandler moved the paper to its even bigger building on Spring Street). Then Brick walked with Bliss *past* the Times building, around the corner to Court Street, where the shabby Civic Center offices of the *Illustrated Daily News* were then standing within sight of the Hall of Records, the Court House and the new City Hall just being built. They went into the building housing this newspaper, this — Brick paused, searching for a good pseudonym — this *Clarion,* he typed. But it was Bliss alone who walked into the office of the managing editor and saw Ted Nielsen behind the desk, the stub of a cigar jammed into his mouth and his pale blue eyes raking Bliss's face in amusement.

Bliss said, "Honest to God, Ted, I didn't know you were here."

"Oh, sure," Neilsen said. "Something good happens to everybody that leaves the Express.*" Neilsen looked at Bliss, and then said wryly. "Just another Kid McCoy. I hear you socked the son-of-a-bitch." He made a half-gesture toward the phone. Bliss didn't know how to answer that one. He couldn't remember what had happened at the last in Larch's office, but his knuckles weren't skinned or anything, and he didn't want to take credit if he hadn't.*

He said, "Naw, it was all a mistake," and Ted said, "The only mistake was I didn't do it myself." Then he shifted back in his chair and said quickly, "No, that's not right either. He's got his job to do just the same as I've got mine, only he's working for a bigger son-of-a-bitch than Bert Birmingham, and so he has to be a bigger son-of-a-bitch than I do."

Brick might have stopped typing there and smiled at the daemon, who was seated on the floor now, her arms wrapped around her knees, staring at him intently. Bert Birmingham. Manchester Boddy. Two cities in England. Not bad. She smiled back.

"Well, I just sort of dropped in," Bliss said, starting to go, and Neilsen said, "Hell, I thought you came over here to work." Bliss said, "Well, Christ, Ted, you know how it is," and Neilsen said, "Well, for Christ's sake, kid, forget it and come on to work tomorrow if you want to."

On Monday he got his Clarion *paycheck for Friday and Saturday, and it was at the rate of fifty a week. He stood studying the check for a minute and finally went into Ted's office and said, "Is this check right? It looks like it's for fifty a week."*

Ted said, "Yeah, it's right. Bert Birmingham don't pay off in peanuts."

Bliss said, "I just wondered . . . ," knowing it wasn't smart to act like he thought he was being overpaid, but just the same wondering why he should get fifty a week for doing exactly the same work he was offered thirty-five for on the Express. *It was more money than he had ever made in his life. He remembered deciding once — years ago — that if he ever got to making as much as fifty a week he'd be on his way to the top. He grinned at Ted. Like the Cheshire cat.*

Chapter Twenty-Six
How to Live Within Your Income

Then the daemon went away. And in came Prospera, the goddess of Commerce. She waddled through the front door, eating chocolates. She licked the goo off her fingers and, being a goddess with a fine sense of irony, told Brick to write a magazine article called "How to Live Within Your Income." So he did, throwing honesty and accuracy to the winds, while Prospera looked on and burped.

Writing under a pseudonym, Michael Armstrong, Brick pretended to be the male half of a young childless couple who could never make ends meet. One day he and his wife, Pete, discovered that the real way to live within their income was to cut each item of expense by a certain percentage. It sold to *This Week,* a national Sunday supplement much like the later *Parade.* The purchase price was seven hundred and fifty dollars.

September 26, 1949

Dear Toni,

I am in a condition of complete mental collapse after your letter. Not that I really doubted it would sell -- sometimes, one knows -- but it has been many years, and I've had so many near misses that I still do not believe it. Nor will I, until I have the check in hand.

Not only that, but the price! I thought maybe $350 if I was lucky. In fact, I went so far as to budget $200 for myself in September for the sale of the article, so you can see I was really pretty confident. But the price! You are the agent of all agents.

Naturally the blurb about me to put with the article is
OK. Any time anybody wants to pay me prices like that for
something, they can put on a blurb calling me the son of
Cardinal Spellman and Clare Boothe and it will be OK by me.[1]

The article was so successful that a Cleveland bank later published 25,000
copies of it in an off-print version, earning Brick (and Toni) another fee, and
for a time sending Brick into unrealized schemes of earning a fortune by
peddling the same piece to other banks around the country.

I had a good idea recently for an article on the S.F.
Bay Bridge and put it aside because it seemed too local. My
title was "The Politest Man in the World," and the opening
gambit is the toll-taker who stands at the tollgate and
takes your quarter and says "Thank you" on an average of
once every three seconds -- twenty times a minute, twelve
hundred times an hour, etc. etc. He has a microphone in his
booth which records how many times he fails to say "Thank
you" and how often he blows his top and calls some driver a
son of a bitch, how many women make passes at him (one gal
grabbed a tolltaker's hand here recently and he was thrown
against the car and had his skull fractured), how long a
guy can work at it without blowing his top. Then I would
move into the internal housekeeping arrangements on the
bridge, still statistical but not dull.

October 29, 1949

The check arrived in the nick of time. I'd bought a
suit and an overcoat and had got behind on my child support
-- and everything turned out just perfectly. Since then
I've been going around in circles thinking of all the
things I want to buy -- and finally putting what is left in
the bank to meet the monthly deficit for the next six
months in the hope that by that time I will have sold
something else.

Soon I'll have outlines for a couple of articles to send
you. After one sale it's a lot easier to see precisely what
is needed. I'm beginning to subscribe to Anne's theory that
in writing it is the daemon that does the work. The only two
things I've ever published were written by the daemon.

Prospera, sitting by the window painting her nails, arched an eyebrow and smiled to herself. Daemon, indeed! She turned herself into a
fat little mouse and went to gnaw on some tasty electrical wiring.

November 18, 1949

Things go reasonably well here. The money from This
Week helps meet the deficit for a couple of months, and

---

[1] Playwright and magazine editor Clare Boothe (1903-1987) became Clare Booth Luce when
she married Henry Luce, the publisher of *Time*. By 1949 she had been a Republican congress-
woman from New York and had converted to Catholicism. Francis Joseph Spellman (1889-1967)
was the Catholic archbishop of New York.

it's nice to have a little relief from strain. In addition,
we had a little fire last month and collected enough
insurance to buy a three-speed record changer and two new
mattresses and a few LP records.

Here are outlines on a couple of articles which you
might consider and see what you can do. The only reason I
don't do better at articles is that I'm too damn lazy. I've
got so far out of the habit of talking to people that I
won't go out and get interviews.

December 11, 1949

I like working with outlines this way; I just start
things and then let you do the rest of the work until we
get a nibble. Then comes the unpleasant part -- I really
don't like to interview, so I keep saying to myself, "Gosh,
I hope Toni doesn't get a nibble on that one."

Do you hear anything from Anne, by the way? I haven't,
for a year or so. Neither directly nor indirectly. Hope she
is working -- Oh, yes, curious; at this point I pick up
your last letter and see you have written: "Any news from
Anne? I haven't heard from her for ages." What sort of game
is this, anyway?

My freshman semester at UCLA was tough; I was only seventeen
and had to hitchhike a dozen miles to school (those were the days when
thumbing a ride was easy and relatively safe). So I chucked college for
six months and moved to Northern California; sometimes I lived with
Brick and Naomi in Richmond, but mostly I lived in San Francisco,
where I worked as a copyboy on the *Examiner* and saved my money to
buy a car upon my planned return to Inglewood in the fall.

Brick finally hit upon a way to live within his own income: He set up
a table in the lobby of a working-class hotel South of Mission and began
to charge people who had even less income than he did to do their tax
returns for them. Sometimes business was slow; he took out the most
recent letter from Toni. Corinne, Toni wrote, had petulantly complained
that Toni hadn't been doing enough to sell Corinne's manuscripts, and
she demanded of Toni that they be sent back. Brick turned to his typewriter.

February 3, 1950

This is being written in the lobby of a fifth-rate
hotel where I pose during the late winter as an income tax
expert. So it is probably disconnected; also, it will serve
to explain why there are no more outlines and things
coming.

I'm surprised at Corinne -- and yet there seems to be
a peculiarity in the family which I find inexplicable. I've
never been able to decide whether it is a type of mental

instability or just simply bad manners. I am reminded of the time we visited Corinne after having been repeatedly urged all summer -- and found ourselves thrown out the first morning of our stay after a big row between the girls over simply nothing. Yet there aren't two sweeter girls in the world -- when they are being normal. For myself, I have had to come to the conclusion that the behavior is that of an ill-trained child of about seven who just simply hasn't grown beyond that in many ways. So, since it's too late to retrain them --

Naomi, incidentally, is in Prescott for a while. Her mother is quite ill, and I imagine she will be there for some time. Patty is with her. In a way, I think the illness came as a good thing because Naomi and I hadn't spoken to each other for about three weeks, and the strain was beginning to wear on me.

(On behalf of Corinne, I should say that she, also, has been suffering with a rather painful illness -- skin ulcers. Marx had it, and it is said to have affected profoundly the pages of "Das Kapital" -- and under the circumstances, a gal is likely to say almost anything. But not, I admit, to the extent of three pages.)

March 17, 1950

The income tax season closed with a terrific rush this year, and I'm a wreck. I did fairly well financially, but coming out of the tax season is like coming out of a dark hole.

Naomi and Patty have been in Arizona for six or seven weeks. I'm going over on April 1 to meet them and take a little train ride.

April 24, 1950

This new one-a-day mail delivery is terrible. Mail arriving in S.F. Friday morning doesn't get delivered until Monday noon!

Another sale: The toll-collector idea to *Nation's Business,* the monthly publication of the U.S. Chamber of Commerce, for five hundred dollars. It was published in February 1951 as "Most Polite Man." Toni also tried to sell some of the service articles he was turning out — one on how to buy a "hand-me-down" home and another on the Permanente Health Plan, one of the country's first HMOs, later to become the Kaiser plan. They were rejected, as was a piece called "What Color Is Your Dirt?"

The idea, borrowed from an interior decorator, is that the dirt in each room in the house is a different color and that, where you want to reduce housekeeping to a minimum, you decorate each room with a complementary color to the dirt. For example, grease is yellow, but you don't paint your kitchen yellow because when the paint gets dirty, you have just a scummy yellow. No, you paint it cocoa or green; then when it gets dirty, you have merely a lighter cocoa or green.

Toni replied that a *Coronet* editor had squelched the idea. "I feel just as he does about the word *dirt*. Somehow it offends me."

Then she moved to a more serious subject: John Clayton's disappointment over the near-acceptance but final turndown of his novel by several publishing houses. "He is a beautiful writer," she said, but the lack of a clear story line in his manuscript hurt its acceptance with the book trade.

May 13, 1950

I don't think you are in any way responsible for anything that happens to Clayton. I didn't know exactly what the situation was -- rather, I didn't know he was on another bender, though I suspected it -- and I think the whole thing is very unfortunate, but I don't think you should feel too bad about it. After all, we do have to be responsible for our own failures, and we can't be responsible for anybody else's.

I talked to John during the preliminaries several times and saw him again soon after he had word of the rejection. I haven't seen him since, so I concluded he had fallen off the wagon -- but I don't think it will be permanently damaging. Anyway, there wasn't anything you could have done about it.

Frankly, though, if I were you, I'd make an iron-clad policy of refusing to encourage any writer concerning a manuscript until you can transmit to him a firm offer from a publisher. If he wants encouragement in the meantime, tell him, as Anne used to write me when I was flat on my back: "Courage, mon ami! Le diable est mort!" Because the only guy who can tell him any more than that is the guy who signs his name to the checks. Until then, let the writer go fishing or get drunk or whatever, but don't expect his agent to wet-nurse him!

It may be that I won't develop the nonfiction business much further. Or anyway not concentrate on it. I used to say that if I could write one article and get out of the hole financially I would be able to concentrate on fiction for a year or so. So I sell two articles and pay off my debts and immediately start planning to sell a dozen articles and get rich. But maybe that would be as much of a rat race as working on the copydesk.

Listen, Toni -- here's another idea. I mentioned it before, but take ten minutes off and think about it. The idea of promoting a pocket book reprint of "You're Paying for It!"

I'm moved to mention it again because they've issued

Ortega y Gasset's "Revolt of the Masses" in paperback.[2] Now "Revolt of the Masses" was a very important book which sold seven hundred copies in the original edition -- and at that, it sold to almost everybody, at two-fifty who would buy it at thirty-five cents. It was a much more important book than "You're Paying for It!" -- but my book would sell to every individual who bought Ortega y Gasset's, and to about nine times as many people who would get nothing from his. I'll gamble that my book is assigned reading in as many college courses as his:[3] again, his audience in that direction is more select but I'd bet that mine is wider. So, I say, there's a possibility.

It isn't primarily a question of money (which, I assume, doesn't amount to much} but sales prestige. Put "You're Paying for It!" on a few hundred thousand news-stands and you're going to find Garrigues articles a lot easier to sell. Right? (Also, the title would have to be changed back to "The Politician's Handbook: A Guide to Graft"; on the stands that would sell like hell.) Well, look, I don't say it could be done, but it is definitely worth thinking about.

June 5, 1950

We spent a couple of weeks looking at new autos and finally decided to get the old one fixed up and use it another year -- it's only a 1938! -- and then I spent ten days taking it to the garage every morning for overhauling.

June 20, 1950

The well is still dry -- and it's a curious psycho-logical experience. If I were trying to live on my earnings I'd go completely nuts and blow my brains out. As it is, I'm rather amused at watching myself. Sure, the beautiful checks are lovely but I find that every time I get one it merely creates the obligation to get another one.

In the summer I was back on the *Examiner* and living with Brick and Naomi in Richmond. Once again my dad and I rode the bus across the Bay to the office, sometimes together, most of the time separately.

One of my morning duties as a copyboy was to walk the several blocks from the Hearst Building at Third and Market to the *Call-Bulletin* on Howard Street, where I picked up a bundle of overnight wire photos. That's how I learned about the June 25 invasion of South Korea by the North, by poring over the photos of men in uniform and the maps of the Korean peninsula as I returned to the office. Later that summer the bay

---

2 The book by José Ortega y Gasset (1883-1955) was published in hard cover in 1929. The Spanish philosopher argued that the masses should surrender social leadership to the cultivated and intellectually independent men among them.

3 Probably not. I did mention to Brick that I had seen his book on the "recommended" reading list for a political science course at UCLA, and he beamed. And perhaps built on the information in this letter to Toni.

was dotted with freighters held back from their voyages in fear of the spread of war. Two months earlier, when I turned eighteen, I had registered for the draft.

Brick and I each read separately a fascinating magazine article by a man named L. Ron Hubbard. Yes, the same Hubbard who that year published a best-selling book called *Dianetics: The Modern Science of Mental Health* and four years later founded the Church of Scientology. The excitement in Brick's letter was typical of many people's that year, but after his initial enthusiasm, he quickly lost interest.

July 3, 1950

Have you heard anything about Dianetics? It will be filling the newsmagazines very soon if it is not already. It is the biggest thing since Technocracy and probably, as an immediate sensation, the biggest thing since Freud.

About two months ago, Astounding Science Fiction (a Street and Smith pulp read almost entirely by adolescents and by graduate physicists and technologists), which occasionally carries rather technical fact articles, and also occasionally carries burlesque hoax articles which can only be appreciated by qualified physicists, printed a long article entitled "Dianetics."

The editor wrote a foreword in which he insisted that the article was no hoax: that this was a straight scientific article reporting the most important psychotherapeutic discovery in history, etc. etc.

The article, by one L. Ron Hubbard, a science fiction writer, claimed that he had discovered a method by which he (or any layman) could accomplish psychotherapy on any patient in a time considerably less than that taken by any form of psychoanalysis.

Apparently every science fiction fan in the country rushed to buy the book. I did. Most of the physics majors and graduates at the University of California atom laboratory did.

The claims made by the author are incredible. He asserts that he has accomplished the complete cure of 272 psychotics and neurotics out of 272 patients. He asserts that anybody, without scientific training, can do the same.

Nevertheless, despite the incredibility of it, one cannot believe that Hubbard is self-deceived. In other words, either he had one hundred percent cures or the whole thing is a book-selling hoax. But it is incredible that it should be a hoax, simply because so clever a hoaxer would have been clever enough not to have made the incredible parts of it quite so incredible.

Anyway, hoax or not, the thing has caught on in San Francisco -- and so I suppose elsewhere. Dianetics cooperatives are being formed -- clubs of from fifty to a hundred people who meet and compare notes on their Dianetics experiences. I suspect that within a few weeks there will be hundreds of such clubs in every large city in the country.

It is one of those curious things which is propagated from person to person. You say: "Do you know anything about Dianetics?" and the other person says, as though secretly ashamed of it, "A friend of mine says he got basic-basic in fifty hours," and you say, "Do you think there is anything to it?" and then you're off.

The technique is on the surface somewhat like that of psychoanalysis. The therapist is called the "auditor." He puts the patient in what seems to be an exceedingly light hypnotic trance (no, it is not that, either: it is lighter than that; I suppose you could say it is no more than directing the patient's attention) and then tells him to "return" to a previous time in his life when he underwent an accident or an operation or an emotional crisis which rendered him unconscious.

One actually relives the experience. If you return to your appendectomy, you actually suffer the pain which your body experienced while you were unconscious. You go over the experience time after time until it is all brought into your consciousness. Ultimately, it is "released," and you can no longer "relive" it; you can now consciously remember it.

And when you have gone over it and completely re-experienced all such experiences in your life (including your prenatal life) you are cured of all your psychiatric and psychosomatic ills.

A person so cured is a "clear." To be a clear is to be almost a superman. Your I.Q. actually increases about fifty points. You have no more ills, no allergies, no common colds. Germs cannot bite you. You are terrific. Probably you don't even need deodorants. To become a clear takes usually from two hundred to five hundred hours of therapy -- usually two hours a treatment about two or three times a week.

But, again, there is no cost involved[4] because anybody can do it. I can audit you for two hours and then you can turn around and audit me for two hours. Husbands and wives can audit one another -- or friends, or parents and children.

A friend of mine has just started to undergo therapy. She is not particularly suggestible but she started re-living her appendectomy, including each slice of the knife and each jab of the needle -- all of which occurred while she was under anaesthesia. She is going to start auditing

---

4 This free ride did not last long. Scientology — the successor to Dianetics — now has different levels of "clarity," all available at different prices.

me later this week (she is already auditing her husband), and I will probably start auditing somebody within a few days thereafter.

The theme of any article would have to be either:

1. How an incredible pulp writer made an incredible success with an incredible theory, or

2. What funny people people are where their minds are concerned.

July 16, 1950

For the last two weeks I've been writing furiously about Dianetics and I wanted to get the article finished. At least it has got me writing again. I want to get it out of the way and go on to something else.

August 2, 1950

Congratulations on selling Clayton to Collier's. I knew you would do it sooner or later.

John Bell Clayton's first story in *Collier's* was "Afternoon in Deer Meadow," published on October 21, 1950. Thereafter, his stories appeared regularly in that magazine.

September 2, 1950

We had quite an amazing vacation -- three thousand miles in two weeks without going out of the state and without sleeping indoors more than once. (Did I tell you we bought a new car: a Nash, with a built-in bed?)

The 1938 Willys had been falling apart. Brick feared that an all-out war would mean an end to consumer goods just as the last war had. He scrounged enough money for a down payment on the Nash and tried to pay off the rest every month.

I will shortly revise the housing piece to bring it up to date and send it to you again. Also the income tax piece as soon as Congress gets off the dime.

One day, Brick and Naomi were fussing with each other while I was having lunch in the house in Richmond before going to work, when a battle erupted over Naomi's invading what my father considered his private space in the garage. There was shouting. He picked her up and carried her, struggling, into their room. I felt as though I had been punched in the stomach. I left the house, my meal unfinished, took the bus to work and wrote out a resignation letter, which I left on my boss's desk. I scarcely spoke to either Brick or Naomi for the next two weeks, and at the end of that time, I packed up my bags and went alone to the Greyhound station in San Francisco to return to Los Angeles. How surprised and affected I was when my father appeared unexpectedly in the waiting room to see me off. We didn't say what we really felt about each other, although I know he sensed my disappointment in him. He gave a deep sigh of regret when he bid me farewell, but I was rather stiff, somewhat formal. I wanted to escape. I didn't like what he and Naomi had done to each other, and I didn't want to be a part of it; I was yet only a teen-ager and unable to bear the thought of parents in physical combat; even now I am upset by the memory.

September 9, 1950

Summer is always such a difficult time to work. Not only are there the usual distractions, but this summer one of the youngsters has been staying with us so I've had no room to work in. This morning, however, he went back to L.A. to school and I've spent the day moving back into my study with my mss. neatly piled and everything to hand, so I no longer have any excuse.

I haven't touched the novel since last January, but I suddenly discovered myself enamored of a minor character (male) who was on the point of emerging when I put it down. I go to sleep dreaming of him. And just at the point where we need some relief from my main character. There's some damn good writing in that novel. If I can only learn to string it together.

October 7, 1950

I observe that This Week, which was interested in service pieces a few months ago, is now apparently concerned chiefly in fomenting war.

October 24, 1950

I've become an irritable old gentleman lately -- I can hardly stand to live with myself. Thought maybe the blood pressure was up (irritability is one of the symptoms), which wouldn't have been a good thing for a guy with a heart condition, but saw the doctor yesterday and he said I was OK. So I guess it's just the world situation.

November 2, 1950

I finally met John Langdon the other day.[5] He really seems to be an unusually nice character, and you unques-tionably made a great impression on him. You must be as beautiful as I remember you. (And, incidentally, I had a shock the other day. I saw a girl who was a double for the Fanny Strassman of the twenties. I walked around and about her. Not just a remembered resemblance but that particular individual glow which I'd long since let slip out of my mind. You know what I mean? I remembered what you looked like but not how YOU looked -- and then I saw it. Curious,

---

5 John Langdon was a thirty-seven-year-old reference librarian with the Mechanics Institute Library who had been publishing short stories since 1943. He later became a television and movie writer and was one of several authors whom Brick referred to Toni for representation.

very pleasant thing.) Anyway, Langdon is a nice guy. Hope he's as good a writer as everybody says.

Brick ran into trouble making payments on the Nash; he even borrowed some money from me to help out after I went back to Southern California, since I had a few hundred dollars saved from my summer job.

November 20, 1950

Dear Lou:

Here is a check for twenty; I think that straightens us up on the loan -- for which I thank you again. It was nice of you, and it is nice to have a car. Come up and see us some time and you can borrow it.

Needless to say, I'd always hoped that when you guys were old enough to go to college I could take care of it. It didn't turn out that way -- through nobody's fault but my own. If my stuff starts selling again, I'll be able to help to some slight degree. Just now it isn't selling and I haven't been in this business long enough to know whether it will again or not. So long as it doesn't sell -- well, I wouldn't have bought the car if I'd known it was going to squeeze so tight, but now that I have bought it, I'm hung up on it until somebody decides to come through with a sizeable check.

Another thing -- by way of a sermon -- I'm anxious to see you do some serious job-hunting because, ultimately, your success in job-hunting (and its affiliated endeavors, such as back-stabbing, apple-polishing, etc.) will determine how far you Succeed in Life.[6] College is all very helpful in some departments, but the advantages it gives you tend largely to be offset by the fact that it conceals these Facts of Life from you for a long time and then dumps you unceremoniously into a world where they pay off on how well you can impress people -- apple-polish people -- instead of how much you know.

Chuck was out the other morning; he was going to borrow the car to go to the Stanford-Army game but, fortunately, his better judgment prevailed and the whole gang sat around some gal's flat in S.F. and played records and stuff. I sat around for a while; it was very pleasant.

1023 Peralta Avenue
Albany, Calif.
January 22, 1951

Dear Toni,

We have been moving. This is the first time I've picked up the typewriter since the deluge started.

The new place was run down -- it had been vacant for

---

6 Advice from a person who wanted to do none of these things himself.

six months, and the owner, who'd moved away, was desperate
to sell -- so there was a lot of work to do. I've discovered an astonishing ability in myself to do plumbing and
stuff; I've put in a furnace and built a tile bathroom and
made a million minor repairs. It is a very satisfactory
place in every way, on a hillside with a slight view of the
Bay and a nice backyard with a fishpond yet! And very quiet
-- quieter than the desert or the mountains even because
there you always have the wind or the sound of insects or
animals. But at night here there is nothing but the gentle
sigh of the refrigerator.

Albany is a little town just north of Berkeley -- and
Berkeley is as Cultural as hell, its chief industry being
the University of California, where Naomi went to school
and where she worked a while and knew lots of professors
and things. So some of the culture seeps across the city
boundary; anyway, to all intents and purposes, we play that
we live in Berkeley. It's the first time Naomi's been
satisfied since I've known her. (She's working, incidentally. And still contented!)

I'm sorry none of the articles sold -- I can't think
what I was thinking of to write them that length! If I ever
get back to articles, I'll write them shorter. Frankly,
though, I don't get much lift out of articles any more;
it's like being an oversized newspaperman. And I suspect
that there are more profitable ways of earning a living.

"As for writing fiction," Toni wrote Brick around this time, "maybe
you can reach down into your basic fundamental self, if you try hard
enough and come up with something."

March 26, 1951

It was good to hear that Clayton is selling so well at
Collier's. He seems at last to have found the way to write
within the slick formula without doing an injustice to his
own way of looking at things. I hope he continues to do as
well.

For me, I know that I will never make a good living
writing slick nonfiction -- simply because I don't have
enough interest. If I'd tried a few years ago, before I
lost the reporter's knack, I might have made a good living
at it. But now there are hundreds who can do it better.

What I really want to do is to finish "Neither Five
Nor Three." It was starting to go beautifully when I was
suddenly interrupted by our move to Albany. But it has to
write itself; there's just no way I can force it or make
decisions about it except at the typewriter. If the garden
wasn't so beautiful and the house so in need of paint (and
a new foundation), I would be reasonably certain to spend
the summer at the book.

April 16, 1951

I seem to be compelled by some neurotic compulsion to slave away at the house and yard. There is such a wealth of things to be done; I could work steadily at it for the next two years and never catch up with even the immediate necessities.

Writing nonfiction is purely a matter of money -- and I'm reaching the place where I'm very rebellious about attempting to make money. One big shock of my life was when I discovered a few years ago that there was no possibility of my ever making enough money to do what I want -- to have a little reserve and not have my nose to the grindstone. If I made a million dollars a year Naomi could spend $1.1 million just as easily as she can spend sixty-six hundred on an income of six thousand. And don't say: "Don't blame it on Naomi," because the only thing which checks her desires is the realization that she can't charge any more until next month because you haven't been able to pay for what you bought three months ago. And it is that particular feeling of being deprived -- of being unable to spend a cent freely because you have already over-spent -- which I have wanted, above all, to get away from.

That realization came years ago. But it is only lately that I have become outright rebellious about making money. Because, now, I find myself doing it. I find myself charging things I can't pay for and, in effect, simply violating every principle of living which, however poor a thing, has always been my own. So I just sit and say stubbornly, "To hell with it. I will NOT go out and gather some dope for an article."

I wrote Curtis Brown a couple of weeks ago, asking them to see what they could do toward selling "You're Paying For It!" for reprint purposes -- two-bit paperbounds -- pointing out that if they didn't want to play with the idea, I'd like a release of their agency rights.

I don't mean to imply that I think there is a great deal of chance of selling this -- nevertheless Mentor and Pelican and Penguin (that's British, isn't it?) and some of the others are putting out stuff with less popular appeal and, in view of the Kefauver hearings, interest in political corruption is at a higher point than it has been in forty years. I don't think the public would be interested in a book that was dull or ponderous or expose-ish; they don't want to be shocked but only to have their worst suspicions confirmed. What do you think? Do you feel like taking a whirl at it?

That novel I've been working on doesn't seem so much as a novel; it doesn't seem to get anywhere. But in going over it, I can't help but feel that I've got some very good chunks which could possibly be turned to account. Naomi started typing it with the idea that I'd send it to you and see what reaction I got.

Only, unfortunately, Naomi's enthusiasm for my work -- boundless as it is -- does not carry her to the point where she is willing to type a ms. And I, in my secret rage, say I'll be damned if I'll send out even one more manuscript and let her spend the money if she won't even type the damn thing after I've written it.

Ain't life hell in a mean, petty way?

I'm much encouraged by Clayton's continued success. I think the last one in Collier's[7] was the best he's done and would seem to dispel the idea that a story has to be lousy to sell to the slicks. I saw the yarn in first draft -- and it's amazing how the guy has learned to handle his stuff.

Sympathize with me. And work a little voodoo or something. I need it.

July 25, 1951

I finally found a copy of "You're Paying for It!" which Naomi has mailed to you on the possibility that somebody might be interested in a thirty-five-cent reprint. Remember, I wrote you about it?

Cornelia visited us. She is working hard but is lost at about the same place I am.

August 23, 1951

I never dared think how completely disrupted I've been -- how completely unlike myself, laboring on the foundations of a house, building a patio, oh, damnation.

As ever,

Brick

---

7 "Phantom of Walnut Spring," April 7, 1951.

Chapter Twenty-Seven
The Boy on the Wagon

Brick sent a fragment of his novel to Toni. She cautioned him: "There are many reasons why it is not for the magazines; it is too long, it has a child as a central character, it isn't tight enough and dramatic enough for magazine use." But, she went on, as a novel, "I liked it enormously. There is warmth and nostalgia and a lovely quality about it. . . . It is really good, Brick, and I really think you should go on working on it." Brick replied:

September 2, 1951

Dear Toni,

First of all, I have a theory that people read a book because they like the storyteller, whether as author or as a narrator -- or even as simply expressed in the point-of-view. You must go along into a book as with a friend.

Specifically, the entire story is told by a narrator, a character who is both outside the story as author (and so, omniscient) and at the same time, for certain periods, within the book as a younger boy who admires and almost worships Bliss, in their high school days. True, many readers and editors object to these obvious mechanics of story-telling in the modern age -- yet it is also true that the device is most effective with the very best story tellers. Kipling used it; Maugham, Conrad. That doesn't mean that I can; it only means that IF I can do it well, it is a good thing to do.

It is by this device that the entire story gains perspective. Bliss Lane, then fiftyish, is brought into a hospital after having been clubbed unconscious by a policeman. He has gone through life valiantly and vainly attempting to convince himself "that two and two make four, and neither five nor three"; he has compromised and resisted, compromised and resisted until, finally, an act of revolt has brought him to disaster.

His childhood friend, Bob Reynolds, now the jail surgeon, recognizes him as his boyhood hero and, suddenly, the earlier identification which Bob had with Bliss comes back so that he -- the surgeon -- understands himself as a failure, a fumbler. Bob feels that if he, at fifty, can KNOW what has happened to Bliss, can understand what life has done to him, he can understand wherein he, Bob, has failed -- where he has missed the boat.

And so, on the basis of his own need, he tries to re-create the story of Bliss Lane -- not as he knows it, but as it must have been. He says in effect to the reader: "This story is not true; this is not fact. It is fiction. It is something I am making up out of my own inner need. Believe it only if it seems to you to be true." And then Bob stops being omniscient within the book to reappear only as a minor character within it.

Because Bob loves Bliss -- loves his own adolescence in the memory of Bliss -- you feel a warm, emotional attachment, an identification with Bliss through Bob, which you could not get any other way.

It is not necessary to stress the pitfalls of this sort of treatment. But the positive advantages are important, too.

The reader will follow the story because he wants to live for a long time with Bliss -- rather than because he wants an outcome. For example, in the fragment you've seen, "The Deadline," the reader doesn't particularly give a damn whether Bliss gets the ranch or whether he proves Jehovah to be a phony. What the reader enjoys is not the goal, but the journey.

The whole story must be written that way -- must be read that way. Now, the place you mention on page 11, where the point-of-view changes from third person to second, well, maybe it doesn't come off -- but it's intended as a shift into a stream of consciousness in which the reader is plunged -- slid, rather -- into identification with the character:

"When the teacher came out on the steps everybody put their hand up," -- you are seeing a small boy, rather bewildered, puzzled -- "over your eyes like you were shading them from the sun and said with the teacher," and suddenly you, the reader, ARE that small boy, puzzled and bewildered -- "except that if you covered up your eyes and then peeked between your fingers like you did in church the teacher would come down and larrup you."

Maybe those things don't come off; that is always the problem that the writer can never answer, but it is those things which give the thing its nostalgic, warm quality.

The First Day at the New School

It had not occurred to Bliss, until now, to doubt that he was the exact geographical center of the physical universe. In Kansas — and even on the O'Connell ranch — the land fell away — fields or hills or rolling plains — equidistant on every side so that: the world was a vast circle, like a plate, and you stood in the center of it. The sun came up on the eastern side of the plate and moved over your head; at noon it seemed to stop, for a little while and stand there and make your shadow very small, and then it moved on and went down in the west, directly opposite where it had come up, and you never thought to question that God had arranged it that way because you were the center of things and the world was something that was around you.

But in Greenstone it was different. There was no order nor symmetry nor sensible arrangement of things. Everything — streets and houses and trees and buildings — was laid out not between you and the horizon but in square lines and blocks in which you existed, squeezed and crowded and cramped — and casual and unplaced like the mites on the undersides of hen roosts.

The first morning he couldn't wait to get out. He pulled on his jeans and shirt and ran out barefoot, without combing his hair, and went down to Whitfield avenue and watched the automobiles chug by and the horses clop-clop with their iron shoes striking hard against the pavement. And after breakfast he went down by the tracks and watched the men load oranges into the waiting cars. But long before noon he was back — in time to hear Mama's argument with Grace about God striking Mrs. McConnell dead — and he sat on the kitchen floor and played with some sticks and wondered what they'd come into this old Greenstone for, anyway.

"Go on out and play," Mama said when she'd stepped over him for the third time.

But he couldn't. "There's nothing to play. Mama," he told her. "There's no place to go."

"Goodness!" she declared. "With all the children there are in a fine town like Greenstone . . ."

"Aw, it's a tacky old town," he insisted. "I don't see who'd want to live here anyway."

That was Saturday. Sunday was Sunday anywhere — except that he went to church three times instead of twice and after evening service he was almost asleep before they got home.

But Monday was school day. Out on the O'Connell ranch there was Cal and Tom and Grace to go to school with and they — together with the Woodses and the Dusseldorfs who lived almost across the road — made up more than half the school. But now Cal and Tom had graduated and Grace went across Whitfield Avenue to the eighth-grade school, and when he took his lunch and went down the sidewalk there were a thousand trillion kids walking and running down the sidewalks and pushing and bouncing at each other and looking at him in a funny way.

It was the first time he had ever seen so many kids. The schoolyard was full of them, and they were leaping and shouting and making so much noise his head swam. After a while a teacher came out and rang a bell and all the kids lined up in different rows and Bliss got into a line of boys about his size and hoped they were third-graders. When the teacher came out on the steps everybody put their right hand up over their eyes like you were shading them from the sun and said with the teacher,

"Ipledgeallegiance — totheflag — andtothecountry — forwhichitstands — one nation — indivisible — withlibertyandjusticeforall."

It was like a prayer except that if you covered up your eyes entirely and then peeked between your fingers like you did when the preacher prayed in church the teacher would come down and larrup you.

Afterwards you filed into the school building in two long rows, one for girls and one for boys. But you had to be on the watchout because the boy in front would sometimes kick back with his foot and slam you in the stomach when the teacher wasn't looking, or the girl opposite you in the other row would reach over and nip you with her fingers when the rows came close together as they went through the big doors. And if you yelled or jumped away to keep from being kicked or nipped the teacher would land on you and give you heck.

I suppose that when it is all done, there will be large chunks which now seem very precious which must be cut out. I am prepared to do that -- if only I can retain the warmth and nostalgia. In fact, I'm deliberately writing it twice too long so I can do that.

After all, I do have to do it myself, don't I? Maybe about all anybody can give at this point is encouragement. Anyway, if you have any suggestions --

We had a marvelous vacation, and I came back fully refreshed for the first time in years. In the Bay district the high fog comes up each June and stays there until September so that each day is duller than the one before; a

cold wind blows around your heart and makes you feel old;
the sky settles down close so that there is no horizon and
you walk with your eyes on the ground and your thoughts in
the past.

Usually we rush madly away and camp somewhere in the
high mountains -- rushing from place to place and trying to
cover as much of the state as possible with the idea that
by covering space we can extend time. But this year I went
alone, at first; we have friends in Clear Lake, where it is
dry and hot; one lies in the lake and cools off and then
crawls out and drinks a bottle of beer and soaks up heat
and then crawls back in the lake.

The wife and I adore each other (platonically, let it
be said with perhaps suspicious emphasis) and the husband
is a nice guy whom I like very much and, amazingly, Naomi
likes them both. We camped a while, the three of us; later
Naomi came up and nobody lived by the clock and we did as
we damn pleased and I feel twenty-five instead of fifty --
only I now get excited only over pleasurable things. It is
a very pleasant world.

Even going back to the office was not intolerably bad.
For years -- ever since I came to realize that my life with
Naomi was going to be what it is -- no worse than most
people's, but definitely what it is -- I have done nothing
more than submit, cheerfully, sometimes, to the intolerable
fact that two and two makes four, and neither five nor three.

I mean, it wasn't really, ever, going to get any
better -- even for a little while. Now, going back to the
office and the grind at home, I am buoyed up by the
realization that, for a little while, it WAS better.

October 10, 1951

I think I am beginning to get the story line of
"Neither Five Nor Three" worked out. If true, that's a
tremendous relief. Up to now, I haven't had any great
trouble writing it, but I've never been more than half sure
that I was writing it in any given direction.

It's been eleven months now since I stopped work and
the time has come when I must either decide to settle down
the way Clayton has been working -- or stop kidding myself.

[Late] November 1951

Recently it has dawned on me that I was no longer
thinking of myself as a writer. For a year at least all my
thoughts had been given to such domestic matters as
carpentry, painting, etc. etc. But it was more than that;
I'd suddenly stopped feeling any necessity to write.

The realization alarmed me. Finally, after considerable negotiation with Naomi, I decided to find myself a
place in town where I could stay at least on my late

nights, coming home on my days off -- or at least on one of
them. I was a little surprised when Naomi went for it; in
fact, it was really her idea. I succeeded in finding a
place for less than twenty dollars a month, and I paid a
month's rent and started cleaning it up -- and Naomi blew
her top at the idea that I would ever consent to do such a
thing! It was not good to point out to her that it had been
her idea all the time.

Finally, after a month of cleaning and painting, I
moved in, despite her protest -- and finally silenced her
only by making it clear that I couldn't work if the
protests continued; so if they did, I'd just move into town
permanently.

Well, anyway, that's the experiment. I expected to
"freeze up" when I tried to work -- and I did. (I've had
that happen before, when I've gone to great efforts to find
adequate time and privacy to write, and then found I
couldn't.) The change of routine is such a violent one that
it is going to take some time to get straightened out.

But it is deeper than that: I feel as though some
permanent psychological change had occurred in me. It is a
little like that which happened when Dickie and I split up
-- except that I don't have the emotional reaction that I
had then. I have no intention of leaving Naomi completely -
- unless she makes it absolutely impossible for me to
write. But at the same time, I have a very strong necessity
not to be dependent on her in the peculiar way I have been
for the last fifteen years.

I was delighted to hear that you've heard from Anne.
None of her closest friends, apparently had heard a word.
Is she still in Southern California?

A friend of mine has just started to work as an
attendant in a state hospital for the criminally insane not
too far from here. This gal is a very fine, sensitive
person; I don't know whether she can write or not, but her
oral descriptions make the interiors of these wards come to
life so that the most horribly deteriorated people become
human, and warm and pathetic. I might do a collaboration
with her if we can work out a good idea.

In New York, Toni pondered Brick's letter. "I was just thinking the
other day," she wrote, "of all the writers in California and how most of
them began with me due to you — Clayton, Anne Hawkins, Cornelia
Jessey, and through Clayton several others I haven't sold yet. Just think
what you started. But most of all I wish I had something of yours, so
unfreeze yourself and let me hear what gives."

April 6, 1952

Honest to God, Toni, I don't know what I've been doing
the last year or so. Nothing, really. But there seemed to

be a time when we moved to the new house when the idea that
I had any writing to do just went out like a light. When
I'd talk to Clayton, for example, about writing, it would
be just as though it were something I knew nothing about,
and I wondered if it would ever come back. Even after I
took the studio last fall, it didn't, and I finally came to
the conclusion that it was just one of the vagaries of my
youth which I had finally overcome.

But now I've just finished doing a query-and-outline
for an article in which I have considerable confidence. It
deals with the results of an experiment in intensive
therapy at Stockton Mental Hospital in which twenty-four
hopelessly insane patients who had been in the chronic
wards from ten to fifteen years were restored to sanity and
released through intensive treatment.

This field is one which interests me very much and I'd
like to see if I can't develop it into something regular, if
the market seems to be there. One reason I stopped writing
before was the realization that I didn't have a wide enough
area of interest to be able to achieve a very large output
of salable stuff. I don't actually like people well enough
to want to spend my time writing about their problems --
unless it is something freakish like the budget piece.

But, ultimately, I remembered that I have always been
interested in wacky people; the most interesting people
I've ever known have either just been going into, or coming
out of, an insane asylum.

Les Jones, the gal I wrote about, has been a good bit
of help in this line and, as I gradually get my brain
cleared, I begin to think I can see possibilities. She's
got enough stuff for a really good book if she would only
do it: for example, the kindly old attendant in the women's
side who says, "Sure, I know how to treat those poor unfor-
tunates. I treat them just like I would my own mother if
she was sick" and then waddles over and clouts a whimpering
senile case on the side of the head and yells, "Shuddup and
siddown, you old son of a bitch!"

April 21, 1952

"Neither Five Nor Three" was, as I think you know,
chiefly a psychotherapeutic, rather than a literary,
exercise. It started the work of uncovering layer after
layer of repressed experiences and compulsions and bringing
them into consciousness and understanding. Under the
circumstances, it was impossible to bring the novel into
one piece; I have the feeling now that when I get back to
it, I may be the master, not IT. (Not that I see around the
corner yet. But I hear sounds from there and they are good
sounds.)

It's such a nice spring day. I feel very happy.

By May 1952, Rena Vale, then some fifty-four years old, had achieved a reputation as a writer of fantasy and science fiction. That month her story "The Shining City" was featured on the cover of the magazine *Science Fiction Quarterly*.

May 19, 1952

So, a writer writes anywhere, does he? That isn't the way I heard it. I heard that writing is such hard work that a man will do ANYTHING -- lift up houses and put new foundations under them, or drink himself to death, or anything -- to keep from doing it.

Congratulations again on Clayton. I hear his second novel has been accepted. I think "Six Angels" is terrific -- the whole thing is now as good as the first section was when I read it in the hospital years ago.[1]

Brick's next sale was "Target Therapy: New Hope for Lost Minds," in the August edition of a pocket-sized mag called *Brief,* about a treatment for patients at Stockton State Hospital. *Brief* that month also featured pin-up pix of Marilyn Monroe, Mara Corday, Terry Moore and Ursula Thiess.

July 28, 1952

I'm still trying to re-organize my life so there will be a certain amount of free time and energy to write. What I've been trying to do is to get Naomi to consent to give me a six-month vacation from any of the responsibilities of marriage except those of earning a paycheck -- so that all I have to do is earn a living for the family and write my little pieces. You would think that such a request would not be unreasonable -- but all I get is kind and sympathetic understanding. Period.

There isn't a day when there aren't a dozen household tasks to be done -- picking up the laundry, getting the car greased, going down to meet an overdraft at the bank and when I get home at night I am regaled by all the childish problems of all the childish people on the street, none of whom strike me as having any dramatic impact -- so that there seems very little adulthood left in my old age.

August 1952

Dear Toni,

Isn't it marvelous about Clayton? I do not believe the rumors going around about the pocket book price he got. I refuse to believe.[2]

Do you know what is wrong with Anne? We have a mutual

---

1 Macmillan published *Six Angels at My Back*. Autobiographical, it received high praise: "A first novel of real talent." — *Chicago Sunday Tribune*. "This is one of those rare books in which there seems not one word too many and hardly one which could easily be changed for the better." — *New York Herald Tribune*. "This is the first novel of an experienced and deft writer. It is very, very good." — *Saturday Review*.

2 Popular Library paid Clayton $21,000 for the reprint rights of *Six Angels at My Back*.

friend -- Andree Clear -- who was to see her and writes
mysteriously about it all. Anyway, I guess I'll know in a
couple of weeks as the Clears are coming to see us soon.

Writers often become interested in psychiatry as a subject because
they recognize the need for seeking psychiatric help for themselves. At
long last Brick consulted a doctor about his own problems.

August 2, 1952

How are you? I am fine. In fact, I'm so fine I
sometimes wonder if I haven't gone slightly batty in the
last year. Shall I tell you the story of my life? Well,
here goes -- No, on second thought, it would only bore you.

I think, though, that starting an autobiographical
novel and working on it from time to time, and then, a
couple of consultations with a psychoanalyst -- no
analysis, just a little chat -- and, finally, a long
session of self-analysis in the Karen Horney fashion -- all
of these, or something, have resulted in what may be called
the "disintegration of a personality."

Karen Horney was the influential dean of the American Institute for
Psychoanalysis. She suggested that environmental and social conditions,
rather than Freud's biological destiny, drive a person nuts. She thought
that people could learn to psychoanalyze themselves. She died on December 4, 1952, at the age of sixty-seven.

You know, damn it, Toni, I just don't feel like the
same sort of person I have been for the last twenty or
thirty years. I seem to have none of the drives, compulsions, inhibitions and few of the obsessions I've had ever
since I was a kid. I seem -- to myself, anyway -- to be
relaxed and in full possession of my faculties.

I know that for years I've been excessively paternal;
I've been ridden by guilt feelings. But now I don't feel a
damn bit paternal and I don't think I have any more guilt
feelings -- at least not any repressed ones.

True, I continue (so far) to lead almost exactly the
sort of life I have led for years -- but I know very well
that I am not that sort of person. Does that make sense?
No?

I remember the last great change that took place in my
life: the last violent, upheaval, I suppose, when I split
up with Dickie and had that wild affair with the manic-
depressive gal; I remember sitting in my little office at
the News in L.A. and writing you to the effect that I was a
new man, a different man, that my life had changed,
thenceforth and forever -- [3]

So I suppose it is only appropriate that I should
write you of this change, too.

---

[3] See his letter of December 10, 1934, pages 118-119.

Because of that last experience, I mistrust this one. I did go through a little manic experience last winter but I leveled off at a level just a trifle above "normal" and have been "coasting high" ever since.

I trace it back to a discovery I made -- intellectually several years ago, and emotionally about a year ago -- that my father is dead. Is that a curious thing to say? I found that when we moved to Richmond about five years ago I had an absolute insane compulsion to dig in gardens, raise flowers, lawns, etc. etc. and, after a while, I realized that the compulsion WAS neurotic.

And then, after a while, I realized that what I was trying to do was to make up to my father for all the furious digging in the ground he had done when I was a kid and he was trying so desperately to make a go of farming in order to send us kids through school. It was a little more than that, of course; actually, it dawned upon me after a while, what I was doing was to obey a sort of posthypnotic command placed upon me by my father: To dig furiously in the earth.

And after I realized that, the compulsion began to lose its power.

But it took more than that. Theodor Reik[4] puts it this way: "The 'I' observes the 'Me' (and hence the Universe) through the eyes of the 'They'" -- the "They" being the significant parent or other person. After a long while, it began to dawn upon me that just as my father's command to dig furiously in the earth was no longer binding upon me, so none of his other commands were binding upon me, either.

In brief, I am under no compulsion to be the sort of man he would approve of. I need not emulate him in any way. I need not try to pay my bills on time, or get out of debt, or take care of my family, any more than I need dig in the ground. In fact, I don't need to do a damn thing. I don't need to write a book, or make a success of writing in order to justify myself for not digging in the ground.

I don't need to write articles; he can't read them; consequently, there is no possible reason why I can't write a book, or articles, if I want to. There is no reason I can't do anything I am capable of doing.

Since then I've been walking around in a sort of a daze. I still go to work every day and come home to my family and act very much as I did before. But I am not the same --

I'm fond of my daughter and of my two sons but they do not dominate me. Because my father does not dominate me.

---

4 The eminent Austrian-born psychoanalyst (1888-1969) wrote popular yet thorough books on psychology. He believed that "all love is founded on a dissatisfaction with oneself. It is an attempt to escape from one's self in search of a better, an ideal self."

The Summer They Sold the Grapes for Wine

They always got up when it was still dark, even on an August morning. Bliss scattered the grain for the chickens, still sleeping on their roosts, and he filled their pans with fresh water while Papa hitched up the team to the lumber wagon. Papa had fed the team even earlier, while Mama, holding her lips tight together, had fixed breakfast and shoved it on the table. When the team was hitched up, Papa told Bliss to get up on the seat and hold the reins, and then he hesitated a minute and went back into the house. When he came back he climbed up and took the lines and clucked at the horses and they started off without a word.

Bliss felt strange. It had been a year-and-a-half since the revival meeting, and it seemed to him he had never been alone with his father in all that time, and he was ill at ease in his presence. Just the same, he wanted to do or say something that would let his father know he was FOR him . . . and he couldn't, because you couldn't ever let either your father or your mother know that you knew they quarreled. You couldn't because, after all, your father and mother were not two persons, but one person; they thought with one mind and came to one decision and did not ever have differences of opinion or even of ambition or desire.

And so Bliss looked straight ahead in the dark, fearful that his father would read his mind and know that he, Bliss, had heard the quarrel about selling the grapes for wine.

"Albert!" Mama had said. "I never thought I'd hear my own husband offer to go in cahoots with winebibbers and saloon keepers. I'd sooner see you tear up every one of them vines than to have them lead some sinner into perdition."

Bliss, coming on the porch to get a drink of water, had known instantly what they were talking about: the zinfandels in the north vineyard. When Albert Lane had bought the ranch, he had failed to discover that ten acres were planted to wine grapes, and he had been sickened when he discovered it because no Christian could possibly sell grapes for wine. Each season the grapes had been allowed to rot on the vine. But now, with money shorter than ever and the shadow of the mortgage looming longer and blacker above them, Papa wanted to sell the grapes to an Italian family that made its own wine. Bliss crept silently against the porch wall to listen.

"It isn't as though they were going to sell them to saloons," his father said. "These Italian people drink wine just like we drink water and never get drunk or anything."

"Just the same, wine is a mocker, and strong drink is raging. Do you want it said that you helped to hasten another mortal soul to hell by looking upon the wine when it is red?"

"They'll pay twenty dollars a ton for them," his father said. "I don't see how we're going to make it if we don't take advantage of every dollar we can squeeze out of this ranch. You know how the commission merchants are . . ."

"You can't!" Bliss sensed that his mother was near tears. "Money received from the devil never helped anybody. So long as we keep the Lord on our side, we know we can trust in him. But when we turn against him. . . ."

There was a long silence, and then Albert Lane said in a tone of discouragement that Bliss had never heard before:

"Ruth, they say the Lord helps those that help themselves, but I'm getting to think he only helps those that help themselves to what belongs to somebody else. He seems to help out the commission merchants, and F. L. E. Skinner, all right, but if a man really gets out and works for a living it don't seem that he gets very much help from anybody. If the Lord don't want me to sell those grapes, I guess he knows how to make 'em dry up and rot before I get 'em picked. But if he don't, I'm going to pick 'em and sell 'em."

"Albert!" the tears had gone from his mother's voice. "Albert Lane, no man is going to stand in my kitchen and blaspheme against the Lord God Almighty. God is not mocked, Albert, he acts in his own good time to punish the transgressor and reward the faithful. He could wither the grapes and he could wither this entire farm. And he visits the sins of the fathers upon the children. . . . Oh, take care, Albert, that he does not wither our children, too. . . . "

Bliss was suddenly frightened, and he crept away as silently as he could and went down to the orchard to think among the peach trees. He was thirteen now, and hellfire was no longer as real as it had been when he was nine; nevertheless he would find himself looking at his hand or arm from day to day to see if they were beginning to wither under the curse which (he half believed without believing) his father had put upon them all. The morning after the quarrel he got down his rifle and went out in the earliest dawn to shoot a cottontail for supper, and he made a point to circle through the north vineyard to see if the zinfandels had been withered on the vine. He half hoped he would find the grapes destroyed; that would mean that God's anger had turned against the grapes instead of himself and his brothers, and he crept away with a little qualm in his heart when he found them firm and full and purple.

After breakfast they started picking: he and his father and Cal and Tom. Grace usually helped pick, but Mama called her back and set her to washing windows so that the menfolks worked alone.

It seemed strange to be picking grapes without Grace, for picking *was really women's work; the sensation of being only among men, and of men handling the unfamiliar dark fruit, and of being in the unfamiliar north vineyard, gave him a sense of doing something shameful or forbidden, even though his father and brothers were working with him. But it gave him a new sort of kinship, too. For the first time since he had been a baby he began to feel himself a member of the mantribe, one who did his work and took his chances even though those chances included the possibility of being blasted to bits by God's anger.*

The feeling stayed during the two days of picking. And now, seated beside his father on the high seat of the lumber wagon, he wanted to tell his father what he felt, and he could not.

It was very early, and the morning chill was still in the air. He got down and ran beside the wagon to keep warm and then climbed up and took the reins while his father got down and walked and swung his arms to warm himself. But it still seemed strange, when they were both on the seat again, to be sitting so close to this stranger: this man whom he intensely loved and whom he had come not to know at all — this man whom he loved and with whom he was self-conscious and uncomfortable so that he took pains never to be alone with him. He smelled so different from his brothers, too: a sour, aging smell not like the sweetish odor of Cal and of Cal's books and clothes and blankets, not like the bright, almost sparkling smell of Tom and Tom's things. And Bliss, watching his father's hands on the heavy knees beside him, saw that they were gnarled and twisted, mottled and scarred and broken with a lifetime of work; he looked at the heavy shoulders and saw that they were drooped with fatigue even at this hour of the morning, and he saw that there were faint lines of gray in the heavy brown mustache that fell over his father's mouth.

He had never thought about his father this way before: As though he were somebody who could be pitied as well as loved and feared and revered and resented. And he saw, too, that he, Bliss, had not done enough; though he had tried, he had not tried hard enough to lift some of the burden from the shoulders beside him. He felt ashamed: not merely for himself but for his father, too, that he should need a boy's help.

He rode swaying on the high seat, thinking that there was no reason why he should have been brought on this trip. There was no work he could do here; he suddenly realized that his father had brought him along for company and to give him a holiday in the city near the sea, and he was suddenly flustered.

The fog began to clear and the sun came near the horizon, and his father pointed out rabbits hidden in the grass and called his attention to the morning feeding song of the quail. And then, as they neared San

Julian they passed a group of laborers about to begin work on a sewer excavation, and his father stopped talking. After a while he said, not to himself, but to Bliss, as though out of some obscure need for justification — speaking one man to another: "There is just one thing I'm afraid of . . . I don't want to end up doing that . . ." His knotted hand made a little gesture toward the laborers, "digging with a pick and shovel in a ditch . . . working for other men. . . ."

Bliss sat silent, not knowing what to say at this signal of his father's impotence in the face of his need.

"I don't ask very much," he was saying, and Bliss saw that he was talking to himself now (or perhaps even talking to God, though he did not put his hands over his eyes or say, "In Jesus' name, Amen.") "Only that I don't end my days working in the ditch. You know I don't mind working harder than the next man if only I can keep a place of my own and raise up my kids the way they ought to be raised."

Bliss saw that his father did not even know that Bliss was there, and he slipped off the wagon and trotted along behind the tailgate, pretending he was running to keep away the cold, lest his father read his face.

Later when the grapes were unloaded in the cool, sharp-smelling cellar of the Italian family, when his father had put the money — yellow gold pieces and bright, round silver dollars — into the leather pouch he carried as a purse, they unhitched the team on a vacant lot and gave them a feed of hay in the wagon bed while they themselves went down to see the town. Bliss, for the first time since he was a baby, put his hand on his father's sleeve as they walked along the main street with its clanging trolley cars and its rush of people going in and out of stores or offices. They got onto one of the streetcars and rode down to the harbor, where there were a few huge, rusty ships tied up at the docks. They ate their lunch (which Mama had prepared and put into a paper bag) among the sharp, sweetish smells of creosote and the alien exciting odors of fish and coal smoke mingled with the reek of the salt flats in the harbor.

"We'll make a day of it," his father said. "I told Mama that Grace could milk and feed if we were not home by four."

They took an interurban car and rode out to the beach, where Bliss went wading and flew in a captive airplane that went round and round a big pole and made him dizzy and finally made him throw up. Afterward, though, he ate a weinerwurst sandwich and an ice cream cone, and they both went down on the wet sand and found flat, round shells they tried to make skip on the water.

But by four o'clock, when they got back to the wagon, the closeness seemed to dissolve. They rode back, silently, side by side on the high seat, as though each was determined to withdraw, to hold himself aloof, and so to give full, unqualified attention to some problem that only he could solve.

After a while he noticed his father's lips moving, ceaselessly, almost soundlessly, yet with a faint sibilance between a whisper and a murmur. At first he was abashed, thinking his father was praying: sitting there in broad daylight, with eyes straight ahead, staring at the horses' ears. And then the faint rhythm of whispered syllables caught his ears and he realized his father was adding up long columns of figures in his head: long columns of receipts and expenditures, trying vainly to seek a surplus which would balance over and against some unavoidable obligation that must be met — yet could not be met. At months' ends he had heard his parents going over their accounts in just this tone. And now, without paper or pencil, Bliss's father was doing the same thing as though the columns of figures he repeated over and over constituted a sort of endless litany that kept disaster at bay.

Bliss sat on the high seat and watched the dry August hills turn purple, watched the rumps of the tired horses pull, forward and back, forward and back, knew the gentle swaying of the seat beneath him, heard the first croak of a frog in the distance, watched the first soft flutter of a nighthawk in the gathering dusk. . . .

The road turned so that in the west he could see a low, bright star, and he thought of the time when he had prayed for his dream ranch and imagined his prayer flying past the star until it reached God; he remembered the other times when he used to lie and say "Star light, star bright" and make a wish . . . and he smiled a little to himself because he understood now that the way to get things was not by wishing for them or praying for them but by working and planning and skimping and saving for them.

But he understood, too, that you had to have something else; you had to have the special quality of being something special: that something which he, Bliss, had and which the others (even his father, he saw now) did not. You had to work hard like Papa and you also had to be a good manager, which Papa was not, but those things alone were not enough. You had to find out what you were because it was the special thing you were which was going to make it different for you from what it was for Papa and Mama.

He sat on the swaying seat, watching the stars and the rumps of the tired horses and the dark outline of his father against the evening sky, and he knew that he forgave his father because he had failed; he knew that his father had failed — that Descanso was lost, now that the last desperate steps of selling the wine grapes had been taken. But it did not matter; in just a few years Bliss would buy it back. He would go in to F. L. E. Skinner and plunk down the money on the desk and take the papers that went with the ranch and go tell his father, and they'd even hire people to help them and install an inside bathroom and a cesspool. He knew that he had to do this, now that his father had failed, because he was, in a way, a part of his father so that Bliss's doing it would be, really, his father doing it. For just a moment he hated his father because he, Bliss, would have to do it; he would have to prove to himself that his father had not failed. And then he forgave him his failure: he knew that everything would be all right because even the failure would be wiped out in just a little while.

He fell asleep thinking about it. When he woke up, the wagon had stopped in the barnyard and Mama had come out with the lantern; Papa climbed down and Mama threw her arms about him and gave him a big hug, and Bliss knew that she had decided: Even if Papa went to hell and burned forever and ever for selling the grapes for wine, Mama would go with him.

Chapter Twenty-Eight
Legacies

I'm more understanding now of what must have been the failings and motives of our parents at various times in their lives. Father's youth is coming out a bit more, and he is so much like you. I feel very cheerful about this; the family seems all to be in good shape, with an amazing amount of humaneness and good intentions.
— From a letter by Chuck, written from Okinawa, 1952

At age forty-nine, Brick again had a Ranch of sorts: A suburban "ranch," a place where he could raise flowers and tend the yard and worry about the fish pond and watch his terrier, Speck, lie in the sun. I spent summer 1951 with him and Naomi and eight-year-old Pat. His enormous energy was focused on jacking up the creaky old flooring of his house so he could put in a new foundation, and he had me working that summer in the crawl space, digging out the soil with a small shovel and a bucket.

If Brick was trying to teach me the virtues of digging furiously in the earth, he failed. I found the work tedious. What I liked were my shifts in the *Examiner's* city room, for at UCLA I was working my way up the ladder of the college newspaper, the *Daily Bruin*. During the past year I had often worked in the Bruin's composing room, getting the cuffs of my white shirts dirty from printer's ink, as Brick did when he worked as makeup editor. Classes were definitely secondary.

Brick wanted me to stay with him and go to the University of California at Berkeley or to San Francisco State College. I said no. Dickie paid my tuition, which was forty-three dollars a semester, and she pitched in for my books. My meals out, my clothing (what few scraps I felt like buying), my car expenses and my social life were on me. Brick had written a long letter, of which this is just a part:

[Fall 1951]

Dear Lou,

I got a letter from your Mom pointing out that it was costing a lot of money to send you through college and asking that I contribute my share. I guess I was a little surprised; I'd got the very definite impression from you that you were self-supporting.

Anyway, I had to write and tell her that I simply hadn't made adequate provision to help out and that for the present there was simply nothing I could do about it.

Don't think I am unaware of how much UCLA means to you -- or, rather, I suppose, how much UC and State repel you. I know that your associations there are pleasant, happy, memorable. I know, too, how determined a character you are in getting what you want; you never want a great deal, but what you want, you are determined to have. (And, usually, rightly so, since you want only that one thing.)

There are a lot of generalities I would like to discuss:

One is the fact that the most important development about growing up -- or maturing, or growing old -- is the ultimate realization that it is useless -- or foolish -- to hurl your will against the universe as though you could, by sheer willpower, compel it to submit to your will. A man is mature when he learns not to do this. Some people learn it at twenty -- and live happily and successfully the rest of their lives. Some learn it at thirty and some at fifty -- when it's too late to do much about it. It is no good to bang your head against a stone wall -- there are other ways of killing a cat than choking it on hot butter. Sometimes you can knock down a stone wall with your head -- but it is a foolish man who tries, simply because there are better tools for the purpose.

You, I regret to say, follow very closely in your old man's footsteps. It took me most of a lifetime to find out how much strength I had wasted. Not only in trying to do impossible things -- but in trying to do things the hard way because to walk around the wall instead of banging it down with my head would have been an admission that the universe had a right to interfere with my private plans.

Another generality is the question of a parent's responsibility in sending a son through school.

My own position (I tried to reason this out with
myself when I was a senior in high school) is something
like this: "If it is at all possible, a parent should
enable his son to go through college -- not primarily for
the pleasure of the son but to enable him to compete better
in the world. Basically, his responsibility is to enable
the kid to leave college as well equipped as possible -- in
intellect, emotional slant, experience -- to compete.
Beyond that responsibility does not go; what does go beyond
that is the pleasure that a parent should get in giving his
kid something he wants. But that other thing is not a
responsibility."

It seemed to me at the time (and still seems, now)
that either UC or State would equip you as well to confront
the universe as would UCLA. It seemed that the experience
of being on your own would be valuable -- would be
particularly valuable in your case because it would, I
hoped, teach you not to bang your head against a stone wall
when it would be just as easy to go around. In other words,
you'd begin learning in college the things most of the kids
wouldn't begin to learn until they were out.

There is the other matter, of course -- the fact that
I'd like to give you something you want very much. That is
the really unpleasant thing about the whole deal, from my
standpoint. I don't feel that I SHOULD necessarily, but I
wish that I COULD so that I could enable you to have what
you want. That's a matter that comes up for parents from
the time a kid is able to look over a dime store counter.
There's always something -- and at any time from the dime
store age to adulthood there's always the question of what
the parent should buy in the way of presents. I guess
there's no rule of thumb; there are none of these things
which are absolutely impossible if the parent is willing to
make a big enough sacrifice. When Patty wanted a bike, we
bought her a bike; when she wanted a TV set, we said "no."
But I know lots of people in our circumstances who have
bought their kids TV sets. Where is the line between a bike
and a TV set or a college education?

In this case, I think the college education is just
outside the line.

So, what do you think? I'd like some definite ideas,
if you have them. If you come up here, you can make it --
there'll be free rent and utilities and groceries at cost
or less and we can get by. And we'd be standing by to help
out if things get too tough. What do you think?

But of course neither the campus of UC Berkeley nor of San Francisco State boasted the presence of a strikingly beautiful green-eyed blonde
named Vivian Shulman. UCLA's did. I stayed at UCLA.

And so in the summer of 1952 I was living with Brick and Naomi for what would be my last summer as a child — a twenty-year-old child, but in Brick's and my eyes a child nonetheless.

Brick and I would sometimes walk to the bus stop together and then ride through the stench of the mud flats and past the driftwood sculptures of the Bay shore, across the massive vaults of the bridge to San Francisco. During the afternoon and evening I would occasionally see the weariness in his face when the chief copy editor would reject one of his suggestions for a banner headline, and he'd turn back to pen another, for he always scribbled his heads in ink. All the Hearst papers liked to use words like *Red* or *Russ* (for Russians), *mull* and *eye* and *probe* (as verbs). His mind once in a while seemed far away, though he traded quips with the other men on the desk and he often was reading a book.

Parents pass their wisdom to their children in a variety of ways, I discovered. Brick tried to teach me to write headlines; I couldn't get the hang of it right away, but he gave me one rule I've followed ever since in my editing jobs: "Never use 'Man' as one of the words in your head. Tell what kind of a man — cop, teacher, husband or whatever."

That summer, Vivian paid us a visit. My father and Naomi and Patty liked her immediately. In one of those curiosities of left-wing Southern California life in the thirties, Vivian's mother, Mollie Prager, had also been an acquaintance of Rena Vale and was "named" by her in the same affidavit in the same year as Brick, though I don't believe either Brick or Mollie was aware of the fact. Vivian and I, then, were both "red-diaper babies." There were unspoken legacies left for both of us.

When the summer was over I took my savings back to Inglewood and Viv and I chose two wedding rings at a wholesale jewelers'.

With that summer at an end Brick resumed his correspondence with Toni, but it was a mellower Brick, a fifty-year-old, more placid Brick.

September 3, 1952

Dear Toni,

This morning's routine was typical. Awake at seven and lie there wondering if, by some chance, Naomi will get up this morning and fix breakfast (I still being under the childhood illusion that wives are supposed to get breakfast for their husbands); then remembering the agreement that I will get mine and let her get theirs; up at seven thirty, feed the dogs (ours, plus a bunch of pups we're keeping for friends), shower, start my own breakfast; Patty comes out and announces she is eating with me and will I fix hers, too?

So I do and while I'm doing it, Naomi comes out brightly and expectantly so I make her toast, too, and finally finish my breakfast by eight-fifteen and do a few chores like writing this week's checks and adding up to see how much we're going to be overdrawn at the bank. And

turning on the sprinkler on the lawn. Then Naomi leads me
aside and says worriedly she is going to take Patty to the
doctor for a sore throat, and while I know and Patty knows
that Patty doesn't have a sore throat, I know there is no
use in arguing about it, so I say, "Courage, my pet; don't
let her bully you," and brace myself for the storm, which
rocks the house when Patty learns that she can't spend all
morning playing with her friends.

So after she has blown off steam for a while, I go in
and calm her down and her mother starts getting her ready
for the trip -- with shouts and yells and threats flying
back and forth through the house -- until, by nine o'clock
they are nearly ready to go, and I am nearly ready to sit
down at the typewriter, so I march about trying to assist
them and, finally, at nine-fifteen, collapse into the
writing chair and pick up the portable typewriter. And
after five minutes the little girl across the street rings
the bell and inquires: "Patty plaaay?"

In other words, just normal family life; good, clean,
wholesome. Last night: home at seven, loud and enthusiastic
greeting from my two feminine darlings; dinner and do
dishes while Naomi types manuscript.

Decide I'll watch wrestling on TV at nine o'clock.

"Oh, Daddy, can I stay up and watch the lady wrestlers? Can I? Can I, Daddy?"

"No lady wrestlers on tonight."

"Oh, Daddy, can I stay up and watch the men wrestlers
throw each other out of the ring? Can I, Daddy? Can I?"

"Okay, I guess so."

So we spend half an hour moving her TV into the living
room and getting it adjusted. Then, "Daddy, when is the man
going to throw the other man out of the ring?"

"I don't know, darling."

"Daddy, what do the people, the spectators, do when
the wrestler gets thrown out of the ring?"

"They just duck, I guess. Anyway, it's time to go to
bed now."

"Naaahhh!"

Ultimately --

She gets off to bed and Naomi comes and stretches out
on the couch (first inquiring as to whether she will be in
the way and of course you say "no" because in fact she
won't) and puts her knees across your lap and watches the
wrestlers (in whom she is not at all interested) while you
divide your attention between her and the screen, wondering
how it fell to your lot to acquire a woman who, at some age
beyond forty has such lovely knees, both to see and touch,

and how much more beautiful she is at forty-plus than at
thirty: how nicely rounded and nicely smooth and fresh and
you get bored with the wrestlers and discover you're very
tired and go to bed -- and lie there, still wondering about
how it is that some women -- some few women -- can become
lovelier and lovelier as they near fifty -- being conscious
of no other thought and yet with no desire to do anything
about it; when you're awakened it's seven in the morning --
and you wonder how some women can be as lovely in the
morning as at night -- and whether this morning, perhaps,
she will get up and fix breakfast.

Idyllic? I don't want to give that impression. I don't
want to give any impression except that of a life filled to
the brim with trivia. Fighting one's way out of it is like
trying to fight out of -- oh, say, a dish of egg whites which
have been beaten into a warm, sweet froth -- cake frosting.

But this was just one of the good evenings. The bad
evenings are filled the same way. Only with violent
recriminations -- ravings -- accusations. You never know
which you will have. All you can be sure of is that you
will have one or the other.

I understand that Anne is in a really bad way. Sits
alone in her house for months at a time, I'm told, and won't
even open her mail. So it is impossible to write her. And
Bob, her husband, has no savvy -- nothing except devotion,
plus awe at the wonderful way his wonderful wife's mind
works. I wish I could get down there and see her at first
hand. Meanwhile, I guess there is little to do.

Toni was worried that *Nation's Business,* which had published Brick's
story on the Bay Bridge toll collectors, would refuse further articles from
him as a tainted "identified former Communist." Brick suggested then
that he do what many other writers had to do during this blacklist period:
write under a pseudonym.

October 6, 1952

You wrote about Nation's Business and the red scare in
a recent letter. How about reviving Michael Armstrong for
them? I have an idea for a piece called "Psychiatry Learns
From Industry" which might go for them.

October 28, 1952

I have been rewriting the entire high school sequence
in "Five Nor Three" in order to eliminate a shift in point
of view and have done a very good job and have been well
pleased with myself, and suddenly I walk into a paragraph
which is building up to the climax of that entire section
and discover that the climax -- and so the entire thirty-
thousand-word sequence -- is meaningless from the changed
point of view!

November 22, 1952

The next project is an interview with a psychiatrist called "Brotherly Love Is Curing the Insane" -- done in a rather sticky, mushy style. It's the sort of goo that Reader's Digest handles. If I can remember how we used to raise all that tall corn in Kansas, maybe I can start selling this stuff.

Vivian and I announced our wedding plans for the next month.

December 17, 1952

[To George Louis]

Well, well, well -- Congratulations!

I am surprised to find myself filled with approval. For which you can blame Vivi. I would have said you were slightly off if you had predicted I would ever view with other than sour resignation (1) marriage, (2) marriage while you were still too young to know better, (3) marriage in college, (4) marriage before you were self-supporting, (5) marriage.

I can only conclude that it's the girl who makes the difference. I am aware that there are very excellent fishes in the sea; nevertheless, I am inclined to share your unexpressed conviction that you would have to search over many mighty oceans before you find the good fortune to be caught by one quite as nice as Vivi.

I think I will spare you the paternal homilies. I find myself growing less and less paternal as I grow older. I will say, though, somewhat against my will, that I'm not so sure I still hold to the theory that people ought to grow up before they get married; I'm inclined to suspect that the chief purpose of marriage is to enable one to get over the last, most difficult, phase of growing up. Sometimes you make it and sometimes you don't; if you make it, and finally do get grown up, marriage doesn't matter so much. And if you don't, that's life.

As a writer on the *UCLA Daily Bruin,* I was vaguely liberal but couldn't get excited by activist politics. But one day I wrote an editorial that flailed the city of Los Angeles for firing people who had refused to sign a loyalty oath. I felt impelled to do so because the father of a good high school friend, George Smart, had been discharged by L.A.'s municipal Department of Water and Power for refusing to sign just such a statement. (I found out years later that the FBI took due note of that editorial.)

The immediate result was that the conservatives on the campus put me on their suspicious-character list, and one of them soon found my father's name in the 1943 Tenney Committee report and told the others. When I was nominated for a top editorial position by the staff, the student council rejected this newest Los Angeles writer named Garrigues. It was a bona fide controversy of the sort then raging at major universities all over the country at the depth of the McCarthy era; the staff threatened a strike on my behalf. Brick's advice to me, I realize now, had an edge of weariness in its obvious sense of deja vu.

[Winter 1952]

Dear Lou,

Congratulations on the nice fight being waged for you on the Bruin. I expect you will probably lose because it looks as though the cards are stacked against you, but it is a good fight -- win or lose.

One thing I do want to say: I hope you don't take it too seriously, no matter how it comes out. It would be just as bad to win and take it too seriously as to lose and take it too seriously. The most valuable thing in the world -- because it is the rarest -- is perspective. Unfortunately, by the time you are old enough to get perspective, you are too old to realize it! Ah, me!

The editorship is important, in a secondary or tertiary sense. If it seems important in a primary sense right now, that is because it seems important to prove to your doubting self that the world is organized along the lines you insist it must be organized on. And there's no use in trying to prove that; it simply isn't so. (Not because your ideas are specifically wrong; simply because the world insists on being organized in its pattern, not yours.) The important thing right now is the long-term endeavor, your marriage, which begins February 1. That means realistic approach to job, future, etc. etc. The Bruin fight is side play.

No, I replied, Age Twenty confronting Age Fifty: There is something deeply important going on here, even though I can't understand what it is. He answered at once:

December 26, 1952

I hope I didn't give the impression it is unimportant because it is trivial or childish. Quite the contrary.

I imagine the editorship seems important right now because, whether you have been aware of it or not, the contest constitutes a test of your ability to make the world conform to your wishes. We think the world "should" be thus-and-so, but we are not usually frank enough to admit that we are simply trying to impose our picture upon the universe.

So we say it is "right" that ability should be rewarded; it is "right" that the press should be "free" (whatever that means). And it seems important to us that the "right" should prevail.

But you cannot impose your will upon the universe. That is a truth that Herbert Hoover never learned. But you can, by diligent attention to the external world, discover interstices in it through which you can make use of some of its more onerous compulsions so you may, in some cases, even direct its course. That was something that Roosevelt always seemed to know.

The reason I am moved to make this point is that it took me most of a lifetime to learn the answer, even though I knew the question at an early age. I was about seventeen or eighteen when a series of severe disappointments set me asking that question: Is it better to accept the fact that the world is a terrible place and go about trying to make the best of it, or is it better to insist that it can be a very fine place (i.e., that it will react the way I want it to) and go about trying to prove it?

I took the second alternative quite consciously. I would have had a lot more fun (and probably have done a lot more to change the world) had I been smart enough to take the first.

So I pass on this bit of philosophizing for whatever good it may do. The opportunity to philosophize is one of the privileges of parenthood which have not been withdrawn -- not since the time of Polonius.

I don't remember that I paid attention to that advice, but in any event, I didn't have any stomach for waging what would be a quixotic battle. I gave up the fight, there was no strike, and Vivian and I concentrated on each other instead of campus politics.

January 2, 1953

Dear Toni,

The holidays have been unusually hectic for me this year. Patty is just the size to fill the house with small friends; Chuck has been back on a thirty-day leave from Pearl Harbor; George (my younger son) has announced his determination to get married on a total income of something like seventy-five dollars a month (he's still going to school), and I have many other troubles of various sorts.

Besides, Naomi and I seem to have developed a lot of friends; the house has been filled with people for two weeks. Curiously enough, I still feel cheerful; it seems like there's an awful lot of fun left in life.

We were married on the last day of January; we moved into a studio apartment in Venice on Westminster Avenue at the corner of Speedway; it had a pull-down bed that filled the whole room and there were tiny recessed bookcases on either side at the head of the bed. No stall shower; we had a tub.

Venice had changed in thirty years. The big indoor swimming pool and the amusement pier, with its Race Through the Clouds, were gone. Most of the canals had been abandoned or were filled with stagnant water. There were still trams that ran up and down the deserted beach walk, carrying a few elderly Jewish passengers, but most shops on Windward Avenue and on the ocean front were empty. The little grocery store on the corner sold maggot-infested meat. The whole neighborhood was so creepily shabby, so oddly macabre that Orson Welles used it as a set for his *noir* movie, *Touch of Evil.* Dickie paid our thirty-five-dollars-a-month rent, and we normally took the Santa Monica blue bus to the UCLA campus for what would be our last semester there. Pregnancy came very quickly.

March 1, 1953

Generally speaking, I've been feeling quite bitter at the world the last few months. One good thing about the income tax business is that it has kept me busy enough so I don't have time to be bitter. I don't feel bitter about any of the things I used to -- I even forgive my wife for being herself instead of somebody else -- I guess it's just the process of growing up. Just the same, I dread the end of the tax season, when I'll have time to sit around and mope. I guess I need a change.

I know what's the matter with me. I am under an increasing necessity of going back to sort of tie my life together from my present to an extreme old age -- attempting to correlate values of today by examining them through the eyes of a 14-year-old kid, and vice versa. It is not exactly the "Conrad in Search of His Youth" process; I've been through that one.[1]

What I miss most in Naomi is a common background through which it would be possible for us to share, in retrospect, common or similar experiences -- of the remote past. Yes, I would like to travel across the continent and spend an evening talking with you just to see how the world looks to you and me in comparison with the way it looked to us when we were kids.

In March Brick showed up unexpectedly in Los Angeles. He had been subpoenaed to appear on the twenty-seventh of that month in a closed session before Congressman Harold H. Velde of the House Committee on Un-American Activities, which was investigating subversion in the Los Angeles area, and Raphael I. Nixon, a staff member.[2]

Brick was happy enough to get a government-paid trip to L.A. to see his son and new daughter-in-law, though he was not happy he had an

---

1 Probably a reference to Joseph Conrad's short story "Youth," in which an old man remembers the adventurous scenes of his early years.

2 No relation to Richard M. Nixon, who had been a member of the committee until he was elected to the Senate in 1950.

odious ritual to perform: the "naming" whereby he earned absolution. He told us that he had identified only those party members who were dead or who had already been identified by others. This was a tactic many ex-party members took; the alternative, Guild or no Guild, would have been loss of his job. (Four years later, a colleague, Jack Eshelman, was fired from his job as an *Examiner* reporter when he refused to answer questions before the same committee. He was never able to work steadily as a reporter again.)[3]

Mr. NIXON: Now, has there been any time . . . that you had occasion to join the Communist Party?

Mr. GARRIGUES: Yes, I did join the Communist Party.

MR. NIXON: . . . You saw William Z. Foster?

Mr. GARRIGUES: I was assigned to go and interview him, which I did. I was rather impressed by the man's attitude, wrote what I would consider a very favorable, honest interview, was quite proud of the fact that it was probably the first honest interview written of a Communist and published in a Los Angeles newspaper.

Mr. NIXON: For what newspaper was this?

MR. GARRIGUES: That was the *Daily News*. . . . At that time I was — you remember that was the depth of the Depression, and one of my jobs was meeting the people who came to . . . the *News* . . . in search of some kind of help. Many people came there very desperate for food or paying their rent — and during many days twenty or thirty sometimes — and I would question them and sometimes, very frequently, call reports in to the WPA. [The Works Progress Administration, one of the New Deal's anti-Depression agencies.] I would very frequently call friends of mine at the city and county offices and ask them to help this particular family or that particular family.

After this interview with Foster, I began to — or the boys came and called me up, several Commies whom I don't now recall, and they made no particular impression on me.

Mr. NIXON: They were known to you as Communists or so identified themselves?

Mr. GARRIGUES: They identified themselves as Communists.

Mr. NIXON: All Communists, were they?

Mr. GARRIGUES: As well as people of all other left-wing political beliefs. And during the campaign I had contact for the first time with what the people called first just "the movement," which consisted of the Communists, Guild Socialists, Walker Socialists, Utopian Socialists, remnants of the old IWW, as well as merely ordinary socialists and left-wing Democrats, and noted trade unionists began to come in later, I think.

They didn't make too much impression on me, except I became aware

---

3 In 1980, Victor S. Navasky, the influential editor of the Nation, in his book *Naming Names* (Viking Press), labeled people who identified others before the name-gathering committees as simple "informers." His dismissal with this mocking word of the anguished little people summoned to testify was glib and cruel. I leave aside the kind of witness like actors Robert Taylor and Ronald Reagan, and Rena Vale, who seemed to relish the idea of turning in their fellows. Brick didn't.

for the first time that there was a good body of political theory which I was not familiar with.

During those times when I was engaged in political work for Mr. Boddy, the publisher of the *News,* as a reform investigator, I had begun to theorize a great deal about the basis of the American Government, municipal and higher governments, and had at various times started preparation of a book relating to some of my experiences as an investigator, and some of the things which I thought could be done and could not be done and should be done or should not be done in order to save the American system from downfall from internal corruption.

As my experience in that direction became wider I began to have more and more definite ideas, and by 1935 they had begun to crystallize in a book in which I set forth quite completely my conclusions as to the relationships between business and government, the genesis of graft, and that sort of thing.

Mr. NIXON: Now, fixing this again in period of time, you just referred to 1935. What was the commencement of this feeling? 1932, 1929? . . .

Mr. GARRIGUES: My interest in the subject began when I was a kid. The first work I did was [as] a newspaper editor in Venice, California, when Venice had a realty boom in 1922. I didn't have any opportunity to do any more investigation probably until 1930, when I assisted in the prosecution, the detection and prosecution of certain people known as the dam graft ring, which sent a couple of men to the penitentiary, and out of that there came not only the political idea, you might say moral idea, of what should be done, but I was interested to see if it was possible to convict a bribery case solely on circumstantial evidence, and they did that in the first bribe case in American jurisprudence with no evidence other than circumstantial, got a conviction and got it sustained by the Supreme Court.

Mr. NIXON: All right. We will get down to the actual period of your joining. You have previously referred to your interview with William Z. Foster. . . . It was not at that time that you actually joined the Communist Party.

Mr. GARRIGUES: No, that was my first contact with it, as I say. Then increasingly during the rest of the Depression I began to come in contact with this segment of society who called themselves "the movement." . . . I had just finished my first book, and it was accepted and I then began to debate the idea of doing another book on the relationship between labor and government, the potentialities in there. At that time . . . I was employed by a committee working for Harlan Palmer for district attorney, and after that campaign ended I went to San Diego.

I was then employed by the King-Ramsay-Connor *[sic]* Defense Committee, investigated a murder trial in Alameda County a couple months, when I met more and more Communists.

I came back to San Diego and went to work for the *San Diego Sun.* That must have been early in 1937. And at that time I decided that I would make a thorough investigation of the potentialities of the labor movement in the same manner that I had previously done with the graft situation, except to approach it on a different angle.

I went down to the Communist Party offices and book shop, headquarters in San Diego, and told them, this man there, that I wanted to join the party. He handed me a card and I signed it. And a couple of months later or possibly a month . . . I had a call from him that I was to meet a certain man at a certain place. I remember who, but where I don't recall.

Mr. NIXON: From that you recruited yourself actually into the Communist Party.

Mr. GARRIGUES: That is right. . . .

Mr. NIXON: Were there any instructions given to you as to future meetings or activities?

Mr. GARRIGUES: Yes. I was told that I was to — the party would keep in contact with me, but that I was to keep undercover, not to expose myself, and they would have more information for me later. . . .

Mr. NIXON: During that period of time were you given any instructions or indoctrination instructions into the party, or Marxism?

Mr. GARRIGUES: Well, by this time I had begun to read theoretical Marxism, which is what I say most interested me, that aspect of it. There was a person who came to me . . . from time to time and [brought] . . . me pamphlets and books. . . .

Mr. NIXON: You were not throughout the period of time assigned to any particular group or anything, but more in a position of a member at large?

Mr. GARRIGUES: Yes, for a little while; I don't remember how long. As a matter of fact, I know I was regarded with considerable suspicion at first.

Mr. NIXON: Why?

Mr. GARRIGUES: Because I had recruited myself. . . .

Mr. NIXON: And then I think you referred to having left San Diego? When was that?

Mr. GARRIGUES: That was in — must have been probably October of 1937. . . . I came up here; they asked me, that is, the Newspaper Guild. Of course, by this time I was a part-time organizer . . . and they were having trouble with the Guild in Los Angeles, and the Guild officers asked me to come up.

Mr. NIXON: In connection with your work in organizing the Guild, did you receive any instructions or directives from the Communist Party as to what action your work should be directed to?

Mr. GARRIGUES: Not in the sense of instructions or directions, no.

Mr. NIXON: Well, would it be on a basis that because of your knowledge of the purposes and your activities in the party, that your direction or the activities that you used in organizing the Guild were influenced by the Communist Party to the extent that you were a member of the Communist Party as well as an organizer for this particular organization?

Mr. GARRIGUES: Well, I think you can go farther than that. I was in the Communist Party, at least in theory, because I believe in the importance of the labor movement as such. The Guild, according to the theory under which we were working, was a very important aspect of that labor movement, and anything I could do to strengthen the labor movement —

Mr. NIXON: By "the Guild," are you referring to the Communist Party?

Mr. GARRIGUES: I am referring to both, although I mean the labor movement particularly.

Mr. NIXON: Particularly in regard to aiding the Communist Party?

Mr. GARRIGUES: Yes; that is right. . . .

Brick and his inquisitor seemed to be talking at cross purposes, with one not really understanding what the other was getting at. (Not much had changed since 1938, when Hallie Flanagan, the head of the Federal Theater Project under the New Deal, made a reference to the sixteenth century English dramatist Christopher Marlowe, and a committee member demanded to know if Marlowe "was a Communist.")

Mr. NIXON: When did you leave the Communist Party?

Mr. GARRIGUES: In 1939. . . .

Mr. NIXON: Was there any occasion or reason for you to feel all the time that you were in the Communist Party that it was a revolutionary party or was a conspiracy in the sense of advocating the overthrow of this Government, as was stated?

Mr. GARRIGUES: No, not in the sense in which the terms are now being used. That was not my experience with it at all. That was the particular point I studied most carefully. I didn't want to be in such a conspiracy.

Mr. VELDE: Mr. Garrigues, on behalf of the entire Committee on Un-American Activities, I wish to express our thanks for your testimony today.

You may be excused.

(Whereupon the witness was excused and the subcommittee adjourned subject to the recall of the Chair.)

He went back to work writing headlines on the *Examiner's* copy desk with scarcely a ripple left behind him in the fight against international communism.

Chapter Twenty-Nine
Running the Eggfield

The war in Korea was in its third year, but it wasn't like the later war in Vietnam. Though there was some opposition to it on the left, there were no protest marches and the campuses were quiet. One reason: In the Korean War, most college students were excused from the draft, and the battles were fought by men lower down in the economic pecking order. I had a student deferment, but Chuck joined the Navy for four years on Brick's advice, "to keep out of the front lines." He was stationed much of that time on Treasure Island, and he could spend his nonduty hours in San Francisco with his friends.

Almost everybody except Brick and me and people like us were scared of communism; we, though, were scared of the Communist-hunters. The death of Joseph Stalin left the world fearful; Czech aircraft shot down two U.S. jets; American soldiers were covered by radioactive dust less than two miles from nuclear tests in the Nevada desert; a stream of refugees was pouring out of East Berlin; band leader Artie Shaw told an investigating committee he had been a "dupe" of the Communists during the 1930s; the State Department was removing from its overseas libraries books that had been written by authors identified by the McCarthy Committee as Communists or their sympathizers. We all felt like we were running through a field scattered with raw eggs.

And in the midst of it, Brick and Naomi received a letter that they would soon be grandparents.

[To George Louis and
Vivian; June 1953]

Much excitement in the Garrigues household. Patty
running excitedly from neighbor to neighbor, shouting, "I'm
going to be an auntie! I'm going to be an auntie!" and all
the little girls saying enviously: "Gosh!" And Naomi
reacting similarly, in slightly more adult fashion. And
even the old man getting out the ancestral pictures and
looking at photos of his grandfather and saying determinedly, "Well, if I'm going to be a grandfather, I'm at
least going to be a foxy one!"

Kids, I oughta say that news such as yours is always
received with a complete welter of mixed feelings. The
dominant one is: "It couldn't have happened to nicer
people" -- and coming close after that is, "How are they
going to get by?" And then, "Will they ever get more than
one jump ahead of the wolf?" Sort of philosophically, one
looks back over his own life to see if there is anything he
can garner from his own mistakes -- and realizes everybody
has to make his own.

My own old man was a very paternal sort of guy -- not
in the dominant, or domineering, fashion, but the sort of
guy who lived exclusively for his kids. It was very fine of
him -- and damn bad for him, too, because when the kids
grew up, he had nothing left. Consciously, I've always
tried to avoid his particular mistake -- and yet I have
always been under a considerable compulsion to be a great
deal more paternal than I would have liked to be. I hope I
haven't passed any similar compulsion on to you; the nice
thing about you and Viv is that you have so much fun -- and
I hope neither of you lets parental compulsions come
between you and fun.

June 2, 1953

Dear Toni,

I had not realized I'd written so many unsuccessful
articles. I think you might give them all to the trash man.

Haven't heard from Clayton since the new book came
out, though we were expecting them to move up here some
time in May. It got excellent reviews, didn't it?[1]

Do you hear anything more from Anne? I wrote her twice
and got no reply. I'm seriously concerned about her.

Anne Hawkins by this time was living with her husband, Bob Cotton, the horn player, at the Willard Hotel in Klamath Falls, Oregon,
where he was managing the bar and grill. She liked the hotel because
everything was taken care of — the cooking, the cleaning, the responsi-

---

1 John Clayton's second book, *Wait, Son, October Is Near,* published by Macmillan in 1953, was
praised as a "distinguished novel" *(New York Herald Tribune)* and "a book of great truth and great
beauty, as unself-conscious in its splendors as the changing of the seasons" *(Saturday Review).*

bility. She had myasthenia gravis, a disease that causes extreme weakness, but in most cases is not fatal. But she had to give up any book projects, although, as she wrote to Toni, "my mind goes right on 'writing' books even though my hands lag behind."

July 31, 1953

I've really been concentrating on the novel. If you remember "The Deadline" -- the fragment I sent you a couple of years ago, the story deals with a kid growing up in the nineteen-hundreds and obsessed, first, by a strong attachment to his father (partly symbolized by the family farm) and second, by his insistence that two and two should make five or three or anything he wanted it to make, in addition to four.

I think, now, that I see an ending point at about 125,000 words, where the kid, in his twenties, has to make an impossible decision.

It is not a final decision; it is not one which, ultimately, answers his question. But the answer is sufficient to determine the course of his life thereafter. And so, in a sense, is determinative.

Many fine, successful novels have ended at that point -- but many have not been as good as they should have been because they were fragmentary and jejune and somewhat naive. But when we look at these, we find that they were written by young men who could not carry on their story after the early twenties because they had not lived beyond their early twenties.

My script, though, will have the freshness of youth and yet will have been written by an old man who, though he stops at twenty, still knows what comes after.

And what comes after? Another book, through the Depression, the political scene, the pseudo-revolutionary movement -- and then still another book where, in middle age, the problem of "neither five nor three" is ultimately solved.

All of which is a very roundabout way for a would-be writer to tell a busy agent that he proposes to write a trilogy. But there it is.

August 21, 1953

Thanks for a look at the letter from Life. It is encouraging -- and would be a lot more so if I had any ideas other than psychiatric. I remind myself of an underworld character we put a microphone on once. He had quite a crime syndicate: a small bunco department, a blackmail ring and several burglars working for him. The first thing we heard after he got the mike hooked up -- we were sitting in an adjoining apartment where we could watch him come and go -- was when he threw himself down in his chair and said: "God damn! When I think of myself sitting here with a million ideas of larceny and not a thing to steal -- and all the stupid sonsabitches sitting around with a million things to steal and not a single idea of larceny, it makes me sick!"

Not an idea -- it makes me sick!

Meanwhile, I have continued to work on the novel. I am amazed at the progress I seem to be making, in the little time I have at hand. Day after day I solve problems that have held me up for years. It may not be as good as I hope, but it is a hell of a lot better than it was.

The only reason I don't say definitely that it will be done in a month or six weeks is that I'm not sure when the character's problem -- Bliss's problem -- will be solved. Actually, it is never solved until late in life; the question is, whether there is enough climax at the end of his boyhood to provide a sort of temporary ending -- a temporary solution which definitely turns his life-efforts into a given direction -- which would leave the reader satisfied but still wanting more in the future.

September 18, 1953

Just a note to say with delight that I have, at long last, finished "Neither Five Nor Three" (which, on account of Helen MacInnes, is now masquerading under the title of "Many a Glorious Morning." Who else has used that title?)

In one of those curiosities of the times, the little couplet by A. E. Housman had also resonated with another writer, Helen Highet (1907-1985), whose pen name was Helen MacInnes. By the early 1950s she had already published five adventure thrillers, including *Neither Five Nor Three,*[2] whose plot was both a symptom and a cause of the twisted anti-Communist hysteria that swept the country in the McCarthy era. The book describes a New York publishing scene in which Communists have infiltrated all the influential magazines of the day and a group of patriotic writers have banded together to block them. In her topsy-turvy version of the 1950s, she even used the word *blacklist:* but in her world it was the Communists controlling the media who punished non-Communist writers and prevented them from holding jobs and earning their living.

I cannot help but feel that it is god damn good.

I know of a couple of serious technical flaws in construction -- but I do not know how I could do precisely what I set out to do in any other way. And I cannot help but believe that there is enough of both warmth and realism in it to over-ride even these serious flaws, I have improved it tremendously in this last writing; I do not

---

2 Harcourt, Brace and Co., 1951. Three of MacInnes' books were made into movies: *Above Suspicion, Assignment in Brittany* and *The Venetian Affair.*

believe that there is anybody, including Salinger,[3] who has
written as discerningly about adolescents as I have done.

True, I'm prepared for a failure. I've had so damn
many near misses in my life -- in everything. So another
will not surprise me. Yet I cannot help but say: This is
what I wanted to do. And so to be satisfied with it, even
if nobody else is. And, also, I have exactly that sense of
excitement, delight, necessity, drive -- almost to a
psychotic degree -- that I had when I wrote "You're Paying
for It!" Fact is, I've been in an intensely nervous state
for the last month or so: nervous, agitated, almost ready
to take off and fly, or jump off the Bridge. Must be hell
for Naomi. Hell for me, too.

October 10, 1953

The second volume of the trilogy is half written.
Writing is such horrid work that I find myself in a
complete psychological state. Living so intensely with the
adolescent Bliss Lane (who encountered many of the same
problems which the adolescent Brick Garrigues did, even
though he, Bliss, came out much better) -- anyway, living
with that guy for so many months seems to have made an
adolescent out of me with the result that, at least as of
now, I bear no possible resemblance even to the just-past-
adolescent Brick Garrigues you knew a long time ago.

Honestly, it is very strange -- I look at myself in
the mirror (or maybe see some snapshot taken a dozen or so
years ago), and I say to myself: "Who in hell is that old
bastard?" because, honestly, I go about my ordinary life
from day to day, thinking of myself as being about eighteen
-- being very proud of myself that the problems which gave
me so much trouble in those days can now be solved without
difficulty! It is a situation which has disrupted my home
life, brought me and Naomi almost to the point of divorce
and, generally, raised hell.

I have an appointment for next Thursday in Sacramento
with the head of the State Department of Mental Hygiene to
start shaping up an outline on that article on psychopaths
for Life magazine. If I could get back to work on some nice
factual article, it would be a godsend. I've been so god
damn busy playing football for El Jardin Union High School.

As ever,

Brick

The Eggfield

When school opened that fall Bliss went out for football. Coach Clark
handed over an ancient, smelly pair of football pants and a freshly washed
jersey, and he put them on and pulled on his tennis shoes, which he wore

---

3 J. D. Salinger had published *Catcher in the Rye* just two years before.

to school because there wasn't enough money to buy him a pair of regular shoes, and he went down to the hard-baked clay football field to run formations with the squad.

After they'd run a few, Coach Clark put him in at tackle on the second team. He was still only fourteen and he hadn't yet begun to get his growth. He had hardly ever seen a football game — and of course he had never been to Los Angeles where the USC Trojans played — and he had never handled a football, he couldn't pass, and he couldn't run very well and he wasn't heavy enough to open a hole in the line. But he knew something that the others didn't know -- he remembered what the Stinker had said and what Cal had taught him, and Tom, and what he had learned from his fight with Harold.

The coach sent Dean Caldwell through the line on a routine line buck; Dean was the toughest line bucker in the league. Bliss went in at his shoe tops and piled him up. There were two men running interference, and Bliss piled all three up because Dean Caldwell wasn't smart enough to go around when his interference was stopped.

Coach Clark, who was playing with the second team to give the first team better practice, stopped the scrimmage and came around and bawled Caldwell out for getting stopped. Caldwell gave Bliss a dirty look, and when they lined up again said, loud enough for the coach to hear: "You little squirt, I'm going to kick your teeth down your throat." He came through again, and this time Bliss went even lower and managed to get through the interference and snag him by the ankles. His cleats caught Bliss in the cheek and ripped down the side of his face; he held on and Caldwell went down for the loss of a yard this time.

Coach Clark came over, lined up the squad again and said: "I been telling you lunkheads for three years now that the reason a shoestring can throw a two hundred pound man was because it got down lower than he was. I never had a human shoestring to show it with before. Now I swear to Goddlemighty, if you lugs are going to let this scrawny sophomore stop you, I'll jerk every man off the squad . . . "

They lined up again, and the quarter sent Hen Penney through on a criss-cross. Hen ran lower than anybody else; he had sharp, bony knees that came up like pistons so you couldn't tackle him or even block him without getting hit in the ribs. Coach Clark yelled "Give'm the shoestring play, kid!" and Bliss went in low and took the knees in the ribs and stopped him.

By the end of the scrimmage he knew he had it made. They were calling him "Shoestring" Lane, the first time he'd ever had a nickname. When he played ball when the season started he was in on almost every play and stopped most runners cold if the guards didn't take Shoestring out first.

He got up before the student body at rallies and had three-times-three given for him and they even yelled "Speech!" when he stood up to acknowledge the cheers, and some times he postured and said loudly what his listeners wanted to hear.

Of course, he knew he wasn't a regular football hero: not like Whitey Lytell and Hen Penney or Dean Caldwell. He wasn't big enough to open a hole for his own backs to go through nor fast enough to go through the line and smear a play before it got started. He was more of a mascot, maybe. Everybody played better because of him; the backs had to run lower to keep him off their shoestrings, and the linemen had to charge faster to keep him from going under them and spilling the play.

On the day before the Bostonia game they had the football parade downtown and Bliss rode up on the truck, right between Whitey and Hen: they rode down Main Street, where the good respectable people lined up on the west side of the street and grinned and yelled at the kids they knew, and the stewbums and saloon keepers and hookers came out of the saloons on the east side of the street and yelled for the team. Bliss was surprised to hear a lot of people on both sides yelling, "Hey, Shoestring!"

That night was the bonfire and rally, and the next day they beat Bostonia 21 to 6. A week later Bliss got his letter, a red block EJHS, which his mother would sew on his white sweater just as soon as the Lanes got the money to buy the sweater. Everybody cheered and yelled "Speech! Speech!" and Bliss stood grinning at them as though he had a speech to make and finally opened his mouth, and the students all grew quiet. "Thanks," he said, and sat down, which made everybody cheer all the louder.

But afterward, when everybody was getting ready to go home, Coach Clark went over to him and said, "Shoestring, I want to see you out on the playing field Monday after school." Bliss said, "Okay, coach," wondering what was up because the season was over and there wouldn't be any more scrimmage until fall.

On Monday he went to the field and saw Coach on the bench with an egg basket between his feet. Coach stood up and walked behind a tamarack hedge with the basket in his left hand and a football tucked under his right arm, and Bliss followed. He saw that the basket was filled with eggs.

"You think you're pretty Goddlemighty good, doncha?" the coach said.

Bliss didn't say anything. He knew the coach was going to ride him and there wasn't anything he could do but take it.

"You got a letter when you're a sophomore, so now you're the school's baby hero," the coach said. "Going to be a star tackle, huh? Hell, I'll lay you two to one you don't even make the team next year."

Bliss said, "Gee whiz, coach, why not? I made it this year, didn't I? What's the matter with me?"

"You're swell-headed. You're slow. You're light. You ain't got guts. But, most of all, you're swell-headed. Because they let you have a letter."

In spite of himself, Bliss felt his face begin to pucker up.

"Sure," the coach said. "Sure, you look like you got guts because you'll go up against a guy twice your size. You're a pint-sized bully and there's nothing worse than a pint-sized bully. He can go up against a big guy and get hell knocked out of him but who looks worse, huh? The big guy. The little guy always looks better. I don't know where you learned it, but it's a trick that got you a letter but it ain't going to get you any letter next year when you're as big as anybody else on the squad. How you going to get a letter then, huh?"

Bliss said, "Gee whiz, coach; I'm willing to work, ain't I? Didn't I work all season? You want me to do some work now?"

Coach gave a half-smile and tossed Bliss the ball. "Go on up there and we'll see how you run the eggfield."

Bliss went up a ways and when he turned around the coach had scattered a couple dozen eggs over the ground where Bliss would have to run. Coach said, "Come on now, let's see how fast you can move," and Bliss started tearing down the field trying to miss the eggs but Clark rolled another and another in front of him so he had to sidestep and he went down with his shoulder plopping, crunching an egg. They were infertile eggs Clark had got from some hatchery, and they stunk, so Bliss got up feeling silly and smelling worse.

"Fine! Fine!" the coach said. "That's what I mean, see? You're so Goddlemighty clumsy you fall over your own feet when you try to run. What you gonna do when that egg's a tackler with two arms?"

Bliss went back up the field and tried it again, and this time he kept his feet but stepped on one egg when Clark rolled another in front of him. It broke all over his tennis shoes — which were the same shoes he wore to class — but he kept at it for a full hour until Coach called off practice until the next day. He went home and took off his tennis shoes and scrubbed them good and washed his jersey and hung it up to dry.

The next afternoon he went out to the field and ran the eggfield until five o'clock and then went home and washed his shoes again.

After a while he began to think he was pretty good. He learned to shift direction and change pace in order to avoid the eggs the coach rolled out; sometimes he'd go through an entire session without stepping on a single egg, but usually he'd get himself all messed up with the stinking stuff and would have to go home and wash his shoes. Even the coach stopped being sarcastic and smiled more; Bliss got a kick out of it because he and the coach had a secret nobody else was in on and because he knew next year he'd be a full-fledged halfback who would really run a broken field.

He'd been running the eggfield a couple of weeks when, one morning in English class Lucille Hardy got up and moved to another seat.

Lucille was the prettiest girl in school. Or, anyway, that was what

Bliss thought that spring. She had long black curls which came down below her shoulders and she had the nicest complexion — some of the girls said she used powder, but Bliss didn't care; he thought the other girls would look a little better if they used powder, too.

When you were a sophomore you didn't go with girls. You didn't even sit beside them in class. You tried, if you could, to sit behind the one you liked best; then you'd put your feet on her chair and jiggle it. Or you'd direct raucous whispers past her at somebody else and try to make her giggle. Or, if you were very bold you'd tap your fingers rapidly over the arm of your chair, making a series of running taps which didn't mean anything but still meant everything you wanted to say. Lucille was a very popular girl; she was one of the most popular girls in the class but she always giggled at Bliss's whispered jokes or said, "Aw, cut it out!" when he jiggled her chair. He couldn't believe it when she moved away from in front of him.

Next morning when he came into class he moved over behind her new position and sat down, trying to appear as unconcerned as he could. This time she turned around and sniffed — then moved up into the front row where only the four-eyes and teachers' pets would sit.

Bliss realized. He knew now. He really could smell it all over himself, all over the classroom. Nobody knew about the eggfield except him and Coach, and he didn't dare tell anybody and didn't even dare ask them if they could smell it, too. He looked straight ahead until class was out and then ducked out and went home and scrubbed the tennis shoes again; he scrubbed them until they were white as snow and hung them up to dry in the hot sun and then he went back and sniffed at them and could smell the rotten eggs and he went back and washed them again.

He didn't dare ask Mama for a new pair of tennis shoes because he knew they cost ninety cents and he was expected to make them last until spring. And he couldn't tell her he'd ruined them by running through rotten eggs; he was pretty sure he'd get a walloping if Papa knew he'd done that. He let them hang out on the line all night, and in the morning he was pretty sure the smell was all gone. So he put them on and went to school but he was careful to sit by himself on the opposite side of the room from Lucille.

He didn't go out to run the eggfield that afternoon; it was the second day he had missed and next morning the coach caught him in manual training class and started to bawl him out for having missed two days in a row. Bliss didn't know what to say; he could feel his face begin to screw up and his throat get tight because he couldn't tell the coach about the shoes. The coach started to talk about swellheads and how they never got any place in football or anywhere else and all of a sudden he stopped and murmured, "Oh, for Goddlemighty sakes!" and walked outside and left Bliss sitting there.

He sat for a long time, at first because the tears wouldn't stop coming and then because, after they stopped, he could smell the eggs again. He could smell them in the narrow little office and he didn't dare go out and go to class. He didn't even dare go home and start scrubbing them because he knew it was no good and he'd never dare wear them to school or anyplace.

After a while the door banged open, and the coach barged in and slammed a package on the desk and said, "Christ sake, squirt, don't be a damn fool all your life. Put them things on and get back to class."

Bliss untied the package, and there was an almost-new pair of tennis shoes. He tried to say, "Gee, thanks, Coach," but he couldn't because he was ashamed to have the coach know that they were so poor he couldn't have regular shoes to wear to school and football cleats to play football in.

After the last period he went out to run the eggfield in his old shoes, but when the coach showed up he was carrying an old pair of cleats.

"Better learn to use these," he said, as though it were the most natural thing in the world for him to be providing cleats and tennis shoes for his players. "Sneakers is all right for dirt, but we might win the league title again and go into the state playoffs and have to play on turf."

Bliss put them on and ran the eggfield; he kept them cleaned and oiled the way he kept his .22. He and the coach worked all spring, and when fall came he knew he was good. He was shifty and fast and he had guts. He had more than that; he had the ability to make an easy play look hard and a hard play look impossible — and to accomplish both. Maybe it was true what Ray McKay said about him, that he was a grandstand player. But he was more than that; he was showy and he always made it look tough when he got that extra foot of gain — but he got the extra foot. He kept behind his interference, too, and whenever one of the other backs would take out a tackler and let him make a good gain he'd always go over and give his arm a squeeze and say, "Good gain, Red," or whoever it was, so the crowd would give the blocker his share of the credit. And the school loved it and ate it up; the town loved it, too. Everybody loved it except Old Bottoms, the principal. Old Bottoms was strong for the school and strong for the team and strong for Bliss — but he wasn't any stronger for Bliss than he was for some guard or tackle that nobody else ever noticed.

That was the year everybody has just one of — only at the time you don't know there's just one such year. You think the next year will be even better and the next and the next and the next . . . that's the pity of it, or maybe it's better that way.

Chapter Thirty
Fathers and Sons

Bad news from Toni. *Many a Glorious Morning* was rejected by Viking. But she would try elsewhere.

November 22, 1953

Dear Toni,

    I'm afraid that what the Viking people say tends to confirm my worst fears about "Many a Glorious Morning." I have always suspected that it didn't quite make a novel.

    However, I think that it comes close enough to be worth trying some more; if all publishers thought alike there would be only one publishing house. And I think it does come very near (like most of the stuff I do). While you're collecting rejection letters for me, I'll be giving some more objective thought to what can be done about it. I have a lot of specific ideas as to how it can be knit closely into a single piece of work; if all the editors are as nice as Viking in pointing out objections I may be able to select the best of these and, if I finally must, knit it together.

January 27, 1954

    I think it is an excellent idea to submit the script to Houghton Mifflin as a novel in progress, and will send back the application blank and other stuff within a few days.

On January 2, Brick's first grandchild, Lisa Gale Garrigues, was born to Vivian in Santa Monica. Brick and Naomi seized the opportunity to travel south to see the baby and to visit the Claytons.

                                        April 21, 1954

We took Easter Week off and drove down to Laguna Beach
to see the Claytons. I had given them the script of
"Morning" when they were up here, and we spent about four
days arguing the damn thing. They are excellent as editors;
rather, I should say that Martha is amazing as an editorial
amateur and that John is very helpful.

They each agree, independently, that the script as now
written falls apart in the middle and that the only
solution is to make two books out of it. The first book I'm
calling, for working purposes, "Three Jousts With God," and
it's quite a different story from the present one, though
it involves much of the present material up to the time the
ranch is lost. But written from a different angle. The
second begins when Bliss is a sophomore in high school and
ends with his graduation.

It is virtually the same story as at present, but the
first half, at least, has to be done over, completely from
scratch, because Bliss must be made to stand alone, without
reference to the now non-existent Bliss of "Three Jousts."
Very simple, eh what?

Only who's going to bell the goddamn cat?

On May 5, 7 and 13, 1954, Brick was interrogated by special agents
of the FBI's San Francisco office. They filed this report:

He was a member of the CP in San Diego, California,
approximately February to October of 1937 at which time he
was transferred to the CP in Los Angeles, California. He
said he only attended two CP meetings in San Diego and one
in San Francisco; that he never held any CP office; and
never served on any CP committee. He said he moved to San
Francisco in the summer of 1939 and dropped out of the CP
because he was not a "dedicated communist"; that he was
more interested in the study of theoretical Marxism and
felt the party had nothing more to teach him. He said he
believed Marx was correct in predicting the inevitable
communist revolution and that in this country the anti-
communist forces would eventually develop a police state
which might lead to a revolutionary situation.

He also stated that when the House Committee on Un-
American Activities and the FBI questioned him about his
political activities, he told them that the police state
was here. He said the classless society advocated by the CP
was a most desirable thing and worth all the struggle
necessary to attain it.

                                        1430 11th Avenue
                                        San Francisco, Calif.
                                        August 7, 1954

No, I didn't exactly drop dead, but I sometimes feel
it would be much better if I had. I've really been -- am

going -- through a time. Sort of an emotional upset and collapse; the sort of thing they used to call a nervous breakdown.

One result is that I've stopped writing and, I think, given up the idea of ever writing again. No, that isn't quite true. I've decided that I have to decide, permanently, whether I want to give up the idea of writing. And I can neither decide, nor write.

I started back to college during summer session. I took one course in psych, with the idea of concentrating my attention on going into psychology professionally, and one in story writing from a very good guy named Arthur Foff who has written at least one novel and quite a number of stories.[1]

The idea of the story class was simply to get some kind of appraisal of my potentialities -- which I didn't get. But I did get the beginnings of a new approach to the problem of writing a story. Consequently, I think I will have two short stories to offer you within the next six weeks. Both are written but can be considerably improved. Remember "The Deadline," which I sent you some time back: the first section of the novel? eighteen thousand words. Martha and I got it down to eight thousand, and the class showed me how to take out another three thousand and it may be a story. I think it will be.

Oh, yes, one result of all the turmoil is that Naomi has moved out. Don't blame her. "We" moved to town, then she moved out, and now she is going to take over this house and I'm going to get a flat with a friend of mine (male). Don't know how permanent this is. But the address will be as above, until further notice.

The Deadline

Bliss decided to ask God to provide the Lanes with a place of their own; a place with a big house, and orange trees and a windmill and perhaps herds of cattle, if not horses. When night came, he hunched himself up on his knees beneath the covers and prayed:

"Our blessed Heavenly Father, we pray that Thou wilt provide us with a great big ranch for our very own so I can show Forrest Bingham that we are as good as he is. In the name of Thy Blessed Son, Jesus Christ, we do ask it. Amen."

He looked through the screen at the star which glowed in the west, and he imagined his prayer being borne faster than light, past the bright star and past all the other, littler dimmer stars to where it was heard by God, sitting on his vast, inconceivable throne in some vast, inconceivable Heaven. But he could not imagine what would happen after that; he was afraid to imagine what God would look like (the preacher said: "No

---

1 At that time Arthur Foff had published a coming-of-age novel, *Glorious in Another Day* (J. B. Lippincott Co., 1947). He was later to publish *North of Market* (Harcourt, Brace, 1957).

man shall see God and live"), and he could not guess whether the prayer would be listened to with a slow smile and nodding of the head or with a blunt, curt refusal. Sometimes he would imagine God sending an angel to look for a ranch for the Lanes to live on, and sometimes he would imagine Him just waving a wand and whisking a ranch out of thin air.

But as the summer vacation grew nearer and nearer, Bliss found himself adding, in his own thoughts, looking at the star, "And, please, God, do it before my birthday. Do it before the tenth of July, God, please do it before that."

That date, he suddenly realized, had become a deadline; it became a deadline which he had set for God. This was a test — in which it was no longer Bliss Lane who was being tested, but God. He knew that if God did not answer his prayer by the tenth of July, then God did not answer prayers and he had just as well forget about it.

He had a scare one night. His mother took him as usual to services in the Pentecostal Mission and, as usual, he sat for two hours through singing and shouting and exhorting-to-repentance, through the altar call and the weeping of sinners as they made their way to the front. Always these services filled him with terror. And on this night, the preacher leaned across the pulpit and shouted, directly at him: "You can't make a deal with God! You can't buy him off; you can't bargain with Him. You rest in the hollow of his hand . . . "

Bliss could feel his heart creep up in his mouth until it almost choked him; he could feel it stop beating as his flesh crawled while he knew that his secret was out. The preacher knew it, and God knew it; they knew that he had been trying to make a bargain with God — he had been trying to say, "God, give me the ranch before the tenth of July and I'll believe in you. And if you don't, I won't!" And he suspected that this was the Unforgivable Sin, for which he might be helplessly and hopelessly blasted forever and ever.

After that he was careful not to add, even in his thoughts, the deadline he had set. Yet he knew that the deadline was there, and he knew that the probing finger of God would reach down and down, deep into his brain and uncover it; he could feel the thought of God reaching relentlessly, remorselessly into his thoughts and uncovering this thought, this deadline, and knowing that he had committed the Unforgivable Sin. He would feel beneath his shirt, holding his hand on his heart to know when it stopped beating as God whisked him away to Hell.

Or he would lie, rigid with terror, staring at his favorite star, not moving, not blinking, lest in a minute of his inattention the star would begin to melt and run down the sky while the trumpet of doom rang out and the moon turned into blood and the sun rose up and turned into ashes and the damned cried out for the earth and stones to swallow them up and the devil reached out and flicked him off to the black pit, the bottomless pit.

So terror held. It was no good to go to services. Either he had committed the Unforgivable Sin or he had not. If he had, then it would do no good for him to seek salvation. All the angels in Heaven would laugh at him because he was already doomed. And if he had not, then, stubbornly he thought there would be time to seek salvation after the tenth of July.

For, he told himself, either God was dependable or he was not. If he was capricious and undependable, there was no use in attempting to follow Him. You'd never know where you were. You wouldn't know what to count on.

Dad was dependable. When you wanted something, he gave you a straight "yes" or "no" — and no amount of begging could get him to change his mind. His commands were straight and to the point. Mama was less dependable; sometimes she'd promise and then forget. People could forget; but God could not.

And so, each night, Bliss hunched himself in his cot and prayed — and it was no longer merely the dream ranch but God himself who depended on the answer to the dream. And on the deadline.

The last day of school came, and Bliss went home and sat in the yard and found that it was no longer fun to play on his dream ranch. It didn't exist, anymore, even in the secrecy of his own thoughts. Somewhere, perhaps, it existed in God's thought; somewhere God was busy materializing it; or perhaps sending angels out to look for it. But he himself had lost it.

He waited. passive and sluggish, squatting out long days beneath a scrawny pepper tree in the backyard or watching a colony of ants on the edge of a dirt path, or just sitting on the worn step humming a tune until his mother would interrupt: "Hmph. Why don't you go out and play?"

But there was nothing for him to play. He hung suspended between the earth of Greenstone and the heaven of the dream ranch. The one he had put behind him, and the other lay somewhere in the future. It did not do to nag God. For then, some evening He would become angry and suddenly whisk away what He had promised: "Don't bully me, young man," he would thunder, and the ranch, which would be half materialized by that time, would fade back into the air, and the Lanes would settle down to live in Greenstone until Bliss was old enough to get a job in the bank so they could get rich.

It was during this time that Albert Lane began to make the slow decision which had never been in doubt in his own mind and which, indeed, could never have been in doubt in the mind of anyone who knew him except, possibly, his wife.

He brought it up tentatively with Ruth as she was darning Grace's well-worn stockings, in that period when the children were in their beds and the husband and wife were yawning their final yawns in the living room before *blowing out the light. "I don't know how I ever come to move into this town and work for wages. I never did think I'd be working that way when I was past forty years old. A man ought to have some independence by the time he's past forty if he's ever going to have. I don't know why we did it."*

Ruth knew. She did not for a moment doubt that God had struck Mrs. McConnell dead in order that the Lanes, being without a ranch or a ranch job, would be compelled to move to town. Privately, she thought that if she had been God she would have managed to do it without killing Mrs. McConnell or anybody at all, but if God had chosen to do it that way it was, of course, his own responsibility. And since God had gone to such ends to provide them with a place that had a toilet and running water it would be the sheerest ingratitude for the Lanes to give it up and move away back into the country.

But, she knew, too, that this was no time to oppose the hunger that was in her husband's heart. She sighed.

"It's nice here," she said. "It would be nice for the children to grow up in a God-fearing town like this. . . . "

"Ruth!" He was as near being short with her as he ever came to be. "I don't want to work for wages all my life. If a man can't stand on his own feet . . ."

They weren't quarrels. Or disputes. But the strain went on week after week, without conflict and without decision so that each week the rut between the Lanes' rented house and the Union oil yards — the visible rut worn by his bicycle tires in the unpaved road, the invisible but not undetected rut worn in Albert Lane's life — each week the rut grew deeper until Ruth Lane felt cautiously that she had won out.

And then Albert quit his job and went into San Julian, and when he arrived, he sat in the hotel restaurant and wrote out a card saying he would be a little longer, that he was thinking also of going to El Centro to look at some places in the Imperial Valley. He mailed it and asked the hotel clerk where he could find F. L. E. Skinner's office. That afternoon he was gazing at a little white house on the top of a hill, surrounded by orange trees. He heard the meadow larks singing.

Bliss saw his mother's lips tighten before she threw the card on the table and walked into the bedroom, where she shut the door and, Bliss knew without asking, informed the Lord that she would not accept a ranch in the Imperial Valley.

Wednesday was the tenth, and it was Bliss's birthday and the deadline set for God. Papa came home on the morning train. He brought a BB gun for the boy. Mama and Grace ran and threw their arms around him and took off his coat and helped him loosen his tie. Bliss was torn between his desire to practice with his air rifle and his need to hear about the ranch — if there was going to be a ranch. But for a while neither

Mama nor Papa said much, so he went outside and set up a target and stood near the window where he could listen even while he was practicing.

"Did you have a nice trip?" Mama said at last, and Papa said, "A very nice trip; it's a beautiful country down there."

"Nice in Imperial Valley?"

Papa sort of laughed and said, "No, it's HOT in Imperial Valley; I almost baked!" — which was not a lie because it was hot in Imperial Valley when they visited Uncle Ed last summer. And he had *thought of looking at a place in Imperial Valley before he set out on this trip even though he hadn't done so. Instead he had spent the two days riding about the countryside near El Jardin in a rented rig, talking with farmers and learning what he could about farming in that coastal, cooler part of the state. But Bliss, carefully cocking his rifle and aiming it and letting the little BB go ping! at the target, could not know this any more than Mama could know it. He could only know that the conflict had deepened and was coming to a crisis, though he did not know what the crisis might be.*

He could tell that neither of them was anxious to talk until Grace burst out with: "Well, Papa, tell us about it!" Bliss came over and listened against the window.

"Well, to begin with, it's a very nice place called 'Descanso,' and it'd be a good place to buy if the price wasn't so high. There's a big house with running water and maybe we could put in a bathtub and a solar heater later."

Mama shifted in her chair, picked up her knitting.

"It's a big white house on a knoll . . ." and as he went on to describe the place, something of the enthusiasm he was trying to hide crept into his voice so that Grace began to catch it, too.

"Oh, Papa, it sounds just wonderful!"

Albert took from his carpetbag an envelope with a photograph, which Mr. Skinner had given him.

Mama accepted the photograph, her face not saying much, and she handed it to Grace.

Grace said, "Ohh, Papa! It seems almost too good for us. Almost too — high class."

Bliss could wait no longer. He shoved the casement window all the way up and climbed in (which was against the rules) and peered over his sister's shoulder. There was the house, quietly opulent, quietly dominant on its knoll in the exact center of the valley. There were the groves and vineyards; there the fields. And beyond, in the distance, other houses, other ranches. And Bliss knew this was it.

His mother sniffed. "Now, don't you go on like that, Grace Lane," she said. "I guess the Lanes are as good as any people in Greenstone. We're entitled to as good as the best . . ."

"Besides," she added, almost as an afterthought, "That house is not so much. There isn't any inside . . . " she hesitated, as always, over the word, then emphasized it as though picking it up distastefully with tongs, "bathroom." A pause. "And it's probably miles from the nearest town."

She broke off, realizing she had said more than she intended. Her prayers of the afternoon before had been directed not against El Jardin, but against the Imperial Valley. She had eagerly agreed in this conference with the Lord to accept a ranch near El Jardin — or any other ranch near a town — if he would save her from the hot and miserable air of a desert.

"Yes, you're right. It's about three miles from town," Albert responded. "And it is pretty high class for Kansas dry farmers. I'm thinking after all maybe we can handle a place in Imperial a little better . . ."

He pulled out another photograph, a smaller one, supplied by another real estate man he had met on the road. "Of course," he said, "it's not so nice. But we could buy it clear without any mortgage . . ."

"Oh, Albert, everybody has a mortgage. I'm sure we could pay off the mortgage. We'll all work hard." And Ruth busied herself with the knitting.

"Sure we could, Papa," Grace joined in. "It's so grand."

Albert Lane put the picture back in his bag. "If people can't afford the best, they have to make do with what they can," he declared. "We'll talk about it tomorrow."

But that night Ruth Lane's prayers resolutely instructed the Lord in the beauties and conveniences of Descanso, reminding him meanwhile of the faithful service rendered in his behalf by the Lanes.

Albert Lane, on his side of the bed, grinned in the darkness and reflected in a surge of tenderness that it was sometimes possible to get ahead of them if you took thought and pains beforehand.

And Bliss, on his own screen porch, looked at his star and thought about God and the deadline. The deadline had come and gone and they didn't actually have a ranch. True, they had a deal for a ranch and Bliss knew enough now to know that his father had won and that, in a few days or weeks, the ranch would be theirs. But not within the deadline.

Did that mean God had kept his promise? Or that he had not? Or that he had skillfully squeezed through Bliss's fingers, avoiding either denying Bliss's prayers or giving in to them: granting the ranch even though avoiding the deadline?

He lay and watched the star, and suddenly he was no longer watching for it to melt and run down the sky like a big white-hot teardrop. He was no longer afraid that God would be so angry at the world he would burn it up. Never mind what the preacher said; how could God be angry at the people whom he could play with so easily?

Suddenly it was just a star to wish on.

August 29, 1954

Hope's about all I have these days -- and damn little of that. On my latest story, I started to use the byline "Juan Hope" but decided that would be just a trifle too damn corny. So corny somebody must have done it before.[2] But I do feel a little more able to work; about half the time I'm almost constructive and quite excited by both (1) the idea of rewriting "Morning" and (2) the idea of going back to school and becoming a master psychologist. Unfortunately, I can't do both.

November 7, 1954

You were quite right. After a couple of months of school, I have decided I must be a writer, after all. I'd like to get to work on the novel again, and may, if my domestic situation ever settles down.

I'm writing to Anne and seem to have lost her permanent address. Would you forward a letter for me? Thanks.

[To George Louis and
Vivian]
November 21, 1954

Dear Kids,

I'm having a very fine time in a semantics course I'm taking at S.F. State. The prof is a genius and instead of teaching in the usual fashion gives a very fine survey course in philosophy from Plato to now.

I plunged pretty actively into being a college boy for a few weeks, but when midterms came along and I got all A's, I decided the payoff was not enough for a guy of my age, so I dropped the idea of getting the degree.

I had told him in a letter that my new job as a reporter on the *Inglewood Daily News* required me to handle a camera as well as write, a double duty that just wasn't done when he was a young reporter.

I will not deny that the purpose of photography is to evoke emotion. But it does so at a very low level.

Why do I always take off on photography at every opportunity? I really don't feel strongly about it. Maybe it's just the after-effect of the old reporter's curse: May all your children be cameramen. Or maybe it's just that, whenever a cameraman and a reporter go out together on a story, it's the cameraman who gets all the attention from the girl.

I do not hear so very much from br'er Chuck. I think he's due to leave the ship in January and gets out of the Navy in late February. At last reports he planned to loaf and be a bum. Or turn into the prosperous and pushing American businessman. Or both, simultaneously. We will see.

---

2 Wanhope = an obsolete word for what is now recognized as psychotic depression. The word was used by Chaucer.

December 1954

We are sorry that Vivi is going to have to quit her job. But there's no doubt it's plenty tough to be a mother and work, even part time. Tough on the mother and on the baby. I'm always burned up at Noma because she hovers over Patty so much, but I'm obliged to confess that one reason Patty seems to be turning out so well, in health and mental and social adjustment, is because Noma has always been on hand -- whether she was wanted or not.

February 11, 1955

Patty is getting to be a very pretty and cute little girl -- though not nearly as cute as Lisa, I hasten to admit. (Secret: Females are cutest and nicest at about eighteen months. Thereafter, they deteriorate definitely but irregularly for about twenty-five years, after which the deterioration becomes acute. That's the period when they find out they can boss men around without being cute about it.)

[Early 1955]

Chuck is here -- more or less. Confidentially, I think the Navy was a very traumatic experience for him. He is anything but his old self. Seems to have the old morale battered down and beaten up and it makes him pretty aggressive and rigid. He needs to float around for a while. He's planning on going down to see you and your mom, maybe next week.

Anyway, he's a very nice guy and one of the nicest things about him is his very honest admiration for you. He thinks you are an exceedingly able and competent character -- which you probably are. Only, it's kind of rare to see two brothers with that idea about one another. One of the nicer things of life is to have a couple of sons who do have that idea.

On February 9, 1955, John Clayton was taken to Hoag Memorial Hospital in Laguna Beach with a virus infection. He died two days later. He was forty-eight years old.

June 9, 1955

Dear Toni,

The fact is, I've been in a Slough of Despond. Sometimes I crawl out on a little hummock and sit there and sun myself for a few days. Then I fall back in.

I think this is probably a period that most men go through at about this age.

I know that Clayton did in the year before his death and I think -- and Martha thinks -- that it was really his depression that killed him. It is a strange thing how little the people closest to us know what is happening to us --

We spent a week with the Claytons a year ago last Easter at Laguna. I was just headed on my downward spiral and I remember observing John and thinking how strange it was that at least one man should have got so precisely what he wanted out of the world. I could remember eight or nine years before when I first met him and Martha how, if he could have described exactly the most he would want out of life, he would have described his life at Laguna: a beautiful house overlooking the ocean, rented, no responsibilities, Martha to look after him and, of course, the ability to sit down, day after day, and write -- fruitfully, successfully, and with the knowledge that he knew exactly what he was doing. That -- as a way of life -- was the pinnacle of success for John.

And he started downward from that point. I saw him a couple of weeks before his death. He didn't look particularly bad and yet, afterwards, looking back, I could realize he was ready to die simply because he was worn out with the effort of trying to convince himself that life was worth living. Martha (who spent a few days with us about a month ago) says that the night he was taken to the hospital -- for only a slight illness, really -- he told her, in all seriousness, "Marthie, if the next ten years are going to be like the last one, I don't think I want to come back."

What was it? Not just that his stuff wasn't selling, nor that he'd got some bad reviews on "Rainbow,"[3] nor even that he felt he had reached the limits of his talent. I think, rather, just that he had reached the limits of his life.

I think this period tends to be worse for people who, like John and me, tend to be rather strongly father-directed. With John, two things: father-directed and teacher-directed. He never sent a story out except with the same feeling he had in school: that some teacher, somewhere, (editor, or critic or general public) would grade him "A" on it. And when he gradually came to realize that there were no teachers and no grades -- that he was the only one who could grade his work because he was the only one who really knew -- well, despite the sense of freedom he derived, there was also a great sense of loss. Without the "A" from the teacher-figure, the work was meaningless.

I think something of the same sort happened in regard to his personal life. There is a sense of unutterable loneliness when one reaches the realization that he is now

---

3 The reviews were mixed, according to those I have seen. Caroline Tunstall wrote in the *New York Herald Tribune Book Review:* "John Bell Clayton has a gift for description that recaptures the Virginia countryside of his youth, the eager sense of discovery that marked his college days, the garish beauty of a sick man's first vision of San Francisco. It is a pity that the substance of his novel is so hackneyed." Pat Frank in the *Saturday Review:* "John Bell Clayton is a deft and able professional who has proved himself in his *Six Angels at My Back,* and his account of the novelist's attempt to hold himself together with Seconal is vivid and real and frightening. One suspects, however, that he would have done better to keep the novelist out of his book and put the book's problems into another character — say a nice banker or a nice real-estate agent."

the father-figure and that there is nobody to whom he can turn for approval. One goes on for a while, attempting to adjust to the realization. And then one quits.

This is the first time I have ever written anybody about John's death. I realize that I am writing of myself, too.

Martha's visit with us was one of the few pleasant spots I've known in recent months. She stayed, I think, three days and there was something so genuinely tragic about her that even to see her sit with the tears suddenly pouring down her face was almost a beautiful experience. She was a pretty girl before but she has become a beautiful woman. And there is no resignation in her; she feels that Fate has played her a dirty trick and she means to fight it and to hate it. She is a little surprised to find that she has emerged stronger and better equipped for life than she was before. Her emotions are all tangled up between grief and despair and resentment and, even a little, hidden, secret sense of joy and relief that she will no longer have to submerge herself in John and John's problems.

Another thing -- perhaps THE thing -- which makes this period so bad for a writer --

A would-be writer lives, throughout his life, almost wholly in the delusion that life can be grasped through words: the delusion that one can take experience and carve it into words (scenes and incidents and stories) and so give it a solidity, a substantiality, a meaning, which it does not have by itself. There comes a time when he realizes that this cannot be done. What one writes about life is not life: Life is unutterable, what the general semanticists call the Un-speakable. Yet the writer's life has been made up of the search for verbal symbols and when he realizes the impossibility of what he is seeking to do, there is no substitute.

If this realization happens to him (as it occasionally does) when he is twenty-five or thirty or thirty-five, there would be time for adjustment. But when it happens at forty-five or fifty -- when his physical powers are weakening and he feels Old Age breathing down his neck -- there is no place to turn, except to Despair. Before, whatever disaster overtook him, he could say: "I am a writer. I will use this experience, and so make myself the master of it." But now he knows he cannot master it in this way. And he cannot turn back and forget the experience by plunging into the activities -- romantic or alcoholic -- of youth.

So there is little left for him to do except to cling on until his fingers tire. And then let go. That is what John did.

(I understand now about the Faust story. I had always missed the point. The point is that when you, at last, have

Knowledge -- as Faust did -- you need Youth to sustain the unbearable shock of it. Faust was right to sell his soul for it -- not for the "pleasures of the flesh", but for the one analgesic for Knowledge -- Youth. If he had not had Knowledge, he would not have needed Youth.)

This last year has been the first time in many, many years when I have been literally unable to find any comfort whatever at the typewriter.

I think I told you; about a year ago I started back to college, to take some writing courses and find whether I could supply the deficiency in my writing, and some academic courses and see whether I could find some other way to occupy myself if I did give up writing. The outcome has been, on the whole, good. I have in some degree escaped from the ivory tower which was cutting me off, more and more, from people. I have made a few friends on the campus.

And I have learned a little about writing -- though not enough either to do it or to give it up. This last semester I signed up for a course of "directed writing," which means that you take your project (in this case, the novel) and work it over with such help from the instructor as you may need. Foff (the instructor) is intelligent enough not to suppose that he can teach anybody to write, but he also has a very fruitful knack of putting his finger on a weakness -- THE weakness -- in a story in such a way that you can't help but see what has to be done with it. The result is that I am attacking "Morning" from an entirely new angle; I don't know how the project is going to come out yet, but it is interesting to attack it in this way -- if only because it makes me realize how slight a story I really have.

June 20, 1955

I'm quite sure of one thing: I should put "Morning" away, perhaps permanently. I have been working on it, from time to time, and it has been rehashed and rehashed so much that it's all criss-cross. Furthermore, it doesn't, now, demand to be written. And it is basically the book that every writer wants to write, rather than the one which every reader wants to read (so that one puts in what one wants, instead of what should be there).

April 27, 1956

I have been saddened by the deaths of many writing friends in the last year or so. First John and then Bernice, who seemed close though it was so many years ago[4] and then Mike Foster ("The American Dream"; "To Remember at Midnight"), whom I roomed with many years ago, and then Rox Reynolds, who was one of the few remaining authentic traditions in San Francisco.

---

4 Bernice Cosulich died in 1956. She was the author of a historical book entitled simply *Tucson* (Arizona Silhouettes, 1953).

Mike's death, I think, hit me harder than any of the others. I hadn't seen him but once or twice since the Twenties, but we were such confident, swaggering young bucks when we started out and he wrote one beautiful novel at least -- perhaps as beautiful a novel as had ever been written in the U.S. I don't think there is a more beautiful chapter anywhere than the opening chapter of "Midnight."

Foster, who had been known to Brick as "Gully" thirty years earlier, was not only a novelist, but also a screenwriter: He worked on the film script for *Gone With the Wind*. One reviewer wrote of Foster's novels that they were "cynical in tone, beginning and ending with suicides and depicting frustrated individuals throughout."[5]

Somehow, for me, Mike's death closed an era. He had been hanging on for years, coming out of an alcoholic haze occasionally long enough to write a story or two, but he was as dead then as now -- as dead as any of us of the Twenties are dead.

Bernice's death hit me in a different way. It was so long ago that I knew her and it came upon me that I knew her so little -- and there was so much to know. I remember her as a person basically and authentically unhappy: one doomed to frustration and disappointment, and I wonder why I never took the trouble to find out why she was that sort of person. It was as though her suicide began on an afternoon we spent together in an old adobe hut she had away out in the desert: it was as though I should have known THEN that her life was to be simply one step after another toward that ending. And there wasn't anything I could have done; it was her problem, not mine. And yet I didn't even trouble to look --

But there must be something more cheerful to write about than death: Langdon's good fortune that you wrote me of; he is a fine fellow and I look for more from him. Or Martha's. She writes that she has sold the compilation, or whatever it is, of John's stories. That is very good. She deserves something like that.

John Langdon's "good fortune" may have been the acceptance of his story, "The Blue Serge Suit," by the *Paris Review*. It was to win him the third prize in the O. Henry competition in 1957.

Well, this note seems to have grown. It is the first time I have tried to collect myself at the typewriter. I have become so thoroughly convinced of the futility of words. But the fact is that for years and years and years and years I have thought of myself (for some reason) in terms of being a writer and then, almost suddenly, there came the realization that I was nothing of the sort and that, really, it didn't

---

5 *Contemporary Authors,* Vol. 110, Page 189.

matter, because writing was not very important (except to one's agent, to whom it is bread and butter).

Which reminds me of a story which I had better tell you because it is about Rox Reynolds, who was a very bitter humorist and, now that he's dead, somebody will put it in a book about somebody else.

Rox was a copyreader on the Examiner, after he quit conducting a humor column. He was a bitter, neurotic character who stuttered and was always ill at ease. And we had -- have -- a very kind, motherly, or grandmotherly advice-to-the-lovelorn editor named Anita Day Hubbard. Nobody really minded handling her copy because she wrote good sense and wrote it interestingly and well -- but we all pretended we did because it is beneath the dignity of a copyreader to handle women's page copy. So, one night Anita came downstairs with her column and gave it to the news editor who, as routine, gave it to the dealer who, as routine, stuck it on Rox's spike, and Rox, looking up and not realizing Anita was standing behind him, exclaimed indignantly:

"G-g-g-god damn it, Kieldsen; do I have to read this s__t?"

So everybody looked up, past him at Anita, who was standing behind him, and he looked up and started to swallow his words and couldn't swallow anything until Anita walked out and said, with great feminine dignity:

"Well, Rox, I ask only one thing. Just remember that it may be s__t to you, but it's bread and butter to me!"

I would like to be able to send you some bread and butter.

1373 17th Avenue
San Francisco, Calif.
July 28, 1956

This letter is about as far as I have gone toward breaking my writing block -- in a long time. Going back to school seems to have been necessary, but from a writing standpoint it was precisely the wrong thing to do. Seeing my work put up against that of non-talented freshmen and sophomores merely convinces me that my stuff is always completely sophomoric and the idea leaves me helpless.

As an example -- I have recently taken on, as a side issue, the reviewing of jazz records for the paper. I find that it now takes me a week -- that is, two or three hours a day for about four days to write a five-hundred-word review which, formerly, I would have dictated extemporaneously on the telephone to a rewrite man. A peculiarly vicious form of perfectionism. It is fun doing the records, though, and I make a few extra dollars out of it.

We recently moved into this new house (which is in the

very coldest, foggiest, most middle-class, white-stucco
district of San Francisco) and I had to lug over all my old
manuscripts -- a lifetime of sometimes hard, sometimes
desultory work -- and it left me thinking: "What the hell?"

We just came back from our vacation. We spent a few
days in Idyllwild (six thousand feet up on the spur of a
beautiful mountain) with Cornelia and Irving. And a few
days in Prescott, where, evening after evening, I went out
on the mesa and saw miles and miles of beautiful sky. And a
few days in Santa Monica, where I wandered about nostalgi-
cally among the scenes of my youth; the Venice area, which
was lusty and vigorous during the early days of Prohibition
(i.e. the early days of Garrigues) has fallen down and
become something between a slum and a ghost town, and it
was pleasant to wander among ancient apartment houses and
remember the lovely, beautifully curved and colored,
delightfully soft and pleasant-to-the-touch girls who (like
me and the apartment houses) have now fallen into ruin --
and whom I used to know in those once-glamorous slums. I
came back feeling better.

Afterwards we went to Reno and put a few dollars in
the slot machines.

June 14, 1957

I've stopped writing not only fiction and nonfiction
but also letters. I think I lost the friendship of Martha
Clayton, which I prized very much, that way. I always felt
very close to her; in some ways closer even to her than to
John. She is a very lovely person. After the acceptance of
John's posthumous book, she wrote to tell me of it: to her
it was a triumph, not only for John, but for herself and,
also, for herself as John's guiding spirit. But more, I
think, for herself.[6]

It was the first time she had really got her teeth into
anything since John's death, and she just opened up -- in the
way she has -- and was ready to be told that she was now
ready to take hold of life again. And, in my utter self-
preoccupation, I simply ignored her letter for months. I
finally wrote, filled with contrition, but received no reply.
Which was only to be expected.

All my life I have been projecting myself -- an image of
myself -- as a writer. Ultimately I began to doubt, and that
was when I went back to S.F. State to study under Foff and
see what was missing. For that purpose, he was a very good
instructor. I saw two things: first, that I wasn't really
interested enough in people to write about them (you showed
me once, I didn't really like them, and that's why my

---

6 Twenty-one posthumous stories of John Clayton's were published in 1957 by Macmillan as
Strangers Were There. Richard Sullivan wrote of Clayton in the *Chicago Sunday Tribune:* "Many
readers . . . must profoundly mourn his passing. . . . he was a writer of high, bright excellence. He
wrote of what he knew with brilliance, honesty, irony, and critical generosity."

characters turned out badly). And, second, that I didn't
really like writers. Or, rather, that I didn't think the
things they did were important enough to justify all the
attention they gave themselves -- and claimed for themselves
from others.

It is strange to be free of the compulsion to be a
writer. (Not the compulsion to write; I suspect that that is
an affectation.) I am like a reformed drunkard who can
honestly take it or leave it alone, but who hates the stuff
so much that he leaves it strictly alone. (And not because,
as you might think, he is afraid he'd fall off the wagon if
he took one drink.)

Aside from that, my life has been almost perfectly
normal. I see people. I have more friends than ever and they
are, for the most part, interesting friends -- under-
graduates, or graduates, or faculty members at State. I study
philosophy -- which means, in terms of modern philosophy,
that I study words: not as weapons, not as tools, not as the
means of illusion, not as devices upon which to cut one's
throat, but as part of the behavior patterns of human beings.

Also, I dig jazz. I review the jazz records for the
paper and so get an unlimited number of them. And modern jazz
is very serious music: much more serious than is "classical."
When I come home at midnight, everybody is asleep and I am
undisturbed; I fill a glass with bourbon-and-water, a plate
with liverwurst and cheese, and the phonograph (or tape
recorder) with records -- usually the soft, quiet, complicated stuff that is known as "West Coast jazz." (I dig your
noisy New York stuff, too; sometimes it's better than ours.)

Then, in the morning, I drag myself out of bed at eight
to have the decks cleared so I can record, on the tape, what
I want from the morning's chamber music program from our
local FM "good music" station -- which is very, very good.
Handel and Haydn, and Mozart and Brahms: the little-known
stuff you'd never think of buying.

If this sounds like an approach to an ideal existence --
it is not. I only got that way because I came to realize that
-- well, I was in such damn bad shape that I either had to
make peace with the world or not live in it at all.

I wrote you once, I think, that the deaths of John and
of Mike Foster made a terrific impression on me. John used to
say that every man had one book in him that he had to write.
For him, his last book was it -- and I am firmly convinced
that he died simply because, having written it, and having
found that the world, for him, was not transformed thereby,
there was nothing left for him to do.

Writing "that one book" is for many of us the ultimate
act of making peace with the universe -- with one's guilt
feelings, one's childhood repressions and frustrations, the
hidden, inner, secret self that you have to placate. If the

act is complete, adequate -- or, put it this way: some writers (e.g. Maugham) have written it and survived, and others, stronger or weaker, have written it and found that when the act of placation had been completed there was no writing left to do.

I'm sure that was true of John. He did not know it until the book was actually published; he thought he had become a craftsman, a professional, who could turn out book after book, year after year. He had the skill, he had the ability.

It was true of Mike Foster, too. He was a better craftsman, and a stronger character, than John, but when he had done penance to his father by "The American Dream," he had done all he had to do. He used to say that he was driven to alcohol by his first wife, for whom he had to make twenty or thirty thousand dollars a year, whether he had anything to write or not.

But that wasn't true. He was a professional writer; he thought that "To Remember at Midnight" was a better book than the other because it was a more professional book. But, craftsman or not, he had written himself out when he made peace with his father, who was dead; after that, he drank himself to death trying to find something that was not in him.

And me? I always understood that the novel I was working on was a job of psychotherapy. Gradually I came to see that it could not be both therapy and a novel. When Foff let me see how it could be made into a novel, I knew that, no, THAT was not the book I wanted to write. But by this time the therapy (not only the script, but professional) had worked so far that I no longer needed to write my book at all.

But therapy is, literally, like surgery. It does not heal; it cuts things out of you -- and I suspect you are never the same again.

We are all Tom Wolfes.

As ever,

Brick

The Man With Bowed Shoulders

Bliss, to whom the memory of his first day at Descanso was so clear, could in later years never clearly recall the day they moved away. One day they were living on the dream ranch and then suddenly in El Jardin, in a rented house found for them by F. L. E. Skinner. He could even look at the calendar and say, "That was the date we moved away" but still he could not envision it.

Probably the furniture was loaded into a lumber wagon and hauled into town, where he and his brothers helped to move it into the rented house. Probably his mother went down to the butcher shop, only a few blocks away now, and brought veal chops home to fry for supper. Possibly he himself went down to the Rexall store and bought a Coca-Cola or a lemon soda and stood around to see if there were any of the kids he knew in school. If so, he could not remember.

He could not remember whether they had the veal chops for supper or perhaps brown beef stew — or whether Cal and Tom were actually there, nor what his father or mother said: whether Papa was resigned or bitter or despondent, or Mama was sympathetic or secretly elated to get back to town. He could not remember whether he knew what his father was going to do to put food on the table; it was not until some weeks later when he was on his way home from high school and saw his father with a group of laborers spreading oil upon the road and scattering gravel over it that he knew what working for the county really meant.

In those later years Bliss would sometimes drive down from the city and stop his car at the edge of the cliff to look over at the ranch house and the land around it which he had seen for the first time when he was a few weeks past nine.

It was the cliff where Old Prince had cramped the wheels and backed him off the road — horse and buggy and boy and lugboxes of grapes going over the sharp embankment in a welter of dust and terror and anger and hatred — and he, the grown and adult Bliss, would pull up his car at the edge of the cliff and sit for five minutes or maybe ten, looking down at the farmhouse, and he'd think of the panic, the terror, as the wheels cramped and the ground gave way and the buggy tipped and went over.

He would never get out of the car, and he would never visit any of the neighbors with whom he had gone to school, and he would never, above all, drive down the dirt driveway and up the knoll to the ranch house itself. With that small part of himself which always kept its fingerhold upon reality, he knew that what he sought to look down upon was not the scene of his childhood but his childhood itself. And that if he did drive or walk down that path the dream ranch would vanish and leave in its place only forty acres of soil and fertilizer and crops and bank interest and taxes.

Once, after rising in the dark quiet of the night and driving furiously along deserted highways, he reached the little cliffside at dawn and looked at the farmhouse while the first breakfast smoke poured from the chimney; then a heavyset man with bowed shoulders walked down from the house and into the barn and soon led two horses to the watering trough. After a minute Bliss shuddered and covered his eyes because for a sharp moment he had seen himself running down the path to where the man stood and crying with suppressed joy, "Here I am, Dad!" and he knew that if he had done that — and if the bowed man had raised his head from his work and shown the face of a stranger, he, the adult Bliss Lane, would have known then, beyond question, that there was nowhere in the world, anything that had belonged to Bliss Lane the child.

But as long as he did not set foot upon the ranch — after driving down from Los Angeles, from that universe so crowded and jammed without order or symmetry except for the artificial rectangular symmetry of houses set in square blocks on city streets — after driving down from that city he could set his universe to order again.

Once more the earth would achieve symmetry: The center of the sky would be exactly overhead and the horizon would stretch away, equidistant on every side, range after range of hills succeeding each other in concentric circles of which the center was a white farmhouse set on a knoll. And after sitting in the car awhile, just looking down at the ranch, he would press the starter button and drive away, trailing his faint cloud of dust, carrying with him the thing he had known on an August afternoon when he was nine; the thing he had been constantly about to forget, or to doubt, or not to know for all the time he had been away.

Perhaps it was that forgetfulness, that amnesia, which forced him to come back, year after year, and park his car on the embankment and look down upon Descanso and try to recall that August day when he and his family had finally left.

The day they moved away was the day of his second birth; once again he left the womb and this time he stood upon his own feet and saw the sharp knife come to cut the cord and he turned away and would not see it fall. He closed his eyes and heart and refused to remember the sweep of the knife nor feel the sharp pain, so that he could not thereafter recall, and in those later years he would be compelled to come back and sit for a little while on the edge of the cliff and look down in a search for the part of him which was no more.

Chapter Thirty-One
The Answer

All the world's a stage, and all the men and women merely players:
They have their exits and their entrances, and one man in his time plays
many parts, his acts being seven ages:
   At first, the *infant,* mewling and puking in the nurse's arms.
   And then the whining *school-boy,* with his satchel and shining morning face, creeping like snail unwillingly to school.
   And then the *lover,* sighing like furnace, with a woful ballad, made to
his mistress' — eyebrow!
   Then a *soldier,* full of strange oaths, and bearded like the pard, jealous in honor, sudden and quick in quarrel, seeking the bubble reputation,
even in the cannon's mouth.
   And then the *justice,* in fair round belly, with good capon lined, with
eyes severe and beard of formal cut, full of wise saws and "modern"
instances — and so he plays his part. . . .
                                        — *William Shakespeare,* As You Like It.

By the end of the 1950s, the Eisenhower era, that age of the Silent
Generation, we were all settling into our parts, all of us in the midst of
learning new roles. Like Dickie and Brick some three decades before,
Vivian and I were learning ours as young parents of a small child, Lisa,
with another baby on the way. Like Brick before me, I, too, was seeking
my bubble reputation as a reporter in Los Angeles — as a writer with the
Times, in that big new building on the corner of First and Spring Streets,
then presided over by Harry Chandler's son, Norman.

I knew that I was, to use a perambulatory cliché, following in my father's footsteps. Sometimes I would send him copies of my feature stories. Once, as I made my rounds in the City Hall, an oldtimer asked me if I was related to Brick Garrigues. "Yes." "He was a helluva reporter," the old guy said.

Chuck had just got out of the Navy, and Patty was creeping very unwillingly through high school, readying herself for her next role, one in which musicians of various kinds would strum guitars for her and, perhaps, croon about her eyebrow.

And Brick? Had C. H. Garrigues been born into a wealthy family, or grown up in some place other than Imperial or lived in a time when free university education was really free, he might have actually become a justice or a lawyer of some kind, but then he wouldn't have been Brick Garrigues.

No, in these days his role was writing about jazz. It was, mostly, a satisfying one. I think of Brick at this time, like one of those big oak trees in Mount Diablo State Park, fully formed, branches radiating outward, roots set solidly into the soil, but buffeted by the winds that constantly whipped around him.

By this time San Francisco and Los Angeles had become the centers of a new kind of music — West Coast jazz, and in the San Francisco Bay Area young jazz musicians were studying at academic institutions like Mills College in Oakland (under Darius Milhaud) and at San Francisco State College (where artists such as Paul Desmond, Cal Tjader and Pete Rugulo were just starting out). Johnny Mathis had given up setting high-jump records at San Francisco State and was beginning his "Wonderful, Wonderful" recording career. The jazz establishment came to San Francisco as well: Louis Armstrong and His All-Stars at Easy Street, 2215 Powell, for example, and June Christy at Fack's, 960 Bush.

C. H. Garrigues: jazz reviewer for the *San Francisco Examiner*. An acquaintance of musicians with a weekly column and a recognized name. Entrée to clubs and concerts. The ability to write about music and the capacity to do it with authority and style. No publishers or editors to say "Not this time!" It was almost like the 1920s, but with jazz, not opera, as Brick's ticket to an arcane world. Another difference from the Twenties: The young woman whom he occasionally took to hear the music was not a girlfriend but his teen-age daughter.

Years later, Patty wrote:

    Yes, the highlight of my teen life was going with
    Brick to the Blackhawk and other jazz clubs. It was fun; I
    felt like a grown up! I was probably about twelve or
    thirteen, though -- any older and I may not have thought it
    was cool. I remember going to the Monterey Jazz Festival
    with Brick and Naomi one year, and we sat near the front
    row because he had a press pass. It was great. We saw Louis

Armstrong, and he was wonderful. I was entranced with how much he perspired, and I counted the large handkerchiefs he used during his set -- thirteen! Never forgot that! Felt proud to be with Brick!

San Francisco Examiner, March 12, 1961. A NEW JAZZ LABEL VOICES A SHOCKING CALL FOR FREEDOM. By C. H. Garrigues. It is a remarkable fact that jazz, though it has grown up in the veritable shadow of social injustice, has had almost nothing to say about the grave blot on our social structure which has made most jazzmen second-class citizens and, in some section of the Nation, deprived them even of the right to be human beings.

Aside from Billie Holiday's "Strange Fruit," there is virtually nothing in the experience of jazz to make one aware that most jazz musicians are Negroes. Nearly a century after the Emancipation, these people still find themselves treated with contempt in almost any town or hamlet in the land, solely on the basis of their race.

True, in recent years a few jazzmen have become somewhat more daring. One went so far as to honor a new African nation by giving its name — spelled backward — to one of his tunes.[1]

And it is a more or less open secret in the jazz world that all the furor about "soul" is code for "the brotherhood of Negroes for Negroes." And "soul music" is a musical assertion of the validity of the Negro's social, cultural and musical heritage.

It is against this somewhat negative background that Candid Records — a new jazz label but already a major force in the jazz world — has issued "We Insist — Max Roach's Freedom Suite" (Candid 8002).

It is an album which may prove to be the most controversial jazz album ever issued.

It starts rationally enough with "Driva Man," a musical reminder of the days of slavery with Abbey Lincoln singing the bitter lyrics in front of Coleman Hawkins, Walter Benton, Julian Priester, James Schenck and Max Roach. Then "Freedom Day" expresses the joy which was to have come (reminding one at the same time vaguely of Ellington's "Emancipation Proclamation").

A triptych opens not surprisingly with "Prayer." And then, without warning, one is thrown into "Protest." — an experience somewhat comparable to that of strolling on a lovely afternoon through a peaceful Southern wood to come upon a lynching, the victim's feet still kicking gently, his slayers vanished.

Miss Lincoln's performance will be attacked upon both esthetic and social grounds.

It will be said that she does not sing but screams — and that is true.

It will be said that the function of art is, as Aristotle saw it, "by imitation, to purge the soul of pity and terror," not to make you want to run home and hide your pale-faced head in terror and shame.

But two other things must also be said:

---

1 Sonny Rollins first recorded his "Airegin" with Miles Davis on *Bag's Groove* for Fantasy Records in 1954. It was also done in 1956 in the LP *Cookin' With the Miles Davis Quartet* on the Prestige label.

That having heard Miss Lincoln singing on this record, you will never forget it.

And that if even a moderate portion of Americans today feel the outrage Miss Lincoln expresses toward the actions of other Americans, then this Nation had very well look to itself, for it will not be Russia which will destroy it.

Brick was finally thinking of himself as a Successful Writer, though his words were in news pulp, not between hard covers. And for the first time in years, thanks to his sale of freebie records and a newspaper pay scale that just kept rising along with the Eisenhower prosperity, money wasn't so much of a problem. But when he and Naomi sold the family Nash they bought an economical Volkswagen Beetle anyway.

2015 17th Avenue
San Francisco, Calif.
January 24, 1958

Dear Toni,

It was nice to get your letter. I am so non-verbose by this time that when I have written "It was nice to get your letter" I have said practically all there is in my head. My neglect of my friends (so far as letter writing is concerned) is shameful. That's one reason I'm answering this immediately; if I put it away I'll slide off into some wordless never-never land.

Did you ever happen to read Raoul Faure's "Spear in the Sand"?[2] (He was a friend of John's, incidentally). The guy was shipwrecked on this desert island and spent his life there, doing nothing -- less and less each year -- until suddenly he woke up and found he was an old man -- but time was going by so fast he didn't have time to do anything but watch the stars go over and the sun, and the tide come in and go out -- not with any sense of haste but just with the feeling that there was never enough time to get all the impressions that impinged upon him (much less make up words for them). That is the way life goes by.

Sometimes I have thought lately of doing some writing again. It is true that I have come through some sort of crisis, or passed some sort of peak, or reached some sort of solution -- or something. I no longer have any need to write -- either in order to "express myself" or to "be a writer." If I ever go back to it, it will certainly be from a different point of view.

But there is a curious thing -- people who are impressed by writing now bug me no end, as we say in the jazz business. Naomi is an example; she has always been impressed by writing to an unwholesome degree, but in the

---

2 A novel published in 1946 by Harper.

last two or three years she seems to be going avidly through an experience where she literally dwells in a world of words so that every minute her nose is in a book from which she lifts it only long enough to shout "Gad! That's a beautiful phrase" (or "sentence" or "story" or "situation" -- or something) and then plunges back into the next one. And me, I get insulting about it: we become like elderly couples whom you've seen walking down the street, one walking bitterly ahead of the other, tossing back insults -- for no reason.

The expression "It bugs me" is, like all jazz phrases, an interesting one. There is nothing which expresses precisely that feeling except precisely that phrase. And devotion to words bugs me in exactly that way.

Particularly, non-professionals who are impressed by writing bug me. (I consider myself a professional, not that I ever made a living out of it, but that I did make a profession out of it -- I professed to be a writer, if I may be permitted a semi-pun). I have seen reformed alcoholics who felt the same way about drinking that I do about writing. I am not the kind of man who can take it or leave it alone; I seem to have been given the "nausea treatment" for verbal addiction as they give "nausea treatment" for alcoholism.

Aside from detective stories, I have read just two books in the last couple of years: "The Jungle," which seems to have been Nelson Algren's first novel,[3] and something called "The Southpaw," by one Mark Harris, a professor at S.F. State. The fact that I was able to read a story about a baseball player from start to finish impressed me very much. Something must have happened to me. If I ever went back to writing a novel I would be a different person.

This is the first time I've ever let myself become verbal about my non-verbalism since I became non-verbal.

I now have a full page every Sunday (in the tabloid section) for jazz and record reviews; usually I manage to expand it to two or three pages. In a few years, if this keeps up, I will be a well-known jazz expert. That fact, and some observations I've made about other great men (Kenneth Rexroth, Henry Miller, et al), shows me the way to greatness: Just live longer than anybody else, continue to be a "character" and the newer generation, having noticed you around for some time, will assume that you wear the marks of greatness.

---

3 Published in 1959 by Avon Books, *The Jungle* (no connection with Sinclair Lewis's book of the same name) was an abridged version of Algren's first book, *Somebody in Boots*. Harris's *The Southpaw* was published in 1953 by Bobbs-Merrill. The writer Henry Miller, 66, was then living with his beatnik entourage in Monterey County's Big Sur. The poet Kenneth Rexroth was only 52; his best work was still ahead of him.

September 9, 1958

Yes, I was shocked at Martha's death; I think I continue to be more saddened by it as the weeks go by. Somehow, I had tended to forget a little what very good friends she and John had always been and how much they (and in some ways, especially Martha) constituted a big chunk in my life even after they had moved south. In one way, I'm not sorry; I think Martha was a very sad person after John died, but for my own sake -- well, Martha is one of the few people I would have liked to take into old age as a friend.

She died quietly and suddenly of a heart attack -- very much as John went. She had not been happy; during recent months she had been living it up and trying to capture the teen years she had never enjoyed as a child. I shall never forget a week she spent at our place not too long after John died: how she went from tears to hope -- hope of a new, more complete life -- time after time, hour after hour, so that she was alternately tragic and gay. There was something so very tragic about the whole thing that it almost ceases to be pitiful. And yet it seems too sad that there is now nothing left of John except the few books -- and so few of us to remember him, as you, and I, and Martha and one or two others knew him.[4]

As for me, I think I have not been so content in years -- thanks to the after-effects of psychotherapy, the present effects of Miltown and the future effects of advancing old age.[5]

The curious part is that I, virtually, no longer read. I finally read Mailer's "Deer Park"; it left me with a feeling that I could have done as well.[6]

November 8, 1958

This mass of newsprint is some tear sheets from our new tabloid section for which I do the jazz page. This

---

4 Martha's body was found on August 6, 1961 by her sister, Georgia, in the Beverly Hills house that Hoagy Carmichael had bought for them. "She'd drunk quite a bit during dinner, and before going to bed had apparently taken a sleeping pill, from which she'd never awakened," wrote Carmichael's biographer, Richard M. Sudhalter, in *Stardust Melody* (New York: Oxford, 2002). "Though no mention was made at the time, family suspicion lingered that her death had not been accidental." Carmichael himself recalled in his *Sometimes I Wonder* (written with Stephen Longstreet; New York: Farrar, Straus & Giroux, 1965) that after John Clayton's death Martha "gathered up his papers and manuscript and made another book for him, and then one night while still young and healthy she quietly let go."

5 Miltown is a trademark for a meprobamate tablet that was introduced in the mid-1950s for treatment of nervousness or tension. It was succeeded in popularity by tranquilizing drugs with fewer side effects. Poet Robert Lowell also took the drug: "Tamed by Miltown, / we lie on Mother's bed," he wrote in his dark sketch *Man and Wife*.

6 The sexually charged *The Deer Park* (Putnam, 1955), received poor reviews from the critics, but it has since developed a cult following. Some say the book by Norman Mailer (b. 1923) was based on film director Elia Kazan's "naming names" before the House Committee on Un-American Activities.

week I also did the cover article on Kid Ory,[7] so I
thought I would send it along.

Somewhere around here I have your last letter which
I should answer, but I can't find it, and the only thing
I remember is that you said you didn't dig jazz -- which
is all right, because very few people do. This Ory piece
isn't designed to make you dig jazz, only to display the
fact that it is now possible for me to write one thousand
consecutive words without falling on my face. Which is
new, for me, in recent months or years.

People do get hung up (the jazz expression for
addiction) on jazz just as people get hung up on
narcotics, and when this happens (ignoring the few for
whom jazz is merely fashionable), they seem to be hung up
pretty well for life. If they are musicians, they drop
into the lower and lower economic strata (few serious
jazz players make as much as five thousand dollars a
year, even the big names). If they are fans they squander
their patrimony upon records and admission to jazz clubs.
They stop reading, lose interest in politics, forget to
look at paintings -- and even stop quarreling with their
wives, as long as their wives don't object to them
playing the hi fi all night, as I do.

Yet the rest of the world continues to exist almost
without knowledge that jazz even exists. For ninety-nine
percent of the population, jazz consists of some such
George Shearing slop as you see on "Jazz Meets the
Classics" or a Time magazine show featuring Louis
Armstrong.[8]

People say, I don't like jazz, and if you ask them,
Did you ever hear any jazz? they will cite you some
Dixieland (which bears about the same relation to jazz
that "Poet and Peasant Overture" bears to Beethoven's
Sixteenth Quartet). And if you sit them down and play
some Charlie Parker (Bird),[9] they will be convinced that
you have gone utterly mad. (I saw on a men's room wall in
a jazz club the other night: "Bird Is God.")

Jazzmen -- especially horn players -- will tell you:
I keep hearing notes and riffs that I can't play; if I
could only learn to handle my horn the way I should, I
think I could play them. Dorothy Baker used that one in
"Young Man With a Horn";[10] the literary tradition is that
because a jazzman can hear it and can't play it, he takes

---

7 Edward "Kid" Ory, the jazz trombonist, was then seventy-two. He is best known as the
composer of "Muskrat Ramble" in 1926. Though he played in the New Orleans style, he was an
early entertainer at California jazz clubs. He died in 1973.

8 Shearing, the English-born pianist, was then thirty-eight years old. Armstrong, the trum-
peter and gravel-voiced singer, was fifty-eight. He died in 1971.

9 Charles Christopher Parker Jr. (1920-55), a saxophonist, composer and bandleader, was
the father of bebop and considered by many the greatest improviser in jazz history.

10 Dorothy Baker (1907-1968) published her book with Houghton in 1938.

to drink or narcotics and so kills himself. And sometimes
that is true, too. The reason Charlie Parker is the god
of all jazzmen is that he did, actually, find out how to
play the notes he was hearing; he taught all the hornmen
later to do it -- and so most of them have been trying to
play Parker's thoughts ever since. (They took him away to
the asylum in the middle of a recording session, but he
never played any better afterwards.)

Brick suggested that he write an article for Toni to market on
Judy Tristano, who

was married for ten years to Lennie Tristano, one of the
real gods of modern jazz people (like being married to
F.D.R., for rabid New Deal Democrats). She had been a
singer, apparently a very good one as jazz singers go,
and she kept hearing these riffs and knew she couldn't
sing them, so she tried playing them on the sax and
studied with Lennie. Now, it's a very firm conviction
among all jazz people that chicks just can't play jazz
(except piano), and this didn't seem right to Judy. When
she and Lennie broke up, she came west and set about to
become a name jazz player, partly because there just
wasn't any life when you weren't playing your horn, and
partly because it was (and is) intolerable to her to be
unable to play simply because she is a woman.

December 26, 1958

I'm still having a ball writing about jazz. In
another three weeks it will be back to the income tax
job.

Life becomes placid as time goes on. Christmas was
nice; I just disassociated myself from it enough so I
didn't bother to dislike it. Then I enjoyed it.

November 14, 1959

I am in comparatively good spirits. I'm just
finishing five weeks in the hospital, in a cast, in bed
at home and am now learning to walk again: surgery for
the removal of a tumor on my knee; non-malignant but
refused to heal. The experience was good for me; when one
has begun the Great Descent, it is good to have these
little ledges on which to pause and contemplate what's
below.

Not long ago, Patty showed me a special copy of *You're Paying
for It!* It had been bound anew and inscribed on the flyleaf: "To my
lovely Naomi — best friend and dearest critic. Brick Garrigues (20
years after)." I assume it was a twentieth-anniversary present; that
would have been in the fall of 1959. And I was reminded of what
Vivian had said: "This man is fascinating, but insensitive and arrogant"; he gave *her* a copy of *his* book! And yet, I don't know what

passed between Brick and Naomi in the quiet times, the good, times;
I don't know what other gifts he had given her, besides the flowers
picked from his garden. But I do feel that, to Brick, a gift of *You're
Paying for It!,* the only thing of his ever printed between hard covers,
represented a gift of the best part of himself. It is telling, though, how
hard he found to write in it the word *love.*

December 18, 1959

Dear Dickie,

Looking back at a long, long span of years (I am
easily a hundred and two these days) it strikes me that as
many of the imperative compulsions we had -- you had, I
had, everybody had -- were so unnecessary. How smooth life
would have been had I never had the compulsion to "be a
writer"! To "make my mark in the world"! (Do you remember
the story in "Figures of Earth"[11] where Dom Manuel went
about carving statues because his mother had put on him the
obligation "to make a fine figure in the world"?)

The other day I was out at San Francisco State, and
then I saw Deneal Amos, Chuck's old philosopher roommate,
and we greeted each other with much affection and sat down
in the warm sunlight to discuss questions of philosophy,
when a young girl sat down and said, rather shyly: "Deneal,
I've been wanting to ask you -- what is the purpose in
life?"

Well, naturally, Deneal and I were both taken aback by
her confidence: we had asked, and been asked, the question
a thousand times, but never with such perfect confidence --
and we tossed it back and forth between us and finally came
up with -- "There is a biological time for everything --
there is a time when a baby is old enough to walk and a
time when it is old enough to climb stairs and a time when
it is old enough to go courtin' and a time when it is old
enough to stop worrying about raising children and start
thinking about grandchildren -- and a time when it is old
enough to die. And the purpose of life is to fulfill each
stage as it comes, naturally and easily and to do in one's
time what is biologically right to do in that time."

It seemed to me when we had finished that we had found
something which it would have been very good to have found
years ago.

(It was interesting, too, that by the time we had
reached that point there was a whole row of youngsters
sitting on the long, long bench, all friends of Deneal's or
Chuck's, or mine, and not taking part in the discussion,
particularly, but pausing a little while in the afternoon
to say "hello" to Deneal, or to Chuck's old man, because it
was so warm and pleasant where Deneal and I sat.)

---

11 Another book by James Branch Cabell.

Maybe that is a true parable --

Ten or twelve years ago I started writing a long autobiographical novel, as much for psychotherapy as out of literary need; I hoped it would wrap up the important points of my life and, in so doing, justify myself -- and answer the question which the little girl asked Deneal. But it didn't; because I was not able to answer that question -- it was impossible to choose which episodes were important so that, after years and years of work, I laid it aside permanently. It seems strange to realize that, now having the answer, I could write the book. Only, now having the answer, I no longer need to write it.

As we grow older (and in waking up in the morning I wonder how a person can be as old as I and still live), we need to commune only with ourselves and with those who knew us in our youth. Not merely to justify ourselves, but to be reminded of who we really are -- not the fat, wrinkled, tired person who can scarcely walk a block and who knows very little, but that other, quite wonderful person who could do everything and knew everything.

All in all, we are quite well. Pat is so much the image of me, temperamentally, that we quarrel furiously -- and I never win. But she forgives me for losing. Naomi, too, feels the need to draw closer to her own childhood; we too quarrel furiously but we don't really affect each other except as one is affected by the frustration of traffic lights turning red against one.

In a way, this is almost Patty's last Christmas with us; underneath she realizes that she is grown up and is clinging feverishly to this one more season of childhood. So it's a sort of sad and still fruitful season. It is as though it were fulfilling another stage in biological development -- that one called aging.

As ever,

Brick

Part Four
Oak

The problem is how to reconcile
the clarity of adulthood,
which is deadly,
with the naivete of childhood,
which is lifegiving.

Chapter Thirty-Two
Chuck

Man, I'm telling you. I got a load of paradoxes from that cat [Brick]. All this good training in being a *human* — human like poetry and art and love, and the life of the mind (which is a *human* life, not a sidetracking as some of your Rousseau types would have it) and Winnie-the-Pooh and music and talk and conversation, and then he cops out. . . . I mean, what happens when you're raised on Thorstein Veblen and one day you catch the old man washing the Nash? — *From a letter by Chuck, 1962.*

Chuck's role in his early twenties was one he had not prepared for, despite those war games he played just a few years before. He was in a war, but he was far from putting himself in front of the cannon's mouth. As a radarman in a destroyer escort, he served duty in what was then called the Formosa Strait. He took part in nuclear bomb testing in the Pacific (perhaps contracting there an occult dose of radiation that, years later, may have sickened his lymph glands and eventually killed him). He wandered the streets of Taiwan and Japan. He counted the days until finally he could leave the Navy. And after all that he enrolled at San Francisco State to study art.

While I was wearing a gray flannel suit and commuting to my job from suburbia, Chuck, pushing thirty, was in the midst of the beatnik movement in San Francisco. Oh, he was no Lawrence Ferlinghetti or Jack Kerouac. He wrote some poetry and worked on his art projects, but mostly he merely lived in the atmosphere of the time, a time when Art and Music and Writing were fueled not by marijuana or cocaine but by cheap Chianti in basket-covered bottles. San Francisco's North Beach still had some inexpensive digs where Chuck could live with his painterly friends and chat with them in City Lights Books or drink in Vesuvio's with various mysterious and compliant women adorned with lots of beads and heavy black eye makeup.

June 17, 1959

Dear Toni,

If, within a week or so, a tall, scraggly man (probably with uncut hair) calls on you and says he is Chuck, it will be my eldest son. He is on his way to Europe, via scooter and steamship. He's really a brilliant youngster who is taking his last (and almost his first fling) before abandoning Bohemia and settling down to something such as teaching -- it says here.

He is with a couple of friends; they're planning to sell their scooters in N.Y. and use the money to buy new ones in Italy, then tour Europe. Chuck is a bit of a sculptor, as well as a painter and a writer; he may possibly stay in Denmark and do some ceramics work.

Chuck's trip to Europe was partially financed by a gift from Dickie.

July 3, 1959

Dear Dickie,

Ever since Chuck left, I have been trying to find time to let you know how very delighted and happy and thankful he was about the money you sent him. I don't think I've ever seen a man so basically happy about anything as he was about that.

It wasn't entirely the money -- although it took a great load off his mind. It was the fact that somebody really solidly approved of what he was doing; specifically, that YOU did. Enough to actually help out. He didn't say a great deal, but he was a much lighter-hearted youngster after he got the check.

I do feel that in many ways I have been a little too non-leading as far as Chuck was concerned. I have been so anxious to let him find his own way, and so confident that he would, that I haven't either approved or disapproved verbally of the things he has decided to do. I know your warm sympathy gave him a great boost; he suddenly found himself about three times as rich in family as he thought he was.

> 1836 Santiago Street
> San Francisco, Calif.
> July 14, 1959

Dear Toni,

The last two weeks we have been moving -- our biennial jump -- and the day after we got moved, Naomi found she had to go to the hospital for an emergency thyroidectomy. They suspected cancer but everything was found to be all right;

she stood the operation well and will be home soon.

It was her first serious illness; she is one of those persons who lives in constant fear of illness -- particularly cancer -- and rushes to her doctor at the slightest lump or sniffle. But this was the first time she ever actually had to go to the hospital -- and it struck me as strange when I realized that I, who think of myself as being strong as a horse, have been in and out of hospitals much during the last few years. And Naomi not at all. But it was a tremendous relief that things turned out well; I had not realized how much I had let her take the initiative on things until I had to take over a little bit.

First, thanks again for helping Chuck. I suspect that it must have been a visual shock to you if he announced himself with his usual bush of hair and (likely as not) some homemade parka that he had worn from Salt Lake without washing -- plus the usual weather-beaten condition of having ridden a scooter 3,000 miles across the continent. I suppose I should have warned you, but the fact is that he is so utterly indescribable that I could only let you see him.

Some time I would like to sit down with somebody who has no emotional involvement at all with Chuck -- and who has, in their own background, some possibility of understanding his curious social and intellectual ungraces -- plus his graces. I remember that you lived in the Village when the Village WAS the Village. I ask you to believe that San Francisco's North Beach is something like a tremendously exaggerated replica of the Village -- minus, if you will, the talent that did flourish there, but not minus that degree of sincerity which was certainly present then. (And, about talent, who of us in the older generation can say?)

I don't think Chuck is as intelligent a man as I thought he would be, but he is a lad of talent as a sculptor. The faculty of S.F. State is fascinated by him, not merely as a good student but as a challenging educator, a man who shortcuts academic nonsense.

I wonder where the time goes? I seem completely disorganized. It is the sort of disorganization exemplified by the absentminded grandfather who goes about looking for his spectacles which are on his nose. A sort of presenility, I suspect. And in trying to keep things organized -- income tax, jazz records, live jazz, personal correspondence, copy reading, etc. it seems that I can never find my spectacles.

All my life (literally and figuratively) consists in looking for something I have just laid down -- or which I am wearing on the end of my nose!

On September 13, Vivian gave birth to our second child, Michael Charles Garrigues, named after her father and my father.

September 18, 1959

Dear Dickie,

Hi. And congratulations on the new grandchild. I think we have to admit, whatever else we may have goofed in our lifetime, we did very well in the offspring department.

Which brings up the real purpose of this letter. I imagine that you, like I, have received a letter from Chuck announcing that he has had a very fine time and has thirty dollars left -- as a sort of preliminary to a second letter we can expect at any time saying, "How am I going to get home?" So I thought maybe we should confer on what each of us intends to do.

I can go down to the bank or credit union and borrow any amount within reason. I confess I don't like to. Do you want to go fifty-fifty on it?

Pat is fine, a very popular success in school and a mess in her studies. But we've stopped bugging her about that; she doesn't want to go to college; she wants to work in an office and then get married, and I think she'll be a success at both.

I still have the jazz page and now have added a weekly hour on the radio, as a sort of promotion venture.

November 13, 1959

Dear Dickie,

It seems strange to think of Chuck kicking around Europe virtually living on his wits, but my own chief thoughts are how he will keep warm now that the weather has turned cool. Plus my own determination, not to send him any money, which I don't have, on the theory that he shouldn't expect either his parents or his casual friends to pay for a European junket.

So, the disapproving parent comes to the surface after all. And with it the feeling that I failed him in some very important way. Because he doesn't actually have the confidence to tackle life. Every detour he makes is an effort to postpone getting his degree. I could psychoanalyze him, but to no good purpose. I only hope he gets back from Europe without freezing to death.

November 14, 1959

Dear Toni,

Thanks for the word on Chuck. I have not heard from him directly for some time; I had not answered his last letter, and I think he thinks I disapprove somewhat of his European junket. Which is true. Curiously, there keeps coming back to me some paragraphs from the last chapter of "The Silver Stallion,"[1] where Dom Manuel gets vague word of

---

[1] By James Branch Cabell. First published in 1926 by McBride & Co.

his once-favorite son grown to manhood and whoring about
the Shores of Barbary, and he wonders half petulantly who
this stranger can be --

[Fall 1959]

[To Dickie From Chuck]
Dear Mom:

Boy, have I got news! I told you I would have some
surprises for you, and here they are!

First, I'm settled in Belgium for the winter. No
more moving. Second, by a near-miracle, I have actually
got everything I came to Europe for. I am enrolled in
ceramics school and I am taking French lessons.

(The trip into Belgium was exciting. We smuggled a
Yugoslav student whose passport was no good across the
border in the middle of the night.)

When the Belgian guy I was traveling with discovered
I had only four dollars left, he took me in immediately.
He feeds me, buys me postage stamps, and this is his
typewriter I am using. I am rather shy about asking for
food, and sometimes I don't eat until five in the
afternoon.

Since I left Denmark I have felt great! I wasn't
doing so well there. Pretty discouraged. But now
everything seems wonderful. Learning French is wonderful,
and it also helps fulfill one of the requirements for the
Ph.D., if I ever decide to try for one.

Any day now I expect your letter responding to what
I wrote you last week. I must confess I feel a bit of
trepidation; I imagine getting a letter from you saying
that there isn't enough money. I hope not, but I am
already preparing myself.

Chuck needn't have worried; the letter he received included a big
money order: Dickie's Sense to Chuck's Sensibility.

December 18, 1959

Dear Dickie,

I was really pleased by Chuck's last two letters. He
seemed at the time to have the situation well under
control and be ready to knuckle down and get something
started when he gets home.

So far as the trip to Europe is concerned, I think
it was a tremendous thing that you helped him. In a
sense, I think I should have done so, too -- for the fact
is, though it may not seem so, that Chuck has been on his
own, depending on nobody for help, since he was out of
high school. When he came up here to go to school I got
him a job at the Examiner and told him: "Son, you can
make it through State on your own. Of course, if it gets

too tough -- " But he was very determined not to lean on
me for a thing during that period and, in fact, saved up
enough money to give his friend Casey Van Duren a trip to
Mexico when he, Chuck, went into the service.

I felt at the time that I was doing him a service by
teaching him young the problems of poverty. But he,
apparently, thought the lesson was that poverty was
something to be courted. (I wrote him recently, "My boy,
when I introduced you to poverty I hoped you would make
her your friend, not your mistress." Which was about as
close as I could come to being the heavy Victorian
father.)

I do think that if any failure was involved with
Chuck, it is my own. I never realized until the last year
or so how heavy a feeling of responsibility rested upon
him during his childhood. When you and I split up, I made
the mistake of telling him, "You're the man of the house
now; you must take care of your mother."

It never dawned upon me how seriously a young boy
might take something like that, yet now I can see that up
until the time he went into the Navy he always felt that
this heavy responsibility hung over him -- not especially
in regard to you, maybe, but to his whole view of life.
After he got out of the Navy he asked me one day -- and
insisted upon having an answer, "How long do you think it
will be before you retire," and it finally occurred to me
that he was thinking (very worriedly) how many years he
would have before he would have to support me -- how many
years of freedom he might still have.

I do think his unwillingness to accept responsibility now is just one of the results of that situation.
Plus several other things. One of these is the fact that
I refused to teach him -- oh, I think the technical term
is that I refused to institutionalize his social
responses.

On the one hand, he saw me living a very normal
middle-class existence (and sometimes revolting against
it) and at the same time I was teaching him that middle-
class social values were not necessarily the ones HE
should accept (certainly not the ones I would accept) --
so that when he grew up he had no hard core of unconsciously accepted beliefs to fall back on.

The one thing I did teach was "a life of reason" --
because I supposed that life could be lived with reason.

When he got in the Navy, though, he found he
couldn't swab a deck with reason -- and this was a
terrible shock to him. It was a complete overturning of
his beliefs: his unquestioned assumptions. He tried to
learn to do things with his hands, because this was
action, not reason; and he did learn these things, too.

What he has been trying to do the last few years is
to find his own institutionalized responses -- in the
institutions which belong to his own generation and
century, not to ours.

(Of course, in this regard, he would have been much
better off had I been able to point determinedly at
something in his life and shout This is wrong! But I have
not been able to do that, and had I been able to, he
would at least have had something to rebel against.)

Everybody knows him at State College, everybody
loves him, everybody respects him highly. So as long as
he can remain an undergraduate he is safe. But he is
afraid to be put in front of a class, as the professor,
as the head of a family, as the father. So he dodges
graduation, financial security, marriage.

I know that both of us tried determinedly when we
split up to avoid a feeling of bipolarity (as between you
and me) in either of the boys -- to keep them from
feeling that they were being tugged between us. But I
didn't realize how exceedingly sensitive a kid --
especially Chuck -- actually is. Where there's a vacuum
-- a lack of explanation, or reason, for something --
they must out of necessity fill it up with explanation,
or feelings, of their own.

I know now (I didn't before) that Chuck thought he
must emulate me -- and in so thinking, I suppose he must
have thought that he had to "put you down" (as the kids
say now) in some way. I'm not sure exactly how or why --
beyond the fact that boys do tend to emulate their
fathers, and to adopt what they suppose are their
fathers' attitudes.

But now! Now, "Dear Old Mommy" suddenly emerges as
the really important person in his life -- not just
because she gave him money for Europe, but because she
COULD. And not merely because she could but because she
WOULD. Suddenly there were connections re-established
which had been, unhappily, cut years before. Suddenly it
appears that his "Dear Old Mommy" was the one who had
something on the ball all the time. And, curiously, that
fact freed him from the necessity to depend, emotionally,
upon his father.

From now on, I'm inclined to believe, he's going to
be capable of being his own man -- though it may not be
exactly the man you or I would choose.

And, after all, isn't that what we mean by "maturity"?

Chuck returned to San Francisco and enrolled again in school. In
Los Angeles, Vivian and I put a thousand borrowed dollars of Dickie's

money down on a three-bedroom tract house in the Northeast San Fernando Valley suburb of Tujunga.

August 23, 1960

[To George Louis and Vivian]
Dear kids:

Well, I can't tell you how delighted I was to hear that you made the big jump to become householders. Somehow there is something very substantial about getting your names on a deed, no matter how many years you have to keep paying rent on it until it is all yours.

We are all well here, except for my usual aches and pains. Naomi gets younger with each passing year, and Pat has now emerged as the butterfly girl of the Sunset District. She's quite a gal; bosses the old folks around as you, my boy, never did get a chance to do! She is tied down the rest of the summer with a job at the Emporium in Stonestown.

You know, your buying a house makes me feel old. Seems like things have really been happening in the last thirty years. Oh, well.

A letter to Grandma Emily would be much, much appreciated. She is practically blind, waiting for her cataract operation and feels very much cut off from the world.

September 28, 1960

Dear Toni,

Chuck is fine; he is busy being himself (there was almost a pun there about "busy bee-ing"). He seems to have made some major adjustments in Europe; I've seen him very little since he came back. He is taking his master's; he got his bachelor's with honors (as his girlfriend said: they honored him because it took him nine years to get through).

In addition he is running a sort of bi-racial boarding house down in the slums; it seems to be an establishment where the owner and inmates assert the value of the individual in some fashion or another. I approve of it quite heartily, especially in connection with his college work. The one to balance the other. But I see him only when we call him up and tell him we have some old furniture or clothing to discard. Come to think of it, maybe he's a sort of private Salvation Army.

(I know that what Chuck and his friends are doing and looking for is not the mere romantic bohemianism of our youth -- any more than it is the necessity to "get ahead," which was also so compulsive to our generation.)

November 26, 1960

Dear Corinne and Irving,

I received a call from Chuck. He said he had given up school, had abandoned definitely the idea of teaching and had firmly made up his mind to spend his life running his beatnik boarding house. He would live, as he phrased it, an interstitial existence -- rejecting all the necessities of a modern Madison Avenue way of life dedicated to the getting of things -- not by fighting against the pressures of Madison Avenue but by simply dropping through the crevices and emerging whole on the other side.[2]

My first reaction was one of shock. How could a son of mine so forget the compulsions of bourgeois existence as to not find somewhere a means of pursuing endlessly the succession of dollars which would give him status and a place in the world? No, he should get that master's, earn that doctorate first; he should succeed, and only then should he permit himself to quit the race.

But then I immediately realized how wrong I was; he, at age thirty, had broken just in time the bond which I had not been able to break until age fifty-eight. Simply by denying the validity of the bond he had achieved his freedom from it.

Yesterday he and his gal friend invited us to turkey dinner. We found a house built in the 1880s, very much falling apart, inhabited by some fifteen or twenty artists, sculptors, poets, philosophers, etc., people all very much involved in the joy of living and doing what they wanted to do.

Each is responsible for his own living space: he can make it as charming or leave it as dull as his taste and energy suggest. All join to some slight degree in the work; some cook, some just carry in the wood and start the fire. They pay some miserably small sum a month for room and board -- I hesitate to tell you how small -- and it is Chuck's job to keep the place going on that small sum.

He is the entrepreneur; it is his place and if anybody is to be tossed out, he must do it. And, in addition, being a skilled critic of the arts, he provides encouragement and moral support for each of the inhabitants, each on his own level.

It is quite impossible to describe the feeling of ease, content and "constructiveness" which pervades the place. For example, Tim (the poet) has discovered that the fireplace was made of metal, painted over -- and he has undertaken the task of restoring it to its primal state --

---

2 The "interstitial existence" practiced by Chuck and his friends included raiding the trash bin behind the Safeway for discarded vegetables.

metal with the patina of age on it. It is going to be beautiful. And so with the furniture monstrosities they have picked up.

They have acquired a whole basement full of other old furniture and plan to rent another big house and start a second establishment. But not as a chain; Chuck will have nothing to do with the second place after he has turned over the furniture. The two houses will have no other link than fraternal. And so, as Chuck says, "We expect the centers of interstitial existence to proliferate!"

I could not help but be reminded of how the early monks fled from "things" into the Thebaid.[3] For this house of Chuck's is essentially a religious endeavor. Only, I believe I would prefer the desert, even though it meant that I would become Garrigues Stylites.[4]

Also I could not help but reflect upon the curious difference between Chuck and George. Or, more properly, upon how neatly I had been divided, straight down the middle, between the two boys. There was half of me which wanted to do -- under a kind of compulsion -- precisely what Chuck is doing (though I would never have had the sense to do it as well as he) and another half which was just as badly hung up on the exurbanite existence which George has chosen. And these two halves have been neatly apportioned, one to each child, so that each seems to be univalent, complete.

(What, I wonder, is left for Patty? My restlessness and unwillingness to accept reality, I'm afraid.)

December 6, 1960

I must hasten to deny that I was putting George down. If it seemed so, I think it was because I was over-correcting a little tendency to put Chuck down for his choice. I take great pleasure in the fact that each of the boys is exactly as he is; my own division is so completely in the middle that I still cannot decide which I admire the most, particularly because I think George is much more whole-hearted in his choice (which is, after all, an easier choice in our society) than is Chuck.

It isn't the eight hours a day which keeps one's nose grindstoned off; it is the failure of capacities within one's own self.

As ever,

Brick

---

3 The Thebaid was a region of Egypt (from *Thebes*), where early Christians established the first communally based monasteries.

4 A reference to early Christian ascetics, or *stylites*, who spent their lives atop a column, open to the elements. Alfred Lord Tennyson wrote an extended verse, "St. Simeon Stylites," about one who lived in the Syrian desert.

Chapter Thirty-Three
I Do Not Know the Truth. Not Yet

"The dreams of the parents can become the nightmares of the children," Brick's brother-in-law, Irving Sussman, once told him.

Irving painted in oils, startling his viewers with broad swatches of color in dream-like scenes that summoned up mysteries of life, death and faith. I have one of his canvases on my wall, captioned

> *Your old men shall dream dreams;*
> *your young men shall see visions.*

In the center, Brick as a young man, in a farmer's coveralls, his arm around Naomi, who is seated demurely on his lap.

Rising like sylphs: graceful figures of the same Brick, with a hoe, and Naomi, with a bouquet of flowers, almost like a bride, separate, but each looking slightly back at the other. Two-year-old Patricia jumping eagerly, with her arms outspread as if to catch the attention of her unobservant parents.

Elsewhere, Brick hugging a viola to his chest (although I had never seen him pick up any musical instrument), his eyes closed in devotion, and a wind-up Victrola with a blossom-shaped horn bearing the legend
> *Music.*

Another figure of Brick, this time as a boy clutching an enormous book and kneeling before a closed orange door; nearby a giant hand writing on a chalkboard

> *There was a door to which I found the . . . .*

In the background, two boys, perhaps Brick's sons, disporting in the branches of a leafless tree.

In another panel a giant oak looming before a blue sky. Brick as a young man with the book, the orange door behind him as though he had just gone through it, the legend on the volume almost obliterated by the bottom leg of a floating isosceles triangle:

$$2 + 2 = 5.$$

Looming behind Brick, as though permanently attached to his body, a mysterious blue shadow, the black shape of its head and figure very much like Brick's.

The only real gaiety in the canvas being that of the children.

Brick and Naomi visited the Sussmans often, and one of them, or most likely both, because their minds worked that way, suggested that Brick send some jazz records so they could find out for themselves just what this *jazz* was he was talking and writing about. This first letter of introduction to jazz ran almost six single-spaced pages.

                              May 27, 1960

Dear Corinne and Irving,

    I've puzzled a lot about how to introduce jazz to people
who know very little about it. There exists as much
difference between jazz and European music as between Chaucer
or Spenser and modern English. If you were to lecture on
modern English to Chaucer, you might give him a look at the
strange modern spelling of the English language. Then you
might call attention to technical devices of modern English
poetry: internal rhyme, klangtint,[1] cadence, such formal
sorts of organization as (for example) the sonnet or the
villanelle. Perhaps even at the first lesson he might feel
the wide variation between "Horatius at the Bridge" and
"Morning Song of Senlin" -- but I think it might be difficult
for him to compare opening sentences of "Lord Jim" with any
given paragraph of "Marius the Epicurean."[2]

Brick sent the Sussmans records like Leonard Bernstein's *What Is Jazz?* and Stan Getz's *Blues for Mary Jane,* and works by Shelly Manne, Shorty Rogers, Dave Brubeck and Chet Baker. Then Dizzy Gillespie, Gerry Mulligan, J. J. Johnson and Kai Winding.

    Finally, there is the "hard bop" or "modern" jazz
which I (and most jazz musicians) consider to be the

---

1 Apparently from the German *Klang,* the general character or style of spoken or written expression, and *Tint,* color. H. L. Mencken used the word in writing about Darrow's oratory in the Scopes trial, but I have seen it in no dictionaries.

2 "Horatius: A Lay Made About the Year of the City CCCLX" was written by Thomas Babington Macauley (1800-1859). "Morning Song of Senlin" was by Conrad Aiken (1889-1973). *Lord Jim* was a novel by Joseph Conrad (1857-1924), published in 1900, and Walter Pater's *Marius the Epicurean: His Sensations and Ideas* was published in 1885.

essence of today's serious jazz. We feel about it like the
honest Methodist farmer does when, coming out of church, he
declares to his wife, "That Reverend Smithers sure preaches
a hell of a sermon!" The essence of this jazz is that the
Rev. Hornplayer gets up there and blows a hell of a sermon,
using all the imagination, all the technique, the virtuos-
ity of which he is capable -- and yet, ultimately, being
concerned only to express what is in his own soul.

Jazz, I emphasize, is something one LISTENS to and
does not use as a background for conversation. But I think
that jazz on this level is also something that one listens
at, finding each time some new hidden phrase, allusion,
assertion -- or something.

The musicians are speaking of all jazz now in terms of
"soul," by which they seem to mean a sort of proud, self-
confident assertion of their (Negro) cultural background --
and this seems to take us into a place where the essential
contradiction of jazz is lacking. But I am not sure how far
that will go.

Also, jazz fans love to compare. I suggest that you
compare Baker's trumpet and Gillespie's; you will also want
to compare Roach's drums with those of Manne (and Krupa).
Only by listening to all men's truths do we find our own --
in jazz.

I would, naturally, be very curious as to your
reactions to this course of jazz study. I don't believe
that jazz can either be taught or explained, either to
musicians or laymen.

On the other hand, I think Vivaldi would have
understood the essence of jazz, and Bach might have done so
had he been compelled to work with clavichord and other
small instruments or groups.

September 8, 1960

Let me start rather tentatively to answer your letter
-- tentatively because I have been for some weeks so
completely off the jazz kick that I don't even want to keep
my column.

First, I think you know precisely what jazz is:
"contemplative prayer -- the soul speaking, complaining,
crying out, adoring, praising, cursing, rebelling, loving,
meditating." You have described it precisely. And doing all
these things, not seriatim, but simultaneously: the two
ends of the stick, the two sides of the apple contemplated
simultaneously.

My present turning away from jazz is caused largely by a
somewhat belated realization that most jazzmen do not, in
practice play this way. They are concerned with technique:
the technique of playing and the technique of improvisation.
It is only rarely that the jazzman gets up on the stand, even

in a recording studio, and plays because he has something he wants to say. For the most part he is concerned with running through a more or less routine set of chord progressions, demonstrating his speed, his control of his reed, his timbre, etc. And of most jazzmen it must be said that when they go beyond this, they do so only by seeking new, strange, outre (the jazzman's "far out") harmonies and progressions and rhythm structures with which to amaze the multitude. In other words, today's jazzmen have missed, for the most part, the whole point of what it is they are doing.

But this is to say only that even in the Twentieth Century with hundreds of millions of people flitting about, there is not a Beethoven behind every street sign. If a jazzman does no more than "blow the changes" in his solo, he still does more than the symphony musician does. And sometimes even the most commercial jazzman does catch fire. Whenever he does, then there IS a Beethoven behind that sign. And if it happens on one track out of a hundred records, jazz has justified itself.

I think your choice of Brubeck to start with was a wise one. Very many jazzmen of today "put down" Brubeck, partly because of his success, partly because he is white (there is a shocking amount of Crow Jimism in the jazz industry),[3] partly because his piano is descended from the classical, not from the honkytonk. But he is a sincere experimenter; even in those albums where he seems most commercial he is often doing a delightful job of lampooning.

I have a letter on my desk from the woman manager of a New Orleans clarinetist named George Lewis. She is a monomaniac and Lewis is her mania; he is a shy, slight, frail, delicate little man who played the clarinet on the waterfront until 1942 when he was "discovered" and had a couple of years of success and since then has been scuffling. He plays the most beautiful clarinet anyone has ever heard, but all the old musicians with whom he played (some date back to the Nineties) are dying on him and George has a really tough time. But his clarinet is beautiful. It is as though a mockingbird inhabited his instrument.

So I reviewed a recent record of his and praised again the beauty of his tone and his phrasing but pointed out in passing, "He is no technician." And I got a furious letter from Dorothy Tait, the manager, demanding to know, what is technique in jazz? She told of an incident where they were listening to the playback of a record session and one of the old, old timers said to him: "You sounds a little flat there, George." And George says: "Huh, did you ever hear a

---

3 "Crow Jimism" was the often sincere but ignorant spiritualization of Negro life by white people, particularly those in the Beatnik movement. This kind of idealization was deflated by poet Kenneth Rexroth (1905-1982), who wrote in his article "The Jazz Novel" that "Anybody who considers the evil effects of discrimination as virtues is pretty silly, and he is unlikely to be a Negro."

woman cryin' on the grave of her husband? She didn't sound
so pretty either, did she?"[4]

Well, on to another subject entirely: When we got Pat
her first TV a few years ago, it was a seven-inch screen
and was bought with the distinct understanding (dictated by
Naomi as well as me) that it must never be brought into the
living room. Now, though, we have a twenty-one-inch monster
in the living room and a marital arrangement whereby I am
permitted to spend the evenings in my office (downstairs)
until it's time for the TViewers to go to bed. So I get
considerable writing done.

(Seriously. I spent two hours the other night looking at
an old movie -- a Fred Astaire thing. He used to be my
favorite. But when the picture was finished I had a curious,
unpleasant sensation as though, by trick and device, I had
been robbed of two hours of my very precious life.)

September 28, 1960

Dear Toni,

I have found that much of my reluctance to write was
caused by a curious inability to punch the keys of a
typewriter. My doctor thought it was probably the other
way: that my inability to use a typewriter was based on a
profound and deep reluctance to write anything. I beat it,
at least partly, by buying one of those beautiful little
Smith-Corona electric portables -- which I have now learned
to use quite well.

My determination not to write again remains firm. How
dreadful a thing it is to be a writer! To drag your
intestines out and expose them to the people and say: "Look
at what I have suffered! And how beautiful it all is!"

Gradually, now that I have my little sky-blue Corona-
doll, I have come to write more and more letters to people
I know. But I do not think my Corona-doll would like it if
I tried to "write" any kind of fiction with her.

Last weekend I went to the Monterey Jazz Festival (as
a critic, of course.) It is the one beautiful place on the
Pacific coast. The festival is held in an open arena in
beautiful and spacious grounds, deep in thick turf, spotted
with ancient live-oaks. From 3,500 to 7,000 people come to
each of the five performances; many of them spend the day,
bringing a picnic lunch or buying sandwiches and coffee or
beer: beatniks, ex-college couples, staid middle-aged
people who have become interested in jazz, kids from the
colleges and high schools.

The sun shines down warmly, and the kids sun themselves; there is a bar for the musicians only, and there
are art exhibits and commercial exhibits and caricaturists
who will draw your picture -- but nothing seems commercial.

4 George Lewis was born in 1900 and died in 1968.

The musicians have never dreamed of a place like this; they were looked upon with near reverence by the multitudes who listened with almost painful sympathy and attention to some of the most extremely experimental works -- and if a player should be performing one of these and a wave of understanding suddenly runs through the audience, it is accompanied by a wave of joy: for the audience because they have understood something new, and for the player because he was understood.

We went down early and got ourselves a motel suite at Pacific Grove on a peninsula running out into the Pacific, atop a cliff, looking across the bay: the most beautiful rocky coast and blue, blue sea. We hoped to spend many hours there while the concerts were not actually on. But we scarcely saw it: three hours immersed in music in the afternoon, then about four hours out to write my review and eat and drive back to the fairgrounds, and then five hours more immersed in music. For three days.

And then to come back to the fog and the offices and the commercialism and the cut-throating. I did understand what the musicians mean when they say that "Jazz is a religious experience."

The strange thing is how many, many people it hits -- and how utterly it is unknown to the great majority whom it has never hit. For example -- I was standing on the grounds the other day when a well-dressed man walked up to me and said: "Mr. Garrigues, I'm Chuck Redlick -- Art Gilbert's friend." I knew who he was; he had called Gilbert (the Examiner's $60,000-a-year advertising director) and had been referred to me because he thought I could help him find somebody to teach him jazz piano.

And he was, quite incidentally, the head of the biggest furniture store in northern California. And beside him was a bearded beatnik sleeping in the sun, and a nice middle-aged couple eating pastrami sandwiches. (The pastrami booth is run by the Monterey Jewish community. Except last year the festival came during the Holidays so they had to hire gentiles to run it!)

Well, I didn't mean to write an essay on jazz. But Monterey was a very profound experiment to one who has become very much fed up with jazz in the last year.

November 20, 1960

Dear Corinne and Irving,

I have been trying to find energy to write you to thank you again for all the care and rest and serenity I found at Palm Springs. I am not exaggerating when I say that it saved my life; though I am not as well as I hoped to be by this time, the visit with you did break the continuing cycle of worsening illness.

I suppose Naomi has told you the news -- that I am on the partially disabled list. When I left Palm Springs I felt good, but a couple of days in L.A. quickly convinced me I needed nothing but more desert. So I canceled all dates and set out early one morning for Borrego Springs, via Julian. It was a wonderful trip and wonderful experience. There must have been an early frost because the leaves of all the sycamores, poplars, etc. in the mountains had turned brilliant reds and yellows -- like you never see in the lowlands.

The desert was wonderful. It is the most unspoiled desert left in California: a beautiful oasis at Borrego Springs and then just miles and miles and miles of pure desert everywhere else. There are two roads paved -- one north and south, one east and west -- but most of the area can only be reached by jeep. The people talk about "jeeping" as the Old West used to talk about riding a horse.

The State Park Department is doing a wonderful job in keeping it unspoiled. There are only two or three camp sites with water in the whole 500,000 acres. But there are "primitive camp sites" here and there -- level places in the desert with a couple of johns set up a canyon, and nothing else. Exactly what I had been looking for -- except that I forgot to bring my camping equipment. But I drove out one night (the moon was nearly full) and sat a whole evening on the ground at one of these places. For the first time since I was a boy there was absolute silence. Not the sound of a distant car, not a cricket, not even the slight whisper of a desert wind!

I drove everywhere you could drive safely without a jeep and one hot afternoon went to the end of the road in a geologically incredible place called Split Mountain and then walked for miles up a flat canyon -- I want to go back next fall. In fact, what I want to do is to retire to a camper-on-a-truck combination which will move from Borrego to Julian and back again as summer and winter succeed one another. Until I'm just too old and weak to drive a truck.

I decided, out of pure cussedness, I'd drive to the top of Mount Palomar. That, too, was a magic drive. There is a beautiful road winding around and around this high mountain which is covered with real Sierra-type trees. The clouds were down close; nothing to see but the trees and the wisps of fog. Sometimes I could hardly see the road.

And finally, at the top, a wind-scarred expanse of brush, a deserted parking area -- long, square or rectangular walks of concrete, then the square white entrance to the museum looming out of the wind-whipped clouds -- I walked through that: spacious, deserted. Then walked on through the wind and fog until the observatory loomed up -- cold, spacious, incomprehensible -- and deserted. It was like a dream trip to the stars.

When I got back to work, I put in three days, then I
came down with some kind of allergy -- either to a new
tooth paste or to a tranquilizer the doctor had been giving
me. My mouth swelled up as though I had been eating a
poison ivy salad. I laid off, saw my doctor; he told me I
should give in and take a six-month leave of absence from
work. That is what I'm doing. However, the office has
consented to let me keep the jazz column and pay me two
days a week for doing it.

The whole experience -- from my trip to Palm Springs
down to the experience of laying off from work -- has been
an emotionally exciting one. In one way, it is such a
complete break with the past that it throws into perspective a whole way of life that I was never satisfied with
but which I kept accepting more and more, while rebelling
against it unconsciously. So far I'm struggling around in a
fog. My doctor is hoping for more results from this change
-- this acceptance of freedom from responsibility -- than
he is from the actual rest.

My first thought when I came home from the office after
asking for leave was: "After thirty-four years, my neck is
out of the yoke!" My second was: "For the first time in
thirty-four years, somebody other than I will have to ask,
'Where's the money coming from'?" Since then I've been
practicing being carefree and irresponsible -- and it hasn't
worked too well. I keep asking myself what it will be like
when I go back to work five months from now, and secretly
I've been telling myself that my subconscious will take care
of me and make me ill again when it's time to go to work.

At the same time, I have a feeling as of a job
completed; it feels as though I were no longer under the
gun -- as though the whole score were in and counted and I
wasn't even concerned enough to look at the totals.

There are curious side effects, too. When I was going
to work at one or two I would often sleep until nine or
ten. Now I don't get enough sleep. I wake up at five or six
in the morning -- not wondering "where the money is coming
from" as I've done for so many years, but either planning
how I am going to spend the day in complete irresponsibil-
ity or (more likely, I suspect) to gloat over poor Naomi's
getting up and going to work!

Yesterday, for perhaps the first time in eighteen or
more years, we just took off for the Russian River without
planning when we would be back. We spent the afternoon with
a friend, took her out to dinner, and drove back. On a
Saturday. I haven't been able to do that before because of
a curious feeling that Saturday was for the masses and that
a proper newspaperman should have his days off in the
middle of the week. Naomi can't understand why I'm so easy
to get along with.

November 26, 1960

My sudden reaction to the theme of my novel was a violent one which came when I accepted the fact that I was no longer, could no longer be, responsible for a family in the way I had been for thirty-four years.

My novel was to have been the story of how a man's nose gets put to the grindstone and stays there -- quite unintentionally -- through a lifetime. All the relations between father and son, son and mother, all the hesitancies and acceptances and ultimate half-rejections which were to have made up the body of the book -- all the story of a person who tried to find his individual self by acting in certain socially dictated ways -- all these were to have involved ultimately the acceptance by the boy of the rules of a game which made him seek to follow in the footsteps of his father, seeking to succeed where his father had failed (he thought) -- and all within a given economic and social milieu.

And then suddenly I found that I myself had passed through to the other side: that the compulsions which had driven me for thirty-four years were no longer Compulsions Felt but only Compulsions Remembered. I suddenly realized that the writing of the book had been a sought means of bursting through, of finding my way through, my maze of often contradictory compulsions -- and then I found that I had come through to the other side.

December 2, 1960

Last night I finally summoned up energy. I rearranged the furniture in my office and crowded all the jazz things into two corners and got an old table and put it into a third corner and then dug deep into the basement and brought up a dozen volumes of a story manuscript now masquerading under the title of "Many a Glorious Morning."

Then, having done so much, I laid it aside, open on the table, where it can stare at me quite reproachfully when I dawdle, as I am doing now. I'm not sure what my next step will be; perhaps I will draw up a cast of the characters and a map of the territory to understand better the action which follows. I have some excellent ideas as to what is wrong but no very excellent ideas as to what to do about it.

But the result of having done even as much as I have is that, for the first time in half a dozen years, I am thinking of myself in terms of writing again. I have really been very much at loose ends for the last six years; I have not known what to do with myself. I do not know yet -- but I do have the feeling that something has subtly shifted and is about to give.

I still have bad bad chunks of chest pain, but today as a whole was clear, happy, fruitful. So I am hopeful that something may come of it.

December 6, 1960

I was made very happy to get your letter yesterday, Corinne; both of you had been much in my thoughts, particularly the last couple of days since I dug out the old mss and re-read all the very helpful suggestions you made. I was much minded to sit down and answer again all those letters of 1949 and 1953 because the eagerness to write the story surged up in me again and once more was frustrated by the same problems which had caused me to lay it aside -- except that because I could see it much clearer it was not quite so painful.

I was much interested in your suggestion that Naomi and Pat move to Tucson and that I get my camper-truck, etc. etc. In a way it seemed such a sensible solution, I wondered if Naomi would mention it (since I wouldn't dare). But she didn't; she asked me if I were quite satisfied with the way I was spending my leave and when I said I was as well satisfied as one could expect she let the matter drop.

As a practical matter, I don't think it would work. Naomi does want to stay in San Francisco; she is completely wrapped up in her job and the people she works with. Patty wants nothing except to get away from her home; she has reached the age when everything she does rubs Naomi the wrong way, and vice versa. She really needs to escape from her mother (and only tolerates me because I try to make her feel welcome in the world of adults without getting in her way). And I, for my part, much as I love the desert, feel I am not quite able yet to let the family shift for itself.

I don't think that Naomi and I get in each other's hair quite as much as we used to. At any rate, with no pressure of work over me I am much less likely to fly off the handle; when I get oppressed I just walk out of that part of the house.

I'm a little afraid Naomi is working too hard; she seems to have reached a period of compulsion such as I was going through when she finds it difficult to relax and so goes to her office to work even on Saturday and Sunday. I think that is partly because she finds she has lost much contact with Pat (as I have, too), and she doesn't really find it possible to pick up the old pre-Pat contacts with me again. We do manage to go out for a while at least once a weekend; last week we went to Muir Woods after a rain and walked in the cold, damp -- but beautiful -- outdoors. But these things are not quite enough for her.

Well, as I said, I finally moved another table into my office and set it up as the auctorial corner. My first task was to go through the two versions of the book. I was surprised, I confess, at how good some of the writing was. Of course, one difficulty with the versions up to date is that I wasn't really concerned with writing a novel. I was concerned with writing a case history, my own. (A case history: how did he get that way? A novel: what's happening to him?)

But, being concerned with how Bliss got the way he was, I was much too involved in episodes of the past; in fact, the whole thing was concerned with the past. Bliss had to leave El Jardin because I had left Imperial. I did learn to reverse episodes so that actual defeats were turned into triumphs (and so improved, dramatically), but the main line of events had to come almost whole out of life.

Now, I think, I may possibly be far enough away from things so I can be concerned, as we said at your place, with the Truth instead of the Facts. But if I no longer have any alley to run in, then neither do I have a set of lines to guide me. I do not know the Truth. Not yet.

December 17, 1960

Dear Toni,

This is my season for reminiscence. It seems that one of the things that got me started on this is the fact that it's almost like an Arizona winter day here: bright and warm (warmer than our July) and still soft.

And yet it seems so many years ago that we were in Arizona. There are very few things in my remote past I would cry about, but it seems to me that I was peculiarly unfortunate in living my Arizona life at a time when I was too young to adjust to it; if I had only been a few years older and had known and experienced a little more of the world, Arizona should have been a peak of my existence.

As it was -- it is nice to look back at -- I remember the girl who was going to be Peter Pan and never grow up (how remote is Barrie now!) and who shocked me one time by asking me seriously if I had ever read a book (I thought of myself then as a tremendous litteratus, though, I confess, I didn't own a book) and who remedied matters by giving me a copy of "Green Mansions" as a going-away present. So it seems that this is my day for nostalgia.

Aside from the lovely weather, I would of course be thinking about you because (somewhat to my astonishment) I have dug the novel out of the dark recesses of our storeroom and have been going through it for the last week, wondering if now I will be able to put it together and make a book out of it. Today it seems that perhaps I can; for the first time since I laid it away in 1954 I feel I have ideas about it that will be fun to play with.

And this ties in to a pilgrimage I made this fall back to my home in Imperial. It was the first time since I last went there about 1926 that I actually got out of the car and went down into the town and visited the school I had written about. The old brick school has been removed and a

bright, modern "education plant" has been built. It was fun
to go in and talk to the principal. He had been doing some
research on the history of the school and happened to have
the 1918 and 1919 school annuals on his desk, so we spent a
happy afternoon looking over pictures and comparing notes.

Now for the first time I feel I can handle the high
school sequence with some degree of professionalism, though
I have not yet mastered some problems of the theme.

The Judge

*Bliss seemed to take more pride in debating than in football; it was as
though debating, being done with words, was somehow more near the real
world. With his gift of gab he made the team right off, in his junior year. Mr.
Sallywalker, the elocution and drama teacher, listened to him in tryouts and
picked him for the team and taught him how to write out his speech and make
his points, one by one, and memorize the speech and get up and deliver it —
the way he taught all debaters at El Jardin. They did fine. Bliss and Agnes
Harker defended the proposition "Resolved: that the unicameral legislature
should be adopted in California" ; he reeled off his speech and they won the
decision.*

*But in his second debate he did something nobody had done before;
he and Agnes were at Hopeville, taking the negative of the question "Resolved: that Universal Military Training should be adopted in the United
States," and Bliss, who had carefully prepared his speech, threw it away
and got up and argued extemporaneously, meeting his opponent's arguments and advancing his own, talking straight down the throats of the
audience. It was a smartalecky thing to do. He could feel Agnes Harker
shooting daggers at his back and when he sat down she whispered furiously at him, "Now you've done it; Mr. Walker will give you what-for!"*

*Even when they got the unanimous vote of the judges he didn't know
for sure that he hadn't let El Jardin down and whether, maybe, it wasn't
Agnes Harker who had saved the team. But the next morning Old Bottoms called him in and congratulated him. It was the first time he'd been
in the principal's office since the time of his fight with Harold, and this
time he had enough sense to keep his mouth shut and not be smartalecky.
He said, Yes, Sir and Thank you, feeling the warmth come up in his chest
and knowing that, from now on, Bottoms could have his right eye or a
quart of his blood or anything he might need.*

*He went home with the warm, good feeling still in his chest; he sat
around and wanted to tell somebody, but there wasn't anybody to tell
except Mama. Cal and Tom were both off, fighting the Hun. Grace was
in Normal School getting ready to be a teacher, and he knew if he told
Mama she'd say, Did you, son? in that usual, affectionate, not-under-
standing tone.*

Bliss sat around not-waiting; he was not-waiting for Papa to come home because he remembered how it had been on football afternoons when he, Bliss, had come home. He would enter the house quietly through the side door, with the cheers of the crowd still in his ears and the solid, bruising thump of hard flesh in his shoulders and legs and the sight of an opponent's twisted face still flashing fitfully before him. He'd come home tired and shining and would sit around until his father trudged up the path, tired and not-shining, a little grumpy, a little indifferent — and Bliss would wait until his Old Man had gone out to the back porch to wash up, and then Bliss would go up and lie down on the cot in the attic. He'd lie face down and feel the shiningness go out and the tiredness come up until he could go down to the supper table and they would all sit eating and nobody saying anything except maybe "Please pass the potatoes."

So tonight he sat, not-waiting, still feeling the warmth in his chest and wanting to share it and not having anybody to share it with until Papa came home from his County job and they were all sitting at the supper table and Papa said, "I hear you had yourself quite a time over at Hopeville last night."

Bliss said, "Yeah," suddenly feeling good again, feeling better than ever.

Papa said, "Your grandfather was a great orator. He debated once with Stephen A. Douglas. That was before he was a judge."

Bliss said, "Oh." He saw now what it was — it wasn't just that he had to be a farmer; not just that he had to get the ranch back. He had to get the Lanes back — back to where they were when his grandfather was a judge.

"They say I got a good gift of gab," Bliss said.

"Your grandfather was a real leader of men," his father said.

So that was the year — the year everybody has just one of. But Bliss didn't know that. He thought the next year would be better. And the next. And the next.

Meanwhile, the jazz job, which started as a hobby, has become just a job -- though a reasonably enjoyable one. It requires very little time; ordinarily I would spend more time on it than necessary in an attempt to justify two days' pay, but the way I feel now I spend as little time as possible. And just potter the rest of the while. I have a nice little office and plenty of time. I have never had it so good for writing.

I remember once before, by dint of great effort I got myself set up where I had solitude, leisure, warmth, a good typewriter -- and spent a week walking the floor in desperation because I couldn't write. (The climax of that week was my heart attack in 1945.) But this time I don't have to prove anything; I am no longer "a writer." If it proves to be fun, I may do it. All I have to do is kick my

rolling chair over to the fiction table, pull the typewriter table after me -- and go to work.

I'm glad, though, I never became a professional
writer. They give too much of themselves; rather, it takes
too much out of them. While in Palm Springs I visited Frank
Scully (we used to know each other slightly in Arizona and
later in L.A.) and saw the outcome of a life spent at being
a hack writer -- not a very good writer but a very good
hack -- the uncertainty, the necessity for pretense to
oneself -- and it confirmed my earlier conclusion that,
whatever I was, I was not a pro, but I have not yet learned
to make writing a hobby.[5]

There is a theory that writing an autobiographical
novel is good therapy. I don't believe it. I think his last
book killed John Clayton, for various reasons, including
the fact that he was incapable of resolving the ultimate
conflict in the book just as he was incapable of resolving
the conflict in his own life. And I'm afraid the same thing
is true of "MAGM." I know pretty well what the conflict is
-- but I am incapable of resolving it so long as it
reflects my own personal conflict. So there is a possibility that this will turn into an entirely different sort of
book. If it turns into a book at all.

January 19, 1961

Dear Corinne and Irving:

My period of detachment from jazz has continued. Since
the Christmas weekend when I heard "Messiah" no less than
eight times. I have been more or less on a classical kick
-- with all my emphasis on the pre-Beethoven periods. Aside
from my own detachment, though, there is a very definite
doldrums in modern jazz. Very little of importance, I
think, is being done; the musicians like Brubeck are being
put down (and, in fact, have long since reached the limits
of their capacity), and all the emphasis is being placed on
bright young Negro players who are very skilled technically
but who went into music more because of its commercial
possibilities than because they had anything to say. They
have crowded the white musicians out of the field of
serious jazz. So that the white man, for the most part,
must content himself with playing arranged, written jazz --
or with competing in an area where he is not really at
home.

Perhaps, too, there is the difference in the social
milieu of the young Negro of today. The Negro musician of
the Thirties and Forties stood alone; whatever indignities
were heaped upon him, within the music world and out, he
felt them as an individual and responded to them with the
cry, the wail, which was not too far removed from the old

---

5 Scully was then writing his autobiography, *This Gay Knight, The Autobiography of a Modern Chevalier*, published in 1962 by Chilton.

folk song, the spiritual, etc. The feeling of ambivalence,
of loneliness, even of hatred, was there.

But today's young Negro musician is, as likely as not,
a member of a picket committee. He is part of a movement
which is remaking the Negro's place in society -- and he is
much more likely to make a speech at a rally than to cry on
his horn. Indeed, his only individual success is not to
express what is inexpressible except in music, but to blow
faster, louder, with more fantastic intervals than any
other young Negro musician who might stand in his way to
material success.

February 17, 1961

The Chronicle, after almost folding a few years ago,
has caught up with the Examiner in circulation, and the Ex
has brought in a Hearst hatchetman to do things over.
Somewhat surprisingly, for a Hearst man, he has been
persuaded that the Chronicle's gain is because of its
status as a newspaper for the intellectual few. So now we
have the curious sight of a Hearst paper trying to appeal
to people of intelligence.

In New York, Toni was depressed; she had run into some personal
and professional bad spots in her life. Brick tried to help her.

May 20, 1961

Dear Toni:

I was terribly sorry to hear that things are still
breaking badly for you and hope that by the time you
receive this something nice will have happened.

I think it is inevitable that we go through these
things, these periods, as we reach our age. If we succeed
in living through them, we survive quite happily to a ripe
old age, which may even be filled with fun.

It is the most difficult thing to learn to drift with
the current and find a nice side-eddy in which to rest and
recuperate. And you, all your life, have been a barrel of
dynamic energy -- and a girl with very firm, fixed and
immovable intentions and values and determinations. Many of
these you have not realized, have not satisfied, and I think
this fact has given you a feeling of increasing frustration
(and desperation) as year gave way to year. I suspect you
have not given yourself time for contemplation; there is much
in your life, as an achievement, to contemplate with joy and
satisfaction. I think you should pay more attention to the
Person Toni and perhaps a little less to the Career Girl Toni
and the Authors Representative Toni.

Nothing I say about myself need apply to you. Yet
perhaps it might, and so I want to recall this one little
thing about myself:

One of the things about me is that I have been very closely tied to my childhood emotionally. Admittedly, that is not good. But it is a fact. A few weeks ago I took time out from thinking about my failures to try and look at myself through the childish eyes of Me at, say fifteen. What did I see? A personality which would have seemed the height of success to the fifteen-year-old me. A writer (!); the author of a column on jazz (!); thoroughly sophisticated (!); a confidant of mayors, judges, senators and governors until I found how empty they were; a friend of musicians, singers, actors, authors (!).

No matter how vapid such descriptions are, in fact, to the mature mind, they are valid in terms of the boy who set out to achieve them. And, basically, they are as valid as any other; as valid as any I, or you, might form in our adulthood. (Maybe there is something of this in the commonly accepted religious idea that it is necessary to go back and be as a little child in order to be saved.)

I cite this experience of my own because, to me, you will always be that very pretty girl a little past twenty who, in those days, was wise enough to insist that she was Peter Pan and would never grow up. (I wonder if you even remember that phase in your life?)[6]

To me, at the time, a brash and unperceptive youth, it seemed a little silly, a little affected though charming. But I can see now that you were wiser then than now. In the harsh, implacable realities of beating the New York career girl racket, you covered yourself with a veneer of disillusion which did not really substitute for the childish naivete which is still you, underneath. And you are con⬜fused because the one does not find adequate reflection in the other. True, we cannot go back and find complete release in observing the ambitions of our twenties. But we need, I think, all of us, some liaison between the Me-Twenty and the Me-Sixty so that we emerge as one person in time, rather than a fractured series of individuals.

In one way, you and I have made identical mistakes: I recently; you for most of your life. That is the mistake of letting your hobby be your livelihood.

Take me, first: me and the jazz column. It was purely a hobby at first, and I was wise enough to insist that I would not get involved with it financially -- would not become dependent upon it. Because I wanted to keep it as a hobby, not to let it become a job. But I have not done so. Small as is the income I get from it, I now do it because I don't want to lose my little income. And so I have no hobby: nothing to turn to for the sheer joy of doing; nothing to escape to on my days off. And this, I think, was at least partly the cause of my recent near collapse.

---

6 Fanny Strassman had actually been about thirty when she met Brick.

Now take you: your hobby, when I knew you, was the collection of brilliant men, particularly writers. You deliberately put yourself in a position where you would meet virtually all of them. They swarmed around like bees, in the years you were with Viking and later when you went into business for yourself. And ultimately you, too, had no hobby. Because, for one thing, you found how dull is the average writer; it was a sillier hobby than collecting old stamps -- and at least the stamps would remain in their albums and not make unreasonable and childish demands upon you.

So you have no hobby, no direction for the pursuit of joy, pleasure, achievement, relaxation.

I remember, once, you said, with awe in your voice: "And that night Maxwell Bodenheim[7] held my hand." And now you wouldn't have that same awe if the nine most distinguished living authors, individually and collectively paid court to you in a gondola. But you were right, then; you are wrong, now. And the problem is how to reconcile the clarity of adulthood -- which is deadly -- with the naivete of childhood, which is lifegiving.

I don't want to overemphasize this thing, but I want to recall a scene in my unfinished novel which has stayed with me throughout these years. It is one of the few scenes I am still happy about. The kids are going down to see the village editor and try to get him to help in their fight with the principal.

They went into the close, airless office smelling of tobacco spit and ink from the print shop in the back room, and told their story to Mr. Rankin. He sat and listened, puffing little puffs of smoke from his crooked-stemmed-pipe until, when Ray McKay had finished, Dub McLain butted in: "Honest to Gawd, Mistah Rankin, that man's so Gawd damn mean he hates himself!"

"I hope you don't forget this."

It seemed a funny thing to say, but Ray McKay, who always knew how to talk to older people, said very sincerely, "Oh no, we won't, Mr. Rankin."

Mr. Rankin smiled at him and said, "Some time, maybe in fifteen, twenty years, maybe when you have kids growing up and raising hell — excuse me, Isabelle — maybe you'll look back at this and get the idea it wasn't so important after all. Maybe you'll have a sort of shame-faced feeling that you were a bunch of smartalecky kids and that it didn't really matter what happened at El Jardin way back in 1917 or 1918."

Ray and Dub exchanged looks. Rankin had said it almost as though he wished he were in the kids' place. "When that time comes, remember it

---

7 Bodenheim, born in 1893, was a noted figure in Chicago's 1920s literary scene and later in New York City. A modernist poet, he also wrote novels.

isn't so. Remember that what happens to you when you're sixteen is a damn sight more important than what happens to you when you're forty-six." After a pause: "Whatever happens to you NOW, don't let them talk you out of it — what you knew to be right, and what you did about it — THEN . . ."

Ray McKay said with just the right air of earnest sincerity:

"Then you will help us, Mr. Rankin? You'll put a piece in the paper?"

Mr. Rankin said "No." . . .

And so I say, Toni: Don't let THEM talk you out of it NOW; what happened to you THEN, my dear Miss Peter Pan, is as much YOU as anything that has happened since. What happened later is not "realer" just because it happened later.

As for me, I am feeling much better than I have felt for years. I think I told you I had to take partial sick leave from the paper. I ran the income tax office as usual (though somewhat less profitably) but instead of putting my money in the bank to be dribbled away during the year I paid off the Volkswagen bug and then made a down payment on a VW camper with the intention of spending at least half my time out in the hills where I could be free from the frustrations and annoyances of (1) my family, (2) the San Francisco weather.

I did manage to get away for three weeks: Palm Springs with Cornelia and Irving and also Borrego Desert. It did marvels for me; for the first time in years I began to look forward to living. Much of the chest pain has disappeared. (The doctors are still unable to diagnose it; after guessing at angina, hiatus hernia, ulcers, gallstones, etc. etc., they have decided it must be "emotional tension.")

I'm looking for more improvement when Naomi and I dissolve what has been a thoroughly unsatisfactory marriage. Pat has grown up; Naomi and I are both adult enough, at last, to realize that we have almost nothing in common; we can be friends at a distance but trying to live in the same house is ulcerous for both of us. A few months ago we decided that on July 1 Naomi would take over the house across the bay in Albany, and I would get an apartment in town and we'd get a divorce. Now she's decided she'd rather live in town so I'm going to move to Albany on June 1, and she'll get a place in town. (Pat, meanwhile, is getting a job and an apartment.) I still can't believe it will work out amicably; it seems too good to be true. But I think my own life depends upon it.

Keep the spirits up, Miss Pan.

As ever,

Brick

Chapter Thirty-Four
There Came a Feeling of Finality
I Cannot Shake

Brick and Naomi did not divorce. Instead, they moved together back to the house in Albany. For the first time in eighteen years, they were alone with each other. Two decades, they finally discovered, had bonded them inextricably. For richer, for poorer, in sickness . . . .

> 1023 Peralta Ave.
> Albany, Calif.
> June 12, 1961
>
> Dear Toni:
>
> Conditions are much better in our new quarters.
>
> I have my desk in my own room, plenty of light, heat and privacy; no records to bother about. The only handicaps are two: I have less freedom of time than I did and my right hand still cannot type (nor handwrite). My doctor says it may be early Parkinsonism which is not fatal unless it becomes late Parkinsonism -- which it doesn't always do. Meanwhile, I've an appointment to see a neurologist. I'm told they have medicines which can ameliorate the symptoms so that perhaps I can write again. If they don't -- I don't know whether I can do a job of writing or not.

James Parkinson was the British doctor who puzzled over the disease and first described it in 1817. Later, other doctors found out that the normal age of onset of Parkinson's disease is about fifty-seven, so

Brick was just about on schedule. The ailment often begins with a slight "pill-rolling" tremor of the hands and slowly progresses over ten to twenty years, ending in the worst cases in paralysis, dementia and death. There is no cure. It affects about half a million people in the United States alone, with about fifty thousand new cases each year. One doctor said he suspected everybody in the world would get Parkinson's if they lived long enough.

"Early symptoms of Parkinson's disease are subtle and occur gradually," says the Web site of the National Institute of Neurological Disorders and Stroke. "Patients may be tired or notice a general malaise. Some may feel a little shaky or have difficulty getting out of a chair. They may notice that they speak too softly or that their handwriting looks cramped and spidery. They may lose track of a word or thought, or they may feel irritable or depressed for no apparent reason. This very early period may last a long time before the more classic and obvious symptoms appear." Over the years, Brick's condition worsened. His speech slurred and he began to shuffle. His conversational powers dwindled.

Nobody knows just what causes Parkinsonism. Some research has pointed to genetic links. At one point it was thought that the widespread outbreak of sleeping sickness in 1918 might have resulted in many cases. And poisoning by carbon monoxide, manganese or cyanide could be the culprit. Perhaps my father's disease could be traced to the calcium cyanide often used on farms to kill rats and mice. Or to the poisons he used in his gardening. "One of the most demoralizing aspects of the disease," says the Web site, "is how completely the patient's world changes."

To add to Brick's depression, in 1961 he was fired from his job as jazz columnist for the *Examiner*. I do not know why. He remained with the paper as a copy editor.

August 10, 1961

Dear Corinne and Irving,

I have been putting off from day to day the enjoyable task of writing to thank you for the warm and productive hospitality and the joy of communing with people who, after all, do speak my language. Somehow, I haven't felt I would deserve the pleasure until I had all my little chores -- business and pleasure -- behind me. Perhaps not even until I should be able to say gruffly "... no time to write; the novel is hatching."

But alas! the novel does not hatch. First because it is a monster and not viable. Second, because nobody's been sitting on it to hatch it.

Item, the loss of the jazz job, though mildly
annoying, was a life-saver for me. I know now I couldn't
possibly begin to get back on my feet until I was rid of
it. Financially it was a loss; I'd counted on that. But
in terms of morale -- well, I was through with jazz
criticism (more: the "role" of the critic) before it was
through with me.

In an obscure, "corner of the cellar" sort of way I
had become a veritable "man of affairs." Telephones
ringing, a huge desk which I vainly tried to get organized
week after week, deadlines, pictures to look up, income tax
customers to reassure and placate. My first reaction of
chagrin was followed by one of amazed relief (amazed that I
was relieved) and then one of positive gloating.

Why? Well, in the long search for the answer to What
is My Name? I had long known the answer was not: "I Am The
Jazz Critic on the San Francisco Examiner." I had known
this but had not utilized my knowledge, so that for months
I went about acting a role which, I knew, had not been
assigned to me. And much of my ambivalence to many things
was based on the fact that I was playing this unassigned
role. The weekly column I could do. But the other jobs, the
side jobs, the prestige jobs left me shivering with
apprehension. Not apprehension that I'd be found out; I
knew I could do as well as the rest of them. But just
simply the feeling that I was wearing the wrong man's
clothes and beard.

It has taken me at least until now to find the little
Me hidden down in the debris of the collapsed Man of
Affairs. But gradually he is emerging; I think, having lost
his own clothes -- rather, his borrowed clothes -- in the
debacle, he is moving about rather tentatively wrapped in a
shred of a horseblanket. But he is at least alive.

I don't know where I stand in regard to jazz right
now. I listen to it, either by records or on one of our
excellent FM stations. And I seem to know so much more
about it than before. But it is not, on the whole, as
impressive to listen to; by and large I get as much
pleasure now from listening to the classics as I do from
listening to jazz. And I do not think that it is imperative
to listen to some particular record, or some particular
solo on it. (In the way I have, at times, thought it was
imperative to listen to Beethoven's Piano Concerto Opus
109, or to his Sixteenth Quartet.)

Item: What Is My Name? As you know, that is the
question which has bugged me quite seriously for almost a
decade. Each person, I think, must have a Name. Only he
knows it -- IF he knows it. Many people know him by a false
name: to one he is "Honey," to another "Daddy," to another
"a copyreader on the 1:30 shift; if he doesn't show up

we'll have to call in a sub"; to many others, perhaps, he's "that brilliant writer they used to have on the News; I wonder if he's still alive somewhere and whether he's sold out to the greedheads."[1]

Parenthetically, I think that is where you mystics -- I might say, "you genuinely religious people" -- have a great advantage over the rest of us: Though this may not be the way to phrase it, I think your Ineffable Name was whispered into your ear at birth or at baptism. And while it may take you a lifetime to find it, you can be serene in your search because you know that it is there.

It isn't, either, just a question of knowing what the Name is; it is a question of knowing how to pronounce it. Sometimes it is a very long and complicated Name, made up, perhaps, of millions of words which, all together, consti- tute The Name. I think (rather, I know) that my novel was an attempt to pronounce The Name. Ultimately, I failed simply because I didn't know what The Name was -- and was unwilling to pronounce those parts of it which I did know.

Before, everything was tangled up. Parts of my Name were "He Who Is a Father and Was Conditioned to be Such- and-Such a Father," "He Who Is a Writer," "He who Is a Political Activist," etc. Time, age and circumstance have erased many of the syllables and The Name, when I find it, will be much easier to pronounce.

Item: I have been much overwhelmed by Things since going back to work. Even the loss of the jazz job was a Thing, and it took time and effort out of all proportion to get rid of that Thing. And the Thing called moving, and the Thing called Your Own Home, and the problem of adjusting to the possibility of, or the necessity to complete, the separation which we had decided was inevitable.

So far as the separation is concerned, we have been content to drift along because we can't see any real practical way of separating without lowering our living standards. Naomi, it seems to me now, has made much more of an effort since coming back from her vacation; I mean she seems consciously to be making an effort toward affability so that I have fewer and fewer things to complain about. Except when one of the children -- Chuck or Pat -- arrives on the scene: either in person or as a subject for conversation. Then, almost invariably, there is another blowup.

I think I understand these things: Both of us are content not to be the head of a House which is a non-House.

---

[1] In 1945 Guy W. Finney published his *Angel City in Turmoil,* a history of Los Angeles County politics in the 1930s. Of Brick Garrigues he wrote, "Garrigues, a fine reporter, did an exceptionally good job in running down the facts in the sensational John P. Mills asserted rape case. . . . Where he has gone since those thrilling days of Los Angeles' 'fantastic era,' the writer does not know. But he is glad to salute his courageous memory, with a like tribute to all newspaper men of his sturdy breed."

We keep it on a non-House level so long as there are just the two of us. But when one of the children appears -- boom! it becomes a Household again. And neither is willing to accept a subordinate place in it.

September 12, 1961

Dear Toni,

The doctor says absolutely no extracurricular activities for a few months at least. I can continue to work the copy desk five days a week -- but even so, I'm badly beat at the end of the week. However, the new regimen seems to be getting results; I am having much less pain than six months ago, and the degree of reduction in pain is almost precisely proportionate to the amount of work I can get out of doing. (Mental work, that is; I can dig moderately in the garden and profit from it.)

My daughter has left home and got a job; my wife works; I have solitude and peace and no compulsion to do anything -- though the yard is there if I want to dabble with it. It has been wonderful having warm, sunny, Indian summer days after the fog we lived in for the last five years or so. The last two weekends have been especially warm and pleasant so that I did nothing except sunbathe. I am as brown as a teen-ager in August. For the first time in a long while, I feel as though I were making something of myself: a contented man.

December 5, 1961

Dear Corinne and Irving,

I continue to feel a little better from week to week. I am really enjoying life for the first time in years -- simply doing nothing except putting in a dull forty hours at the office. Curiously, jazz seems to have deserted me. I can hear it, I occasionally play it, but I cannot, as of now, understand why it was so important to me for so many years.

November 19, 1962

Dear Toni,

This is to inquire about another possible client for you. As to whether you think it's worth while.

A Marguerite Walker, an old, old friend from college days, has recently been retired (she's the country's first woman electronic engineer). She has been planning in retirement to try to fatten her income by doing illustrated travel pieces, with special emphasis upon fine photography.

She was a newspaperwoman before she took up engineering and can write well enough to satisfy professional needs. Her photography is professional in quality.

In the last couple or three years she has spent her

vacations in the most remote sections of Utah, Arizona, New
Mexico (packing in by jeep and Indian guides) and in
equally remote areas of the Canadian Rockies -- gathering
photos, Indian legends, etc. She plans to have two types of
material: the picture-article depending as much on text as
on pictures and the picture-in-itself with nothing except
the pix and the caption.

I told her I would ask you if you cared to handle her
stuff. Since I know less than nothing about the market for
this sort of thing, I don't know whether you will have time
to handle it at all.

On May 9, 1963, Brick's mother died at the age of ninety-three in
Santa Barbara. But a new life was to take her place.

August 15, 1964

My daughter Pat has a baby, almost a year old now.
(Her husband is a struggling, promising and not wholly
destitute folk singer. A pro, I mean; not just a sandal-
wearer.)

And Chuck, whom you'll remember, has at last got his
first job -- at thirty-four. Of course, he's had jobs
before but they have been temporary affairs like delivering
papers or painting the inside of a house or something else
where he felt he couldn't get caught in the economic trap.
But now -- well, he got his bachelor's degree in Art, then
didn't like that so went back to school and got one in
Language Arts (prerequisite to teaching writing, etc.) and
then realized that was hogwash and went back for a degree
in Psych with the idea of doing postgraduate work. So now
he's starting as a research assistant at U.C.'s Langley
Porter Clinic (the top psychiatric research center of the
West), at a good salary plus academic credit. He's really
quite a lad.

By this time, Chuck had also been married for more than three years—
to a girl he met at San Francisco State, Ann-Marie Bleher. And they had
a boy, two-year-old Christopher William.

In this year also the two remaining San Francisco daily newspapers
merged in the nation's first newspaper joint operating agreement, with
separate editorial staffs but with combined advertising and circulation
departments. The *Examiner,* which had been going head to head with the
Chronicle in the mornings, moved to an afternoon publishing schedule.
But the *Examiner* was definitely the weaker partner in the arrangement.

February 18, 1966

One fact is that the merger of the two papers set me
on my ear. I had been coasting along beautifully on the
a.m. Examiner, boasting to myself that nobody had ever
arranged a more peaceful old age for himself when wham!

here I was working 8:30 a.m. to 5 p.m. again -- bank
clerk's hours -- riding commute buses once more instead
of driving to town, eating lunch out of a paper sack,
working in an assembly-line newspaper plant down on Skid
Row[2] -- and in general doing all the things I had known
I'd never have to do again.

My M.D. attributes my great increase in angina to
what he calls "unconscious resentment," to which I say:
"Hell, doc, you think it's unconscious? What do you think
I talk about all the time?" But he says it's harmless if
I keep myself filled up with nitroglycerin -- which I do.
(I've been having these angina pains for ten years now
and they still don't show any damage on my EKG so I guess
he's right. Only I've got to find some way to get away
from these bank clerk hours.)

Of course, just to add to it, there's this
Parkinson's disease, which is as yet very slight but does
make my writing completely illegible and even typewriting
very difficult on a manual machine. But they do let me
use a typewriter for heads at the paper.

And, by the way, where did 1965 go? That was where I
stopped counting; it wasn't that I planned to stop living
at the end of 1965; it was just I never thought of
anything as existing or persisting after that date. And
here it is like being in an unknown country, well into
1966, and I don't feel any responsibility about it or
anything. It's just a year that doesn't belong to me and
I don't have any responsibility for it.

But I have been thinking a lot again about when we
were virtually kids in Tucson -- very wise and knowing
(or at least I thought I was) -- and I've been thinking
that the nicest thing a person can take with him into the
state of being a Senior Citizen is the ability to look
back at some particular time of his youth and say: "That
was wonderful!" And the brief time we spent in Tucson was
wonderful -- the more so because I hated Tucson at the
time.

(Remember how we all used to go out into the desert
after work and play records on a hand-crank portable
phonograph? I wish my library of tapes sounded as good
now as those records did then.)

In November 1966, Brick's remaining brother, George, died in Santa
Barbara at the age of seventy-three.

Vivian and I had divorced, and I had moved with the children from
Los Angeles to an old frame house about a mile from the University of
California in Berkeley, where Chuck was then studying psychology. I
had consciously fled L.A. to be close to him and to my father, the impor-

---

2 Near Fifth and Mission; a definite comedown from Third and Market.

tant older men in my life. Those being the days when Lyndon Johnson was trying to combine guns in Vietnam with butter at home, and with a sudden upsurge of hiring by anti-poverty organizations, it was easy for me to get a job with a state agency as a publicity writer. Vivian, left alone in Los Angeles without her children nearby to anchor her life, felt herself drifting. Within a few months, she, too, left Southern California behind and had taken a job in San Francisco and an apartment in the East Bay, to be close to her kids.

January 3, 1967

Dear Dickie,

It was nice seeing you during the holidays but I was sorry we didn't have more time to chat. It seems that the younger generation(s) is (are) crowding us into the corners, doesn't it?

I must admit, though, that they are doing much better than I had expected. Last night we went over to George's for Lisa's gift-opening ceremonies on her thirteenth birthday. It was the first time I'd seen George at home when he wasn't being harassed by children -- but it really was nice. The old house sparkled and shone, and the kids were at their best and everybody was cousinish or uncle-ish etc. It struck me that George's family had much more sense of being family than anybody else I know. The kids have a proper amount of sibling rivalry but they are actually very devoted to one another and have a sense of belonging together which is going to do them good in the long run. I'm very much delighted with the way things are turning out though I'd like for Lisa to have a little more supervision at the teenybopper stage. (Don't tell her I said "teenybopper"; she'd teenybop ME.)

It seems very strange to realize that after Saturday I won't have to go into the Examiner any more. The last couple of weeks I have been counting: "One more 4 o'clock; three more 8:15's; one more 3 p.m.'s." Then "No more 6 o'clocks; two more 8:15's," etc. etc. Now there are only three more to go!

I'm going to miss those nice paychecks, though. Since Patty got married and Bill got steady work it has been nice to have an extra twenty or so in the paycheck every week -- something that wasn't already spent before I got it. I'm going to miss that!

But for the first time I've been feeling that grandparents are superfluous; all the kids have such a feeling of belonging together, in family units, that I have no hesitancy about taking a back seat. Even so, isn't it true that Youth is much too fine to waste on the young?

May 14, 1967

Dear Toni,

You have been considerably in my mind during recent days -- partly, I suppose, because Naomi and I had just come back from Prescott and had toyed considerably with the idea of making a visit to Tucson. Somehow, it seemed that if we just went to Tucson (and perhaps drove out at sunset to look at the Mission) something of those days we enjoyed so many years ago would return. But better thoughts prevailed, especially when I was told that Tucson now has a population of 300,000. Where, in the name of the gods, could one recapture even the briefest memory in a bustling little city of 300,000?

But it was nice to think about. I don't have many memories of Tucson, but the few I do have are linked with the long afternoons we spent together, and a few trips out on the desert to play our few but priceless records.

I think you were the first "intellectual" woman I ever met. I put the word in quotes because I don't mean that exactly -- and yet I do. You were an education to me (and have remained so, I'm afraid). Also there was "Jean-Christophe," a much better book than the Russians everybody was reading then. Yes, I think I was more than a little frightened of you. Did you know that?

Well, it would be easy to over-sentimentalize those days. But they were very beautiful -- I'm glad I had them.

Yes, I've retired -- and I'm not sure how I'm going to like it. From what I've seen of it, I'd say one would be wise to approach it with caution. Of course, women do stand retirement better than men. At least it seems so. But for me there came a feeling of finality that I cannot shake. It's a curious combination of feelings: I feel lost at the feeling of having nothing I have to do and at the same time, if there is anything I do have to do I resent it bitterly. Gradually I'm learning how to live with these conflicts -- but it isn't fun.

Once upon a time I started to write a science fiction novel. It was about a time when Man had achieved Immortality, at least in the sense that he need not either die or grow old unless he chose. Science had found for him not only the Elixir of Life but the Elixir of Youth. The gimmick of the story was the question: "How can man tolerate Eternal Youth? Wouldn't he just die of sheer boredom?"

What would it mean to him to meet the ninth wife before the last? Could he even remember her over all the hundreds of years in between? Worse, wouldn't he confuse her with the eleventh wife before the last, who gave him such a bad time? etc. etc. It might have been a good story. I invented the "mnemonic pause." (This was in the days when the general semanticists were talking about the "semantic pause.") One practiced certain mental exercises ten minutes every morning in order to avoid that sort of confusion.

But Eternal Youth remained intolerable so everybody had to have Infinite Wealth, too. With this it was possible to "travel in time" -- not literally, as in a time machine, but people set up colonies based on various periods of the past and then traveled between them, or stayed more or less permanently in one era which they liked, and so restricted their memories to one or another set and thus saved themselves from falling into Mnemonic Confusion.

It was a great idea. And it seems to apply somehow to the problems of retirement, now.

I'm doing no writing. Except for income tax, this is about the second time I've touched a typewriter in the last six months. I'm astonished that I type so well; the Parkinson's disease has been progressing very slowly.

I do have a feeling of uncertainty -- a feeling that I no longer communicate very well, either orally or in writing. As though things keep going around and around in my head but don't entirely make sense when I try to verbalize them. I've seen so many people to whom that happened, at a certain age.

From that point of view, the sort of cloistered life I live now is not at all good. But I don't socialize too well so I engage seldom in conversation. Naomi and I have our little routine patter, morning and evening, but I'm never quite sure I'm saying anything.

Maybe that's one reason for the length of this letter. I'm trying out my conversational powers. (I notice, too, that the typing gets worse as my uncertainty gets deeper.)

Aside from such minor complaints, things go well with us. Naomi's rather precarious health holds up well. I have two new granddaughters -- Tauni Lynn from Patty and Bill, Leonie from Chuck and Anne-Marie. That makes seven altogether; I'm beginning to look guilty whenever anybody mentions "population explosion." (But where does the new generation get the names they apply to the next generation?)[3]

In the summer of 1967 I was appointed a public information officer with the International Labor Organization, an agency of the United Nations, in Geneva, Switzerland. Despite the fact that (1) my father was an ex-Communist, (2) I had written an anti-loyalty oath editorial in my college newspaper and (3) I had attended a get-together sponsored by the Socialist Party a few years before, the FBI — which seemed to know all

---

[3] The seven at that time were Lisa Gale, Michael Charles, and Rica Liane from Vivian and me, Christopher William and Leonie Marie from Anne Marie and Chuck, who had moved to Ukiah in Northern California, and Tony and Tauni Lynn from Patricia and Bill Collins.

this and more about me — said I wasn't a security risk and could go shuffle papers in Geneva.

The weekend after I had told Brick and Naomi my news, the phone rang at my Berkeley house, which I shared with my children and a male housekeeper and the dog. It was Brick; he and Naomi wanted to see me.

They came in hesitantly, he dressed somewhat formally in a jacket and tie, his figure rather bent, slightly crippled by his Parkinsonism; his lips bore traces of the white antacids he took for his pains and his hair was thinning. She was wearing, I think, a simple cardigan sweater, a blouse and a skirt. Her hair was gray, and they were two individuals of another generation. They were familiar to me of course but also distant figures, people who by that time were living lives entirely separate from my own and whom I didn't know well at all, for I hadn't yet read my father's novel nor his letters, and we never talked about much of consequence.

They had by this time lived together for twenty-eight years; I rarely saw them separately, and when I mentioned them to Chuck or to my kids it was always "Dad'n'Noma this" and "Dad'n'Noma that." Whatever rough surfaces had existed between them had been rubbed away by time; and by the narrowing of their options and a focus on what remained of a very short passage through life.

"I wish you wouldn't go," my father said in that soft voice made softer by his progressive illness.

"Why?" Surprised.

"We would miss you." It was a simple statement. I didn't realize that there might have been another reason, one very particular to Naomi.

But I was young — thirty-five — and my options were unlimited and life would go on forever. I told them that my dream had been always, it seemed, to live and work in Europe, that I had studied French in high school and Russian and international relations in college and now the dream was going to come true.

I think they sighed, or at least my present image of them is of two old people sighing — though they were both younger then than I am now. They had come to make their case, but the only solace I could give them was that the children would not be going with me to Europe — that they would stay close to them, with their mother.

In the fall, just before taking the airplane for Europe, I made my last visit to Brick and Naomi's house on the hill in Albany. As I walked down the outside stairway, I looked back at them standing on the porch, and Naomi had an odd, wistful expression, as though she were seeing me for the last time. Suddenly, she called goodbye and turned away, went inside, and with a kind of finality closed the door behind her.

January 20, 1968

Dear Toni,

I suppose Cornelia told you that Naomi has an
inoperable cancer. They are trying chemotherapy in the hope
of slowing the spread, or possibly inhibiting it. But it is
only a question of time. Meanwhile she has good days and
bad days; this is one of the bad ones. She is not, for the
most part, in great pain, yet. But we're just sweating it
out.

Fortunately, all the kids are living out of town, now.
I mean, that leaves me free to act as nurse without
worrying about the kids' worrying. We don't know how much
longer it will last.

As ever,

Brick

Chapter Thirty-Five
What Clarale Typed at the Big Desk

Corinne Sussman drew upon her life for her novels and essays. In an unpublished novel, this is what she wrote about Naomi, whom she called Nomie in the manuscript. In the work Clarale (Corinne) is examining family photographs and keepsakes, and they bring back visions of the sisters' childhood, of their growing-up together. Clarale's mind wanders from one scene to another.

Clarale and Nomie

She saw the two children there in the Old West, in Arizona, Jewish children where there were no Jews. She could hear the winter storms beating on the wall of their gray frame house. The children sat close beside the big black stove reading aloud: "Wuthering Heights," or "Jane Eyre." They read too many books about fated lovers; they were forever doomed to seek romantic love because of Charlotte and Emily Bronte.

Clarale turned the page of the album. There was Papa and the silk flag he was given when he got his citizenship papers, and there he was with the brown velvet case where he kept his blue and white prayer shawl.

Nomie married a writer who came from Anglo-Saxon Kansas pioneers; no prayer shawl, but always a family Bible. They moved to San Francisco, where in their living room the couch, reupholstered many times, had a soft shabbiness, as did the big overstuffed chair. Here was a picture of Nomie and her husband in that house.

In the dining room a large mahogany table took up most of the space.

Nomie and Brick had searched for it every weekend. They found a big one, really an old-timer, with leaves to make it even bigger at family reunions — Thanksgiving, Christmas, birthdays. The table represented Nomie's dream of family all around the table, happy, eating and drinking, in joyful harmony. Where she got this idea of joyful harmony around the family table Clarale could never imagine, since it had not been so in Arizona — not since the girls became adolescents and began demanding their rights, always at the family table. It was some kind of dream Nomie needed to reach for. As she had always reached for the flowers.

When Nomie bought large bouquets of flowers from the vendors on San Francisco streets, her husband would become angry, because the blooms cost more than groceries, and newspaper writers didn't make much money. But it wasn't just that. He also had the farmers' heritage of planting and reaping; you didn't buy flowers, you planted seeds and grew them. She would always be an "alien Jewish girl" to him, as he would always be an "alien Goyish man" to her.

Above the fireplace in Brick's and Nomie's living room was a reproduction of Andrew Wyeth's painting, "Christina's World." "Is that Nomie?" visitors would say when they came into the house. Actually it showed only the back of the woman, but there was something about her that was Nomie, perhaps just that love of earth, while simultaneously trying to let go, lift off. There was an awkward grace, as if she needed a helping hand. Nomie had that grace, that stubborn sense of trying to lift herself up without asking for help. Nomie had bought a frame that was too large for the picture. So she painted two more inches of sky. Now the painting fit the frame, but the sky was a different color. She said, "Nobody can match a Wyeth sky, so it's my own kind of sky." She did her own thing whether anybody liked it or not.

Clarale let the album drop and stared absently; in her mind she heard Nomie's voice on the telephone, crying in anguish — she and Brick had terrible arguments, inflicting suffering on each other, especially he on her, that seemed to Clarale demonic — and always over small things. Once it was because she put the clock on the kitchen wall and he didn't want it there. But mostly it was over money. Clarale came to dread the ringing of the telephone, because she knew it would be Nomie needing to share her anguish. Then a few days later, a letter would come, reassuring: Everything was fine, the storm had blown over; they loved each other and had a beautiful marriage.

Once he came alone to visit and poured out the story of their great differences and the tensions between them. Clarale, hearing his side for the first time, exclaimed: "You can't go on tearing at each other — I'm going to try and persuade her to leave!"

His hands began to tremble and he said: "What I've told you I've said in confidence. Please don't say a word to her, don't do that — we love each other — we don't want to break up."

There was a picture of Brick and Nomie with their dog Speck, in back of the house, she in shorts and halter, he standing with one arm around her, the other holding a rake. They looked attractive and in love, young and busy making a home.

He was holding the rake because of the garden. A large old apricot tree spread its twisted branches over the brief hill. Large, golden, rosy apricots year after year bowed down the branches. Nomie made apricot jam, preserves, jelly, and still there was bounty left over to give to neighbors. Bit by bit Brick had terraced that stony hill and planted each terrace, thinking out the colors he wanted to look at, the harmonious, intense, vibrant colors. Some years he planted only blues and purples, the masses of flowers rising up from terrace to terrace, beginning with transparent larkspurs, and going on to irises, and even purple roses. And by summer, anyone looking at the terraced hill was looking at a Van Gogh.

The Death of Nomie

There was a letter from Nomie. She was dying of cancer. She was climbing her mountain.

"This world, this life is frightening, sister. But I love it, love it, the beautifulness and the ugliness, too, because I can't have one without the other. I am glad I have been in this life and I wouldn't have missed a minute of it, though so much was too terrible to bear, and it takes courage. Remember, sister, courage, hang in there; believe that love is what will remain at the end, even in the fire, the terrible fire of pain.

"I am climbing this mountain and I've taken John Muir for my partner because he loved his mountains, even in the storms; he said the mountains welcome the storms. He was a man close to God, sister, and he said that even the terrible storms are part of the grand scheme. The storms feed the springs and the falls, so with us, the storms in our lives feed the springs and the falls. I try to meet the storms of pain with outflung arms, darling, and sometimes when I do the storm passes over my head. It leaves me battered, but calm and enriched in so many ways. I tell you this because I want you to know that is my philosophy of life."

Clarale and Nomie had been brought up in an era when it was important to have a philosophy of life. Nomie's philosophy of life was like a great painting, a composition she herself was painting in which animals, old people, family, babies, poor people, especially those who suffer in-

justice — for she had a painful awareness of injustice all her life — were surrounded by fields of flowers. Life!

Yet the very intensity of her feeling for life made her impatient to get it over with, especially when she knew that the top of her mountain was near. So she took a long drink of water to wash down the twenty-five pills she had saved, and wrote her sister and her husband and all her children:

"I write this letter to you all, my darlings. I pray you understand and forgive me, if you feel I do wrong. But I have thought and thought about this. As you know, for many years I've had cancer and God has given me, in his mercy, many years free of pain, and the joy and delight of a devoted husband, the joy of watching my daughter grow up, get married, give birth to beautiful children; what lovely babies my grandchildren are! And my stepsons, I've watched them grow up to be good men. I have been blessed. Thank God.

"I've thought and thought about what I'm doing now, but lingering on in a hospital or rest home would cause agony and suspense to all of us. I believe God doesn't want a person to die that way. So now the time comes when I feel I must take the responsibility, with God's help, and 'go to sleep' here in my own home, uplifted by your belief in creative love, and I believe it too.

"Life is rich, with the ups and downs, and I've reached sixty. I've had sixty years of deep appreciation for life and for my chance to experience being a human being. I have faith and I feel I should die as I have tried to live, with courage. You will grieve, I know, but go on bravely and keep creating something good out of all this. I need not say more. I feel this with my heart, thankful for all of you, and God bless and keep you and me, too."

In her mind she heard the typewriter clicking out Nomie's story. It began with her deathbed letter.

"I'm not afraid to die because I wasn't afraid to live. I'm glad I lived, even though it costs to live, but it's something I wouldn't want to miss, except for the cancer. But even the marriage troubles, the fights, the times of poverty, I fought to get all I could out of life; I fought for my marriage, for my child."

Clarale recognized the Nomie she knew —a fighter, intense, passionate, wanting to eat the fruit.

Clarale had fallen into a heavy sleep on that stormy night her sister died. She heard Nomie's voice: "Forgive me, sister, don't be hurt; I know you will understand and forgive me, because I can't wait for you to

come so we can say goodbye in person. I have to take my leave now. I just daren't wait any longer, you will understand someday, forgive me."
There was the clink of the glass.

Clarale thought it was because it was night that the sad dreams came and went, so that there was no end to them, no end to the dreamers and the dreams.

The darkness was not just a sensation, it was a sound, many sounds, respirators, machines beeping, machines breathing hard down her ears; it was jazz. It was Nomie's house after Nomie died. The sound of jazz all night filling the house because her husband couldn't sleep no matter how many sleeping pills he took; he played his jazz tapes all night, shoring up the ruins with the abstract, sad, yet personal beat of jazz.

The Celebration

Before she died Nomie had looked in the yellow pages and found a rabbi. She drove in her little Volkswagen, alone, to Berkeley and rang the bell, hoping he would be an elderly rabbi even a little like Papa, who had been a cantor. But a young man answered the door. He was the rabbi. He invited her into his office. She sat down and he sat down behind his desk. "I'm dying of cancer and I want to make my funeral arrangements so my family won't be bothered." Suddenly she began coughing and couldn't stop. The young rabbi jumped up and put his arm around her shoulders, "There now, just relax, you try to relax; I'm bringing you a glass of water." He went out and returned quickly, not with just a glass of water but with a tray holding two glasses and a bottle of schnapps. "One for you and one for me," he said. "I need it, too! I'm new at this."

"Don't cry," said Chuck, Nomie's stepson, driving Clarale to the mortuary, "she wasn't killing herself; she loved life. She was killing the cancer."

Her coffin was a plain wooden box like a poor nun's. Bouquets of beautiful flowers stood on the floor all around it, and one red rose which Clarale had put on top of the box. The rabbi said:

"Who can find a virtuous woman! Far above pearls is her value. The heart of her husband safely trusts in her, she treats him well and not ill all the days of her life. She rises while it is yet night and gives provision to her household. Her lamp goes not out by night and she spreads wide her open palms to the poor; her hands she stretches forth to the needy. Strength and dignity are her clothing and she smiles at the coming of the day. Her children rise up and call her blessed and her husband also, he praises her."

It was all true of her sister, Clarale knew. She could be safely trusted by her husband, she treated him well all the days of her life, she rose early to go to work in pouring winter rains, crossing the Bay Bridge in her little car, to give provision to her household, and at night her lamp went not out until her man returned from the late night shift on the paper; she spread wide her open palms to the poor; her hands to the needy, and she had strength and dignity of spirit and soul, and smiled at the coming of the day, for she loved the sun as only a child who had grown up in Arizona knew how to love the sun.

Chuck walked to the coffin to give the homily. But as soon as he began to speak, he, too, got a catch in his throat, coughed and the rabbi gave him a glass of water. Then at last, composed, he began again. He said: "Nomie!" He slapped the coffin, as if trying to wake her up. Clarale watched the rose leap up in the air and fall. Perhaps he would wake her up! Everyone waited, watching for the coffin lid to lift slowly up. But all was utterly still.

"Listen, Nomie, when I was a little kid I'd come home from school depressed, feeling like a loser, feeling I was nobody, poor and not even a good athlete and for me it was the end. You'd sit me down at the kitchen table and stay there until I poured out my unhappiness. I'd tell you everything that got me down, how I felt like a failure all the time. But you'd say in a strong voice: 'You are good! You've got brains. You are very intelligent. You'll see. You can do anything. You are very smart and you will never be a loser.' Nomie, you'd say it with so much power, so much confidence in me, that I began to believe you. You believed in me. I will never forget. I hear you right now, Nomie, saying: 'Believe in yourself, kid, because I believe in you, and if you want to know why I believe in you, I'll tell you — it's because I really know you as you cannot possibly know yourself. I know what talents you have. As for those who don't know you, forget them; they don't count. You can do anything you want to do.'

"I remember your words, Nomie. You talked so convincingly, you convinced me. You knew what a very confused little boy needs. Then, after we talked you'd get that big fat cookie jar you always kept full of big fat cookies and you'd feed me cookies. So now I want to know who you are, Nomie, because you helped me know who I am. You were the person who helped me, who said the right words and backed them up with sweet cookies."

Clarale felt a needle go into her heart, sharp, quick, the seismographic needle. She thought, "It is measuring my earthquake, it is shaking me apart, I am cleft, I am cleft by death, death is my earthquake, the epicenter is my heart, my hardworking heart is shaking; oh sister heart, you are riven."

The Quiet House

Clarale could see the front door slightly ajar. She pushed it open. Silence. There had always been sound, a high vibration of sound; she had always known she was in her sister's house by the music, the inten-

sity of sound, and it was Mozart. Now when she pushed the door open and stepped inside all was silence. In Nomie's room the bed was stripped. Her letters, the letters Clarale had written on desert stationery with pictures of smoke trees in bloom, were stuck with Scotch tape all over the headboard. On the bare mattress Nomie's large brown leather handbag lay open, her dark glasses, her black kid gloves, her embroidered hankie fragrant with Coty's L'Amant, her driver's license with the picture where she looked like an older version of a young singer named Cher, her doctor's appointment card for next week, and scores of snapshots of her daughter, and her daughter's husband, and her grandchildren, had fallen out all around.

Clarale went into the next room and sat down at the big desk where Nomie's husband wrote in times past when he had tried to make it as a writer. She typed on that typewriter

HERE LIES NOMIE ON THIS PAGE.
SHE HAS NO OTHER TOMBSTONE, ONLY A SCATTERING OF ASHES.
BUT HER NAME WAS MADE FLESH AND SHE IS IMMORTAL.
SHE LIVES, FOR HER NAME WAS SPOKEN.
PUT ASTERISKS AROUND FOR STARS.
PUT STARS AROUND NOMIE.
THE ASTERISKS SAY THAT THERE IS MORE.
* * * *NOMIE* * * *

Part Five
Ivy

I had always wished
for solitude — and
when I finally got it,
I found I couldn't take it.

Chapter Thirty-Six
Grieving

When Naomi died I was in my fifth month at the International Labor Organization. Snow was falling and the valley was enveloped in that murky gloom that covers Geneva all winter long. Brick's cable came to the tiny post office in the old gray building hard by the lake:

"Naomi died yester. Letter follows."

I block-printed my reply and handed it over to the clerk to be sent:

"How I wish I were with you now."

February 8, 1968

Dear Corinne and Irving,

I want to get at least a few lines written and on their way today though, for some reason, chores, particularly paper chores, seem piled up about my ears.

Everybody has been wonderful; Pat has called up at least every other day and so has Chuck, and this morning I had a warm and wonderful letter from George. But the fact is that I have not begun to adjust yet. It seems impossible that she is gone, and I still find myself reacting to events with the old thought, "She'll get a kick out of that when I tell her." It is as though she had died suddenly and unexpectedly. As though I had made no preparation for it. Because, even in the last few days, she was still so vividly alive. I find myself still eating food which she had asked me to buy for her, and each bite is an unconscious denial of her passing.

I realize that this is something that has to be gone through and that there is no use in trying to avoid it. Indeed, I want to get through it as quickly as possible. I know that in many ways I have it much easier than other bereaved people do. There is no thought of guilt to increase sorrow; I know that there was nothing left undone which could have made things easier for her. Under the circumstances things were done exactly as she wanted them. We were very close during the last few years, and particularly the last few months. I have that to look back upon.

I still cannot plan for more than a day ahead. I think I have to live through this present period first. Until that is a little past I cannot make any adjustment to the future. I don't really want to stay in this house (I don't want to raise flowers for anybody else) but I am reluctant to make any change from here.

So far, Naomi's room is just stripped and bare with her photos still up around her dresser -- all the pictures of the people she loved most. I'm going to have to change that; it's too much like a memorial. But I don't want to move into that room; I want to keep it available for Patty and Bill or Chuck and Anne-Marie to use on weekends. And for you two; somehow I think that you should spend considerable time here during the next few months.

I was delighted to get the clipping about "Christina's World." Naomi and I used to disagree about that picture; I maintained that, beautiful as it was, it was an illustration rather than a painting: there was a story there which needed to be told before the picture meant anything. Naomi disagreed. I said that there had to be some reason why a girl would sit down in the midst of a field, in that particular position, and unsuitably dressed as she was. I even said that Wyeth was a poor draftsman because he drew her right arm as though she had polio. But of course the fact that she did have polio and was unable even to walk does explain the "story," the position, the dress, the leaning-forward-longingly, of the picture.

Now I must run and do some of the chores I promised myself to start today. Your letters do help, very much.

February 15, 1968

Dear Dickie:

Naomi's death was very sad but everybody felt glad that she had chosen her own time and place to go. She had consulted all members of the family privately in advance so none of us was shocked and we all felt she had done a brave and sensible thing in saving herself months of pain.

You would have been proud of Chuck. I was. Months before, Naomi and I had discussed the funeral and she had asked if I thought he would be willing to deliver the

eulogy. At first I felt it would be fine but later got to
thinking that it would be a lot of strain for a kid (at
thirty-seven!) and we finally decided to have a rabbi.
Then, the night before the funeral Chuck asked if he might
say a few words. He got up and made the most beautiful
speech, touching upon the things Naomi would have been
happiest to hear: not only about the family relationships
but about her paintings and the other things she would have
been proudest of. It was very moving -- and satisfying.

I'd like you to know, too, that two things in your
mimeographed holiday letter helped to make her final days
happier. The first was your reference to her as Brick's
"lovely wife"; somehow this seemed to move her very much.
And the second was your reference to Tauni as "the cutest,
prettiest, daintiest baby" you've seen since your sister
Vesta was a baby. She couldn't get over that; she kept
repeating it to everybody she saw -- because of course, you
confirmed her own judgment. (And you are right, of course,
except that I think Chuck was an even prettier baby.)

Though we were prepared for Naomi's death, it is still
difficult to adjust to. It seems incredible that we should
have been married for thirty years; in living that half-
lifetime it had seemed as though all that time was just a
footnote of the years when I was married to you. Only now
do I come to realize how deep my roots were dug into the
later years with Naomi.

It has been impossible to make any plans for the
future. First must come this present period of getting used
to being alone in the old scenes; then must come a transfer
to new scenes. Chuck and Pat both want me to live with them
-- and I could live with either of them equally well since
I am good friends with each. I'm quite sure I want to sell
this house; I cannot imagine myself with enough energy to
take care of the flowers and weeds and lawn for another
summer. In other words, I think I will address myself
exclusively to being a grandfather with, perhaps, a cane.
But no beard.

I don't see George's family often enough but they
seem to be doing very well with Vivi to care for them.
Sunday Mike and Lisa came over but I was in the city so
they left a greeting carefully chalked on the front
porch. Lisa came to visit again Monday but I was on my
way to a doctor's appointment and saw her only a few
minutes. She is really very beautiful though being so
tall at her age, fourteen, frets her.

March 3, 1968

Dear Corinne and Irving,

I want to write at least a few lines today to let you
know I'm still among the living. It seems very difficult to

force myself to the typewriter these days, possibly because I cannot yet distinguish between me-gardener, me-housekeeper, and me-etcetera. So I stand in the middle and do nothing.

So far, I find it difficult to do even those things which I have told myself I must do to break the pattern of my days here. Such things as seeing people, spending weekends with Chuck, etc. etc. What I'm doing is simply to stay in the same old rut which I have been digging for myself for a long while -- except that, now that I'm alone, there's no profit in it. One gets up in the morning, plots out his day all pointing to the climax of evening, and when evening comes -- what?

I thought that my planned trip to Southern California might serve to break the pattern. But no, now I don't think so; after being in the South for five days I'm certain I would get all uptight and then have to rush back here to be sure the sun was still rising in the east and water was still running downhill.

Anyway, I'm making progress today -- having dinner with Ruth. I think she is fun; we should have a lot of things to talk over.

Ruth, a widow, was a friend of both Naomi and Brick.

Like you, I still suffer from that incurable impulse to say "There! That's something I must tell Naomi about." Or to look in the mailbox for an airmail letter. I think part of that is because there have been so many times that Naomi was away for a few days or a few weeks so that this absence, too, seems like a temporary one, soon to be ended. Solitude itself I do not mind; I have always enjoyed much solitude. Only there is always that compulsion to look over one's shoulder and find her still there.

March 9, 1968

Yesterday was a beautiful day, warm, sunny and spring-like. I went out and worked in the garden -- digging at towering weeds -- and forgot for a little while that there was nobody there to take the cut flowers to, nobody to look out of the window and say, "The garden looks beautiful!"

Then I found myself counting the days -- as I used to do when she'd go on a trip -- until she would come back. She made many trips in the last thirty years -- visits home, or to Palm Springs, sometimes at the climax of a quarrel, sometimes just to visit. And I enjoyed the solitude because I always knew I could pick up the phone and call her and then start counting the days until I'd be driving to the airport or the depot to meet her. So I find the greatest shock when I start counting the days -- and find them infinite.

I think that this is why I've been waiting, delaying my trip south. This is something I can't run away from; I mean it has to happen to me and I guess it has to happen to me here, at home. Maybe by the time it's over I'll be ready to pick up and go. I couldn't face the trip south with it hanging over me. I couldn't even make new friends to fill in the time. Ruth was fun to have dinner with and watch the Smothers Brothers with, and I hope we're going to be good friends. But as yet no friendship can be a shield against the present sense of loss.

I cannot see myself living on here in this vacant house and yet I fear to be cast adrift to float down slowly but inevitably toward lobby and room space in a cheap San Francisco hotel. I've seen so many old people waiting out their time in those little hotels where I've had my income tax offices. And I feel that if I do get rid of this house I will have lost my anchor. Yet, again, the house was Naomi's and there will be no constructive new pattern here.

I can't quite see myself as living with either Pat and Bill or Chuck and Ann-Marie. If there were an "in-law" apartment, yes. Because the one thing I do cling to is the kids. But I'd hate to go gentle into that dark night.

Meanwhile, I've been experiencing a strange contradiction between belief and knowledge. I do not, never have and cannot believe really in -- you know -- immortality -- the survival of the soul -- life after death. I still don't believe, but I know, completely nonobjectively, that Naomi still exists, very close. Here is a case where belief is stronger than knowledge -- yet does not eclipse it. It is the first experience that I've ever had where Belief and Knowledge kept each to his own side of the room.

And now I must turn to a bit of humor. Joe Dolan, the radio talk show man, was being given a bad time by a caller this morning when he at last said:

"You are the final proof of the transmigration of souls."

"I am?" demanded the caller, flattered a little. "How do you figure that out?"

"Because nobody could become as big a fathead as you are in one lifetime," said Dolan, pulling the switch on him.

I guess that's enough for today. The next letter, I promise, will be more cheerful. Write soon.

April 2, 1968

I got a little delayed, but I think I'm now ready to embark, tomorrow, on the long-planned trip to the South. I think it's high time I took it, just to get away from the familiar scene. I'm really surprised to find just how difficult a bereavement this is: As long as I stay here I will continue to exist as only half of an individual -- and the missing half will be as painful as can be. This trip is, I think, sort of symbolic of my former trips when I went out into the desert to be by myself, except that now I go there so I won't be by myself.

I'm surprised at myself. I've always considered myself quite self-sufficient, but I seem to be less so than most. Ruth described her reactions as being precisely like mine -- and after three-and-a-half years! I don't think at this rate it is worth it!

Ruth, though, has been, and is, a great help. She is such an outstandingly outgoing person, and we usually manage an hour-long conversation once or twice a week.

I wonder if anybody ever did a real fictional study of bereavement? From the outside, yes. But a stream-of-consciousness account which would avoid the sentimental. Dreiser did one in a very early short story called "Old Rogum and His Lost Theresa," which related the outward behavior very revealingly. But not the inward.

May 8, 1968

I am very glad that you have Naomi's little black notebook and that you dip into it from time to time and send me messages because it is those contacts which I miss the most. That little thing about keeping the house or letting it go was just what I needed -- not that I'm nearer making a decision but rather that I know I'll have an OK from her when I do. It seems that I always had to have an OK from her before a thing could feel right.

Besides, Naomi would be very happy to know that her notebook was being read and cherished. She loved the business of writing -- just getting words on paper -- so much that she would never think of putting her thoughts on paper for the public to read, and yet she wrote very well whenever she was writing for just herself and her family. It would please her to know that we are enriched by the things she wrote.

At last my second trip south is about to begin -- unless something unexpected happens. I've purposely left my plans very loose, and it seemed for a while I'd never get around to starting but apparently, now, I'm going to take off tomorrow morning and probably arrive in Palm Springs some time Sunday or Monday.

On the way down I want to stop to see my friends in L.A. But I will probably take about three days to make the trip. I only hope I won't hit a hot spell; after I arrive I won't mind, but I can still remember too well those trips across the desert I made in an old Model T Ford -- and it was HOT.

Chuck was by this time a psychiatric social worker, and his first posting was at the state hospital in Ukiah, where he ran an anti-drug program that was cited as a model of its kind in *Life* magazine. I have heard some of these addicts say that Chuck saved their lives.

The trip to Chuck's was quite a success. Everybody from grandson Chris to German shepherd Johnny was very glad to see me. They are living in a fabulous house with a beautiful big swimming pool. Ann-Marie is a wonderful cook, and one night we went to the hospital for a dinner being given by Chuck's patients in honor of his first "graduating class" -- three former addicts who were being discharged as cured and set to running a community center for teenagers at Fort Bragg (the theory apparently being that they, having been hooked themselves, were in a better position to keep pot-smoking school kids from graduating to heroin). It was a very enjoyable evening.

For me, I haven't worked out any satisfactory way of living, as yet. I do think that things are going to be a little more flexible from now on, but I don't think the time has come to make any decided step.

May 25, 1968

I haven't called Ruth since I got back; I think when I start to call I'm always checked by the thought "Oh, she's probably in San Jose visiting her granddaughter" so put it off until the next day, and then the next and the next. She is, though, the only person around here with whom I can communicate with ease; other people just don't seem to be worth the effort.

I finally got a copy of "Soul on Ice"[1] this afternoon and find it all the reviewers said it was. It would be a good thing if all white liberals were required by law to read it at least once. I can hardly see how anybody, even a white conservative, could fail to understand "What do THEY want now?" after reading this book. And he writes so well.

I was delighted to hear that the writing business seems to be turning out so well, with both of you working at it. I don't think you are "loners" at all. I have always envied anybody -- especially husband and wife -- who can sit down in the same room at the same time and actually get some writing done. One would think that a reporter, at least, would learn to write in public. But I never could; a closed door was always an essential.

I still don't feel, though, as if I would ever start writing again. Partly, it's the lack of motivation, partly the insistence of my fingers in finding the wrong keys. And partly the feeling that I don't really have anything worthwhile to say.

---

1 The autobiography of Eldridge Cleaver (1935-98), a militant whose 1968 book, published by McGraw-Hill, is considered a classic statement of black alienation in the United States.

I was at my desk in Geneva when the door burst open. Another expatriate American poked his head in. "Martin Luther King has been killed, and the blacks are rioting all over the country!" That had been April 4. And on June 5 there was another death. I still have a copy of the next day's *Tribune de Genève* with the big picture of Robert Kennedy lying crumpled on the floor, his eyes staring glassily, a Filipino busboy kneeling in confusion at his side.

June 10, 1968

It was a terrible week, wasn't it? I turned off the TV about the middle of the week and refused to watch any more. It had only been a few weeks since we watched the King funeral at your house. And it seemed scarcely longer than that when we saw the JFK funeral. It seems that we have already come to the era of government by assassination -- even though this most recent one seems to have no domestic political overtones.

And the sad part of it is that nothing good can come of it. Almost certain for now we'll have to choose between Humphrey and Nixon. Oh, well, we can vote for Peace and Freedom anyway.[2]

Friday night Chuck came down with his family. They spent Saturday at the movies (all four of them), then I babysat with the two little ones (and the dog) Saturday night, and they all went out to make the Haight-Ashbury scene before going back to Ukiah. It was lots of fun; Chris is very self-sufficient; he is a builder and will amuse himself for hours with a set of blocks or perhaps a piece of chalk and a sidewalk. Leonie is a doll; she has a terrific Garrigues temper and, in general, acts more like a Garrigues than any of the others.

As ever,

Brick

---

2 The Peace and Freedom Party was a progressive, anti-war party on the California ballot.

Chapter Thirty-Seven
Peggy

11651 Gorham Avenue
Los Angeles 90049
December 17, 1968

Dear Toni,

A letter this year instead of a card because I must
tell you what's happened to me.

Chiefly, what's happened is that I've married again --
to my astonishment. There are several contributing causes,
but I guess the chief one was that I found I couldn't live
as a "loner"; I had always wished for solitude -- and when
I finally got it, I found I couldn't take it.

Actually, this is the culmination of a romance that
began in 1920; Peggy -- or Marguerite; do you remember? She
was the woman engineer who was thinking of marketing her
photographs; I wrote you about her a couple of years back.
Anyway, Peggy was the first girl I dated when I was a
freshman at USC a whole lifetime ago, and we have remained
warm friends ever since, despite a couple of marriages on
my part and one on hers.

As you may imagine, I did find it very difficult to
adjust after Naomi's death. As long as there were things to
do I managed to keep going and tried to carve out a life
pattern which would include frequent visits to the homes of
my children, etc. etc. But it gradually dawned upon me that
this was no life; coming and going I would be constantly
interrupting the lives of my children or, if I chose to

live with any one of the three families I would necessarily throw their own lives out of balance "taking care of Grandpa." Still that was the way things seemed to be shaping up until I went to the Motor Vehicles Department to have my driver's license renewed. There the man at the window said: "So sorry. You have Parkinson's disease? No driver's license!"

That put me in the hole. I did get a temporary license pending a hearing on my contention that I was able to drive a car. But I learned that there was little chance I would ever get a license so long as I had Parkinson's. I knew there was some kind of operation to cure it, so I tried the neurosurgeon at Kaiser Hospital but he didn't want to do it -- and I got the impression that he wasn't very skilled at that sort of thing.

But fortunately, I'd been in touch with Peggy, who lives in West Los Angeles (the Brentwood district, actually), and her doctor (a childhood friend of hers) was in close contact with the neurosurgeon at UCLA who is one of the top men in the country on this sort of surgery -- so Peggy said, "Come down and see what we can do," and so I came down and eventually one thing led to another, and Peggy and I got married and we did get me an appointment with the neurosurgeon, and we did set up an appointment to have this surgery done, and I went to the hospital and was all set when my heart started kicking up, and they postponed the whole business until they were sure my heart was strong enough to take it.

So, meanwhile, after a lifetime of knowing each other, Peggy and I have started to get acquainted and are learning to live without overcrowding in a small apartment.

It's a topsy-turvy sort of living for me, but Peggy is a warmly devoted person who busies herself about the apartment, drives the car (I now have no license), does the Christmas shopping and, generally, keeps things running smoothly most of the time. My own activities are limited to taking a four-block walk in the morning and an eight-block walk in the evening and carrying the household trash out once a day.

Besides sitting and counting my pulse and wondering how it's going to be when (and if) they start drilling holes in my head. (You've read about this operation. It's the one where they open your skull -- a little -- under a local anesthetic, then probe your brain with a cold probe, while the patient tells them how the stiffness gives way in the muscles when the probe reaches the right place in the brain.)[1]

---

[1] Called pallidotomy, the operation — in a vastly improved form — is still used despite its early incidence of complications. It was even more common before the appearance of L-dopa, the first medication to be truly effective against Parkinsonism.

Actually, I'm in no worse health than I was a year or
two ago. I could still do many things if I had to. But
among the things I can't do is drive a car and use a pen or
pencil -- I can't even take an address or phone number on a
phone call and write it down. So I'm practically incommuni-
cado. The electric typewriter I can still use -- up to a
point. But by the time I get this far in a letter the
frustrations of having to send an independent message to
each finger, saying "Hit that m-key" or what ever key it is
-- the frustration ratio gives me the screaming meemees.

Under the circumstances, I think I'm pretty fortunate.
Peggy and I come from the same background; we were born
within 100 miles of one another in the dreary heart of
Kansas. But whereas I have in some degree escaped from
mine, she clings to her WASPish (White Anglo-Saxon-
Protestant) opinion to the point where we have to bar all
political discussion. And I normally do a lot of political
discussion. But she is a warm and devoted person, which
makes up for a great deal.

What life holds in the near future depends, I guess,
on what the surgeon does, if anything. So we wait, from day
to day, not knowing exactly what is coming up the next day.
The surgeon says that there is a one-in-a-hundred chance of
the operation turning out badly and about one chance in ten
I'll be no better -- and no worse -- than I am now. So
those are pretty good odds. But he won't operate until my
heart man gives him an OK -- and we just don't know how
that is going to turn out.

I'm hoping that when the surgery is over I will be
able to get another driver's license. I think that, living
in New York, you can scarcely imagine how impossible life
is without a car. I mean, in N.Y. you just have to get
along on public transportation. But neither Los Angeles nor
the S.F. Bay Area is laid out that way. In Albany I was in
the heart of suburbia yet had to walk six blocks to a
store, a pharmacy, a bank or the bus. Here in Brentwood all
those things are a couple of blocks away.

I've been promising myself I would try a whirl at
writing if I get the use of my right hand back. Nothing
very important to say, but at least it would keep me from
the TV set. And TV, it is a horrid affliction.

Despite all this, I will be lonely at Christmas this
year. I do miss my grandchildren; this will be the first
Christmas since Chuck was born that I haven't been a pater-
familias. But I'm glad it isn't worse, as it well could be.

In Inglewood, Dickie wrote in her datebook: "Dreamed about Brick
and Peggy's wedding last night. Was I jealous! *Almost fifty years, and I
still can't get over him!*" The last sentence was underlined three times.

At age seventy-three, Toni thought it was time to come to Califor-

nia to see some of her authors. It had been forty-two years since Brick
had last touched Toni's hand, and he was nervous about doing so
again. But all went well, very well.

                                      January 4, 1969

```
Dear Corinne and Irving,

     How nice that Toni could come and see you after all;
or, at least, I hope she did -- that nothing came up to
prevent it at the last minute.

     My own meeting with her was delightful -- at Farley
and Emma O'Briens' cocktail party for her. I had been very
much of two minds about going; it seemed much better that
Toni and I remember one another just as a squiggle of a
signature at the bottom of a letter, plus the dim memories
of the days when we were both young and strong, and, as
Toni says, incredibly naive and unsophisticated.

     But the meeting turned out very nicely; Toni was at
least fifteen years younger than I had imagined her to be,
and we did get a while to compare notes on the past. (I
hadn't seen her since 1927 or so -- which is a long time.)
Anyway, I was delighted to find that somewhat acrid tone
which I had noticed in her letters in recent years was no
more than the maturing of a certain acrid tone which was
there when she was, as she phrased it, "a snotty kid from
Noo Yawk who knew everything." In other words, she seemed
not to have changed.

     Oh, yes -- very nostalgic. When I saw Toni I was re-
reading "A Moveable Feast,"² and it all brought back so
vividly the years when we were going to write the great
American novel -- the years when writing was a compulsion
and writing well was a goal. It all seemed so far away and
yet so vital -- and still seems so, I guess. How else can
one justify one's losses in other areas?

     And it was all very nice except for the fact that we
will probably never see one another again.
```

Since 1936, when Brick had last lived in Los Angeles, the city had
changed. The big red cars were gone from Venice Boulevard, and the yellow
streetcars no longer criss-crossed the downtown area — nor indeed any area,
and most non-Hispanic Angelinos didn't go downtown any more anyway,
unless they were called for jury duty. The city was interlaced with freeways.
There was only one city-wide newspaper left, the *Times,* which, to its credit,
was no longer the one-sided champion of the status quo; it developed fairly
progressive views after Norman Chandler handed the reins to his young son,
Otis. Manchester Boddy had died, and so had the *Daily News.*

At the City Hall there was a new cast of characters: a black mayor, Tom
Bradley, and Jewish and Latino council members. It was a city of neighbor-

---

2 The memoir by Ernest Hemingway of his early years in Paris.

hoods, and one of them was Brentwood, which was divided between the estate homes of the rich and the more modest apartments housing the middle class and a smattering of students who attended UCLA, about three miles away. Brick was sharing a double bed with Peggy in her two-story apartment house in Brentwood; the other bedroom was given over to his desk, his hi-fi system and his music. His gardening was limited to the narrow earthen border down one side of the building, which had an open carport in the front and a narrow alley in the back, yet there was something about the bright sun and the birds singing that made him happy. When he had the strength, he still typed his lengthy letters, but they were marred by many strikeovers and faulty words blotted out with a line of X's.

With me, most things go well. I was very reluctant to let 1968 get away this year. Not that it was any good, but I didn't see how 1969 could fail to be worse. But the old year went, and the new year came, "what without asking hither hurried whence," etc., and I didn't even try a glass of wine to drown the memory of that insolence,[3] so that when I woke up, it was 1969, and I decided to ape Lucy Brown, the little girl in "Peanuts," and make 1969 "my" year. So far it has worked very well.

I find that I move very slowly as I get older. But Peggy races about through her household chores as though her life depended upon it. So there's a little discrepancy because she really shouldn't move so fast. Whereas I do enjoy moving slowly and cautiously. So, when I finish this letter (my usual 1-1/4 pages before I tire out), I will take my morning walk to the store and mail this and walk back and loaf until nearly evening, then take another short walk and come back prepared to listen to Huntley-Brinkley and then to resist turning on the other TV junk. I wish I were not too tired to write in the evening but, again, I am. Which is not a productive state for one who thinks best on the typewriter.

January 12, 1969

The news here is that I'm scheduled to go into Santa Monica hospital again tomorrow with surgery scheduled for next Friday. I confess, I'm a little nervous about it -- more, I think, about the time between than I am about the surgery itself. Last time was so very unpleasant, fighting to get enough nitroglycerine to keep me going until the doctor had finally impressed on the nurses that I was to have all I wanted, by my bedside. But this time I'll know more how to go about it.

The other big news is that I had a chance to visit

---

3 Brick's reference was to the *Rubaiyat* of Omar Khayyam, Edward Fitzgerald's translation: "Into this Universe, and why not knowing, nor whence, like Water willy-nilly flowing: And out of it, as Wind along the Waste, I know not whither, willy-nilly blowing. What, without asking, hither hurried whence? And, without asking, whither hurried hence! Another and another Cup to drown the Memory of this Impertinence!"

with George last week. He and Lisa flew home (to Albany) for Christmas -- over the polar route. I haven't seen Lisa yet; she is coming down from Berkeley this week to visit two of her grandmothers, and I expect to see her at least briefly at the hospital. After which she flies back alone to New York where she will join George on the flight back to Geneva. When I think of my little fifteen-year-old jetting about the world --

I was delighted with George. His experience abroad has matured him immeasurably; he seems to have got a lot of foolishness out of his system and is prepared to settle down and attach himself to some good job someplace and live sensibly.

Not very sensibly, actually. I was already making plans to leave the International Labor Organization and return to the United States to study for a master's degree and become a college journalism teacher.

I had a couple of very delightful evenings watching some avant garde plays on KCET, the PBS station here. Friday night there were three plays from the downtown Center Theater, a special group called New Theater for the Now. Most impressive was a five-minute subliminal montage effect consisting almost wholly of newspaper headlines and pictures of Vietnam, etc., people dead and dying, bombs dropping, while a voice asked, over and over, "Do you feel safe now?"

It was terrifying. And at the same time it recalled most forcibly what you said about the necessity for obscenity to encompass the contemporary world. Certainly these things are the essence of obscenity.

Saturday night KCET showed another group of experimental films.

One of these, which I'd seen before, dealt, too briefly, with Bob Dylan. But one was a prize-winning film called "THX-1138-4EB," which you may get to see some day even if you have to drive in to L.A. to see it. To films, it must have been what "The Trial" was to the novel.[4] It probably ran thirty minutes or more; there was no dialog, no subtitles, no characters; just shots of a "control center," with anonymous voices coming out of nowhere, with subliminal bits and fragments of mechanized voices (like voices from space ships), and anonymous (but numbered) "scientists" operating the controls, and long shots of blank, sterile passageways -- and a white-clad figure running, running, running, not merely in terror nor with hope, but in desperation, which never showed except in the two or three times he paused and looked back -- or looked back without pausing.

---

4 The film, *Electronic Labyrinth: THX-1138-4EB,* was the 1967 project of the young George Lucas when he was a cinematography student at the University of Southern California. With the financial backing of Francis Ford Coppola, it was made into a feature-length movie, *THX 1138,* released in 1970. Franz Kafka's *The Trial* (1925 in German) was a chilling story of a young clerk who is judged for a crime that is never explained to him.

It was a stimulating experience and one which I needed
badly. Intellectual stimulation here is, believe me, at a
minimum. And television is not wholly a wilderness. And it
is as important to see this film as it was to read Kafka.

June 13, 1969

Dear Toni,

Just a few lines to let you know that I'm still among
the living. Even if the spelling done by this typewriter is
really rather weird. I'm good for about three lines of
fairly competent spelling; then the typewriter goes wild
and hits any key that it fancies. I mean my fingers do.

Chiefly I've been trying to get well, conquer the
typewriter, learn to talk again, and learn to sign my name
-- in that order. This is by far the best letter I have
typed, so you'll know what the others have been like.

It seems that the surgery I had doesn't usually cure the
condition I had; it just makes it better, and there is a
maximum that one can do, no matter how hard he tries. Only, I
suspect, the doctors won't tell you this because they want
you to be reaching for that maximum. So that's what I'm doing
now. I go to physical therapy three mornings a week to try to
learn to walk better and spend another session, morning and
evening, at the typewriter, writing about the quick brown fox
or asserting that now is the time for all good men, etc., and
my typing is gradually improving.

I often think of Anne Hawkins and how it must have
been for her to have been cut off so early in her career.[5]

On July 20, 1969, Chuck's boyhood fantasy finally came true. Like
Buck Rogers, a man flew through space and then walked on the moon.
Chuck had never owned a television set, so on that day he and Ann-
Marie rented a motel room with a TV in Ukiah so they and their two kids
could watch the historic event. That summer I moved with Lisa back to
Los Angeles.

October 12, 1969

George and Lisa are here; they have rented an
apartment in the apartment house which Peggy's family owns,
where we stay, that is, so they are our closest neighbors.
But I don't see very much of them; as George is going to
school -- and so is Lisa, for that matter. But I look
forward to knowing them better. They have been away so
long, and I never really knew them. I'm sure of one thing:
George is of all my offspring the most like me. I don't
know whether that is good or not.

Two decades after I first set foot on the UCLA campus as a freshman, I was back as a graduate student, thirty-seven years old. Times had

---

5 Anne's lengthy bout with myasthenia gravis had rendered her incapable of writing.

changed. In 1949 no one could so much as pass out a handbill, on pain of expulsion. But the Free Speech Movement at Berkeley had brought a permanently open political life to the University of California. In my first week back I gave a quizzical look to a group of young women with banners: "Women's Liberation." How bizarre, I thought; what do women have to be liberated from?

I enrolled Lisa at University High School in West Los Angeles. Michael, ten, and Rica, seven, were with their mother in the San Francisco Bay Area. Patty was getting ready to divorce Bill and marry a young attorney, Rod Shepherd. Brick was busy putting his large collection of jazz records onto reel-to-reel tape. He watched professional football and documentaries on television, went with Peggy to visit her family and, for exercise, shuffled through the neighborhood. Despite his frailty, he gladly took on the burden of caring for his old friend, who was his new wife.

December 6, 1969

Dear Corinne and Irving,

I'm afraid I am going to have to remain absent from the desert for a while yet. The fact is that Peggy has been having trouble with her heart, and I'm afraid to take the long trip until (if ever) I get my driver's license back. Please don't say anything about this in future letters, as I don't want her to know how worried I am, but her blood pressure has gone back up to a quite high figure, and last night after dinner she had a very difficult time to stop the pain in her arm and chest.

For the first time, she had a spasm on the freeway, and I had to feed her nitroglycerine as we went along past an accident. I can't keep her as quiet as she should be, but I'm determined to keep her from long trips.

December 12, 1969

Peggy is in the hospital with a bleeding ulcer. She is still very weak but is looking forward to coming home early next week.

Believe me, I've missed her while she was gone, as she has become a sort of third hand to me in the last year, and I have come to depend a great deal on her doing things that I should be doing myself. Fortunately, George was here and offered to drive me around. I also found out it is possible to take the bus to Santa Monica, and in a way I like the bus very much. But I still depend on Peggy for most things.

As ever,

Brick

Chapter Thirty-Eight
Letting Go

December 17, 1969

Dear Corinne and Irving,

Peggy is home, but is very weak, yet still insists that she must carry on as usual, although I manage to take over a little of the household chores.

I am feeling fine. Peggy really opened the right doors for me. I am now able to walk almost without impairment at all. I still have trouble with my talking; the words just won't come.

Last night we saw the Modern Jazz Quartet at Tanglewood on Channel 28. It was marvelous. They are really twice the artists they were ten years ago, which is about when I heard them last. I've always respected their work but seldom played their records -- except for three or four things I liked. But last night was marvelous -- particularly the "Concierto de Aranjuez," which as you remember, Miles Davis did on one track of the "Sketches From Spain."

I am reading "Letting Go" by Philip Roth[1] and am determined to finish it. It goes on and on -- but does have an interesting bunch of characters. But they do at last reduce everybody to a least common denominator.

---

1 Letting Go was the first novel for the 36-year-old Roth; 630 pages long, it was published in 1962 by Random House. It told the story of a newly discharged Korean War veteran striving to live seriously and act generously.

January 10, 1970

Tell me, what do they mean by a "cinema verite" method? Do they mean a documentary, or fiction, or what? It was a program on Channel 2 the other night, a CBS Special called "The Battle of East St. Louis." It picked up a bunch of cops and a bunch of militant blacks and showed them in their natural habitat and then in a three-day "encounter" in which they met and talked things over with psychiatric help -- such things as reverse role playing, etc. It was very moving -- you just couldn't help but feel that this was real, because nobody could be acting and be so free of ham as these people were. Then the horrible thought that these were actors. I looked up the program, and it says, "Cinema verite techniques were used." So I ask, "What are these? Were they actors or were they real?"[2]

Oh, incidentally, that baby on Patty's Christmas card was not Tauni but the child of a friend of theirs. I think my favorite card, though, was one I got from Ruth: "War is not healthy for children and other living things."[3]

January 26, 1970

The fact is that I do begin to feel some urge to attempt to write. But I cannot master this typewriter; the things I have to say are not strong enough to force their way through. I'm not sure whether some of this is due to brain damage or not. I think clearly, but in conversation I find myself grasping for the most common words after I've finished a couple of sentences. So I find it easier to be silent than to carry on a conversation, and Peggy, I must admit, finds herself capable of carrying on enough conversation for both of us.

If I ever get my driver's license back, I want to drive around the place where my book is located; I feel that I can divorce myself from the real background enough so that I can write it as fiction and not as history-turned-around. Or so I think. Yet it is going to be difficult unless I can conquer this typewriter.

The American Way of Life

The night before school opened in the fall, some of the seniors and juniors got together on the steps of the Carnegie Public Library to decide what they were going to do about the new principal, a man named Atterbury. Nobody had seen him yet except Dick Steele, who said he was big as hell and a mean-looking bastard. Somebody had heard he'd come from being principal at a reform school in the Sierra where he'd been fired because the kids caught him and stripped the clothes off him, tied

---

2 "The Battle of East St. Louis" aired on December 30, 1969. Cinema verité techniques involve the use of hand-held cameras and other techniques in dramas and documentaries to convey candid realism.

3 Created in 1969 by Lorraine Schneider for the anti-war group Another Mother for Peace.

him to a flagpole and left him there. Mote Salisbury said, "We ought to tie him to the flagpole at the start, just to show him."

But Ray McKay said there were a lot of things to be thought about the situation, but it wasn't Atterbury's fault the school board had fired Old Bottoms, so they ought to greet him with a real welcome — "Whyn't we give him a good rousing yell at the assembly tomorrow morning to show we don't hold any hard feelings?" Dick Steele, the yell leader, finally agreed. And Mote kept quiet.

The new principal was big and mean-looking. He moved up the aisle the next day like an elephant in bad temper, like he was stepping on trash. But Dick spread his arms for the yell anyway: "Atterbury, Atterbury, attaboy, Atterbury! Rah! Rah! Rah!"

The principal reared up, then stood still for maybe ten seconds. "No more such demonstrations will be tolerated! Dismiss!" He didn't bother with the last syllable. There was stunned silence, then they all went to class without gathering in knots in the hall, as they usually did. "Gawd damn!" muttered Dub McLain at Mote Salisbury's back. "I don't see how a man can be so Gawd damn mean!" Mote just looked sick.

On Friday there was a notice on the bulletin board saying the school board had canceled permission to use the buses to take the football team and the rooters over to San Benito for the opener. And afterward El Jardin lost 13-7; the spirit had gone out of the players and the few students who had been able to make the trip.

Monday was Student Assembly day; usually during football season the meetings turned into rallies. Not this time: Instead, Ray McKay immediately stood up and moved that the school board be asked to give the kids and the team the buses again. The motion would have carried instantly if Agnes Harker had not moved to refer the matter to the principal. That was a surprise; nobody had ever referred anything to Old Bottoms; he was usually right in the room, and if he had anything to say, he said it. But everybody knew Agnes was a sneak and her old man was president of the school board.

What also surprised everyone was Bliss Lane's seconding Agnes's motion in a loud, clear voice, and of course there had to be a debate between him and Ray.

Ray talked about democracy and the defense of the American way of life and about orderly, constitutional processes. It was stuff he'd heard at home and picked up by reading the war news. He argued that the school constitution didn't require consultation with the principal before the students took a vote, that there should be no knuckling down in advance. From the chuckles and applause, it looked liked he would carry students with him.

But Bliss walked to the front of the room and began talking: He recalled the spring night on Old Bottoms' lawn, before the former principal moved from town, and he reminded the students of what Old Bottoms had said then.

Bob Reynolds, in awe, thought it was the most effective speech he had ever heard. Mr. Watkins, the English teacher who'd been assigned to handle the meeting, started taking notes. Bliss didn't notice, and he summed up with the words that drifted out of quiet memory: "In all things where the honor of El Jardin is involved . . . do the right thing." There were murmurs of recognition.

"Besides," he added slyly, "no reform school principal could ever be expected to know the meaning of the traditions of El Jardin." There was laughter and loud applause.

After that, Agnes's motion passed on a shouted voice vote, and Mr. Watkins got up to walk cautiously toward the principal's office.

Atterbury came out, and Bliss could sense what might happen. Bliss licked his lips and tried to think of what he could say. But he needn't have bothered. The man with the elephant skin took most of the space at the front of the room. He was quiet, almost pleased.

"I have warned you young ladies and gentlemen that no more noise would be permitted at student body assemblies." The room was chillingly silent. Atterbury went on:

"If there is one bit of advice I can give you, it is this: 'If you want anything in this world, take it; but pay for it.' You have chosen to take a few minutes to disrupt school affairs by unseemly conduct. You will now pay for it. Assemblies are suspended for one month."

Everybody stared at Bliss. To Bob Reynolds Bliss looked like a prize fighter who'd been knocked down and then tried to stand up again on the count of seven. He rose slightly, then sank to his seat again. Atterbury glowered around the room.

"Dismiss!"

On February 24, 1969, Earl Warren's Supreme Court, in a decision written by Abe Fortas, decided in *Tinker v. Des Moines Independent Community School District* that high school students did not "shed their constitutional rights to freedom of speech or expression at the schoolhouse gate." The students in Des Moines, and all over the country for that matter, were free now to wear black arm bands to protest the Vietnam War.

The war, the war . . . It was everywhere.

On May 4, 1970, national guardsmen killed two students at Kent State University during an antiwar protest. At UCLA the next day a group of students threw rocks and Molotov cocktails at a line of university police guarding the ROTC headquarters, their batons in hand, plastic shields covering their faces. Helicopters chattered overhead.

On Sunset Boulevard, hundreds of motorcycle police gathered out of sight, and when they were ready, they advanced down the hill, dismounted and drove all the students in front of them. I got up from a bench near Janss Steps, where I had been observing the spectacle and took the blue bus back to Brentwood.

Later that week I flew to Western Washington State College in Bellingham, Washington, where classes had been suspended in protest over Kent State. A group of professors interviewed me for a journalism teaching job. They hired me, and by September Lisa and I were living in the little town near the Canadian border, known both for its smelly paper mills and its steady stream of young Americans heading north to avoid the draft.

Chuck and Ann-Marie and their two kids were in the Mendocino County forest, in a cabin with no running water. Their marriage was falling apart. Patty and Rod and her family were in Carmichael, a small town outside Sacramento. Dickie gave up her secretarial service and took up retirement. She was still active in the Soroptimist Club, and she traveled to Europe, where she went to a tea party with the Queen. Vivian and our two younger children were living in Brick's and Naomi's old house in Albany.

Brick — well, Brick wasn't doing too well. His remaining sister, Eleanor, was close to death. Brick and Peggy went several times to Santa Barbara, where Eleanor lived in a teachers' retirement home.

March 16, 1970

Peggy has really been marvelous over the whole thing; she has taken on the full responsibility for Eleanor, and you'd think that Eleanor, whom she didn't know at all a year ago, was her own blood sister.

Of course, I had to handle Eleanor's financial affairs, including income tax and health insurance -- and she really couldn't tell us a thing -- she'd get nervous and upset as soon as we asked her anything about them. So we had to dig it out ourselves.

Meanwhile, I have been too busy to get my driver's license or even take a driving lesson. But I start that again tomorrow.

March 25, 1970

I flunked my driving test and, frankly, I don't know whether I will pass it the next time or not. At first I was really burned up -- it was ridiculous that after driving for 55 years (and since 1926 without an accident) I should be unable to drive a car!

The main thing they flunked me on was failing to look back when making a lane change. I swore I had looked back

every time, but yesterday, on practicing a little bit, I
suddenly realized that I had just made a lane change
without looking in the mirror. Then I remembered a lane
change I had made during the test where I had used only the
mirror -- and the fact dawned on me that I had probably
done it at least twice more.

So now I'm not burned up any more.

November 10, 1970

I've been feeling a little less than my best for the
last few days. I don't know what's the matter; my bodily
functions all seem to be performing at top level, and the
doctor can find nothing wrong with my EKG but I walk around
like a zombie most of the time. My doctor tends to pass it
all off as a result of the operation, which it well may be.
In that case there is nothing to do but accept it. Because
obviously I don't want them unscrambling my brains again.
So anything they did wrong the first time is just going to
have to stay wrong.

But the fact that I felt better yesterday and today is
something to be encouraged about. Yet it makes me wonder --
to feel so mentally decrepit while appearing so normal, and
not to find any ache or a pain that I can identify with. It
makes me look again at people in jails or mental hospitals
and wonder if they, too, are undergoing something of this
sort.

I haven't heard again from Patty but know she will
write -- or call -- when the spirit moves her. I think the
most difficult thing for a parent is to realize that a
child has grown up and that any resemblance between what
the child is and what you wanted it to be is purely
coincidental.

The things that children attribute to their parents!
Your story of Patty's having been left at the park reminds
me of the time we were living at the ranch and Louis (as he
was then) woke up with a nightmare about me standing up and
hurtling him out of the rumble seat of the old Ford. How he
could ever have dreamed that is beyond me -- and yet
children do live in that sort of fantasy world which is
beyond belief. I cannot believe that anything like that
Golden Gate Park episode happened -- but Patty, I suppose,
must have thought that it did.

I had my own introduction to life-as-it-is with Chuck.
He was, I think, about fourteen and we were having a big
row about something, and suddenly I realized that the
little baby I had adored and played with and petted and
taught was gone as literally and completely as though he
had died. In fact, for all practical purposes he had died.
I remember that I burst into tears at the realization.

I told him that henceforth he was on his own. I was

willing to advise him if he wished. I might even give him an order or two. But he was not expected to obey and I would not be angry with him if he did not.

I'm afraid, though, that the upshot was not as favorable as might have been expected. For the fact was that he did not have anybody to rebel against and it was not until he got in the Navy that he began seriously to go through the period when one dislikes one's father.

I was delighted with the election. Even Tunney. After all, a guy who roomed with Ted Kennedy can't be all bad. I did vote for him on the basis of having another Democrat, even a bad one.[4] But the rest of the ticket I pretty well voted for the Peace and Freedom candidates.

But all in all, it was a delightful election. Whether it will give the fascists a setback is another thing.

February 11, 1971

We had a little earthquake the other morning. At least it was a little quake for us veterans of 1933, etc. It was quite a shock, though. I woke up right in the middle of the floor and then, realizing there was no place to run to, I just stood until it was all over.[5]

August 24, 1971

I think that what gets me down as much as anything is the smell of death all around. It seems that everyone I know is on the verge of dying -- of old age, or bad hearts or something. I suppose one must get used to this when he reaches a certain place in life, but it is troublesome nevertheless. I think that is partly due to the fact that I live among people of my own age instead of seeing my children and grandchildren a part of the time. When Peggy gets better, I hope we can spend some more time with them. As indeed we have plans to do.

September 23, 1971

The last few weeks have been sort of grim. I think the L-dopa is working and producing some side effects. Several weeks ago I fell into a brief period of deep despondency, and my doctor cut down my dose. That cured the depression, but the last week or so I've been very tired like I had iron-poor blood or something horrible like you see in the TV ads. I'm so weak I can scarcely get out of bed in the morning, and I drag around all day without getting any stronger.

I'm glad summer is over because we can start planning on going to Palm Springs again. It really has been a good

---

4 The Democrats increased their margin in the House and retained control of the Senate. John Tunney, son of the former heavyweight champion, was elected U.S. senator from California on the Democratic ticket. Edward M. (Ted) Kennedy had been senator from Massachusetts since 1962.

5 The Sylmar earthquake of February 9, 1971, killed fifty-eight people, about half of them in a Veterans Hospital in the San Fernando Valley.

summer in spite of all the bad things that happened to our
health -- and to Eleanor. One of the most remarkable things
has been the weather. As though Mother Nature wanted to
remind me what it was like in my youth -- almost every day
has been bright and clear and non-smoggy, like it used to
be fifty years ago. And the mockingbird sang from early
spring until July with an astonishing variety of songs.

[Carmichael, California]
October 12, 1971

I am at Pat's, writing this on Rod's electric
typewriter so this may be even less legible than usual.

The big news around here is Patty's pregnancy. She has
been shouting it, pridefully, from the house tops, even
though she hasn't had it confirmed as yet; she is pretty
sure. And she and Rod are as proud as though they had
invented it. They are very nice kids, both of them, and
they're going to be very happy when the new baby comes.

The bad news is that Chuck and Ann-Marie have split
up -- again. They broke up first when Chris was about two
years old, but this one seems to be more permanent,
according to Chuck. I was in town yesterday and talked
with Ann-Marie. Apparently it is entirely Chuck's fault.
He just out and announced he didn't want to be married
any more. And apparently he doesn't. He has always been
ambivalent about marriage and this seems to be it. Ann-
Marie is very sweet and, incidentally, very beautiful and
I wish they would reconcile.

Their little Leonie, my granddaughter, has grown
into a beautiful, beautiful girl. She's about five, I
think, and has the most beautiful eyes. It is strange how
much more beautiful my grandchildren are than their
immediate ancestors.

October 31, 1971

Yesterday I took Peggy for a little drive out to
Topanga Canyon. It was very nice and brought back memories
of when I was a newspaper reporter here. It seems that the
old Topanga Canyon has fallen prey to developers less than
most other parts of L.A. and we could even find a place to
park the car and go for a little walk -- twenty feet or so.
That is a major accomplishment for us these days. Anyway,
there is a small hippie colony there (with some small
hippies, about fourteen, I would guess.) It was lots of fun
and served to stir up hope for "The Greening of America."

I'm sorry to say I tuned out the Dick Cavett program
with the kids. I was tired and it didn't seem to me they
would have anything to say. So I skipped them -- much to my
later regret. Because Charles Reich is right: either you
have a revolution which will transform America from within
or you will have no America at all. And no revolution,

either. (I heard David Harris say something to the same effect not long ago.)[6]

I didn't tell you about the airplane trip to Sacramento, did I? It was marvelous. I finally decided to go by plane when I was feeling so depressed that I figured a nice airplane crackup was something which would end all my troubles. Rather, I felt that going by plane was safer than going by car since you can count the number of near-misses you have on the freeway and you never know the amount you have in going by plane. It made a jet setter out of me. Not a bump all the way and we slipped in smoother than a Greyhound bus. Or a train. I plan to do all my travel by air after this.

Last night I had a long phone talk with Dickie. It was the first time I'd spoken with her in a couple of years, but she had just finished a three-week tour up north, visiting the kids and she was full of conversation so it just went on and on. She saw George in Bellingham, then she visited Chuck and later, on the way home, Ann-Marie. She reports nothing in sight in the way of a reconciliation. Ann-Marie is very sad about it. But Chuck seems to have made up his mind. I'm glad to have Dickie to talk to, from time to time. She is really quite a woman.

December 27, 1971

Dear Toni,

It was nice to get your Christmas note. I have to answer it on the typewriter because, bad as my typing is, it's still legible. Which my handwriting is not. And never was, for that matter.

I hope you're feeling better. Maybe I wish I were religious so I could say, "I'll pray for you," like Cornelia does. Not that it does any good, but it's a lot nicer thing to say.

I have been feeling quite well lately. Which reminds me that I always put the year on the date of letters, not because I expect anybody to save them but to remind myself how late it is. Like 1972 is borrowed time; I always told myself I should live so long. But now that 1972 is just around the corner, I still cling to what there is left.

Keep in touch -- there's a popular song which has a refrain: "But I always thought that I'd see you again."[7] We cannot afford to have our friends feel bad; there are so few of them left.

---

6 The popular television interviewer, Dick Cavett, had just had several students on his program as representatives of their generation. Charles Reich's book *The Greening of America: How the Youth Revolution Is Trying to Make America Livable* was published by Random House in 1970. David Harris was a former student president at Stanford University who served nearly two years in prison for draft evasion. He was at that time married to singer Joan Baez.

7 "Fire and Rain" by James Taylor.

March 13, 1972

Dear Corinne and Irving,

Eleanor died last week, and while we were prepared for
her death, something like that comes as a shock. We drove
up to see her two days before her death, and one could tell
then that the end was near. That leaves me as the sole
survivor of our generation. And it's a lonely place to be.

Eleanor was a woman who lived solely for others -- our
father, our mother, my brother. Even in funeral arrangements she did all the work in advance; arranged with the
undertaker, paid him in full, decided what sort of funeral
she wanted, etc. etc. Only then -- but this was a year ago
-- did she call me in and ask me to take over. So there was
a minimum of trouble. All her life she has been acting like
that, and I think that she has never given a thought to any
other way of existing.

There is a will to be probated so I'll have to go up
there again. But the long chain of visits will be ended:
first to see my father decline and die, then my mother,
then my brother -- there is forty-five years of driving to
Santa Barbara on such unhappy errands. Yet Santa Barbara
was never "home" to any of us.

As ever,

Brick

Chapter Thirty-Nine
Period Pieces

Western Washington State College in the early 1970s was astoundingly beautiful. Surrounded by stands of pines and firs, its red-brick buildings lay sprawled on the brim of a hill overlooking the busy harbor of Bellingham, which is in the northwest corner of the mainland U.S., eighty miles from both Seattle, Washington, and Vancouver, British Columbia. The students came from both farming towns and what passed for big cities in the state. There were a few Lummi Indians and Canadians and a noticeable presence of antiwar protesters, feminists, Jesus freaks, vegetarians and hippies, both real and wannabe. It was the last stop on the way out of the country for draft evaders. On Wednesdays a group of solid Bellingham citizens would stand silently in front of the Whatcom County courthouse to protest the war, while others scurried by, busy making money from it.

Overcast day, chilly. I rush across the Main Quad on my way to teach a class. I see in the center of the broad open space: Women and girls waving signs and chanting, something to do with feminism. Lisa is there, too. She has dropped out of the local high school and is living in a women's collective. I stop and talk to her. They're all wearing dungarees or jeans or bib overalls. No makeup within a hundred yards.

"What's going on?"

"Demonstration, can't you see?" Typical teen talk.

"Be careful." Typical dad talk.

Off to class. Me. Not her. Things are different from when I was a kid.

April 22, 1972

Dear Corinne and Irving,

Last night I did something I've planned to do for a long time. I got out the hundreds of pages which go to make up the novel and read them over to see if inspiration would come -- but it didn't. I've been troubled a little by that fact; this morning I woke up in profound depression which lasted several hours -- and even yet there is a gnawing sensation down inside myself that I should do something about it. The worst shock, though, was that I have not worked on it for some eighteen years. You'd think, wouldn't you, that in so many years one would learn to leave it alone?

I thought for a long time that I was free of it -- especially when the people concerned all began to die off. As though at last I was going to have the last word. But the characters and events, even if wholly imaginary, still haunt me and demand to be set on paper.

Then, too, there is the fact that so many years have intervened so that what was once a contemporary story has become a period piece -- a costume piece which makes entirely different demands on the writer -- and I suppose on the reader. Imagine how today's sophisticated reader would react to one of the few sex scenes in the book. At the same time, there is a cry for nostalgia.

Or take the high school scenes: Could a graduate of a modern high school of, say, 3,000 kids, most of whom smoke pot and call policemen "pigs" (and whose athletic events have been canceled because of a lack of funds in the budget) find any importance in Bliss Lane's one-man revolt against authority? Perhaps they could, but I doubt it.

Of course, the change in the world makes some parts of the book easier to handle. I imagine that the whole first section, the subject of Bliss's revolt against his parents, especially their religion, would have a costume-piece sort of relevance. But it still seems a very untimely thing to attempt, now, to write for a generation which has become accustomed to "Myra Breckinridge" or "Rabbit, Run."[1]

The Strike at El Jardin High School

 . . . *"Then you will help us, Mr. Rankin? You'll put a piece in the paper?"*

Mr. Rankin said "No."

Dub McLain butted in: "I don't get it, Mr. Rankin," and the editor said in a very formal voice, "I mean that the Journal *is not in a position to intervene in the matter at this time."*

There wasn't much to say. Dub McLain opened his mouth but Ray

---

[1] *Myra Breckinridge,* by Gore Vidal, was published in 1968 by Little, Brown. *Rabbit, Run* by John Updike, was published in 1960 by Knopf.

shushed him and they all got up from their chairs. It wasn't until they were out on the sidewalk that Mr. Rankin, who had come to the door with them, said: "Of course, the Journal *is always glad to publish correspondence from its readers in 'The People's Voice.'"*

Ray McKay said, "Yes, thank you, Mr. Rankin."

The kids went back to school. That night they met again in Pink's barn and everybody was pretty discouraged. Finally Bliss said, "What was that about putting something in the Letters Column?" and Ray McKay said, "Yeah, I guess he would if anybody could get his old man to write one." Nobody said anything for a minute, nobody wanted to have his old man fight his battles for him. Bliss said, "What if we wrote one ourselves?" and Pink said, "I expect they could get you for that."

Bliss asked, "Why? It's a free country, isn't it?" And Ray said, "Not that free." Finally Bliss said, "I think we ought to do it," and Ray shook his head and said, "That's what I used to think, too. Then look what happened." Bliss lounged back against the manger, sort of grinned and said, "So what?"

But the week after that the Journal *carried a long letter from a local businessman in 'The People's Voice,' urging everybody to get behind Atterbury for County Superintendent. It criticized the laxness of discipline at the high school under Bottoms and claimed that Atterbury had saved the taxpayers a bundle and made him sound, as Dub McLain said, like a little tin Jesus on ball bearings.*

It made everybody sore, and some of the kids wanted to go down and talk to Mr. Rankin about it again and show him how wrong it was, but Ray pointed out that they'd already been to see him once and the best thing they could do was to keep out of it. Bliss Lane didn't say anything at all.

A couple of days later, Bob was sitting at the breakfast table. His father exploded into a cough and a choke so that his coffee went all over the Journal *and dribbled down his shirt.*

"Bob," he demanded when he got his breath back and wiped his eyes and replaced his glasses, "isn't this Bliss Lane the boy that goes to school with you?"

Bob said he was, and craned to see what his father was reading, but he needn't have bothered. His father cleared his throat again and said, "Listen to this." He read aloud:

"'To the Editor, Sir: A correspondent in a recent letter to the Journal *wrote that he was pleased with the "improved discipline" at El Jardin High School since the replacement of the former principal by A. H. Atterbury. He seriously urges that Principal Atterbury should be elected as County Superintendent of Schools, so that the same influence which has been exerted over El Jardin High may be extended over all the schools in the county.*

"*The author of that letter is not the parent of any boy or girl now attending El Jardin; hence it may be assumed that his statements are based upon simple ignorance rather than a desire to break down our public school system by foisting the policies of Principal Atterbury upon the other schools. Had he been more familiar with the deterioration of El Jardin High, he would have known that the facts are exactly the opposite.*

"*El Jardin students were formerly devoted to their school and to their principal, Mr. H. L. Bottoms, because they understood that the devotion was returned. No repressive measures of discipline were necessary because the students strove to carry out the adjuration of their principal: "In all matters where the honor of El Jardin is at stake, do the right thing!" No less faithfully do they now attempt to carry out the advice of Mr. Atterbury: "If you want anything in this world, take it — but pay for it."*

"*Formerly students of El Jardin were expected to act like honorable men and women and they did so. Today they are expected to act like reform-school inmates: should it be wondered that they actually do so?*

"*It's true there are many students at El Jardin who might short-sightedly agree that it would be well for their school if the present principal were promoted to the position of County Superintendent so that El Jardin might be freed from his direct control. But isn't this a selfish point of view? Isn't it true that El Jardin has a greater responsibility to the other schools of the county than simply to beat them each year in athletics as we formerly did, under Mr. Bottoms? Doesn't El Jardin's traditional position of leadership carry with it the responsibilities of noblesse oblige? Could we honorably confront our opponents of the future, knowing that we have weakened them by exporting to them our own special illness?*

"*I don't believe we could. Heavy though our cross may be, let's not ask our neighbors to help bear it. In this matter, where the honor of El Jardin is at stake, let us all — students and parents and friends to the school — make every effort to assure that the disaster which has come upon us shall not be spread to the other schools of the county. Respectfully, Bliss Lane.*'"

"*Do you suppose he really wrote it?*" Bob's mother demanded. "*Maybe it was his father.*"

"*No,*" Bob's father said. "*His father is Albert Lane. It's the boy, all right. There'll be trouble about this.*"

Bob stopped to show the paper to Pink Stephenson, so that the nine o'clock bell was ringing when he got into the auditorium. There were several copies of the Journal stuffed into desks. Bliss was in his seat. Bob gave him a quick look. The teachers were hurrying up and down the side aisles; some scurried into the principal's office, as though there was going to be a faculty meeting.

Everybody sat still, and there was hardly any whispering, until Miss Lundeen, who taught drawing and singing and was not considered exactly a member of the faculty, came out and made the announcement.

"Our regular schedule is disrupted this morning, boys and girls," she said. *"For the first period we will have community singing. All except Bliss Lane, that is. He is required to go to the principal's office."*

Bliss got up from his seat and looked around the room with a sort of mock-serious terror as though to say, "Now I'm in for it!" and then walked into Atterbury's office.

That night, lying in the grass in front of the Carnegie Library, talking with Bliss, Bob Reynolds remembered how the rubber soles of Bliss's tennis shoes had squeaked on the polished floor. "I was scared," said Bliss, "because I didn't know what I'd done wrong. I wrote the letter in my own house with my own pen on my own paper and walked down to the post office and mailed it with my own stamp, and I just couldn't see where it ever came under Old Atterbury's jurisdiction."

"Nobody else could either," Bob said. "We were really burned up. Some wanted to go home and get their parents and bring them down to see what Old Atterbury and the faculty were doing."

Bliss said, "I was scared I would knuckle under."

He was rolling it over in his mind, trying to get things straight, because it was important to know who Bliss Lane was and what he really wanted and what he was capable of — but he hadn't knuckled under. "You didn't," Bob reminded him.

Bliss gave a little laugh, "I would have, only two things happened. The first was they'd stuck Miss Alsop with her shorthand books and pencils over at a table half-hidden in the coat closet. I guess they had the idea of getting her out of sight, but there wasn't enough room, and they didn't have enough nerve to say, 'Bliss, we're going to take down everything that is said here so the school board will know.' They had to pretend to hide her. I thought of a silly-looking ostrich sticking its head in the sand, and all of a sudden I wanted to laugh. I could see, even before I sat down, what Old Bullneck was up to."

"Up to?"

Bliss stood and began pacing. "He didn't have the nerve to kick me out himself; he had to call in the whole faculty and get them to do it. I just looked them over and realized there wasn't brains enough in the whole bunch not to half-hide Old Lady Alsop and her notebooks, and I remembered — well, you know — Atterbury's favorite saying. And I said to myself, 'Okay, kid, you'll have to pay for it — but take it.'"

Bob just lay there and listened. It was like Bliss was running for office.

Mr. Watkins had opened the questioning.

"We were all of us shocked, Bliss, by this letter we found in the

Journal *this morning. Your name appears to be signed to it. I suppose
there is no possible doubt that you did write it?"*

"*There could be no possible doubt,*" Bliss said. "*I'm sorry anyone
was shocked by it.*"

*Bliss wondered if they could punish him for something he did on his
own time. He thought they were trying to get him to repeat the same thing
on the schoolgrounds so they could kick him out for saying what he had a
right to say elsewhere. He grinned at them, or tried to, and said: "Mr.
Watkins, it might not be wise to discuss our private opinions of El Jardin
High School at this time."*

*And all that time, Bliss told Bob, "I kept feeling that music, like it
was coming from the rooting section and I held on; maybe it was a grandstand play, but dammit, what isn't a grandstand play that amounts to
anything?"*

Bob thought about that morning; it seemed so long ago.

*The kids saw the principal's door open and Pink Stephenson called
out, "Here he comes!" Isabelle Heard, at the piano, struck up the opening chords of "El Jardin Forever," and they all stood and sang while
Bliss walked down the hall and out the front door without looking back.*

*Then Atterbury came out and stood before them, and Isabelle, flustered,
stopped playing. The song died out quickly. "I regret to tell you that your
colleague has been sent home to await action by the school board. Let me
suggest that each of you hasten to dissociate yourself from him in order that
your graduation may take place according to schedule."*

*He stood looking at them a minute as though to let them know exactly
what he meant. Then he said, "Dismiss!" dropping the final consonant as
he always did, and they went out, half-cowed and half-defiant, knowing
they would have to do as much for El Jardin as Dick Angell or Bliss Lane
had done.*

*By the time classes were over that afternoon it was all arranged. Nobody
in El Jardin had ever seen a strike or even read much about one, but they
knew what to do: those bankers' sons and the children of the town merchants
and the kids from the country whose fathers ran wandering Wobblies off the
place with a pitchfork. The school board was to meet that night and everybody agreed that if they expelled Bliss, nobody would go back to school. They
would have picket lines; anybody who crossed would be made pretty unhappy
afterward. Ray McKay, as always, organized things, and everybody felt good
because they knew that if Ray McKay, who had never much liked Bliss Lane,
stood behind Bliss the school was really united.*

*Ray said they had to go to see Bliss, so they went over to his house
and sent in Bob Reynolds to bring Bliss outside, and they asked how it
went and what his old man had said.*

Bliss wasn't smiling anymore. "He took it kind of hard," he said. "He didn't get tough about it or anything. Said it was up to me; I'd have to make my own decision about things like that. Said nothing like this had ever happened to a Lane before. I feel kind of bad about it."

They couldn't tell whether he was weakening or not. Ray McKay broke in: "We want you to know, Bliss, that we're behind you absolutely one thousand percent. If they kick you out tonight we're going to walk out in the morning. Either you graduate with us or there won't be any graduation."

"Gee, that's swell," Bliss said. Then he added, "But I don't think any of us really got anything to worry about. They can't kick you out for speaking your mind off the school grounds. And I was careful in there this morning not to say anything they could expel me for."

"Wait a minute," Ray said. "You mean you think the board will let you get away with that letter just because it was written off the school grounds."

"Sure," Bliss said. "They can't stop it. The Constitution guarantees free speech and free press."

"And you think that means kids."

"Sure," Bliss said again. "It means everybody, niggers, chinamen, kids — everybody. The Constitution is there to protect them . . . "

"Not around here," Ray said.

May 27, 1972

There is one thing I have to say about the campus riots: Everybody says, "Oh, the riots are counter-productive; force and violence never helped anybody yet." Peggy says it, and I know both of you say it, and at times I've thought it myself.

But it simply isn't true. If there weren't people who, however foolishly, were willing to put their lives on the line, the more "moderate" of us wouldn't even take the trouble to vote. Only the courage of the extremists spurs the lesser courage of the non-extremists into action. Not that I think the little people's windows should be broken. For that matter I hardly doubt that rioters are being financed secretly by the CIA. Or whoever. But it remains a fact that no revolutionary movement was ever carried out except by force and violence. If we except India, of course. But India is a special case. When we reach the place where we can worship a cow while our children starve, than we will be ready for Gandhi. And that time may come. But it is not here yet.

As a matter of fact, on the surface the world situation is much better than it has been any time in the past. The mere fact that there are campus riots -- well, is it better for them to be waving "Stop the War" flags or to be swallowing goldfish?

And while it's true that Nixon's Supreme Court seems determined to undo all the good that Warren's did, it is still true that they will not quite accomplish this. And while we will undoubtedly go into a New McCarthyism, there are forces to fight against this which did not exist at the time of the old McCarthy.

The trouble with the revolutionary movement today is that it is so completely "anti." It has no "pro." No shining example to which it can point a finger and say, "We want that." Yesterday's revolutionaries could point to the Soviet Union, but no more. So the youth movements of Germany, France, Italy, Japan, the United States all have nothing to revolt for; they are only against. And consequently they find it impossible to seize power. They stand helpless.

As ever,

Brick

How the Strike Was Ended

Nobody went through the picket lines next morning except Agnes Harker, who had to because her old man was president of the board, and maybe a few other kids. It was like a vacation. They hung around just off the school ground and stopped any other kids that came along and then, when the teachers had all gone into their empty classrooms, everybody went out on the athletic field and had speeches and a bonfire and, at noon, a wiener bake. Walt Kendricks, the day marshal, came out and stood around; he could have run them in, maybe for building a fire on school property, but he joshed them a while and then went back to his office. In the afternoon they held a parade downtown; they'd made some banners calling for "Free Speech and a Free Press" and asking "Are Students People?" and proclaiming "It Is The School Which Is Public, Not The Student."

They stuck it out through Thursday and Friday and Saturday and Sunday. On Monday they held another parade down Main Street and a rally at the ball field; Ray McKay made a fiery speech in which he pledged that El Jardin would rot before any man or woman of them would ever set foot in its halls again and everybody cheered and gave a triple three for good old Bliss.

But afterwards Ray privately asked several of the leaders, even juniors and sophomores and the president of the freshmen class, over to Pink Stephenson's carriage house to discuss strategy. When they got there, he told them how he had the real dope from his old man; he said his old man had talked to the members of the school board and that they had decided that under no circumstances could Bliss be reinstated. The kids just as well better make up their minds to give up the idea of graduating.

Pink Stephenson suggested that if Bliss knew it was really hopeless, he'd be the first one to want them to go back. Ray McKay said they shouldn't put it up to Bliss that way, but there was something about the idea of going back and getting their diplomas which kept getting bigger and bigger. The girls' mothers had already made their graduation dresses and the boys had bought their special outfits; it was the biggest event in their lives. Ray suggested that since they were going to lose the strike anyway, maybe a committee should call on Bliss and discuss strategy. Nothing was said about telling him the strike was lost and asking him to approve calling it off. But they picked Ray McKay to head the committee.

And Ray did it very well. They sat around a while on Bliss's screen porch, talking about the last four years, and what they were going to do next year, since none of them was going to graduate. They all vowed that none of them would go back next year if Atterbury were still there so that, ultimately, the school board would have to give in. And some talked of going over to Bostonia to finish, and others about getting a job; they were talking about the things kids talk about before graduation, with this difference, that none of them was going to graduate.

But Ray stirred up the talk more and more until finally he said: "You know, my old man and I are pretty close. I think I could get him to go to the board with a compromise. And I think he could put it across, Bliss, if you wanted him to."

Bliss looked at the kids and saw what was in their minds and asked, speaking the words very distinctly, "What kind of a compromise would you suggest, Ray?" He could see, then, what was coming, and Ray got red and said, "Oh, any kind of compromise that you want, Shoestring."

Bliss felt like El Jardin had just called a time-out on the football field, one point behind on the thirty-yard line and only three minutes in the game, with the players all gathered around and eying the goal posts. Finally, he said: "Look, fellows, this is a strike for El Jardin, isn't it? Not for me and not for the class of 1919 but for El Jardin? To get the old school spirit back and get rid of Atterbury and have the kind of school we had when old Bottoms was here.

"Because if we don't get it back — we who were here when Bottoms was here — then the new kids will never know what it is, isn't that right?"

Nobody said anything for a minute; they didn't know what was coming next.

"Well," Bliss went on. "Here's the dope. Let Ray's dad tell the school board that you'll all go back on condition that Atterbury is fired from his job as principal and that Watkins is reduced from his job as vice principal and that student government is restored as it used to be and that the kids can use the buses to go to games again. And that phys ed credits be given for athletics again just like they were before. Otherwise. . . ."

It was as easy as that. Everybody knew that Atterbury's contract *would not be renewed anyway and that he had already dropped his plan to run for County Superintendent of Schools. They knew they could figure on a new principal deposing Watkins and putting football back on its feet — because the town had shown that football was important. They knew that Bliss's terms were complete surrender. But they shouted, "Attaboy, Bliss! That's the ticket, kid!" "We'll show 'em, won't we, Shoestring!"*

Bob Reynolds felt sick, and he blurted out, "But how about you, Shoestring? What'll you do?" Ray McKay's heel hit Bob's shin in the dark. But Bliss was ready for him. "Me?" he grinned. "Oh, I'll go down in history as the first student at El Jardin who ever got a principal expelled."

And so they graduated, the class of 1919 — the boys in their sharply pressed ice cream pants and blue serge coats; the girls in their frilly, lacy dresses, made for them with infinite labor by their mothers.

Bob still felt queasy about it all, and he did the one thing he could do as chairman of the Committee on Arrangements. This meant he had to see that the stage was set with chairs for the graduates and the visitors and the table and pitcher of water and drinking glass for the speakers. So before the curtain went up, he set an extra chair in the semicircle of seats for the seniors. It stood there empty during all the proceedings.

Ray McKay was salutatorian; when he got up to speak, all the kids stood up and applauded and the parents did, too, because there was no doubt he was the nicest boy and one of the finest and had led their children with intelligence and skill. But Gertrude Offenheimer was valedictorian; she was one of the girls who had gone through the picket line, and when she gave her speech nobody applauded except the parents and visitors. And then she began to cry and ran from the stage without waiting for her diploma.

Bliss sat at home, turning the pages of a Liberty magazine. His father sat too, not reading, as he usually did, but staring at the opposite wall. His mother had come over and put a hand on Bliss's shoulder but then looked at his father, dropped her hand and went into the bedroom.

After a long while, his old man went to bed. He got up and stretched, just as he did on other nights, and Bliss thought he was going to say something and he knew that if he did, Bliss would start to cry. He couldn't help it; there wasn't anything to cry about, but the old man had been so god damn fine about it. He knew in a way it didn't make any difference; he'd get his diploma next year. But it would delay things — getting back to the dream ranch and everything.

His old man stretched and put down the unread book and walked into the other room, carrying his shoes. Bliss sat there with his magazine.

Two or three times he started to get up and go up to his own room, but he didn't. Once he heard voices and the sound of footsteps outside and waited self-consciously. Maybe they were coming to gather in front of the house and sing "El Jardin Forever" like when they lost a football game. But then the voices died away and the steps moved on.

At ten, he told himself the commencement must be over. At ten-thirty, he went out and looked down the street. At eleven, even the crickets and frogs were silent. At twelve, he went to bed.

Chapter Forty
Neither Five Nor Three

In fall 1972 I returned to Los Angeles, to teach at the University of Southern California: news reporting ("Follow the money") and copy editing ("Never use 'Man' as one of the words in your headline.") Lisa, at eighteen, was on her own. I traded visits occasionally with Brick and Peggy. They'd show up on my doorstep, Brick looking very natty in the shirt and tie Peggy had obviously picked out for him. He no longer wore a hat, and of course no topcoat in Southern California. He spoke very little; my dad, whose mind was a dictionary of words and their meanings, could no longer easily say aloud what was written there. He still kept up with the news, but mostly on television, so he might have missed the story in the *Times* on March 30, 1973, that his old nemesis, former Los Angeles District Attorney Buron Fitts, had committed suicide the day before at his home in Tulare County.

                              May 4, 1973
Dear Corinne and Irving,
      We had a wonderful trip, no part of which was more
wonderful than the evening's conversation at your place —
for which we are eternally grateful.
      San Diego was nice, but once again we got so mixed up
on the east side of town that we never got to see the
downtown area, or Coronado or anything. But we drove out
around the old homestead again, and this time we drove into
the old farm (Dad's place) and parked on the old dirt road,

where Peggy took some pictures. The old white house is still glittering with bright, fresh paint and, despite the fact that the homestead has been subdivided, there is something very nice about it. Apparently it is never going to be just a tract. Little parcels have been sold here and there about the eighty acres of ground so it retains its individuality. Everybody builds his house just as they want to, though most of the houses are small and rather mean-looking.

We drove over to my old place in Spring Valley, too, and Chuck was enraptured. He made us park the car while he got out and hiked over the creek and the other places he knew from his childhood and renewed what must have been to him a sort of dream experience. And came back very happy. That place is being subdivided, too, but the houses each seem to have a little ground and look very nice.

I have been feeling rather depressed lately, but not for any particular reason at all. It seems as though one goes only downhill after a certain age. And of course that is true, but since there is nothing to be done about it, there is no use being depressed about it. And, as you say, there is the example of Picasso.[1]

And there is Duke Ellington. The first time I heard him, he was down and out, looking old, looking sick, playing the same old stuff. That was ten or twelve years ago. Suddenly he regained his youth and (I saw him on TV the other night) is doing it all again as he never did it before.

September 13, 1973

I feel that I haven't been a very good correspondent lately; in fact, I haven't been much good at anything. There is a little jingle in my speech therapy which goes:

> Sometimes my thoughts are just cocoons,
> All cold and dull and blind;
> They hang from dripping branches
> In the gray woods of my mind.

And I guess that just about says it. All cold and dull and blind.

Meantime, I have my new hi fi system to get acquainted with. I think it is by and large the best set I have ever seen. With phonograph, FM and AM radio -- one can lock oneself up and play anything one wants -- it sent my thoughts back to the time when everybody had a precious little collection of Victor Red Seal records and invited his friends over maybe once a week to spend an hour listening to music, and it seemed that music was the most important thing in the world. (As indeed it was!)

---

[1] Pablo Picasso died on April 8, 1973, at the age of ninety-one. Ellington was then seventy-four. He died on May 24 the next year.

It seems almost criminal for me to now have such a collection of records and tapes! In addition to which there are KFAC, KUSC and KSLU (I think those are the call letters of Loyola University) and KPFK -- all playing classical music most or all of the time.

I think, now, that the boy I should have written about should have been the boy who borrowed a book from the retired gentleman farmer who lived in the big house on the hill, who was the same boy who sneaked down from the upper balcony to sit with his friend, the girl usher at the opera house. He was a much more interesting character than the one who got tangled up in politics.

Perhaps I see it clearer now than I did then. In fact, though, it's a question of it-might-have-been, and I don't want to spend too much time in regret that I didn't do it another way.

The association with Peggy is rather a peculiar thing. When I first knew her many years ago our backgrounds were so similar that now it hardly seems we have been apart. So we can fight (about Governor Reagan, for example)[2] without really losing our tempers, because each of us knows that -- well, I don't know that I can explain it, but I suspect that you know what I mean.

It has something to do with the business of growing old. One by one your friends drop off, and your circle narrows -- and those you don't see any more you don't know whether they are living or not.

But more than just people: the things around you have changed. Perhaps most of anything, the demise of the newspaper business -- all the things you knew about -- have ceased to exist anywhere. You literally know almost nothing about the business of gathering news and writing it, or editing copy because everything is done electronically, and what skill one had is a lost skill, and there is nobody in the world today that needs to know what you know.

Love,

Brick

The Heart of Man Has Long Been Sore

He had the good sense, or the good fortune, to go away for the summer. He got a job on a ranch back in the hills, and when he came back in September he got a haircut and a new suit of clothes and registered in high school under the new principal. Everybody was glad to see him. Maybe time had worn some of the rough edges off everybody: teachers and pupils and townspeople and Bliss himself. Everybody yelled, "Hiyah, Shoestring!" and he waved and called back and grinned. Not

---

2 Ronald Reagan was governor of California from 1967 to 1975.

only in school but in the town, the merchants and townspeople and Dr. Edwards and Joe Bishop, who managed the Standard Oil works, everybody would see him on the street and say, "Good morning, son," or "Hey there, Shoestring!" depending on who they were, and Bliss would grin back or wave and say, "Good morning, doctor," or "Hi, Joe."

Of course he had been a football hero in the town as well as in the school, but it was different now; being in school had set him apart, but now he was a young fellow who had already made a mark and was going to get ahead in the world and everybody wanted to give him a hand, they wanted to show that now it was all over, they were FOR him. He didn't stop to wonder why that was.

Joe Bishop came around to his house the second night he was back. Joe had been out of high school six years. He had played quarterback and was still a football fan. He asked, "You want a job, kid?" Bliss said no, he was going back to school and get his diploma, and Joe said, "Well, God damn, that's all right, too, if you want to do it, but you don't need no damn high school diploma to work for Standard Oil, and if you say the word I'll put you on driving a truck in the morning, and, hell, kid, I bet you'll be plant manager before you're twenty-one."

Bliss said, "Gee, thanks, but I gotta finish school." And Joe said, "Well, sure, that's all right, too, but remember, Standard promotes from the bottom. Time you get outa school I'll be division manager, I bet, and I'll keep an eye on you 'cause I know you've got the kind of stuff Standard needs."

Even Richard Wiley, Neil's old man, sent for him; he had a chain of department stores in El Jardin and Bostonia and Hopeville and two or three other towns. He sent Bliss a note asking him to call at the office. Bliss went around and Mr. Wiley talked to him about the future and offered him a job clerking in the hardware department of one of his stores at sixty dollars a month.

Just the same, he knew he had to go back to school. He did. It wasn't the same; he was not exactly a visitor: the fellows yelled "Hiyah!" and the girls (with a note in their voices he had never noticed before) cooed "Hel-l-l-l-o-a, Bli-i-i-ss." But it was not the same. From the first he could see Mr. Engelhardt watching him; on Friday morning the new principal called him into the office and asked him to sit down in the leatherbacked chair in front of the desk and told him, in that somewhat stiff and formal way he had, that Bliss no longer need attend classes.

"It would be foolish to ask you to repeat a year's study because of an unfortunate incident," he said. "I am sure that everybody regrets the mistakes of the past. I suggest you get yourself a job and prepare to go to college next year. Come back in June and graduate with the class; everybody should have the experience of graduation."

Bliss thanked him and went out and walked by the Carnegie Public Library and then went home and sat under the chinaberry tree in the front yard. After a while he could smell veal chops frying in the kitchen, and he went in and told his mother he didn't have to go to school but would get a job and help pay expenses so things would be easier for Papa. Mama said, "My, that will be nice," and went on frying the veal chops.

He went to his room and sat there, feeling his school days were really over, and wondering why he didn't feel better now that he had won out. Because, in effect, the school had admitted that he had been right and it had been wrong. He wasn't even going to lose any time; he'd be a year behind in college but he'd have some money to go on, which he wouldn't have had before.

When Papa came in, Bliss told him what had happened and what he was going to do about getting a job. Papa brightened and said, "Good boy!" It was almost the first time he'd seen Papa look cheerful since they'd left Descanso. They sat quietly at the table a few minutes, but Bliss found he couldn't taste the veal chops nor the canned corn his mother had heated up. He said: "Gosh, Papa, if we all pitch in and work together for two or three years, maybe with Cal and Tom getting out of the Army, we can all save our money and move back to the ranch."

But Papa shook his head and said, "No, I guess your Mama and I are getting too old to be farmers. You can pay board if you want to, but you better save your money so you can go to college next year." The look on his face made Bliss feel good; he got up from the table knowing he was going to be doing his share for the first time since they'd lost the ranch.

Just the same he wasn't satisfied; he put on his new suit and went downtown to Mr. Engelhardt's house and rang the bell and asked if he could come in and talk a minute. Mr. Engelhardt said, "Certainly," and led him into the parlor, and Bliss found himself suddenly tongue-tied; the two sat there facing one another. Finally, Mr. Engelhardt broke the ice by asking him what he intended to do with his life.

Bliss said he wasn't sure; he had thought of studying law and maybe going into politics. "There seems to be a great deal of injustice in the world," he said. "Maybe that would be a good field for me."

Mr. Engelhardt smiled. He looked at Bliss with curiosity, the way Bottoms had done, but at the same time there was something cautious about him. He said he thought that anybody with a gift of gab like Bliss's would probably do very well in politics. He said he understood that Bliss had a good, logical mind; that was necessary in law, though not necessarily helpful in politics, but he was sure Bliss had the stuff in him to go a long way.

Bliss sat listening and gaining confidence. Finally he looked up and demanded: "Look, Mr. Engelhardt, I wonder if you could tell me something? I've had two principals before you. The first one used to say, 'You can do anything in the world if you want to badly enough.' And the second one, 'If you want anything in this world, take it — but pay for it.' I wonder what I would have learned from you if I had spent the rest of the term in school?"

Mr. Engelhardt leaned back in his chair and smiled at Bliss and said: "I don't think life can be reduced to a formula like that, Bliss. I think most of our troubles come from attempting to reduce life to a formula. But if I had some word of wisdom to pass on to you, particularly, I think it might be this: 'Pride and anger are both unwise; vinegar never catches flies.' "

Bliss thought a minute, then got up and said, "Thank you, Mr. Engelhardt; I'll keep it in mind."

They said good night, and he went on downtown and into the Palace Pool Hall and watched a game of pool and thought it over. He didn't like it. Finally he went home. A few days later he got into his new suit and went to Mr. Engelhardt's door again and asked him if he could come in and talk a little more.

"Maybe I'm reading too much into it," he said. "But it seems to me that if what you say is true, then a fellow has to be a sneak and a hot-air artist and a hypocrite to get anyplace in the world. Is that what it means? We had a guy here last year — I guess every class has one — who was very popular and had a great gift of gab and was always buttering up everybody, even his worst enemy. Do you mean you've got to be like that? 'Pride and anger,' you say, but where would Honor be without Pride, or Justice without Anger?"

He was all wound up. The words flowed out in a torrent after having been dammed up all summer, and Mr. Engelhardt let him talk it out until he had finished. "It can't be like that, Mr. Engelhardt, it just can't be!"

The principal leaned back and asked: "And why can't it be?"

"Because there would be no sense in life," Bliss insisted. "No honor, no justice, no right or wrong. It would be a heck of a life, Mr. Engelhardt, honest it would!"

"Do you like poetry, Bliss?" Mr. Engelhardt asked.

"Yes," wonderingly. "Of course."

The principal swung around to his typewriter and tapped out a few lines on a sheet of paper and folded it up and handed it to Bliss.

"There's a poet," he said, "who is little known in this country as yet. Later you may come to appreciate him a great deal. He has written my answer to your objection; I know you won't like it: there it is, as it stands. Put it in your pocket and read it when you get home."

Bliss said, "Thank you," and got up and said good night. Under the first street light he unfolded the paper and read:

> To think that two and two makes four
> And neither five nor three,
> The heart of man has long been sore,
> And long 'tis like to be.

He folded it up again; at home he went to his room and took off his good suit and lay down, looking into the autumn darkness. There were a million stars and yet he couldn't see the star he used to wish on when they were living on the ranch. He knew now that you had to do more than wish; you had to be able to know and to plan; you had to know who you were and then you'd know what you wanted and then, if you wanted it badly enough, you'd get it — even if you had to pay for it.

Of course it was silly to think you could make two and two equal five or three, but then maybe, in a way you could at that — if you wanted it badly enough. He remembered how he'd made up his mind he was going to be somebody when they moved to town, and how he'd got the name Shoestring and how he'd run the eggfield, and how, even, he'd turned last spring's defeat into a victory. Because there wasn't any doubt now whether he or Ray McKay was biggest. Of course Ray was away at college and Bliss was right here in town, but when people said "Hiyah, Shoestring," or "Hello, Bliss," they meant it; they didn't just mean how's your fat-assed father sitting in his cage in the bank.

And that proved maybe, in a way, you could make two and two be five.

Chapter Forty-One
The Name, When I Finally Find It,
Will Be Much Easier to Pronounce

We all have our stories. Some are told between the covers of a book. Others exist only in fragments of memory, perhaps in legends of our ancestors; still others through a necklace with a broken clasp, a box of books, a faded photo of a young soldier (was that Uncle Samuel in his doughboy's uniform?), a newspaper clipping. I told you before I sometimes think of Brick as Everyman. His successes were the successes that any of us might attain; his failures were not unique to him. And yet his story is his alone. He did, as we all do, often make wrong choices and often those that were right. Sometimes they were made for him by somebody else. By a teacher, by a parent, by a publisher, by a school board, by a U.S. senator with a list in his hand, by a madman on a distant continent. The choices tally the sum of a person's life.

Having passed my seventieth birthday, I catch myself reading the *Times* obituaries more than I used to, wonderingly, fascinated by the idea that so many rich lives are summed up in just a few meager lines. "What *is* the meaning of life?" the college girl asked on that long bench many years ago. Perhaps part of the answer can be found in today's newspaper —

"Despite her lifelong battle with diabetes, she was adventurous and courageous throughout her life and enjoyed sailing and traveling the world. She had a great love for her chihuahuas, Sylvia and Woofie, her parrot, Pete, and for all beings whose lives she graced."

"Served in the Navy Air Corps in the Pacific Theater, WWII, and was awarded the Silver Star and two Distinguished Flying Crosses."

"A survivor of the Holocaust and the child of Holocaust survivors, he will be missed deeply."

Nothing is any less "real" because it happened thirty years ago. Or a hundred years ago. Or because it happened to someone else.

This book is Brick's Book, my father's story. I said at the outset that I saw ghosts, but in discovering the bits and pieces and yes, the secrets, of my father's life in his letters, in metal filing cabinets and on strips of microfilm, or in the old records at Imperial's Carnegie Library, the ghosts took shape and became embodied again. They still exist, very close.

October 31, 1973

Dear Corinne and Irving,

Just a few lines to let you know that we are still alive, even if it doesn't seem like it.

Peggy has had a very tough time of it for the last couple of weeks. She got what she thought was the best surgeon in Los Angeles -- and she's had nothing but trouble. It started out with a big row over the anesthetic; she told them in advance that she wanted the scopolamine, as she was allergic to everything else, with the result that she spent six days (count 'em) vomiting, violently ill, and she damn near died.

I was trying to get her to eat, and she was refusing. She couldn't swallow because her throat was sore from throwing up and for the first week at home I managed to get possibly two bites of food down her every two hours. Well, gradually she got better and is determined to get dinner tonight. She is the stubbornest woman I ever did see. I confess I didn't feel too well myself. I dropped the speech therapy for at least two weeks and, instead, have spent most of the time resting in the afternoons and doing household chores in the morning.

Meanwhile, I've been living on Watergate. As the whole comic interest of an ill-spent life. How could one man have surrounded himself with so many corrupt incompetents? He seems to be keeping it right up until he has everybody included -- not excepting Gerald Ford.

(See "The Washington Payoff" by Robert N. Winter-Berger. I don't know where I got this book; I think Dickie may have brought it over to the apartment, having noticed that it was dedicated to Toni Strassman. Anyway, it takes care of Gerald Ford, and that was all done in advance of his selection as the Heir to the Throne.)[1]

I find I must close. Forgive me for not writing. At this point the typewriter always seems to fail me.

---

[1] Richard Nixon nominated Gerald Ford as vice-president on October 6, 1973, to succeed the disgraced Spiro Agnew. *The Washington Pay-Off; an Insider's View of Corruption in Government* was published in 1972 by Dell.

In November, Brick fell ill and was taken to the hospital, where he suffered a massive heart attack. His heart stopped beating; he stopped breathing. To all intents, he was "dead." But within two minutes he had been taken to the emergency care unit and he was hooked up to several life-support systems.

When they called me in to look at him, he had a tube down his throat and his nose and some kind of device stuck into his chest to maintain his lung pressure. He was conscious, and he looked at me and held out his hand, then he collapsed.

I thought he was dying, and so did everyone else. I called Patty and Chuck, and they arrived in Los Angeles along with Rod and Lisa the next day, Saturday afternoon.

Chuck sat with him. The two were alone, and they talked; or rather Chuck talked and Brick whispered. "I hope I live long enough to write the story of my life," he told Chuck.

Chuck took out a notebook and wrote that down.

Brick said he was ready to die. "When you've been about it for seventy-one years, when it finally comes what is there to kick about? Six months, six years, six days, I'm ready."

"Are you afraid?"

"No."

"Angry?"

"No."

Brick said he was resigned, accepting.

"There's something about watching Eleanor, George, Pat . . . my brothers and sisters . . . " He was silent a while. "Death is no big deal."

He thought about his grandfather, who had sent cards to all his grandchildren just before his death, to say goodbye.[2]

"I hope you will tell George and Patty I'm sorry I couldn't write myself." Later: "Patty will have little trouble. George will take it harder. George and I have gotten very close the last few years. I'm sorry I can't spend more time with him."

And then an odd prediction: Patty would live as long as her mother did, I would live to seventy-one. As for Chuck, "I don't know about you."

A long pause.

"The thought came to me: There is no life after death, because I've been dead, and there is no life there. I'm just glad it's the last time around."

He was tiring. "I want to keep talking, but it's time to stop."

---

2 The message, sent from Utica, Kansas, on February 10, 1909, to six-year-old Harris Garrigues, said simply, "I would love to see my sorrel top little grandson." And to little Jessie Patricia: "Do not forget that away off in Kansas you have an old grandpa that loves you dearly."

After Chuck left, Brick, as though he had planned it, went into a crisis. The doctor said all the signs pointed to his imminent death. Peg called me to say there was "no hope."

We all began to talk of Brick in the past tense and to think of such things as funerals and other so-called "arrangements." Lisa and I went to the apartment to look for his will and other instructions in the event of his death. I found some letters from a woman named Billie. She lived in the middle of America, in Grundy Center, Iowa.

On Monday evening, though, Brick was a bit stronger. Chuck was surprised to see him sitting in a chair, cutting his fingernails. Chuck wrote that Brick "Didn't look like he was dying. Nurses put him back to bed. Me sad, and with nothing to say, kept yawning."

Tuesday afternoon: "Father looked great. Dickie had visited. His speech was clear." That evening: "Saw him with George. He talked about the nights seeming long now that he is able to understand his surroundings."

He was taken to Peggy's family home in Pacific Palisades, and, when he felt better, somewhat later, he underwent exploratory surgery for suspected intestinal cancer, and then they took him to a convalescent hospital.

I went to visit him there; he was a shadow, drawn and haggard.

"They're keeping something from me," he mumbled, Parkinson's-like.

"What?"

"They're not telling me what they found." He didn't like being treated like a child.

"Do you want me to ask the doctor?"

"Yeah. Will you?"

"Sure."

He looked around him, at the sterile hallways, the nurses hastening on their errands. Men and women in bathrobes slumped in wheelchairs in the hallways.

"My mother died in a place like this," he said.

I went home and phoned the doctor, who told me that the cancer had spread so much there was no point in fighting it.

"Do you want me to tell him?" the doctor said.

"No, I will."

I did.

Brick looked shocked, then subdued.

"I want to call Nom . . . I mean Peggy," he said. He was wheeled back to his room and he made the telephone call.

They took him back to Peggy's home. I visited him several times; once I nudged him and told him to wake up. From his slumber, a big smile crossed his face, and he said, "What for? I'll just have to go to sleep again." I never realized a dying man could be so content with his fate, as though he had finally found his Truth. We held hands.

He died on March 8, 1974. I wrote his obituary, took it down to the *Times* and it was printed the next day — not in the tiny agate type used in the ads, but as a news story under a three-line, twenty-four-point head, a tribute to a remembered Los Angeles newspaperman. Chuck and I did the funeral, there was Beethoven and jazz, and among the mourners for the man who had mistrusted marriage were two of his wives and the sister and brother-in-law of another. His ashes were mixed with the Pacific waters that swept the California coast.

Peggy notified Toni, and I wrote to Billie. She replied that their friendship dated back twenty-seven years, when, as a raw seventeen-year-old just out of a high school in Ohio, she was a copy girl on the *Examiner* and he "slaved on the copy desk and dreamed of turning out the Great American Novel. He had his heart attack while I was out there, and I took him in a taxi from the emergency room to St. Luke's Hospital. We have corresponded over the years. So now you understand how I fit into the jigsaw. He was a rare and wonderful man. Long ago we argued about whether love could last forever — semantics, perhaps, but I assured him it could."

I expect that he signed his letters to her

As ever,

Brick

Chapter Forty-Two
There's Not Enough Time

A week later Bliss was sitting at the counter in the Rexall store, sipping a Coke, and not paying any attention to a bunch of kids at the tables in the back when he saw the Reynoldses' car pull up, slow and careful at the curb. Bob was driving. He pulled on the hand brake and sat there a minute, then got out and pushed his way through the swinging screen door. "Hey, Shoestring, I got the car. How about us getting a couple of girls and going for a joyride?"

Bliss said, "Sure, Bob, I'd like to," just as though the two were always calling up girls and going out with them. "Who'll we get?" and Bob said, "Oh, I dunno, who'd you like to get?"

For half a minute Bliss had the idea that maybe Bob expected him to ask somebody like Claire Morrison or Hazel Kinney, somebody who was really fast. He sipped his drink, then — "Well, how'd you like to try . . ." — he sought furiously for someone who was cute but not so cute she wouldn't say "Yes" — ". . . Ava Johnston and maybe she could get her cousin or somebody?"

Bob said, "Sure, Ava's O.K." And Bliss, realizing he'd never called a girl in his life, said to Bob, "O.K., call her up." Bob said, "No, you call her; you know her better than I do."

That wasn't true; neither knew her at all except to sit near at school or Sunday school parties. But Bliss saw there wasn't any way he could admit he'd never called up a girl before, and besides, it was Bob who had the car, so he'd have to get the girls for them to go out with.

The nickel in his hand was sweaty as he dropped it into the pay phone near the magazine rack, and he could feel his tongue thick with embarrassment, but luckily Ava answered so he didn't have to talk to her folks. She said, Yes, she'd like to go out with them and would get another girl and they could go over to Bostonia for ice cream — but they'd have to be in by ten.

It was the first time he'd ever been out on a real joyride. Ava got Wendy Cox for Bob. As Bob drove along the empty road, the wooden fence posts and eucalyptus windbreaks whipping by in the moonlight, Bliss put his arm around Ava in the back seat and tried to kiss her but she wouldn't let him. At the end of the evening Bliss walked with her from the car to the gate, and he stood there awkwardly. She smiled then, stood tiptoe and kissed him quickly, full on the lips, opened the gate and ran onto her porch.

After they dropped off Wendy, Bob put the car in the garage and walked with Bliss to the high school, where they stretched out side by side on the warm grass. Bliss didn't talk about the girls; he wasn't going to admit he'd never been out with a girl before. They spoke of other things: Bob was working for F. L. E. Skinner, who thought he was there to learn real estate, though Bob had already been accepted at the Medical School in San Francisco. Bliss was putting in six days a week at Standard, paying his folks for room and board and saving the rest for a car and college. They talked also about this business of two and two making four; of course two and two made four but couldn't you make it five (or even six) if you wanted something badly enough?

Walking home it came to Bliss that he could make friends with the very best people. It meant a lot to him to know that he was liked and respected by the Reynoldses because there wasn't any doubt Foureyes and his folks were the very best people. He thought of how much the world had changed since the Lanes had moved into town. He was best friends with the banker's son, could ride in the banker's car, be invited to the banker's house. And that was just a start — and it was more important than the girls. Bob was his friend, and Bliss felt good to have a friend who thought you were important and could lie there and listen to you all night, about everything that was ever important to you, even including Plato.

All that year and into the spring, when Bob had the car on Friday nights, they would take girls out, to Bostonia for sundaes or just for rides on narrow country roads. Once they stopped late at a little country store, rousing the owner out of bed to serve them some of his home-made root beer. But on their free nights when they did not go joyriding, they would stretch out on the high school lawn or sit bundled up against the cold on the steps of the Carnegie Public Library and talk until their throats were dry and their brains were dry, too, and their muscles were stiff. Sometimes they would talk until the sun was about to come up. Then they would separate, and the only words of affection passed between them were: "So long; don't take any wooden nickels." And it meant, "Be safe; stay away from the bad guys, don't make any wrong choices, but if you do, I love you anyway."

Bliss talked about life being too short. "Life's terribly short when you are eighteen; there won't be enough time to do all the things I have to do, and think all the thoughts I have to think and say all the words I have to say. There aren't enough hours in the day or night — you can't go to bed until sunrise, because there might be something you'd miss, something that would escape you forever. There's not enough time."

As they talked, the two of them came to understand that the world was organized differently for Bliss than it was for most other people. Bob's world was a lot of good things: His dad's car, his job, his future. The world of Bliss had some good things, too, but for Bliss there was another world, so the world of THINGS wasn't real. There was another world for him, and it was that one, the unattainable one, which was real for Bliss.

As Bliss and Bob talked in that last year in the little country town where they had gone through high school together, as they talked through those nights while the moon and stars dimmed in the sky, those long fall and winter and early spring nights, Bliss saw himself going away to college and going away forever, to enter that unattainable world, to begin his life. And as they parted each night, Bliss heard Bob say, as always,

"So long, kid; don't take any wooden nickels."

Chapter Forty-Three
Nineteen Years Later

**Fragment of a Requiem Spoken by
Lisa Garrigues
at the Memorial Service for Her Uncle,
Chuck Garrigues,
Who Died in San Francisco, May 12, 1993,
at the Age of Sixty-Two**

Go now, my uncle . . .
Go through the old gate,

where your father, my grandfather,
went before you,

where perhaps you will meet him
in an old Bohemian cafe
filled with jazz and mystery
and you will sit down at the table in the corner,

and maybe there will be answers,

at the end

of the long conversation.

Index

African Americans
  "Crow-Jimism," 463
  discrimination against, 441–442
  and jazz, 462, 473–474
  militancy of, 515
Aging, 99, 404, 442, 448, 474, 520, 537
Aikman, Duncan, 107
Albany, California, 259, 375–376, 478, 518
American Army of Rehabilitation, 108
American League Against War and Fascism, 137
Amos, Deneal, 447
Angell, Ephraim Grant, 19, 37
Angel's Camp, California, 221
Arizona Daily Star, 5, 34
Armstrong, Louis, 440
Ashurst, Henry F., 106–107

Baldwin, Al, 293
Barnes City, California, 37
Bates, Edwin, 107
Beatniks, 450, 463
Beckh, Walter, 288
Bellingham, Washington, 518, 524
Berkeley, California, 150, 152, 182, 183

Big Sur, California, 443
Billie, 545–546
Boddy, Manchester, 62, 87, 90, 108, 110, 114, 133, 136, 363–364, 406, 509
Book and Magazine Guild, 244
Borrego Springs, California, 466
Bowron, Fletcher, 106, 114, 122, 136
Brinig, Myron, 90, 95, 99, 102
Buck, Verne, 41
Buckley, John P., 116, 122
Burnham, Addison, 301

California Reserve Company, 106, 115, 157
Calipatria, California, 42–43
Camp Roberts, California, 239
Carmichael, Hoagy, 286, 338
Carnegie Library, 18, 143, 515, 528, 539, 543, 548
Caselotti, Louise, 75–76, 102, 273
Cathedral City, California, 291
Cavett, Thomas L., 173
Christina's World, 491, 499
Clayton, John Bell
  Brick "discovers," 286
  Brick's help to, 316, 318
  suggestions on Brick's novel, 321, 420

wins O. Henry Award, 322
death of, 428–430, 434–436, 473
Clayton, Martha Carmichael, 286, 291, 311, 318, 420–421, 428–430, 432, 434
death of, 444
Clear, Andree, 387
Clear Lake, California, 383
Collins, Bill [son-in-law], 487
Collins, Tauni [granddaughter], 487
Collins, Tony [grandson], 483, 487
Committee on Un-American Activities in California, 171–173, 258–259, 277
Coronado, California, 291
Cosulich, Bernice, 6–9, 431–432
Covici, Pascal "Pat," 242–247, 250, 340
Cromie, Robert, 120
Culver City, California, 34, 37–39, 50
Curtis Brown agency, 243, 245, 247–249, 377

Daemon, iv, 338
Davis, James E., 135–136
Davis, Lambert, 290
Dianetics, 371–373
Dickey family, 62, 71
Eaphraim, 28, 35
Ella Gertrude Eskridge, 27–29
Florence (Mrs. Henry Hubbard), 32
Harold, 29
Hubert, 29
Jesse Bryan, 28
Mabel (Mrs. Howard Glass), 10
Maude, 35
Vesta Vae (Mrs. Bill Jolley), 29
William Bascomb, 28–29
Woodrow Wilson, 29, 30

Edgar, W. A., 22–23, 25
El Cerrito, California, 258
Epic News, 135–136, 144
Everest, Nathan Wesley, 192

Fabian, Mary, 78, 84, 86
Fell, Donald, 276
Finney, Guy W., i, 73, 115, 481

Fitts, Buron, 114–117, 119, 122, 133, 136–137, 142–145, 151, 172
hires Brick as investigator, 89
indicted for perjury, 116–117
acquitted of perjury, 134
shot by gunmen, 157
joins the Army, 236
death of, 535
Foff, Arthur, 421, 434, 436
Foster, Michael "Gully," 54, 56, 191
death of, 431–432, 435–436
Foster, William Z., 103–104, 405
Franklin, Benjamin, 11–13, 47

Gadsden, Arizona, 29–30
Garrigues family
Eleanor (Beyer) [sister], 13, 194, 228, 518, 523
George William [brother], 12, 288, 322, 334, 484
Jessie Patricia [sister], 13, 17, 256, 341
Samuel C. [brother], 13, 25, 86, 542
Samuel Pierce [grandfather], 12
Garrigues, Ann-Marie Bleher [daughter-in-law], 483, 521–522
Garrigues, Beulah M. "Dickie" [first wife]
birth of, 29
arrives in California, 30
graduates from high school, 32
picks cotton in Imperial Valley, 35
meets Brick, 36
in Oracle, 6
marries Brick, 50
and Marianne, 118–120, 122–123, 127, 128
divorce, 144, 159, 253
moves to Inglewood, 176
moves to San Francisco, 273–278
returns to Inglewood, 280–281
establishes secretarial service, 327
jealous of Peggy, 508
retires, 518
Garrigues, C. H. "Brick"
birth of, 13
childhood, 227–228
relationship to his father, 388
at Imperial High School, 19
letter to Imperial Enterprise, 22–23
expulsion from high school, 23
first newspaper job, 25
graduates from high school, 26

attends University of Southern
    California, 34
meets Beulah Dickey, 36
reporter with *Hemet News*, 34
editor of *Venice Vanguard*, 34
reporter with *Arizona Daily Star*, 34
copy editor with *Los Angeles
    Express*, 39
marries Dickie, 50
reporter with *Daily News*, 62
becomes *Daily News* music critic, 71
becomes grand jury investigator, 88
Daily News political editor, 95
attacked on stairway, 141-142
beaten in courtroom, 115, 141
begins interest in labor movement, 192
takes a room in which to write,
    132, 383-384, 472
and ranch, 144-146
divorce, 144, 159, 253, 344, 384
joins Communist Party, 173, 405-
    407, 420
Newspaper Guild organizer, 163
starts political publicity bureau, 167
marries Naomi, 176
works for *San Francisco Examiner*,
    184, 336
quits Communist Party, 206, 420
listed by Tenney Committee, 258
heart attack, 282, 546
tenth anniversary of marriage, 314
buys a house, 325
tax preparation business, 335, 343-
    345, 367
and his psychotherapy, 387, 436,
    444
HUAC testimony, 404-408
questioned by FBI, 420
at San Francisco State, 421, 427,
    434-435
as jazz reviewer, 433, 435, 440-
    443
traits divided among his children,
    459
leave of absence, 467, 469
onset of Parkinsonism, 464
loses job as jazz reviewer, 479-481
retirement of, 486
death of Naomi, 492-496
marries Peggy, 506-508
his old farm, 535
death of, 546

Garrigues, Charles Louis [father], 13-
    14, 173
sings to his son, 63
lived for his children, 410
gives up farming, 26
death of, 173, 209-210
Garrigues, Charles Samuel "Chuck"
    [son]
birth of, 86
on the ranch, 153-155, 159, 536
first trip to Bay Area, 212-213
nickname, "Slats," 213
and Naomi, 295-298
nervous breakdown, 343
in Navy, 409, 427-428, 440, 450,
    455, 520
after Navy, 450-459
Europe trip, 451, 453-455
communal boarding house, 457-
    459
as psychiatric social worker, 503
at Langley-Porter, 483
Naomi's funeral, 494-495, 499
end of marriage, 521-522
death of, 550
Garrigues, Chris [grandson], 483,
    487, 504-505
Garrigues, Emily Young
    [mother], 14, 173, 194-195,
    224, 228, 322
death of, 483
Garrigues, George Louis [son]
birth of, 102
on the ranch, 154-155, 159
first trip to Bay Area, 212-213
copyboy, 324-326, 338, 367, 370
at UCLA, 367, 395-397
rejected for *Daily Bruin* managing
    editorship, 402-403
marriage, 403
as newspaper reporter, 427, 439
in Geneva, 487, 505
returns from Europe, 511-513
graduate student, 512, 518
as journalism professor, 518, 535
Garrigues, Leonie [granddaughter],
    487, 505, 521
Garrigues, Lisa [granddaughter], 419,
    485, 487, 511-513, 524, 535,
    550
Garrigues, Michael [grandson], 452-
    453, 487, 513

Garrigues, Naomi Silver [second wife]
  meets Brick, 150
  letter to family, 157
  marriage, 176
  death of father, 198, 210
  moves to Prescott, 268, 274
  returns to Brick, 288–289, 299
  death of, 492–494, 498–500
Garrigues, Patricia "Pat" [daughter]
  birth of, 255–257
  as a teenager, 440, 448
  leaves home, 477, 482
Garrigues, Rica [granddaughter], 487,
  513
Garrigues, Vivian Shulman [daughter-
  in-law], *iii–vi*, 258, 397–398,
  401, 485
  marriage, 403
Gentle, Alice True, 78
Gilbert, Art, 465
Globalization, 242
Golden, Bill, 104
Graves, Sidney T., 89, 91, 106, 133, 140
Gray, Russell E., 176, 205, 302–303
Green Mansions, 7, 470
Gregory, George, 115
Grossman, Aubrey, 150, 157

Harris, Frank, 66–68
Hartmann, Sadakichi, 68, 71
Hawkins, Anne, 295, 299–300, 333
  corresponds with Brick, 285, 289,
  293, 301, 369
  first letter to Toni, 287–288
  Pony Express novel, 316, 322, 344
  illness, 410, 512
Hollywood Tribune, 192
Hosmer, Helen, 181, 182
House Committee on Un-American
  Activities, 404–408
"How to Live Within Your Income,"
  365–366
Hubbard, Anita Day, 433

Idylwild, California, 434
Imperial Enterprise, 21, 36, 50
Imperial High School, 19, 23–24, 26,
  37, 470
Imperial Valley, California, 19, 33–
  36, 42, 53, 110, 143, 291, 293
  vigilantes, 183, 192

Inglewood, California, 205, 213, 224,
  274, 281, 293, 343, 346

James, Thomas H., 135–136
Janet (pseud.), 78–87, 200–201, 203,
  271–272, 293
Jazz, 440–442, 445–446, 461–463,
  482, 514
  at Brick's funeral, 546
Jean-Christophe, 7, 47–48, 100, 131,
  486
Jews and Judaism, 7, 47, 91, 93, 102,
  151, 180, 197–198, 244, 270,
  279, 312, 323, 346, 353, 465,
  490–491
Johnson, Grover C., 143–145, 173
Julian, California, 466
Julian Petroleum fraud, 89, 133

Keyes, Asa, 89, 133
King-Conner-Ramsay case, 150, 152
Korean War, 370, 409

Laguna Beach, California, 291, 428
Langdon, John, 374, 432
Lee, Floy, 52
Lincoln, Abbey, 441–442
Long Beach, California, 106, 174,
  185
Los Angeles, 70
  Belasco Theater, 69
  Biltmore Hotel, 77
  Biltmore Theater, 76
  Brentwood, 507–508, 510, 518
  Bunker Hill, 50–51, 359
  City Hall, 61, 364, 440, 509
  compared with San Francisco, 211,
  279
  Exposition Park, 44
  Greek Theater, 100
  Hollywood Bowl, 54, 61, 63
  in the 1920s, 50–51, 59, 61–62, 70
  in the 1930s, 77
  in the 1960s, 509
  Los Angeles River, 70
  MacArthur Park, 355
  Million Dollar Theater, 51
  Morosco Theater, 355
  newspapers, 62, 74, 78, 95
  Opera, 72, 74–76, 85, 100
  Orpheum Theater, 355

Pacific Palisades, 545
Pantages Theater, 355
Pershing Square, 68
Philharmonic Auditorium, 56, 356, 361
Playa del Rey, 147
the Plaza, 103
Polytechnic High School, 62
Public Library, 77
"Red Hill," 70, 359
Shrine Auditorium, 48
springtime, 204
Symphony Orchestra, 44, 69, 76
Taylor Yard, 70
Trinity Auditorium, 133
Union Station, 212, 288
on V-J Day, 282
Westlake Park, 355
Wrigley Field, 44
Los Angeles Illustrated Daily News, 405–406, 509
founding of, 62
fighting graft, 80
Los Angeles Newspaper Guild, 163, 167, 171, 407
Love
as a madness, 124, 127
between men, 549
denoting selfishness, 82
hard to write the word, 447
lasting forever, 5, 546
romantic, 5
"those whom we help," 128

Manuscripts
article on postwar inflation, 278
article on semantics, 287–288, 291
article on spiritualism, 280
The Eclipse of Democracy, 247
how to buy a "hand-me-down" home, 368
The Imaginary Revolution, 260, 265–266, 268, 275–277, 282, 285, 290, 299, 301, 304, 309, 327, 352
The Immediate Future of Man, 240–246, 248–250, 254, 256, 260
"Money Makes the Mayor Go," 177
Permanente health plan, 368
"Psychopathology of Love," 127
This Grim New World, 260, 265–266, 277, 340

"What Color Is Your Dirt?" 368–369
"Without Capitals," 344
Many a Glorious Morning (excerpts)
the Lanes move from Kansas, 14–16
how Mama got her way, 195
Bliss's first day at the new school, 381
Bliss finds out he is poor, 17
Bliss rejects religion, 96–97
Bliss dreams of having a ranch, 147–148
Bliss sets a deadline for God, 421–426
Albert Lane buys his ranch, 328–333
tending the chickens, 230–231
the preacher couple, 347–351
Bliss learns to shoot for food, 138
Albert Lane sells his grapes for wine, 389–394
on "Moonlight Bay," 266–267
the Ames girls, 18
"You can do anything," 187–189
Bliss as a football player, 413–418
the kids serenade Old Bottoms, 319–320
pride in his grandfather, 471–472
Dick Angell's foot race, 19
the kids meet the new principal, 515–517
editor Rankin refuses to take a stand, 476–477
Bliss, his father and the School Board, 235–236
how the strike was ended, 531–534
the summer after the strike, 537–541
Bliss and Bob plan for the future, 547–549
Bliss's affair with Nelia, 357
Bliss's marriage to Marj, 358–361
Mama's method of dealing with money, 312–313
Bliss remembers his father, 436–438
Many a Glorious Morning (writing of)
advice from Anne, 333
as a "period piece," 525
as a trilogy, 411, 413, 420
as autobiography, 314, 347, 448, 473
as psychotherapy, 385, 436, 448, 468, 473
"boy I should have written about," 537
character problems, 322, 374
completion, 412–413

difficulty of, 324, 339, 345, 376–377, 468–470
ease of, 337, 351, 354–364
high school sequence, 400
plot of, 319, 337, 352, 379–381, 411, 468
point-of-view problems, 321, 337
rejections, 419
shown to John Clayton, 316, 318–319, 321
Marianne (pseud.), 113, 117–130, 164, 192, 197–199, 202, 211, 273, 322, 356, 358
Matrimony, 5, 52, 60, 197, 202, 267, 315–317, 401
McCarthyism, 171, 258–259, 409, 412, 531
Meagher, Paul, 281
Means, Beverly "Bevo," 50
Meliorism, 175
Mill Valley, California, 184
Mills College, 440
Mills, John P., 115–116
Minute Men, 114–115, 119
Miriam, 167–168, 170, 186, 191, 356
Monterey Jazz Festival, 464–465
Montrose, California, 109–110, 185
Morgana, Nina, 72
"Most Polite Man," 366, 368
Mount Diablo State Park, 208, 221, 276, 440
Mount Palomar, California, 466
Mulholland, William, 63, 65
Munson, Mary L., 39, 41–42, 50

Neither Five Nor Three, 310, 412
Non-Aristotelian logic, 285

Oakland, California, 198, 204, 212, 240, 440
O'Carroll, Joe, 46, 73, 83, 273
Oracle, Arizona, 2–4

Pacific Grove, California, 465
Palm Springs, California, 465
Palmer, Harlan G., 62, 143–146
Pantages, Alex, 73, 115
Parkinson's disease, 478–479, 484
pallidotomy, 507–508, 510, 512
symptoms, 464, 519–520
trouble in speaking, 514–515, 535

Patriotism, 215
People's Progress and The Utopian News, 134–135, 137, 139, 142–143, 172, 229
Perkins, Elizabeth or Louise (pseuds.), 34, 131–132, 139, 144–146, 153–157, 199, 202, 322
Piatigorsky, Gregor, 76
Pizza, Phil, 78, 80, 90
Prescott, Arizona, 209, 262, 284, 346
Provincetown Players, 73–74, 77

Rage, 65, 186–187, 204, 219, 252, 317, 341, 357, 362, 378
Ralph, James, 11–12, 143
Ramsay, Ernest, 150, 152
Redlick, Chuck, 465
Religion, 93, 95–96, 98, 199, 205, 352, 459, 502, 522
Reno, Nevada, 434
Reynolds, Rox, 433
Richmond, California, 325, 328, 367, 370, 373
Rochester, George W., 136, 143–146
Rolland, Romain, 7, 47, 100–101, 170
Roma, Lisa, 78, 85–86, 91–92
Roman, Gerardo G., 19
Rosanoff, A. J., 123–126
Russian River, 467

Saint Francis Dam collapse, 64–65, 185
Salton Sea, 291
San Clemente Island, 291
San Diego, California, 149
San Diego Federated Trades and Labor Council, 158, 160–161
San Diego Newspaper Guild, 161
San Diego Sun, 154, 156, 406
San Francisco, 246, 262, 291
Alpine Terrace, 208–209
Barbary Coast, 190
Breen's, 190
California Labor School, 277
Coit Tower, 190
Dudley Stone Grammar School, 277
Golden Gate Park, 92, 277
Greyhound station, 211, 373
Haight-Ashbury, 261, 277, 505